WITHDRAWN FROM
MACALESTER COLLEGE
LIBRARY

AFRICAN HISTORICAL DICTIONARIES
Edited by Jon Woronoff

45. *Tunisia,* 2nd ed., by Kenneth J. Perkins. 1997.

46. *Zimbabwe,* 2nd ed., by Steven C. Rubert and R. Kent Rasmussen. 1990. *Out of print. See No. 86.*

47. *Mozambique,* by Mario Azevedo. 1991.

48. *Cameroon,* 2nd ed., by Mark W. DeLancey and H. Mbella Mokeba. 1990.

49. *Mauritius,* 2nd ed., by Sydney Selvon. 1991.

50. *Madagascar,* by Maureen Covell. 1995.

51. *The Central African Republic,* 2nd ed., by Pierre Kalck; translated by Thomas O'Toole. 1992.

52. *Angola,* 2nd ed., by Susan H. Broadhead. 1992.

53. *Sudan,* 2nd ed., by Carolyn Fluehr-Lobban, Richard A. Lobban, Jr., and John Obert Voll. 1992.

54. *Malawi,* 2nd ed., by Cynthia A. Crosby. 1993. *Out of print. See No. 84.*

55. *Western Sahara,* 2nd ed., by Anthony Pazzanita and Tony Hodges. 1994.

56. *Ethiopia and Eritrea,* 2nd ed., by Chris Prouty and Eugene Rosenfeld. 1994.

57. *Namibia,* by John J. Grotpeter. 1994.

58. *Gabon,* 2nd ed., by David E. Gardinier. 1994.

59. *Comoro Islands,* by Martin Ottenheimer and Harriet Ottenheimer. 1994.

60. *Rwanda,* by Learthen Dorsey. 1994.

61. *Benin,* 3rd ed., by Samuel Decalo. 1995.

62. *Republic of Cape Verde,* 3rd ed., by Richard Lobban and Marlene Lopes. 1995.

63. *Ghana,* 2nd ed., by David Owusu-Ansah and Daniel Miles McFarland. 1995.

64. *Uganda,* by M. Louise Pirouet. 1995.

65. *Senegal,* 2nd ed., by Andrew F. Clark and Lucie Colvin Phillips. 1994.

66. *Algeria,* 2nd ed., by Phillip Chiviges Naylor and Alf Andrew Heggoy. 1994.

67. *Egypt,* 2nd ed., by Arthur Goldschmidt, Jr. 1994.

68. *Mauritania,* 2nd ed., by Anthony G. Pazzanita. 1996.

69. *Congo,* 3rd ed., by Samuel Decalo, Virginia Thompson, and Richard Adloff. 1996.

70. *Botswana,* 3rd ed., by Jeff Ramsay, Barry Morton, and Fred Morton. 1996.

71. *Morocco,* 2nd ed., by Thomas K. Park. 1996.

72. *Tanzania,* 2nd ed., by Thomas P. Ofcansky and Rodger Yeager. 1997.

73. *Burundi,* 2nd ed., by Ellen K. Eggers. 1997.

74. *Burkina Faso,* 2nd ed., by Daniel Miles McFarland and Lawrence Rupley. 1998.

75. *Eritrea,* by Tom Killion. 1998.

76. *Democratic Republic of the Congo (Zaire),* by F. Scott Bobb. 1999. (Revised edition of *Historical Dictionary of Zaire,* No. 43)

77. *Kenya,* 2nd ed., by Robert M. Maxon and Thomas P. Ofcansky. 2000.

78. *South Africa,* 2nd ed., by Christopher Saunders and Nicholas Southey. 2000.

79. *The Gambia,* 3rd ed., by Arnold Hughes and Harry A. Gailey. 2000.

80. *Swaziland,* 2nd ed., by Alan R. Booth. 2000.

81. *Republic of Cameroon,* 3rd ed., by Mark W. DeLancey and Mark Dike DeLancey. 2000.

82. *Djibouti,* by Daoud A. Alwan and Yohanis Mibrathu. 2000.

83. *Liberia,* 2nd ed., by D. Elwood Dunn, Amos J. Beyan, and Carl Patrick Burrowes. 2001.

84. *Malawi,* 3rd ed., by Owen J. Kalinga and Cynthia A. Crosby. 2001.

85. *Sudan,* 3rd ed., by

86. *Zimbabwe,* 3rd ed., by Steven C. Rubert and R. Kent Rasmussen. 2001.

Historical Dictionary of Zimbabwe

Third Edition

Steven C. Rubert and R. Kent Rasmussen

African Historical Dictionaries, No. 86

The Scarecrow Press, Inc.
Lanham, Maryland, and London
2001

SCARECROW PRESS, INC.

Published in the United States of America
by Scarecrow Press, Inc.
4720 Boston Way, Lanham, Maryland 20706
www.scarecrowpress.com

4 Pleydell Gardens, Folkestone
Kent CT20 2DN, England

Copyright © 2001 by Steven C. Rubert and R. Kent Rasmussen

All rights reserved. No part of this publication may be reproduced,
stored in a retrieval system, or transmitted in any form or by any
means, electronic, mechanical, photocopying, recording, or otherwise,
without the prior permission of the publisher.

British Library Cataloguing-in-Publication Information Available

Library of Congress Cataloging-in-Publication Data

Rubert, Steven C., 1947–
  Historical dictionary of Zimbabwe / Steven C. Rubert and R. Kent
Rasmussen. — 3rd ed.
      p. cm. — (African historical dictionaries ; no. 86)
Rasmussen's name appears first on the earlier edition.
Includes bibliographical references.
  ISBN 0-8108-3471-5 (alk. paper)
  1. Zimbabwe—History—Dictionaries. I. Rasmussen, R. Kent. II.
Title. III. Series.

DT2925 .R83 2001
968.91'003--dc21   2001032211

∞™ The paper used in this publication meets the minimum requirements of
American National Standard for Information Sciences—Permanence of
Paper for Printed Library Materials, ANSI/NISO Z39.48-1992.
Manufactured in the United States of America.

In memory of

my father,

Jack A. Rubert,

and

my first African History Professor,

David Chanaiwa.

Figure 1: Map of Zimbabwe

TABLE OF CONTENTS

LIST OF MAPS

EDITOR'S FOREWORD

This is the third edition of the *Historical Dictionary of Zimbabwe*. Each edition has appeared in a rather different climate. The first edition, in 1979, was published just before white-settlers dominated Rhodesia and became independent under the country name Zimbabwe. The second edition, in 1990, could look back on a decade of independence and a certain degree of political and economic progress. Since then, the movement forward has become extremely tentative and, in some areas, there has been backsliding. The divisions within the population, already noticeable during the struggle for independence, have not been healed and there are serious problems in the economic field, although Zimbabwe is much better endowed than other African countries. Thus, the undertones of hope and then expectations of progress have dimmed and Zimbabwe is still seeking its way.

This book, which has been revised to reflect the recent events, builds on strong foundations since the previous edition already included considerable material on the first decade of independence and its predecessor described not only the situation of Rhodesia (and Southern Rhodesia) but early colonial and precolonial periods. It contains numerous entries on significant persons, places, institutions, events, ethnic groups, and political parties. The coverage is not only historical and political but, now more than before, economic, social and cultural. This long history is also summed up in the introduction and chronology. An impressive bibliography then provides access to a multitude of other works on these various aspects.

Most of the dictionary's material on the precolonial period was written by Dr. R. Kent Rasmussen, the author of the first edition. He is also the author of several books on Ndebele history. Much of the material on the colonial period was co-authored, and the material covering the liberation struggles and independent Zimbabwe comes from Dr. Steven C. Rubert, who authored the second and this third edition. Professor Rubert, who was formerly a research associate at the University of Zimbabwe, is presently with the Department of History at Oregon State Uni-

versity. He is author of a study of the labor conditions and moral
economy that developed on tobacco farms in colonial Zimbabwe.

Jon Woronoff
Series Editor

ACKNOWLEDGMENTS

Let me reiterate what I stated in the acknowledgments of the second edition of the *Historical Dictionary of Zimbabwe*, I want to thank Kent Rasmussen for giving me the opportunity to revise the first edition. To the people who encouraged and supported our earlier editions, I want to add my thanks to my colleagues at Oregon State University, in particular Jon Katz and Paul Farber.

The first edition of this work was completed in 1978, prior to independence. In the second edition we updated old entries, revised our interpretations of several others, deleted some, and wrote many new ones. I want to thank the reviewers who believed that we did a good job in accomplishing our task with that edition. Because the changes in that edition were so extensive, the ones in this edition are fewer. Again we have updated and revised several entries and added several. In addition we have added approximately 300 new entries to the extensive bibliography that follows the dictionary. The goal of this third edition is the same as with the first two editions, to help identify individuals, events, and organizations that have been involved in the history of Zimbabwe.

Steven C. Rubert
Oregon State University

NOTES ON USE OF THE DICTIONARY

ALPHABETIZATION OF ENTRIES

All entries are alphabetized by individual words, not whole phrases, as in this simplified sequence:

RHODESIA RAILWAYS COMPANY
RHODESIAN AFRICAN RIFLES
RHODESIANA

Personal names take precedence in any given sequence. Thus, HARTLEY, HENRY precedes HARTLEY (the town). No distinctions are made between "first" and "last" names of pre-20th-century Africans with obviously non-Christian names. A name such as MBIGO MASUKU is therefore entered under MBIGO. Prefixes are dropped from Bantu proper names; e.g., for MASHONA see SHONA. Non-proper Bantu nouns are entered under their singular forms; e.g., IBUTHO (pl., *amabutho*). To aid in the understanding of prefixes, the dictionary contains individual entries on important class prefixes, such as ABA-, BA-, CHI-, MA-, and many others. Broader discussions of prefixes can be found in the entries on BANTU, CHISHONA, and SINDEBELE.

CROSS-REFERENCES

In the interest of making information as easy to locate as possible, several forms of cross-referencing are employed throughout the dictionary. Names and terms of special pertinence to the entries in which they appear are set in boldface. Additional cross-references are occasionally enclosed in parentheses with the words "see" or "see also."

DATES

Wherever possible, exact dates are given. Unqualified dates may be regarded as firm. Dates qualified by *c.* (*circa*, "about") are informed approximations. Dates divided by slash lines, such as

"1824/5," represent "either/or" estimates. Rougher estimates of dates are generally given as decades, such as "1790s." Note that an expression such as "1800s" indicates the first decade of the 19th century, not the entire century. In biographical entries the abbreviation "fl." (*flourit*, "flourished") indicates the period in which the person is known to have been alive. In most such cases it can be assumed that the person was actually born several decades earlier than the dates given.

The distribution of firm and approximated dates presented in the chronology reflects the availability of written documentation for the country's history as a whole. With isolated, and perhaps tenuous, exceptions, the written record begins in the early 16th century, with significant gaps until the 1850s. Dates for earlier archaeological findings are generally derived from radiocarbon tests and other techniques.

GEOGRAPHICAL REFERENCES

Unless otherwise stated, place names used in the dictionary are those current to the periods under discussion. Wherever possible, exact longitudinal and latitudinal coordinates are provided.

Figures for altitudes are taken from a variety of government yearbooks, travel guides, and other publications. These sources are not always consistent, so altitudes given in the dictionary are generally rounded off to the nearest five meters. Figures for the areas of districts and other regions are also rounded off for this reason.

VARIANT FORMS AND SPELLINGS

Every attempt has been made to enter names and terms under their most widely accepted spellings and forms, but it should be recognized that consistency is impossible. Different authorities often disagree or change their minds on what these forms should be, and orthographies of African languages are far from fully settled. The variant forms given in parentheses in dictionary entry headings often represent only a small sample of the variations that have been used. Two examples illustrate the dimensions of this problem: historians have compiled more than 100 forms of "munhumutapa" and more than 300 forms of "mzilikazi" alone.

Some help in spelling Bantu words is offered in the note on alphabetization, above. The dictionary also contains special entries on important letters and combinations of letters which present regular problems. For example, Chishona orthography once rendered the *ch* sound simply a *c*. See the entries C, L, Ǫ, SW, TSH, U, and X. Other spelling shifts are too numerous to discuss fully in a book of this nature, but a recurrent problem to watch for is use of the aspirant -*h*- after consonants, as in MHONDORO and NHOWE. Unfortunately, few authorities agree on when this letter should or should not be used, so one can only be alert to its possible absence from a word.

ABBREVIATIONS

ABC	American Board of Commissioners for Foreign Missions
a.k.a.	also known as
alt.	altitude
AMEC	African Methodist Episcopal Church
ANC	African National Congress; African National Council
b.	born
BBP	Bechuanaland Border Police
BSAC	British South African Company
BSAP	British South African Police
c.	*circa* (about)
CA	Central Africa
CAF	Central African Federation
CAP	Central African Party
CAS	Capricorn Africa Society
CAZ	Conservative Alliance of Zimbabwe
cf.	*confer* (compare to)
CP	Confederate Party; Centre Party
d.	died
DP	Democratic Party; Dominion Party
DRC	Dutch Reformed Church
ESAP	Economic Structural Adjustment Program
fl.	*flourit* (flourished)
FRELIMO	Front for the Liberation of Mozambique
FROLIZI	Front for the Liberation of Zimbabwe
HMC	Historical Monuments Commission
ICU	Industrial and Commercial Workers' Union
IDAF	International Defence and Aid Fund
IMF	International Monetary Fund

Legco	Legislative Council
LMS	London Missionary Society
MDC	Movement for Democratic Change
MFF	Mashonaland Field Force
MNR	Mozambique National Resistance
MRF	Matabeleland Relief Force
NAZ	National Archives of Zimbabwe
NCA	National Constitutional Assembly
NDP	National Democratic Party
NIBMAR	"No independence before majority African rule"
NPU	National People's Union
NRZ	National Railways of Zimbabwe
OAU	Organization of African Unity
PCC	People's Caretaker Council
PEA	Portuguese East Africa (Mozambique)
PF	Patriotic Front
RAP	Rhodesian Action Party
RAR	Rhodesian African Rifles
RBVA	Rhodesian Bantu Voters' Association
RF	Rhodesian Front Party
RH	*Rhodesia Herald*
RICU	Reformed Industrial & Commercial Workers' Union
RISCO	Rhodesian Iron & Steel Company
RP	Rhodesia(n) Party; Reform Party
SA	South Africa
SADCC	Southern African Development Coordination Conference
SLA	Sabi-Limpopo Authority
SPG	Society for Propagation of Gospel
SR	Southern Rhodesia(n)
SRMC	Southern Rhodesian Missionary Conference
Tilcor	Tribal Trust Land Development Corporation
TTL	Tribal Trust Land
UANC	United African National Council
UCR(N)	University College of Rhodesia (& Nyasaland)
UDI	Unilateral Declaration of Independence
UFP	United Federal Party

UMC	United Methodist Church
UN	United Nations
UP	United Party
UPP	United People's Party
UPZ	United Party of Zimbabwe
URP	United Rhodesian Party
US$	United States Dollar
UZ	University of Zimbabwe
WMMS	Wesleyan Methodist Missionary Society
YL	Youth League
Z$	Zimbabwe Dollar
ZANLA	Zimbabwe African National Liberation Army
ZANU	Zimbabwe African National Union
ZAPU	Zimbabwe African People's Union
ZBC	Zimbabwe Broadcasting Corporation
ZIPA	Zimbabwe People's Army
ZIPRA	Zimbabwe People's Revolutionary Army
ZNA	Zimbabwe National Army
ZNP	Zimbabwe National Party
ZPDP	Zimbabwe People's Democratic Party
ZUM	Zimbabwe Unity Movement
ZUPO	Zimbabwe United People's Organization

CHRONOLOGY

Headings of relevant dictionary entries are printed in capital letters here. Within each chronological period, the least precisely dated entries are given first.

c.100,000 B.C. Beginning of Early **Stone Age**

c.35,000 B.C. Beginning of Middle Stone Age

c.9000 B.C. Beginning of Late Stone Age

c.5000 B.C. Earliest possible date for extant **Rock Paintings**

c.A.D. 200 Introduction of **Iron Age** cultures

c.900 Rise of **Leopard's Kopje Culture**

947 al-Masudi chronicles of **Sofala** gold trade

c.1100 Settlement initiated at site of **Zimbabwe Ruins;** Sofala founded at present site

c.1200-50 Substantial stone building begun at Zimbabwe Ruins

c.1300 Radiocarbon date for **Monk's Kop Ossuary**

1331 Ibn Battuta mentions **Yufi**

c.1400 Zimbabwe state at its peak

c.1450 Mutota and **Matope** establish **Munhumutapa** state in the north

c.1494 Changamire and **Togwa** states separate from Munhumutapa state; **Chikuyo Chisamarengu** becomes Munhumutapa

1505 (Sept. 19) **Portuguese** occupation of Sofala

1506 (Nov. 20) Diogo Alcacova writes to Portuguese king, giving first description of Munhumutapa state

c.1511 Antonio **Fernandes** becomes first European to visit present Zimbabwe

c.1530 Neshangwe becomes Munhumutapa

c.1547 Neshangwe expels Changamire from Mbire region

c.1550 Chivere Nyasoro becomes Munhumutapa

c.1560 Negomo Chirisamhuru becomes Munhumutapa

1561 (March 15/16) Gonçalo da **Silveira** killed by **Shona**

1570 Barreto/Homem expedition sent against Munhumutapa by Portugal

1575 Mutasa Chikanga signs treaty with Homem; numerous trade **Fairs** opened in northeast

c.1589 Gatsi Rusere becomes Munhumutapa

1597 Zimba people enter Shona territory

1607 (Aug. 1) Gatsi Rusere signs treaty with Diogo Simões **Madeira**

1623 Nyambo Kaparidze becomes Munhumutapa

1629 (May) **Mavura II** becomes Munhumutapa after Portuguese help to oust Nyambo; Mavura signs treaty with Portuguese

1633 First documentation of **Maungwe** people; founding of **Mangwende** dynasty

1644 Bayão expedition into **Butua**

1652 (May) **Siti Kazurukumusapa** becomes Munhumutapa

1663 Siti assassinated; **Kambarapasu Mukombwe** becomes Munhumutapa

1693–5 Changamire armies under **Dombo** drive Portuguese out of country; Munhumutapa state goes into decline

c.1714 Zumbo trading fair founded on Zambezi River

1769 Portuguese fail in effort to reopen **Dambarare** fair

1790s Birth of **Mzilikazi** in Zululand

c.1816 Mzilikazi succeeds **Mashobane** as **Khumalo** ruler

1820s Beginnings of **Mfecane** invasions in country

c.1821 Mzilikazi leads Khumalo out of Zululand, founds **Ndebele** kingdom in the **Transvaal**

c.1828 Ngwato ruler **Kgari** killed during foray into **Kalanga** territory; **Shangwa** drought afflicts much of country

1829 Robert **Moffat** among the first Europeans to visit Mzilikazi near present Pretoria

1831 Kaliphi commands first Ndebele foray into present Zimbabwe from central Transvaal

1830s Ngoni of **Zwangendaba** attack Changamire centers, killing **Chirisamhuru**

1835 (Nov. 20) Solar eclipse over country, associated in traditions with Zwangendaba's crossing of the Zambezi into present Zambia

1836 (March 3) **Mncumbathe** signs treaty with governor of the British Cape Colony, in the name of Mzilikazi; **A. H. Potgieter** et al. scout north of the Limpopo River; first **Afrikaner** clashes with Ndebele around the Vaal River

1837 Ndebele centers in western Transvaal attacked by Afrikaners, **Griqua, Sotho,** and **Zulu;** Ndebele begin to migrate north

1838 (c.March) Ndebele divide unto two main migration parties in Ngwato territory; Kaliphi's division goes directly to present **Matabeleland**

1839 (c.June) Mzilikazi's division of migrants arrives in Matabeleland; **Nkulumane** and dissident Ndebele *izinduna* executed in political crisis

c.1840 Nxaba Msane killed in western Zambia

1841 Ndebele begin raiding Sotho/Tswana territories from their new base in Matabeleland

1840s Ndebele-**Kololo** wars along the Zambezi

1847 Potgieter raids the Ndebele

1851 Kololo king **Sebitwane** dies shortly after visit by David **Livingstone**

1852 Establishent of South African Republic in the Transvaal

1853 Ndebele kill **Nanzwa** ruler Lusumbami; (Jan. 8) Ndebele sign treaty with Transvaal Afrikaners

1854 Robert Moffat and Samuel **Edwards** visit Mzilikazi, opening Ndebele communications with south; Mzilikazi releases **Truey the Griqua** to Moffat

1855 (Nov.) Livingstone visits and names **Victoria Falls**

1857 Moffat revisits Ndebele, arranges for release of Ngwato royal heir **Macheng**

1859 (Dec.) **London Missionary Society** opens **Matabele Mission** at **Inyati**

1860s–1870s Peak of **ivory trade**

1862 Mzila becomes **Gaza** king

1863 (March) **Mangwane** leads Ndebele attack on Ngwato

1864 Lozi overthrow Kololo rulers, refugees flee south

1866 (c. Oct.) Ndebele capture Tohwechipi, ending **Rozvi** resistance

1867 Karl Mauch begins publishing discovery of **gold** in **Mashonaland**

1868 (Sept.) Mzilikazi dies; **Mncumbathe** becomes Ndebele regent

1869 (July) **South Africa Gold Fields Exploration Co.** expedition into Shona territory

1870 "**Fever Year**"; Cecil **Rhodes** arrives in South Africa; (Jan.) **Lobengula** installed as Ndebele king; (June) Lobengula suppresses rebels at **Zwangendaba**

1871 Mauch visits and describes **Zimbabwe Ruins;** establishment of first **Bulawayo;** raising of **Imbizo** *ibutho;* (Aug. 29) Lobengula signs **Baines Concession**

1872 (Jan.) Mangwane leads "**Nkulumane**" coup attempt against Lobengula

1875 Thomas Morgan **Thomas** founds independent mission

1876 (Dec.) Alexander **Bailie** attempts to recruit mine laborers in Matabeleland

1877 François **Coillard** attempts to start mission among Shona; British occupy the Transvaal

1878 (Sept.) Massacre of **Patterson** expedition

1879 (Sept.) Jesuit **Zambezi Mission** arrives in Matabeleland; Lobengula marries **Xwalile** and Gaza princesses; (Oct.) Ndebele kill **Chivi** Mazorodze

1880s Manuel de **Sousa** advances into Shona territory from northeast

1880 (April) Execution of Lobengula's sister, **Mncengence;** (Nov. 25) Augustus **Law** dies while attempting to open Jesuit mission among Gaza

1881 Bulawayo moved to new location

1883 (April) **Gampu Sithole** commands Ndebele attack on **Tawana;** (May) Ndebele kill **Chaminuka** medium

1884 Gungunyane becomes Gaza king

1885 (March 14) **Bechuanaland Protectorate** declared over present **Botswana;** (April) **Lotshe** commands disastrous Ndebele attack on Tawana

1887 (July 30) Lobengula signs treaty with the Transvaal's **P. Grobler**

1888 (Feb. 11) Lobengula signs **"Moffat Treaty"**; (Oct. 30) Lobengula signs **Rudd Concession**

1889 Gungunyane moves Gaza capital to lower Limpopo; **Portuguese** sign treaties with northern Shona rulers; (Jan.) Lobengula repudiates Rudd Concession; (March) formation of **British South Africa Co.**; (Oct. 29) BSAC incorporated by royal **Charter**

1890 (June 28) BSAC's **Pioneer Column** enters country; (Sept. 12) Column founds Fort **Salisbury**; (Sept. 14) Archibald **Colquhoun** obtains treaty from **Mutasa**; (Nov. 15); **P. W. Forbes** arrests Portuguese agents **J. C. P. d'Andrada** and **Sousa** at Mutasa's

1891 (Feb. 15) Temporary frontier with Portuguese territory established in **Manicaland**; (May 9) British Order-in-Council declares protectorates over Bechuanaland, Matabeleland, and Mashonaland; (May 11) British and Portuguese clash at **Maçequeçe**; (June 11) **Anglo-Portuguese Convention**; (June 24) BSAC disperses **Adendorff** trekkers at Limpopo; (Nov.) Ndebele kill reigning **Nemakonde**; (Nov. 17) Lobengula signs **Lippert Concession**

1892 First **Pass Laws** issued in Salisbury; (Oct.) first section of **Railway** from **Beira** opened

1893 (July 18) Ndebele raid Shona near Ft. Victoria in "Victoria Incident"; (Sept.) beginning of **Ndebele War**; (Oct. 24) Battle of Shangani; (Nov. 1) Battle of Bembezi; (Nov. 4) British occupy Bulawayo; (Dec. 4) Ndebele annihilate **"Shangani Patrol"**

1894 (Jan./Feb.?) Death of Lobengula; British work to dismantle Ndebele kingdom

1895 (Jan.) Native Department created in Matabeleland; (May 3) Territory proclaimed **"Rhodesia"**; (Dec. 29) **Jameson Raid** leaves Mafeking

1896 (Jan. 2) **Jameson** surrenders in Transvaal; (Feb.) **Rinderpest** breaks out in Matabeleland; (March 20) Ndebele **Revolt** begins; (June 14) Shona **Revolt** begins; (June 25) **Nyamanda** made Ndebela king; (Aug. 21) first of Rhodes' five **Indabas** with southern Ndebele rebels; Ndebele Revolt ends

1897 (July) Last Ndebele rebel, **Mpotshwana**, captured; (Oct. 27) Shona Revolt pronounced ended; (Nov.) railroad to Bulawayo opened

1898 (Feb.) Beira to **Umtali** railroad opened; (April 27) **Kaguvi** and **Nehanda** mediums executed

1899 (May 15) First session of **Legislative Council;** (May 22) Beira railroad reaches Salisbury; (Oct. 11) outbreak of **South African War**

1901 Mapondera's revolt begins; administrations of Matabeleland and Mashonaland combined under **W. H. Milton; East Coast Fever** hits cattle

1902 Death of **Chioko Dambamupute,** the last Munhumutapa; (March 26) death of **C. J. Rhodes;** (May) end of South African War

1903 New **Chaminuka** medium emerges; **Coal** production begins at **Wankie**

1904 Government eases mining restrictions on **Small-Workers;** (June 19) railway reaches **Victoria Falls**

1906 Formation of **Southern Rhodesian Missionary Conference;** beginning of commercial **Copper** production; appearance of new **Nehanda** medium; publication of **Randall-Maciver**'s *Medieval Rhodesia* opens **Zimbabwe Controversy**

1907 Beginning of commercial **Chrome** production; establishment of **Harare** township

1908 Charles **Coghlan** and others attend **South Africa**'s national Union Convention

1910 Formation of Union of South Africa

1914 Creation of **Matabele National Home Society**

1915 Matthew **Zwimba** founds Church of the White Bird; Clements **Kadalie** arrives in country; (March 13) **BSAC Charter** extended 10 years

1918 Influenza Pandemic hits country

1919 Passage of **Women's Franchise Ordinance**

1920 Cave Commission recommends cash settlement for BSAC assets in country

1921 Buxton Committee makes recommendations on country's constitutional future; **Bantu Women's League** founded

1923 (Jan. 20) **Rhodesian Bantu Voters' Association** launched; (Sept. 12) great Britain annexes Southern Rhodesia as a Crown Colony, with **J. R. Chancellor** as first **Governor;** (Oct. 1) **Responsible Government** established, with **Coghlan** as first premier

1924 (May 30) New **Legislative Assembly** opens

1925 Establishment of Department of Native **Education**

1927 Industrial & Commercial Union founded in Bulawayo; (Sept. 2) **H. U. Moffat** succeeds Coghlan as premier after latter's death; (Sept. 12-17) African miners strike at **Shamva**

1928 First government **Game Reserve** established in Wankie

1929 Gertrude **Caton-Thompson** excavates at Zimbabwe; foundation of **Ruwadzano** Methodist women's organization; (Jan. 24) **Hilton Young** Report on eastern African closer union; (Aug. 31) **Beit Bridge** opened in Limpopo

1930 Beginning of **Strip Road** construction; (Oct. 10) promulgation of **Land Apportionment Act**

1931 Godfrey **Huggins** founds **Reform Party**

1932 Johane **Maranke** founds independent church

1933 Creation of **African Farmers' Union;** (June 29) government buys BSAC's **Mineral** rights; (July 6) George **Mitchell** replaces Moffat at **Prime Minister;** (Sept. 6) Huggins' party carries general election

1934 Aaron **Jacha** founds Bantu Congress, predecessor of **African National Congress;** after split in Reform Party, Huggins carries new election at head of new **United Party;** promulgation of **Industrial Conciliation Act**

1935 Creation of **National Archives**

1936 Creation of **Historical Monuments Commission**

1939 (March 21) Publication of **Bledisloe** Report respecting **Amalgamation Of The Rhodesias;** (April 14) Huggins' party again carries general election

1940 Rhodesian African Rifles raised

1943 African Newspapers Ltd. enters country

1944 (Oct. 18) Establishment of **Central Africa Council**

1945 Karoi made center of resettlement scheme for European war veterans; (Oct. 20) African railway workers strike

1946 Native (Urban Areas) Accommodation and Registration Act passed; (Feb. 10) **Reformed** ICU founded in Salisbury; (April 25) Huggins' party wins general election in which **Liberal Party** shows major gains

1947 (July) Benjamin **Burombo** founds African Voice Association

1948 (April 14-22) African general strike in major urban centers; (Sept. 15) Huggins' party again wins general election, in which Ian **Smith** enters Legislative Assembly

1949 Foundation of **Capricorn Africa Society;** Doris **Lessing** emigrates to England; creation of **Rhodesia Railways Co.;** (Feb.) first Victoria Falls conference on federation; (late) **National Park** Act

1950 Robert **Tredgold** made chief justice of country

1951 Formation of **All-Africa Convention;** passage of **Native Land Husbandry Act**

1953 (April 9) European voters ratify federation in general referendum; (Sept) inauguration of **Federation Of Rhodesia and Nyasaland** with Huggins as federal prime minister; Garfield **Todd** succeeds Huggins as Southern Rhodesian prime minister

1954 (Jan.) First federal elections put Federal Party in power; Todd retained in power in territorial elections

1955 Mai **Chaza** founds independent church; **Chishona** orthography standardized by government; new railway line to Lourenzo Marques opened; work begun on **Kariba Dam;** (Aug.) **Youth League** founded in Harare

1956 Formation of **Dominion Party,** predecessor of **Rhodesian Front;** (Aug.) Youth League organizes Salisbury bus boycott; (Oct. 31) Roy **Welensky** succeeds Huggins (now Lord Malvern) as federal prime minister

1957 (March) **University** College of Rhodesia and Nyasaland opened to students in Salisbury; (Sept. 12) founding of new **African National Congress**

1958 (Feb. 18) Edgar **Whitehead** replaces Todd as Southern Rhodesian prime minister after cabinet revolt; (June 5) Whitehead retained as prime minister after UFP barely carries general election

1959 (Feb. 26) Government declares state of emergency, prescribes ANC; passage of **Unlawful Organizations Act**

1960 (Jan. 1) Formation of **National Democratic Party;** (May 17) Kariba Dam formally opened; (July 19) arrest of NDP leaders leads to bloody rioting; (Oct.) **Law and Order (Maintenance) Act** introduced; **Monckton Commission** Report issued on future of federation; (Dec.) Federal Constitutional Review Conference opens in London

1961 Council Of Chiefs created; (June) **Zimbabwe National Party founded;** (July 26) public referendum approves proposals for new **Constitution;** (Dec. 9) NDP banned; (Dec. 18) **Zimbabwe African People's Union** founded

1962 (March) **Rhodesian Front** founded; (April-May) first full census of African **Population;** (April) federal election boycotted by Africans; (Aug. 14) **T. S. Parirenyatwa** dies under mysterious circumstances; (Sept. 20) ZAPU banned; (Dec. 14) Rhodesian Front wins Southern Rhodesian election, Winston **Field** becomes prime minister

1963 Beginning of **Tangwena Land Dispute;** (July) ZAPU leaders split in Dar es Salaam; (Aug. 8) **Zimbabwe African National Union** founded; (Aug. 10) **People's Caretaker Council** formed as ZAPU front; (Dec. 31) federation officially dissolved

1964 ZANLA founded as military wing of ZANU; (April 13) Ian **Smith** displaces Field as prime minister; (April 16) government detains Joshua **Nkomo;** (Aug. 26) government bans ZANU, PZZ, and *African Daily News,* and declares **Highfield** an emergency area; (Oct. 21-26) **"Domboshawa Indaba"** of government chiefs endorses independence; (Oct. 24) Northern Rhodesia becomes independent as Zambia; (Nov. 5) public referendum by **European** voters endorses independence

1965 ZIPRA founded in Lusaka, Zambia, as armed wing of ZAPU; (Jan.) creation of **Sabi-Limpopo Authority;** (May 7) Rhodesian Front wins all 50 European seats in general election; (May 31) **United People's Party** founded; (Sept.) British government articulates **"Five Principles"** respecting Rhodesian independence; (Oct. 26-30) Harold Wilson visits Salisbury to discuss independence; (Nov. 5) state of emergency declared; (Nov. 11) **Unilateral Declaration of Independence** issued; **Constitution** revised, press **Censorship** instituted; Britain applies economic **Sanctions**

1966 (April 28) ZANLA combatants engage **Rhodesian Security Forces** at **Battle of Chinhoyi;** (Dec. 2-4) Wilson and Smith meet off Gibraltar in **"Tiger Talks";** (Dec. 16) United Nations votes selected mandatory economic sanctions

1967 (Aug.) ZAPU and South African ANC launch guerrilla campaign in northwest

1968 (May 29) UN votes comprehensive mandatory sanctions; (Aug.) **Centre Party** formed by Rhodesian Front opponents; (Aug. 28) Abel **Muzorewa** made UMC Bishop of Rhodesia; (Sept.

30) Bechuanaland becomes independent as Republic of **Botswana;** (Oct. 10-13) Wilson and Smith meet in **"Fearless Talks"**

1969 Land Tenure Act passed; (April-May) census of African **Population;** (June 20) European electorate votes in favor of a **Republic** in referendum; (June 24) H. V. Gibbs resigns as governor; (Nov. 29) new **Constitution** becomes law

1970 (March 2) Rhodesia declared a republic; (April 10) Rhodesian Front sweeps European seats in general election; (April 16) Clifford **Dupont** sworn in as first **President;** (June 15) Leopold **Takawira** dies in prison

1971 ZANLA adopts guerrilla tactics, increases infiltration into northeastern districts; (May 8) death of Lord Malvern (**G. Huggins**); (April) informal British-Rhodesian talks begin in Salisbury; (Oct.) **Front For the Liberation of Zimbabwe** (FROLIZI) formed; (Nov. 17) U. S. President Richard Nixon signs bill containing **"Byrd Amendment"**; (Nov. 24) Ian Smith and Sir Alec Douglas Home sign Anglo-Rhodesian Settlement Proposals; (Dec. 16) **African National Council** formed

1972 (Jan. 11-March 11) **Pearce Commission** in Rhodesia; (May 23) Commissions's Report published in London; (Dec. 21) **Altena Farm** attacked by ZANLA combatants, marking beginning of new stage of large-scale guerrilla war in northeast

1973 (Jan. 9) Rhodesia closes border with **Zambia;** (Feb.) Rhodesia reopens border, but Zambia keeps its side closed; (July) **Muzorewa** and Smith begin talks that last almost a year; (Dec.) government raises a second battalion of **Rhodesian African Rifles** to combat increasing guerrilla activities in northeast

1974 **"Protected Village"** program begun by government; Ndabaningi **Sithole** ousted as leader of ZANU; replaced by Robert **Mugabe;** (April 25) **Portuguese** government falls in coup d'état; new government pledges independence for African colonies; (May) **Gonakudzingwa** detention camp closed; (July) Rhodesian Front sweeps general election; (Sept. 15) direct **Railway** link to **South Africa** opened through **Beitbridge;** (Dec.) Organization of African Unity Committee creates **Frontline States** Presidents' Committee; (Dec. 8) leaders of ZANU, ZAPU, and FROLIZI announce acceptance of ANC as "umbrella" organization with Muzorewa as head; (Dec. 11) Ian Smith announces agreement with nationalists for cease-fire in civil war, release of political prisoners, and plan for new constitutional conference; Ndabaningi **Sithole, Nkomo, Mugabe,** and others released

1975 (Feb.) Smith meets with **Nkomo, Muzorewa,** Ndabaningi **Sithole,** and others to set up formal constitutional conference; (March 19) Herbert **Chitepo** assassinated in Lusaka; (June 25) Mozambique becomes independent, with Samora Machel as president; (July) ZANLA allowed to establish forward camps in Tete Province; (July 8) Rhodesian government announces set-up of anti-guerrilla campaign after failure of cease-fire; (Aug) **South Africa** announces pull-out of its military forces from Rhodesia; (Aug. 25-26) abortive **Victoria Falls Conference;** (Oct.) **Mgagao Declaration** circulated and approved by ZANLA filed commanders in Tanzania and Mozambique; Edson **Sithole** disappears from streets of Salisbury; (Dec. 10) **J. J. Wrathall** succeeds Dupont as president; (Dec. 15) Smith and Nkomo begin weekly talks in Salisbury

1976 (Feb.) **Rhodesian Security Forces** begin making "hot pursuit" forays into Mozambique; (March 3) Mozambique closes its borders to Rhodesia; (March 19) Smith-Nkomo talks break down; (April 26) government publishes regulations increasing **Censorship;** (April 27) Smith announces addition of government chiefs to his cabinet; (Sept. 19) Smith and U.S. Secretary of State Henry Kissinger meet in Pretoria; (Sept. 24) Smith announces willingness to bring about African majority rule within two years; (Oct. 9) Nkomo and Robert **Mugabe** announce formation of **Patriotic Front;** (Oct. 28) **Geneva Conference** opens; (Dec. 9) conference adjourns for holidays, never to reopen; (Dec. 29) government chiefs found **Zimbabwe United People's Organization**

1977 Robert **Mugabe** elected president of ZANU during party meeting at Chimoio, Mozambique; (Jan.) Presidents of **Frontline States** pledge support for Patriotic Front; (Jan. 22) letter bomb kills Jason **Moyo** in Lusaka; (March) Donal **Lamont** deported; (March 18) U.S. President Jimmy Carter signs repeal of "**Byrd Amendment**"; (April 1) amendments to **Land Tenure Act** lift some color bar laws; (April 13) British Foreign Secretary David Owen presents new Anglo-American constitutional proposals to Ian Smith in Cape Town; (April 16) Owen consults with Smith in Salisbury, becoming first British cabinet-level official to visit country in six years; (April 18) emergency Rhodesian Front convention endorses principle of eventual majority rule; (April 29) Smith expels hard-line opponents from the Rhodesian Front; (May 16) President Kaunda announces that **Zambia** is "in a state of war" with Rhodesia; (May 27) UN Security Council tightens mandatory sanctions; (July 4) **Rhodesian Action Party** formed; (July 5) general meeting of OAU endorses **Patriotic Front** as sole representative of people of Zimbabwe; (Aug. 31) Rhodesian Front sweeps European seats in general elections; (Sept.1) British Foreign Secretary Owen and U.S. Secretary of State Cyrus Vance announce proposals acknowledging that the Patriotic Front must play a leadership role in any future government, and that armed forces of an independent **Zimbabwe** should be based upon ZANLA and ZIPRA forces; (Sept. 224) Frontline Presidents group endorses Anglo-American plan; (Sept. 28) Britain presents Anglo-American proposals to UN Security Council; (Nov. 23-28) Rhodesian Security Forces mount major raids into Mozambique (Nov. 24) Smith announces conditional acceptance of "one man, one vote" principle; (Dec. 2) Smith opens new round of internal negotiations with **Muzorewa,** Ndabaningi **Sithole,** and Jeremiah **Chirau;** (Dec. 7) **Zambia** announces withdrawal of support for Anglo-American plan.

1978 (Jan.) David Owen, Andrew Young, Robert **Mugabe,** and Joshua **Nkomo** meet for **Malta Talks;** (March 3) Smith, N. Sithole, Muzorewa, and Chirau sign **Internal Settlement Agreement;** (April) Ministerial Council, with African and European co-ministers for each government ministry, selected; (May) Executive Council announces amnesty for guerrillas who lay sown their arms; ban on African political parties, including ZANU and ZAPU, lifted; (Aug.) Ian Smith and Joshua Nkomo hold secret talks in Zambia; (Sept.) government reimposes bans against ZANU and ZAPU

1979 (Jan.2) government announces plan for new **Constitution** to implement Internal Settlement; (Jan. 30) European electorate approves referendum on new constitution; (Feb. 21) UN Human Rights Commission rejects the internal settlement; (Feb. 28) Smith dissolves Rhodesian Parliament, officially ending 88 years of minority white rule; (April 17-21) first general elections held in which Africans vote for government officials, 64 percent of African electorate votes; Rhodesian Front wins all 28 seats reserved for European, while UANC under **Muzorewa** wins 51 of 72 seats elected by African voters; (May) Conservative Party, led by Margaret Thatcher, wins general election in Britain; (May 25) OAU announces its opposition to Muzorewa's government and lifting of sanctions; (May 28) Muzorewa sworn in as first African prime minister of country; (May 30) **Zimbabwe Rhodesia** declared an independent republic; (Aug.) British Prime Minister Thatcher agrees to **Lusaka Accord;** (Sept. 10-Dec. 21) **Lancaster House Conference** convened; (Dec. 7) Lord **Soames** appointed as **Governor;** (Dec. 12) Zimbabwe Rhodesia **House of Assembly** votes to return country to colonial status; later that day Lord

Soames arrives in Salisbury to take office, officially marking end
of UDI; (Dec. 28) cease-fire takes effect

1980 (Jan. 13) Joshua **Nkomo** returns to country; (Jan. 27)
Robert **Mugabe** returns to country; (Feb. 27-29) general elections, 94 percent of the African electorate votes; ZANU wins
election with 63 percent of the African vote and 57 of 80
parliamentary seats; ZAPU receives 24 percent of the vote, and
wins 20 seats; (March 5) Mugabe agrees to form a coalition
government; (April) Mugabe sworn in as first **Prime Minister** of
Zimbabwe; (April 18) independent Republic of Zimbabwe declared; (May 16) first session of independent Zimbabwe's Parliament opens; (July) Parliament extends state of emergency for six
months; (Sept.) Mugabe orders **Zimbabwe National Army** and
police to act against **Dissidents;** Mugabe orders closure of the
South African diplomatic mission in Zimbabwe, charging Pretoria with recruiting and training dissidents

1981 Mugabe announces that he hopes to create a one-party
state in Zimbabwe; (Feb.) government creates **Mass Media Trust**
and takes control of the country's five major newspapers; (March)
Zimcord conference held in Salisbury

1982 (Feb.) Nkomo rejects proposal to merge ZAPU with ZANU;
Nkomo accused of plotting to overthrow the government and
dismissed from government by Mugabe; (April) government officially changes name of Salisbury to **Harare;** (June) government
mounts campaign against dissidents in Matabeleland; government forces accused of harsh treatment of people in rural areas
of Matabeleland; (Aug.) first post-independence **Census** conducted

1983 (Jan.) **Mozambique National Resistance** rebels sabotage
oil pipeline from **Beira** and cut Zimbabwe's main energy supply
line; (Feb.) price of gas goes up 40 percent; (Aug.) twentieth
anniversary of founding of ZANU, Mugabe again pledges to create
a one-party state

1984 Zimbabwe's economy suffers due to third year of drought;
(Feb.) government imposes dusk-to-dawn curfew in Matabeleland; (April 9) curfew regulations eased following Mugabe
visit to region; (June) government imposes ban on meetings by
opposition parties in central **Provinces;** (July) Rhodesian Front
changes its name to "Conservative Alliance of Zimbabwe"; (July
24) Parliament extends state of emergency for an additional six
months; (Aug.) curfew in Matabeleland lifted; Second Zanu Party
Congress held in Harare, Mugabe is reelected party president;
(Oct.) government lifts ban on opposition party meetings; Zapu

holds party congress, Nkomo is again elected leader; (Nov.) following the assassination of Moven Ndlovu, a ZANU senator from **Beitbridge,** Mugabe dismisses ZAPU members from the cabinet

1985 (Jan.) government postpones elections until July; (June 27) European voters reelect Ian Smith and 14 other members of the Conservative Alliance; (July 1-2) ZANU wins the African general election and increases it total number of parliamentary seats to 63; ZAPU wins 15 seats; (Aug.) unity talks between Mugabe and Joshua Nkomo begin; (Nov.) Abel **Muzorewa** announces his retirement from politics; (Nov. 29) D. C. "Boss" **Lilford,** former chairman of the Rhodesian Front, is found murdered on his farm outside Harare

1986 Negotiations regarding the amalgamation of ZANU and ZAPU continue throughout the year; (May) South African commandos attack houses owned by the South African ANC in Harare; Mugabe becomes one of the major leaders of the Commonwealth campaign to impose economic sanctions against South Africa; (July) state of emergency is renewed for six months; (Sept.) Mugabe becomes chairman of the Nonaligned Movement; (Oct.) Justice Minister Eddison Zvobgo announces government plans to alter its Westminster-style parliamentary system in 1987

1987 (Jan. 20) National state of emergency is extended for an additional six months, partly in response to increasing incursions by the MNR into Zimbabwe; (March) President Joaquim Chissano of Mozambique requests that Zimbabwe continue its military assistance to Mozambique; (April) Mugabe announces that talks aimed at uniting ZANU and ZAPU are being suspended; President Canaan **Banana** intervenes and persuades Mugabe to continue the negotiations; Ian Smith is suspended from the House of Assembly for one year after returning from a trip to **South Africa,** where he encouraged white South Africans to unite against sanctions; (May 13) Smith resigns as leader of the Conservative Alliance (formerly Rhodesian Front), a post he had held for over 23 years, and retires from politics; (July 15) government publishes a bill meant to abolish racial representation in Parliament; (Aug. 21) the House of Assembly approves bill abolishing 20 seats in the House and 10 in the **Senate** reserved for Europeans; (Sept.) Senate approves bill abolishing European reserved seats; (Oct.)Parliament approves a constitutional amendment abolishing the office of prime minister and creates an executive presidency; (Dec. 22) Mugabe and Nkomo sign **Unity Pact;** (Dec. 30) Mugabe, the only candidate, is elected by Parliament to be the country's first executive president; (Dec. 31) Mugabe is inaugurated

1988 (April) Mugabe announces a general amnesty for all dissidents; (April 2) a specially called ZAPU party congress approves the Unity Pact and the party is officially amalgamated by ZANU; (April 9) ZANU party congress unanimously approves the Unity Pact and officially absorbs ZAPU; (May) the government announces the success of its dissident amnesty program and declares that dissident activity in Matabeleland is no longer a national problem; (Oct. 21) Edgar Tekere expelled from ZANU

1989 (Jan. 13) In response to growing criticism, Mugabe appoints commission, headed by Judge President of Zimbabwe Wilson Sandura, to investigate allocations of government ministers using their positions to illegally obtain automobiles from Zimbabwe's only assembly plant; (Feb.) 23-year-old state of emergency renewed for six months; **Willowdale** publicly exposed by opposition newspaper; Frederick Shava, minister of labor, admits to giving false testimony in Willowdale investigation; (March 10) Enos Nkala, minister of defense, becomes second government minister to resign after admitting to perjury before the commission investigating Willowdale; (April 14) Three additional government ministers resign after being accused of corruption as part of growing Willowdale scandal; (April 20) Maurice Nyagumbo, senior minister for political affairs, commits suicide after being implicated in Willowdale scandal; (April 30) Edgar Tekere announces formation of the **Zimbabwe Unity Movement;** (June) Mugabe announces plans to abolish Senate, adding its 40 seats to House of Assembly; (Sept.) Government announces additional plans for abolishing clauses in Constitution of 1980 which entrenched European minority rights for 10 years; (Dec. 19) ZANU Party congress held in Harare, officially unites with ZAPU

1990 Senate abolished; **House of Assembly** membership increased to 150; (March 28 and 29) Second general election since independence; only 56 percent of registered electorate votes, ZANU wins 117 seats, ZUM polls 20 percent of popular vote, but wins only two seats; (April) ZUM accuses government of rigging recent elections; (July) Mozambique border closed to all traffic, except cargo trucks and trains, in an attempt to stop MNR incursions into Zimbabwe; state of emergency lifted; (Aug. 22) ZANU politburo votes against formalizing one-party state; (Aug. 27) Mugabe grants amnesty to 200 former combatants jailed as **Dissidents** in early 1980s; (Nov. 4) Sir Humphrey **Gibbs** dies;

(Dec.) Approximately 8,000 Zimbabwe National Army troops reported to be stationed in Mozambique

1991 (Jan.) **Mugabe** announces his acceptance of ZANU's majority opinion, and will abandon the idea of a one-party state; (June) ZANU announces it has decided to renounce Marxism, Leninism, and scientific socialism; (Aug. 15) **N. Sithole** announces plans to return to Zimbabwe; (Dec. 5) Roy **Welensky** dies in London

1992 N. Sithole returns to the country, forms Zimbabwe African National Union-Ndonga party; (March 19) Parliament approves **Land Acquisition Act** allowing government to nationalize lands owned by European farmers at prices set by the government, act also bars owners from suing for unfair compensation

1993 (March) **Forum Party of Zimbabwe** created under leadership of Enoch Dumbutshena, former chief justice of Zimbabwe; (April) **Zimbabwe National Army** withdrawn from Mozambique; (May) Defense Ministry announces the merger of the army and air force under one command; (July) Health officials announce that **AIDS** (Acquired Immune Deficiency Syndrome) is leading cause of death in Bulawayo

1994 (April) Following first all-race elections in South African history, Zimbabwe establishes diplomatic relations with the government of newly elected South African President Nelson Mandela; (May) Mugabe makes first state visit to Britain since independence; (Aug.) Mugabe makes state visit to South Africa, becoming first African leader to address newly elected South African Parliament; government announces plans to increase acquisitions of European-owned farmlands; (Sept.) ZANU holds second National congress since independence and officially abandons Marxism; Mugabe declares that government will abandon policy of reconciliation between Europeans and black Africans; short-lived **United Party of Zimbabwe** created when UANC and ZUM merge under announced leadership of Edgar **Tekere** and Abel **Muzorewa;** (Oct.) ZUM resurrected by Edgar Tekere after split with Muzorewa; **N. Sithole** and 1,000 ZANU-Ndonga followers evicted from a farm by police; (Dec.) **Federal Party of Zimbabwe** founded

1995 (April 8 and 9) third general elections since independence held, with ZANU winning 63 of 65 contested Parliament seats; 55 seats won by ZANU in uncontested district elections; opposition parties polled 16 percent of the vote, with ZANU-Ndonga gaining two seats in opposition; (Oct. 7) **N. Sithole** arrested in connection with an alleged plot to assassinate Mugabe; (Oct. 21) N. Sithole released from custody without being charged

1996 (March 16 and 17) Mugabe reelected President; (June) Joshua Nkomo announces his retirement from politics due to ill health; (August–Sept.) nationwide strikes by civil servants; (Oct.) ZANU(PF) officially drops Marxism-Leninism as guiding principle; (Dec.) government announces agreement with Malawi, Mozambique, and Zambia to establish Beira Development Corridor

1997 National Constitutional Assembly founded; (March) mutual defense agreement signed with South Africa; (Oct.) Mugabe announces acceleration of national land resettlement program; (Dec. 9) nationwide general strike to protest new taxes led by Zimbabwe Congress of Trade Unions, marks entry of its leader, Morgan **Tsvangirai,** into national politics

1998 (Jan.) Government announces an increase in cost of maize meal; announcement followed by riots in major urban centers; (June) University of Zimbabwe temporarily closed by government after anti-government demonstrations; illegal occupation of white-owned commercial farms begins; (Aug.) Zimbabwe National Army troops sent to Democratic Republic of Congo; (Oct.) gvernment enters into discussions with National Constitutional Assembly on altering Constitution; end of year sees the rapid devaluation of national currency

1999 (March) Mugabe appoints a commission of inquiry to investigate changing Constitution following the NCA's withdrawal from bilateral discussions; (April) Mugabe announces Zimbabwe will sever relations with the International Monetary Fund and World Bank after they threaten to suspend payments because of government corruption and mismanagement of the national economy; (July 2) Joshua **Nkomo** dies; (Sept. 11) **Movement for Democratic Change** (MDC) launched

2000 (Feb. 12 and 13) National referendum on new constitution defeated, with opposition groups polling 55 percent of the vote; (March) veterans of war for independence greatly increase pace of occupation of white-owned commercial farms; (June 23 and 24) Parliamentary elections, ZANU(PF) wins 62 seats while opposition MDC wins 57

INTRODUCTION

Zimbabwe is a completely landlocked country, located between the Zambezi and Limpopo rivers in southern Africa. It shares its borders with four larger neighbors: Botswana, Zambia, Mozambique, and South Africa. Its area of 389,370 square kilometers (150,333 sq. mi.) is roughly the same as that of Japan or California. In 2000 it had a population of approximately 13 million people.

Modern human beings have been present in Zimbabwe for at least 100,000 years. Their hominid antecedents existed in the region for perhaps an additional million years. Because of this long heritage, the country possesses a wealth of Stone Age remains, the most striking of which are the nearly 1,500 rock painting sites of the Late Stone Age, which commenced around 9000 B.C. In the early centuries of the modern era, intrusive Iron Age cultures began absorbing and displacing the Stone Age peoples, giving rise to the first metal and ceramic industries and to agriculture. These earliest Iron Age peoples were most probably Bantu-speaking immigrants from the north. By around A.D. 1000, the ancestors of the modern Shona-speaking peoples were in the ascendent throughout Zimbabwe. Cattle-keeping became important, and a trade in gold and ivory was initiated with Indian Ocean ports.

The early centuries of the second millennium saw the rise of a purely indigenous stone-building tradition, originating in the southeastern part of the country at the place now known as Great Zimbabwe. Great Zimbabwe, magnificent in its stone architecture, became the political, religious, economic, and cultural center of a large state system that flourished until the mid-15th century. The impressive city-state was then abandoned and the stone-building tradition shifted west to focus on a site now known as Khami, near present Bulawayo. The apparent political heirs of the Great Zimbabwe state moved north, however, founding the famous Munhumutapa kingdom in the Zambezi Valley.

By the 16th century the Munhumutapa kingdom dominated the northern part of Zimbabwe and parts of Mozambique. There it controlled the trade routes to the Muslim ports of the east coast. During this same period Portuguese forces displaced the Muslim rulers and traders of the coast, and began attempting to control the inland sources of gold. Contacts between the Shona and the Portuguese were alternately cooperative and hostile. In the 17th century the Portuguese made increasingly aggressive attempts to control Muhumutapa commerce directly. Their efforts brought them little success, but nevertheless contributed to the weakening of the Munhumutapa state. The resulting disorder allowed independent Shona dynasties to increase their autonomy at Munhumutapa's expense.

In the late 17th century a southwestern Shona state known to historians both as "Changamire" after its rulers and as "Rozvi" after a nickname for its peoples, rapidly developed into a major power. Changamire forces drove the Portuguese out of the country in the northeast and reduced the Munhumutapa and many other Shona states to tributary status, becoming Zimbabwe's dominant political and military power through the 18th century.

By the early 19th century the Changamire empire was in internal disarray. Before these political problems could be resolved, the country was invaded by a succession of more militaristic Nguni-speaking bands from South Africa. These bands were spawned by the upheavals known as the *Mfecane*. During the 1830s several different bands known as Ngoni passed through Zimbabwe. Before crossing the Zambezi River to the north, some of these Ngoni killed the reigning Changamire ruler, sacked population centers, disrupted trade patterns, and left the region in political and commercial chaos. These transient invaders were soon followed by other Nguni, who established permanent homes in Zimbabwe. The Ndebele (or Matabele) of Mzilikazi occupied the center of the former Changamire state, where they eventually made Bulawayo their capital. Meanwhile, the Gaza (or Shangane) of Soshangane settled in the border region east of the Sabi River. These two intrusive groups prevented the vastly more numerous Shona peoples from reorganizing large-scale polities by raiding their communities, disrupting trade, and manipulating local politics. In no sense did the Ndebele and Gaza "conquer" the entire region of present Zimbabwe, but throughout the rest of the 19th century these new invaders—particularly the Ndebele—dominated the region's politics and commerce.

The mid-19th century saw a resurgence of European interest in the region of present Zimbabwe. This time Europeans entered not from the east, but from the south. Hunters in search of ivory, missionaries, traders, and concessionaries were among the first Europeans into the region. The Ndebele rulers monopolized European access to the country, giving outsiders an exaggerated impression of their control over the Shona. Thus, when the region began attracting the attention of the European imperial powers in the late 1880s, the Ndebele kingdom became the focus of diplomatic rivalries.

In 1888 agents of the South African financier and politician Cecil Rhodes obtained a mining concession from the Ndebele king Lobengula. Known as the Rudd Concession, it provided the legal basis for the new British South Africa Company (BSAC) to obtain a British Royal Charter, which it did in the following year. In 1890 the BSAC sent a small occupying force into Mashonaland, the eastern part of the country, establishing its headquarters at Fort Salisbury (now Harare). European settlement developed rapidly, extending into the western half of the country (Matabeleland) after a brief war was fought against the Ndebele in 1893.

Few Africans recognized British sovereignty in Zimbabwe during this period, despite BSAC claims. Africans bitterly resented cattle seizures, land alienations, forced labor recruitment, and other abuses forced upon them by the European occupiers. In early 1896 the majority of subjects of the then-dormant Ndebele kingdom rose in revolt. They were soon followed by many Shona in the central and northeastern parts of the country. The British were not able to suppress these uprisings until late 1897. Though badly shaken, the BSAC retained its Royal Charter. It reorganized its administration, granting limited reforms that gave Africans some relief from prior abuses. Africans, however, remained virtually excluded from the legislative representation granted to European settlers in 1898. It was during this period that the territory was officially designated Southern Rhodesia.

Over the next 25 years European mining interests were paramount in the country's colonial economic development. In 1923 the BSAC turned over responsibility for the country to the British imperial government, but the settlers were granted a form of self-government under a constitution that remained in effect for the next 38 years. Although Britain officially retained reserve powers over African affairs in the country, in practice the local government arrogated to itself increasing authority for all local matters. The settler-dominated government was thus able to enact discriminatory laws affecting land allocation, labor rights, and other important matters, with little regard for either British imperial oversight or local African opinion, though the latter grew increasingly outspoken. The country, economically and politically dominated by its European minority, was a British "colony" in name only.

From 1953 through 1963 Southern Rhodesia, Northern Rhodesia (now Zambia), and Nyasaland (now Malawi) joined together to form the Federation of Rhodesia and Nyasaland. Southern Rhodesia dominated the federation, reaping the largest share of the economic benefits that it generated. Many Southern Rhodesian settlers hoped to transform the federation into a white-controlled dominion within the British Commonwealth, but they were met by vigorous African opposition. African protest eventually doomed the federation, forcing a reevaluation of Rhodesia's (as the country was called from 1963 to 1979) own constitutional future.

Negotiations between Britain, the Rhodesian government, and African nationalists produced a new constitution in 1961. However, while this document theoretically recognized the eventuality of majority rule in the country, it actually granted Africans only limited parliamentary representation through a complex double-roll voting system. Britain refused to grant Rhodesia full independence until the settler government provided satisfactory guarantees that majority rule would in fact be attained. The settler government refused to provide these guarantees, and thereby created a constitutional impasse. In November 1965 Prime Minister Ian Smith issued the Unilateral Declaration of Independence (UDI), in an effort to overcome that impasse by asserting his government's de facto independence from Britain.

World criticism of UDI was immediate and harsh. The United Nations soon began voting increasingly strong economic sanctions against Rhodesia, and the Smith government failed to gain international political recognition. The Smith government had planned for the possibility of sanctions, and although some export-oriented industries, such as tobacco, suffered greatly the short-term effect of sanctions were generally minimized. The government also promoted greater crop diversification in the commercial agricultural sector of the economy, and organized sanctions-busting strategies for both export and import commodities—particularly oil—which helped to reduce the economic impact of sanctions through the mid-1970s. The sanctions-busting strategies were able to succeed largely because of the continued support of Rhodesia by the governments of Portugal and South Africa. Both countries—Portugal through its colony of Mozambique—consistently channeled trade to Rhodesia, and South Africa assisted the Smith government with financial and military support.

Meanwhile, important developments had been occurring within the nationalist movement. The National Democratic Party (NDP), the successor to the African National Congress (ANC), had been formed in January 1960 to actively demand more rapid constitutional change aimed at greater African political participation in the country. The NDP organized a June 1961 referendum among Africans, and a series of mass meetings throughout the remainder of that year, to demonstrate opposition to the limited changes embodied in the 1961 constitution. The government responded to this growing opposition by banning the NDP in early December. African nationalist leaders then formed the Zimbabwe African People's Union (ZAPU) on December 17, 1961, and while they adopted the NDP's general policies and strategies, they also called for increased "action programs" designed to bring about majority rule. ZAPU's call for increasingly more militant programs resulted in its banning in September 1962. A split developed within ZAPU over the issue of tactics to be used in confronting the government. ZAPU leader Joshua Nkomo wanted to form a government in exile, while dissident members under Ndabaningi Sithole argued for a policy of mass organization and political action within the country. On August 8, 1963, these dissidents formed the Zimbabwe African National Union (ZANU). The settler government again responded to this continued call for African opposition to its policies by banning ZANU and the People's Caretaker Council (PCC)—a ZAPU front organization—and arresting nationalist leaders in the country. The majority of these leaders from both ZAPU and ZANU spent most of the next decade in detention camps and prisons.

In response to the persistent repression of African political activities and the arrest of their leaders, both ZANU and ZAPU established externally based political headquarters and created military organizations in Zambia between mid-1964 and mid-1965. The armed struggle to liberate Zimbabwe was launched on April 28, 1966, when members of ZANU's military wing—the Zimbabwe African National Liberation Army (ZANLA)—engaged Rhodesian security forces in what has become known as the Battle of Chinhoyi. Within several months this was followed by engagements between security forces and members of the Zimbabwe People's Revolutionary Army (ZIPRA), the military wing of ZAPU. These early skirmishes were generally decided in favor of the government security forces, and both ZANLA and ZIPRA were forced to cut back operations inside the country and reevaluate their tactics. With the liberation of the northwestern provinces of Mozambique in 1972 by FRELIMO—Mozambique's liberation movement—the armed struggle intensified, as ZANLA increased infiltration into the northeastern districts of the country and utilized guerrilla warfare tactics. With the independence of Mozambique in 1975, the entire eastern border of the country was opened up to increased ZANLA activity. Beginning in late 1976,

ZIPRA, responding to Zambian criticism of its apparent hesitancy to operate inside Rhodesia, stepped up its activities in the western districts of the country. The Rhodesian government was forced to respond with larger call-ups of European males to active military service, and increasingly allocated more of the national budget into military expenses.

By the mid-1970s, as a result of a combination of the escalation of the military conflict, sanctions, and increasing international—including South African—diplomatic pressure, the Rhodesian government agreed to participate in a number of diplomatic efforts to peacefully end the constitutional impasse, but every international effort failed. Then in late 1977, Smith initiated contact with African leaders inside the country. In March 1978 Smith announced that the meetings with Abel Muzorewa, Ndabaningi Sithole, and Jeremiah Chirau had culminated in agreement on an internal settlement that would end European minority rule and institute a new government based on the principles of majority rule. The internal settlement was denounced by the Patriotic Front (PF), a political alliance between ZANU and ZAPU, the leaders of the country's African-ruled neighboring states (known as the frontline states), and the United Nations. Nevertheless, in April 1979, after the four internal leaders took nearly a year to agree on a new constitution, elections were held in which African voters were eligible for the first time to vote for national leaders. The United African National council (UANC), under the leadership of Abel Muzorewa, won a majority of seats in the national parliament. On May 30, 1979 the Republic of Zimbabwe Rhodesia was officially declared, ending nearly 90 years of European minority rule of the country.

With the single exception of the white minority ruled government of South Africa, the Muzorewa government failed to gain international recognition. Sanctions were maintained and the liberation war continued. Simultaneously, the newly elected British government of Margaret Thatcher was subjected to mounting pressure from British Commonwealth nations to find a diplomatic solution to the constitutional impasse that had existed for nearly 15 years. The Thatcher government responded by issuing invitations to the Patriotic Front and the government of Zimbabwe Rhodesia to a conference at Lancaster House in London. The conference lasted form September 10 to December 22, 1979, and by its conclusion the parties had agreed to a new constitution, free elections, a British-administered transition period, and a cease-fire. Near the end of the conference, on December 12, the Zimbabwe Rhodesia parliament voted to cease its existence as an independent state and return to colonial status. Later that day, the newly appointed British governor, Lord Christopher Soames, arrived in the country and officially took charge of the government—the constitutional impasse had ended.

In internationally monitored elections held in February 1980 ZANU, led by Robert Mugabe, won a commanding majority of seats in the new Parliament. On April 18, 1980 ceremonies in the capital officially marked the inauguration of the Independent Republic of Zimbabwe.

The government of Prime Minister Mugabe (the office was abolished in 1987 and replaced with the office of executive president, which Mugabe has held since that time) announced a policy of reconciliation toward his political ZAPU opponents in Parliament and with the whites who had remained in the country. He offered government ministerial positions to members from both groups, increased spending on education and health services (particularly in the rural areas), granted material and financial support to African farmers, and raised the minimum wage for the majority of African workers. Due to a combination of increased agricultural and industrial production as a result of the ending of fighting and the ending of international sanctions, the economy soared. It was a strong beginning for the newly independent republic.

However, the national exhilaration did not last long. A severe drought in the early 1980s, coupled with the continuation of civil warfare in Mozambique and open hostility by the minority government in South Africa, adversely affected the economy. In addition, the rivalry between ZANU and ZAPU supporters reemerged into open conflict throughout the country. There was a resurgence of guerrilla activities in Matabeleland. In an attempt to eliminate the so-called "dissidents," the newly created Zimbabwe National Army (ZNA) scoured the rural areas of Matabeleland—in the process, several thousand civilians in the region were killed. Nkomo fled the country, claiming that government troops had tried to murder him during an early morning raid on his home. Political conflict between the two parties and their supporters reached a climax immediately prior to the 1985 elections. Although ZANU again won a majority of seats in Parliament and Mugabe was easily re-elected, the fears of a civil war were extremely high. At that point, under the moral persuasion and political savvy of President Canaan Banana, Mugabe and Nkomo entered into negotiations to end the contentiousness between ZANU and ZAPU. These negotiations resulted in the 1987 Unity Pact, in which the two parties merged and agreed to create a new executive presidential form of government. In early 1988 Mugabe was elected by Parliament to fill the position of executive president and, to officially mark the ending of the conflicts between the two former opponents, Mugabe appointed Nkomo a co-vice president in the newly formatted presidential system and issued a general amnesty to all ZAPU dissidents.

While open armed opposition ended with the merger of ZANU and ZAPU, political opposition did not. With the ZANU-ZAPU merger, Mugabe announced that he planned to fulfill his long-held goal of creating a socialist inspired one-party state in Zimbabwe. In response, his onetime colleague Edgar Tekere announced the formation of the Zimbabwe Unity Movement (ZUM). Under Tekere's leadership, ZUM called for an open market economy and a multiparty democracy. He ran for the presidency, in opposition to Mugabe, in the July 1990 elections but lost by a ratio of five-to-one. Despite Tekere and ZUM's electoral losses, there was a growing opposition to the creation of a one-party state in Zimbabwe. In August, a large majority of the central committee of Mugabe's own party, ZANU, voted against the policy. Citing the end of the Cold War, they argued that the idea of a one-party state was passe and that continuing the policy would harm Zimbabwe's international standing and negatively impact the possibility of international financial assistance and aid.

During the early 1990s the country suffered through yet another devastating drought. The resulting economic slump caused people to begin to increasingly question ZANU's, and in particular Mugabe's, ability to continue to govern the country. To try to offset the declining popularity of ZANU and his presidency, Mugabe announced in 1991 that the government had accepted an Economic Structural Adjustment Program (ESAP) formulated by the World Bank and the International Monetary Fund. Government ministers argued that this would eventually strengthen the economy, thereby creating economic stability and greater employment. Initially the results of ESAP, particularly on the country's poor, were quite the opposite. In turn, this increased the growing disillusionment with Mugabe and the general apathy toward the government. To ameliorate the impact of ESAP, Mugabe announced in early 1995 that the government was instituting a series of programs aimed at developing the rural areas and improving the lives of the country's poor. However, the disillusionment and apathy remained, with the turnout for the 1995 elections being extremely low.

The trends of the early 1990s were further exasperbated in the second half of the decade as economic conditions continued to worsen and political turmoil increased. Although it initially appeared that the economy was recovering, government policies announced in early 1997 began to drastically undermine its vitality. In that year the government made a series of unbudgeted payments to several groups in attempts to silence their criticisms of its financial policies. For instance, in response to criticisms that it had not done enough to help war veterans, the government promised to pay out nearly Z$4.5 billion in unbudgeted funds as pensions. The economy was further destabilized in mid-1998 following President Mugabe's announcement that Zimbabwe would send ZNA troops to the Congo to support that country's embattled president, Laurent Kabila. The ensuing increased spending on military hardware and other war costs were reportedly averaging US$1 million a day by the end of the decade. These unsound economic policies eventually resulted in the World Bank and International Monetary Fund suspending their ESAP payments. Their actions were quickly followed by drastic reductions in other foreign investments in Zimbabwe.

By late 1998 the government was faced with a generalized decline in both domestic and foreign confidence in the economy. By the end of the decade some financial observers were saying that the economy was collapsing, citing high, and rising, unemployment levels and increasing inflation rates as evidence. In addition, by the end of the decade the Zimbabwe dollar had devalued seventy-five percent from its 1996 level. Government critics pointed to this precipitous decline of the national currency as the greatest indicator that the economy was in free fall.

Politically, the government's mismanagement of the economy and its unpopular involvement in the war in Congo added to the view, particularly among those people living in the country's urban centers, that ZANU had lost touch with the needs of the people. In particular, the belief that President Mugabe was no longer up to the task of leading the nation intensified. In response to the rising level of criticism of both his government and himself, President Mugabe heightened his attacks on his opponents. While he verbally assaulted those who publicly spoke against his policies—for instance, editors of the country's few independent newspapers and leaders of the nation's largely urban based labor unions—police and ZANU supporters began to disrupt public rallies where criticisms of President Mugabe or the government were voiced.

However, despite these disruptions a popularly backed opposition movement began to develop in Zimbabwe for the first time since the 1987 Unity Pact had been signed. Led by Morgan Tsvangirai, formerly the general secretary of the nation's largest trade union organization, the Movement for Democratic Change (MDC) was launched in late 1999. Its founders argued that a new voice was necessary in order to contest national policies they claimed were evidence of ZANU's corruption and President Mugabe's increasingly autocratic rule. In early 2000 the MDC led the opposition to a national referendum on changing the Constitution that had been called for by Mugabe. He argued that a "yes" vote would make it easier for the government to confiscate land owned by the country's white farmers, thereby providing land to the county's poor and finally ending the century-long control of the economy by whites. The MDC argued that the changes would further entrench President Mugabe's personal control of the government. In a February election, the referendum was defeated and many critics of the government were quick to infer that the vote had also been a referendum on Mugabe's presidency. While MDC did not publicly agree with that inference, it did announce that it would challenge ZANU candidates for every constituency in the parliamentary elections that were scheduled for later that year. In the months leading up to the elections thousands of squatters, led by Chimurenga war veterans, began to systematically invade hundreds of white-owned farms. The country's courts repeatedly declared the farm seizures illegal and ordered the squatters evicted. However, President Mugabe expressed his support of the squatters' actions and consistently ignored the courts' rulings. He argued that the farm invasions were a popular expression of the people's frustration over the outcome of the referendum. Despite a campaign often marred by violence, primarily aimed at MDC candidates and their supporters, in June elections the MDC won 57 of 120 contested seats, thereby becoming the first major parliamentary opposition in the country since independence.

THE DICTIONARY

A

ABA-. Sindebele class prefix for the plural forms of many nouns and names for people (sing., *um-*, or *umu-*). In accordance with modern English usage, such prefixes are dropped from proper names in this dictionary. Thus, e.g., for Abananzwa, see **Nanzwa.** Note that before stems with the initial *e*, *aba-* becomes *abe-*. Thus, for *abenhla*, see **Enhla.** (see also **Ama-**.)

ABERCORN. James Hamilton, the 2nd Duke of Abercorn (1838–1913), was the first president of the BSAC (1889–1913). The present town of **Shamwa** was originally named after him.

ABRAHAM, DONALD P. British historian. He came to the country in 1947 to work for the Native Department, later becoming a research fellow at the **University College** (1960–67). During this period he collected an immense body of Shona oral traditions and did archival research on Shona history in Portugal. His scattered articles on Shona history, though full of contradictions, remain seminal works on early Shona history (see **Bibliography**).

ABUTUA see **BUTUA**

ADENDORFF TREK (a.k.a. Banyailand Trek). In August 1890 Louis Adendorff and several other Transvaal **Afrikaners** obtained a written land concession from two **Karanga** chiefs. These chiefs, Chivasa (Sebasa) and Nyajena Musavi (Mazobi), wished to enlist Afrikaner mercenaries to help defend their people against Ndebele raids. When Cecil Rhodes later visited the transvaal, he met Adendorff, who tried to sell him the concession. Rhodes rejected the offer as worthless, on the grounds that because the chiefs were vassals of the Ndebele, their territory was covered by the BSAC's **Rudd Concession**, which the company was using as a legal pretext for occupying **Mashonaland.** Adendorff then advertised widely in South African newspapers for Afrikaners to form a 2,000-man trek to create a "republic" in "Banyailand" (see **Nyai**). The BSAC regarded this venture as a serious threat to British predominance north of the Limpopo

River and persuaded the **Transvaal**'s President Paul Kruger to oppose the trek. On June 24, 1891, about 100 trekkers appeared at the Limpopo. A heavily armed detachment of the BSAP prevented their crossing and **L. S. Jameson** persuaded them to disperse. Some of the trekkers, including their commander, a Col. Ignateus Ferreira, accepted the BSAC's offer to settle in Mashonaland as individuals (see also **Moodie Trek**).

ADMINISTRATOR OF BSAC GOVERNMENT (1890–1923). During the 33 years that the BSAC ruled the country, the senior official in the government was the administrator. Organization of the government was rather haphazard until 1898, when the British government issued an Order-in-Council. This edict created an **Executive Council** and **Legislative Council**, with the administrator presiding over both. The administrator also served as secretary for native affairs, appointing magistrates and native commissioners. Although ultimate authority lay with the British government and the BSAC board of directors, in practice the administrators exercised considerable local power. *Administrators of Mashonaland, 1890–1901*: 1890–91 A. R. Colquhoun; 1891–94 L. S. Jameson; 1898–1901 W. H. Milton. *Administrator of Matabeleland, 1898–1901*: 1898–1901 A. Lawley (subordinate to Milton). *Administrators of Southern Rhodesia*: 1894–96 L. S. Jameson; 1896–97 A. H. G. (Earl) Grey; 1897–98 W. H. Milton (acting); 1901–14 W. H. Milton; 1914–23 F. P. D. Chaplin.

AFRICAN DAILY NEWS **(ADN).** Perhaps the most important newspaper published in the country for African readers prior to independence, *ADN* was issued from Salisbury between 1956 and 1964. **African Newspapers, Ltd.** founded the paper in response to urging by **Garfield Todd,** who was anxious for a propaganda vehicle to help counter a developing African miners' strike. The government initially subsidized and helped to distribute *ADN,* giving the paper a progovernment stigma that lasted until 1962. In that year the new management of African Newspapers changed the *ADN*'s editorial policy to a strongly pro-African stance. *ADN* then became the only nonparty paper in the country that voiced African nationalist opinions. It relentlessly criticized the new Rhodesian Front government, calling attention to a wide variety of issues ignored by the rest of the country's **press.** On August 26, 1964, Ian Smith banned *ADN,* terminating its publication. (See **Censorship**).

AFRICAN FARMERS' UNION. Organization established in 1933 under the leadership of **Aaron Jacha** to represent the interests of African private farmers in **Purchase Areas**. Following independence and the incorporation of Purchase Areas into **Communal Lands,** the organization's name was changed to Zimbabwe National Farmers' Union.

AFRICAN LAND HUSBANDRY ACT. Name by which the **Native Land Husbandry Act** is retrospectively known.

AFRICAN METHODIST EPISCOPAL (AMC) CHURCH. American-based black church with worldwide mission program. Richard Allen, a freed slave, founded the church in Philadelphia in 1816 because of racial discrimination in the established Methodist Church. AME church leaders and missionaries came to South Africa in the late 1890s in response to interest by African independent church leaders, many of whom quickly affiliated with AME. American AME officials tried to enter Southern Rhodesia, but were kept out by the administration. South African AME missionaries then entered the country. The most important of these pioneers was Moses Makgatho, a Sotho who bought a farm outside of Bulawayo. Makgatho's farm remained the center of AME operations in the country for the next 25 years. In 1927 Zephaniah Cam Mtshwelo, a South African Thembu, was appointed head of the AME Southern Rhodesian church. Under his leadership the church expanded rapidly, building missions and schools throughout the country. The government prohibited AME from working in the **reserves,** so it operated mainly in urban areas and in African mine compounds. The church's purely black leadership and urban emphasis contrasted sharply with the rural emphasis of white-dominated missions.

AFRICAN NATIONAL CONGRESS (ANC). The country's modern congress movement started in 1934, when **Aaron Jacha** founded the Bantu Congress. Though this organization had been inspired by the large ANC of South Africa, it attracted a small membership through the 1930s. Its political goals were modest, mainly featuring appeals for exemption of educated Africans from discriminatory laws. Its leaders protested the **Industrial Conciliation Act**, but registered approval of the **Land Apportionment Act** before the **Bledisloe Commission**.

Under the leadership of **T. D. Samkange**, the movement experienced a minor resurgence after the Second World War, by which time it was known as the Southern Rhodesian African National Congress. The ANC failed to catch on as a national mass movement, however, and was moribund by the early 1950s. Only the Bulawayo branch of the ANC survived the defection of leaders to multiracial, Federation-oriented parties and societies, and that branch operated mainly as a social organization. This early phase of ANC became known, retrospectively, as the "Old African National Congress."

On September 12, 1957—a date chosen because of its significance to settlers as "Occupation Day"—the ANC was reformed by the leaders of the **Youth League**, which it effectively replaced. **Joshua Nkomo** was made president, and **James Chikerema**, vice-president. Other early leaders included **Jason Moyo** and **George Nyandoro**. The new ANC quickly attracted mass support in both urban and rural areas throughout the country. Employing strictly constitutional means of seeking redress, ANC protested the **pass laws, Native Land Husbandry Act**, and other discriminatory laws, and demanded universal adult suffrage. Its leaders wrote letters and petitions to the government and organized large public demonstrations. By 1959 the government estimated ANC membership at 6,000 to 7,000 people, while ANC supporters claimed a membership of 30 to 40 times greater. Nonracial in orientation, ANC attracted more than a hundred European members, including Guy Clutton-Brock, who later became the only European arrested because of ANC activities.

Alarmed by civil disturbances north of the Zambezi and by the supposed subversive influence of ANC—particularly in rural areas— Edgar Whitehead's government declared a state of emergency and arrested nearly 500 ANC leaders in a sudden morning sweep on February

26, 1959. The government banned ANC, later passing the **Unlawful Organizations Act** further to restrict ANC leaders. The government's ruthless and largely unexpected action demoralized nationalists during the remainder of the year and caused a further revulsion against the concept of **"partnership."** The **National Democratic Party** was founded as a successor organization on the first day of 1960.

AFRICAN NATIONAL COUNCIL (ANC). The African National Council was founded in December 1971, as a temporary pressure group opposing the Anglo-Rhodesian Settlement proposals. To avoid government reprisals, it was organized as a public interest council, rather than as a political party. Two Methodist ministers without prior political reputations, **Abel Muzorewa** and **Canaan Banana**, headed the council. Other leaders, mostly veterans of ZAPU and ZANU, included **Edison Sithole, Josiah Chinamano,** and **Michael Mawema**. The name of the council was consciously chosen to recall the ANC acronym of the older and highly respected **African National Council**.

ANC branches arose spontaneously throughout the country. By the time the **Pearce Commission** arrived in early 1972, the ANC was well represented in both urban and rural areas. While its central executive served primarily to disseminate information, it has been given major credit for convincing the Pearce Commission of African hostility to the settlement proposals. Following the Pearce Commission's hearings, the ANC merged with the internal branches of **ZANU, ZAPU,** and **FROLIZI** and reconstituted itself as a permanent political organization. It favored a negotiated settlement with Britain that would be acceptable to all citizens of the country. Muzorewa was retained as president.

The **Ian Smith** government never moved to proscribe the ANC, but severely hindered its organizing efforts by banning the sale of membership cards, prohibiting acceptance of foreign funds, and arresting and generally harassing leaders. Nevertheless, the ANC remained officially committed to nonviolent change, calling upon the government to participate in a national constitutional conference in order to bring about majority rule. By late 1972 Muzorewa was rumored to be holding secret negotiations with Smith. Further meetings in 1973 were more openly acknowledged.

In late 1974 changing international conditions forced the Smith government reluctantly to accept the demands of both the leaders of the **Frontline States** and South Africa to release several detained nationalist leaders and to begin negotiations. In December, the external leaders of the formerly rival ZANU, ZAPU, and FROLIZI announced that they had united under the "umbrella" of the ANC, and agreed to join in negotiations with the Smith government. The agreed-upon constitutional negotiations finally began at the **Victoria Falls Conference** in August 1975. The conference was a complete failure, and was followed by a split of the ANC into two factions, one led by **Joshua Nkomo**, and the other by Muzorewa. Nkomo returned to the country under the banner of ANC (Zimbabwe), and held private talks with Smith in early 1976. Muzorewa and his faction, renamed the United African National Council (UANC), remained outside the country.

In October 1976, following an initiative by U.S. Secretary of State Henry Kissinger, the British government convened the **Geneva Conference**. The UANC delegation was headed by Muzorewa, who insisted that in any transitional government, whites be barred from retaining any form of control over ministries concerned with defense and internal security. This condition, along with additional disputes by other delegations (which included the **Patriotic Front** and the Smith regime), caused the conference to be adjourned in December, never to reconvene. In early 1977 Muzorewa and the UANC leadership returned to the country. In December, **Muzorewa; Ndabaningi Sithole,** who headed a group known as UANC (Sithole); **Chief Jeremiah Chirau,** leader of ZUPO; and **James Chikerema** joined in negotiations with the Smith government. These talks were the result of a government strategy to bypass the more militant and radical external liberation organizations of ZANU and ZAPU, and reach a settlement with the more conservative internal nationalist leaders. These negotiations culminated with the signing of the **Internal Settlement** on March 3, 1978. Muzorewa was officially to share power with the other four men as a member of an executive council. Also based upon this agreement, elections were held in April 1979. The UANC garnered 68 percent of the total vote and won 51 seats in the new **Assembly**. Muzorewa was asked to form a government, and the country was officially renamed "**Zimbabwe Rhodesia**." He then appointed a coalition cabinet with **Rhodesian Front** and **United Federal Party** members. This UANC government was never officially recognized by any other country; as a result, diplomatic and economic **sanctions**, as well as the war inside the country, continued.

Following the Commonwealth Heads of State and Government Conference held in Lusaka in August 1979 the British government issued invitations to a Constitutional Conference to be held in London. The **Lancaster House Conference** began on September 10 with Muzorewa and Smith representing the Zimbabwe Rhodesia government, and Joshua Nkomo and **Robert Mugabe** speaking for the Patriotic Front. By October 22 an agreement had been reached. The UANC was one of nine political parties that contested 80 Assembly seats in the elections of April 1980. Mugabe's ZANU (RF) won 57 seats, Nkomo's ZAPU (PF) won 20, and the UANC under Muzorewa won only three. In the general elections of July 1985 the UANC was unable to win even a single seat.

AFRICAN NATIONAL YOUTH LEAGUE see YOUTH LEAGUE

AFRICAN NEWSPAPERS, LTD. (ANL). White-owned and -managed group of newspapers published between 1943 and 1964 (see **Press**). Publication of newspapers for African readers had begun with the *Bantu Mirror* in the 1930s. In 1943 ANL was started in Southern Rhodesia by B. G. and C. A. G. Paver, South African brothers who managed Bantu Press in Johannesburg. With the encouragement of the Southern Rhodesian government, ANL acquired control of the *Bantu Mirror* in Bulawayo, and started *African Weekly* in Salisbury. Publications later added included *The Harvester* for African farmers and *The Recorder* for teachers. In 1956 *African Daily News* was begun. Although the management of the ANL cooperated closely with the government to make its publications politically innocuous, the mainly African editorial and writing staffs were allowed considerable freedom through the 1950s.

The ANL group was owned by a consortium comprising the Anglo-American Corporation, Rhodesian Selection Trust, Imperial Tobacco, and the BSAC, but these companies are said to have interfered less in editorial policy than did the government. In 1962 the consortium sold ANL to Lord Thompson, the owner of London's *Sunday Times* and other papers. Under the new ownership, *African Daily News* began developing a strongly pro-African-nationalist editorial policy. This change increasingly irritated the Rhodesian Front government, which had come in about the same time. In August 1964 the government banned the *Daily News*. It and other ANL publications then ceased publication. (See also **Argus Group; Censorship.**)

AFRICAN PURCHASE AREAS (APA) see **PURCHASE AREAS**

THE AFRICAN TIMES. Biweekly government-published newspaper, distributed free to Africans by the Ministry of Information. The Rhodesian Front government started the paper in 1965, after it had effectively suppressed the **African Newspapers, Ltd.** group. By the mid-1970s the government was circulating c.500,000 copies of the propaganda sheet, which it claimed were being read by 2,000,000 Africans. A parallel publication, *Rhodesian Commentary,* was also being published for recent settlers in six different European languages. (N.B.: an independent commercial newspaper named *The African Times* was briefly published in **Fort Victoria** in 1963.)

AFRICAN WEEKLY. An **African Newspapers, Ltd.** publication started in Salisbury in 1943 as a Mashonaland counterpart of the older *Bantu Mirror,* published in Bulawayo. In 1962 it and the *Mirror* were merged in the *Daily News* weekend edition.

AFRICAN WORKERS' VOICE ASSOCIATION see under **BUROMBO, BENJAMIN**

AFRIKANER PEOPLE (a.k.a. **Boers;** South African or Cape Dutch). South African people of Dutch, French, and other non-English European descent who speak Afrikaans as their first language have been known as Afrikaners since the early 19th century. The Afrikaners originated in the Cape Colony (now South Africa's Cape Province) in the 17th century, spreading throughout the South African interior only since the 1830s. Afrikaner migrants of the 1830s, known as Voortrekkers, clashed with the **Ndebele kingdom** then in the **Transvaal**, helping to drive the Ndebele into present Zimbabwe (see **Potgieter, A. H.**). Afterwards the Voortrekkers established many small republics and two large ones: the Transvaal and the Orange Free State.

Transvaalers began hunting and trading in the Matabeleland during the 1860s (see, e.g., **Viljoen, J.**). By the 1880s the possibility of Afrikaner expansion north of the Limpopo River was a real threat, providing Cecil Rhodes with one of his main incentives for acquiring **Mashonaland** and **Matabeleland** for Britain (see **Adendorff Trek**). Nevertheless, during the 1890s hundreds of Afrikaner families migrated into Mashonaland, where they became the majority white populations in many rural districts (see, e.g., **Moodie Trek**). Between the 1920s and the 1950s Afrikaner settlers constituted roughly one-sixth to one-fifth of the country's whole white population, making them the most important white ethnic group, aside from British-derived settlers.

AGRICULTURE. Agricultural activity apparently began in the region of present Zimbabwe with the arrival of **Iron Age** peoples early in the first millennium A.D. By the 19th century the **Shona** peoples were primarily farmers, with some **cattle** and smaller livestock. The main Shona crops were **millets, maize**, and sorghums—all of which were also grown extensively by the **Ndebele** after their arrival in the country. Other crops included **groundnuts, yams, pumpkins, beans, rice**, and **citrus fruits**, as well as **cotton** and **tobacco**. The Ndebele kept more cattle than did the Shona, but these were used largely for social rather than purely economic functions. No draft animals were used, and plowing was done by hand.

Production figures for the precolonial era are not obtainable, but the Ndebele are known to have produced sufficient grain surpluses to export sizable quantities outside the country. When Europeans began occupying the country in the 1890s, they found that African farmers were able to expand production of food crops to meet the needs of the new mining compounds and emerging urban centers. This emerging African peasantry remained viable in only a few areas of the country through the late 1920s.

In 1907 the directors of the BSAC issued a report stating that income from the country's **gold** resources was not sufficient to support the administration of the territory. The directors stated that to ensure the country's long-term survival, a new policy based on the promotion of European commercial farming was necessary. Over the next three decades, both the BSAC administration and the settler-controlled governments after 1923 (see **Responsible Government Movement**) actively intervened in the country's economic development in order to establish and support settler commercial agriculture over African peasant production. Government support for settler farmers came in many forms, including recruitment and financial assistance to immigrate and purchase farms through settlement schemes; low-cost development loans through a government sponsored Land Bank; crop research to develop both better farming methods and better yielding varieties of crops; African labor recruitment; government assistance in establishing foreign markets; and legislation beneficial to European farmers such as the **Land Apportionment Act** of 1930, and the Maize Control Act of 1931. African peasant producers were not benefitted by any of these developments, which were specifically directed at weakening, if not destroying African competition for domestic markets, particularly in maize production.

The Second World War revolutionized European commercial agriculture by greatly expanding markets within the British Empire. After the war a rapid influx of new immigrants increased the numbers of European farmers, stimulating more efficient organization of commercial farming, increased mechanization, and continued scientific research. During the 1950s the most intensive development occurred in the **Mashonaland** provinces, where tobacco production in particular boomed, while the drier provinces developed ranching and extensive maize production. By the early 1960s commercial agriculture accounted for one-third of the country's total foreign exchange and nearly 35 percent of all people employed in the wage economy.

International **sanctions** instituted in response to **UDI** affected European commercial agriculture more severely than any other economic sector. By 1975 over one-half of the country's tobacco growers, producers of the main export crop at UDI, were forced out of business. One of the more important aspects of sanctions was the government's encouragement and support of crop diversification by commercial farmers. As a result of both sanctions-busting and crop diversification, the commercial sector emerged from the war of liberation period in a strong position. It was able to meet domestic needs, as well as produce large surpluses for export. In 1985 this sector produced records in both yield and value in the tobacco and maize crops. White commercial farmers also produce beef, wheat, tea, coffee, cotton, sugar, and soybeans. In early 1988, about 3,400 commercial farmers owned approximately 34 percent of the land in the country.

Since 1980 the government's official agricultural policy has been to stress the need for achieving and maintaining national self-sufficiency in food production, as well as increasing African farmers' overall participation in total crop production. The total number of white farmers remained around 5,000 between 1980 and 1986, while the number of small scale (100 to 300 acres) commercial farms owned by blacks rose from c.9,000 to 10,000. In 1990 about 4,000 white commercial farmers still owned nearly 12 million hectares of land, while approximately 750,000 African farmers occupied 15 million hectares in the country's **communal lands**.

Following independence in 1980 the government continued to support the white commercial agriculture sector, but it also greatly increased the number of financial and material assistance programs available to African farmers. The importance of these programs was proven with the 1984–1985 harvest following the end of three years of drought when black farmers were expected to produce about 100,000 tons of maize and instead produced nearly 400,000 tons. In addition, African farmers produced a small percentage of the total maize and cotton crops in 1980, but by the 1987–1988 season they were producing nearly 50 percent of those crops. According to government statistics covering the period of the mid-1990s, nearly one-half of the country's work force was employed in agriculture.

By the late 1980s the greatest problem facing the agricultural sector of Zimbabwe's economy was soil erosion. The ministry of agriculture estimated that as a result of overplanting and overgrazing, topsoil in some areas of the country was being washed away at the rate of about 40,000 pounds per acre per year.

AIR TRANSPORT/AIR ZIMBABWE. Air transport began in the country when a South African plane landed in Bulawayo in 1920. In 1932 Imperial Airways (the predecessor of British Airways) extended its service to Cape Town, with stops in Southern Rhodesia. The next year this airline and the **Beit Trust** helped to found Rhodesia and Nyasaland Airways, or **RANA**, which the government took over in 1940 and renamed Southern

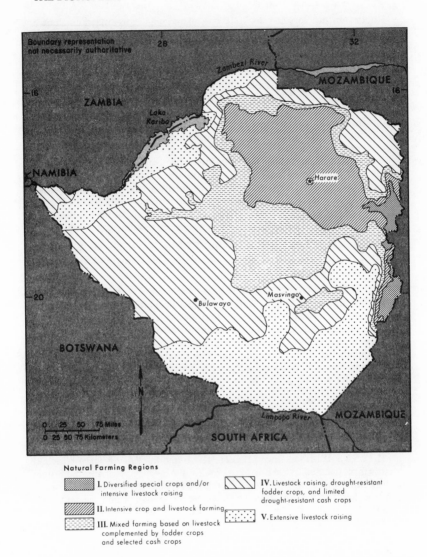

Natural Farming Regions

I. Diversified special crops and/or intensive livestock raising

II. Intensive crop and livestock farming

III. Mixed farming based on livestock complemented by fodder crops and selected cash crops

IV. Livestock raising, drought-resistant fodder crops, and limited drought-resistant cash crops

V. Extensive livestock raising

Source: Based on information from I. M. Hume, *A Strategy for Rural Development and Whitsun Data Bank No. 2: The Peasant Sector*, Salisbury, October 1978, p. 53.

Figure 2: Farming Zones

Rhodesian Air Services. In 1946 the airline was reorganized as Central African Airways Corporation (CAA), under the control of the three territorial governments (see **Central African Council**). CAA operated as an international airline through the years of **federation**, and then divided into separate national airlines: Zambia Airways, Air Malawi, and Air Rhodesia. The last was officially formed in 1968. In 1980 the airline became known as Air Zimbabwe.

Air Zimbabwe has a monopoly of domestic services and also operates international flights to South Africa, Botswana, Zambia, Kenya, and other African countries. In addition, the airline has regularly scheduled flights to London, Frankfurt, and Athens in Europe and to Perth and Sydney, Australia (in association with Quantas, that country's airline). In 1992, Air Zimbabwe operated four B707-300s, three 737-200s, and two other aircraft. In 1994, Air Zimbabwe announced a new airline, Zimbabwe Express Airlines, that would take over domestic services between **Harare** and **Bulawayo,** to **Victoria Falls.** It later added routes to Blantyre, Malawi, Lusake, and Maputo. This new carrier began flying in mid-1995.

ALDERSON, EDWIN ALFRED HARVEY (April 8, 1859–Dec. 22, 1927). British Army officer. Formed and commanded **Mashonaland Field Force** during the **Revolts of 1896–97.**

ALL-AFRICAN CONVENTION. Short-lived political organization formed in 1951 to cooperate with Northern Rhodesian and Nyasalander groups opposing **federation**. The convention joined together representatives of older organizations, such as the **African National Congress, Reformed Industrial and Commercial Union**, and trade unions. **Charles Mzingeli** was made interim president. Other leaders included **George Nyandoro, Joshua Nkomo, Benjamin Burombo,** and **Stanlake Samkange**. The body faded quickly after the creation of the federation in 1953.

ALOES. Succulent plants of the lily family that have a rosette of leaves at their base but no stem. Most of the 30 species of this plant that occur throughout Zimbabwe can be found at **Ewanrigg Aloe Gardens National Park**, about 40 km east of Harare.

ALTENA FARM. On December 21, 1972, a small **ZANLA** force attacked this farm (located in the northeastern Zambezi valley area, approximately 240 km from Harare). Although the attack lasted only about 30 seconds, it marked the beginning of ZANLA's second phase of activity, in which guerrilla warfare tactics were emphasized over direct confrontation with **Rhodesian security forces** (See **Chinhoyi, Battle of.**). Exactly seven years later (December 21, 1979), the **Lancaster House Conference** agreement was signed.

ALTITUDINAL ZONES. Most of the country lies more than 1,000 meters (m) above sea level. Its lowest point, where the **Sabi River** exits the country in the southeast, is 168m. Its highest point, **Mount Inyangani,** is 2,594m. The country as a whole is generally seen as dividing into three altitudinal zones, which occasionally meet in escarpments.

The *High Veld* includes land over 1,220m (4,000 ft), comprising about a fifth of the country. Most of this land forms the Central Plateau, a ridge that runs approximately southwest to northeast, with important exten-

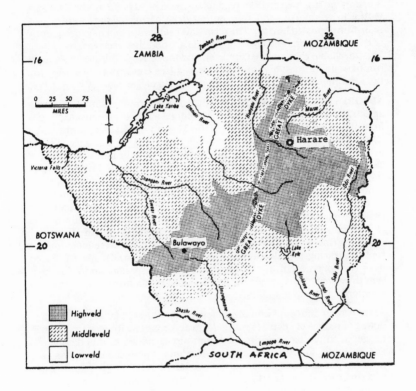

Figure 3: Altitudinal Zones

sions northwest and east of Harare. Although the term "high veld" is sometimes treated as synonymous with "central plateau," it also properly applies to the **Eastern Highlands**, which include the country's highest points. The high veld areas contain the country's most developed regions and most of its important towns.

The *Middle Veld* is variously defined as land over 2,000 or 2,500 ft (600 to 760 m), but below 4,000 ft. This land forms a penumbra around the high veld regions, except in parts of the west, where it rises alone.

The *Low Veld* makes up the remaining, lower parts of the country. It is separated into two distinct regions by the central plateau: the **Zambezi Valley** in the north, and the southeastern corner of the country (see **Sabi-Limpopo Authority**). The term "low veld" is applied most frequently to the latter region. The low veld regions are hot, they receive mostly light and unreliable rainfall (see **Climate**), and they harbor the country's most troublesome human and animal diseases (see **Health**). Hence, they are the least populated and least developed parts of the country.

ALVORD, EMORY DELMONT (March 25, 1889–May 6, 1959). Pioneering agriculturalist. Born in Utah, Alvord obtained a B.S. degree in agriculture from Washington State College (1915). Though raised as a Mormon, he joined the Congregationalist Mount Silinda Mission in Chipinge District in 1919. His success in teaching agricultural techniques to Africans caught the attention of the government, which appointed him "Agriculturalist for Instruction of Natives" in 1926. His basic system emphasized centralization of arable lands and their isolation from grazing animals, heavy use of steer for manure, crop rotation, and soil conservation. The system was well suited for small plots and was easily taught with the use of demonstration farms. Greatly increased crop yields encouraged many African farmers to follow the system, but these gains were offset by the rapidly growing **populations** in the **Tribal Trust Lands**. Alvord retired from the government in 1950 and returned to mission work. The next year the government passed the **Native Land Husbandry Act**, in an effort to enforce many of his ideas.

AMA-. Common **Nguni** and **Sindebele** prefix (Class 3) for plural forms of nouns or names of people (sing., *i[li]-*). In accordance with modern English usage, such prefixes are dropped from proper nouns in this dictionary. For example, for Amandebele, see **Ndebele**. For ordinary nouns, see under *i-*. For example, for *amadlozi*, see **Idlozi**. Note that the *ama-* prefix is frequently shortened to *ma-*, as in Mandebele, and that *ma-* also happens to be a **Chishona** prefix. (See also **ABA-**.)

AMALGAMATION MOVEMENT. Thirty-five years before the creation of the **Federation of Rhodesia and Nyasaland**, a movement arose to amalgamate Southern and Northern Rhodesia (the latter is now **Zambia**) integrally. The initial proponents of this movement were mainly BSAC officials who hoped to achieve some administrative economies and to strengthen the economic position of the BSAC's central African territories in relation to **South Africa.** At first most Southern Rhodesian settlers opposed the plan, for fear that amalgamation would delay achievement of **Responsible Government**. The British government acquiesced to settler pressures, so the idea temporarily died. Amalgamation again became an issue in the mid-1920s, when new mineral discoveries on Northern Rhodesia's Copperbelt offered the prospect of much-needed economic stimulation to Southern Rhodesia's government. Northern Rhodesian settlers also began pushing for amalgamation, in the hope of breaking free from Colonial Office control. Britain responded to settler pressures in 1927 and in 1938 by setting up the **Hilton Young** and **Bledisloe Commissions** to investigate the issue. By then some attention was being paid to African opinion, which in Northern Rhodesia strongly opposed any form of merger with Southern Rhodesia. The commissions' negative reports killed the amalgamation idea, but a new movement, this time for federation, arose after the Second World War. (See also **Unionist Movement.**)

AMANDAS. Village located c.55km north of **Harare**, on the **Shamva** railway line (at 17°22′S, 30°57′E).

AMERICAN BOARD OF COMMISSIONERS FOR FOREIGN MISSIONS (ABC). Based in Boston, the **Congregationalist** ABC is the oldest foreign mission body in the United States. It began work in Southern Africa in 1835, when it sent mission parties to labor among the Zulu of **Natal** and the Ndebele of **Mzilikazi**, then living in the western Transvaal. The American Zulu Mission eventually prospered, but the Ndebele mission, known as the "Inland Zulu Mission," was abandoned when Afrikaners attacked the Ndebele in early 1837.

In 1893 representatives of the Zulu mission were granted large tracts of land in **Gazaland** by the BSAC. That year they founded the **Mount Silinda Mission** in Ndau territory. They soon expanded their operations around the **Sabi River** and Southern Mozambique. During the present century they have made a major contribution to African **education** in the southeastern part of the country through the creation of numerous primary schools and an industrial school at Mt. Silinda.

"ANCIENT." Chronological term frequently applied by archaeologists and antiquarians to virtually all precolonial sites and artifacts in the country. The Southern Rhodesian Monuments and Relics Act of 1936 formally defined as "ancient" all historical sites existing prior to 1890. (See **Historical Monument Commission.**)

ANCIENT PARK NATIONAL MONUMENT see **MONK'S KOP**

ANCIENT RUINS COMPANY see **RHODESIA ANCIENT RUINS**

ANDRADA, JOAQUM CARLOS PAIVA DE (Nov. 29, 1846–April 1928). Portuguese soldier and official in Mozambique. Between 1878 and 1890 d'Andrada attempted to extend Portuguese authority inland from Mozambique. Arrested, along with **M. A. de Sousa**, by **P. W. Forbes** at **Mutasa**'s town in late 1890, by the time he was released in Cape Town most of **Manicaland** had been secured by the British (see **Anglo-Portuguese Convention**).

ANGLICAN MISSIONS. The Church of England entered the country mainly through the efforts of its semiautonomous Province of South Africa, but its own Society for the Propagation of the Gospel (SPG) supported mission work from the start. In 1876 a South African priest,

W. Greenstock, visited **Lobengula** in the hope of staring a mission, but the effort came to nothing. Twelve years later **G. W. Knight-Bruce**, the Bishop of Bloemfontein, visited Lobengula and traveled extensively throughout **Mashonaland.** When the British occupied Mashonaland in 1890, Canon F. R. T. Balfour (1846–1924) accompanied the **Pioneer Column** and established the first Anglican church in Salisbury. Meanwhile, the Province of South Africa created the Diocese of Mashonaland, making Knight-Bruce its first Bishop (January 1891). The new diocese included all of present Zimbabwe and parts of Botswana and Mozambique. Knight-Bruce returned to the country with **Bernard Mizeki** and other African catechists and opened mission stations at Penhalonga and elsewhere in Mashonaland.

Progress was slow until after the 1896–97 **Shona Revolt**, when Knight-Bruce's successors put mission work on a firmer footing. Mission stations, schools, and parishes were gradually extended throughout the entire country. The first local African priest was ordained in 1923. Two years later **E. F. Paget** began three decades of service as bishop. By the late 1950s the church claimed 28,500 African members—the second largest number of any Christian church in the country. (See **Missions**.)

The Mashonaland Diocese was renamed Diocese of Southern Rhodesia in 1915. In 1953 separate dioceses of **Matabeleland** and Mashonaland were created. Two years later these dioceses fell under the newly created Province of Central Africa, which included present Zambia and Malawi. (See also **A. S. Cripps**.)

ANGLO-AMERICAN CORPORATION. South Africa's largest mining finance house. It was founded shortly after the First World War by Ernest Oppenheimer, a diamond magnate, in cooperation with the National Bank of South Africa and two American-owned companies—Morgan Guaranty Bank and Newmont Mining Company. By the 1980s it was an international conglomerate and had become the largest private foreign investor in Zimbabwe. Whether directly or through subsidiaries, Anglo-American controls nickel, copper, and coal mining in country, and is involved in iron, steel, and ferrochrome production. It is also heavily involved in commercial agriculture, owning the **Hippo Valley** sugar estates and **Mazowe Estates,** the country's major citrus producer. Through its subsidiary, National Foods, it is Zimbabwe's largest miller and food processor.

ANGLO-NDEBELE WAR (1893) see **NDEBELE WAR**

ANGLO-PORTUGUESE CONVENTION (1891). **Portuguese** claims to parts of present Zimbabwe go back to the time of their earliest explorations there, but only became concerted in the late 1880s, when it was clear that the British were beginning to regard the region as falling within their own "sphere of interest." The Portuguese government reluctantly conceded that the **Moffat Treaty** of February 1888 gave the British priority over **Matabeleland,** but it then acted to make good its long-standing claims over **Mashonaland** and **Manicaland** (see also **Andrada**). Meanwhile, the government negotiated with the British in an effort to preserve the old Portuguese-British alliance in the face of the mounting competition in Africa. On August 20, 1890, a Portuguese envoy signed a draft convention in London. This document defined the British-Portuguese borders in southern Africa, guaranteeing British railway access from Mashonaland to the Indian Ocean, and promising to keep the **Zambezi River** open to foreign navigation. The agreement was so unpopular in Portugal that it contributed to the fall of the government in Lisbon and the document was not ratified.

The BSAC occupied Mashonaland a few months later (see **Pioneer Column**), and then obtained a grant to Manicaland from chief **Mutasa** and made efforts to secure an Indian Ocean port in **Gaza** territory. Anti-British feeling mounted in Portugal and Mozambique. Incidents at Mutasa's in November (see **P. W. Forbes**) and at **Maçequeçe** the following May brought tensions to a peak. Nevertheless, continuing negotiations in Europe led to the signing of a somewhat modified Anglo-Portuguese Convention in Lisbon on June 11, 1891. This document was ratified by the Portuguese Cortes. It fixed the approximate modern **borders** of Mozambique, forever ending Portuguese ambitions of linking that territory with Angola, and it effectively ended Portuguese-British rivalry in southern Africa.

ANGLO-RHODESIAN SETTLEMENT PROPOSALS (1971) see **PEARCE COMMISSION**

ANGONI see **NGONI**

ANGWA RIVER. Rises just southwest of Chinhoyi, whence it flows north, then northeast, before joining the **Hunyani** in Mozambique. The Angwa separates the **Hurungwe** and **Makonde** districts.

ANTELOPE MINE. Village c.100 km south of **Bulawayo,** on the **Shashani River** (at 21°3'S, 28°27'E). It is named after a gold mine which operated there between 1913 and 1919 on the site of earlier African workings.

ARABS see **MUSLIMS**

ARCHAEOLOGY see **IRON AGE; STONE AGE**

ARCHIVES see **NATIONAL ARCHIVES OF ZIMBABWE**

ARGUS GROUP OF NEWSPAPERS. Unofficial name for publications of the former Rhodesian Printing and Publishing Company, which controlled five of the country's major newspapers prior to early 1981. The Argus Printing and Publishing Company was founded in South Africa in 1889, 32 years after the *Cape Argus* commenced publication. **Cecil Rhodes**, a shareholder in the company, invited Argus to start a newspaper in Mashonaland shortly after his BSAC had occupied the region. In 1891 Argus sent **W. E. Fairbridge** to Salisbury (now Harare), where he immediately started the forerunner of the *Herald*. In 1894 Argus entered Matabeleland and started the *Bulawayo Chronicle*. The company's papers came to be known as the "Argus Group."

The editorial policies of these papers reflected those of their South African counterparts. During the early 1920s they ran strongly counter to settler opinion by supporting the **Unionist Movement**. Settler resentment against South African control of the press led to the formation of the Rhodesian Printing and Publishing Company, Ltd., in 1927. Majority control of the new company was vested in Southern Rhodesians, but the Argus company sold its papers to the company while retaining a nearly 50 percent interest.

In early 1981 the newly independent black majority government announced that it was purchasing controlling interest in the country's five major papers (the *Herald, Chronicle,* Harare's *Sunday Mail,* Bulawayo's *Sunday News,* and Mutare's *Post*) from the Argus Group. The government then created the **Zimbabwe Mass Media Trust** to oversee the operation of the five papers. (See **Press.**)

ASBESTOS. Zimbabwe's third most important mineral in export value, asbestos was first mined near Mashava in 1907. Since the Second World War the country has been one of the world's leading asbestos producers. **Sanctions** did little harm to the asbestos industry, with production increasing during the mid-1970s to an all time high of 281,000 tons in 1976. Production then began to slowly decrease in late 1970s, totaling 173,000 tons in 1985, 160,000 tons in 1990, and 170,000 tons in 1995. The country's largest mines are located near **Zvishavane.** While over 90 percent of asbestos production continues to be for export, building materials such as roofing sheets and water pipes made from a mixture of asbestos and cement are produced in both Harare and Bulawayo. The government announced in 1997 that production had dropped by 21 percent over the previous two years.

ASIANS. During the 1890s a small but steady stream of Asians began immigrating into the country. Most were Hindus from British India. By the mid-1920s, when the government began discouraging Asian immigration, there were about 1,500 Asians in the country. By 1993, Asians in the country numbered approximately 19,000.

AYRSHIRE. Farming region c.15 km north of **Banketi,** taking its name from the former Ayrshire Mine. The mine opened in 1900 to exploit a major **gold** working previously abandoned by the Shona. The mine was closed in 1911 after being worked out.

B

BA-. Common Bantu prefix for the plural names of people. English usage normally drops such prefixes, e.g., for Banyai, see **NYAI.** (See also **ABA-; AMA-; MA-.**)

BABA. Common Bantu word for "father"; used as a polite form of address when speaking to any older man. (See also **Mama.**)

BABAYANE (variant: Babyaan) (fl: 1880s–1890s). A senior Ndebele *induna* by the late 1880s, when he was estimated to be about 65 years old. In late 1888 **Lobengula** named Babayane and **Mshete** emissaries to London, where they met with Queen Victoria the next year. Although the British made a particular effort to impress the Ndebele emissaries with armaments and military installations, Babayane was an active leader in the anti-British **Revolt** of 1896. He fought mainly in the central **Matopo Hills** in association with **Mlugulu** and was one of the *izinduna* who supported the installation of **Nyamanda** as king. In the negotiations with Cecil Rhodes that ended the Matopos fighting, Babayane emerged as a leading spokesman of Ndebele grievances.

BADEN-POWELL, ROBERT STEPHENSON SMYTH (Feb. 22, 1857–Jan. 8, 1941). British army officer of 20 years' experience but with little reputation before serving in the **1896 Ndebele Revolt.** Then a colonel, Baden-Powell arrived in Matabeleland with General **Carrington** in June 1896. As staff officer he and **Colonel Plumer** planned most military operations. As the Ndebele campaign wound down, he and Carrington went to Mashonaland to assist **E. A. H. Alderson** against the Shona.

BAINES, THOMAS (Nov. 27, 1820–May 8, 1875). English painter and explorer. Born in Norfolk, Baines went to South Africa in 1842 and began a long and productive career as a painter. In 1858 he joined **David Livingstone's** Zambezi expedition but was soon dismissed by the latter because of personal differences. He returned to the Zambezi in 1863 and painted the first full-color pictures of the **Victoria Falls**.

After a sojourn in England, Baines returned to southern Africa in 1869 in the employ of the recently formed **South African Gold Fields Exploration Company**. He negotiated several times with **Lobengula** and traveled and painted extensively in northern Mashonaland. In late 1871 he obtained Lobengula's first written **concession** to mine for **gold** in Shona territory. He then returned to South Africa to paint but died before he was able to exploit his mining concession personally.

BALFOUR, F. R. T. see under **ANGLICAN MISSIONS**

BALLA BALLA see **MBALABALA**

BAMANGWATO see **NGWATO**

BAMBATA CAVE. Major archaeological site located in the **Matopo Hills** (at 20°39′S, 23°24′E). Archaeologists have turned up important artifacts representing the middle and late **Stone Age** and the earliest local **Iron Age**. The cave also contains fine examples of **rock paintings** representing an unusually broad range of styles. The cave's name has been given to a major phase of the middle **Stone Age Stillbay** industries.

BANANA, CANAAN SODINDO (b.March 5, 1936). First president of the independent Republic of Zimbabwe (1980–87). An ordained Methodist minister, Banana was born at Esiphezini, east of Bulawayo. He studied at Mzinyati Mission and Tegwani High School, and from 1960 to 1962 at Epworth Theological College near Harare. In 1970 he studied at the Kasai Industrial Centre in Japan, and from 1973 to 1975 at the Wesley Theological Seminary in Washington, D.C., where he obtained a master of theological studies degree. In 1979 he received a Bachelor of Arts (Hons) in theology from the University of South Africa.

Banana's nonpolitical career included posts as the manager of Methodist schools in Plumtree and Hwange from 1963 to 1966, being appointed principal of Maatjinge Boarding School in 1965. During the years 1969 to 1971 he was chairman of the Bulawayo Council of Churches, and from 1970 to 1973, chairman of the Southern Africa Content Group at the Urban/Industrial Mission of the All-Africa Conference of Churches. Since 1970 he has been a member of the Advisory Committee of the World Council of Churches.

His entry into nationalist politics came in 1971 when he became a founder-member and first vice-president of the **African National Council**. In early 1972 he played a major role in organizing opposition to the Anglo-Rhodesian Settlement proposals during the visit of the **Pearce Commission**. His passport was withdrawn by the government in August 1972, but he nevertheless went to the United States the following May to study theology. When he returned to the country in 1975 he was arrested and sentenced to three months' hard labor for leaving the country without travel documents. He was released in January 1976 but restricted to his home in Bulawayo. Later that year he was allowed to travel to the **Geneva Conference** as a member of Bishop **Abel Muzorewa**'s delegation. While at the conference, he joined the **ZANU** delegation under **Robert Mugabe**. He was elected publicity secretary of the People's Movement Internal Coordinating Committee of ZANU (PF) in late 1976. When he returned to the country from the Geneva Conference in January 1977, he was once again arrested and was not released until November 26, 1979. Following nomination by **Prime Minister** Robert Mugabe, Banana was elected the new independent republic's first **president** by a combined vote of both houses of **Parliament** on April 11, 1980.

While the office of president was primarily ceremonial, Banana played a crucial role in the negotiations leading to the **Unity Pact** of 1987. When the talks between Prime Minister Robert Mugabe and opposition leader **Joshua Nkomo** were suspended by Mugabe in April 1987, Banana reportedly used his prestige as president to chastise Mugabe and urged him to reinstate the talks for the good of the country. Following the successful completion of the talks in late 1987, Banana retired from public office in December.

BANKET (formerly Banket Junction). Town located c.25 km east of **Chinhoyi** on the main road and railway line to Harare in eastern Makonde district (at 17°23′9, 30°24′E; alt. 1,300 m). Banket is the center of a prosperous farming area featuring **grains, cotton,** and **tobacco.**

BANNINGS see **CENSORSHIP; LAW AND ORDER (MAINTENANCE) ACT; UNLAWFUL ORGANIZATIONS ACT**

BANTU. Although this term is commonly used in southern Africa as an ethnic or racial identification, it is properly only a linguistic term. Bantu languages occupy a unique place in Africa. Though they constitute only a sub-subgroup of the Niger-Congo family of languages (which also extend through West Africa), they are spoken by almost all the peoples south of a line between Cameroon and central Kenya. The historical spread of Bantu languages remains controversial, but it is generally agreed by historical linguists that proto-Bantu originated in southeastern Nigeria more than 5,000 years ago and then spread comparatively rapidly throughout central, eastern, and southern Africa. Bantu-speakers appear to have first entered present Zimbabwe sometime early in the first millennium A.D. Their arrival in southern Africa appears also to have coincided with the start of the **Iron Age**.

Among the characteristics shared by the 300 or so classified Bantu languages are the division of nouns into classes and the use of prefixes to inflect nouns and verbs (see, e.g., AMA-, ISI-, MA-, etc.). The name "Bantu" itself derives from a word for person which appears in many of the languages. The stem of the word is -*ntu*. The addition of prefixes creates such forms as *muntu* ("person"), *bantu* ("people"), *kintu* ("thing"), etc. These prefixes vary from language to language. Since variations create obvious problems in alphabetizing Bantu words, language dictionaries typically list the words by their stems, and the prefixes are normally dropped altogether in European use of proper names (see note on alphabetizing in this dictionary).

Bantu languages spoken south of the **Zambezi River** are usually called "southeast African Bantu." Their exact interrelationships have not been fully worked out, but certain broad patterns have been recognized. One cluster includes the various Shona or **Chishona** dialects which are spoken throughout Zimbabwe and central Mozambique. A second, broader group of less closely related languages includes **Nguni, Sotho, Tsonga, Venda**, and Chopi. Dialects of all but Chopi are spoken in Zimbabwe. Shona languages predominate in Zimbabwe, accounting for about 75 percent of the population. In the mid-19th century a second major Bantu language was introduced from the south by the intrusive **Ndebele** people, whose Nguni tongue is known as **Sindebele**.

BANTU CONGRESS. Original name of the "old" **African National Congress**.

BANTU MIRROR. Started as a mission quarterly called *Chiringiro* ("The Mirror"), this publication became the country's first African newspaper, *The Native Mirror*, in 1931. In 1943 the paper was taken over by **African News-papers, Ltd.** and was used by the government to disseminate wartime propaganda. Through the 1950s, by which time it was known as the *Bantu Mirror*, the weekly paper published considerable general-interest news but it failed to develop into a significant African political voice. (See **African Weekly; Press.**)

BANTU VOTERS' ASSOCIATION see **RHODESIAN BANTU VOTERS' ASSOCIATION**

BANTU WOMEN'S LEAGUE. Organization established in the **Bulawayo** location in the 1920s. It was organized by respectable African married women in an attempt to protect their economic interests. The women were permanent residents of the location, and the majority owned market stands. The Bantu Women's League is considered to be one of the first women's organizations in the country.

BANYAILAND TREK see **ADENDORFF TREK; NYAI**

BAOBAB (Chisona: *muuyu;* Sindebele: *umkhomo*). Large tree native to tropical Africa, characterized by enormous girth, moderate height, smooth bark, and few leaves. The tree stores considerable water which can be tapped during drought, and it bears edible fruit. Baobabs are found mostly in low-lying savanna and grassland regions, particularly in the Limpopo and Zambezi valleys. (See **Forests.**)

BARING, EVELYN (Sept. 29, 1903–March 10, 1973). Fourth **governor** of Southern Rhodesia (1942–44). During his brief tenure of office, Baring gained the respect of the African population because of his close attention to conditions in the reserves. Afterwards he served as British high commissioner to South Africa (1944–51) and as governor of Kenya Colony (1952–9). He was later created Baron Howick of Glendale.

BARRETO, FRANCISCO (1520–June 1573). **Portuguese** military commander. After serving as governor of Portuguese India (1555–58), Barreto returned to Lisbon, where he became influential at the royal court. In the late 1560s he persuaded the young king Sebastian to appoint him head of a punitive expedition against Munhumutapa **Negomo** to avenge the murder of **Gonçalo da Silveira.** His expedition attracted numerous volunteers anxious to pillage the wealth of the supposed **"Ophir."** Barreto set sail in 1569 with three ships and 1,000 men. He reached **Mozambique** in May 1570 but then dallied along the eastern coast for almost a year. Pressured by Jesuit members of the expedition, he finally selected the **Zambezi Valley** as his route to the interior. The choice proved disastrous. Most of his men and his horses succumbed to **malaria** and **trypanosomiasis.** He suffered further losses in major campaigns against Africans in the valley, turning back before he reached present Zimbabwe. He died at **Sena** and was replaced as commander by **Vasco Homem.**

BARWE (variant: Barue). People living along the border areas of the **Mutoko** and **Nyanga** districts and mostly in Mozambique. The Barwe are frequently described as **Shona**, but they speak a non-Shona **Bantu** language belonging to the Nyanja (or Cewa) group spoken mainly north of the Zambezi River. Since about the 15th century the Barwe have lived under the **Makombe** dynasty, which was imposed by an offshoot of the Shona **Munhumutapa** state.

BATOKA GORGE. Located c.48 km below the Victoria Falls, this gorge severely contracts the flow of the **Zambezi River** into a narrow defile about 90 km long which now meets the southeastern end of **Lake Kariba**. The name "Batoka" derives from the **Sotho** pronunciation of "Batonga" (see **Tonga**).

BATTLEFIELDS. Village in the **Kadoma District** located on the railway line between Kadoma and Kwekwe (at 18°38'S, 29°50'E; alt. 1,115 m). The name "Battlefields" derives form the many local mines named after famous European battles.

BAYÃO, SISANDO DIAS (variant: Baião; fl. 1640s). **Portuguese** trader. As a youth Bayão settled at **Sena**, where he became the leading trader, landowner, and military commander. During the 1640s he was appointed to command Portuguese forces in **Manicaland**. There he is said to have met a deposed **Changamire** ruler who requested Portuguese military aid to regain his power. In 1644 Bayão led a large force deep into **"Butua."** His exact route is unknown, but he may have reached the present **Bulawayo** region. He seems to have died around 1645.

BEADLE, THOMAS HUGH WILLIAM (b. Feb. 6, 1905). Born in Salisbury, Beadle studied law in England and returned to practice in **Bulawayo**. **Godfrey Huggins** made him parliamentary secretary in 1940 and minister of justice and internal affairs in 1946. In 1961 Beadle succeeded **Robert Tredgold** as chief justice. He initially resisted UDI in 1965, but later passed down a series of court decisions legalizing the independence of the regime within the context of Rhodesian law.

BEATRICE. Town located 50 km south of Harare, where the road to Chivhu crosses the Umfuli River (at 18°16′S, 30°52′E). The town arose by the Beatrice Gold Mine, which was started in 1894. The mine was once a leading **gold** producer in the country, but has since been closed down.

BECHUANA see **TSWANA**

BECHUANALAND BORDER POLICE (BBP). Parliamentary force organized by the British Imperial government shortly after present **Botswana** was made into the **Bechuanaland Protectorate** in 1885. Col. **F. Carrington** was the first BBP commander, with his headquarters at Mefeking in South Africa. Some members of the BBP served in the **Pioneer Column**, which occupied **Mashonaland** in 1890. In May 1893 Lt.-Col. **H. Goold-Adams** became BBP commander with his headquarters on the Macloutsie River, just southwest of present Zimbabwe. Later the same year Goold-Adams led a BBP contingent against **Bulawayo** in the **Ndebele War**. At the end of 1895 the BBP was disbanded. Many of its members then served in the **Jameson Raid**, the **Matabeleland Relief Force,** and then the BSAP.

BECHUANALAND PROTECTORATE. In March 1885 a British military expedition under **Charles Warren** declared most of present **Botswana** a British protectorate. The British had acted in response to appeals for protection issued by the **Ngwato** and other peoples, and in order to block **Afrikaner** expansion from the **Transvaal**. An immediate effect of the declaration was the circumscription of **Ndebele** raiding activity in the west and increased Ndebele willingness to negotiate with the Transvaalers (see **Grobler, P.**). The gradual demarcation of the protectorate's northeastern boundary essentially defined what was to become the western **border** of present Zimbabwe.

During the mid-1890s the British government considered turning over the protectorate's administration to the BSAC, which by then was attempting to administer colonial Zimbabwe. In 1895 the Ngwato chief **Khama III** and two other **Tswana** rulers successfully protested the plan in London. The British instead ceded to the BSAC a narrow strip of protectorate land for construction of the main **railway** line to Bulawayo. On September 30, 1968, the protectorate became the independent Botswana Republic. (See also **Tati Concession.**)

BEIRA. Now the second largest city in **Mozambique**, Beira arose in the early 1890s as a **railway** line was being built from the Indian Ocean to **Umtali.** The line reached Umtali in 1898 and was extended to Salisbury the next year. Until the closing of the Mozambique-Rhodesia border in 1976, Beira handled much of the latter's export traffic. The town is located on the northern shore of the **Pungwe River**'s estuary, across the inlet from old Sofala (at 19°51'S, 34°52'E). In 1996 Zimbabwe, with Malawi, Mozambique, and Zambia, created the Beira Development Corridor in an effort to diminish their dependence on South African ports.

BEIT, ALFRED (Feb. 15, 1853–July 16, 1906). Financial partner of **Cecil Rhodes**. Born in Germany, Beit came to South Africa in 1875 as a representative of a Dutch diamond company. He soon went to the Kimberley diamond fields, established his own company, and became a British subject. There he joined with Rhodes to form the De Beers Consolidated Mines and built a vast fortune with diamond and gold mining interests in South Africa. He supported Rhodes' efforts to expand British power north of the **Limpopo River,** concentrating on the financial aspects while Rhodes worked in politics. In 1889 he became a founding member of the BSAC board of directors, later using his private wealth to help see the company through occasional difficulties. Because of his close association with Rhodes, he resigned from the BSAC board in the aftermath of the **Jameson Raid**. He rejoined the board in 1903 and became the company's vice-president.

Although Beit is closely associated with the founding of British rule in Zimbabwe, he visited the country only briefly, in 1891 and in 1903. Beit was one of the trustees of Rhodes' will. On his own death, he bequeathed much of his fortune to the **Beit Trust**.

BEIT TRUST. Philanthropic trust fund created with a £1,200,000 bequest made by **Alfred Beit** on his death in 1906. Since then its trustees have multiplied the size of the fund several times, while dispersing money over a wide variety of projects throughout central Africa. Through the 1920s the money was used mainly to improve **transport** facilities, most notably bridges (see **Beitbridge; Birchenough Bridge; Otto Beit Bridge**). After 1927 an increasing share of the money was used for **education**, particularly private schools in Southern Rhodesia. More recently, funds have been channeled through mission schools for Africans. Other contributions have gone to hospitals, museums, charities, and sports facilities.

BEITBRIDGE. Town (at 22°13'S, 30°E; alt. 500 m) serving as the main port of entry into the country from South Africa, and the headquarters of the district of the same name. It was founded in 1929 with the opening of Beit Bridge (a.k.a. Alfred Beit Bridge; see **Otto Beit Bridge**) over the **Limpopo River**. In 1974 a new **railway** line between Beitbridge and **Rutenga** was opened, giving the country its first direct rail link to South Africa.

BEITBRIDGE DISTRICT. A region of 12,920 sq km in **Matabeleland South Province**. The district was originally part of **Gwanda District** and is used mainly for ranching. The **Limpopo River** runs the entire length of the district's southern border and separates it from South Africa. The northwest border is with Gwanda District, while the northeastern border is shared with **Mwenezi** and **Chiredzi**. Before 1980 the district was divided almost evenly between Tribal Trust Lands and land reserved for Europeans. District population in 1992 was 80,946.

BELINGWE see **MBERENGWA**

BEMBEZI RIVER (variants: Imbembesi; Bembesi). Rises c.40 km northeast of Bulawayo, whence it flows northwest to join the **Gwai** near Lupane. The British and the Ndebele fought the "Battle of Bembezi" near the river's headwaters during the **1893 Ndebele War**.

BENT, JAMES THEODORE (March 30, 1852–May 5, 1897). English antiquarian and traveler. After doing archaeological fieldwork in the Middle East, Bent was invited by Cecil Rhodes to investigate the **Zimbabwe Ruins**. In 1891 he, his wife, and R. M. W. Swan undertook the first systematic survey and excavations of the ruins. Bent's expedition cleared away much of the plant overgrowth, produced the first accurate plans of the ruins, and collected artifacts—notably the **Zimbabwe "Birds."** Publication of Bent's book, *The Ruined Cities of Mashonaland* (1892), aroused worldwide interest in Zimbabwe. The book is a mine of information on artifacts, the layout of the ruins, and contemporary Shona life, but it lacks the kind of rigorous analysis of fieldwork demanded by modern archaeology, and it propounded the untenable hypothesis that the ruins were of ancient Semitic origin (see **Zimbabwe Controversy**). Bent unfortunately kept poor records of his digs, which destroyed much irrecoverable stratigraphical evidence on the site. (See also **Hall, R. N.; Rhodesia Ancient Ruins, Ltd.**)

BERLIN MISSIONARY SOCIETY (a.k.a. Berlin Society). Founded in 1824, by 1860 it was operating in the **Transvaal**. During the 1880s BMS made tentative ventures into Shona territory north of the Limpopo River. In 1882 it founded a mission station in the **Gutu** chiefdom. By 1907 BMS had abandoned its Mashonaland stations, turning over its interests to the **Dutch Reformed Church**.

BIKITA. Administrative center of the district of the same name in **Masvingo Province** (at 20°5′S, 31°38′E; alt. 1.065 m).

BIKITA DISTRICT. Originally the northeastern part of the old **Ndanga District**, from which it was separated in 1920. It now covers 6,925 sq km in the southeastern low veld. The **Sabi River** separates it from the **Chipinge District** in the east. It also borders the districts of **Chiredzi** on the south, **Zaka** and **Masvingo** on the west, and **Gutu** and **Buhera** on the north. The district's Bikita Mine is the largest **lithium** producer in the country. Prior to 1980, the eastern part of the district was reserved for Europeans, while the western part comprised Tribal Trust Land. District population in 1992 was 154,429.

BILHARZIA (a.k.a. *schistosomiasis*). Infectious disease transmitted by waterborne parasites that enter mammalian bodies through unbroken skin. One variety of the disease damages the bladder, kidneys, and genital organs; another damages the large intestine, liver, and sometimes the lungs. Both prevention and treatment are difficult, making the disease a particularly dangerous one in rural areas, where small snails carry the parasites. Although the disease is believed to have entered the country only during the 20th century, it now ranks as one of the most serious endemic **health** problems.

BINDURA. Located 86 km north of Harare in the Mazowe Valley (at 17°18′S, 31°20′E; alt. 1,100 m), Bindura is a mining center that also serves as the administrative center for both **Mazowe District** and **Mashonaland Central Province.** Formerly known as Kimberly Reefs, Bindura has in recent decades expanded rapidly, along with **nickel** production at the nearby Trojan Mine. Population in 1992 was 21,456.

BINDURA DISTRICT. Containing 2,140 sq km, this area was carved out of the eastern part of the **Mazowe District.** It is a rich, mixed farming region in which commercial farmers produce two crops annually, using irrigation from the Mazowe River. The district was reserved entirely for Europeans until 1980. It borders the districts of Mazowe on the west, **Mukumbura** on the north, **Shamva** on the east, and **Goromonzi** on the south. District population in 1992 was 119,770.

BINGA. Fishing and resort village on the southeastern end of **Lake Kariba** (at 17°37′S, 27°20′E) and headquarters for the district of the same name.

BINGA DISTRICT. Covering 15,070 sq km, it is carved out of the former **Sebungwe District** in **Matabeleland North Province.** Except for several game reserves, the district comprises only **Communal Lands.** It borders the districts of **Hwange** on the west, **Lupane** on the south, **Gokwe** on the east, and **Kariba** on the northeast. District population in 1992 was 87,802.

BINGAGURU. Prominent 1,800 m peak north of **Mutare,** near the Mozambique border (at 18°46′S, 32°037′E). Until 1902 the **Manyika** rulers of the **Mutasa** dynasty maintained their headquarters atop Bin-gaguru. In 1891 Portugal and Britain were nearly brought to war when **P. W. Forbes** arrested two important **Portuguese** officials on the mountain.

BIRCHENOUGH BRIDGE. Large, single-span suspension bridge built over the **Sabi River** on the Mutare-to-Masvingo **road** in 1935 (at 19°58′S, 32°20′E). Financed by the **Beit Trust,** the bridge was named after Henry Birchenough (1853–1937), who was president of the BSAC from 1925 to 1937.

BIRWA. Section of **Sotho**-speaking people living around the **Tuli River** in the southwestern part of the country.

BLEDISLOE COMMISSION (1938–39). In response to renewed settler demands for **amalgamation** of Southern and Northern Rhodesia, the British government created an investigatory commission under Charles Bathurst Bledisloe (1st Viscount Bledisloe), a former governor-general of New Zealand. The commission, which comprised representatives of three different British parliamentary parties, also considered inclusion of

Nyasaland (now Malawi), collecting evidence in all three territories during 1938 and 1939. It found settlers generally in support of amalgamation, with Africans strongly opposed. Africans north of the Zambezi River feared extension of Southern Rhodesia's land and tax laws, its **pass laws**, and its political emasculation of traditional chiefs (see **Council of Chiefs**). By contrast, Southern Rhodesian Africans feared increased competition from northern migrant laborers and a weakening of the country's comparatively good **educational system**. The report of the commission, issued in 1939, concluded that closer union was a worthwhile goal but not politically acceptable at that moment, largely because of the restrictive nature of Southern Rhodesia's labor laws, notably the **Industrial Conciliation Act**. The report recommended creation of an interterritorial council and further investigation of the issue. These plans were interrupted by the Second World War, but a **Central Africa Council** was created in 1944, becoming the first tangible step in the movement towards actual **federation**.

BOARD OF CENSORS see **CENSORSHIP**

BOER. Dutch word for farmer; used to describe the people who now generally prefer to be called **Afrikaners**. In many **Bantu** languages "Boer" is rendered *bunu.*

BOER WAR (1899–1902) see **SOUTH AFRICAN WAR**

BONDA (d. 1897). **Shona Revolt** leader. Originally a head man in a **Rozvi** chiefdom in the **Chikomba District,** Bonda is said to have become a "priest" in the **Mwari cult**. In May 1896 he and emissaries of chief **Mashayamombe** consulted with **Mkwati** at **Ntabazikamambo** in **Matabeleland.** Bonda is said then to have returned to Mashayamombe's country and to have helped organize the Revolt there and to the south. Throughout the rest of 1896 and early 1897 he moved about rebel territories constantly, attracting the pursuit of British forces. In July or August 1897 he was shot to death in the **Chegutu District.**

BORDERS. The present shape of Zimbabwe somewhat reflects European interpretations of the extent of **Ndebele** rule during the late 19th century. King **Lobengula** claimed all territory between the **Shashi** and **Zambezi** rivers, as well as hegemony over the **Shona peoples** to the east. The Ndebele actually controlled only the southwestern part of the present country. In any case, the notion of fixed boundaries was alien to most African societies, whose spheres of sovereignty often overlapped physically. Nevertheless, the BSAC used **concessions** wrested from Lobengula as its main legal basis for carving out the entire country.

In 1890 the British reached accords with Germany and the **Transvaal** acknowledging the purported Ndebele domain as falling within the British sphere of interest. The agreement with the Transvaal effectively fixed the **Limpopo River** as the future border between South Africa and Zimbabwe. In September 1890 the BSAC occupied and claimed **Mashonaland** by virtue of its own generous interpretation of the **Rudd Concession** granted by Lobengula. In October, BSAC agents got the Manyika chief **Mutasa** to sign a treaty giving the company a claim to **Manicaland**. Meanwhile, the **British Bechuanaland Protectorate** was being extended north to the Chobe River, thereby creating the future border between Zimbabwe and Botswana.

The BSAC then attempted to extend its domain east to the Indian Ocean by treating with the Gaza ruler **Gungunyane**. The **Portuguese** successfully resisted this British intrusion, and a temporary frontier between Portuguese **Mozambique** and British Mashonaland was created through Manicaland in February 1891. The **Anglo-Portuguese Convention** of the following June detailed the complete border, and further adjustments were made in 1897.

After **L. S. Jameson**, the **administrator** of Mashonaland, decreed an arbitrary border between British Mashonaland and Ndebele territory, the BSAC used Ndebele violations of the border as provocation for the **Ndebele War** in 1893. The British won the war, occupying **Matabeleland** and thereby rounding out colonial claims to the entire territory of present Zimbabwe. The Zambezi River seems always to have been regarded as the natural northern boundary of the colony.

Zimbabwe is now separated from **Zambia** by a c.715 km stretch of the Zambezi. The **South Africa** border extends along c.217 km of the Limpopo River. The c.790 km border with **Botswana** follows an arbitrary line running nearly straight from **Kazungula** to **Plumtree**, whence it follows the **Ramaquabane River** south to the **Shashi** and from there to the Limpopo, except for the **Tuli Circle**. The c.1,165 km border with Mozambique is the longest and most arbitrary. Except for a few short stretches of rivers, the **Eastern Highlands** provide the only natural features forming this border.

Clockwise from **Beitbridge** on the Limpopo River, important border posts are located at, or near, Plumtree, **Pandamatenga, Kazungula, Victoria Falls, Kariba, Chirundu, Mutare,** and **Sango**.

BOTSWANA. Nearly 50 percent larger than Zimbabwe but containing only about a tenth of the latter's population, Botswana shares a c.790 km **border** with Zimbabwe stretching from the **Zambezi** to the **Limpopo**. Except for a few moderate-size rivers in the southeast, no natural features separate the two countries, and the border region has long been a zone of free movement for **San, Sotho-Tswana,** and **Kalanga** peoples. In the 19th century Botswana served as the main approach route for visitors to the region of present Zimbabwe from the south. In the late 1830s the **Ndebele** entered **Matabeleland** by way of Botswana. Later Sotho, Griqua, and European hunters, traders, and missionaries passed through eastern Botswana to Zimbabwe, mostly by way of the **Ngwato** capital of Shoshong (see **Hunters' Road**). The Ndebele regularly raided the predominantly Tswana peoples of Botswana, reaching as far west as Lake Ngami, where the **Tawana** lived. Ndebele and **Ngwato** sovereignty overlapped around the present southeastern part of the border, producing conflicting territorial claims, particularly after the discovery of gold at **Tati** in the 1860s.

Declaration of the **Bechuanaland Protectorate** in 1885 began the formation of Botswana, which became an independent republic in 1968. In the meantime, the external economy of Botswana became inextricably tied to South Africa when a **railway** line was constructed through the eastern part of the country linking Mafeking and **Bulawayo** in 1897.

In the 1970s Botswana became an important refuge for Zimbabwean nationalists and refugees fleeing the war inside present Zimbabwe. The Botswana government, under the late President Seretse Khama, was openly committed to supporting the struggle for majority rule in Zimbabwe and in 1975 became a member of the **Frontline States** organization. An independent Zimbabwe was seen by Khama, and his successor Quett Masire, as a means of lessening Botswana's economic dependency on **South Africa.** Keeping that goal in mind, following Zimbabwe's independence, Botswana joined the Southern Africa Development Coordinating Conference (**SADCC**) in 1980.

BRITISH SOUTH AFRICA COMPANY (BSAC; a.k.a. "the Chartered Company"). London-based commercial organization that colonized the country and administered it from 1890 to 1923. In 1888 **Cecil Rhodes, C. D. Rudd,** and **F. R. Thompson** formed a syndicate, the Central Search Association, which obtained the **Rudd Concession** from the **Ndebele** King **Lobengula.** This group then amalgamated with a similar body, the Exploring Company, Ltd., to form the BSAC in March 1889. Rhodes became the company's managing director in Africa and was its guiding force through the remainder of his life.

In London Rhodes and his financial partner **Alfred Beit** got five prominent British financiers and politicians, including **A. H. G. Grey,** to join them in forming the company's first board of directors. The Duke of **Abercorn** served as the first BSAC president (see list below). The prestige of this body of men, as well as an exaggerated interpretation of the rights conferred by the Rudd Concession, enabled the BSAC to obtain a **Royal Charter** of incorporation on October 29, 1889. The charter conferred upon the BSAC sweeping rights over a vast but undefined territory north of the Limpopo River and west of present Malawi and Mozambique, excluding the **Tati Concession** area. The company eventually carved out the colonies that became present Zimbabwe and Zambia.

Through its charter the company was empowered to make treaties with African rulers, form banks, own and distribute land, and create its own police (see **British South Africa Police**). In return it promised to develop its territories economically, respect existing African law, allow free trade, and tolerate all religions. The British secretary of state for colonies retained supervisory powers over administration, and the charter was set to run for 25 years.

To avoid competing with other imperialist powers, notably the **Portuguese** (see **Anglo-Portuguese Convention**) and Transvaal Afrikaners (see **Adendorff Trek**), the BSAC claimed that the Ndebele ruled all the **Shona** and that the Rudd Concession therefore conferred upon it the right to occupy **Mashonaland.** This the company's **Pioneer Column** did in mid-1890. Once in Mashonaland, the company proceeded to distribute land and mining claims to settlers and missionaries and establish an admininstration (see **Administrators**). With the notable exception of **Mutasa,** few Shona were consulted.

In 1893 the BSAC administrator **L. S. Jameson** provoked the **Ndebele War,** which the British quickly won. Afterwards the company began occupying **Matabeleland,** laying the basis for the country's modern **borders.** Up to this point few Africans recognized company rule. Nevertheless, the BSAC appropriated land and livestock and attempted to assess taxes. Administrative abuses were a prime contributor to the large-scale **Ndebele** and **Shona Revolts**, which erupted in 1896. After the revolts were suppressed, the company reorganized its administration and brought the whole country under more systematic government, but Africans were granted very little additional participation. In 1898 European settlers gained a voice in the government through the establishment of a **Legislative Council**. Meanwhile, the company established separate administrations over the territories north of the Zambezi.

In 1915 the British Crown granted the BSAC a supplemental charter to run an additional ten years. By then, however, settlers were growing tired of the company administration. They formed the **Responsible Government Movement** to demand self-government. Anticipating a change of administrations, the British government created the **Cave Commission** in 1919 to determine the amount of compensation to be paid to the company for its administrative assets in the country.

In 1922 the company's shareholders accepted a cash offer from the government of South Africa to assume control of the country, but the settlers rejected this proposal in a referendum in October of that year (see **Unionist Movement**). A year later administration was turned over to the settlers (see **C. P. J. Coghlan**) and the country became a British Crown Colony. At the same time the company surrendered its administration of Northern Rhodesia to the British Colonial Office. Thereafter the company's interests in central Africa were only financial.

The BSAC had been incorporated in 1889 with a capitalization of only £1 million. Unlike other chartered companies, it did not engage directly in trading or mining operations, but concentrated on investments and financial operations. Heavy expenses incurred during the 1890s wars and the costs of administrative and economic development prevented the company from paying any dividends to shareholders until 1924. By then its worth was estimated at £9 million. In 1933 the company sold its **mineral** rights in Southern Rhodesia to the settler government for £2 million, while retaining its more valuable mineral rights in Northern Rhodesia. Over the ensuing decades the company flourished while developing a network of subsidiary companies controlling vast interests in **mining, railways, agriculture,** real estate, **forestry,** and various secondary industries. The company received a setback in 1964 when it was forced to relinquish its mineral rights in Zambia to that country's newly independent government. The next year the BSAC merged with two other companies to form Charter Consolidated, Ltd., which has since been closely associated with the **Anglo-American Corporation,** also based in London.

BSAC Presidents, 1889–1937: 1889–1913 Second Duke of Abercorn; 1913–17 L. S. Jameson; 1917–1920 (vacancy); 1920–23 Philip Lyttelton Gell; 1923–25 **J. R. Maguire;** 1925–37 Henry Birchenough. (See also list of **Administrators.**)

BRITISH SOUTH AFRICA POLICE (BSAP, or BSA POLICE). Former name of the country's paramilitary police force. In July 1980 the name was officially changed to the "Zimbabwe Republic Police."

The force was first organized as the "British South Africa Company Police" when the BSAC received its charter in 1889. The police served in the **Pioneer Column** the following year and then went through a succession of reorganizations under such names as Mashonaland Mounted Police, Matabeleland Mounted Police, and Southern Rhodesian Constabulary. An African contingent was organized as the Native Police Force in 1893. After the **Ndebele Revolt** in 1896 these forces were combined under a single command as the British South Africa Police, a name retained after the BSAC relinquished authority for the force to the British government in 1909.

Until the creation of the **Federation** in 1953, the BSAP was the country's only standing security force (see **Rhodesian Security Forces**). Following the declaration of UDI, the BSAP initially retained its primary responbilities for criminal investigation and internal security. However, it increasingly took on a more paramilitary role, working very closely with the armed forces, and eventually came under the authority of Combined Operations Command. The force grew to 11,000 regulars (about two-thirds African), with nearly 35,000 reserves (mostly European).

Following independence, the force instituted a policy of "Africanization" in which black officers were appointed to top ranking positions. In late 1982 Wiridzayl Nhuruve, a 22-year veteran who had enlisted as a constable, was appointed the country's first black police commissioner, the force's top post. In 1982 the force had 9,000 regulars (about one-third white) and was divided into nine police provinces throughout the nation. The total number of regular male and female officers grew to nearly 15,000 by the early 1990s.

BROADCASTING see **ZIMBABWE BROADCASTING COMPANY**

BROWN, WILLIAM HARVEY "CURIO" (Aug. 22, 1862–April 5, 1913). American settler. A member of the Pioneer Column, Brown later farmed in **Mashonaland**. Brown served on the Harare town council for nine years including two as the town's mayor (1908–10).

BUBI DISTRICT. A 6,960-sq km section of **Matabeleland North Province**. Most of the district is given over to extensive ranching, and prior to 1980 most of it was reserved for Europeans. **Inyati** is the administrative center. Bubi borders the districts of **Bulawayo** and **Nyamandhlovu** on the west, **Lupane** and **Nkayi** on the north, **Kwekwe** and **Gweru** on the east, and **Insiza** and **Umzingwane** on the south. District population in 1992 was 36,614.

BUBI RIVER. Rises in the Mchawacha Hills near **Inyati**, flowing generally northwest before meeting the **Gwai River** near **Lupane**. The river cuts through the northern part of the district of the same name.

BUBYE RIVER. Rising about 40 km northeast of **West Nicholson**, the Bubye flows southeast before joining the **Limpopo River** c.25 km west of the Mozambique border. It has several large **dams** that collect irrigation water for the region. Part of its course separates the **Mberengwa** and **Mwenezi** districts.

BUDJGA (variants: Budga, Budja, Budya). Major Shona groups speaking a dialect of **Korekore** in the present **Mutoko District**. Budjga settlement there goes back at least several centuries. In more recent times the paramount chiefs have taken the hereditary title of *Mutoko*. During the 19th century the Budjga frequently had to fight to maintain their independence, particularly against Portuguese-African incursions led by **Manuel de Sousa** in the 1880s. In 1890 the *Mutoko* signed a **concession** for the newly arrived BSAC, but thereafter resisted paying taxes. In early 1895 the British mounted a major punitive expedition against the Budjga, but the Budjga did not join in the general **Shona Revolt** which erupted the next year.

BUFFALO RANGE. Village with an airport serving the southeastern low veld region, located near **Chiredzi** (at 21°1′S, 31°32′E). The airport was opened on a ranch of the same name in 1965. In 1977 its landing facilities were expanded to accommodate military aircraft used against guerrillas based in **Mozambique.** (See **Air Transport; Zanla.**)

BUHERA. Village serving as the administrative center for the district of the same name in **Manicaland Provinc**e (at 19°20′S, 31°26′E).

BUHERA DISTRICT. Originally the southeastern section of **Chikomba District**, the entire district is now **Communal Land**. It is separated from the **Mutare District** on the east by the **Sabi River.** It also borders the districts of **Chimanimani** on the southeast, **Bikita** on the south, **Gutu** on the west, and **Wedza** on the north. Most of the inhabitants are **Hera** people. District population in 1992 was 203,909.

"BUILD A NATION." Name of a campaign launched by the government of **Edgar Whitehead** in order to increase the number of registered African voters. Whitehead hoped to enhance the electoral strength of his **United (Federal) Party** against that of the more right-wing European parties and to lure Africans away from the growing nationalist movement (see **African National Congress; National Democratic Party**). Less than a quarter of the anticipated 50,000 new African voters registered, and most of these boycotted the 1962 election.

BULALIMA-MANGWE DISTRICT see **BULILIMAMANGWE DISTRICT**

BULAWAYO (Sindebele locative: *Gubulawayo*). Historically, there have been three distinct Bulawayos.

(1) In 1871 the **Ndebele** king **Lobengula** raised the Bulawayo **ibutho,** making its town his chief headquarters in place of **Gibixhegu**. This town—later known as "Old Bulawayo"—was located c.5 km southwest of present **Hope Fountain.** It is said that Lobengula chose the name **Bulawayo,** "place of killing," to commemorate casualties in the battle of **Zwangendaba** fought in June 1870. "Bulawayo" had also been the name of two of the Zulu king Shaka's chief towns in the early 19th century. (Note that the belief that **Mzilikazi** founded Bulawayo is incorrect.)

(2) In 1881 Lobengula relocated Bulawayo farther north, at a site in the northern part of the modern city (20°9′S, 28°35′E; alt. 1,350 m). Over the next 13 years Bulawayo was the chief gathering place for the Ndebele during religious festivals (see **Inxwala**) and military reviews, and it was

the main center for European and other non-Ndebele hunters and traders. It was not a "capital" in the Western sense, however. Lobengula moved about the kingdom frequently, holding court where he happened to be (see **Umvutsha**). During this period Bulawayo had a fixed population of several thousand people.

(3) Towards the end of the 1893 **Ndebele War,** Lobengula set fire to Bulawayo and fled north. On November 4, 1893, British forces under **L. S. Jameson** occupied the site. European settlement began immediately. Occupation of the town was the most striking British achievement during the war. To symbolize British conquest, Government House was erected on the site of Lobengula's former home. The new **European** town grew rapidly. It soon displaced Fort Victoria (now **Masvingo**) as the major transport link between South Africa and Salisbury (now **Harare**). The outbreak of the **Ndebele Revolt** in 1896 gravely threatened British occupation of the region. For several months Ndebele forces beseiged the Europeans concentrated in Bulawayo, until British imperial troops put the Ndebele on the defensive. After the Revolt, Bulawayo's growth resumed, accelerating even further when the **railway** line to Mafeking was opened in 1897.

During the present century Bulawayo has grown into the country's second largest city with a population in 1992 of 620,936. The city is the country's leading commercial center with more than 1,800 industrial and commercial establishments, over 700 of which are factories producing in excess of Z$700 million worth of goods annually. Bulawayo is the headquarters of the **National Railways of Zimbabwe** and stands at the junction of railway links with Harare, **Victoria Falls**, Mafeking, and **Beitbridge**. The city is also the administrative center for **Bulawayo District** and for both **Matabeleland** provinces.

BULAWAYO CHRONICLE (a.k.a. *The Chronicle*). Second largest of the country's two daily newspapers (see **Press**), with about half the circulation of the *Herald*, the *Chronicle* was started by the **Argus Group** as a weekly in October 1894. It became a daily in 1897.

BULAWAYO DISTRICT. Surrounding the city of the same name, Bulawayo District is the country's second smallest, with an area of only 1,675 sq km. Prior to 1980 virtually all the land in the district was reserved for Europeans. Ranchers and farmers in the district specialize in intensive **cattle** ranching, dairying, and **maize** and **cotton** production. District population at the time of the 1982 census was 396,500.

BULAWAYO FIELD FORCE (BFF). Volunteer military force raised in April 1896 at the start of the **Ndebele Revolt**. It comprised about 850 Europeans and South African nonwhites. The BFF was reinforced by the **Matabeleland Relief Force** in May and was itself abandoned on July 4.

BULILIMAMANGWE DISTRICT (Bulalima-Mangwe District until 1985). West-central border district in **Matabeland South Province** roughly bisected by the **railway** line between **Francistown** and **Bulawayo**. The district covers 12,205 sq km and is separated from the **Nyamandhlovu District** in the north by the **Nata River**. It borders Bulawayo district on the east and shares a long north-south border with the **Matobo District**

on its southeast. The district's entire western border is with Botswana. **Plumtree** is its administrative center. Other centers include **Mphoengs, Figtree,** and **Mangwe**. Prior to 1980 the central area of the district was reserved for Europeans, while both ends of the district were **Tribal Trust Lands**. Animal husbandry is the dominant commercial industry. District population in 1992 was 156,641.

Bulalima is a locative form for "country of the Lilima," a branch of the **Kalanga-speaking people**. The district also contains many **Ndebele**.

BULLOCK, CHARLES (1880–1952). Amateur ethnographer and African administrator. Bullock began his career in the Southern Rhodesian Native Department in 1902, serving in many of the country's districts before retiring as chief native commissioner in 1940. He wrote several standard books on the **Shona** and **Ndebele peoples;** edited the journal **Nada** (1944–45); and wrote *Rina* (1949), a novel dealing with local miscegenation.

BUMBUZI RUINS (variant: Bumboosie). Group of megalithic ruins in the **Hwange District**. Similar to, but widely separated from, the **Zimbabwe** and **Khami-type ruins** of the rest of the country. The origin of the Bumbuzi ruins is in doubt, but they are generally attributed to **Rozvi** offshoots from the **Changamire state** who may have entered the region in the late 18th or early 19th century. **Nanzwa** traditions hold that the main ruin, Bumbuzi proper (at 18°30'S, 26°11'E), was built and occupied by their first **Zanke** (ruler) around the early 19th century. Nearby is an unrelated cave filled with sandstone **petroglyphs** of animal spoor believed to have been fashioned by **Stone Age** hunters. Sandstone is also the main building material of the ruins. Other complexes in the group of ruins include Halfway House Ruin (18°44'S, 27°21'E), and Mtoa Ruin (18°42'S, 26°41'E).

BUMI RIVER (a.k.a. Ume; Omay). One of the **Zambezi River**'s main southern tributaries in the country, the Bumi rises c.30 km north of **Gokwe**, flowing roughly north. It now enters **Lake Kariba** just east of the Bumi Hills.

BUNGA FOREST. Evergreen forest, now part of **Vumba National Park**.

BUNDU. Term for wild bush country. Bundu may be related to such Bantu words as **Chishona**'s *bundo*, for "grazing grass."

BUNU (variants: Bhunu, Vabunu, Amabunu, etc.). Widely used **Bantu** form of **Boer**.

BURANDAYA (pl. *Maburandaya*). **Chishona** term for a person from Malawi; derives from the name "Blantyre," the commercial capital of Malawi.

BURMA VALLEY. Located just south of the **Vumba Mountains**, Burma Valley is the center of year-round intensive agricultural production on commercial farms. The valley's Nyamataka River flows east into Mozambique.

BUROMBO, BENJAMIN B. (c.1909–1959). Variously said to have been born in the **Buhera** or **Shurugwi** districts, Burombo came to **Bulawayo** during the early 1940s after having worked in Johannesburg, South Africa. There he ran a small store and began assisting farmers to resist government destocking measures. Around July 1947 he organized the (British) African Workers' Voice Association—an organization now regarded as an important forerunner of modern nationalism. He played an active role in organizing and in negotiating the general strike of 1948 in Bulawayo. Afterwards he used his organization to concentrate on rural issues. He attained notable successes in opposing implementation of the **Land Apportionment Act** and the **Native Land Husbandry Act**, but the government merely responded by amending the laws to overcome the loopholes which he found.

In 1952 his Voice Association was banned under the terms of the Subversive Activities Act of 1950. Burombo was a dynamic and charismatic leader, but his health was always poor and he succumbed to cancer.

"BUSHMAN." Popular but pejorative name for the **San** people in southern Africa. From the Dutch word *boschjesman.*

BUTUA (variants: Abutua, Butwa). **Portuguese** name for the southwestern part of the country which lay just beyond their penetration (see **Bayao, S.**). The same part of the country is known in Shona tradition as **Guruhuswa**. The word "Butua" is apparently a Portuguese contraction of "Gunuvutwa," the **Tavara** pronunciation of Guruhuswa.

BUXTON COMMITTEE (1921). Once it was certain that the BSAC would be ending its administration of the country, the question of the colony's future constitutional status arose. In March 1921 Winston Churchill, then secretary of state for colonies, set up a committee to investigate the feasibility of the settlers' assuming power in a **Responsible Government**. The committee was headed by a former governor-general and high commissioner of South Africa, Lord Buxton (1853–1934). The committee's report, dated April 12, 1921, recommended an immediate referendum on the issue among the settlers and outlined a **constitution** based on that of the former colony of Natal. An important further recommendation was that the British government retain the same reserve powers over legislation affecting African rights that it held over the BSAC regime.

"BYRD AMENDMENT." Popular name for Section 503 of the Armed Forces Procurement Appropriations Authorization Act passed by the U.S. Congress in November 1971. Senator Harry F. Byrd (Virginia) introduced the section to prevent the president of the United States from prohibiting importation of designated strategic materials from any noncommunist country so long as such materials were being imported from a communist country. The law, signed by President Nixon on November 17, 1971, therefore allowed the United States openly to import **chrome** from Rhodesia in violation of United Nations **sanctions** because the country was already importing chrome from the Soviet Union.

The United States had imported $5 million worth of Rhodesian chrome in 1965, but it ceased all imports the next year. In 1972 the U.S. imported $13.3 million worth of Rhodesian chrome, **nickel**, and **asbestos**, even though large domestic stockpiles of chrome were reported as available. Rhodesian chrome imports rose to $45 million in 1975, and by the next year Rhodesia was estimated to be supplying 17 percent of U.S. imports of the metal. Other major American suppliers included the Soviet Union, South Africa, and Turkey.

Implementation of the Byrd Amendment caused the United States to be repeatedly condemned at home and abroad for flouting the sanctions policy that it had previously endorsed. Under the pressure of newly elected President Jimmy Carter, Congress repealed the amendment on March 14–15, 1977. The Rhodesian government then announced that loss of the American market would have little impact on the country's economy, but it is clear that the change of American policy was a blow to Rhodesian morale.

C

C-. In **Sindebele** orthography the letter *c* represents the dental **click sound**, as in Mncumbathe. In **Chishona** orthography, *c* occurs only in the *ch* digraph, which was formerly often written simply as *c*, as in "Cishona."

CAM AND MOTOR MINE see EIFFEL FLATS

CAMPBELL, ARCHIBALD ANDREW (Oct. 11, 1863–1946). Early African administrator and amateur historian. Born and educated in Natal, Campbell came to **Mashonaland** in the early 1890s to prospect. He joined the **Matabeleland** Native Department in 1896, serving for 23 years before becoming manager of the labor compound at **Shabani.** During his Matabeleland service he pioneered the collection of **Ndebele** traditions, which he used to write a book in 1911. He later published the volume under the pen name "Mziki" ("reedbuck") as *Mlimo: The Rise and Fall of the Matabele* (1926). Campbell's book was not the pure compilation of authentic traditions it purported to be, but it has had a major impact on later writings on Ndebele history. An early draft of his work was used by D. F. Ellenberger in the latter's account of Ndebele history in *The History of the Basuto* (London, 1912). A. T. Bryant in turn borrowed from Ellenberger in his own monumental **Nguni** history, *Olden Times in Zululand and Natal* (London, 1929).

CAPRICORN AFRICA SOCIETY. Multiracial organization founded in 1949 by Col. David Stirling (b. 1915), a postwar immigrant who had been a British commando leader in the North Africa campaign. The society's main goal was to foster a sense of nonracial African identity throughout central and east Africa. After several years of formulating principles, the society issued a manifesto and attempted to recruit members of all races. A handbook issued in 1955 pronounced a doctrine of racial equality, calling for an end to all racial discrimination as well as an abandonment of black African nationalism. It further proposed a franchise system in which multiple votes would be awarded to citizens on the basis of civic contributions—a system recognizing the ideal of universal suffrage while assuring that whites would retain political dominance. Unique multiracial study groups were formed throughout the country, but the society's identification with the **"partnership"** principles of **federation** made "Capricornist" a dirty word among Africans north of the Zambezi. In 1956 the society held a large conference in Nyasaland (now Malawi) but failed to develop into a significant mass movement. Leading African members, such as **Leopold Takawira**, drifted into more militant African organizations. In 1957 European members of the society launched the Constitution Party in Northern Rhodesia, but the party won no elections. The same year society branches began folding up throughout operations, turning over its records to the **National Archives.**

"CAPTAIN OF THE GATES" see **MASAPA**

CARNEGIE, DAVID (Nov. 26, 1855–Jan. 1910). An agent of the **London Missionary Society**, Carnegie worked as an interpreter during the **Ndebele Revolt** of 1896 and helped bring about the negotiations that ended the Matapos fighting. He later founded **Centenary Mission** at **Figtree.**

CARRINGTON, FREDERICK (Aug. 23, 1844–March 22, 1913). British army officer of considerable experience in minor South African campaigns after 1875. Between 1885 and 1893 Carrington commanded the **Bechuanaland Border Police** and then served as military advisor to H. B. Loch, high commissioner of South Africa, during the **Ndebele War.** After the 1896 **Ndebele Revolt** erupted, Carrington was named supreme commander of British forces in **Matabeleland**, where he arrived on June 2. There he commanded about 2,000 white and 600 black troops, including **H. C. O. Plumer**'s **MRF**. His subordinates, Plumer and **Baden-Powell**, pursued an active campaign of using mounted patrols to keep the rebels in motion, building forts, seizing cattle, and burning crops to disrupt Ndebele supplies. By August they had succeeded in neutralizing most rebels in the hills themselves. The theater of the war was ended by negotiation when **Cecil Rhodes** met Matapos leaders in famous *"indabas."* After the outbreak of the **Shona Revolt** in late June, Carrington was designated supreme commander for the whole country, with **E. A. H. Alderson** directing the **Mashonaland** campaign. During the **South African War** Carrington commanded the **Rhodesia Field Force.**

CARTER COMMISSION see **MORRIS CARTER COMMISSION**

CATON-THOMPSON, GERTRUDE (1888–April 18, 1985). British archaeologist commissioned in 1929 to investigate the dispute over the origins and dating of the country's **stone ruins** begun a generation earlier by **D. Randall-MacIver** and **R. N. Hall**. Only the second professional archaeologist to work in the country, Caton-Thompson conducted digs at **Zimbabwe, Dhlo Dhlo**, and other ruins, undertaking her most thorough investigation in the Maund Ruin at Great Zimbabwe. She published her findings in *The Zimbabwe Culture: Ruins and Reactions* (London, 1931), which contains one of the most detailed inventories of artifacts yet presented. She unequivocally supported Randall-MacIver's conclusion that the country's ruins were strictly African in origin, but departed from her predecessor in pushing the date for Great Zimbabwe's beginnings back to the 8th or 9th century. Except for her early Zimbabwe dating, her work has stood up well against more recent investigations, but it failed to settle the **Zimbabwe Controversy** among the lay public.

CATTLE. Animal husbandry, like plant cultivation, is reckoned to have begun in the country in the early **Iron Age**, though cattle-keeping apparently did not become a significant economic activity until late in the first millennium A. D. Clay figurines of cattle appear at both the **Leopards Kopje** and **Gumanye** cultures; remains of cattle bones have been found at **Zimbabwe** and **Khami** sites; and trade in cattle dating from the sixteenth century from the southwest of present Zimbabwe to the **Zambezi** valley is well documented. All these indicate that the **Shona** people have a long record of cattle-herding in the country. When the **Ndebele** arrived in the country around 1839, they brought South African breeds with them. They were able to increase the size of their herds by acquiring local animals, raiding outside the country, and restricting their slaughter for beef.

As in many African societies, cattle played an important social role among both the Shona and Ndebele. They provided an index for personal wealth and prestige, acted as currency for important social transactions such as marriage (see **Lobolo**), and perhaps most importantly were a form of insurance against crop failures and drought. By the late 19th century, just prior to the **European** occupation of the country, the African-owned cattle herd for the country has been estimated at c.500,000, with nearly 200,000 owned by the Ndebele. European occupation of **Matabeleland** after the **Ndebele War** of 1893–4 was accompanied by a vigorous effort to confiscate Ndebele herds on the pretext that all cattle had belonged to the king and were therefore the property of the BSAC by right of conquest. Confiscation was followed by **rinderpest** and enforced destocking throughout the country, and further confiscation and losses during the **1896–7 Revolts**. By the turn of the century it was estimated that only c. 55,000 head were still in the hands of the entire African population. Recovery was rapid, however, and by 1913 African-owned cattle had risen to nearly 400,000 head.

Meanwhile, European farmers were developing a commercial beef and dairy industry. African participation in this commercial cattle industry has always been limited. Two main reasons have been the above-mentioned social value cattle have for most Africans in the country, and the government enforced destocking of African-owned herds has limited the number of cattle owned by any individual family, enhancing their reluctance to sell stock for cash. The commercial beef and dairy industry greatly developed in the 1950s and early 1960 as domestic demands increased. Following UDI, the number of cattle owned by commercial European farmers increased, as many white farmers sought alternatives to **tobacco**, which had been their chief export crop but was greatly effected by international **sanctions**.

The shift to cattle-raising was made partly because beef proved to be a particularly successful sanctions-busting commodity. Beginning in the mid-1970s, African and European-owned cattle herds increasingly became the targets of guerilla forces. Dipping tanks, water sources, and fences were destroyed, **tsetse fly** eradication programs were disrupted and eventually discontinued in much of the country, and animals were maimed or killed. The result was that an estimated 170,000 European-owned, and over one million African-owned cattle died during the war for independence. Since 1980, the national herd has recovered and in 1997 was estimated to be at about 5.4 million head.

CAVE COMMISSION (1919–20). When it appeared likely that the British Imperial government would take over responsibility for the country from the BSAC, the question of compensating the company for its local assets arose. The company claimed assets worth £8 million, but members of the **Legislative Council** protested the amount. To resolve the dispute the British government appointed a cabinet minister, George Cave (1856–1928) to head a commission of investigation. The commission held hearings in London and Salisbury in 1919, issuing its report on January 15, 1920. The report suggested a compensation of £4,435,225—somewhat more than the company actually received four years later. (See **Buxton Committee; Responsible Government.**)

CAVE OF HANDS see **MCHELA CAVE**

CENSORSHIP. The various European governments of the country were sensitive to criticism after the establishment of the BSAC administration in **Mashonaland** in 1890. It is said that **Cecil Rhodes** threatened **W. E. Fairbridge** with deportation shortly after the latter had started the forerunner of the *Rhodesia Herald* in 1891. Fairbridge then toned down his editorial criticisms of the administration. Until the **Rhodesian Front** came to power in 1962, the **European press** tended to identify closely with the interests of the government, so overt censorship was rarely a problem. By contrast, the majority African population—whose interests have almost always conflicted with those of the government—have never established anything like an independent press (see **African Newspapers, Ltd.**). Papers such as *African Daily News, Chapupu*, the *Zimbabwe Sun*, and others were quickly suppressed when they expressed overtly African nationalist sentiments.

Shortly before UDI in 1965, Ian Smith's government promulgated emergency regulations allowing for wide press censorship. One month after UDI the government officially instituted censorship, arguing that the country was virtually at war. Censorship was directed mainly against the **Argus Group** newspapers, which editorially opposed UDI. Government censors inspected newspaper galley proofs and stopped publication of considerable material. The newspapers responded by leaving large blank columns and printing notices calling attention to the fact of censorship. In February 1966 new regulations forbade these practices, but were generally ignored. The government overlooked these offenses, apparently because it feared having UDI challenged in the courts.

In April 1968 censorship restrictions were formally lifted. It is said that the government worked out a secret accommodation with the newspapers calling for self-censorship. Whatever, press criticism of the government was subsequently muted. In December 1967 the government established a permanent Board of Censorship to examine publications and films of all kinds. It frequently banned importation of foreign materials for political or moral reasons. Among the banned authors were James Baldwin, Norman Mailer, Henry Miller, Frank Harris, and Kenneth Kaunda.

Censorship of the country's **press** did not end with independence in 1980. Particularly since its acquisition of the Argus Group in 1981, the government has repeatedly been accused of censoring the nation's press. There was only limited reporting about the **ZNA**'s actions in **Matabeleland** in the early 1980s, and during the **elections** from 1985 to 2000 opposition candidates were noticeably ignored by both the country's newspapers and television news. In addition, individual reporters and editors have claimed that there have been repeated attempts to intimidate them by government agents and **ZANU-PF** supporters. In September 1999, for instance, Mark Chavunduka, the editor of an independent newspaper, and one of his reporters were arrested by the military after reporting that 23 members of the ZNA were plotting a coup.

CENSUSES see **POPULATION**

CENTENARY. (1) LMS mission station founded near **Figtree** in 1898 by David Carnegie. The station was closed in 1913 because encroaching European-owned farmlands cut it off from African communities. (2) Village in the **Mukumbura District.** 132 km north of Harare, named in 1953 to commemorate **Cecil Rhodes'** birth. Prior to 1980, it was the center of a European tobacco farming region. During the mid-to-late 1970s many European-owned farms in this region were attacked by **ZANLA** forces

CENTENARY DISTRICT see **MUZARABANI DISTRICT**

"CENTRAL AFRICA." At one time or another this term has been applied to almost every part of Africa between the Western Sudanic region and present Zimbabwe. During the 1890s Malawi had been known briefly as "British Central Africa." Later "Central Africa" was increasingly used to refer to present Malawi, Zambia, and Zimbabwe. Perhaps the best claimant to the term, however, is the former French Equatorial African territory renamed the Central Africa Republic in 1960. (See **"Southern Africa."**)

CENTRAL AFRICA COUNCIL. Advisory and consultative body created by the British government in October 1944 for the purpose of stimulating interterritorial cooperation among Southern Rhodesia, Northern Rhodesia, and Nyasaland (see **Bledisloe Commission**). The **governor** of Southern Rhodesia was made chairman. The governors of the other territories and the Southern Rhodesian **prime minister** were made ex officio members. Each territory also supplied three common members. The council met twice yearly, beginning in June 1945. Although it had no powers of enforcement, its recommendations to the territorial legislative bodies led to the mergers of **air transport**, meteorological, statistical, and archival services (see **National Archives**) and to formation of a commission to investigate building the **Kariba Dam**. The council provided an institutional framework that facilitated establishment of the **federation** in 1953.

CENTRAL AFRICAN AIRWAYS see **AIR ZIMBABWE**

CENTRAL AFRICAN EXAMINER. Monthly newspaper published in Salisbury from 1957 to 1965, when government pressure shut it down. (See **Press.**)

CENTRAL AFRICAN FEDERATION (CAF). Popular but unofficial name of the **Federation of Rhodesia and Nyasaland.**

CENTRAL AFRICAN PARTY (CAP). Short-lived multiracial party formed by **Garfield Todd** in 1959. The party attracted such African leaders as **Leopold Takawira, Stanlake Samkange,** and **Ndabaningi Sithole** but lost many African supporters to the new **National Democratic Party** the next year. Todd himself resigned his leadership in July 1960. The remaining party leaders supported the proposals for the 1961 **constitution** but failed ever to score an electoral victory.

CENTRAL AFRICAN POWER CORPORATION see **ELECTRICAL POWER**

CENTRAL PLATEAU. The main watershed of the country, the Central Plateau runs southwest to northeast, separating the **Zambezi** and **Limpopo** basins. It is also known as the "high veld," but this term also appropriately applies to any land over 1,220 m (4,000 ft). (See **Altitudinal Zones; Rivers.**)

CENTRE PARTY (CP). Moderate multiracial political party formed in August 1968 by opponents of the **Rhodesian Front** government, such as T. H. Patrick Bashford (b. 1915). The CP favored gradual African political advancement along the lines of the **"Tiger Talks"** proposals, and it attracted some middle-class African support. In the 1970 election the party won seven of the eight African parliamentary seats it contested (see **National People's Union**), but all its white candidates were badly defeated despite support from the **Argus Group** newspapers. In early 1972 the CP reluctantly advocated acceptance of the Anglo-Rhodesian Settlement terms in the absence of any apparent alternatives (see **Pearce Commission**).

CHAKAIPA, PATRICK F. (b. June 20, 1932). One of the most popular novelists writing in Chishona, Chakaipa attended primary school at Saint Michael's in Mondoro Tribal Trust Land (now **Communal Land**) and Minor Seminary in **Chishawasha** from 1950 to 1956. From 1958 to 1966 he studied at the provincial secondary school in Chishawasha. He also took a teaching course at **Kutama** College, where he began his writing career. He was ordained a Roman Catholic priest in August 1968, and in 1973 was appointed auxiliary bishop of Salisbury (now Harare). Chakaipa has used his own homeland of Mhondoro as the main setting in all of his books. His first two books, *Karikoga Gumiremiseve* ("Karikoga and the

Ten Arrows," 1958) and *Pfumo Reropa* ("The Spear of Blood," 1961), are historical romances based on traditional stories. Three later novels (1961 to 1967) with modern settings are moralistic tales attempting to reconcile Western notions of individual liberty with traditional African community values (see **Literature**).

CHAKARI. Town in the **Chegutu District** located c.25 km northwest of the main road between **Kadoma** and **Harare** (at 18°4'S, 29°51'E; alt. 1,160 m). The town arose to support the Dalny Mine, begun in 1908. This mine is now the country's leading producer of **gold**.

CHAMINUKA. Name of the most famous Shona "lion spirit," or *mhondoro*. The identity of the historical Chaminuka personage is uncertain, but is believed to go back several hundred years. The Chaminuka spirit appears to first have entered a medium during the early 19th century—possibly after the arrival of the **Ndebele** in the country. According to a recent Chaminuka medium, the spirit entered a **Korekore** man named Mutota at Great Zimbabwe and then abandoned him to reside near Bulawayo. It then followed a **Zezuru** man named Kachinda to **Mashyamombe's** chiefdom, where it possessed him. From Kachinda the spirit switched to Pasipamire (a.k.a. Tsuro), the son of the Zezuru chief Rwizi. Pasipamire used his personal charisma to develop Chamunuka, his alter ego, into a famous rainmaker and the center of Shona resistance to the Ndebele. Operating from a group of villages known as Situngwiza (**Chitungwiza**) between the **Umfuli** and **Hunyani** rivers, Pasipamire developed a wealthy and influential cult associated with that of **Nehanda**.

During the 1870s the Ndebele king **Lobengula** paid tribute to him and exempted his region from raids. By the early 1880s "Chaminuka" was behaving so independently that he was seen as a challenge to Ndebele authority throughout central Shona country. In May 1883 an Ndebele *impi* (in which the Imbizo *ibutho* participated) attacked the Chaminuka headquarters and had Pasipamire killed. The medium's death later became the subject of many popular legends, some of which include the apocryphal claim that Chaminuka personally confronted Lobengula before being tried and executed. More likely, he was killed near the **Shangani** River while being brought to Bulawayo. The Chaminuka spirit is not known to have possessed another medium until 1903, so it did not figure into the **1896–97 Revolt**. A female medium emerged in 1903, but she soon committed suicide while being held in a British jail. Later 20th century mediums have revived the Chaminuka cult and restored the spirit's reputation as a rainmaker in Zezuru country. The 19th-century medium, Pasipamire, is now regarded as a major symbol of African resistance and is venerated by many modern nationalists.

CHANCELLOR, JOHN ROBERT (Oct. 20, 1870–July 31, 1952). A Scot, Chancellor had a military background before entering the colonial service as governor of Mauritius (1911–16) and than of Trinidad and Tobago (1916–21). In 1923 he became the first governor of Southern Rhodesia. He is said to have exercised considerable influence over the inexperienced government of **Charles Choghlan** and somewhat less influence over **H. U. Moffat**. He was succeeded by **C. H. Rodwell** in 1928. He later served as British high commissioner in Palestine.

CHANGA (fl. late 15th cent.). The son, or perhaps son-in-law, of Munhumutapa **Matope**, Changa was made a district chief over an area around present **Guruve** when the Munhumutapa state was established in the **Dande**. In the 1480s Changa rebelled against his relative **Mukombera**, killing him in a battle in c.1490. For about four years Changa held the Munhumutapaship himself. By this time he had adopted the name "**Changamire**," apparently bestowed upon him by **Muslims**, who called him *amir*. Changa was in turn killed by a son of Mukombero, **Chikuyo Chisamarengu**, who reclaimed the kingship (c.1494). Changa's son (name unknown) then adopted "Changamire" as a title and moved south, where he allied with **Torwa** in defiance of the Munhumutapa state.

CHANGAMIRE. Dynastic title of the rulers of the Shona state variously known to historians as the Changamire Kingdom or the **Rozvi** Empire. Its rulers were also known by the generic Shona title *mambo*. The Changamire state dominated most of the country from the late 17th century to the early 19th century, but its history is poorly known, in contrast to that of the older **Munhumutapa** state.

Changamire history divides into at least two distinct periods separated by a long gap about which little is known. The first person to hold the title "Changamire" was **Changa**, who briefly usurped the Munhumutapaship in the early 1490s. After his death, his son adopted the name Changamire as a dynastic title and apparently retreated south. In c.1547 Munhumutapa **Neshangwe** is said to have expelled the reigning Changamire from the **Mbire** region where the formerly allied **Torwa** dynasty ruled. Some authorities, however, suggest a 17th century Changamire intrusion into **Guruhuswa**. Whichever, it is fairly clear that its main centers were at **Dhlo Dhlo** and **Ntabazikamambo (Manyanga)**. There the Changamires ruled mainly **Kalanga-speaking peoples**.

The second phase of Changamire history began in the 1680s, when Changamire military campaigns began attracting the notice of **Portuguese** traders and missionaries in the northeast. In the early 1690s Changamire forces under **Dombo** swiftly advanced into Munhumutapa, **Manyika**, and other territories. It was apparently then that the people earned the nickname Rozvi, "the destroyers." From then until the *Mfecane* era the Changamire state ruled most of the country directly, or through tributary chiefdoms. Rozvi officials sanctioned chiefly succession in many societies—a practice which persists today.

The 18th century is the country's "dark age" in modern historiography. Dombo's campaigns expelled most of the Portuguese from the country, thereby isolating the state from literate observers. Traditional evidence has been collected, but has not yet been fully worked out. Consequently, there is not yet even a satisfactory list of 18th century Changamires.

By the early 19th century the state appears to have been in disarray. Internal succession disputes, wars with **Karanga** and **Ngwato** (see **Kgari**), and droughts were breaking down central authority. In the early 1830s the *Mfecane* brought a succession of South African invaders to the country. The most important of these were the **Ngoni** of **Zwangendaba** and **Nyamazana**, who killed the reigning Changamire, **Chrisamhuru**, at Ntabazikamambo. An attempt at recovery was made, and Chirisamhuru's son **Tohwechipi** was made king at Dhlo Dhlo after the Ngoni had left.

Soon, however, **Mzilikazi's Ndebele** invaded the country. The Ndebele invasion was initially less violent, but most of the Rozvi leaders fled. A section under Mutinhima, a rival claimant to the Changamire title, resisted the Ndebele in the nearby **Mulungwane Hills**, but he was driven further east. Tohwechipi resisted the Ndebele successfully from a place near Great Zimbabwe into the 1850s, but was captured farther east, in 1866. His capture effectively ended any pretensions the Rozvi had to be sustaining the Changamire state. It did not, however, end the succession. The titular *mambo*-ship has remained a lively focus of political contention into the 20th century.

CHANGANA. Variant of **Shangane**.

CHAPLIN, FRANCIS PERCY DRUMMOND (Aug. 10, 1866–Nov. 16, 1933). Last BSAC **administrator** of the country. Chaplin left England for Southern Rhodesia in 1897 but decided not to enter the country because of the **Revolts** then active. Instead, he became a correspondent for the London *Times* in South Africa. In 1898 he briefly visited Southern Rhodesia, but disliked what he saw there. After a stint as a correspondent in Russia, he returned to the Transvaal and became a manager of Consolidated Gold Fields of South Africa, Ltd. He soon became one of the most influential people in the mining industry and was elected to the Transvaal Legislative Assembly (1907) and then to the Union House of Assembly (1910).

In late 1914 he succeeded **W. H. Milton** as administrator of Southern Rhodesia. Fearful of **Afrikaner** domination in southern Africa (see **Unionist Movement**), Chaplin advocated **amalgamation** of Southern and Northern Rhodesia to strengthen their economies. In the face of strong settler opposition, he abandoned this goal but, ironically, later assumed the additional responsibility of administering Northern Rhodesia in 1921. His later appointments ended in September 1923, when the BSAC turned administration of the country over to the settlers (see **Responsible Government**). Chaplin retained extensive mining interests in central Africa. He returned to South Africa, where he reentered national politics. In 1925 he was made a director of the BSAC.

CHAPUPU (*The Witness*). African newspaper started in Salisbury by the **Youth League** and **African National Congress** in 1957. One of the few attempts at a truly independent African **press**, the paper was banned by the government in 1958 and 1962, when a revival was attempted. (See **Censorship**.)

CHARTER, ROYAL (1889). Document signed on October 29, 1889, by Queen Victoria, officially incorporating the BSAC and granting it wide rights over the territories of present Zimbabwe and Zambia for a period of 25 years. In 1915 a supplemental charter extended these rights an additional ten years. During the 1880s the British Crown granted similar charters to the Imperial British Africa Company, which operated mainly in Kenya; the Royal Niger company, operating in Nigeria; and the British North Borneo Company.

CHARTER DISTRICT see **CHIKOMBA DISTRICT**

CHARTERED COMPANY (a.k.a. "the Charter"). Popular name for the **British South Africa Company**.

"CHARTERLAND." One of the unofficial names by which the country was known in the early 1890s.

CHAZA, MAI (d.1960) A famous faith-healer, Mai ("Mother") Chaza began her brief but spectacular religious career as a member of the Methodist Church. Around 1953-54 she became ill and was believed mentally deranged. When she fell into a coma, she was thought to have died. Her recovery was thus interpreted as a return from the dead—an idea she corroborated with her announcement that she had a vision in which God instructed her to become a faith-healer. In this capacity her fame grew rapidly; she was particularly successful in curing barren women. She found refuge in the **Seke** Reserve, just south of present Harare, calling it *Guta ra Jehova*, "City of God." In 1955 she broke from the Methodists, forming her own independent church variously known to her followers as Guta ra Jehova, or the Mai Chaza Church. She received thousands of supplicants at Seke, including many from outside the country. Additional refuges were established throughout the country. Little is known about the membership of the church, except that it apparently numbered tens of thousands at her death in 1960 and that most of her followers had little education. The next year a Malawian, Bandal Mapaulos, assumed leadership of the Mai Chaza Church. Thereafter membership is believed to have declined.

CHEGUTU (Hartley until 1982). Chegutu is the commercial and administrative center for the **Chegutu District** and is located in the Hartley Hills (at 18°12′S, 30°23′E; alt. 1,190 m), about 100 km southwest of Harare on the main road and railway line to Bulawayo. The hills were named for Henry Hartley and the present town was founded in 1901— relocated from a site c.29 km further east. The town is the site of one of the country's largest textile mills and is the center of an important agricultural area. The population in 1992 was 30,122.

CHEGUTU DISTRICT (Hartley District until 1985). The district covers 7,345 sq km in a region rich in **gold, nickel,** and other minerals, as well as **maize, cotton,** and **cattle.** The district also borders the **Makonde District** on the north, where the boundary is defined by the **Umfuli River,** and the **Harare District** on the east. Prior to 1980, most of the district was reserved for Europeans. District population in 1992 was 191,909.

CHI- (former variant: *ci-*). **Chishona** noun prefix (Class 7) for things (pl. *zvi-*). The *chi-* prefix is also used for nouns denoting language, culture, or style, as in *Chishona* itself. Except for the Chishona entry below, prefixes for the languages are dropped in this dictionary unless they are used as locatives in proper place names, as in Chishawasha. (See **Sindebele.**)

CHIBAMBAMU (variant: Sibambamu) see **TOHWECHIPI**

CHIBERO COLLEGE OF AGRICULTURE. Government agricultural training center for Africans, located in a rural area c.50 km southwest of Harare (at 18°4′S, 30°39′E). The college was opened in 1961 to provide a three-year practical training course leading to the Diploma in Agriculture for up to 80 students. (See **Education; Gwebi Agricultural College.**)

CHIBI. Village serving as the administrative center for the **Chivi District.** The village was originally the center of the Chivi chiefdom of the **Mari** people (located at 20°19'S, 30°31'E).

CHIBI DISTRICT see **CHIVI DISTRICT**

CHICUALACUALA. Mozambique border post opposite **Sango.** Prior to Mozambican independence in 1975, this village was known as "Malvernia" in honor of **Lord Malvern**.

CHIDZERO, BERNARD THOMAS GIBSON (b. July 1, 1927). Born in Salisbury, Chidzero was educated at **Kutama**, where he received a scholarship to Marianhill in Natal, South Africa. He graduated in 1949 and earned a scholarship to Roma University College in Lesotho. In 1955 he received a B.A. from the University of South Africa. He then traveled to Canada, where he earned an M.A. from Ottawa University and in 1958 obtained a doctorate in political science from McGill University, followed by a postdoctoral research grant at Nuffield College, Oxford.

He returned to Zimbabwe in 1959 to conduct research into political developments in the **Federation** and was offered a teaching post at the University College of Rhodesia and Nyasaland that was withdrawn because he was married to a French-Canadian. In 1960, Chidzero accepted a post as an assistant research worker with the United Nations Economic Commission for Africa in Addis Ababa. Three years later he was appointed representative of the UN Technical Assistance Board and director of the Special Fund Program in Kenya. In 1966 he became the resident representative of the UN program in Kenya. In 1968 he moved to Geneva, where he became the director of the Commodities Division of the UN Conference on Trade and Development (UNCTAD). Prior to 1976, his only political activities involving Zimbabwe where when he joined the **National Democratic Party** in 1960 and in the following year was a member of that party's delegation to London which called on the British government to retain its reserved powers in any new **constitution** granted the country following the break-up of the Federation. He was a strong supporter of **ZANU** since 1963 and in 1976 was elected as an economic and political advisor to that party's delegation at the **Geneva Conference**.

In 1980, after being released from his position with the UN, he returned to Zimbabwe and was elected to Parliament as the representative for Harare. He joined Prime Minister **Robert Mugabe's** first cabinet as minister for economic planning and development; this was later combined with finance and provided him with a preeminent position to help direct Zimbabwe's economic development following independence. Under his management, the government in the late 1980s was able to slow the decline in foreign exchange and reduce the negative ratio in the country's balance of payments. In January 1988 Mugabe shuffled his cabinet to mark the merger of ZANU and **ZAPU**, and Chidzero was named one of the three senior ministers and placed in charge of Zimbabwe's national finances and economic development programs. In 1990 he was given the added responsibilities of heading the newly formed Ministry of Trade. Later that year, with the full backing of Mugabe and the Zimbabwe government, he was a candidate for the position of UN Secretary-General. Starting in 1993, his health began to deteriorate, and he retired from government following the 1995 elections.

CHIEFS, AFRICAN see **COUNCIL OF CHIEFS**; see also under specific dynastic titles, e.g., **Makoni** or **Mangwende**; and under the generic titles, **Induna; Inkosi; Mambo.**

CHIKEREMA, JAMES ROBERT DAMBAZA (b. May 1925). Born at **Kutama**, where his father was a teacher, Chikerema began his education there, later attending the University of Cape Town in South Africa. While in South Africa he helped found the Central African Social Club, designed for the political education of Zimbabwean blacks living at the Cape. Club activities, including a demonstration opposing the establishment of the **federation**, led to his deportation in 1953. In 1955, he helped to launch the **Youth League** and became its first president, as well as editor of *Chapupu*. Two years later he became vice-president of the revived **African National Congress**. He was arrested in early 1959.

While in prison in 1961, ZAPU was formed and he was appointed a member of the executive. Released in 1963, he helped **Joshua Nkomo** form the **People's Caretaker Council** and then left the country later the same year. In October 1971, in a proclaimed attempt to unite the different external factions, he created **FROLIZI**, becoming its president in the following year. In August 1975 he attended the **Victoria Falls Conference** as a member of the **African National Council**'s negotiating team. In 1976 he joined with **Abel Muzorewa**'s ANC and participated in the **Geneva Conference**. In 1977 he returned to the country and worked with Muzorewa's faction, later becoming vice-president. In April 1979 he was elected to the short-lived **Zimbabwe Rhodesia Parliament** as a member of the UANC, but in June he broke with Muzorewa over accusations of Shona tribal factionalism and led seven UANC parliamentarians out of the party. Chikerema contested the 1980 elections as head of the Zimbabwe Democratic Party, but failed to win any seats.

CHIKOMBA DISTRICT (Charter District until 1985). Easternmost district in **Midlands Province**, Chikomba covers 6,670 sq km. Its original headquarters was established at Ft. Charter (18°36'S, 31°4'E), but that site declined rapidly after the **railway** was extended from Bulawayo to Harare and the administrative center was shifted to **Chivhu**. The original southeastern section of the district was separated to form the **Buhera District**. The remaining parts of the district were, prior to 1980, divided roughly evenly between European-reserved land, **Purchase Area,** and Tribal Trust Land (now **Communal Land**). District population in 1992 was 124,745.

CHIKUNDA (Bachikunda). People speaking an Nsenga, or Sena, branch of **Bantu**. Most Chikunda are in **Mozambique**, but several thousand live in the extreme northern part of Zimbabwe, around the **Hunyani River**. Chikunda society appears to have coalesced from diverse Bantu groups during the 19th century, when the Chikunda played an active role in **Zambezi River** trade with the **Portuguese**.

CHIKUYO CHISAMARENGU (a.k.a. Kakuyo Komunyaka) (c.1475–c.1530). Early **Munhumutapa** ruler. While he was still a youth in c.1490, his father **Mukombero** was killed and displaced as Munhumutapa by **Changa**. After Chikuyo became an adult, he organized a counter-coup and regained the Munhumutapaship for himself (c.1494). Thereafter his reign was troubled by intermittent wars with the rebellious **Torwa** and **Changamire** dynasties to the south. Meanwhile, the **Portuguese** occupied **Sofala** (1505) and began penetrating the interior. In c.1511 Chikuyo was visited by **António Fernandes**, the first European known to enter the country. The meeting was a mutual success, beginning an era of Portuguese-Shona trade. On his death in c.1530 Chikuyo was succeeded by a nephew, **Neshangwe Munembire**. Later his own son **Chivere Nyasoro** became Munhumutapa.

CHILIMANZI DISTRICT see **CHIRUMANZU DISTRICT**

CHIMANIMANI (Melsetter until 1982). Eastern border town that serves as the administrative headquarters for **Chimanimani District** and is located near the **Chimanimani Mountains** (at 19°48'S, 32°52'E; alt. 1,555 km). The original settlement was first established by members of the **Moodie Trek** near **Chipinge**, 65 km to the south, and was moved to its present site in 1895. In June 1982 the town was renamed Mandidzudzure, but in September 1982 was officially given its present name.

CHIMANIMANI DISTRICT (Melsetter District until 1985). Eastern border district covering 3,345 sq km in **Manicaland Province**. The district was originally more than twice as large but lost its southern part to form **Chipinge District**. The western part of Chimanimani is **Communal Land**, while the eastern part is Chimanimani National Park and commercial farming lands that were reserved for Europeans prior to 1980. In addition to Chipinge, the district borders **Buhera** on the west and **Mutare** on the north. The district population in 1992 was 110,836.

CHIMANIMANI MOUNTAINS (a.k.a. Mawenje Mountains). Southern-most part of the **Eastern Highlands**, the Chimanimani Mountains straddle the **Mozambique** border just east of **Chimanimani**. An 8,180-hectare section of the range along the border was set aside in 1950 as the Chimanimani National Park, featuring dense flora, trout **fishing**, and mountain climbing.

CHIMURENGA (pl. *zvimurenga*). **Chishona** word for resistance or rebellion, used especially to refer to the **Revolts** of 1896–97 and the modern liberation struggle. (See **Chindunuma; Murenga**.)

"CHIMURENGA NAMES." Pseudonyms taken by many freedom fighters during the 1970s to conceal their true identities. This was done in the belief that they were protecting families and friends from possible interrogation by **Rhodesian security forces**. The taking of pseudonyms was also a conscious attempt at national unity, in that Chimurenga names were often chosen from names common to other regions of the country, thereby blurring differences in tribal identities. The practice lasted throughout the war for national liberation, with some ex-combatants keeping their new names after independence.

CHIMWENGAS. Term meaning "Little Lights" and used in the mid-1990s to describe armed groups reportedly operating in some southeastern districts of the country. They supposedly operated from bases located in the Manica Province of **Mozambique** and were said to be loyal to **Ndabaningi Sithole** and his **ZANU-Ndonga party**. While reports of their activities inside Zimbabwe were generally discounted by the government, their existence inside Mozambique was confirmed by Mozambican defense authorities in July 1995.

CHINAMANO, JOSIAH MUSHORE (Oct. 29, 1922–Oct. 1, 1984). Educator and nationalist leader. Born at **Epworth Mission**, Chinamano was educated in Methodist missionary schools, and he briefly taught at **Waddilove**. In 1953 he returned to the country after teaching in London and became headmaster of a mission school. Later he founded the country's largest nongovernment school in **Highfields**. In 1960 he and his wife Ruth (b.1925) were among the founders of the **National Democratic Party**. Later they stayed in **ZAPU**. Constantly harassed by the government because of their political activities, the Chinamanos were arrested in the government sweep of April 26, 1964, and their school was closed. They both spent most of the next 11 years in detention or prison. Chinamano became treasurer of the **African National Council** in December 1971 and was vice-president of **Joshua Nkomo**'s branch of the ANC through 1976. From 1978 to 1979 he worked with ZAPU in **Zambia**, maintaining his post as second-in-command to Nkomo. In 1979 he joined Nkomo at the **Lancaster House Conference** in London. In 1981, after being appointed minister of transport by Prime Minister **Robert Mugabe**, he was nominated to fill a vacant seat in Parliament by ZAPU. However, in February 1982 he was dismissed from the cabinet, along with Nkomo and Joseph Msika, following the discovery of hidden arms caches on a farm that belonged to ZAPU supporters. Following his death in 1984, Chinamano was declared a National Hero by the government and buried at **Heroes' Acre**.

CHINAMORA. Dynastic title of the rulers of the most important **Shavasha** chiefdom. The dynasty was established just northeast of present Harare in the mid-18th century. The Chinamoras remained independent through most of the 19th century, despite invasion by the **Ngoni** in the 1830s and occasional later **Ndebele** raids. In c.1888 Kuvimadzama became Chinamora and was visited by the **Portuguese** agent **Manuel de Sousa**. The British established Salisbury in 1890 and then granted part of **Shavasha** land at **Chishawasha** to Jesuit missionaries two years later. The Shavasha participated in the **Revolt** of 1896–97. The Chinamora himself surrendered in September 1897 but was retained in office. He later converted to Catholicism. After his death in 1907, Shambare (d.1916) became the first of the government-appointed Chinamoras.

CHINDUNDUMA. Chishona term for uprising or riot; one of the names by which the **Revolt** of 1896–97 is known. (See **Chimurenga**.)

CHINHOYI (Sinoia until 1982). Administrative and commercial center of both the **Makonde District** and **Mashonaland West Province** (at 17°22′S, 30°12′E; alt. 1,390 m). The original town was founded in 1895. Chinhoyi is c.115 km northwest of Harare near the terminus of a major branch **railway** line. It is an important center of **tobacco, maize, copper**, and wheat production. In 1992 the town had a population of 42,946. The name "Chinhoyi" derives from a **Zezuru** chief, Chinhoyi. During the 19th century Chinhoyi and his people barricaded themselves inside the **Chinhoyi Caves** complex for protection against occasional **Ndebele** raids and against the British in the **1896–97 Revolt**.

CHINHOYI, BATTLE OF. On April 28, 1966, an armed band of **ZANLA** combatants engaged elements of the **Rhodesian Security Forces** in a battle near the town of **Chinhoyi**. The fighting lasted several hours, with the immediate result being the death of seven ZANLA combatants; but it had a greater impact in the long view. Following this battle and several smaller encounters with Rhodesian forces in the ensuing year, ZANLA and its parent organization **ZANU** rethought their military policies and tactics. ZANU leadership concluded that military warfare tactics were not applicable to the military situation they faced, and they were therefore changed to guerilla warfare tactics based on examples of China and **FRELIMO** in Mozambique. ZANU considers this battle the official beginning of the armed struggle, and the site has been officially commemorated by being declared a Heroes' Acre for the **Mashonaland West Province**.

CHINHOYI CAVES (Formerly Sinoia Caves). Subterranean limestone caverns located 8 km west of **Chinhoyi**. The caves—known as the "Dark Cave" and "Light Cave"—include stalactite formations and the "Sleeping Pool," which has a depth of at least 91 m.

CHINODYA, SHIMMER (b. May 30, 1957). Born in Gweru, the son of a shop salesperson, Chinodya was educated at **Goromonzi** Secondary School and the **University of Zimbabwe**, where he received a B.A. in literature in 1979. The following year he earned a graduate certificate in education. In the early 1980s he went to the United States where he gained a M.A. in creative writing from the University of Iowa. In 1990, his novel, *Harvest of Thorns,* won a Commonwealth Writers' Prize. His other works include three novels, *Dew in the Morning* (1982), *Farai's Girls* (1984), and *Child of War* (published under the name B. Chirasha, 1985). Chinodya has won considerable international acclaim as one of the best of the younger generation of Zimbabwean writers who grew up during the war of liberation and write about the social and political impact of that war on Zimbabwean people. (See **Literature.**)

CHIOKO DAMBAMUPUTE (d.1902). Last titular **Munhumutapa**. The son of Munhumutapa Kataruza (d.1860s?), Chioko became Munhumutapa in c.1887. He ruled only a small branch of the **Tavara** along the present Zimbabwe-Mozambique border near the **Mazowe** River, but his title still carried considerable prestige among the other Shona. During the 1890s he refused to acknowledge **Portuguese** sovereignty and also encouraged Shona in Southern Rhodesia to defy the British administration. From 1900 to 1902 he was the focus of a small revolt, in which he was aided by **Mapondera**. After his death in 1902 the Portuguese defeated his people, finally bringing to an end more than 400 years of Munhumutapa independence.

CHIPINGA see **CHIPINGE**

CHIPINGE (Chipinga until 1982). Town at the southern end of the **Eastern Highlands** founded by members of the **Moodie Trek** in 1893. It now serves as administrative center (at 20°12'S, 32°37'E; alt. 1,135 m) of **Chipinge District**. The village was originally called **Melsetter**, but that was soon transferred to another settlement 65 km to the north.

CHIPINGE DISTRICT (Chipinga District until 1985). Originally the southern part of **Chimanimani District,** it now covers 5,260 sq km between the **Sabi River** and the **Mozambique** border. Besides Chimanimani, the district is bordered by **Bikita** and **Chiredzi** districts to the west. The Sabi River runs the entire length of the district's western border. A well-watered area, the district is a center for **tea, coffee,** mixed farming, and timber production. Prior to 1980, most of the northern end of the district was reserved as Tribal Trust Land (now **Communal Lands**). District population in 1992 was 336,890.

CHIPURIRO (variant: Sipolilo). Dynastic title of the rulers of a small **Korekore** chiefdom in the **Guruve District**. The Chipuriros maintained their independence through the 19th century until British occupation in the 1890s.

CHIRAU, JEREMIAH (c.1924–January 26, 1985). Nationalist leader. Born in **Makonde District,** Chirau joined the **Rhodesian African Rifles** in 1941 and fought in World War II. In 1946 he left the army and joined the prison department in Bulawayo. Appointed as a chief in the Lomagundi District (now Makonde) in 1961, he served as president of the **Council of Chiefs** from 1973 through 1979. He was elected to the **Senate** in 1970 and 1974 and in 1976 served as deputy minister of development. From 1976 to 1982 Chirau headed the Zimbabwe United People's Organization (**ZUPO**). From December 1977 into 1978 he represented ZUPO in negotiations with **Ian Smith, Abel Muzorewa,** and **Ndabaningi Sithole** and along with them signed the **Internal Settlement** agreement in March 1978. After joining **ZANU (PF)** in 1981, he served as a provincial secretary for production.

CHIREDZI. Town founded in 1961 about 15 km west of the **Chiredzi River** on the **railway** line that connects low veld farms to the main railway line (at 21°3'S, 31°40'E). The town serves as the administrator center for the district of the same name. At the time of the 1982 census, the town's population was 10,300.

CHIREDZI DISTRICT. Carved out of the southern parts of the old districts of **Chivi, Masvingo, Zaka,** and **Bikita**. On its northeastern border, Chiredzi is separated from **Chipinge District** by the **Sabi River**. The district is an important center for game ranching and **sugar** cane production. **Cotton,** citrus, and wheat are also grown in the area. The district's longest borders are on the west with **Mwenzi** District, and with Mozambique to the east; while in the south, the **Limpopo River** separates it from South Africa. Except for the **Communal Lands** on the district's eastern and western borders, the entire northern half of the district was reserved for Europeans prior to 1980, while the southern part was divided between former Tribal Trust Lands and **Gonarezhou** game reserve. The district administrative center is at the village of Chiredzi, with additional centers important to the district being at Buffalo Range and Triangle. District population in 1992 was 183,228.

CHIREDZI RIVER. Rising c.50 km east of **Masvingo**, the Chiredzi River flows southeast to join the **Lundi** about midway between the latter's connections with the **Mtilikwe** and **Sabi** rivers. In 1966 Manjirenji Dam was built at about the midpoint of the Chiredzi, creating Lake MacDougall.

CHIREMBA (pl. *zviremba*). **Chishona** word for doctor or healer; title by which *nganga* healers are addressed. *Zviremba* are usually specialized herbalists, in contrast to most *nganga*, who specialize in divining.

CHIRINDA FOREST (variant: Silinda Forest). Located on the slopes of **Mount Silinda** in **Gazaland**, the 640-hectare Chirinda Forest is an unusual remnant of a prehistoric tropical forest. It contains over a hundred species of trees, including ironwoods and mahoganies, as well as a large variety of birds. The smaller Bunga Forest in the **Vumba Mountains** is the only other significant stand of trees like it in the country (see **Forests**). During the mid-1970s **ZANLA** guerilla fighters began using the forest's dense vegetation as cover while infiltrating the country from bases in neighboring **Mozambique**.

CHIRINGIRO. Original name of *Bantu Mirror*.

CHIRISAMHURU (a.k.a. Rupengo; Dhlembewu) (d.1830s). The reigning **Changamire** ruler at the time of the *Mfecane* invasions, Chirisamhuru was killed by the followers of **Zwangendaba** and **Nyamazana**, then traveling together, at **Ntabazikamambo**. One line of tradition holds that Chirisamhuru died when he hurled himself from a precipice overlooking the invading throng of **Ngoni**. Another tradition claims that he was captured and skinned alive. Chirisamhuru is usually described as the last Changamire ruler in the **Matabeleland** region, but traditional evidence indicates that his son, **Tohwechipi**, was installed as his successor at **Dhlo Dhlo** before the arrival of the **Ndebele** in 1838 drove the Changamire leaders east. (For Chirisamhuru Negomo, see **Negomo Chrisamhuru.**)

CHIRUMANZU (variant: **Chilimanzi**). Dynastic title of the Govera branch of the **Karanga-speaking Shona** in the Chirumanzu District. The dynasty appears to have been established in the mid-18th century by a man named **Mhepo**, connected with the **Mutasa** dynasty of the **Manyika**. Mhepo is said to have been nicknamed *Chizimuhanzu*—later contracted to "Chirumanzu"—because he wore a *hanzu* robe obtained from **Muslim** traders. During the 19th century the **Govera** responded to the **Ndebele** occupation of **Matabeleland** by aggressively raiding Ndebele cattle. The Ndebele successfully retaliated in the mid-1850s, making the Chirumanzu chiefs their tributaries for the next 35 years. Chirumanzu Chatikobo briefly revolted against the Ndebele in 1889 but was overthrown by Chinyama with the aid of the Ndebele two years later. Chirumanzu Chinyama nevertheless lent men to the British in the **Ndebele War** of 1893. He also collaborated with the British against the Ndebele in the **Revolt** three years later.

CHIRUMANZU DISTRICT (Chilimanzi District until 1985). Covering 5,305 sq km near the center of the country in the eastern part of **Midlands Province**, its administrative center is **Mvuma**. Before 1980, the northern three-quarters of the district were reserved for Europeans, while the southern quarter was Tribal Trust Land. The district borders the **Chikomba** and **Gutu** districts on the east; **Masvingo** on the south; **Shurungwi**, **Gweru**, and **Kwekwe** on the west; and **Kadoma** on the north. The main industries of the district are cattle-ranching and **tobacco** growing. District population in 1992 was 69,974. In 1985 the district was renamed "Chirumanzu," taking the dynastic title of the Govera branch of the Karanga-speaking Shona who live in the district.

CHIRUNDU. Northern port of entry into the country from Zambia on the main road between Lusaka and Harare. The town stands on the south bank of the **Zambezi River**, just above the river's confluence with the Kafue River. The crossing is made on the **Otto Belt Bridge** (at 16°2′S, 28°51′E).

CHISAMHURU NOGOMO see **NEGOMO CHIRISAMHURU**

CHISHAWASHA MISSION. Roman Catholic mission station just east of Harare (at 17°47′S, 31°14′E). The station was founded in 1892 on a 5,665-hectare tract of **Shavasha** and granted to the Jesuits by the BSAC. **Andrew Hartmann** and **Peter Prestage** organized the station before returning to **Matabeleland** in 1896. The station subsequently developed an agricultural and industrial training center dominated by the strict supervision of the Jesuit priests.

CHISHONA. By far the most widely spoken language in the country, Chishona is the language of the **Shona peoples** and stands apart as a major cluster of southeastern **Bantu**. The above equation might well be more appropriately reversed, as it is primarily commonality of language which has given the Shona their collective identity. Six main dialects of Chishona are generally recognized as distinct. These are, in order of the number of speakers within the country: **Karanga, Zezuru, Korekore, Manyika, Ndau,** and **Kalanga**. Zezuru is the dialect around which "standard Shona" has been built since the 1930s. A unified orthography was fixed by the government in 1955. Kalanga is the most distinct of the dialects and is sometimes described as a separate language. The unifying features of Chishona dialects are considerable shared vocabulary; similar phonology, including tonal vowels and "whistling fricatives"; and common grammar, which features monosyllabic noun prefixes such as *chi-, ma-, mi-, mu-, u-,* and *va-*. (See also **Literature; Sindebele**.)

CHITEPO, HERBERT WILTSHIRE TFUMAINDINI (June 5, 1923–March 18, 1975). The country's first African lawyer, Chitepo was born in the **Inyanga District** and educated at mission schools and in Natal before taking his B.A. degree from Ft. Hare University College in South Africa in 1949. Afterwards he worked at the School of Oriental and African Studies in London while qualifying as a lawyer at King's College and Gray's Inn, London. When he returned home in 1954, the government amended the **Land Apportionment Act** to allow him to open a law office in Salisbury.

He entered politics in 1957 by joining the new **African National Congress**. He later served as **Joshua Nkomo**'s legal counsel in the **National Democratic Party**. In 1962 he went to Tanganyika (now Tanzania) and became that country's first African director of public prosecution. Following the split between **ZANU** and **ZAPU** in 1963, Chitepo sided with **Ndabangini Sithole** and was asked to lead the external wing of that party. In 1966 he moved to Lusaka and became the chairman of the Revolutionary Council of ZANU. In 1968 he reorganized the Revolutionary Council into the **Dare re Chimurenga**, which became the central council for the prosecution of the ZANU element of the liberation struggle. Chitepo was assassinated in Lusaka, Zambia, when a bomb exploded in his car. Following his death it was thought that he had been the victim of factional disputes within ZANU, but a recent study by David Martin and Phyllis Johnson has argued that Chitepo was assassinated by an agent of the Rhodesian Central Intelligence Organization. Chitepo was reburied at **Heroes' Acre** in August 1981.

CHITEPO, VICTORIA FIKIKLE (b. March 28, 1927). Born Victoria Mahamba-Sithole in Dundee, Natal, South Africa. She was educated in South Africa, eventually earning a B.A. degree from the University of Natal, as well as a postgraduate degree in education from the University of Birmingham (U.K.). It was during her attendance at Adams College in South Africa that she met her husband, **Herbert Chitepo**. She began her teaching career in Natal from 1946 until 1953 and following her marriage moved to **Southern Rhodesia** in 1955, when her husband worked as a social worker in Salisbury until 1958. With the founding of the **National Democratic Party** in 1960, Chitepo became involved in the country's nationalist politics. In 1961 she led the "Women's Sit-In" at the Magistrate's Court in Salisbury to demand full citizenship rights for the country's African majority. She later accompanied her husband to Tanganyika (now Tanzania) in 1962. She worked from 1966 to 1968 as a social worker in Dar es Salaam before returning to teaching, and lived in Tanzania until 1980. She returned to an independent Zimbabwe and was elected to the **House of Assembly,** then appointed minister of natural resources and tourism by Prime Minister **Robert Mugabe**. In the 1985 general election she was returned to **Parliament** from Mutasa and retained her cabinet portfolio.

CHITUNGWIZA. Located southeast of Harare, Chitungwiza was established as a separate urban area by government proclamation in 1977 and subsequently as a Town Council in 1981. Following the general movement of rural peoples to the urban centers of the country following independence in 1980, Chitungwiza grew tremendously. By the time of the 1992 census it had become the third largest urban center in the country, with a population of 274,035. By 1987 there were over 29,000 fully developed housing units, and 13 of the 129 industrial sites had been occupied by developers.

CHITUPA (pl. *zvitupa*). **Chishona** forms of *situpa*, a term for registration certificate (see **Pass Laws**).

CHIVERO, LAKE. Previously known as Lake McIlwaine (See **Hunyani River**).

CHIVERO NYASORO (d.c.1560). Early **Munhumutapa** ruler. The son of Munhumutapa **Chikuyo Chisamarengu**, Chivero succeeded his cousin **Neshangwe Mumembire** as Munhumutapa in c.1550. He established his headquarters just west of the **Musengezi River** in the **Dande** and devoted much of his reign to driving local **Tonga** people out of the northeastern part of the country to make room for his own people. He was succeeded by his son **Negomo**.

CHIVHU (Enkeldoorn until 1982). The main commercial and administrative center of the **Chikomba District**, Chivhu stands between the headwaters of the **Umniati** and **Sebakwe** rivers (at 19°1'S, 30°54'E; alt. 1,480 m). **Afrikaners** founded the town in 1897 and have remained its predominant European community. Nearby is the **Maronda Mashanu** mission.

CHIVI (variants: Chibi; Tschibi). Title of the paramount chiefs of the **Mari** (or Mhari) chiefdom. The Mari are a branch of the **Karanga** cluster of **Shona** and were often called "Banyai" (see **NYAI**) during the 19th century. The Chivi paramountcy seems to have originated in **Manyika** country in the early 18th century and to have been established between the **Tokwe** and **Lundi** rivers of the present Chivi District in the early 19th century, when it was loosely associated with the **Changamire** state.

CHIVI DISTRICT (Chibi District until 1985). Originally covering more than 27,000 sq km, it lost most of its area to the later **Mwenezi District**. Still later, the southern wedge of Chivi was separated to form the **Chiredzi District**. By the 1970s the district covered just 3,775 sq km within **Masvingo Province**. Its longest borders are with the districts of Masvingo on the east and **Zvishavane** on the west. Virtually the entire district is made up of **Communal Lands**. District population in 1992 was 157,277.

CHROME. The country is said to have the world's largest known reserves of high-grade chrome ore. Mining of chrome ore began in 1906 near Shurugwi, but it was not until World War II that the country became one of the world's main producers. Production prior to UDI was about 500,000 tons a year, but following the imposition of **sanctions**, production dropped to a low of 370,000 tons in 1969. After the passage of the **Byrd Amendment** in 1971, chrome production increased yearly until 1977, when the U.S. Congress repealed that legislation. Production in the late 1980s began to decline, reaching a low of 230,000 tons in 1996. The Peak Mine at **Shurugwi** is the country's largest single producer. Most of the chrome ore produced is exported, but some goes to two large alloy refineries located at **Gweru** and **Kwekwe,** which by 1982 had annual capacities of 163,000 and 180,000 tons, respectively.

CITY YOUTH LEAGUE see **YOUTH LEAGUE**

CLAN-NAMES see **ISIBONGO** (Ndebele); **MUTUPO** (Shona)

"CLICKS." Explosive consonant sounds made by suddenly drawing air across the tongue while it is pressed against the inside of the mouth. The three basic clicking sounds are (1) dental, represented by the letter *c*; (2) palatal, represented by the letter *g*; and (3) lateral, represented by the letter *x*. Spelling variations in African words frequently derive from shifting or misunderstood clicks, as in the name **Nxaba**, variously spelled "Ncaba," "Ngaba," or "Nxaba." Clicking consonants are the most outstanding characteristic of the **Khoisan languages**, from which they have been introduced into all **Nguni** dialects, including **Sindebele**. **Chishona** languages do not have clicks.

CLIMATE. (1) *General overview.* Although the country lies entirely within the southern tropics, most of it enjoys an equable climate comparable to the temperate regions because of the ameliorating influence of the country's inland location and generally high **altitudes**. The most temperate regions are the **Central Plateau** and the **Eastern Highlands**, and these are also the most densely populated parts of the country.

(2) *Rainfall.* A dominant climatic feature is concentration of almost all rainfall within a five-month "wet season" between November and March. Less than 3 percent of the annual rainfall occurs outside of this period, except in the Eastern Highlands, which sometimes receive up to 10 percent of their precipitation during other months. The rains are brought by the Inter-Tropical Convergence Zone, which sends moist air inland from the Indian Ocean. Precipitation is thus greatest in the eastern parts of the country, diminishing as the moist air moves west. The Eastern Highlands and the northeastern section of the Central Plateau receive more than 750 mm of rain per annum. Stations recording more than 1,250 mm of rain are rare. More than two-thirds of the country receives less than 750 mm of rain per annum, with the **Limpopo** basin receiving the least. Also important is the erratic and unreliable rainfall in many areas. Further, loss of water to evaporation and rapid runoff is great, so conservation of surface water is critical to development. (See **Dams and Water Supply; Rivers.**)

(3) *Temperature.* The sun passes directly over the entire country twice between late September and late March, but heat is severe only in the Zambezi Valley and in the southeastern low veld during these months. The highest recorded temperature was 45.6° C (about 114°F), set at **Kariba** in 1955. As a general rule, each 300-meter rise in altitude reduces temperatures by 2°C. Temperatures are further ameliorated by the correspondence between the months of most intense solar radiation and the rainy season, during which rainfall and cloud cover greatly cool the air. The lowest temperature on record was -9.5°C (about +14.9°F) set at **Matopos** in 1968. Such cold is highly unusual, as freezing temperatures rarely occur anywhere in the country. Groundfrosts develop occasionally, but snowfall has never been recorded.

(4) *Seasons.* The distinction between "summer" and "winter" seasons means little in the country, as its seasons are reckoned around the dominant rainy season. Outside that important period, however, climatic changes are not sharply divided, and wide fluctuations can occur from year to year. A typical year follows this pattern, however: November—hot,

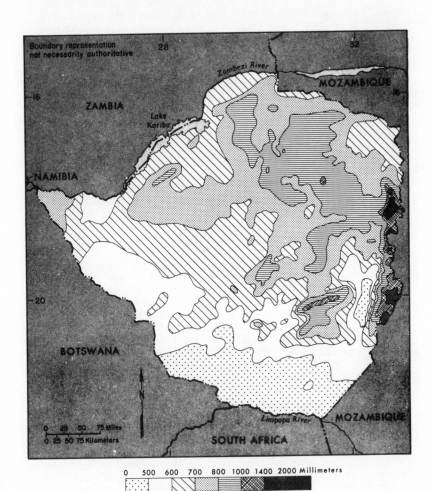

Source: Based on information from George Kay, *Rhodesia: A Human Geography*, New York, 1970, p. 17; and I.M. Hume, *A Strategy for Rural Development and Whitsun Data Bank No. 2: The Peasant Sector*, Salisbury, October 1978, p.47

Figure 4: Mean Annual Rainfall

beginning of rains with storms; December–February—warm, steady rainfall; March—warm, rains begin to abate; April–May—cooler, occasional showers; June–July—cool and dry; August–September—warmer, but dry; October—hot and dry, with storms sometimes beginning late in the month.

COAL. The country's coal reserves have been estimated at 30 billion tons. Major coalfields have been found in both the **Limpopo** basin and in the southeastern low veld, but commercial exploitation has been undertaken only at **Hwange**. Coal mining was first begun at Hwange in 1903 by the Wankie Colliery Company, Limited. Second and third collieries were opened in 1927 and 1953. Total production first topped a million tons per annum in 1927 and, following a slight slump, rose to 2 million tons in 1949, and then to 4 million tons in 1957. Following UDI and the imposition of **sanctions** coal production dropped, and from 1965 to 1980 annual production was slightly over 3 million tons per annum. The lifting of sanctions following independence helped to revive coal mining in the country, with production reaching 5 million tons in 1990 and 5.8 million tons in 1996.

Hwange's bituminous coal is ideal for steam raising. Until activation of the hydroelectric facilities at **Kariba Dam** in 1961, coal-burning thermal plants generated virtually all the country's **electrical power**. Coal also fueled the country's **railways**, as well as much of those of Botswana, Zambia, and parts of Mozambique and Zaire. Coal is so bulky it can be transported economically only by rail. The decision to route the main northern railway line through **Victoria Falls** was reached in order to make Hwange accessible to rail transport. Since then Hwange's productive capacity has consistently outstripped the country's capacity to carry its coal by rail. Until the opening of Kariba, as much as a third of the country's railway capacity was used to move coal to thermal plants. Kariba's hydroelectric output allowed most thermal plants to be shut down, freeing considerable rail capacity and obviating the need for further expansion of coal production. However, increased electrical consumption since the mid-1960s revived the need for thermal power generation. To help meet that growing need, a new thermal power plant was opened at Hwange in the mid-1980s.

COFFEE. Production of coffee began in the **Chimanimani District** around 1900. Beginning in the 1950s, the region between **Vumba** and **Mount Silinda** was developed into a major center of Arabica coffee production. Production rapidly increased throughout the 1970s and early 1980s, with 374 tons being sold for export in 1970, 4,106 tons in 1980, and 11,354 tons by 1985. However, due to extended drought conditions in the early 1990s, production in 1992 dropped to about 4,000 tons, but rose to approximately 10,000 tons in 1997.

COGHLAN, CHARLES PATRICK JOHN (June 24, 1863–Aug. 28, 1927). First **prime minister** of Southern Rhodesia (1923–27). Born in King William's Town, South Africa, Coghlan came to **Bulawayo** in 1900 after having practiced law in Kimberley. He soon established a reputation as a vigorous defender of the rights of settlers, especially miners, against the unpopular BSAC administration. In 1908 he was elected to the

Legislative Council, in which he quickly rose to leadership of the unofficial members. The same year he attended the national union convention in South Africa (see **Unionist Movement**).

Back home, the Legislative Council wrung enough concessions from the BSAC for Coghlan to support renewal of the company's **charter** in 1914, but he soon found himself clashing with the administration again—particularly over the issue of **amalgamation**, which he vigorously opposed. Coghlan lost his initial enthusiasm for union with South Africa and joined the **Responsible Government Movement** in 1919. Over the next several years he put increasing pressure on the British government to grant the settlers self-government. In 1921 he led a delegation to London to negotiate the question. When self-government was achieved in September 1923 the new governor, **J. R. Chancellor**, invited him to form a government as premier. He was sworn in on October 1, when he also assumed the "Native Affairs" portfolio. He then reorganized his party as the **Rhodesian Party**, leading it to victory in a general election the next year. Favorable world prices for the country's exports made Coghlan's term of office a relatively prosperous and undramatic era within the context of settler politics. His main concerns were fiscal problems. The **Morris Carter Commission** recommended discriminatory land-tenure laws during Coghlan's administration (1925), but he died in office, leaving the problem for his successor, **H. U. Moffat**.

COILLARD, FRANÇOIS (July 17, 1834–May 27, 1904). French missionary. After two decades of mission work for the Paris Evangelical Missionary Society, Coillard crossed the **Limpopo River** in 1877 in an attempt to start a mission among the people of **Chivi**. There his party was arrested by **Ndebele** scouts and taken to King **Lobengula**. After his release in 1878 he visited the **Lozi** people north of the **Zambezi**. There he founded a successful and influential mission station. His book, *On the Threshold of Central Africa* (London, 1897), contains one of the rare written accounts of the Shona during the 1870s.

COLENBRANDER, JOHANNES WILHELM (Nov. 1, 1855–Feb. 10, 1918). Born in Natal, where he later served with the colonial army against the **Zulu**, Colenbrander was fluent in the Zulu language (closely akin to **Sindebele**) and very knowledgeable about northern **Nguni** culture. He came to **Bulawayo** in 1888 and made a favorable impression on **Lobengula**. Later that year he acted as an interpreter for **Babayane** and **Mshete**, Lobengula's emissaries to Queen Victoria. He returned to **Matabeleland** as official representative of the BSAC. Despite his intimacy with the **Ndebele**, Colenbrander advocated British conquest of Lobengula. He himself got out of the country just before the **Ndebele War**, returning later as a native commissioner in the BSAC administration. He then played a leading role in the collection and redistribution of loot **cattle**. During the **1896 Revolt** he raised and led a corps of South Africans to fight the Ndebele. He also served as **Cecil Rhodes**' interpreter during the *"Indaba"* peace negotiations. Two decades later he accidentally drowned while playing the role of Lord Chelmsford in a film about the Zulu War, which he had earlier survived.

COLLEEN BAWN. Village on the **railway** line between **Gwanda** and **West Nicholson** (at 21°S, 29°13′E; alt. 90 m). The local Colleen Bawn **gold** mine was established atop early African workings in 1905. The village's main modern industry is cement, with one factory supplying most of the country.

COLOURED PEOPLE. From the beginning of the 20th century the white government of Southern Rhodesia—later Rhodesia—followed South African precedent and designated as a separate "race" people of mixed African and European or Asian descent, whom they classified as "Coloured." These people were legally placed in an ambiguous position between the European and African populations and were subject to discriminatory laws.

COLQUHOUN, ARCHIBALD ROSS (March 1848–Dec. 18, 1914). Early administrator. After a varied career in Asia, Colquhoun came to South Africa in 1889 and met **Cecil Rhodes.** Rhodes made him civil administrator of the **Pioneer Column** which occupied **Mashonaland** the next year. During the column's advance, Colquhoun and **F. C. Selous** went to **Manicaland,** where they obtained chief **Mutasa's** signature to a mining concession. Colquhoun finally arrived at Salisbury in October 1890, when he took up office as the first BSAC resident commissioner for Mashonaland. Frustrated with the rough-and-ready exigencies of frontier administration, he resigned on the pretext of ill health and was replaced by **L. S. Jameson** in September 1891. Colquhoun later wrote his autobiography and several books on British imperialism in southern Africa. His wife was the later **Ethel Tawse-Jollie**.

COMMUNAL AREA MANAGEMENT PROGRAM FOR INDIGENOUS RESOURCES (CAMPFIRE). Government sponsored program established in 1987 in an attempt to diminish the growing problem of African peasant farmers moving onto wildlife game reserves and thereby endangering both the local wildlife and national tourism revenues. Campfire promotes localized participation in wildlife conservation by allowing local people to benefit directly from tourism on their lands. By granting proprietary rights to local wildlife resources, as well as a greater share of local tourism revenues, to the local people the government hoped to encourage local people to see wildlife as a resource and thereby be willing to actively protect it from both illegal poaching and domestic squatters. By 1990, 12 Campfire districts had been created around several national parks and **reserves** throughout the country. This innovative program has been cited by environmental groups worldwide as a model for wildlife conservation.

COMMUNAL LANDS. Since independence in 1980, this name applies to those rural areas formerly known as "Tribal Trust Lands" (TTLs) and prior to 1970 as "Native Reserves." After the conclusion of the **Ndebele War** in 1894, a land commission was formed by the BSAC administration to investigate the problem of relocating the **Ndebele** people. This commission created two large reserves in **Matabeleland,** establishing the principles that African needs had to be met before land could be alienated to Europeans. A British order-in-council in 1898 reiterated this principle and made the BSAC administration responsible for assigning land to

Africans. However, no guidelines for determining African land needs were established, so the administration simply passed its responsibility on to its district commissioners to enforce (see **Districts**). The result was piecemeal allocation of African reserves based on situations pertaining in individual districts. By 1913 more than a hundred separate reserves of vastly different sizes had been designated throughout the country. These were consolidated somewhat over the next decade, and the basic pattern of land allocation was firmly set by the 1920s. The 1923 **Constitution** formalized the existing reserves, and the 1930 **Land Apportionment Act** enlarged the reserves' total area slightly, so they accounted for approximately 22.4 percent of the whole country.

After the **Rhodesian Front** came to power in 1962, it began to articulate a policy of achieving "parity" between European and African lands. This policy was formalized in the **Land Tenure Act** of 1969. Under this act European and African lands were equalized, with African lands, designated as TTLs, fixed at 16,151,520 hectares, or 42.4 percent of the total land in the country. Most of the remaining African lands were divided into noncommunally owned **Purchase Areas**. The **president** of the country was empowered to transfer pieces of land among categories while retaining the basic overall proportions. One result of the act was to fragment African lands into more than 160 units, which were generally the least productive agricultural lands and were overpopulated by both people and cattle. During the war for independence, these areas were often infiltrated by **ZANLA** and **ZIPRA** forces. The African populations were subject to government raids and concentration into **"protected villages."** As a result, many of these areas were ravaged and suffered the closing of many small businesses and schools, as well as heavy war casualties. Following the war, the government of Zimbabwe consolidated the former TTLs and Purchase Areas into Communal Lands, and it has made the development of these areas one of its main economic objectives.

CONCESSION. Village immediately south of **AMANDAS** on the Shamva **railway** line (at 17°12′S, 30°57′E). It is the commercial center for a mainly agricultural region.

CONCESSIONS. During the late 19th century European entrepreneurs and adventurers known as "concessionaires" beleaguered African rulers throughout southern Africa for concessionary rights to mine, to monopolize trade, to cut timber, etc. Concession gathering was the technique used by the BSAC to gain control of present Zimbabwe. (For examples, see **Adendorff Trek; Lippert Concession; Rudd Concession; Tati Concession.**)

CONFEDERATE PARTY (CP). Successor to the **Democratic Party**, the CP was formed in 1953 to oppose **federation**. It was the only party to oppose the **United (Federal) Party** in both territorial and federal elections that year, but it won no seats in either assembly. The party broke up the next year when English-speaking members quit to protest **Afrikaner** domination.

CONGREGATIONALIST MISSIONS see **AMERICAN BOARD OF COMMISSIONERS FOR FOREIGN MISSIONS; LONDON MISSIONARY SOCIETY**

CONICAL TOWER. Descriptive name for the imposing 10-meter-high structure in the southern end of the Elliptical Building in the **Zimbabwe Ruins**. Built with an even-coursed stone facing over a solid core, it was apparently erected when the nearby adjacent outer wall was constructed. Similar but much smaller towers are found in some of the nearby valley ruins and elsewhere. The tower, like the **"Zimbabwe Birds,"** has come to symbolize the ruins. Its superficial resemblance to ancient Near Eastern structures fueled arguments for non-African origins of the ruins (see **Zimbabwe Controversy**). The tower has been popularly interpreted as a phallic symbol associated with some unknown fertility rites. A more plausible interpretation suggests that it and similar towers simply symbolized **Shona** grain bins, and that they were used as tribute collection centers.

CONSERVATIVE ALLIANCE OF ZIMBABWE see **RHODESIAN FRONT**

"CONSOLIDATED VILLAGES" see **"PROTECTED VILLAGES"**

CONSTITUTION PARTY see under **CAPRICORN AFRICA SOCIETY**

CONSTITUTIONS. Formal constitutions were promulgated in 1923, 1961, 1965, 1969, 1979, and 1980.

Constitution of 1923. In September 1923 Britain annexed Southern Rhodesia as a Crown Colony, replacing the **BSAC** government while granting **Responsible Government** to settlers under a loosely outlined constitution (see **Buxton Committee**). This constitution created a **Legislative Assembly** elected by a nonracial franchise effectively limited to Europeans because of high property and income qualifications. A British **governor** was placed at the head of the government. Britain retained important reserve powers over entrenched portions of the constitution; it could, theoretically, legislate for African affairs itself, as these were seen as falling outside the jurisdiction of the local Assembly. In practice, however, the Assembly and its **prime ministers** arrogated increasing powers to themselves, legislating for Africans as well as settler affairs. The British government neither legislated for Southern Rhodesia affairs, nor did it overrule Assembly decisions affecting Africans. It instead amended its own reserve powers while permitting the settler government greater autonomy.

Constitution of 1961. This document was drafted by a convention held in London and Salisbury (now **Harare**) in 1960 and 1961. Settler representatives sought to safeguard their control of the government, while African representatives (see **National Democratic Party**) fought unsuccessfully for majority rule. The result was a compromise constitution which created separate voter rolls giving Africans their first seats in the **Assembly.** It also contained complex provisions for attainment of majority rule in the remote future. Britain retained ultimate sovereignty but relinquished its reserve powers over local legislation. In place of British oversight, the constitution contained a bill of rights and created a Constitutional Council meant to safeguard African rights. Existing legislation which contradicted the new bill of rights was unaffected, and the settler-dominated Assembly effectively nullified the Constitutional Council, which it was empowered to overrule with a two-thirds majority vote on any challenge. The British Privy Council remained the ultimate court of appeals. During the period of **UDI**, Britain and most other nations regarded this as the legal constitution for the country.

Constitution of 1965. Promulgated shortly after UDI, this constitution essentially modified the 1961 constitution. It still recognized Queen Elizabeth as the country's sovereign, but replaced the British governor with an **"Officer Administering the Government."** It also eliminated all vestigial British reserve powers. The new constitution and subsequent legislation gave the government wide discretionary powers to declare states of emergency, arrest and detain opponents without trial, and **censor** publications.

Constitution of 1969. Approved by public referendum in June 1969 and passed by **Parliament** in November, this constitution renounced British sovereignty altogether and made Zimbabwe a republic, effective March 1970. It created the office of **president**, divided **Parliament** into two chambers, and instituted loyalty oaths for government officials. For the first time voter rolls were defined on an explicitly racial basis, and the possibility of eventual majority rule was denied. The government was granted still wider powers to restrict civil rights, and the power of the judiciary to rule on the constitutionality of legislation was given to the legislature itself.

Constitution of 1980. The product of the **Lancaster House Conference** negotiations of October 1979, this constitution took effect in April 1980 with the independence of the Republic of Zimbabwe. It also retained the office of president and a bicameral Parliamentary form of government. In addition, it contained a "Declaration of Rights" which called for the protection of minority rights and was entrenched for a period of ten years. The constitution provided for special legislative representation for Europeans for a period of seven years. It guaranteed that all government obligations of previous regimes would be respected, and that fair compensation would be paid for any lands acquired by the new government for redistribution. The constitution was amended in 1987 to create a unicameral **House of Assembly**, and in March 1992 the newly enacted **Land Acquisition Act** once again amended the constitution by allowing the nationalization of privately owned lands at prices established by the government, and barred owners from suing the government for higher compensation.

COPPER. Archaeological evidence indicates that copper has been mined in the country for almost as long as **iron**, i.e., from about the A.D. 100s. Almost all modern copper mines are sited over old African workings, more than 150 of which have been identified. There is also evidence of early bronze casting, but is believed that the **tin** employed in this alloy was imported—probably from present Zambia. Modern copper production began in the **Gwanda District** in 1906. The industry rapidly developed in the mid-1950s, thereafter maintaining steady growth, reaching a production high of 51,900 tons in 1973. International copper prices began to greatly fluctuate downward after that, and production slowly decreased to a 1985 level of 20,700 tons. By the mid-1990s production had dropped even further, reaching a low of 8,900 tons in 1995. There are about 20 operating mines in the country, the largest being the Mhangura Mine, located c.150 km northwest of Harare. This single mine produces approximately one-half of all Zimbabwe's copper.

COSGRAVE, MARY ANN (Mother Patrick) (May 22, 1863–July 31, 1900). Pioneer Roman Catholic nun. Born in Ireland, Cosgrave came to South Africa as a youth and entered the Dominican Order in King William's Town, South Africa. In 1890 she volunteered to accompany the **Pioneer Column** into **Mashonaland**. The **BSAC** would allow no European women in the country, so she and four other nuns ran a nursing station for the column just southwest of **Ft. Tuli**. In July 1891 she accompanied Father **Peter Prestage** to Salisbury, where she helped to establish the first hospital, a school, and a convent. In 1899 she was made Dominican prioress for the whole country.

COTTON. The **Shona people** have long grown cotton, and weaving is one of the crafts associated with the development of the **Zimbabwe culture** before the 15th century. Demand for cloth outstripped local production, however, making Indian cotton cloth a major import item during the period of the **Munhumutapa** state.

During the 20th century, cotton has ranked as a major secondary **agricultural** product among both African peasants and European commercial farmers. Following UDI and the imposition of international **sanctions**, cotton became an even more important crop to the European commercial farmers, as they diversified their production away from an overreliance on **tobacco.** By the early 1980s, as a result of increased assistance from the government, African peasant producers had increased their overall share of the cotton crop. This represented a substantial development, both in terms of production for export and income for the rural peasant producers, as the total amount of cotton being grown was nearly 45 times that grown at the time of UDI (1965: 6,767 tons, 1986: 297,538 tons). The major cotton producing areas are found around **Banket, Gokwe, Kadoma, Mutare, Sanyati,** Tafuna, southwest of Mutare, and southeast of **Masvingo.**

While cotton remains one of Zimbabwe's chief export crops, it is also the foundation of a large textile industry in the country. There are ginneries in Banket, **Chegutu, Glendale,** Kadoma, Mutare, Sanyati, Tafuna, and **Triangle,** and more than 150 clothing factories throughout the country. Since independence, the export of clothing and other textiles has slowly been increasing.

COUNCIL OF CHIEFS. Following the suppression of the 1896–97 **Revolts** the white governments largely controlled the nomination and installation of African chiefs, whom they used as paid government servants to administer rural areas. Traditional ethnic boundaries were frequently realigned in order to consolidate and rearrange chiefdoms. The chiefs were originally stripped of their traditional political and judicial powers. However, beginning in the 1920s there was a consistent trend toward increasing the range of the chiefs' functions while further co-opting them into the white power structure. In 1961 the Council of Chiefs was created to represent African concerns in the Tribal Trust Lands (see **Communal Lands**) within the government's Ministry of Interior Affairs. The council normally comprised of 26 seats, 10 of whom were selected to sit in the **Senate** after 1965. When the **Rhodesian Front** assumed power, the government frequently used the council to elicit manifestations of African support for its actions (see **Domboshawa Indaba**.) After independence the council was retained and technically its members can advise the **president** on matters relating to African cultural and rural matters. In reality, however, the government virtually ignores its existence and it exercises no influence on government policy.

CRIPPS, ARTHUR SHEARLY (June 18, 1869–Aug. 1, 1952). English missionary and poet. After studying at Oxford, Cripps trained for the **Anglican** clergy and served as a vicar in Sussex. In 1901 he came to **Mashonaland** as a missionary for the Society for the Propagation of the Gospel. He was stationed at Wreningham, just northeast of **Chivhu**. During World War I he served as a chaplain to British forces in East Africa, returning to Wreningham in 1916. Through this period he acquired grants of land closer to Chivhu, on which he built **Maronda Mashanu** as a mission substation. In 1926 he returned to England because of homesickness and mounting disagreements with mission authorities. He particularly opposed the mission's policy of accepting government financial support.

After doing parish work in east London slums, he returned to Maronda Mashanu permanently in 1931. There he set himself up as an independent missionary, selling some of the mission's land to support its work. Under the terms of the new **Land Apportionment Act** the government could have expelled him from the site, but it left him alone to avoid trouble with his many supporters. During the late 1930s Cripps' health deteriorated and his sight began failing. By 1941 he was completely blind. Thereafter he resided mostly at Chivhu, while its unpaid secretary, Leonard Mamvura, supervised the mission's operation. Cripps' impact on African attitudes was profound. In contrast to other missionaries, he shunned Western materialism and lived much as an average African. He championed African rights, relentlessly criticizing European settlers and the government. An admirer of **Clements Kadalie,** he supported the latter's **ICU**. He was a prolific writer and correspondent, using his pen to condemn every policy inimical to African interests, from the hut tax raise in 1903 to the establishment of **Federation**, which came a year after his death. Often described as a "Utopian socialist," Cripps' apparent goal was to see a merger of true Christian ideals and the traditional African way of life. He expressed his philosophy in pastoral poetry, fiction, and pamphlets. (See also **White, J.**)

CRIPPS, LIONEL (Oct. 11, 1863–Feb. 3, 1950). First speaker of the **Southern Rhodesia Legislative Assembly**. Born in India and educated in England, Cripps came to South Africa in 1879. In 1890 he participated in the **Pioneer Column** as a trooper. He then prospected in the **Mazowe** area, eventually settling near present **Mutare**, where he was a pioneer **tobacco** farmer. In 1914 he was elected to the **Legislative Council**. On the achievement of **Responsible Government** in 1923 he was elected speaker of the new Assembly. He retired from politics in 1935 and then helped to establish the **National Archives**.

CROONENBERGHS, CHARLES (1843–1899). Belgian Jesuit priest. As a member of the **Zambezi Mission**, Croonenberghs ran the Jesuits' **Matabeleland** stations from 1879 to 1884.

CURRENCY. During the early years of the BSAC administration, the country officially adopted the Cape Colony's currency. After 1910 both British and South African currency were used in the country. Southern Rhodesia began issuing its own coinage in 1932, dropping South African coins the next year. Commercial banks issued Southern Rhodesian paper currency until 1940, when the government took over. The previous year both British and South African currency ceased to be legal tender in the country. Southern Rhodesian currency was based upon British sterling and was similarly divided into pounds, shillings, and pence. Between 1955 and 1965 currency issued by the **Federation government** was also used locally. After **UDI** in 1965, the Rhodesian pound was disassociated from the British pound and placed on its own gold standard. In 1970 the government decimalized the currency, making the new "dollar" equivalent to one half a former Rhodesian pound. Following independence in 1980, the government adopted the "Zimbabwe dollar" (Z$) as the official currency of the country. The dollar is divided into 100 cents, with coins of one cent, five, ten, twenty, fifty cents, and one dollar; with paper currency issued in various denominations. In 1994, US$1 = Z$8.12. In the mid-1990s, as a result of high inflation rates, the value of Zimbabwe's currency was greatly diminished. In 1999 the government set an official exchange rate of US$1=Z$39.25.

D

DABENGWA, DUMISO (b.December 6, 1939). **ZIPRA** commander. Born at **Ntabazinduna**, the son of a **Purchase Area** farmer, Dabengwa received his primary education at Ngwenya and Cyrene Mission schools. He then attended **Kutama** Mission in 1955 and Tegwani Mission in 1957 and taught at Cyrene in 1958. He moved to Bulawayo and worked as a clerk for the municipality in 1959, and from 1960 to 1962 worked for the Barclays Bank. He first became involved in political activities while working in Bulawayo and joined **ZAPU** in early 1962. In September 1962 he was arrested when ZAPU was banned by the government and charged under the **Law and Order Maintenance Act** with making subversive statements. He served six months in prison. In September 1963 he left the country and went to the Soviet Union for military training. In 1965 he returned to Zambia and assisted **Jason Moyo** in forming **ZIPRA's** first command structure, ultimately serving in ZIPRA's war council as secretary for warfare from 1972 to 1980.

He returned to the country in December 1980 and, with **Lookout Masuku,** participated in the cease-fire agreement. After independence he helped implement ZIPRA's integration into the new **Zimbabwe National Army**. Dabengwa retired from the ZNA in September 1981 and started a private company with several other ex-combatants. In March 1982 he was arrested with a number of other ZAPU leaders and charged with conspiring against the government of Prime Minister **Robert Mugabe**. He was tried and acquitted in 1983 but held in prison under a government detention order until December 1986. In May 1987 he established an import/export company in Bulawayo. Following the **Unity Pact**, he re-entered politics and participated in the 1990 **elections**. Following his election to the **House of Assembly**, he was appointed assistant minister in the Ministry of Foreign Affairs and State Security, and in 1993 was named minister for home affairs, continuing in that post following the 1995 elections.

DAGA (variant: *daka*). Translated literally as "mud," *daga* is a common **Bantu** word for plastering and building material made with powder from termite hills. Mixed with water and various other ingredients, the resulting compound dries to varying degrees of hardness. *Daga* has long been one of the most important building materials used in the country, even in the construction of **stone ruins**. An unrelated word, *dagga*, for hemp or marijuana, derives from a **Khoi** language.

DAILY NEWS see *AFRICAN DAILY PRESS*

DALHOUSIE, SIMON RAMSAY (Lord Dalhousie from 1950) (b.Oct. 17, 1914). Second and last governor-general of the **federation**, Dalhousie succeeded **J. J. Llewelin** in 1957.

DALNY MINE see under **CHAKARI**

DAMBARARE. Portuguese trading **fair** located near the present **Jumbo Mine** c.32 km north-northwest of Harare. Dambarare appears to have been established around 1580 and to have become the dominant Portuguese center in the **Munhumutapa** state during the 17th century. It was apparently destroyed by a **Changamire** army in 1693. Portuguese attempts to reestablish the fair in 1769 failed. The site now consists only of ditches and foundation structures.

DAMS AND WATER SUPPLY. An enormous number of dams and weirs have been built throughout the country to enable the development of intensive **agriculture** and industry in the face of an endemic water shortage situation (see **Climate**). Most parts of the country receive only sparse, irregular, and short-term rainfall. And much of the rain that falls comes in brief heavy storms, resulting in rapid runoff (see **Rivers**). Considerable water is lost to evaporation and to seepage into underground reserves. Some underground water can be easily retrieved from *vleis*, but to obtain large quantities thousands of expensive bore-holes have to be drilled. Only more efficient retention of surface water is economical on a large scale.

Construction of dams, weirs, and irrigation ditches was begun at least several centuries ago by the builders of the **Inyanga Ruins**, where some water furrows still function. Elsewhere, African agriculturalists seem not to have employed irrigation systems. When Europeans began settling the country in the 1890s, dam-building began in earnest. Private farmers and government agencies built thousands of small weirs and dams, but large projects were restricted mostly to the rivers around major urban centers. The uneven distribution of water supplies has influenced the distribution of industries, favoring the larger centers such as **Harare, Gweru, Bulawayo,** and **Mutare**. In the mid-1960s the government shifted emphasis from small dam building to large-scale regional projects such as the vast **Sabi-Limpopo Authority** in the southeastern low veld (see **Kariba Dam**; individual dams are discussed mostly under the names of their rivers; see also **Lakes**).

DANCING see **INXWALA** [Ndebele "Great Dance"]; **MUSIC**

DANDE. Traditional **Shona** name for the region circumscribed by the **Zambezi River** on the north, the **Zambezi Escarpment** on the south, and the **Angwa** and **Muzengezi** rivers on the west and east, respectively. Originally the home of the Tande (Vatande) branch of **Korekore-speaking people**, the Dande was occupied by the early **Munhumutapa** kings from the mid-15th to 17th centuries. (See **Guruhuswa; Mbire**.)

DANGAREMBGA, TSITSI (b.1959). Playwright, novelist, and filmmaker. while born in Zimbabwe, Dangarembga spent many of her early years in England, where her parents earned degrees in higher education. In 1965 her family returned to the country and she briefly attended a mission primary school in **Umtali,** then completed her secondary schooling at an American-sponsored convent school. In 1977 she returned to England to study medicine at Cambridge University, but returned to Zimbabwe in 1980, shortly before independence. After briefly working at an advertising agency in Harare, she entered the **University of Zimbabwe** to study psychology. During this second period of higher education, she began to write, contributing three plays to the university's drama workshop group. She published a play, *She No Longer Weeps* (1987), and in 1989 received a Commonwealth Writers award. She then left Zimbabwe to study filmmaking in Berlin. She earned international attention and critical acclaim with the publication of her first novel, *Nervous Conditions* (1988). (See **Literature**.) By the early 1990s, she had begun to direct films. Her first film, "Everyone's Child," dealt with the issue of women's continuing inequality in modern Zimbabwean society. (See **Film Industry**.)

DARWENDALE. Village c.60 km west of Harare on the Zawi **railway** line (at 17°43′S, 30°33′E). It is a center of **tobacco, cattle,** and **chrome** production.

DARWIN DISTRICT see **MUKUMBURA DISTRICT**

DAWSON, JAMES (Nov. 1852–Oct. 7, 1921). A Scottish trader, Dawson came to **Matabeleland** in the 1870s. On the eve of the **Ndebele War,**

Lobengula asked Dawson to take three chiefs to Cape Town to meet with the British high commissioner in the hope of averting war. On the way south the party met British soldiers at the **Shashi River** and two of the Ndebele men were killed in a misunderstanding because of Dawson's negligence. Dawson returned to Matabeleland after the war and then commanded a troop of the **Bulawayo Field Force** during the **Ndebele Revolt** of 1896. Thereafter he farmed around Essexvale (now **Esigondini**) until 1905, when he went to western Zambia to trade. Accumulated financial difficulties were the apparent cause of his suicide years later.

DEMOCRATIC PARTY (DP). Of the many political parties with this name, the following stand out: (1) Strongly pro-**Afrikaner** nationalist party founded in 1948 by members of the country's Association of Afrikaners (Afrikaner Genootskap). In 1953 it became the **Confederate Party**, with DP dissidents forming a new "Rhodesian Party," which was soon absorbed by the **United Party**. (2) African political party that broke away from the **United People's Party** in August 1969. Chad Chipunza was the party's only member of Parliament. In June 1969 the DP reunited with the UPP to form the **National People's Union**. (3) Rightwing European political party founded in 1972 by C. W. Phillips, a defector from the **Rhodesian Front**. (See also **National Democratic Party**.)

DEMOCRATIC PARTY OF ZIMBABWE. Opposition party formed in 1991. Its leadership was made up of individuals who broke away from the Zimbabwe Unity Movement and its leader **Edgar Tekere**. In March 1994 the DP's leader, Davison Gomo, publicly charged that **ZANU** was planning to rig the upcoming 1995 **elections**. It did not participate in those elections, pulling out two weeks before the elections after contending that it was virtually impossible for an opposition party to win.

DE SADELEER, FRANS (Dec. 8, 1844–Jan 20, 1922). A Belgian Jesuit missionary, De Sadeleer joined the **Zambezi Mission** to Bulawayo in 1879. During the next several years he participated in several unsuccessful attempts to launch new missions at **Pandamatenga** and in **Barotseland**.

DETE (Dett until 1982). Headquarters of the **Hwange National Park**, this village is located on the Bulawayo-to-Victoria Falls railway line (at 18°37'S, 26°52'E; alt. 1,080 m).

DETT see **DETE**

DHLISO MATHEMA (variant: Hliso) (fl.1890s). Ndebele *induna* associated with the Nqama *ibutho,* quartered just north of the **Matopo Hills**. During the 1896 **Revolt** Dhliso was a major rebel leader in the Matopos fighting and was one of those who installed **Nyamanda** as king. He participated in the peace negotiations with Cecil Rhodes and was then made a salaried chief in the **Matobo District**.

DHLO DHLO (a.k.a. Danangombi). Important **Khami culture** ruins located in the northern **Insiza District** (at 19°57'S, 29°20'E). The complex comprises a number of buildings, the most important of which is built around two platforms containing an estimated 10,000 tons of rubble fill.

The enclosure's well-built retaining walls are noted for their varied and colorful decoration.

Known to the **Rozvi** as Danangombi, Dhlo Dhlo was one of the main **Changamire** administration centers until it was sacked by the **Ngoni** in the early 1830s. Rebuilding then began, and **Tohwechipi** was apparently installed there as the new Changamire. The subsequent **Ndebele** invasion of the late 1830s caused the Rozvi to abandon the site.

Europeans first discovered the ruins during the **1893 Ndebele War**. The following year Europeans ransacked the ruins for **gold,** carrying off nearly 18 kg in ornaments. W. G. Neal and others (see **Rhodesia Ancient Ruins, Ltd.**) took an additional four kg of gold ornaments in 1895. Virtually all these artifacts soon disappeared without record. Also found by early pillagers were two **Portuguese** bronze canons and a number of Roman Catholic relics. These items have been interpreted as indicating a Portuguese presence in the area during the 16th and 17th centuries, but they more likely were obtained through trade or raids into the northeast.

The Ndebele knew the ruins as *Imithangala ka Mambo,* "the Mambo's Stone Walls," giving rise to the early 20th century name "Mambo Ruins." This name was, however, soon dropped to avoid confusion with the **Mtabazikamambo ruins.** The site was renamed "Dhlo Dhlo" after a local 19th-century Ndebele settlement which had nothing to do with the original ruins builders. Archaeological digs at Dhlo Dhlo have been undertaken by **D. Randall-MacIver** (1905), **G. Canton-Thompson** (1929), and **R. Summers** (1959).

DIAMONDS see **GEMSTONES**

DIANA'S VOW CAVE. Located c.30 km from **Rusape** (at 18°21′S, 21°18′E), this cave contains some of the finest and most unusual **rock paintings** in the country. A complex frieze features a large reclining human figure believed to be the center of a burial ceremony. Detailed smaller figures that surround it represent many cultural features associated with the **Iron Age** peoples, such as baskets, **cattle,** and a leashed dog. The paintings are now interpreted as an outstanding example of a **Stone Age** artist's depiction of a **Bantu** culture.

"DISSIDENTS." Term used by the government during the 1980s to describe persons engaged in violent antigovernment activities, primarily in the **Matabeleland provinces.** The government of Prime Minister **Robert Mugabe** generally claimed that "dissidents" were supporters of **ZAPU,** an allegation consistently denied by **Joshua Nkomo** and other ZAPU leaders. The government produced evidence to show that some dissidents received training and material support from **South Africa.** In April 1988, in conjunction with the signing of the **Unity Pact** agreement, Mugabe declared a general amnesty that covered the dissidents, and the government claimed in mid-1988 that this national problem had finally been controlled.

DISTRICTS. The basic territorial unit through which the country had been administered during the 20th century has been the district. The **BSAC** administration began creating "Native Districts" for the purpose of

African administration during the mid-1890s. Each district was headed by a native commissioner, later called a district commissioner, who was responsible for the implementation of virtually all laws and policies affecting Africans. By 1923 there were 32 such districts. The number has steadily increased as established districts have been divided and completely new districts have been assembled from sections of older districts. By 1979 there were 55 districts, virtually all of which had undergone at least slight boundary changes in previous decades.

A new system of district administration was introduced through the **Districts Councils Act** of 1980. Districts are administered by district administrators who are the senior local government officials of the Ministry for Local Government and Urban Development and are charged with the responsibility of coordinating government policies in the districts. At the same time they act as the chief executive officers of the district councils. The district councils are elected political bodies, and their primary function is to ensure coordinated development in the district. The council is assisted by a district development committee made up of heads of ministries and departments at the district level and chaired by the district administrator. Magisterial and electoral districts generally conform to the same district boundaries but are administered by the Ministry of Justice, Legal and Parliamentary Affairs and the Ministry of Home Affairs, respectively.

All present and former official districts are entered in this dictionary; complete lists of their most current names are found under the entries for the individual provinces which they define (see **District Councils Acts, Land Apportionment, Land Tenure,** and **Provinces**).

DOMBO (a.k.a. Dombolakonachingwano) (d.1695). Outstanding **Changamire** ruler. Although **Portuguese** records show that the Changamire dynasty was established in the late 15th century, Dombo is one of the earliest Changamires remembered in traditions, which credit him as the "founder" of the state. Dombo emerged suddenly in Portuguese records of the 1680s, when he began a wave of conquests from his base in **Guruhuswa**. In the early 1690s he was apparently invited by the reigning **Munhumutapa** to ally against the Portuguese. Between 1693 and his death in 1695 Dombo directed campaigns against the Portuguese **fairs** in the northeast and against the **Manyika** and other previously autonomous Shona states. The full extent of his conquests remains controversial, but he clearly initiated a major expansion of Changamire authority that made his **"Rozvi"** empire the single greatest power in the country in the early 18th century. He was apparently succeeded by a son Negomo, who died between 1704 and 1710.

DOMBO (pl. *madombo*). **Chishona** word for large stone or rock, such as a *kopje* (cf. **Dwala**). The word appears in many place names, such as *Dombo ro Mambo,* "Mambo's Hill" **(Ntabazinduna)**.

DOMBOSHAWA. Chishona for red (*kopje*), this place name occurs in at least six places in **Mashonaland**. The most important of these is located c.30 km north of Harare in the present Chinamora Communal Lands (at 17°36′S, 31°8′E). This hill is a massive granite dome containing several shelters with notable **rock paintings**. These include fine animal and human depictions of several different styles. Some of the human figures are believed to be **San** representations of **Bantu-speaking peoples.** Another of the many important rock painting sites in the area is the **Makumbe Cave** to the north. The nearby town of Domboshawa contained an industrial school for Africans established by the government in 1920.

"DOMBOSHAWA INDABA" (1964). In order to convince Britain that Africans supported its plans for **UDI, Ian Smith**'s government assembled 600 government chiefs and headmen at **Domboshawa** school to discuss the issue "according to tribal custom and tradition" (see **Indaba**). The convocation was not publicly announced until it opened on October 21, 1964, when the area was sealed off by military forces to avoid interference from African nationalists. On the last day, October 26, the chiefs announced unanimous acceptance of government plans to declare independence. (See **Council of Chiefs.**)

DOMINION PARTY (DP). (1) Short-lived political party that unsuccessfully contested two **Legislative Assembly** seats in the 1948 election. (2) Forerunner of the **Rhodesian Front Party** founded in 1956 out of the disparate opponents of the **United (Federal) Party.** Drawing upon the growing European reaction to African nationalism and European dissatisfaction with government policies, the DP built a strong grassroots organization and rapidly developed into the strongest opposition party. It won 13 of 30 legislative seats in the 1958 election, which the UFP won only because of complex vote-counting technicalities. **William Harper** became the leader of the opposition in the **Assembly,** and a Federal DP was formed with the help of Northern Rhodesian settler politicians. The Federal DP sought to create a white-dominated dominion comprising Southern Rhodesia and the most developed parts of Northern Rhodesia. The two DP branches split in 1960, with the southern branch concentrating on achieving dominion status for Southern Rhodesia alone. In March 1962 the DP merged with other rightwing groups to form the Rhodesian Front, which won the next election under the leadership of **Winston Field.**

DONGA. Widely used southern African term for a ravine or gully cut by running water, though dry most of the year. Introduced into English usage from Zulu, the word is also found in **Sindebele.**

"DOUBLE PYRAMID POLICY" see **"TWO PYRAMID POLICY"**

DRUMS. The Shona people use a wide variety of drums (*ngoma*) in their **music.** Most are carved from solid blocks of wood, with one or both ends covered with stretched hide. The Ndebele people have historically made little use of drums. They have, however, introduced to the country the earthenware "pot drum" (*ingungu*).

DUMA. (Vaduma). Branch of the **Karanga** cluster of Shona with unclear connections with the **Rozvi.** A belt of Duma communities has occupied the region between present **Masvingo** and **Chipinge** since at least the mid-19th century.

DUMBUSEYA. Shona group of obscure but apparently recent origins. The Dumbuseya appear to have coalesced from various refugee Shona groups after the **Ngoni** invasions of the 1830s. The original Dumbuseya may have included some Ngoni people, for Dumbuseya culture is said to have included some **Nguni** elements. By the mid-19th century the Dumbesaya were settled near present **Zvishavana**, where they were harassed by **Ndebele** raids. During the 1870s two of their chiefs, Wedza and Mazeteze, allied with the Ndebele in raids against other Shona. In 1896 the same chiefs joined the Ndebele in the anti-British **Revolt**.

DUPONT, CLIFFORD WALTER (Dec. 6, 1905–June 28, 1978). Born in London, where he practiced law, Dupont came to Southern Rhodesia in 1948. Despite his previous inexperience in agriculture, he became wealthy as a **tobacco** farmer. In 1958 he entered politics and was elected to the Federal Assembly. In 1962 he helped to organize the **Rhodesian Front Party**, becoming its first chairman. The same year he was elected to the **Southern Rhodesian Legislative Assembly** and was appointed minister of justice, law, and order by **Winston Field**. In August 1964 he resigned his seat in order to challenge **Roy Welensky** in a by-election. The main issue was independence, which Welensky opposed. Dupont's easy electoral victory strengthened the Rhodesian Front's position on **UDI**. Dupont is credited with having been the legal expert behind UDI. Because of this contribution and because of his ill health, he was appointed to the post of **"officer administering the government"** on November 17, 1965, effectively replacing **H. V. Gibbs** in the role of **governor**. Dupont caused an international outcry in September 1967 when he signed death warrants for three Africans convicted of offenses prior to UDI. On April 16, 1970, he was sworn in as president of the country under the terms of the 1969 republican **constitution**. In December 1975 he retired from public life and was succeed by **J. J. Wrathall**.

DUTCH REFORMED CHURCH (DRC; a.k.a. Nederduits Gereformeerde Kerk). Calvinist Protestant sect which has been the dominant church in South Africa since the 17th century and is also the main church of Zimbabwe's **Afrikaner** population. The DRC became the second Protestant denomination to field missionaries in the country in 1872, when European and African evangelists based in the **Transvaal** began making tentative forays into southern **Shona** territory. A more formal start was made in 1891, when the Rev. A. A. Louw (1862–1956) founded **Morgenster Mission** near Great Zimbabwe. Under Louw's direction seven other missions, as well as schools and medical facilities, were established around the country. By 1959 DRC missions—by then known as the African Reformed Church in Southern Rhodesia—claimed nearly 28,000 African members and ranked first in mission school attendance (see **Education**) and out-patient medical treatments (see **Health**). The DRC's popularity among Africans has suffered because of the church's austere liturgy and its identification with South Africa's **Afrikaner** minority. DRC missions are consequently said to have lost considerable numbers of their members to African independent churches.

DWALA. Term from **Sindebele** for a large, dome-shaped granite *kopje* such as **World's View** in the **Matapos**. Also known locally as "whaleback *kopjes*." (See **Dombo**.)

DZIMBABWE see **ZIMBABWE**

DZIVAGURU. Shona spirit medium or **mhondoro** in the **Korekore** area of the northeastern part of the country. The Dzivaguru spirit is said to antedate the arrival of the Korekore people. During the early 20th century the medium representing Dzivaguru traveled extensively in the northeast, establishing a wide reputation as a rainmaker and playing an active role in the revolts of **Mapondera**. *Dzivaguru*, "the Great Pool," is also a praise-name for the high god, **Mwari**, among some Shona groups.

DZVITI (pl. Madzviti; variants: Mazwiti; Madviti; etc.). **Shona** name for *Mfecane* invaders, including the **Ndebele, Gaza,** and **Ngoni**. The name derives either from the **Chishona** verb -*dzvita*, "to disturb," or from the name of the Ndwande king **Zwide**, whose wars helped to set the *Mfecane* in motion. (See **Matabele; Rozvi**.)

E

EAST COAST FEVER (a.k.a. African coast fever). **Cattle** disease transmitted by ticks; endemic to the eastern coast. In 1901 infected animals from present Tanzania were brought into the country by way of **Beira.** Within a year the disease spread through the entire country and entered the **Transvaal.** The epidemic posed a major threat to the country's already much reduced cattle herds and killed enough oxen to retard the incipient transport industry. Localizing of herds and dipping of animals were employed to combat the epidemic. By the 1950s the disease was virtually eradicated, but vigorous countermeasures have been continued to prevent a recurrence (see **Health**).

EASTERN HIGHLANDS. Series of mountain ranges running along the eastern border with **Mozambique** from the **Nyan District** in the north to the **Mount Silinda** area in the south. Among the constituent ranges are **Inyanga, Vumba,** and **Chimanimani**. (See **Altitudinal Zones**.)

ECONOMIC STRUCTURAL ADJUSTMENT PROGRAM (ESAP). Publicly revealed in 1991, the ESAP was formulated by the International Monetary Fund (IMF) and World Bank and accepted by the Zimbabwean government in an attempt to increase foreign investments and aid. Under the program, Zimbabwe would liberalize its economy by instituting a new, "realistic" exchange rate, lifting price controls, and largely eliminating practices that restricted imports from competing with locally produced goods. The immediate result of the implementation of these measures was a drastic rise in prices. It was generally reported that as poorer Zimbabweans were hit hard by the rise in prices, they increasingly demanded that the government nationalize **European**-owned farmlands. In addition, the popularity of the government, and of President **Robert Mugabe** in particular, plummeted to an all-time low. By the late 1990s, ESAP had been blamed, in part, for the decline of the national economy and of specific social programs such as the primary health care system and the inability of rural parents to pay primary education fees. (See **Health, Education.**)

EDUCATION. Prior to independence in 1980 the country's school system was racially segregated, with about 92 percent of expenditures going to the minority of non-African students. In 1977, the government was spending over ten times as much on the annual education of a single European student as it did for an African student—R$557 and R$46 per student, respectively. Education for non-Africans (Europeans, Asians, and Coloureds) was both free and compulsory. The education that was available to Africans placed a heavy emphasis on agricultural and industrial training.

The origins of that system were to be found in the early **BSAC** administration's reliance on Christian **missions** to provide African education. From the early 1890s the BSAC encouraged missionary societies to come to the country by providing generous grants of land. After 1899 it began subsidizing mission schools while encouraging their industrial orientation and discouraging integration. The stated policy was to educate Africans to work for and serve the European minority. By the early 1920s African school attendance was well over 40,000 pupils, but total expenditures in 1923 amounted to only $70,000, of which the BSAC contributed only 28 percent.

The first government primary schools were opened in the 1920s, and a Department of Native Education was established in 1925. This agency was shifted around frequently, finally emerging as the Department of African Education in 1964. Under the **Rhodesian Front** the government gradually assumed control of most mission schools and promulgated a policy of pegging African educational expenditures at 2 percent of gross national product, despite the disproportionate rate of African population growth relative to economic development. As a result of these early policies, by the 1970s it was estimated that about 30 percent of the total African population of the country was functionally illiterate.

For most of the 20th century, although African education focused on primary education, the vast majority of African children did not attend school even at that level. In 1976 over one-half of the African population of 6.6 million were under 15 years of age, yet only 846,260 were enrolled in primary schools throughout the country. Of that number, it was estimated that over half dropped out before completing their primary education, with only 0.5 percent reaching the sixth form.

During the 1970s, as the liberation war intensified, the government closed many African schools for security reasons, particularly mission schools in operational war zones. Attendance was also greatly affected as African students boycotted government schools as a form of protest against policies of the **Ian Smith** regime in general and against the segregated status and disproportional funding for African education specifically.

At independence in 1980, the restructuring of the country's educational system was one of the new government's primary objectives. The Ministry of Education, no longer divided by racial lines, initiated a series of reforms aimed at revolutionizing the system. Free primary education was introduced in 1980, with secondary education at minimal tuition (Z$8–Z$25 per term) being made available to all primary graduates who wanted to continue. The racial segregation of public schools was abolished in 1981, and sexual discrimination in course selection was also abolished. In addition, the Ministry of Education began to transform curriculum and teaching materials from a foreign content to one with a local orientation.

The government also initiated building and teacher training programs in attempts to meet the extraordinary increase in student population brought about by these reforms. In 1979 there were 2,401 primary and 177 secondary government-supported schools, with 18,483 and 3,534 teachers, respectively. None of the secondary schools were located in the rural areas of the country, and only 18 percent of primary school graduates went on to secondary schools. Within four years of independence there were 4,161 primary and 1,129 secondary government supported schools, with 54,424 and 14,644 teachers, respectively. By 1986 there were 54 secondary schools in the rural areas and approximately 83 percent of primary school pupils went on to further their educations. In 1990 there were 2,274,000 students in primary schools and 951,300 pupils in secondary schools, comprising nearly 85 percent of the population between 5 and 19 years of age. In an attempt to curb an increasing dropout rate among primary school students, in May 1994 the government introduced legislation to make primary education compulsory for nine years. By 1996, there were 4,659 primary schools with 63,718 teachers and 2,493,800 students. There were also 28,254 teachers and 751,349 students in secondary schools.

By the mid-1980s, the major problem facing the new national education system was the availability of qualified teachers. It was estimated that over 40 percent of the teachers were unqualified. The government tried to remedy this weakness through increasing enrollments in teacher training colleges—in 1986 there were ten, eight of which were associated with the **University of Zimbabwe**—and the creation of four special training centers for teachers under the Zimbabwe National Integrated Teacher Education Course. By 1998 there were 18,901 students at 15 teachers' training colleges and 14,602 students enrolled at technical and vocational colleges.

EDWARDS, SAMUEL HOWARD (Nov. 27, 1827–June 21, 1922). South African hunter, trader, and concessionaire. Edwards began his interior career at Mabotsa, a mission station his father and **David Livingstone** had founded in former **Ndebele** territory in the western **Transvaal** in 1843. After several hunting and trading expeditions into **Botswana,** he accompanied **Robert Moffat** to **Matabeleland** in 1854. During this trip he conducted a profitable trade in **ivory** and became the first European trader to enter the new Ndebele domain. In 1869 Edwards returned to Matabeleland as guide for the **London and Limpopo Mining Company** expedition. After this company lost its mining **concession, Lobengula**

awarded it to Edwards and several associates in 1881. Edwards then resided mostly at what became the **Tati Concession** until his retirement to Port Elizabeth in 1892. Edwards also is credited with having assisted **Cecil Rhodes'** party in the negotiations that led to the **Rudd Concession** in 1888.

EIFFEL FLATS. Mining town located c.7 km northeast of **Kadoma** on the main road to Harare (at 18°19'S, 29°59'E). Most working residents have been employed by the nearby Cam and Motor Mine. This mine, formed out of an amalgam of small mines in 1909, is the country's largest **gold** producer (see **Chakari**). Since the late 1960s the mine has also processed **nickel** and other minerals.

ELDORADO. Village just east of **Chinhoyi** on the site of the former Eldorado **gold** mine (at 17°21'S, 30°14'E). The site was one of the last major gold mines worked by the **Shona** up to the late 19th century. Shona production apparently ceased after 1892 when the local ruler, **Nemakonde**, was killed by the **Ndebele**. The mine was reopened by Europeans in 1904, causing a minor gold rush. The next year a narrow-gauge **railway** line was extended from Salisbury, further accelerating local development. The mine itself shut down in 1928.

ELECTIONS. Since the granting of **Responsible Government** in 1923, general political elections have been held in 1924, 1928, 1933, 1934, 1939, 1946, 1948, 1954, 1958, 1962, 1965, 1970, 1974, 1977, 1979, 1980, 1985, 1990, 1995, 1996, and 2000. In addition to these elections, there was a nationwide referendum, on changing the constitution, in early 2000. Only since 1980 has the African majority been eligible to participate.

ELECTRICAL POWER. The first generation of electricity in the country was begun by a private firm in **Bulawayo** in 1891. Two years later the operation was taken over by the municipality, setting the pattern for other towns. **Harare** got its first municipal power station in 1913. In 1936 the government created the Electrical Supply Commission, which erected transmission lines and built new power stations throughout the country in an effort to provide service to wider areas. Through the 1950s virtually all electrical power in the country was generated in thermal plants burning **Hwange's** coal. By the mid-1950s *coal* shipments were creating a serious bottleneck in the country's **railways**. Rapid industrialization made development of new sources of electrical power imperative. By this time technological advances made possible much longer-distance power transmissions, making feasible the development of a major hydroelectrical project. Under the aegis of the new **Federation** government, **Kariba Dam** was built during the late 1950s. While power from Kariba Dam was initially sufficient, by the late 1960s further industrial demands necessitated the reopening of many thermal power plants. Following independence in 1980, the government began a program of expanding electrical power to the rural areas. In an attempt to meet increased demands brought about as a result of this program, as well as increased production by the country's industries after the liberation war, a major new thermal power plant was built at Hwange in the mid-1980s. By 1996, the country's total electrical production had reached 7.8 million kilowatt hours.

ELEPHANTS. Although elephant populations were greatly reduced by 19th-century **ivory hunters**, remnant herds are still found throughout the country's rural regions, notably in **Hwange National Park**.

EMERALDS see **GEMSTONES**

EMPANDENI MISSION. Jesuit mission station founded in 1887 near the site of present **Plumtree** on the site of the Impande *ibutho* of the **Ndebele** (20°45′S, 27°58′E). Under the leadership of **Peter Prestage** and **Andrew Hartmann**, the mission labored with little success and was closed in 1889. Prestage reopened the mission in 1895, however. (See **Zambezi Mission**.)

EMPRESS MINE. Of the several mines with this name, the most important is that located c.30 km west of **Kadoma** in the northern **Kwekwe District** (18°27′S, 29°26′E). **Nickel** has been mined extensively there since 1955.

ENHLA (pl. *abenhla*). **Sindebele** term meaning, literally, "north" or "upcountry." Within the context of **Ndebele** society, the term was applied during the 1820s to people from the north, or South African high veld, to distinguish them from the *zansi*—the people from the south, or Zululand. By the time the Ndebele migrated from the **Transvaal** to **Matabeleland** in the late 1830s, *enhla* outnumbered *zansi* roughly two to one. This ratio remained similar over the next century. Popular views of Ndebele society hold that the people were rigidly divided into three "castes" and that the *enhla* occupied a middle position between the *zansi* and the *holi*—the latter being mainly **Shona**. Regardless of the accuracy of such views, it is clear that the *enhla* were, and are, Ndebele who trace their ancestry to the mainly **Sotho-speaking peoples** of the South African high veld.

ENKELDOORN see **CHIVHU**

EPWORTH MISSION. Wesleyan Methodist mission station and theological college located just east of Harare (at 17°52′S, 31°8′E). **Isaac Shimmin** (1860–1933) and another South African missionary founded the station in 1892 on land granted by the BSAC. The station developed into one of the country's most important mission and training centers. Many Africans have resided on the mission's farms, which from the late 1950s were increasingly surrounded by European settlements. Under the provisions of the 1969 **Land Tenure Act**, the government attempted to evict the African residents.

ESIGODINI (Essexvale until 1982). Located just southeast of **Bulawayo** on the main road to **Beitbridge** (at 20°18′S, 28°56′E; alt. 1,165 m). This village was established in 1894 at the center of a depleted mining area and is at present a small commercial center within the **Umzingwane District**.

ESSEXVALE see **ESIGODINI**

EUROPEANS. According to custom in most of southern Africa, a "European" is any person of purely European descent, regardless of place of birth. The term is often used synonymously with terms such as "white," "settler," "commercial farmer," etc. By the end of 1975 the European population of the country peaked at 278,000. Although this number constituted only 4 percent of the country's total population, Europeans had for nearly 90 years monopolized political and economic control and held lands equal in size—but superior in quality—to that of the entire African population (see **Land Apportionment** and **Land Tenure Acts**). Despite their vast land holdings, most Europeans lived in the urban centers, particularly **Harare**.

The **Portuguese** were the first Europeans to enter the country. During the 16th and 17th centuries they played active commercial and military roles in the northeastern parts of the country from bases in **Mozambique**, but by the early 18th century they were largely gone from Zimbabwe. The next Europeans to arrive entered from the south, mainly by way of **Botswana**, during the 1850s. From that point increasing numbers of **missionaries, hunters**, and traders entered the country. Few settled permanently, however, and significant European settlement began only in the 1890s, when the **BSAC** occupied the country and established a European administration.

There were an estimated 1,500 European residents in 1891. This figure rose to 11,000 in 1901; 23,600 in 1911; 33,600 in 1921; 49,900 in 1931; and 69,000 in 1941. The Second World War created a boom in European immigration, particularly from Britain, raising the number to 82,400 in 1946 and to 136,000 in 1951. The figure topped 200,000 in 1959 and then diminished slightly in the early 1960s, as fear of an African political takeover stimulated emigration. Net European immigration gains again rose in 1966, with the total European population reaching 228,300 in 1969, 41 percent of whom were native-born. Starting in the mid-1970s, net emigration increased as the war for independence continued and increased in intensity. By 1981 it was estimated that as a result of independence and African majority rule, more than one-half of the European population had emigrated. The total European population for that year was estimated to have been 110,000. By 1992 the European population was c.80,000.

EWANRIGG ALOE GARDENS NATIONAL PARK. Botanical gardens located c.35 km northeast of Harare (at 17°41'S, 31°20'E). The 24-hectare **national park** features **aloes** and cycads.

EXECUTIVE COUNCIL. In 1894 the British secretary of state for colonies issued an Order-in-Council creating an advisory council for the **BSAC's** administration in Southern Rhodesia. The council included a high court judge, three BSAC appointees, and the BSAC **administrator**, who presided. The council as a whole was responsible for the routine governing of the country. Another Order-in-Council in 1898 recreated the body as an Executive Council and added a **Legislative Council** with elected settler members. A nonvoting British resident commissioner sat on both councils, reporting on their actions to the British high commissioner for Southern Africa.

When **Responsible Government** was achieved in 1923, the Executive Council became the government's cabinet and was formally presided over by the British **governor**. Membership comprised the **prime minister** and the heads of the various ministries. Over time the influence of the governors diminished and the Executive Council evolved into a cabinet in the more truly parliamentary sense.

F

FAIRBAIRN, JAMES (1853–April 11, 1894). A Scottish trader, Fairbairn first came to **Matabeleland** in the 1870s. In 1881 he formed a concessionary company with Thomas Leask, **George Westbeech**, and **G. A. Phillips**. Three years later **Lobengula** awarded this company a mining **concession** between the **Gwelo** and **Hunyani** rivers, which they sold to the BSAC for a large sum in 1889.

FAIRBRIDGE, WILLIAM ERNEST (Nov. 2, 1863–Oct. 5, 1943). South African journalist. In 1891 the **Argus Group** of newspapers sent Fairbridge to Salisbury, where he almost immediately started the *Mashonaland Herald & Zambesian Times*, the forerunner of the *Rhodesian Herald*. Argus then made him their manager in the country until his return to South Africa around 1904. Between December 1897 and July 1898 he also served as the first mayor of **Salisbury**. (See also **Censorship**.)

FAIRS (Portuguese: *Feiras*). Markets or trading centers established in **Shona** territory and the **Zambezi** Valley by coastal-based **Muslims** at least as early as the 14th century. The fairs were set up in the interior to buy **gold** dust, **ivory**, and **iron** goods from African producers who had insufficient quantities to merit transport to coastal ports such as **Sofala**. After the **Portuguese** occupied Muslim ports in the early 16th century, they gradually recognized the necessity of establishing their own network of fairs. By the early 17th century they had opened at least a dozen fairs in Shona territory—mostly in the **Munhumutapa** and **Manyika** regions. Each fair typically contained a market center, small fort, Dominican mission church, and a few Portuguese houses. Among the most important fairs in the country were **Dambarare, Luanze, Maramuca,** and **Masapa.** In the early 1690s the **Changamire state** expanded into the northeast and destroyed most of the fairs. Thereafter Portuguese traders were largely kept out of the country and had to work indirectly through African employees or slaves known as *musambazes*. The Portuguese retained their bases at **Tete** and **Sena** on the Zambezi River and opened a fair at **Zumbo** in c.1714 in order to have a closer link with the Changamire state

FAKU NDIWENI (fl. 1870s–90s). Ndebele **induna**. In 1872 Faku is said to have informed on a brother who supported the abortive coup attempt of **"Nkulumane"** and **Mangwane**. After his brother was executed in early 1875, Fahu became regent of the Ndiweni chieftaincy centered by the headwaters of the **Gwai** and **Khami** rivers. When his nephew, the rightful chief, came of age in the early 1890s, Faku refused to give up his position. **Lobengula** was about to intervene in the dispute, but the **Ndebele War** interrupted him, bringing the British to power. The new **BSAC** administration recognized Faku as Ndiweni chief, and he became one of its strongest supporters in **Matabeleland**. His collaboration with the company seriously divided his people during the **1896 Revolt**, in which he was made a salaried chief. Later his own descendants were confirmed as heirs to the Ndiweni chieftaincy in the Kezi area, south of the **Matopo Hills.**

FALCON MINE see **UMVUMA**

FANAKALO (variant: Fanagalo; a.k.a. Chilolol; Chilapalapa; "Kitchen Kaffir"). A pidgin language, Fanakalo is an amalgam of Afrikans, **Sindebele, Chishona**, English, and other African languages. It is used widely throughout the country as a simplified mode of European-African communication. The name derives from a similar lingua franca developed in the South African mines. (See also **"Kaffir"; Language.**)

"FEARLESS TALKS" (1968). Two years after the abortive agreement produced by their **"Tiger Talks," Ian Smith** and British Prime Minister Harold Wilson met again (October 9–13, 1968) off Gibraltar, aboard the warship H.M.S. *Fearless.* Although Britain dropped the demand for a return to "legality," no agreement was reached. The next Anglo-Rhodesian settlement agreement was reached in November 1971 (see **Pearce Commission**).

FEDERAL PARTY see **UNITED PARTY**

FEDERAL PARTY OF ZIMBABWE (FP). Political party created in December 1994 by former members of the **Forum Party of Zimbabwe.** Reportedly suspicious of the increased dominance of the national government of **President Robert Mugabe** over local issues, the leadership of the FP called for the establishment of five federal provinces, each with an elected prime minister. Under this plan the central government would maintain control over national defense and foreign affairs, but the powers of the executive president and **House of Assembly** would be greatly reduced.

FEDERATION OF RHODESIA AND NYASALAND (a.k.a. Central African Federation [CAF]). From 1953 to through 1963 Southern Rhodesia, Northern Rhodesia (now Zambia), and Nyasaland (Malawi) were linked together by a self-governing federation dominated by white Southern Rhodesian politicians.

(1) *Creation of the Federation.* **Amalgamation** of the two Rhodesias was first proposed during the First World War as an alternative to the **Unionist Movement** proposals to link Southern Rhodesia to South Africa. The idea was opposed by Southern Rhodesian settlers until after the achievement of **Responsible Government** in 1923. Then the British

government's **Hilton Young Commission** (1929) and **Bledisloe Commission** (1939) issued reports rejecting the idea. The latter report did, however, pave the way for creation of the **Central African Council** in 1944 to stimulate international cooperation. After the Second World War **Godfrey Huggins'** government abandoned the idea of amalgamation in favor of federation—a looser form of union. **Roy Welensky** became the leading advocate of federation in Northern Rhodesia.

Settler motives for creating a federation were primarily economic. They wished to tap the wealth generated by Northern Rhodesia's Copperbelt, to create a larger and more diversified national economy, and to attract foreign investments away from South Africa. Federation was also seen as a more promising vehicle to attain autonomous dominion status, although many settlers feared being politically overwhelmed by the larger African majorities north of the Zambezi River. This risk was enhanced by the need to persuade the British government that federation would not retard African political advancement. Huggins and his supporters met this challenge by articulating the concept of federal **"partnership."**

The CAF was planned in a series of conferences between territorial representatives and British government officials from 1948 to 1953. The British government committed itself to the scheme only after 1951, when the Conservative Party took power. At British insistence Nyasaland was included in federation plans, though that country had little to contribute but migrant laborers. Africans north of the Zambezi strongly opposed federation, for fear of falling under the domination of white Southern Rhodesians. African opinion in Southern Rhodesia was divided. Most Africans there recognized that federation meant enhanced white power, but many saw closer union with South Africa as an even more unpleasant alternative (see **All-African Convention**). In any case, Africa objections were largely ignored and the British Parliament approved a federal constitution in March 1953. On April 9 a Southern Rhodesian referendum ruled in favor of federation by a vote of 25,580 to 14,929. Only a few hundred Africans were able to vote on the issue. A British Order-in-Council created the CAF on August 1. By October the Federation was in full operation.

(2) *Federal structure.* The federal constitution created a Federal Assembly with 35 seats (later raised to 60), including six reserved for Africans. Southern Rhodesia had 14 seats open to all races, but in practice these were held only by whites. A fifteenth European was elected to represent African interests. The two initial African seats were won by **M. M. Hove** and **J. Z. Savanhu**, who were elected by predominantly European constituencies. After the first general election in December 1953 Huggins became Prime Minister. His new Federal Party, an offshoot of the **United Party**, was never seriously challenged during the life of the Federation. After Huggins' retirement in 1956, Welensky became the second and last prime minister.

A British governor-general became head of state (see **S. R. Dalhousie** and **J. J. Llewellin**). He signed all federal legislation but exercised almost no discriminatory powers. A special body, the African Affairs Board, was created within the Assembly to guard against discriminatory legislation. The board was to report to the British government, which had reserve veto powers. The board's ineffectiveness was proven when Britain refused to block discriminatory federal franchise legislation in 1957.

Existing territorial institutions, including Southern Rhodesia's **Legislative Assembly** and **governor**, were retained. The federal government assumed jurisdiction only over specified government functions, including external affairs, customs and immigration, non-African and general higher education, and public health. Southern Rhodesia's government retained sole responsibility for its African affairs, local government, police, and various internal economic sectors. Revenues were shared among the three territorial and the federal governments, with Southern Rhodesia generally expending more than it contributed.

(3) *Developments and dissolution, 1953–63.* It is generally recognized that the period of federation was one of increased economic prosperity, but authorities disagree on the contribution the federation itself made to this state of affairs. The federation's economy was built largely around Northern Rhodesian copper exports, and copper happened to enjoy a worldwide price boom in the mid-1950s, thereby stimulating the entire federation economy. The most obvious economic benefits that the federation itself produced were those arising from the construction of the huge **Kariba Dam** hydroelectric scheme. Southern Rhodesia was the clearest beneficiary of federation. It received a disproportionate share of federal revenues; it contained the federal capital, Salisbury (now **Harare**); and it experienced a rapid period of industrial expansion. In 1955 the federation extended a new **railway** line through Southern Rhodesia to provide a connection with Lourenzo Marques (now Maputo). In 1957 the federally sponsored **university** was opened in **Mt. Pleasant.** On the dissolution of federation, Southern Rhodesia inherited these facilities and others, including most of the federal army equipment (see **Military**).

Although the federation government was dominated by Southern Rhodesian settlers who hoped to make it an independent dominion (see **Dominion Party**), its eventual dissolution was almost foreordained by its inherent structure. The federal government had no control over constitutional advances within constituent territories, and Britain was already committed to bringing African majority rule to the two northern territories. It was only the speed with which this happened that was unexpected. In 1959 Britain set up the **Monckton Commission** to make proposals respecting constitutional changes. This commission found opposition to federation so well organized among the Africans north of the Zambezi that it technically exceeded its own instructions by recommending that the individual territories be given the right of secession. When the ensuing Federal Review Conference, which met in London in late 1960, became deadlocked, it deferred decision-making until the attainment of responsible government in Northern Rhodesia and Nyasaland. When this was achieved, Britain granted both territories the right to secede from the federation (December 1962). Both did so quickly, and the CAF was formally terminated on the last day of 1963.

Welensky's ruling party regarded Britain's condoning of territorial secession as a betrayal, but by then the government of Southern Rhodesia itself was in the hands of the **Rhodesian Front Party**, which opposed federation for reasons of its own.

FEIRAS. Portuguese term for trading **fairs.** For Feira town, see **Zumbo.**

FERNANDES, ANTONIO (fl.1506–1520s). The first European known to have entered the country, Fernandes is an elusive character in **Portuguese** records, partly because his name was a common one. He apparently came to **Sofala** in 1506 as a *degredado* (perhaps an exiled criminal) after seeing service in the Kongo kingdom of west-central Africa. Though described as a carpenter, he was commissioned by the commander at Sofala to discover the **gold** fields in the interior. He apparently made his first journey in 1511, traveling inland from Sofala to **Manyika.** By mid-1513 he had made a second longer journey, this time meeting **Munhumutapa Chikuyo Chisamarengu** and traveling widely in the northeastern section of present Zimbabwe. The reports of his trips were recorded by a clerk in Sofala. His later activities are unknown, but Fernandes was reported as dead by 1525.

FIELD, WINSTON (June 6, 1904–March 1969). Seventh **prime minister** of Southern Rhodesia. Born in England, Field came to the country in 1921. He became successful as a **tobacco** farmer in the **Marondera District** and served as the president of the Rhodesian Tobacco Association from 1938 to 1940. During the Second World War he served in the British army. Afterwards he returned to the country and initiated an unsuccessful scheme to settle Italian peasant farmers (1952). He entered politics in 1956 as the leader of the new **Dominion Party.** The following year he was elected to the **federation** Assembly in a **Murehwa** by-election. As the leader of the opposition to the **United (Federal) Party** government, Field advocated dissolution of the federation and creation of a white-dominated dominion which would include the main European areas of Northern Rhodesia, as well as all of Southern Rhodesia. In 1962 he became leader of the DP's successor party, the **Rhodesian Front,** leading it to victory in the December election. As new prime minister he surprised Africans by releasing political detainees in January 1963, but he then quickly toughened the **Law and Order (Maintenance) Act.** RF hardliners became impatient with his leadership because of his failure to press the British government sufficiently hard on the independence issue (see **UDI**). In April 1964 a party congress forced him to resign in favor of his deputy, **Ian Smith.** Field then retired from politics.

FIGTREE. Village 38 km southwest of **Bulawayo** on the main road to **Plumtree** in the **Bulilimamangwe District** (at 20°22′S, 28°20′E; alt. 1,380 m). Figtree is a commercial center in a mainly **cattle**-keeping region.

FILABUSI. Mining village and headquarters for the **Insiza District,** of which "Filabusi District" was formerly a separate part (at 20°32′S, 29°17′E on the **Insiza River**). Filabusi experienced a brief boom during the Second World War, when military demand for tungsten increased local scheelite production.

FILM INDUSTRY. Film production in the country dates to 1960 and the establishment of the Central Film Unit, which was operated by the **federation** government. With the dissolution of the federation, 51 percent ownership passed to the government of **Rhodesia,** while 49 percent of the Film Unit was sold to two private individuals who changed the name to Central Film Laboratories and ran it as a private company. In 1980 the newly independent government of Zimbabwe acquired the minority shares and the company came under the control of the Ministry of Information, Posts, and Telecommunications. However, though it is a parastatal, it still operates as a private company and must show a profit to continue operating.

Film production during the 1970s was virtually nonexistent due to the war, but following independence in 1980 some small-scale documentaries were produced. Since 1984, Zimbabwe has been used as the location for a number of major international feature films, including "King Solomon's Mines," "Cry Freedom," "Mandela," and "A World Apart." In addition, a growing number of Zimbabwean-produced documentaries and educational films have been made in the country. All projects must be submitted to the ministry for approval, and the government has stipulated that foreign production companies set up training programs for Zimbabweans.

FINGO LOCATION. Special area granted to **Mfengu** immigrants who entered the country between 1898 and 1902. It is located near the junction of the **Bembezi River** and the Bulawayo-to-Harare Road (at 19°56'S, 28°55'E).

FINGOS see **MFENGU**

"FIRST FRUITS FESTIVAL" see **INXWALA**

FISHING. More than 100 varieties of fish are native to the country. The most important of these are members of the carp family (*Cyprinidae*), bream (*Cichlidae*), and catfish (*Siluridae*). The **Shona, Tonga,** and other peoples—excepting many South African-derived **Ndebele**—have long caught fish to supplement their diets. The development of modern **dams** has greatly enlarged the country's fishing waters, particularly in **Lake Kariba**, which has the country's only commercial fishing industry. Many dams on European farms are stocked with fish to feed African workers, and the government has a program of introducing fishing dams to African areas. Sport fishing is an important feature of the tourist industry. Exotic fish such as black bass and trout are bred locally and stocked in **national parks**. Rainbow, brown, and American brook trout thrive in the rivers of the **Eastern Highlands**. An unusual native variety, the Tiger Fish (*Characidae*), is regarded as the most exciting sport fish and is found in the larger lakes. It grows up to 15 kg and is noted for its long razor-sharp teeth, which can destroy ordinary fishing gear.

"FIVE PRINCIPLES." Conditions cited by the British government as essential to any Anglo-Rhodesian constitutional settlement. The five principles were first expressed in a letter from the British secretary of state for commonwealth relations to **Ian Smith** in September 1965. They were (1) unimpeded progress toward majority rule, (2) guarantees against retrogressive constitutional changes, (3) immediate improvements in the political status of Africans, (4) progress toward ending racial discrimination, and (5) acceptance of any Anglo-Rhodesian settlement terms by the people of Rhodesia as a whole. Shortly after **UDI** a sixth principle was added to ensure that there was no oppression of the majority by the minority, or of a minority by the majority.

FLAGS. The **BSAC** and Southern Rhodesian governments flew the British Union Jack with their respective coats of arms added in the center. The **federation** government used a flag combining the symbols of each of its constituent territories. The Rhodesian government in April 1964 adopted a light-blue British ensign with the Union Jack in the canton and the shield from its own coat of arms on the fly. The **UDI government** in 1969 adopted a flag with three equal-size vertical stripes. Two green stripes surrounded a central white stripe dominated by their coat of arms. The government of Zimbabwe in 1980 adopted a flag with seven horizontal stripes and a white triangle. The central stripe is black and symbolizes the African majority; the next two stripes on either side of the black are red and represent the blood of the people spilled during the armed struggle for independence; the next stripes are yellow; and the last two are green, representing the mineral, and vegetable and agricultural wealth of the nation, respectively. The white triangle along the left-hand edge stands for peace; and in the center of this triangle is a gold **"Zimbabwe Bird"** superimposed over a red star. The red star symbolizes the nation's aspirations, and the bird is a national emblem.

FLAME LILY (*Gloriosa superba*). This perennial flower appears in December and January, and is red and yellow, orange and yellow, yellow, or magneta brown in color. The red and yellow form, common in the high and middle veld regions of the country, is Zimbabwe's national flower.

FLEMING, ANDREW MILROY (Jan. 28, 1871–1954). Early **health** officer. A Scottish physician, Fleming came to the country in 1894. During the **1896 Revolts** he was made principle medical officer to **BSAC** forces. Afterwards he became the country's first director of the Public Health Department (1898–1931). His early researches into **malaria** made a major contribution in combating this disease around the world. He retired to Scotland.

FORBES, PATRICK WILLIAM (Aug. 31, 1861–May 27, 1923). British army officer with service in South Africa during the 1880s. In 1889 he joined the forerunner of the **British South Africa Police**, with which he served in the 1890 **Pioneer Column**. In November he was sent by **Archibald Colquhoun** to Chief **Mutasa** in **Manicaland** to prevent **Portuguese** infiltration into BSAC-claimed territory. Although Forbes commanded only 15 troopers, he boldly arrested two important Portuguese officials there, **J. C. P. d'Andrada** and **M. A. de Sousa**, whom he sent to Salisbury (November 15, 1890). He then began a push to open a route to the Indian Ocean but was recalled by the government. In July 1893 **L. S. Jameson** named Forbes commander of BSAC forces while preparing for the **Ndebele War**, which began in October. Forbes commanded the Salisbury Column through two major battles and the occupation of **Bulawayo.** He then led a column north in pursuit of **Lobengula**. Forbes then fought Ndebele skirmishers while retreating to Bulawayo, with his own military reputation thereafter tarnished. In 1895 he became BSAC administrator of North-Eastern Rhodesia (now eastern Zambia). Poor health caused him to retire to Southern Rhodesia in 1898, but he later became staff officer for the Southern Rhodesian Volunteers in the **South African War**. He returned to England in 1902 and later served in the First World War.

FORESTS/FORESTRY. The country's indigenous woodlands are of limited economic potential, except in the dry region of **Matabeleland North Province**, where teak and other native hardwoods are profitably exploited (see **Sawmills**). Most hardwood production is exported. The **Eastern Highlands** are ideally suited for rapid tree growth, but indigenous trees of commercial potential are concentrated in a few small areas which are now protected as reserves (see **Chirinda Forest; Vumba**). A commercial forestry industry began in the early 20th century with the importation of pines and Australian wattles to the Eastern Highlands. More than 800 sq km of land are given over to intensive plantation cultivation, supplying most of the country's internal demand for softwood and paper products. (See also **Baobab; Mopane; Savanna**.)

FORT CHARTER see under **CHIKOMBA DISTRICT**

FORT SALISBURY see **HARARE**

FORT VICTORIA see **MASVINGO**

FORUM PARTY OF ZIMBABWE (FPZ). Opposition political party founded in 1992 and led by the former chief justice of Zimbabwe, Dr. Enoch Dumbutshena. In 1994, the FPZ claimed to have 36,000 dues-paying members throughout the country. The FPZ was created when two quasi-political groups, the Forum for Democratic Reform and the Open Forum, merged memberships. Those groups had been established in the early 1990s as political discussion groups by prominent intellectuals, church leaders, businessmen, and several liberal **European** politicians, all of whom were concerned by President **Robert Mugabe**'s continued calls for the formalization of a one-party state in Zimbabwe.

In December 1993, the FPZ charged the government and **ZANU** with election fraud during the 1990 presidential **elections**. In May of the following year, the local **press** reported that the FPZ was in disarray as a result of internal disagreements over how, or whether, to contest the 1995 elections. The press also reported that Dumbutshena had been expelled from the party, although party officials later stated that he had not been expelled. They claimed that a small group of government-sponsored "provocateurs" had called a meeting of no more than 300 disgruntled members and attempted to discredit the party by reporting Dumbutshena's expulsion. The leadership claimed that all the party's provincial executive committees continued to support Dumbutshena. Two weeks prior to the 1995 elections, the FPZ withdrew from the campaign and the elections to protest what its leaders called "an uneven playing field." However, the leadership reversed its decision and 26 seats were contested by FPZ candidates, winning 16 percent of the vote in those constituencies. In 1996 Dumbutshena stepped down and was replaced by Washington Sansole.

FRANCISTOWN. Botswana town on the Mafeking-to-Bulawayo **railway** line in the former **Tati Concession** area (at 21°12′S, 27°31′E). In the mid-1970s Francistown became an important base for anti-Rhodesian nationalists who used local broadcasting facilities to communicate propaganda to the southwestern districts of the country.

FRONT FOR THE LIBERATION OF MOZAMBIQUE (FRELIMO). A dual political-military organization in **Mozambique.** FRELIMO was founded on June 25, 1962, in Dar es Salaam, Tanganyika (now Tanzania) under the leadership of Eduardo Mondlane. After a little more than two years of organizing and formulating strategy, FRELIMO launched its war of liberation against the **Portuguese** colonial government on September 25, 1964, in northern Mozambique. Following the assassination of Mondlane in February 1969, Samora Machel was elected to lead FRELIMO in May 1970. After more than a decade of sustained armed struggle, FRELIMO led Mozambique to independence on June 25, 1975. Machel then became the country's first president.

The contributions and sacrifices made by FRELIMO's leadership in support of the liberation of Zimbabwe were great (see **ZANLA**). In 1972 FRELIMO established a "liberated zone" in northwest Mozambique, bringing all of **Tete** Province under its control. FRELIMO then allowed ZANLA to open forward camps and infiltrate its forces into northeastern **Rhodesia** from this region. Following Mozambican independence FRELIMO allowed **ZANU** and ZANLA to establish additional camps throughout the country's borders to Rhodesia, an act that cost Mozambique up to $57 million a year in lost revenues from 1976 to 1980. It also forced Rhodesia to send its **railway** traffic through South Africa at much higher transit costs. These acts of solidarity with ZANLA weakened both the Rhodesian economy and the government's ability to counter the infiltration of ZANLA combatants into the country.

Ties between the leaders of ZANU and FRELIMO have stayed close following Zimbabwe's independence in 1980. In addition to its own economic needs, one reason given by President **Robert Mugabe** for the presence of Zimbabwean troops in Mozambique throughout most of the 1980s was to repay FRELIMO and the people of Mozambique for the sacrifices they made in support of the Zimbabwean struggle for independence (see **Mozambique National Resistance**).

FRONT FOR THE LIBERATION OF ZIMBABWE (FROLIZI). In October 1971 nationalist leaders resident in Lusaka, Zambia, announced the formation of FROLIZI as a merger of **ZAPU** and **ZANU**. It appears, however, that FROLIZI was simply a new organization formed by dissident leaders from the two rival parties. Skilkom Siwela and Godfrey Savanhu, the titular leaders of the new organization, were ousted early in 1972 by **James Chikerema, George Nyandoro,** and **Nathan Shamuyarira**. FROLIZI never established itself within Rhodesia, but instead attempted to ally with the **African National Council**. The party gained considerable outside support in 1972, but early in 1973 it was officially ignored by the Liberation Committee of the OAU. Thereafter it faded in importance.

FRONTLINE STATES. In December 1974 the Liberation Committee of the Organization of African Unity created a "Frontline Presidents' Committee" to coordinate external support and strategy for the African liberation of Zimbabwe. The original members of the group were Kenneth Kaunda of **Zambia,** Seretse Khama of **Botswana,** Samora Machel of **Mozambique,** and Julius Nyerere of Tanzania. President Augustino Neto of Angola joined later. This group, from its beginning, was referred to as the "Frontline States." A study by Carol Thompson demonstrates that this group assisted the Zimbabwean natiionalist movements in three primary ways: (1) they provided rear-base logistical support, helped to train guerrilla fighters, and established and maintained refugee camps; (2) they provided both a diplomatic base for the **Patriotic Front** liberation movements, and international diplomatic support for those groups; and (3) they played a key role in keeping the nationalist movements united in their demands. The Frontline States provided this support at a heavy cost—both in terms of lost capital and civilian casualties—to themselves. After the failure of the **Geneva Conference** in 1976, both British and American governments regarded the participation and support of the Frontline States' presidents as crucial to any settlement negotiated between the Patriotic Front and the **Ian Smith** government.

Following Zimbabwe's independence in 1980, the country became the sixth member of the Frontline States. In a somewhat reduced capacity, these six Southern African states provided the same basic forms of support to nationalist movements involved in the liberation struggle in **South Africa.** Beginning in 1980, the six Frontline States joined with Malawi, Lesotho, and Swaziland to form the **Southern African Development Coordinating Conference,** in an attempt to strengthen themselves economically and lessen their overall economic dependence on South Africa. This was a direct outgrowth of the initial political support of the Zimbabwean liberation movements, and was consciously seen as a continuation of the struggle to free themselves from external political and economic forces.

FYNN, PERCIVAL DONAL LESLIE (Aug. 16, 1872–April 25, 1940). Born in the Transkei, Fynn joined the Cape civil service in 1889. In 1897 he followed **W. H. Milton** to Southern Rhodesia, where he held a series of important posts in the **BSAC** government. He joined **Charles Coghlan's** government in 1923 and thereafter dominated finance for a decade. He initially opposed **Godfrey Huggins** in 1933, but then led the opposition members who helped to form the **United Party.** He retired from the cabinet the year before his death.

G

GAIREZI RIVER. Flows north from the eastern slopes of the **Inyanga Mountains** to form an 80 km stretch of the **Mozambique border** before joining the **Ruenya River.**

GAME RESERVES. Conservation of the country's vast wildlife resources was initiated by European landowners in the **Hwange District**, part of which became the first government-designated game reserve in 1928. Efforts to protect game were intensified after the creation of the Natural Resources Board in 1942. This led to the National Parks Act in 1949 and the Wildlife Conservation Act of 1960. Some reserves, such as Hwange, became **national parks**, which differ from nonpark reserves in that they are developed to accommodate vacationers and tourists. By the early 1970s 14 game reserves proper had been designated, including six open to the public on a limited basis. Sites are selected only if they have poor agricultural potential. The largest reserves are Chete, Chizarira, and Matuasadona—all near **Lake Kariba** and Chewore, north of the **Zambezi Escarpment**; and **Gona-re-Zhou** in the southeastern low veld. (See also **Hunting.**)

GAMPU SITHOLE (variant: Gambo Sithole) (c.1840s–1916). **Ndebele induna** whose father, Magekeni (d.1870), was one of **Mzilikazi's** original followers in Zululand. Gampu inherited his father's leadership of the Igapa **ibutho** in the southwestern section of the kingdom after having supported **Lobengula's** accession to the kingship in 1870. His influence became great, but in 1887 he was charged with seducing one of Lobengula's daughters and had to flee to the **Transvaal** (apparently with **P. D. Grobler**) to avoid punishment. He returned home the next year, but his position remained insecure. During the 1893 **Ndebele War** he commanded the force guarding the southern approach to the kingdom. His standing among the Ndebele was further compromised when his force was easily pushed aside by **Goold-Adams'** invasion column.

The next year Gampu became one of the most prominent Ndebele leaders openly to support British occupation of the country. The British rewarded him with land and **cattle,** which eventually made him wealthy. Over the next two years he opposed attempts to make **Nyamanda** king, and then sided with the British in the *Revolt* of 1896 (see also **Faku**). He fought rebel forces in several engagements which gave the Revolt the character of a civil war and helped to keep open the British supply route in southwestern **Matabeleland.** After the Revolt he was one of the first *izinduna* whom Rhodes made a salaried chief. He settled down to become the British ideal of a loyal and progressive African leader.

GANN, LEWIS H. (b. Jan. 28, 1924). A German-born, English-educated historian, Gann began his productive career in central African history in Northern Rhodesia (now Zambia) after the Second World War. He came to Salisbury in 1954 and became publications editor in the **National Archives**. A firm supporter of the **federation**, he used his immense skills as a professional historian to defend the role of Europeans in building a multiracial society by writing the first thoroughly scholarly histories of the region. He was commissioned by the federation to write major histories of each territory, but completed only the volumes on Northern and Southern Rhodesia before the federation collapsed. Disenchanted with Rhodesia's retreat to territorial nationalism in the mid-1960s, Gann joined his frequent coauthor, Peter Duignan, at the Hoover Institution in Stanford, California.

GATHS MINE. Major **asbestos** mine just north of **Mashaba** in the **Masvingo District** (at 20°1'S, 30°31'E).

GATOOMA see **KADOMA**

GATSI RUSERE (variant: Gassi Lusere) (c.1560–1623). Perhaps the best documented of the early **Munhmutapas**, Gatsi Rusere unintentionally initiated a major era of **Portuguese** influence in the country. The grandson of Munhumutapa **Neshangwe**, Gatsi Rusere succeeded **Negomo** as ruler in c.1589 as the result of an earlier agreement with the latter's rival ruling house. Beset with rebellions in his eastern provinces, he achieved order with the help of Portuguese forces. On August 1, 1607, he signed a treaty with **Diogo Simões Madeira** theoretically ceding all his country's mines to the Portuguese. Conflict over implementation of these cessions led to a war with the Portuguese after his own passing. He and some of his sons (see **Dom Miguel**) accepted Christian baptism. On his death in 1623 he was succeeded as Munhumutapa by his son **Nyambo Kapararidze**.

GAZA KINGDOM (a.k.a. **Shangane**; Vatua; etc.). One of the most important of the *Mfecane* era states, the Gaza kingdom was created in southern **Mozambique** in the early 1820s by **Soshangane** and **Nguni** refugees from Zululand. In the 1830s the Gaza (who took their name from Soshangane's grandfather) established their headquarters by **Mount Silinda**, in the southeastern part of present Zimbabwe. Soshangane moved back to the lower Limpopo basin after a few years, but his son **Mzila** returned to Mount Silinda in the early 1860s. In 1889 Mzila's son **Gungunyane** made the final move back to southern Mozambique (see **Manhlagazi**). Throughout this entire period the Gaza raided African communities and **Portuguese** posts between the Zambezi and Limpopo rivers. They raided the **Ndau** especially intensively, but their impact on other Shona-speaking peoples of the country was much less disruptive than that of the similar **Ndebele kingdom** in the west. The Gaza state was brought to an end by Portuguese conquest in 1895, when Gungunyane was sent into exile. An unsuccessful revolt two years later brought down strong reprisals. Although the Gaza parallel the Ndeble in many ways, they did not have the latters' success in imprinting Nguni culture on their subject peoples. *Gaza kings,* c.1820–95; c.1820–c.1859 Soshangane; c.1859–62 Mawewe (usurper); 1862–84 Mzila; 1884–95 Gungunyane.

"GAZA QUEENS" see under **XWALILE**

GAZALAND. European term for the area dominated by the **Gaza kingdom** during the late 19th century. The region roughly encompassed the territory east of the **Sabi River** and south of present **Chimanimani** and southern **Mozambique**. Gazaland was effectively partitioned between Britain and Portugal by the 1891 **Anglo-Portuguese Convention**. Within present Zimbabwe, "Gazaland" has since been applied loosely to refer to the Chimanimani and **Chipinge** districts. The **Portuguese** made "Gaza" the official name of an administrative district south of the Sabi (Save) River. (See **Manicaland; Mashonaland; Matabeleland**.)

GEMSTONES. Although the country is a major producer of precious gems, production accounts for only a minor part of the total value of the **mineral** production, and is undertaken mostly by **"small-workers."** Nearly all varieties of gemstones are found in the country. Most occur in alluvial deposits in the **Somabula Forest** area. Diamond production began there in 1906 and accounted for the largest part of the gemstone production until the late 1950s, when production virtually ceased. Ruby, sapphire, and other gem deposits have been found mainly in association with diamonds. In 1965 emeralds were first discovered in the **Belingwe District**. These now account for the bulk of gemstone production, much of which goes into local jewelry markets. (See also **Mtorolite**.)

GENEVA CONFERENCE (1976). The first major attempt at a negotiated constitutional settlement after the abortive August 1975 **Victoria Falls Conference**, and the first settlement attempt in which Britain was directly involved after the 1972 **Pearce Commission**, the late 1976 Geneva Conference was the product of a direct American diplomatic initiative. On September 19, 1976, U.S. Secretary of State Henry Kissinger met with **Ian Smith** in Pretoria, outlining to him a settlement proposal, which the Rhodesian government accepted under apparent pressure from the South African government. On September 24, Smith publicly announced his government's willingness to negotiate a settlement leading to African majority rule within a two-year period. This was a major retreat from his 1964 vow never to permit majority rule within his lifetime, but the announcement was greeted skeptically by nationalist leaders, and it appeared that there were some discrepancies between the plan Kissinger presented to Smith and the proposals he communicated to the presidents of the **Frontline States** group. Despite African reservations, a conference to discuss the settlement proposals was convened at Geneva on October 28, under the chairmanship of British UN Ambassador Ivor Richards. Five official delegations attended: Smith's government; **Ndabaningi Sithole**'s branch of **ZANU**; **Abel Muzorewa**'s branch of the **African National Council**; **Joshua Nkomo**'s wing of **ANC**; and **Robert Mugabe**'s branch of **ZANU**. The last two men announced formation of a **"Patriotic Front"** on the eve of the conference. The conference quickly became deadlocked over the issue of a timetable for transition to majority rule. The African nationalists agreed on a one-year deadline, but Smith demanded at least 23 months. Richards got the nationalists to compromise on a March 1, 1978, deadline, but the Smith government demurred and the issue was deferred. The next dispute centered on the composition of office-holders in any transition government. The Smith government insisted on adherence to the Kissinger proposals, which called for a complex two-tiered, multiracial council system, but the nationalists rejected the Kissinger proposals altogether, citing special objections to control of the police and military by the Europeans. In the second week of December the conference adjourned for the Christmas holidays without having achieved any substantive accords among the white and black delegations. Smith's increasing intransigence was attributed to his government's apparent successes in the anti-guerilla campaigns. In January 1977 the British government attempted to reopen the conference, but the Smith government refused to participate. A new British initiative was made by Foreign Secretary David Owen in April, but through July this came to nothing. Smith meanwhile dissolved **Parliament** and announced his intention to achieve an **internal settlement** on the basis of the original Kissinger proposals.

GIBBS, HUMPHREY VICARY (Nov. 22, 1902–Nov. 4, 1990). Eighth **governor** of Southern Rhodesia (1959–69). Born in London and educated at Eton and Trinity College in Britain, Gibbs came to Southern Rhodesia in 1928 and began farming near **Bulawayo.** He became prominent in national farming organizations and represented Wankie (now **Hwange**) in the **Legislative Assembly** from 1948 to 1953. In 1959 he succeeded **P. Williams-Powlett** as governor. Gibbs was knighted in 1960 for his service to the British Empire and in late 1963 served briefly as acting governor-general of the **Federation**. After the **Rhodesian Front** government proclaimed **UDI** in 1965, Gibbs attempted to dismiss **Ian Smith**, calling upon the population not to support the regime because UDI had made it illegal. Smith then tried to force Gibbs from the Government House residence by cutting off the utilities, but Gibbs held firm for more than three years. Britain cited Gibbs' continued residence as evidence of its authority in the country. Meanwhile, the government disregarded his office, creating its own **"Officer Administering the Government"** with all the functions and perquisites of the governorship. After settlers voted to create a **republic** in June 1969, Gibbs resigned and returned to Britain where he was feted. He later returned to the country and retired to his farm. In 1983, following an incident in which his wife's car was shot at by a deranged farm employee, Gibbs moved to **Harare,** saying it was no longer safe to continue to live at his farm.

GIBIXHEGU. Once the name of Shaka's chief town in Zululand, South Africa, this name was briefly used for two Ndebele towns in **Matabeleland** in the 19th century. The first town, established in the **Mulungwane Mountains**, was abandoned in mid-1839. When **Lobengula** became king in early 1870, he established a new Gibixhegu at the headwaters of the **Umzingwani River**. A year later he either abandoned this town or renamed it "Bulawayo," which he located a little to the north.

GLOBE AND PHOENIX MINE. Third largest **gold** mine in the country, ranking after mines at **Chakari** and **Eiffel Flats**. The mine is contiguous with the town of **Kwekwe,** which has essentially arisen around it. Its gold-bearing ore is particularly rich. It is estimated that in precolonial times Africans extracted more than 1,400 kg of gold there. The modern mine has been in continuous production since 1902, producing more than 100,000 kg of gold.

GOKOMERE. Term for an early **Iron Age** culture, or industry, named after a site found near **Masvingo** in the early 1920s. Many Gokomere culture sites have since been found throughout **Mashonaland** and southern **Matabeleland**. The culture featured cultivation, livestock-raising (but without cattle), metalworking, and "stamped ware" pottery. It flourished from c.A.D. 200 to about the 10th century, when it was displaced by the **Leopard's Kopje** culture. The latter half of the Gokomere period has recently been divided into separate Zhizo and Malatapi cultures. (See **Ziwa**.)

GOKWE. Administrative center for the district of the same name, Gokwe stands on the Northern edge of the **Mafungabusi Plateau** (at 18°13'S, 28°56'E; alt. 1,285 m).

GOKWE DISTRICT. Covers 23,030 sq km, making up the northwestern section of **Midlands Province**. It previously was the largest section of the former **Sebngwe District**. Except for the **Mafungabusi** forest area, the district is made up almost entirely of **Communal Land**. Gokwe is bordered by **Kariba District** to the north, **Hurungwe** to the northeast, **Kadoma** and the panhandle section of **Kwekwe** to the east, **Nkayi** to the south, **Lupane** to the southwest, and the **Binga** to the west. The district population in 1992 was 403,136.

GOLD. It would be difficult to exaggerate the role gold has played in the country's history. It appears to have first been mined in the northern areas around the 7th century. By about the 11th century mines were operating throughout most of the presently known gold-bearing areas, which correspond, very roughly, to the **Central Plateau**. The identity of these **"ancient"** miners is often treated as a mystery, but they were almost certainly **Shona-speaking peoples.** Trade with **Muslim** settlements on the east coast may have started as early as the 10th century. It clearly was flourishing by the 12th century, when monumental stone-building commenced at **Zimbabwe**. By the late 15th century the **Munhumutapa** state in the northeast was controlling most of the coastal trade for the country. Rulers taxed production heavily and most of the output was traded for cloth and luxury goods. Muslim traders entered the country from **Sofala** in order to facilitate the trade, but production remained firmly in Shona hands. **Portuguese** penetration into the country from the early 16th century was motivated largely by desire to monopolize the gold trade. Although Shona miners occasionally worked in shafts more than 30 m deep, most extraction was limited to surface deposits. It appears that these were largely worked out by the 18th century. The *Mfecane* invasions of the early 19th century greatly disrupted mining, and most remaining workings were then abandoned. The newly arrived **Ndebele** were not gold miners. Further, they actively inhibited Shona trade and vigorously attempted to prevent Europeans from prospecting in the country. Despite their efforts, Henry Hartley and **Karl Mauch** identified old gold workings during the 1860s. After Mauch publicized his findings, a minor European gold rush began. **Concession**-hunters flocked to **Lobengula**'s court in the 1870s and 1880s. Lobengula reluctantly awarded concessions to the **Tati** and **Northern Goldfields** regions, but no significant production was achieved before the 1890s.

Exaggerated descriptions of the country's gold prospects and romantic notions about "King Solomon's Mines" and **"Ophir"** greatly stimulated fresh European interest in the country, especially after the major gold discoveries in the **Transvaal**'s Rand in the mid-1880s. **Cecil Rhodes' BSAC** gained entry to the country with Ndebele concessions, and recruited settlers and mercenaries through promises of generous mining claims. European prospectors swarmed over the country in the 1890s, most simply looking for signs of abandoned Shona gold workings. More than 150,000 claims were registered before 1900, but only 2,259 kg of gold were extracted, and only a fraction of the early miners made any profits. (See also **Rhodesia Ancient Ruins, Ltd.**) From the 1890s to the 1930s gold mining was the country's most important industry. Production generally rose until 1940, when it reached 23,533 kg. Most of this gold was exported, accounting for nearly 60 percent of the country's export trade. Thereafter gold production gradually declined. In 1952 it was displaced by **asbestos** as the leading **mineral** product. During the **UDI** period production dropped again as mines closed due to increased guerrilla activities. However, as a result of the rising price of gold in the late 1970s, production was increased and in 1982 gold once again became the country's most valuable mineral. Total gold reserves have been estimated at c.788,000 kg, and since the early 1980s the government has provided assistance to mining operators in order to stimulate production. In 1990, production had reached c. 17 tons, with an approximate value of Z$505,200,000. By 1996, production had risen to nearly 27 tons. Thousands of **"small workers"** dominated the gold production during the early decades of European occupation, but they were gradually replaced by larger operations which could afford the capital equipment necessary to work increasingly deep large mines. By the late 1970s there were about 260 mines in production, but 10 percent of them accounted for over three-quarters of total production. The country's leading mining centers are located near **Kadoma, Chegutu, KweKwe,** with the largest being at **Eiffel Flats**. The Cam and Motor Mine at Eiffel Flats is the country's largest and deepest, descending to nearly 2,000 meters.

GOLDEN VALLEY. Mining town located 20 km northwest of **Kadoma** (at 18°13'S, 29°48'E). Golden Valley **gold** mine was opened there in 1899. Tungsten is also produced locally.

GOMBWE (pl. *Makombwe*). **Shona** name for a type of "lion spirit" medium similar to, and sometimes synonymous with, the more important *mhondoro*. Like *mhondoro*, the word *gombwe* refers both to the spirit and to its medium (see **Svikiro**). Unlike most *mhondoro* mediums, however, the Makombwe tend to lack territorial bases and to work more frequently as professional healers and diviners. The mediums represent the spirits of long-dead ancestors, but usually their own personal reputations are more important to their success. (See **Religion—Shona**.)

GONAKUDZINGWA. Former government detention camp for political prisoners, located in the extreme southeastern corner of the country near the **Limpopo River**. Through the 1960s the camp was used primarily to hold **ZAPU** supporters, including **Joshua Nkomo**. It was closed in May

1974 in anticipation of difficulties with the new regime in neighboring **Mozambique**.

GONAREZHOU. Game reserve covering c.1,370 sq km along the southeastern border with **Mozambique**. It stretches between the **Sabi River** on the northeast and the **Nuanetsi River** on the southwest, and makes up about one-third of the **Chiredzi District**. During the 1970s, **ZANLA** forces made incursions into the country through this region.

GOROMANZI. Administrative center of the district of the same name, located directly east of Harare (at 17°51'S, 31°23'E).

GOROMONZI DISTRICT. An area of 2,805 sq km, formerly part of the **Harare District**, which now forms its western border. It is a well-watered region, with important agricultural and mining industries. Except for some Tribal Trust Land (now **Communal Land**) territory on the east, the district before 1980 was reserved for Europeans. The district borders the districts of **Murehwa** on the east, **Marondera** on the southeast, **Seke** on the south, **Harare** on the west, and **Mazowe, Bindura**, and **Shamva** on the north. District population in 1992 was 147,126.

GOULDSBURY, HENRY CULLEN (May 9, 1881–Aug 27, 1916). A popular writer within the country's early European community, Gouldsbury wrote stories and verse about European life in **Mashonaland**. He left 10 published novels and volumes of poems, including a posthumous collection of his best verse, *Rhodesian Rhymes* (1932). (See **Literature**.)

GOVA. Several otherwise unrelated **Shona** groups share this name. The Gova branch of **Korekore** live in the Zambezi Valley near **Kariba**. The Gova branch of **Zezuru** live in **Mazowe District**, north of Harare. The **Karanga** Gova live in the **Shurugwi District**.

GOVERA. A branch of the **Karanga** cluster of **Shona**. (See **Gutu**.)

GOVERNORS. When the British government took over responsibility for the country from the **BSAC** in 1923, the colony's new **constitution** established the office of governor as local head of state and representative of the British Crown. The British government had sole right to select the governors, but in practice it consulted with the leaders of the local settler government. In 1942 such consultation was formalized, and by the 1950s the local **prime ministers** were nominating the governors themselves. Under the original constitution the governor was vested with enormous reserve powers over the local government, but these were almost never exercised. Nevertheless, the governors wielded significant influence over government policies and ministerial appointments, particularly in the early days of the **Responsible Government**, when the local officeholders were inexperienced. Until **UDI** in 1965, the governors were noted for working closely with the prime ministers, and no significant conflicts ever developed, a state of affairs made more possible by the gradual curtailment of the governors' reserve powers. By the late 1950s the governors' duties were mostly perfunctory and ceremonial. After UDI the **Rhodesian Front** government replaced the governor with its own **"officer administering the government,"** who assumed the former's duties and perquisites. Britain retained its governor in **Harare** until June 1969, when the settlers voted to create a **republic**. The governor resigned and no replacement was officially named until 1979, following the **Lancaster House Conference** agreement. The appointment of the new governor marked the official end of the rebellion of the UDI government against the British government. This last governor served for only four and one-half months and presided over the official transfer of power from the British to the newly formed Republic of Zimbabwe. *Governors, 1923–80*: 1923–28 **J. R. Chancellor**; 1928–34 **C. H. Rodwell**; 1935–42 **H. J. Stanley**; 1942–44 **E. Baring**; 1945–46 **E. C. Tait**; 1947–54 **J. N. Kennedy**; 1954–59 **P. B. R. W. William-Powlett**; 1959–69 **H. V. Gibbs**; 1979–80 **A. C. J. Soames**.

GREAT DYKE. Natural geological formation, so named because of its distinctive appearance on geological maps. Not a true "dike" in a geological sense, the Great Dyke is a narrow mass of ultra-basic and basic rocks, stretching in a nearly straight line c.515 km long, from **Mberengwa** in the south to **Guruve** in the north. **Chrome** and other **minerals** are mined from it at many points.

GREAT ZIMBABWE see **ZIMBABWE RUINS**

GREY, ALBERT HENRY GEORGE (4th Earl Grey from 1894) (Nov. 29, 1851–Aug. 29, 1917). After serving in the British Parliament (1880–86), Grey was asked by **Cecil Rhodes** to become a founder-director of the **BSAC** when it got its **charter** in 1889. Grey visited Southern Rhodesia in 1894, and then returned there in April 1896 to replace **L.S. Jameson** as **administrator**. His arrival coincided with the outbreak of the **Ndebele Revolt**, and Grey later participated in Rhodes' negotiations with rebel leaders in the **Matopo Hills** (see **Indaba**). From Bulawayo, Grey went to Salisbury to assist in putting down the still active **Shona Revolt**. He resigned his administrative post in June 1897, leaving the country for good. He retained his seat on the BSAC board until 1903, and then began a seven-year stint as governor-general of Canada.

GROBLER, PIETER D. C. J. (variant: Grobelaar) (May 2,1855–1888). **Afrikaner** hunter, trader, and diplomatic agent for the South African Republic of the **Transvaal**. After several commercial trips to **Matabeleland** during the 1880s, Grobler was sent back there by the Transvaal government to negotiate a treaty with **Lobengula**. On July 30, 1887, he got the **Ndebele** king to sign what became known as the "Grobler Treaty," a rather one-sided document reaffirming the treaty **A. H. Potgieter** was said to have made with **Mzilikazi** in 1853. Although the treaty acknowledged Ndebele independence, it called Lobengula a Transvaal ally, binding him to assist the Republic militarily. It also required the Ndebele to extend considerable rights to Transvalers in Matabeleland, as well as to accept a consul at **Bulawayo.** The existence of the treaty was not announced until after the signing of the **Rudd Concession** the next year. Lobengula denied having signed the treaty, and the British government discounted its authenticity. Grobler himself was shot by an **Ngwato** patrol while traveling to take up the post of consul; he later died from his wound. The whole episode helped to quicken the pace of British involvement north of the **Limpopo.**

GROOTBOOM, JOHN (fl. 1890s). South African scout. An enigmatic figure, Grootboom was evidently a Southern **Nguni** man, for he was variously described as either a Xhosa, a Thembu, or a **Mfengu**. He came to **Matabeleland** in the 1880s as a wagon driver for **Charles Helm**. During the 1893 **Ndebele War** he served as a scout for **BSAC** forces. At the end of the war he carried a message from **L. S. Jameson** to the fleeing **Lobengula** asking for the latter's surrender. During the Revolt of 1896 he was the best known African scout working for the British. He helped to arrange the first *indaba*, which he attended. Afterwards he accepted only a horse from **Cecil Rhodes** as payment and then disappeared from historical record.

"GUERILLAS." During the period of the war for national liberation (mid-1960s to 1979) soldiers of both the Zimbabwe National Liberation Army (**ZANLA**) and the Zimbabwe People's Revolutionary Army (**ZIPRA**) were commonly referred to as "the boys," "freedom fighters," "combatants," "guerillas," "comrades," "**vakomana**," or "terrorists." Throughout this edition the terms "guerillas," "freedom fighters," and "combatants" are used to refer to these men and women.

GUEST, ERNEST LUCAS (Aug. 20, 1882–Sept. 21, 1972). Born in South Africa, Guest came to Zimbabwe as a high court solicitor in 1910. Elected to the **Legislative Assembly** in 1928, he rose to cabinet rank under **Godfrey Huggins** in 1938. He later opposed Huggins' pet project, **federation**.

GULUBAHWE CAVE (variant: Gulabahwa). Located just east of the **Matopo Hills** National Park, Gulubahwe contains **rock paintings** which feature an unusual picture of a snake 4.5 m long, with small human figures on its back.

GUMEDE, JOSIAH ZION (b. 1919). **President** of **Zimbabwe Rhodesia**, May 29 to Dec. 11, 1979. A Zulu, born and educated in South Africa, Gumede apparently came to the country sometime in the 1940s. He served as a Rhodesian diplomat during the period of the **federation**, and later worked for the Rhodesian government as a township superintendent in the 1970s. He was elected president by the Zimbabwe Rhodesia **Parliament** in May 1979.

GUNDWANE NDIWENI see **KALIPHI**

GUNGUNYANE (variants: Gungunhana; Ngungunyana) (c. 1850–1906). Last king of the **Gaza**, Gungunyane illegally seized power on the death of his father **Mzila** in 1884. In many ways his reign parallels that of his contemporary, the Ndebele king **Lobengula**, whose daughter he married. The two **Nguni** rulers found themselves the last major independent African rulers in southern Africa during the era of rapid European takeover. Further, Gungunyane also found his military position relative to his African neighbors deteriorating. His armies could not overcome the **Manyika of Mutasa** to his north and his Chopi tributaries in the south were successfully defying him. In 1889 he shifted his capital **Manhlagazi** from **Mount Silivda**, in the present **Chipinge District,** to the lower **Limpopo** Basin in southern **Mozambique**. As the Gaza were still the major power, the **BSAC** negotiated with him in the hope of obtaining a seaport in the future. On October 4, 1890, Gungunyane signed a **concession** with a BSAC agent very similar to the **Rudd Concession**, which Lobengula had signed two years earlier. The company's efforts to carry through with the deal collapsed, however, when the British and **Portuguese** governments partitioned their southern African spheres of interest in such a way as to leave Gungunyane in the Portuguese domain (see **Anglo-Portuguese Convention**). In 1895 the Portuguese finally conquered the Gaza kingdom, effectively destroying it. Gungunyane was exiled to the Azores Islands, where he died a decade later.

GUNUVUTWA see **BUTUA; GURUHUSWA**

GURUHUSWA (variants: Guruuswa; Gunuuswa; Gunuvutwa; etc.). Traditional **Shona** name for the southeastern part of the country—the same region known to the early **Portuguese** as "**Butua**." Guruhuswa was the center of the **Torwa** and **Changamire** states, and is believed to have correspond roughly with the region known as **Matabeleland** in the 19th century. (See **Dande; Mbire**.)

GURUVE DISTRICT (Sipolilo District until 1985). Northern border district, covering 8,830 sq km of what was once the northeastern corner of the original **Makonde District**. Administrative center is the village of Guruve, located just northwest of the **Umvukwe Hills** (at 16°40′S, 30°42′E; alt. 1,180 m). The district's northern panhandle just touches the **Zambia border**. The district also borders **Mozambique** on the north and the districts of **Muzurabani** on the east, **Mazowe** on the southeast, **Makonde** on the south, and **Hurungwe** on the west. The sparsely populated northern two-thirds of the district are **Communal Lands**; while the southern one-third is dominated by commercial farms. District population in 1992 was 135,637.

GUTSU. Ndebele name for the sandy-soiled country northwest of central **Matabeleland**.

GUTU (variant: Mukutu). Dynastic title of the rulers of the **Govera** branch of **Karanga** in the present **Gutu District**. During the 19th century the Govera were caught between **Ndebele** and **Gaza** raids. They managed to expel the Gaza in 1880, but afterwards they became reluctant tributaries to the Ndebele. Although the Ndebele assisted Gutu Makuvaza to attain his position in 1892, they raided him the same year. The next year Gutu allied with the British in the **Ndebele War**.

GUTU DISTRICT. Originally the northeastern part of **Masvingo District**, Gutu became a separate district in 1906. It now covers 5,780 sq km in the extreme northern part of the **Masvingo Province**. It borders **Chikomba District** on the north, **Buhera** on the northeast, Masvingo and **Bikita** on the south, and **Chirumanzu** to the west. The administrative center is at the village of Gutu (19°38′S, 31°10′E), while other important centers for the district are at Chatsworth and Felixburg. Prior to 1980, the upland western section of the district was reserved for Europeans, while the eastern region was divided between Tribal Trust Land (now

Communal Land) and **Purchase Area** lands. District population in 1992 was 195,364.

GWABALANDA MATHE (variant: Kabalonte) (fl.1830s–1860s). **Ndebele** *induna* said to have been one of **Mzilikazi's** most influential chiefs during the 1830s. When the Ndebele migrated to **Matabeleland** in 1838–39, Gwabalanda traveled with Mzilikazi's division. In the political crisis which ensued (see **Kaliphi** and **Nkulumane**) he is said to have saved the young **Lobengula** from execution. Thereafter his influence in the kingdom seems to have declined, though he was the *induna* of the important Mhlahlandhlela *ibutho* during the last years of Mzilikazi's life in the 1860s. His position was inherited by his son Luthuli, who became one of Lobengula's top advisers during the late 1880s.

GWAI RIVER (variant: Gwaai). One of the **Zambezi River's** main southern affluents, the Gwai rises near **Figtree**, flowing northwest to join the Zambezi c.130 km below the **Victoria Falls**. The Gwai's chief tributaries are the **Umguza, Bembezi, Bubi,** and **Shangani,** all of which enter it from the east.

GWANDA. Administrative center for the district of the same name (at 20°56'S, 29°E; alt. 985 m). Founded as a mining center at the beginning of the 20th century, Gwanda developed into an important livestock shipping depot as well after a **railway** line was extended to it from **Heany** in 1905.

GWANDA DISTRICT. A Y-shaped region covering 10,875 sq km in the central part of **Matabeleland South Province.** The district was formerly more than twice as large, but it gave up its southeastern section to form the **Beitbridge District.** It now borders **Botswana** on the south and the districts of **Matobo** on the west, **Umzingwane, Insiza,** and **Mberengwa** on the north, and **Mwenezi** on the northeast. A poorly watered region, the district's main industries are **cattle** and **mining.** Before 1980, its lands were divided roughly equally between Tribal Trust Land (see **Communal Lands**) and land reserved for **Europeans.** District centers include **West Nicholson** and **Colleen Bawn.** District population in 1992 was 123,791.

GWEBI COLLEGE OF AGRICULTURE. Government agricultural school located on a large farm just west of Harare, astride the road to **Chinhoyi** (at 17°41'S, 30°50'E). The site was originally established between 1906 and 1915 as a government demonstration, experimental, and training farm for European settlers. In 1950 it was transformed into an agricultural college restricted to Europeans only; since independence that official restriction has been removed.

GWELO see **GWERU**

GWELO RIVER. Rises just south of **Gweru,** flowing northwest to join the **Shangani River** southwest of the **Mafungabusi Plateau.** The name derives from the **Sindebele** description of the river's steep banks.

GWERU (Gwelo until 1982). Administrative center of both **Gweru District** and **Midlands Province,** Gweru is one of the largest towns in the country with a 1992 population of 124,735. It is located near the intersection of the **Gwelo River** and the main road between **Bulawayo** and **Harare** (at 19°27'S, 29°48'E; alt. 1,415 m). It was founded in 1894 amid a thriving goldmining area, but eventually developed into one of the country's most important commercial and industrial centers. It enjoys the advantages of good water, electrical supplies, and a location at the junction of many **roads** and **railway** lines in the very center of the country. It has both light and heavy industries and is one of the most important stock and dairy centers of the country.

GWERU DISTRICT (Gwelo District until 1985). Located at the center of the country in **Midlands Province,** Gweru District covers 6,795 sq km between the upper **Shangani** and **Umniati** rivers. It was formerly more than twice as large, but the northern section was separated to help form the newer **Kwekwe District.** Other neighboring districts are **Chirumanzu** on the east, **Shurugwi** on the southeast, **Insiza** on the south, and **Bubi** on the west. Gweru is rich in **gold, chrome,** and other **minerals.** Prior to 1980, with the exception of some small Tribal Trust Land territory, the entire district was reserved for Europeans. District population in 1992 was 213,545.

GWINDINGWI HILL. Site of the chief town of the **Shona** ruler **Makoni** during the 19th century. The hill, which is honeycombed with deep caves, served as the Makoni's stronghold during the Revolt of 1896–97until British forces used dynamite to blast out resisters (at 18°55'S, 32°26'E).

H

HAGGARD, HENRY RIDER (June 22, 1856–May 14, 1925). English novelist. Haggard did not visit present Zimbabwe until 1914; however, he worked for the British colonial government in South Africa between 1875 and 1879 and gathered information on Zimbabwe that he later used in romantic adventure in his fiction—most notably *King Solomon's Mines* (1885). This classic story was clearly inspired by rumors he heard in South Africa connecting **"Ophir"** with the then little-known **Zimbabwe Ruins.** Haggard not only modeled the novel's violent "Kukuana" people on the **Ndebele,** he has King **Lobengula** and the real Ndebele appear briefly as characters. His colorful hunter-adventurer "Allan Quartermain" was said to be inspired by **F. C. Selous**. More interesting, however, is "Umbopa," no doubt based on the pretender to the Ndebele throne, **Nkulumane**, the former gardener of Theophilus Shepstone, Haggard's boss in the **Transvaal**. Haggard's *Benita* (1906) is a later reworking of the *Mines* theme, but unlike the earlier romance, it makes more extensive use of Ndebele and **Kalanga** characters in a **Zambezi** Valley setting.

HAKATA. Shona divining "dice." Of several types used, the most important are carved wooden, ivory, or bone pieces. Each piece is typically inscribed with a special symbol, and the diviner—usually an *nganga*— throws them in multiples of four. The diviner interprets the throws according to established formulae similar in principle to Tarot card reading.

HALFWAY HOUSE RUIN. Ruin site in the **Bumbuzi group** named after a local hotel.

HALL, RICHARD NICKLIN (1853–Nov. 18, 1914). Pioneer archaeologist and journalist. An English lawyer, Hall came to the country around 1897 to work for a farmers' association and the **Bulawayo** chamber of commerce. He edited some local newspapers (see **Press**) and helped to publicize the country in London, but he somehow ran afoul of the **BSAC** administration. Around 1900 W. G. Neal, a director of **Rhodesia Ancient Ruins, Ltd.**, turned over to Hall his company's descriptive records of the many **Iron Age** ruins its prospectors had ransacked. The two men used this and other data to write *Ancient Ruins of Rhodesia* (London, 1902), a massive compendium which immediately attracted considerable popular attention. With his reputation somewhat restored, Hall was made "Curator of Great Zimbabwe," a post he held for most of 1902 to 1904. Although he was assigned merely to prepare the ruins for tourists, he undertook large-scale excavations of the site. A completely untrained archaeologist, he destroyed deep stratigraphical layers in order to remove evidence of what he regarded as "degenerate" African occupation over presumably alien ancient deposits. In 1905 he published *Great Zimbabwe*, using his new findings to elaborate on the theories of ancient Near Eastern builders he had presented in his first book. He was removed from his curator post, and the administration brought in **D. Randall-MacIver**, a trained archaeologist, to conduct proper investigations. Randall-MacIver condemned Hall's techniques and completely overturned his interpretations by conclusively demonstrating that the country's megalithic ruins had purely African origins. An acrimonious debate ensued, in which the embarrassed Hall was supported by his fellow settlers. In 1909 Hall published an emotional rebuttal to Randall-MacIver, *Prehistoric Rhodesia*, in which he introduced the explicitly racialist argument that Africans were incapable of sustaining a nondegenerate culture. Though Hall is damned by modern archaeologists for his destructive digs and unfounded interpretations, his books remain useful for their reliable descriptive material—especially of structures which no longer stand.

HAMPDEN, MOUNT (Shona name: Musitikwe). Located 16 km northwest of **Harare**, Mount Hampden rises 1,600 m. It is adjacent to a small town that shares its name. The mountain was designated as the destination of the **Pioneer Column** when the **BSAC** occupied **Mashonaland** in 1890.

HARARE (Salisbury until 1982). (1) National capital, and the largest city in the country. It is a leading commercial, financial, and industrial center, as well as the administrative center for the **Harare District** and is located on the northeastern part of the **Central Plateau** (at 17°50′S, 31°3′E; alt. 1,500 m). The town was established as "Fort Salisbury" when the **Pioneer Column** halted there on September 12, 1890. The **BSAC** named the site in honor of the British prime minister Lord Salisbury in order to build goodwill with the imperial government. The name became "Salisbury" in 1897, when it was declared a municipality. In June 1982 the name of the city was officially changed to "Harare" after a local ruler whose people inhabited the area prior to European settlement. Harare's location was chosen somewhat arbitrarily, as a practical high veld site suitably distant from the potentially hostile **Ndebele** kingdom. Harare's growth experienced a brief setback in 1894 after **Bulawayo** was occupied by the British, but **Cecil Rhodes** quickly promised that the city would remain the country's capital, and its growth has since been continuous. It was linked with the **Beira railway** line in 1899 and to the **Bulawayo** line in 1902. In 1935 it was proclaimed a city. Between 1953 and 1963 it served as capital of the **Federation**. Harare has always been the predominant center of European settlement. Before 1979 residential segregation was formalized with virtually the entire area north of the city center reserved for Europeans, who lived in mostly low density suburbs, such as **Mt. Pleasant**, Highlands, Greendale, and elsewhere. While a large number of Africans lived in these areas, mostly as servants, the great majority of Africans who worked in the city were forced to live in townships in the southwestern sector of the city. Harare draws most of its **electrical power** from **Lake Kariba**, but also has its own coal-powered thermal plant. The city's water supply comes mainly from **dams** on the nearby **Hunyani River**. The city's population in 1982 was 656,011, but nearly doubled over the following decade, reaching 1,478,810 in 1992. (2) (variant: Harari). The capital city's oldest and largest African residential area; located immediately south of the city center between two industrial areas. Established as a township in 1907, Harare developed into one of the country's most important African centers. A large percentage of its population are single men, and almost all of its residents are renters. In 1973 its population density was estimated to be 15 times greater than the rest of the capital as a whole.

HARARE DISTRICT (Salisbury District until 1985). Shaped like a crude number "7," this district is the furthest west in **Mashonaland East Province**. **Goromonzi District**, which was once part of the district, now borders the district on the east, as do **Seke** and **Marondera** districts. Harare also borders the districts of **Mazowe** on the north, **Bindura** on the northeast, **Chikomba** on the southeast, **Kadoma** on the southwestern tip, **Chegutu** on the west, and **Makonde** on the northwest. Prior to 1980, except for two small **Purchase Areas**, the entire district was reserved for Europeans. Outside its capital city of **Harare** the main industry is **agriculture**, with some of the best farming lands in the country within the district's boundaries. District population in 1992 was 1,204,775.

HARPER, WILLIAM JOHN ("Wild Bill") (b.July 22, 1916). Born in Calcutta, India, Harper came to Southern Rhodesia in 1949 after service in the Royal Air Force. In 1958 he was elected to the **Legislative Assembly** for Gatooma (now **Kadoma**) on the **Dominion Party** ticket. The next year he became president of the DP and emerged as a leading spokesman for white supremacy. He joined **Winston Field**'s cabinet in 1962 and was made minister of internal affairs by **Ian Smith** in 1964. Adamantly opposed to any kind of direct African parliamentary representation, he split with Smith in July 1968 over the terms of the new draft **constitution**, resigning from both the cabinet and the ruling **Rhodesian Front Party**. During the **Pearce Commission** investigation in early 1972 he briefly reemerged to criticize Smith and to help found the ultraright-wing United Front Party.

HARTLEY see **CHEGUTU**

HARTMANN, ANDREW (1851–Dec. 27, 1928). An Austrian Jesuit missionary, Hartmann came to **Bulawayo** in 1888 as a priest in the **Zambezi Mission**. He later served as Roman Catholic chaplain with the **Pioneer Column** and helped establish the **Chishawasha Mission**.

HEADLANDS. Railroad siding village roughly midway between **Harare** and **Mutare** in the **Makoni District** (at 18°17′S, 32°2′E; alt. 1,570 m). Nearby is the **Inyati** Mine, one of the country's major **copper** producers.

HEADRINGS. (Sindebele: sing. *isidlodlo*; pl. *izidlobo*). Mixture of natural growing hair and gum, sewn into tight rings on the heads of **Ndebele** and other northern **Nguni** men during the 19th century. (See **Ijaha; Indona**.)

HEALTH. (1) *Human Health.* Prior to the 20th century the country was relatively free of many endemic diseases widespread in areas north of the Zambezi River. **Malaria** has historically afflicted people in regions below 1,000 meters, and it remains a major health problem. Other maladies, such as **sleeping sickness, bilharzia, typhoid**, and tuberculosis, became local threats only with the development of international labor migration in the 20th century. Epidemic diseases, such as **smallpox** and **influenza**, have invaded the country at various times in recorded history. (See **Leprosy; Trachoma**.)

Prior to the advent of **European** settlement in the 1890s medical treatment was largely in the hands of healers and diviners who treated patients with herbal medicines and psychosomatic cures closely tied to traditional religious beliefs (see **Religion—Shona**). These were often efficacious against mental illness and mild physical ailments, but mortality rates were high and life expectancies short. **Christian missionaries** began offering Western medical treatments to Africans during the 1860s, but such services had a negligible impact, except among a small **Ndebele** elite.

Following the European colonization of the country in 1890, the **BSAC** administration established a civil medical department in 1897, with **A. M. Fleming** as the first director. In 1923 this agency became the Public

Health Department. In 1948 the department was made into a separate Health Ministry, which fell under the aegis of the **Federation** government between 1953 and 1962.

The health services in the country originated from a network of hospitals which served the European community. Early health services for Africans were initiated largely in response to settlers' fears that epidemic disease like smallpox among Africans would spread to the European community. In addition, a healthy African labor force was necessary for the efficient operation of settler owned mines and farms. The government responded by opening fever hospitals in the larger towns and by establishing mine hospitals. As early as 1909 missions and the government had established rural hospitals and clinics, but most lasted only a few years. In 1927 the government began to issue grants to mission hospitals for the employment of qualified doctors to treat rural Africans. In the early 1930s the government began to institute a rudimentary health service by dividing the country into large rural areas, each with a hospital surrounded by a network of clinics. This rural clinics building program lasted until 1945.

Throughout the period of European rule in Zimbabwe the main problems facing the rural health system were a lack of trained personnel and insufficient government funding. The main portion of the national health care budget went to the major urban hospitals which served the European community. In 1971 it was estimated that there was only one doctor for every 45,556 Africans in the rural areas of the country. In 1976 the government provided only one hospital bed for every 1,261 Africans, but one bed for every 255 Europeans. The main focus of the health system was the treatment of endemic (and epidemic) diseases, not the prevention of those diseases.

Since independence in 1980, the Ministry of Health has moved away from its predecessor's policies and has attempted to increase health services available in the rural areas. In addition, it has shifted general policy to an emphasis on preventative health care. In 1980 the ministry established a department of health education and in 1982 initiated an expanded program of immunization and a program to train and deploy Village Health Workers. In addition, the government abolished the racial segregation of hospitals and the major urban institutions opened to Africans for the first time in 1980. The government also passed legislation implementing free health care to all Zimbabweans earning less than Z$150 per month.That minimum income level was raised to Z$400 per month in the 1990s. In addition to upgrading nearly 150 rural clinics which had been basic out-patient centers, the government also began a major health clinic building program. By the mid-1980s there were 1,062 static rural clinics and health centers and 32 mobile rural clinics operated by the Ministry of Health. However, a large discrepancy in budget allocations between urban and rural areas continued to exist. In 1987, there were 1,243 physicians (one per 6,951 persons) and nearly 20,000 hospital beds (one per 411 persons) in the country.

The government initiated the use of rural self-help health care programs. One of the best examples of this type of program is in family planning. Started in hopes of slowing Zimbabwe's very high birth rate, the program is locally controlled. Rural villages select two-thirds of the staff from among local residents, who are then trained in Harare before returning to their local area to distribute contraceptives and help educate their fellow villagers about the importance of family planning. Begun in 1983, the family planning program stresses birth spacing rather than limitation, and thereby has overcome much of the resistance to family planning faced by programs in other areas of sub-Saharan Africa. The program has gained high praise from many international health care organizations. It has been estimated that by the late 1980s, 38 percent of the country's married women were practicing some form of birth control—a rate four times higher than the average for sub-Saharan Africa. Partly as a result of this program, the country's crude birth rate fell from 53 (per 1000 women) in 1970 to 41 in 1990 and 39 by 1995.

In 1987, life expectancy at birth was 57.9 years for men and 61.4 years for women. By 1990 the country had an annual rate of population increase of 3.5 percent—one of the highest in the world. In the early 1990s, the largest health care problem facing the country was that of malnutrition. Even with increasing national crop production (see **AGRI-CULTURE**), the Ministry of Health at the time estimated that 36,000 Zimbabweans die annually and that about 500,000 have suffered some form of mental or physical underdevelopment as a result of malnutrition and related diseases. By the mid-1990s, the problem of malnutrition had been surpassed by Human Immunodeficiency Virus/Acquired Immune Deficiency Syndrome (**HIV/AIDS**) as a national health concern. In 1992 government health authorities estimated that 60 percent of Zimbabwean soldiers and 30 to 50 percent of hospital patients were HIV positive. In 1994, the World Bank estimated that 17.4 percent of the adult **popula-tion** were HIV positive; that number had risen to 25 percent by 1999. In 1995, it was reported that 90 percent of all deaths in Zimbabwe were AIDS-related, and that life expectancy at birth had dropped to 52.4 years for men and 55.1 for women. These numbers continued to drop in the late 1990s.

(2) *Animal health.* Disease has also played a major role in the breeding of domestic animals in both the **agricultural** and transportation indus-tries. The country's indigenous and imported **cattle** have been peri-odically devastated by epidemics of **lung-sickness, rinderpest, East Coast Fever**, and hoof-and-mouth disease—particularly in the 1930s. An endemic disease, **nagana,** has long inhibited the raising of livestock in the country's **tsetse fly** areas. These diseases and **horsesickness** have also made **horses** particularly difficult animals to raise in Zimbabwe.

HEANY JUNCTION. Village 25 km east of **Bulawayo** on the main **railway** line and road to **Gweru** (at 20°5'S, 28°47'E, alt. 1,360 m). In 1905 a branch railway line was extended south from Heany Junction to **West Nicholson** to serve mines in the **Gwanda** Valley. Since World War II Heany has been an important military training center.

HELM, CHARLES DANIEL (1844–Jan. 1915). A South African-born agent of the **London Missionary Society**, Helm joined **J. B. Thomson** at **Hope Fountain** in 1875. In 1888 he acted as interpreter and interme-diary during **Lobengula**'s negotiations with **Cecil Rhodes'** repre-sentatives. Helm is said to have advised Lobengula to sign one sweeping **concession** rather than many small ones, and he himself signed the resulting **Rudd Concession** as a witness. He retired from mission work in 1914 and was replaced at Hope Fountain by **Neville Jones**.

HERA (Vahera). **Shona**-speaking group usually classified as a branch of the **Zezuru**, though some Hera regard themselves as **Karanga**. By the 19th century there were several autonomous Hera chiefdoms. One has been ruled by the **Hwata dynasty** in the southern **Mazowe District**. Branches under the Mutekedzi and Nyashanu dynasties are in the **Buhera District**, which is named after the Hera. These chiefdoms apparently split off from the **Munhumutapa** state about 300 years ago. Living near **Mount Wedza**, the Hera and their neighbors, the **Njanja**, became famous as iron-workers.

HERALD (Formerly *RHODESIA HERALD*). Published in Harare, the *Herald* is the country's largest-circulation daily newspaper. It began publication on June 17, 1891, as the *Mashonaland Herald and Zambesian Times*, a handwritten and crudely duplicated paper completely produced by **W. E. Fairbridge**. It became the *Rhodesia Herald* in October 1892, when its first printed copies were issued. From its inception through 1981 it was a member of the **Argus Group** of newspapers. It and its co-publication, the **Sunday Mail**, have been the country's most influential newspapers. Like their fellow Argus papers, they consistently supported the European governments while maintaining a paternalistic attitude toward Africans through 1962. From 1962 until independence, they were often outspoken in opposition to the **Rhodesian Front** government. In 1981, the independent government of Zimbabwe bought out the Argus Group's interest in all of its newspapers in the country, turning their operation and editorial policy over to the newly formed **Mass Media Trust**.

HEROES' ACRE. The national memorial of Zimbabwe, built by the government in the mid-1980s to honor those who died in the struggle for national liberation. Located seven km west of **Harare** on the main road to Bulawayo, since 1986 this 57-hectare site has become the final resting place of many men recognized by the government as national heroes, including: **Josiah Chinamano, Herbert Chitepo, Robson Manyika, Simon Mazorodze, Jason Moyo, Masotsha Ndlovu, Joshua Nkomo, George Silundika, Leopold Takawira, Rekayi Tangwena,** and **Josiah Tongogara**. There are also two provincial Heroes' Acres: the site of the **Battle of Chinhoyi** in Mashonaland West and a site situated at **Gweru** in Midlands Province.

HIGH VELD. Land over 1,220 m, including the **Central Plateau** and the **Eastern Highlands** (see **Altitudinal Zones**).

HIGHFIELD. Former African **"township"** located 8 km southwest of **Harare**'s city center, just west of the main road to Masvingo. (N.B.: the similarly named "Highfields" is a railroad siding located 58 km northwest of Bulawayo.)

HILTON YOUNG COMMISSION (1927–28). British Imperial commission created to investigate the possibilities of closer union between the British territories of east and central Africa. Sir Edward Hilton Young chaired the body. After collecting evidence in the various territories, the commission issued its report in 1929. The report recommended against immediate **amalgamation** of Southern and Northern Rhodesia, but the commission members differed on future recommendations. While the chairman suggested later partitioning Northern Rhodesia to enlarge Southern Rhodesia, the majority rejected adding any territory to Southern Rhodesia. The majority opinion was upheld by the British government and was reiterated in the report of the **Bledisloe Commission** a decade later.

HIPPO VALLEY. Center of a major **sugar** estate in the southeastern low veld near the confluence of the **Mtilikwe** and **Lundi** rivers (at 21°10′S, 31°33′E). Hippo Valley Estate was established by local Europeans in 1956. With the help of government-assisted irrigation schemes, Hippo Valley and neighboring **Triangle** developed into the country's foremost sugar producers by the early 1960s. The loss of export markets after **UDI** hit the industry hard (see **Sanctions**). The estate has since diversified its crops, but sugar remains predominant.

HIPPOPOTAMUSES. Once common throughout the country, these amphibious pachyderms were extensively hunted during the late 19th century for their edible flesh, hides (see **Sjambok**), and teeth (see **Ivory**). The animals are now largely restricted to the Zambezi and Limpopo valleys, and are hunted on a very limited basis (see **Hunting**).

HISTORICAL MONUMENTS COMMISSION (HMC). In 1936 the Southern Rhodesian **Legislative Assembly** established the HMC, entrusting it with the tasks of designating, controlling, repairing, restoring, and investigating pre-1890 African sites and pre-1910 European edifices (see **"Ancient"; Ruins**). Belated creation of the HMC helped to preserve what was left of the many battered megalithic ruins which had suffered in the well-meaning but ignorant hands of the public works department (see **Hall, R. N.; Rhodesia Ancient Ruins, Ltd**). By 1975 the HMC had designated 140 National Monuments on both public and private lands. The most important of these are **Stone Age** sites; **rock paintings**; **Iron Age** sites and ruins; early **Portuguese** sites, including **fairs**; 1890s-era **"pioneer"** and **Revolt** sites; and graves, such as **World's View**. The HMC exercises exclusive control over all archaeological digs, and it employs the only resident professional archaeologists in the country. The scientific integrity of the HMC has not been questioned, but its position as a government agency with monopolistic control over archaeological research has compromised its independence. In 1973 the HMC was incorporated into the National Museums and Monuments Administration.

HLENGWE (Bahlengwe). **Bantu**-speaking people of the **Tsonga** (or Thonga) group who occupy the southeastern districts of the country, most of southern **Mozambique**, and parts of the northern **Transvaal**. Only a small part of the nearly two million Tsonga live in present Zimbabwe. Tsonga is sometimes described as a Mguni language, but it occupies an independent, intermediary position between **Nguni**, **Sotho**, and **Venda**, and is more distantly related to **Shona**. During the early 19th century, Hlengwe country was occupied by the **Gaza** state, to which Hlengwe chiefdoms paid tribute. The Hlengwe absorbed some Nguni vocabulary and cultural features from the Gaza, and have since also been called

"Shangane," like other southeastern peoples. (Note that the Tsonga— sometimes written "Tonga"—have no connection with other **Tonga** groups.)

HOLE, HUGH MARSHALL (1865–1941). Early **BSAC** official and amateur historian. Born in England and trained in law at Oxford, Hole came to South Africa in 1889. He went to work for **Cecil Rhodes** just as the BSAC was obtaining its charter, and then commenced a long career in the company's administration, holding posts in Salisbury, Bulawayo, and London. He had considerable experience in African administration, and he fought in the **1896–97 Revolt.** In 1926 Hole published the first standard history of the country, *The Making of Rhodesia.* Two years later he retired from the administration and devoted his energies to writing, turning out personal reminiscences, histories, and even a fictionalized biography of **Lobengula.** His books set a standard for the developing tradition of amateur historical scholarship in the country, but his bias was overwhelmingly pro-imperialist. (See **Bibliography.**)

HOLI (variants: *Maholi; Roli;* etc.). Poorly understood **Sindebele** term used to refer to the local peoples of neither **Nguni** nor **Sotho** origin (sing., *iholi;* pl., *amaholi).* The **Ndebele** tended to call all neighboring **Shona, Venda,** and other **Bantu**-speaking peoples, as well as local peoples incorporated into Ndebele society, **amaholi.** Derivation of the term is controversial, but it appears not to have been used before the 1840s or 1850s. According to 19th century European observers, the Ndebele people were rigidly divided into three "castes," with the *amaholi* at the bottom, below the *zansi* and *enhla.* Europeans no doubt exaggerated the degree of *holi* degradation in describing them as "slaves," but it is clear that the term carried pejorative connotations which the people themselves wished to shake off (cf. **Swina**). Whatever their precise status, the *amaholi* formed a strong majority within the Ndebele kingdom by the 1890s. Use of the term *holi* has persisted into the 20th century, but the people themselves prefer such terms as *lowzi* or *abantu ba ka mambo* ("people of the mambo"), which stresses pre-Ndebele roots in the **Rozvi** state system.

HOLIDAYS, PUBLIC. The Zimbabwean government recognizes five official holidays, in addition to the standard Western holidays of Christmas, Easter, and New Year's Day. They are: Independence Day (April 18); Armed Forces Day (April 19); Workers' Day (May 1); Africa Day (May 25); and Heroes' Days (August 11 and 12).

HOMEM, VASCO FERNANDES (fl.1560s–1570s). **Portuguese** military commander. In 1569 Homem was made a subcommander of **Francisco Barreto's** expedition against **Munhumutapa Negomo.** He took command of the expedition in early June 1573, when Barreto died at **Sena.** By then only 180 men were still alive, and Homem himself had just recovered from a near-fatal illness. He retreated to the coast to recuperate. There he received fresh Portuguese reinforcements. In early 1575 he launched a new expedition, this time taking the healthier route from **Sofala** to **Manyika.** After surveying the local goldfields, he again retreated to the coast. The Barreto/Homem expeditions achieved tacit recognition of Portuguese privileges from the Munhumutapa state.

HONDE RIVER. A tributary of the **Pungwe**, the Honde River rises just north of the **Odzani Falls**, flowing north, then northeast into **Mozambique**. The river drops off the **Eastern Highlands** quickly, flowing through the broad Honde Valley, where **tea** and tropical fruits are grown intensively. During the mid-1970s the valley became a major area of armed clashes between African nationalist and government forces.

HOPE FOUNTAIN. **London Missionary Society** station located 16 km southeast of modern **Bulawayo** (at 20°16′S, 28°39′E). It was founded in late 1970 by **J. B. Thomson**, who was anxious to conduct mission work at a site closer to **Lobengula**'s new Bulawayo center than the existing LMS center at **Inyati**. **C. D. Helm** and **David Carnegie** later joined the station. As at Inyati, the work of converting the Ndebele to Christianity moved slowly until the **Ndebele Revolt** of 1896. In 1912 Shishi Moyo (d.1938) became the first African minister ordained by the LMS in **Matabeleland** at the station. **Mtompe Kumalo** followed suit in 1917. Under the direction of **Neville Jones**, an African girls' institution was opened at Hope Fountain in 1916.

HORSES. The only equine animals indigenous to southern Africa are zebra, which are not amenable to domestication. Horses were first introduced to the country, on a small scale, by **hunters** and traders during the mid-19th century. Their high susceptibility to endemic diseases such as **horsesickness** and **nagana** made even local breeding almost impossible until well into the 20th century. Even now the country contains relatively few horses. Donkeys, however, are much hardier, and many are owned by Africans. Although horses have never been particularly numerous, they have affected the country's history in several ways. During the 19th century their speed and agility gave riders many advantages in hunting and in fighting. The country would probably not have been opened up to European occupation quite so soon, had not hunters had horses with which to pursue elephants. Hunter penetration of the country led to the discovery of **gold**, drawing into more intensive European activities. Further, it was largely horses that gave **Afrikaners** and **Griqua** military advantages over unmounted African spearmen in early encounters. **Ndebele** setbacks at the hands of mounted enemies in the **Transvaal** greatly contributed to their migration to present Zimbabwe in the late 1830s. The Ndebele themselves acquired some horses as early as the 1830s, but they had little success in keeping them alive. During the late 19th century **Lobengula** acquired about a hundred horses from hunters and traders, but the Ndebele did not use them for military purposes. By contrast, the British combined horses and advanced firearms to good advantage in both the 1893 **Ndebele War** and the **1896–97 Revolts**.

HORSESICKNESS (*Oedema mycosis*). Serious infectious equine fever, unique to Africa. It is usually fatal to domesticated **horses**, but only affects mules and zebras mildly and has little effect on donkeys. The disease's mode of transmission is poorly understood, but it is endemic to the country's warmer regions, particularly during the wet season (see **Climate**). Horsesickness has inhibited the use of horses in eastern and southern Africa since it was recognized by Arabs in East Africa in the 14th century. **Hunters** and traders who entered the country during the 19th century lost most of their horses to this disease very quickly. Animals that survived infection carried an uncertain immunity for several years and were known as **"salted horses."** Since the 1920s, increasingly effective antitoxins have greatly reduced mortality of horses locally. (See also **Health.**)

"HOTTENTOT." European term for **Khoi** people; coined in South Africa by the Dutch in the 17th century. The name is now regarded as pejorative.

HOUSE OF ASSEMBLY. Formal name of the lower chamber of the **Parliament** established in 1970 by the 1969 **Constitution**. As the successor to the **Legislative Assembly**, the House is the main lawmaking body of the government. The 1980 Constitution provided for 100 members, 80 to be elected by Africans registered on a common role, while the 20 remaining seats were reserved for members to be elected by whites, **Asian**, and **Coloured** voters only. The reserved seats were entrenched for a period of seven years. This provision of the Constitution was amended and the reserved seats abolished by a unanimous vote of the House in late 1987. In 1990, the **Senate** was abolished and membership in the House was increased to 150. 120 members are elected by universal suffrage, 10 are chiefs elected by the country's traditional chiefs, 12 are appointed by the **President**, and 8 are provincial governors. The House is elected for five-year terms.

HOVE, CHENJERAI (b. 1956). Novelist and poet. Born in Mazvihwa, he attended local secondary schools, then earned a B.A. by private study from the University of South Africa. He held a variety of jobs—including teaching literature at a secondary school, editing for Zimbabwean publishing houses, and working for a cultural news agency which covered the **SADCC** countries—before turning to writing full time. He has published several collections of poems, including *And Now the Poets Speak* (1981), *Up in Arms* (1982), and *Red Hills of Home* (1983). He has two works published in **Chishona**, *Matende Mashama* (1981), a collection of short stories, and a novel, *Masimbo Evanhu* (1986). He also has two novels in English, *Bones* (1989), winner of the 1989 Noma Award, and *Shadows* (1991). *Bones* won international critical praise for its portrayal of the lives of farmworkers in Zimbabwe, while *Shadows* is a sensitive examination of the emotional suffering experienced by a peasant family during Zimbabwe's war for liberation. Hove, along with **Shimmer Chinodya** and **Tsitsi Dangarembga**, is considered one of Zimbabwe's best young writers. (See **Literature.**)

HOVE, MICHAEL MASOTSHA. One of the first two Africans to represent Southern Rhodesia in the **federation** Assembly (see **Savanhu, J. Z.**), Hove entered politics after having been a teacher and the editor of the *Bantu Mirror*. He won his seat in the Assembly by defeating **Joshua Nkomo** in a 1953 election. A faithful supporter of the ruling **United (Federal) Party**, Hove was rewarded with the post of federation high commissioner in Nigeria in 1962. After the breakup of the federation in late 1963, he entered the African administration in the city of **Bulawayo.**

HUGGINS, GODFREY MARTIN (Viscount Malvern of Rhodesia from 1955) (July 6, 1883–May 8, 1971). Fourth **prime minister** of Southern Rhodesia (1933–53), and the first prime minister of the **Federation of Rhodesia and Nyasaland** (1953–56). Born in England, where he qualified as a medical doctor, Huggins came to Southern Rhodesia in 1911 to practice medicine temporarily. He liked the country and found his profession placed him in an elite group, so he stayed. In 1924 he entered politics and was elected to the **Legislative Assembly** from Salisbury as a member of the ruling **Rhodesian Party.** By the late 1920s he stood out as a strong advocate of racial segregation as the best means of securing the settlers' future in the country. After pushing **H. U.** Moffat's government on the issue, he broke from the ruling party to form the **Reform Party** in 1931. Increasing economic difficulties brought on by the world depression added fuel to his criticisms of the government, bringing his party to power in the 1933 election. Within a year of taking the office of prime minister, he enlisted the aid of **P. D. L. Fynn** to merge the main leaders of the Rhodesian and Reform parties into the new **United Party,** which he led to victory in a fresh general election in 1934. He retained his premiership without interruption for more than 21 years—a period said to be a record within the British Commonwealth countries. Although Huggins had been an early supporter of the **Unionist Movement,** he became a strong advocate of **amalgamation** of Southern and Northern Rhodesia during the mid-1930s. Frustrated in this ambition by the report of the **Bledisloe Commission** in 1939, he later became the leading advocate of **federation.** Meanwhile, he articulated his segregationalist ideas, which he called the **"Two Pyramid" policy** and promoted passage of the **Industrial Conciliation Act** in 1934. During the 1940s Huggins retained control of the government against strong challenges from the **Labour** and **Liberal** parties, even though he emerged from the 1946 election with only a plurality of Assembly seats. The same year he introduced the **Native (Urban Areas) Accommodation and Registration Act,** which extended the principles of the **Land Apportionment Act** to the towns. The 1948 election restored his strong Assembly majority, giving him the opportunity to push plans for federation. With the support of **Roy Welensky** from Northern Rhodesia, he began federation discussions with the British government in 1950. In 1952 he obtained the British agreement to his federation plans, despite the opposition of **Joshua Nkomo** and **J. Z. Savanhu,** who had participated in London talks with him. By the 1950s Huggins had abandoned the "Two Pyramid" concept in favor of **"Partnership,"** an equally hazy concept expressed in order to satisfy the British that federation would not merely benefit settlers. He obtained settler support for federation by promising that prosperity would ensue without the possibility of Africans ever achieving political power. When the federation was created, he resigned his Southern Rhodesian premiership in favor of **Garfield Todd** and took up the leadership of the new federal government. After his pet project, the **Kariba Dam** , was launched in 1956, he retired from active politics and was succeeded as federation prime minister by Welensky.

HUMAN IMMUNODEFICIENCY VIRUS/ACQUIRED IMMUNE DEFICIENCY SYNDROME (HIV/AIDS). A viral disease which attacks the human immune system, making it difficult, if not ultimately impossible, for an infected person to fight off life threatening illnesses. HIV may develop into AIDS, but the exact process is not completely understood. A growing health problem worldwide, the disease apparently spread to Zimbabwe along commercial trucking routes from East Africa in the mid-1980s. Virtually ignored and publicly downplayed by government officials until the early 1990s, in July 1993 **Bulawayo** health officials reported that AIDS-related deaths were the top cause of death in that city. An official ministry of health press release that same year stated that there had been 25,300 reported cases of full-blown AIDS in Zimbabwe and estimated that the total number was about 55,000, with over 700,000 additional people infected with HIV. In 1995 it was reported that as high as 90 percent of all deaths in Zimbabwe were AIDS-related. In response to the 1993 reports, the government initiated an AIDS education program, which by 1995 had gained momentum and has been described as one of the best AIDS programs in Africa. (See **Health.**)

"HUMBUG CONCESSION" (1891). Nickname for the **Lippert Concession.**

HUNGWE (Bahungwe; Wahungwe). Variant of Maungwe, the name of a **Shona** group ruled by the **Makoni dynasty.**

HUNTERS/HUNTING. During the **Stone Age** hunting was the principle means people had of obtaining meat, but techniques and human needs were too limited to have a significant impact on the country's game populations. Later **Iron Age** herders and cultivators such as the **Shona** and **Ndebele** peoples supplemented their diets with feral animal flesh and hunted **elephants** for **ivory** to trade. Large-scale hunting began only in the 1860s, when European hunters and traders began entering the country in increasing numbers (see, e.g., **Edwards, S. H.; Selous, F. C.**). Europeans hunted primarily to obtain ivory. Using firearms and **horses**, they turned hunting into systematic slaughter. The Ndebele kings attempted to control hunting throughout the country, mainly to protect their monopoly over the ivory trade. Nevertheless, increased African acquisitions of firearms by the 1880s greatly reduced the populations of large animals, such as **elephants, hippopotamuses, rhinoceroses,** and **ostriches.** During the 20th century the country's governments have exercised increasingly strict controls over hunting, while protecting remaining animal herds in **game reserves** and **national parks.** Hunting is now tightly regulated through licensing laws. Hunting for "sport" is restricted mainly to private farms and Controlled Hunting Areas in the **Tuli** Block and in the **Zambezi** Valley. (See also **Fishing.**)

HUNTERS' ROAD. Europeans and other South Africans who visited **Matabeland** after the early 1860s entered the country almost exclusively from the southwest. The **Ndebele** kings carefully controlled foreign access to their country, and the southwestern approach had the further advantage of circumventing the **tsetse fly** regions around the **Limpopo River** to the east. Soon a clear wagon track known as "Hunters' Road" was established between the **Ngwato** town Shoshong in **Botswana** and the mission station at **Inyati**. Later the road was extended northeast to the **Hunyani River** in **Mashonaland**. A modern village named Hunters' Road now stands midway between **Gweru** and **Kwekwe** on the main road.

HUNYANI RIVER (a.k.a. Manyame or Mhanyami River). Rises just west of **Marondera**, flowing generally northwest before turning north near **Chinoyi** to join the **Zambezi River** in **Mozambique**. The Hunyani is well fed by tributaries, including the **Angwa**. Its main **dams**, Prince Edward (built in 1928) and Hunyani Port (1952) supply Harare and other towns with water. The latter dam forms Lake Chivero (formerly Lake McIlwaine), which is surrounded by the 57-sq-km Lake Chivero Recreational Park, just west of Harare.

HURUNGWE DISTRICT (Urungwe District until 1985). Northernmost district, covering 18,235 sq km that were once the western half of the original **Makonde District**. The district borders **Zambia** along most of the entire stretch of the **Zambezi River** between Lake **Kariba** and **Mozambique**. The district of **Guruve** borders it on the northeast. The **Angwas River** separates it from the Makonde District on the southeast, and the **Umniati** River separates it from the **Gokwe District** on the southwest. Hurungwe also borders **Kariba District** on the west. It is mostly a low veld area, and is relatively undeveloped, except around **Karoi**. **Mana Pools** National Park is situated in the northwest of the district, while the remainder of the district is made up of a patchwork of **Communal Land**, game reserve, and commercial farming lands. District population in 1992 was 246,902.

HWANGE. Originally named "Wankie," this town is the largest urban center in the western part of the country, serving as headquarters of the **Hwange District** (at 18°22′S, 26°29′E; alt. 760 m). The town took its name from the title of the local **Nanzwa** rulers, the *Zanke*. It was founded early in the 20th century as an adjunct of the Wankie Colliery, which taps the region's vast coal reserves. The colliery administers most of the town and provides employment for the majority of the adult male population. Hwange's population in 1992 was 42,214.

HWANGE DISTRICT (Wankie District until 1985). Westernmost district in the country, Hwange covers 27,835 sq km in **Matabeleland North Province**. The district was formerly somewhat larger, but gave up its northeastern corner to help form **Binga District**. Hwange also borders the districts of **Lupane** on the east and **Nyamandhlovu** on the southeast, as well as **Zambia** on the north and **Botswana** on the west. The southern half of the district comprises **Hwange National Park**. The northern half of the district is a patchwork of national land, a large block of **Communal Land**, and land formerly reserved for Europeans. District headquarters are at **Hwange**, and other centers include **Victoria Falls** and **Kamativi**. Population in 1992 was 113,921.

HWANGE NATIONAL PARK. Located on the **Botswana** border, this **national park** covers 13,470 sq km between **Pandamatenga** and the **Nata River**, accounting for half the **Hwange District**. Most of the present park became the country's first protected game reserve in 1928. In 1949 the area was augmented and made one of the first national parks. The northern edge contains the **Bumbuzi Ruins.**

HWATA (variant: Wata). Dynastic title of the rulers of an independent **Hera** chiefdom located at the headwaters of the **Mazoe River** just north of present Harare. By the early 19th century the Hwata chiefdom held a dominant position in regional trade. Apparently for this reason, the Ndebele strove to subjugate the Hwatas from the middle of the century. In 1864 an Ndebele *impi* captured Hwata Gwindi and brought him to **Mhlahlandlela,** where he was kept prisoner for six months. Gwindi was released on the promise of paying tribute regularly, but he was soon behaving independently. In 1868 another Ndebele *impi*—in which **Lobengula** personally participated—again raided the Hera. Afterwards the Hwatas were nominally tributary to the Ndeble until 1889, when the reigning Hwata signed a treaty with **Portuguese** agents in return for firearms. In 1896 the Hwata—who is said to have had a special relationship with the **Nehanda** medium—was one of the first **Shona** chiefs to rise against the British in the **Revolt.** The Hwata himself was eventually captured and hanged. Subsequent Hwatas were government-appointed chiefs.

I

I- (variant: *ili-*). **Sindebele** prefix (Class 3) for singular forms of nouns and proper names, mainly pertaining to words for people (pl., *ama-*). The prefix is dropped for **Ndebele** personal names in this dictionary but is retained for ordinary nouns, e.g., *idlozi*. (See **U-**).

IBUTHO (variant: *ilibutho*; pl., *amabutho*). **Sindebele** term for a group of men of roughly the same age organized into a unit which was given an individual name, e.g., **Mhlahlandlela.** During the 19th century the **Ndebele** kings periodically raised new *amabutho*, which were given an older leader (*induna*), **cattle** to tend, and a town in which to live. The *amabutho* could be mustered for military or police work and were periodically moved to new locations within the kingdom. Since the early 19th century, Europeans have consistently described the *amabutho* as "regiments," but this description is appropriate in only the loosest sense. The Ndebele did not possess a true standing army. The towns that arose around the *amabutho* carried the *amabutho*'s names but were essentially nonmilitary in character. Between the early 1820s and 1893 roughly 70 *amabutho* were formed, each containing from 50 to several hundred men.

Amabutho with as many as 1,000 men were rare. (See also **Imbizo; Zwangendaba.**)

IDLOZI (variants: *ilidlozi; idhlozi;* pl., *amadlozi*). **Ndebele** name for ancestor spirit. The *amadlozi* are said to stay near their descendants, whose welfare they watch over. They act as intermediaries between individual mortals and the high god **Nkulunkulu**. Typically, these spirits reside in the bodies of living animals. They require prayers and propitiation. During the period of the 19th-century Ndebele kingdom, the royal (**Khumalo**) spirits were thought to look over the welfare of the whole nation, and they played a special role in the annual *inxwala* festivals. (See **Religion—Ndebele.**)

IJAHA (variant: *ilijaha;* pl., *amajaha;* variants: *majaha; machaka*). **Sindebele** term for young man. Under the military system of the 19th century **Ndebele kingdom** an *ijaha* could join an *ibutho*, but he normally had to see active service before gaining the status of an adult (*indoda*). The *amajaha* thus constituted a naturally militaristic faction within the kingdom, particularly during the reign of **Lobengula**.

IMBIZO (variants: Mbizo; Imbezu; etc.). Most prestigious of **Lobengula**'s *amabutho* (see **Ibutho**), the Imbizo was raised in 1871, and its manpower was constantly renewed over the next two decades. Lobengula groomed the Imbizo as an elite unit, and occasionally used it as his bodyguard. Through the 1870s the Imbizo saw action in most major military campaigns, including the 1879 siege of **Chivi**. At an apparently early date Lobengula made his cousin **Mtshani Khumalo** the *induna* of the Imbizo, but by the early 1890s Mtshani was assuming much wider command responsibilities as well. During the 1893 **Ndebele War** Lobengula held back the Imbizo and two other *amabutho* as a reserve until the battle at Bembezi, in which the Imbizo suffered the largest Ndebele losses. Some Imbizo members accompanied Lobengula on his flight north and saw action against Wilson's **"Shangani Patrol."** Afterwards the unit broke up. Many members joined the **BSAC** administration's Native Police (see **BSAP**), but then went over to the Ndebele rebels during the **1896 Revolt**.

IMPI (pl., *izimpi*). **Sindebele** term for a military force or expedition. It is frequently used incorrectly to refer to standing military units (see **Ibutho**).

IN- (variant: *im*). **Sindebele** prefix (Class 5) for the singular forms of many kinds of nouns (pl., *izin-*, or *izim-*). The initial *i-* is frequently dropped in English usage but is retained in this dictionary for the sake of consistency. (See *I-*; *U-*.)

INDABA (pl., *izindaba*). Widely used **Nguni** word for "meeting" or "discussion" also carrying the more general meanings of "affair," "news," "or story." A tree under which the **Ndebele** king **Lobengula** frequently held meetings became known as the "Indaba Tree." It is now protected as a National Monument.

The word *indaba* has found its way into southern African English usage. The name "great Indaba" has been popularly applied to the peace negotiations held between **Cecil Rhodes** and a number of **Ndebele Revolt** leaders in the **Matopo Hills**. There were actually four such meetings in 1896, on August 21 and 28, September 9, and October 13. Although these negotiations clearly helped to end the Revolt, it should be realized that most rebel leaders, including **Nyamanda**, did not participate.

INDEPENDENT INDUSTRIAL AND COMMERCIAL WORKERS UNION OF RHODESIA see **INDUSTRIAL AND COMMERCIAL WORKERS UNION (ICU)**

INDIANS see **ASIANS**

INDODA (pl., *amadoda*; variant: *madoda*). **Sindebele** term for adult man or husband. During the 19th century **Ndebele kingdom** the *amadoda* were entitled to wear **headrings**, to marry, and to serve as *izinduna* (see **Induna**). A younger man was known as an *ijaha*.

INDUNA (pl., *izinduna*). **Nguni** term of such widespread usage in southern Africa that it has virtually become an English synonym for "chief." In literature pertaining to the 19th-century **Ndebele kingdom** and similar Northern Nguni-derived states, the term *induna* is frequently used in the sense of military commander or head of a "regiment" (see **Ibutho**). In actual **Sindebele** usage, however, the term *induna* was applied to a wide variety of officeholders who had mainly nonmilitary functions.

INDUSTRIAL AND COMMERCIAL WORKERS UNION (ICU). Now regarded as perhaps the most important forerunner of modern mass nationalism in the country (see **African National Congress**), ICU was founded as the Independent Industrial and Commercial Workers Union of Rhodesia in 1927. In response to Southern Rhodesian African appeals for assistance in organizing a trade union movement, **Clements Kadalie**, the head of the then enormously powerful South African ICU, sent Robert Sambo and Mansell Mphamba, two fellow Nyasalanders, to **Bulawayo** to start the movement there. Sambo was soon deported and Mphamba left on his own account, but ICU leadership was quickly taken up by local workers. The first chairman was Thomas Sikaleni Mazula, but **S. Masotsha Ndlovu, Charles Mzingeli**, and Job Dumbutshena were the most assertive and powerful leaders by 1929.

ICU attracted a mass following in Bulawayo by holding frequent public meetings in which speakers boldly denounced the white government, missionaries, African elitist organizations, and ethnically based social and welfare groups. Despite its name, ICU never developed into a true trade union organization, but instead grew as a quasi-political movement, calling for united African resistance to white oppression and demanding higher wages and better working conditions generally. In late 1929 Mzingeli founded a Salisbury branch of ICU. By the next year ICU was active in the main urban centers throughout the country. Efforts to recruit agricultural workers were abandoned early, however, and ICU achieved no success in reaching workers in the tightly controlled mining compounds, despite Dumbutshena's earnest efforts.

ICU grew rapidly for several years but soon withered under the combined pressures of government harassment, missionary opposition (only **A. S. Cripps** supported ICU), and the conservatism of workers unprepared to commit themselves. Finances were also a chronic problem, and the organization's image was badly damaged by destructive splits in the South African ICU leadership. Several ICU leaders were imprisoned in the mid-1930s. By 1936 ICU had vanished in Southern Rhodesia. A decade later, however, Mzingeli revived the movement as the **Reformed ICU.**

INDUSTRIAL CONCILIATION ACT (1934). Law passed early in the **Godfrey Huggins** administration to provide conciliation machinery for European labor disputes, particularly in the building and printing trades. In response to pressures from both European employers and employees, the law specifically excluded "natives," i.e., Africans, from its definition of "employees." This exclusion effectively barred Africans from forming their own trade unions, from striking, and from obtaining apprenticeships in skilled trades. A 1937 amendment required that the government set minimum African wages at no lower a level than those of their European counterparts in order to prevent cheaper African labor from competing with European labor. The law thus severely restricted African entry into skilled labor. Its harshly discriminatory nature was cited by the 1939 **Bledisloe Commission** Report as a particularly objectionable feature of the country's African policy.

While the law stimulated European trade unionism, it left African workers with little opportunity to voice grievances. An African **railway** workers' strike in 1945 and a general African strike in 1948 led to some improvements in African working conditions, but Africans were not granted the right to organize unions until this act was completely rewritten in 1959. A 1971 amendment to the act reimposed government restrictions on striking and gave the **president** power to declare any strike illegal. The act was finally repealed by the **Labor Relations Act** of 1984.

INFLUENZA PANDEMIC OF 1918 (a.k.a. *furuwenza*). The "Spanish Flu" pandemic, which is believed to have killed as many as ten million people worldwide in late 1918, entered Southern Rhodesia from South Africa in early October 1918. The viral disease raged locally for about five weeks, virtually bringing commerce to a halt. Africans living in crowded urban areas and mining compounds were especially hard hit. An estimated 2 to 3 percent of the rural population died. Afterwards measures were taken to relieve overcrowding and to improve government health services. (See **Health.**)

INGEZI see **NGEZI**

INKOSI (pl. *amakosi*). **Sindebele** term for "king" or "ruler"; also widely used in other **Nguni** languages. The locative form is *enkosini*, "at the king's place." During the 19th century the **Ndebele** had two reigning *amakosi*: **Mzilikazi** and **Lobengula**. In modern usage the term *inkosi* is used in three ways: (1) as a respectful form of address to an important man; (2) as the title by which Christ is known; and (3) to refer to an employer or supervisor, particularly on European-owned farms prior to independence.

INKOSIKAZI (pl. *amakosikazi*). Female equivalent of **inkosi**, meaning "queen" or woman of high rank (**Chisona** form: *hosikadzi*). The term "queen" is misleading in the context of the 19th-century **Ndebele kingdom**, as the many wives of the king had no formal political powers. For examples of "royal wives," see **Lozigeyi; Xwalile**. Lobengula's sister **Mncengence** was also known as an *inkosikazi*.

INSIZA DISTRICT. Northernmost district in **Matabeleland South Province**, covering 8,700 sq km. The district borders the districts of **Gwanda** on the southwest, **Umzingwane** on the west, **Bubi** and **Gweru** on the north, and **Zvishavane** and **Mberengwa** on the east. Prior to 1980, most of the northern area of the district was reserved for European ranchers, while the southern part of the district was mostly Tribal Trust Lands (see **Communal Lands**). **Filabusi** is the district's administrative center. The village of Insiza stands on the main Bulawayo-to-Gweru road, where it is intersected by the **Insiza River**. District population in 1992 was 78,134.

INSIZA RIVER. Rises by the village of Insiza (at 19°47'S, 29°12'E; alt. 1,413 m) and flows almost due south within the **Insiza District**, joining the **Umzingwane River** just north of **West Nicholson**.

INTERNAL SETTLEMENT. An agreement signed on March 3, 1978, by **Ian Smith, Ndabaningi Sithole, Chief Jeremiah Chirau**, and **Abel Muzorewa**. The agreement followed three months of negotiations and ostensibly accepted the concepts of free elections and majority rule, while representing the hopes of the signatories that it would lead to ending of the war, the lifting of economic **sanctions**, and international acceptance of an independent **"Zimbabwe Rhodesia."**

Following the failure of the **Geneva Conference**, Smith was faced with rising international—including South African—pressures to end the war and accept the idea of majority rule and African participation in the governing of the country. In April 1977 a new set of Anglo-American proposals was announced, calling for a conference to draw up plans for a majority-rule constitution and free elections. Following a series of meetings between British foreign secretary David Owen, American UN representative Andrew Young, and African leaders, a revised set of these proposals was made public. Although falling short of the **Patriotic Front's** positions demanding the end of white rule and the disarming of the **Rhodesian security forces**, the PF did approve several sections of the new proposals. However, the Smith government rejected all the proposals, stating that they did not go far enough to protect the rights of the **European** minority.

Late in 1977, in an attempt to gain international respectability by appearing to be willing to negotiate with African nationalist groups, Smith initiated contact with several African leaders within the country. In December he then began negotiations with Muzorewa, leader of the **United African National Council**; Sithole, who called his group the **African National Council (Sithole)**; and Chirau, president of the **Zimbabwe United People's Organization**. None of these African leaders had command of any military forces, nor did it appear to most observers that they represented any major organizations or even larger blocks of individual followers. Smith also tendered invitations to the Patriotic Front during the three months that the negotiations were in progress. The PF refused to participate and rejected the negotiations on the grounds that the three internal leaders did not represent the people of Zimbabwe and that questions regarding land redistribution, changes in the country's political structures, and continued European control of the security forces and police, as well as the government bureaucracy, were not being discussed. In addition ZANU's **Robert Mugabe** believed that a military victory was possible, and therefore negotiations to share power were counterproductive.

After a series of often acrimonious meetings, Smith, Muzorewa, Sithole, and Chirau reached agreement on a set of proposals to end European minority rule and institute a new government based on the principals of majority rule. The agreement called for the writing of a new **constitution** by the end of the year and the creation of a transitional government headed by an executive council, which would govern the country until the promulgation of the new constitution. The executive council would be made up of the four signatories to the agreement—who would rotate chairmanship of the council each month. In addition, there would be a ministerial council with African and European co-ministers sharing portfolios. The transitional government took over operation of the government in April and began almost immediately to remove legal restrictions based on race, to commission African officers in those units of the security forces and police which were predominantly African, and to release about 800 political prisoners. The executive council also announced plans for an amnesty to **ZANLA** and **ZIPRA** guerrillas who defected to the government side.

The new constitution was not approved by the **Rhodesian Front**-controlled **Parliament** until February 1979. Its clauses indicated that the three African leaders had acceded to nearly every demand made by Smith. Requirements for high office in the police, security forces, civil service, and judiciary virtually guaranteed that no African would assume any position of power in the new government in the foreseeable future. Twenty-eight seats in Parliament were reserved for the European electorate, while 72 were given to Africans. A proportional system for allocating ministerial posts meant Europeans would maintain control of several important ministerial portfolios. In total, the constitution included more than 120 "entrenched" clauses which, in effect, guaranteed the continued political and economic control of the country by Europeans.

Elections were held in April, with about 64.5 percent of the eligible electorate voting. The UANC won 68 percent of the vote and a majority of 51 seats, and Abel Muzorewa was asked to form a government by the newly elected president, **Josiah Gumede**. The republic of **Zimbabwe Rhodesia** was officially declared on May 30, 1979. The new constitution, the elections, and the Muzorewa government were all denounced by the Patriotic Front, the presidents of the **Frontline States**, and the United Nations. No country, except South Africa, officially recognized the new government. Critics maintained that the constitution reenforced European dominance, the elections had not met standards called for by either Britain or the UN, and free participation was not allowed to all political groups, specifically the Patriotic Front. As a result of this almost universal condemnation of the new constitution and elections, the initial hopes of the four signatories to the internal settlement—that **sanctions** would be lifted and the guerrilla war could be terminated—were not realized.

Within five months of the declaration of Zimbabwe Rhodesia, a new conference at **Lancaster House** had been convened, in which all parties to the question of an independent Zimbabwe would participate.

INTERNATIONAL DEFENSE AND AID FUND (IDAF). British organization founded to provide legal aid for South Africans. After 1958 it extended its services to Southern Rhodesia. In 1972 an IDAF legal team followed the **Pearce Commission** to the country to assist Africans in presenting evidence, to press the government to clarify its definition of acceptable "normal political activity," and to reveal the activities of the security police. From that time until independence in 1980, the IDAF provided legal assistance to Zimbabwe's nationalist organizations.

INXWALA (pl. *izinxwala*). Annual **Ndebele** religious festival celebrated during the 19th century. Variations of the *inxwala* have long been celebrated by most **Nguni-speaking peoples**. The Ndebele began observing the *inxwala* as soon as **Mzilikazi** founded their kingdom. The festival quickly became one of the kingdom's most important unifying forces, as it regularly brought most of the people together in one place. After the start of the long rains, usually around January, the Ndebele gathered for a complex series of rites which lasted several weeks. The *inxwala* proper, known as the "great dance," lasted about five days during the middle of the sequence and was the most important part. The personal participation of the kings was crucial. They led the dancing and some prayers, and symbolically ate from the first harvested crops—hence the popular name "first fruits festival." The most significant rites included ceremonies of national thanksgiving, reaffirmation of allegiance to the king, and honoring of the royal ancestors, whose spirits (see **Idlozi**) were thought to be contained in black oxen which were paraded (see, e.g., **Mashobane**).

After the Ndebele left the **Transvaal** in late 1837, they celebrated an *inxwala* in eastern **Botswana**. Afterwards they were separated in two main parties for over a year. Mzilikazi's party celebrated the next *inxwala* north of present **Matabeleland**. The other migrants apparently made Mzilikazi's son **Nkulumane** acting king in order to celebrate their *inxwala* in Matabeleland, where they arrived first. In 1870 **Lobengula**'s installation as king was incorporated into the regular *inxwala*. Two years later his half-brother **Mangwane** attempted to invade the kingdom in January, hoping to catch Lobengula off guard during the *inxwala*. The death of Lobengula in 1894 effectively ended *inxwala* celebrations, but an abortive attempt to revive them was made in 1896 during the **Revolt**.

INYANGA see **NYANGA**

INYANGA MOUNTAINS. The highest range in the country, the Inyangas form the northernmost part of the **Eastern Highlands**. The range runs from Mount Nyangui (17°53′S, 32°44′E; alt. 2,228 m) in the north to **Mount Inyangani** in the south. The southern part of the range falls within the 35,225-hectare Rhodes Inyanga and **Mtarazi** National Park.

INYANGA RUINS. Covering most of present **Nyanga District** and extending into **Makoni** and **Mutare** districts and a small part of **Mozambique**, the Inyanga Ruins are the largest single concentration of stone **ruins** in Zimbabwe. They appear to have developed independently of the **Zim-**

babwe and **Khami-type** ruins characteristic of the rest of the country. Recent linguistic and archaeological research indicates that they were built by **Sena-Barwe-Hwesa** peoples prior to **Shona** immigration into the region in the early 18th century.

The ruins fall into two main complexes: an early "upland" (above 1,500 m) group in the southeast and a late "lowland" group toward the northwest. The **Van Niekerk Ruins** are the largest complex of the later group.

The Inyanga Ruins are characterized by a number of features rarely found elsewhere in the country. The most outstanding feature is an extensive system of cultivation terraces and irrigation ditches (see **Dams**). The lines of terraces, many of which have stone retaining walls, extend over several thousand km. Their only southern African parallels are found in the Transvaal. **Stone-lined pits** are another characteristic. Less common, but equally characteristic of the group, are massive "forts," of which **Nyangwe** is the best-known example.

In contrast to the stone ruins associated with ruling minorities elsewhere in the country, the Inyanga Ruins are mostly remains of ordinary people's buildings. Nyanga District is not a mining region, and the ruins have produced few metal artifacts or imported luxury goods. Even midden dumps are rare. Pottery finds have been plentiful, but ceramic workmanship is considered inferior to that of the earlier **Ziwa culture**. Most of the sites appear to have been abandoned by the early 19th century—perhaps in response to the *Mfecane* invasions.

INYANGANI MOUNTAIN. The highest peak in the country, rising to 2,595 m; located at the southern tip of the **Inyanga Mountains** (at 18°18'S, 32°51'E).

INYATI. The first permanent mission station and European settlement in the country, located 80 km northeast of **Bulawayo** (at 19°41'S, 28°51'E), Inyati was founded as an **LMS** station by **Robert Moffat** in late 1859. The station took its name from the nearby Inyathi ("buffalo") *ibutho*, in which the **Ndebele** king **Mzilikazi** was then living.

The **Matabele Mission**, as it was called, became the center of European activities in the country for several decades, but its agents had little success in gaining converts. After Mzilikazi moved to **Mhlahlandhlela** in 1861, the mission's links with the king were weakened, and six years later the Inyathi *ibutho* itself moved to another site. The increased isolation of the station from the Ndebele people gave **J. B. Thomson** the incentive to found a second station at **Hope Fountain** in 1870.

After British occupation of Matabeleland in the mid-1890s, Inyati became the administrative center of the **Bubi District** as well as the commercial center of a developing goldmining region. More recently the area's importance has been enhanced by the development of **nickel** mining. LMS work at the station has continued, and an African secondary school was founded there in 1953. (For Inyati copper mine, see **Headlands**.)

INYAZURA see NYAZURA

IRON. This important metal is the earliest **mineral** known to have been mined in the country (see **Iron Age**) and is widely distributed. Precolonial workings are numerous, but almost all were small. While iron smelting and smithery were highly esteemed skills in local African societies, production was generally limited to weapons and tools. No significant long-distance trade in iron goods seems to have developed, in contrast to that for **gold** and **copper**. Local trade was, however, important, and by the 19th century the **Hera** and **Njanja** peoples were particularly famous as ironworkers.

Modern iron production has been important but unspectacular. Most iron ore is now mined at **Redcliff** and is used in local industries. Iron pyrite (FeS_2), mined mainly north of **Harare,** makes an important contribution to the country's chemical industry.

IRON AGE. The first Iron Age culture was introduced into the country by at least the end of the A.D. 100s. The arrival of iron-using peoples also heralded the beginnings of **agriculture**, livestock-raising (see **Cattle**), and pottery. The connection is not proved, but it is highly likely that the Iron Age was introduced by **Bantu-speaking** immigrants who gradually absorbed or displaced the earlier **Stone Age** peoples.

Both classification and periodization of Iron Age cultures within the country are far from settled. New archaeological finds and radiocarbon dates have regularly inspired reclassifications and new periodizations. The terminology applied within the field is thus everchanging. The most important historical problem to be resolved is determining whether the appearance of major cultural innovations—which archaeologists typically associate with pottery styles—represent local changes or intrusions of new societies. Generally, archaeologists have attributed innovations to new peoples from the north, but such peoples are rarely identified.

The earliest-known Iron Age culture has been called **Gokomere. Ziwa** was once regarded as an independent contemporary culture, but is now treated as a Gokomere variation. Gokomere flourished from about A.D. 200 to c.900. Its latter phases are now called Zhizo and Malapati. The 10th century introduced the "late" Iron Age, represented by **Leopard's Kopje** culture. The culture that developed stone building techniques at the **Zimbabwe Ruins** has been regarded as either an offshoot of Leopard's Kopje or a separate tradition. In the west the early and later phases of Leopard's Kopje are now called Mambo and Woolandale, respectively. Monumental building in stone (see **Ruins**) began around the 12th century, during the late Zimbabwe periods. The late 15th century heralded the beginnings of the **Khami culture** throughout the southern parts of the country. Around the same period a major independent stone-building culture arose in the **Inyanga Ruins** region to the northeast. (See also **Monk's Kop.**)

The 19th century is regarded as an era of sweeping Iron Age culture convergence, brought about by the disruptions and population movements caused by the *Mfecane* invasions. Occupation of the country by Europeans in the 1890s terminated many traditional Iron Age industries by introducing the Western industrial Iron Age.

ISI-. Sindebele prefix (Class 4) for many kinds of nouns (pl., *izi-*). The initial *i-* is frequently dropped in English usage, as in "Sindebele" itself. (See **CHI-.**)

ISIBONGO. Term whose meaning varies somewhat among **Nguni** languages. In **Ndebele** usage it means family surname or clan name. In its plural form, *izibongo*, it also means praises or praise-name (the latter being distinct from a "surname"). An *imbongi* (pl., *izimbongi*) is a poet, or praise-singer—someone who is well versed in traditional history.

The Ndebele term for "clan" is *usendo* (pl., *izinsendo*). Ndebele clans are patrilineal. Among the **zansi** and **enhla** members of Ndebele society, possession of a common *isibongo* implies descent from a common ancestor, precluding intermarriage. The Ndebele consider it rude to address an adult by other than his surname. If this is unknown, then the honorifics **baba** or **mama** should be used. During the 19th century all subjects addressed the Ndebele kings by the latters' royal clan name, **Khumalo.** (See **Shona Mutupo.**)

IVORY. Until the late 19th century vast herds of **elephants** roamed the country, particularly in the western regions. From early times ivory ranked only behind **gold** as a **Shona** export item to **Muslims** on the east coast. The **Portuguese** continued the trade from the 16th century, but allowed it gradually to taper off until the early 19th century. In the mid-19th century renewed **European** interest in ivory products brought British and **Afrikaner hunters** and traders to the country from the south. This time traders dealt primarily with **Ndebele** rulers. In 1854 **S. H. Edwards** bought a large amount of ivory from **Mzilikazi,** who thereafter maintained a formal, but loose, monopoly over Ndebele trade. Mzilikazi also controlled the entry of hunters into the country, charging irregular fees for hunting licenses. His successor **Lobengula** exercised more systematic controls over hunting and preferred to have his own men hunt so he could sell the ivory directly. Statistics on the ivory trade are imprecise and irregular, but it is clear that the 1860s and 1870s were the peak years. Thousands of elephants were killed annually. Each animal bore about 35 to 55 kg of ivory, fetching 8 to 11 shillings per kg in South Africa. On top of this, a smaller trade in **hippopotamus** teeth was also conducted. By the 1880s the surviving elephant herds had been driven into **tsetse fly** regions, beyond the reach of professional hunters using **horses,** and the ivory trade largely ended.

For most of the 20th century, the ivory trade in the country was controlled by limiting access to the areas occupied by elephants. However, that changed in the 1970s. As international prices for ivory soared, the country's elephant herds were increasingly subject to illegal poaching. While never as great a problem as in other parts of Africa, where at least half the total number of elephants were killed in the 1970s and 1980s, Zimbabwe's herds were included in an international ban of the trade of ivory. Organized by the United Nations' Convention of International Trade in Endangered Species (CITES) as a means of protecting elephants from extinction, this policy went into effect in 1989. By the mid-1990s, Zimbabwe's government was beginning to petition CITES to be allowed to sell ivory under heavily monitored conditions. The govenment claimed that the country's elephant populations had recovered and that a controlled ivory trade would allow them to fund larger conservation projects. In the face of international opposition to the resumption of an ivory trade, Zimbabwe, and other Southern African nations making the same request, agreed in April 2000 to not sell any ivory until CITES members met in general conference in 2003.

IZI-. Sindebele prefix for plural forms of Class 4 nouns whose singular prefix is *isi-* . *Izim-* and *izin-* are variants of the plural prefix for Class 5 nouns with *im-* or *in-* as singular prefixes, and for plurals of Class 6 nouns with *u(lu)-* as the singular prefix.

J

JACHA, AARON RUSIKE (b. Oct. 1899). Raised and educated at **Epworth**, Jacha taught in **Methodist** schools before turning to political activism in the early 1930s, when he organized the Bantu Congress. The Congress was essentially an elitist organization, and by the early 1940s was being led by **T. D. Samkange**. Jacha later became the leader of the **African Farmers Union**. In 1952 he became the first African appointed to an official government policy-making body when he accepted a post on the Native Land Board.

JAMESON, LEANDER STARR (Feb. 9, 1853–Nov. 26, 1917). **Cecil Rhodes'** confidant and agent in Rhodesia. Born in Scotland and trained as a doctor in London, Jameson came to the Kimberley diamond fields in South Africa in 1878—a year after taking his M.D. There he became a trusted friend of Rhodes. After **Lobengula** repudiated the **Rudd Concession** in 1889, Jameson went to **Bulawayo** as Rhodes' agent to persuade the **Ndebele** king to reconsider. During three visits to **Matabeleland** in 1889 and 1890, he got Lobengula to concede a few minor points in the dispute. These Jameson exaggerated in his reports, giving the false impression that Lobengula had reconfirmed the Rudd Concession and that he had become amenable to the passage of a British occupation force into **Mashonaland**. Armed with Jameson's reports, Rhodes obtained British government permission to organize the **Pioneer Column**. Jameson then accompanied the Column as Rhodes' personal representative. Afterwards, he and **Frank Johnson** made a dramatic trip down the **Pungwe River** in an attempt to find a practical route to the sea.

The following year, 1891, Jameson succeeded **A. Colquhoun** as the **BSAC** administrator of Mashonaland. He exercised much firmer control over the incipient administration than had his predecessor, and he worked to find excuses for invading Matabeleland (see **Lippert Concession**). In 1893 he arbitrarily designated a "boundary" line between

Matabeleland and Mashonaland. He then charged the Ndebele with having violated the boundary when they raided Shona villages near present **Masvingo** in mid-July. He thereby instigated the ensuing **Ndebele War**. With the addition of Matabeleland to its territories, the BSAC made Jameson the first **administrator** of the whole country. Jameson lost this position to **A. H. G. Grey** in early 1896, after leading the abortive **"Jameson Raid."** Jameson surrendered to Transvaal authorities during the raid; they turned him over to Britain for trial and imprisonment.

Jameson was released from prison in December 1896, returning to South Africa to begin a new career in Cape politics. There he inherited Rhodes' party leadership and became prime minister of the Cape Colony (1904–08). He retired to England in 1912 and was elected president of the BSAC early the next year. He was particularly interested in the question of joining Southern Rhodesia either with South Africa (see **Unionist Movement**) or with Northern Rhodesia (see **Amalgamation Movement**), and he made several trips to Southern Africa before his death from accumulated tropical ailments. His body was interred at **World's View** in the **Matopos** in 1920.

"JAMESON RAID" (1895). In the hope of overthrowing the **Transvaal**'s Afrikaner government, **Cecil Rhodes**—then prime minister of the Cape Colony—secretly commissioned **L. S. Jameson** to organize an invasion force in eastern **Botswana**. Jameson took most of the European police out of Southern Rhodesia for this purpose (see **Bechuanaland Border Police; British South Africa Police**). On December 29, 1895, he advanced into the Transvaal with just over 500 men. The expected uprising of expatriate Transvaal miners (*uitlanders*) did not materialize and the raid was a fiasco. Disgraced, Rhodes resigned his premiership and his seat on the BSAC board of directors. Jameson was tried and imprisoned in England, and he too resigned all his official positions. The removal of most of the police from Southern Rhodesia contributed to the timing of the **Shona** and **Ndebele Revolts**, and the raid itself helped to bring about the **South African War** four years later.

JESUIT MISSIONARIES see **SILVEIRA, G. DA; ZAMBEZI MISSION**

JOHNSON, FRANK WILLIAM FREDERICK (1866–Sept. 6, 1943). Born in England, Johnson came to South Africa when he was 16. In 1884 he joined the British army and served in Warren's Expedition into **Bechuanaland**. Afterwards he joined the BBP. In 1887, he, H. J. Borrow, and M. Heany formed a syndicate to seek mining **concessions** in **Matabeleland**. Johnson met Rhodes at Kimberley in 1889 and obtained from him a contract to command the "Pioneer Corps" section of the **Pioneer Column** which occupied **Mashonaland** the next year. After arriving at Salisbury in September 1890 he joined **L. S. Jameson** in an expedition down the **Pungwe River**. He then returned to Mashonaland to consolidate mining interests and other commercial activities. He left the country before the outbreak of the **Ndebele War** in 1893 but retained active control over his financial interests there. After the First World War he returned to the country and was elected to the **Legislative Assembly** in 1927. In that body he led the opposition against **C. P. Coghlan**'s government, but was turned out of office the very next year. He returned to Britain permanently in 1930 and later published his autobiography, *Great Days* (1940).

JOLLIE, ETHEL MAUDE see **TAWSE-JOLLIE, E. M.**

JONES, NEVILLE (1880–1954). English missionary and archaeologist. In 1912 Jones came to the LMS **Hope Fountain** station in **Matabeleland**, where he worked for the remainder of his life. Meanwhile, he trained himself in archaeology and investigated traces of **Stone Age** occupation, particularly in the **Matopo Hills**. His fieldwork led to several books and numerous articles in which he developed the basic sequences of Stone Age cultures in the country. From 1936 to 1951 he served as secretary of the **Historical Monuments Commission**, becoming its chairman in 1951. Jones also wrote several books on modern African life. Most notable was *My Friend Kumalo* (published under the pen name "Mhlagazanhlansi"), recording **Mtompe Kumalo's** views of **Ndebele** life and history.

JUMBO MINE. Gold mine and town located just west of **Mazowe District** (at 17°28'S, 30°55'E). Pegged in October 1890, the mine is said to have been named after the famous elephant in the London Zoo. Nearby is the site of the old **Portuguese** trading fair **Dambarare**.

K

KABALONTA see **GWABALANDA**

KADALIE, CLEMENTS (c.1896–1951). Malawi-born labor leader whose Industrial and Commercial Workers Union (**ICU**) became the largest African organization in South Africa during the late 1920s. After a brief stint as a teacher in Nyasaland (now Malawi), Kadalie started for South Africa in 1915, unexpectedly remaining in Southern Rhodesia for three years along the way. There he held clerking jobs in many different places, including **Bulawayo** and the **Shamva** mining compound. His experiences in the country sensitized him to racial discrimination and European mistreatment of African workers—evils he vowed to correct in South Africa. Later, during his meteoric rise to prominence in South Africa, he remained concerned with Southern Rhodesian problems. He corresponded with the missionary **A. S. Cripps**, and in 1927 he responded to an appeal for assistance from Southern Rhodesia workers by sending Robert Sambo and other fellow Nyasalanders north to help organize the Southern Rhodesian ICU.

KADOMA (Gatooma until 1982). The administrative and commercial center of **Kadoma District** (at 18°21'S, 29°55'E; alt., 1.165 m), as well as the center for the country's **cotton** industry. The town arose on the main road between Bulawayo and Harare amid a cluster of small European **gold** mines in the late 19th century and was formally organized as a town in 1907. In 1992 the town had a population of 67,750. The name "Kadoma" is derived from the **Chishona** word *Kusadoma*—"don't speak about it because it is inhabited by spirits"—which refers to a past **Shona** battle site on a nearby hill.

KADOMA DISTRICT (Gatooma District until 1985). Covering 6,864 sq km, it originally formed the southwestern part of **Chegutu District**. The banana-shaped district is roughly bisected by the main road and **railway** line, and prior to 1980 was mostly reserved for Europeans, except for **Purchase Area Land** in the northwestern corner and Tribal Trust Land in the southeastern corner. It borders the districts of **Gokwe** on the west, **Kwekwe** on the south, **Chirumanzu, Chikomba,** and **Harare** on the east, **Chegutu** on the northeast, and **Makonde** on the north. District population in 1992 was 222,567.

"KAFFIR." Term for African widely used by white southern Africans; it is today regarded as highly pejorative. The term derives from Arabic *kafir*, for "infidel" or "nonbeliever." **Portuguese** explorers adopted the word from east African **Muslims** in the early 16th century, thinking it meant simply "black African." However, it was from 19th-century South Africa that the word found its way into modern usage. The Portuguese, as the first Europeans to encounter the **Nguni**-speaking peoples of the southeastern coast, called these peoples "Caffres." The term was later adopted by Dutch and English-speaking settlers. By the late 19th century whites tended to call all **Bantu**-speaking peoples "Kaffirs," and it was in this sense that the word was introduced into present Zimbabwe.

"KAFFIR BEER." European term for fermented African beverages, usually made from eleusine (finger millet).

"KAFFIR CORN." European term for sorghum, an important African grain crop (see **Agriculture**). Sometimes also applied to **millet**.

"KAFFIR-FARMING." Pejorative term used during the period of **BSAC** rule to refer to a system of tenant farming in which Africans paid rents to work and to live on European-owned land. The practice was abolished by the **Land Apportionment Act**.

KAGUVI (variant: Kagubi). Shona "lion spirit," or *mhondoro*, whose medium, Gumporeshumba, was a leader during the 1896–97 **Shona Revolt**. Unlike other famous *mhondoro*, Kaguvi has had no known mediums (see **Svikiro**) other than Gumporeshumba, who rose to fame suddenly as "Kaguvi" during the Revolt. Gumporeshumba is believed to have been a member of a **Zezuru** chiefly family and possibly to have been the brother of Pasipamire—the most famous **Chaminuka** medium. Gumporeshumba's prominence as a Revolt leader appears to have rested on his own charisma, not on the prior reputation of the Kaguvi spirit.

Early in 1896 "Kaguvi" joined chief **Mashayamombe**, making the latter's town his Revolt headquarters. From April to October he sent out messengers to surrounding chiefs, issuing instructions, collecting loot, and distributing captured firearms (see **Nehanda**). The extent of his actual authority over other rebels is now being debated, but his reputation was clearly great. Europeans called him the "Lion God," but he titled himself simply *Murenga*, "The Resister." After **Alderson's** forces began blowing up Mashayamombe's shelters, "Kaguvi" began a long period of moving about the country. At this time he was joined by Mkwati from Ndebele country, and the two exhorted Shona chiefs to continue their resistance against Europeans. By early 1897 Europeans concluded that killing "Kaguvi" would end the Shona Revolt, so they began a concerted effort to get him. His prolonged success in evading capture increased his fame, but the Revolt was meanwhile breaking down as other leaders either surrendered or were killed. Finally, in late October 1897, "Kaguvi" himself surrendered in the **Guruve District**. The following March he and the Nehanda medium were tried for murder. On April 27, 1898, "Kaguvi," "Nehanda," and Chief Mashanganyika were hanged in Salisbury. Under the pressure of a Roman Catholic priest and one of his daughters—who, remarkably, attended the **Chishawasha Mission** school—"Kaguvi" accepted baptism while "Nehanda" was being hanged. Christened Dismas, "The Good Thief," he thus became one of the first Shona converts to Catholicism since the early days of **Portuguese missionaries**.

KAKUYO KOMUNYAKA see **CHIKUYO CHISAMARENGU**

KALANGA (variant: Kalaka). One of the six main clusters of **Shona** languages, Kalanga—or "Western Shona"—stands apart as both the most isolated and the most different form of **Chishona**. Some authorities have even classified Kalanga as a non-Shona language.

Kalanga-speakers (called Va-, or Makalanga) have inhabited the western and southwestern parts of the country, as well as eastern **Botswana**, for at least a millennium (see **Leopard's Kopje Culture**). They have seen a succession of **Shona** and non-Shona invaders, many of whom have adopted the Kalanga form of Chishona. These invaders have included **Karanga** from the **Zimbabwe** culture in the 15th or 16th century and the **Ndebele** in the early 19th century. Ndebele occupation of present **Matabeleland**, which corresponds roughly with Kalanga territory, further isolated the Kalanga from other Shona and resulted in many Kalanga adopting the **Sindebele** language. Today about 5 to 6 percent of the country's Shona-speakers speak Kalanga. Among the surviving distinct Kalanga groups are the **Nanzwa** and Lilima (see **Bulilimamangwe District**).

KAMATIVI. Mining town east of **Hwange** on the lower **Gwai River** (at 18°19'S, 27°4'E). Since the mid-1950s Kamativi's **tin** mine has become the country's largest. Mining and smelting operations occupy most of the adult population. **Lobengula's** grave is nearby.

KAMHARAPASU MUKOMBWE (variant: Kambarapasu; a.k.a. Affonso) (d. 1690s). The son of **Mavura II**, Kamharapasu was described as a "young man" when he succeeded his brother **Siti Kazurukumusapa** as **Munhu-**

mutapa in 1663. The last Munhumutapa to rule from the **Dande region**, he was perhaps also the last truly effective ruler of the kingdom. Although he was baptized "Affonso," he worked to turn back **Portuguese** influence in the country. In this he was aided by tropical diseases which greatly reduced the number of resident **Portuguese** in the late 17th century. He resecured the homage of **Manyika, Barwe**, and other former provinces, but was defeated in a war against the **Changamire** state in 1684. He died sometime the next decade. He was succeeded by an uncle, Nyakunembire, who called in Changamire aid against the Portuguese. A rapid succession of new Munhumutapas then followed, and the state was reduced to tributary status by **Changamire Dombo**.

KAPARIDZE see **NYAMBO KAPARARIDZE**

KARANGA (a.k.a. "Southern Shona"). According to linguistic classifications, the Karanga (or Chikaranga) dialect of **Chishona** is spoken by about one-third of all **Shona** people in the country. Its speakers are concentrated in a compact area between, roughly, **Gweru** in the northwest, **Bikita** in the northeast, **Chiredzi** in the southeast, and **West Nicholson** in the southwest.

Karanga (or Ma-, or Vakaranga) is also used as an ethnic identification which includes not only the Karanga-speakers but also other Shona, notably some of the **Kalanga**-speakers of the west. Some authorities use "Karanga" as a synonym for "Shona" itself, arguing that the term is the original name of the Shona-speaking peoples. Within the Karanga dialect cluster are included such important chiefdoms as the **Mari** of Chivi, the **Govera** of Chirumanzu, the **Duma, Gova**, Jena, Nyubi, and others.

KARIBA. Town serving as the administrative center of the district of the same name; located on the promontory (at 16°31′S, 28°48″E) that separates **Kariba Gorge** from the eastern bulge of **Lake Kariba** very near the dam. The town arose after construction began on **Kariba Dam** in 1956. Now a major tourist center for lakeside recreation, the town has its own international airport (see **Air Transport**). Its **border** post by the dam is one of three major crossing points into **Zambia**. In 1992 it had a population of 21,039.

KARIBA, LAKE. One of the largest artificial bodies of water in the world, Lake Kariba began to form in 1959 when the retaining wall of **Kariba Dam** was completed. By the early 1960s it stretched more than 280 km: from the **Kariba Gorge** in the northeast, up the **Zambezi River** to near the **Batoka Gorge** in the southeast. As wide as 40 km in places, the lake covers c.5,200 sq km. At its completion, Kariba ranked as the world's largest manmade lake, with a volume of c.160,400 million cu m (130,100 acre-ft), but it has since been slightly surpassed by new lakes in Egypt and Russia. The area along the southern shore of the lake is relatively wild and inaccessible (see **Game Reserves**), but the eastern part of the lake has developed into a major tourist area centering on **Kariba** township. The government has stocked the lake with several varieties of **fish**, and the country's only commercial fisheries have developed at both ends of the lake. Easily navigable, the lake offers cheap water transport, but the areas surrounding the lake are insufficiently developed to promote significant shipping. (See also districts of **Binga** and **Kariba**.)

KARIBA DAM. Interrupting the flow of the **Zambezi River** at **Kariba Gorge**, Kariba Dam is a massive concrete arch structure 128 m high and 579 m wide (at 16°32′S, 28°46′E). It is the product of the largest single construction project in which the country has ever participated. After World War II it was generally recognized that the greatly increasing **electrical power** needs of both Southern and Northern Rhodesia would best be met by the development of a cooperative large-scale hydroelectric scheme. Indeed, the need for such a project was an incentive for creating the political **federation**, which eventually undertook the project.

The first problem faced was choosing between the Zambezi River and Northern Rhodesia's Kafue River for a dam site. At first federal Premier **Huggins** favored the Kafue, but Southern Rhodesia Premier **Todd** and other politicians pushed for a site on Kariba Gorge. The Southern Rhodesians prevailed, causing considerable resentment among Northern Rhodesian politicians. A French consulting firm reported on the advantages of Kariba, which offered much greater hydroelectrical energy potential than Kafue. The topography of the Zambezi Valley and the river's proven low siltage were factors that bode well for the long-term operation of a dam at Kariba. After the federal Assembly voted 25 to 7 in favor of Kariba in 1955, the next problem was the major one of financing the huge project with the relatively small resources of the federation. Huggins quickly committed federation funds to undertake preliminary construction work and was personally vindicated when the World Bank announced it would underwrite part of the project. Northern Rhodesian copper companies, the **BSAC**, and British banks also invested. Of the estimated £78 million which the project eventually cost, about 59 percent originated outside of Central Africa. By 1956 French, Italian, and British firms were at work on the dam.

The relative remoteness of the dam site from established population centers required building new access roads, airstrips, and the town of **Kariba**. Salisbury served as the administrative center for the whole project. Brush had to be cleared away where the new lake was to rise, and more than 20,000 **Tonga** people living on the southern banks of the river had to be relocated. In 1958 nearly disastrous floods did considerable damage to the dam site, but the main retaining wall was nevertheless finished the next year. As lake waters rose, thousands of animals were ferried to the main shores in **"Operation Noah."** In May 1960 the dam's hydroelectric generators began supplying power. A large road atop the dam created a new link across the river.

Placement of the underground power-generating facilities on the southern side of the dam caused considerable resentment in Northern Rhodesia, although the siting was defended on purely technical grounds. The issue later became an important sore point in Zambian-Rhodesian relations. At the time **UDI** was declared in 1965, Zambia was receiving 68 percent of its electrical power (including 90 percent of Copperbelt power) from Kariba Dam. Shortly after UDI President Kaunda unsuccessfully appealed to the British government to protect the dam with ground troops, but Zambia's electrical services from the dam were never interrupted. Since 1965 Zambia has developed its own **coal** resources for emergency thermal power generation and has undertaken to build a second hydroelectric facility on its side of the dam.

KARIBA DISTRICT. Covering 3,200 sq km, Kariba was created out of the northern part of the former **Sebungwe District** and a section of the western part of **Hurungwe District**. It now borders the districts of Hurungwe on the east, **Gokwe** on the south, and **Binga** on the west. Except for a small area north of Kariba township, the district is separated from Zambia by the lake. Prior to 1980, the land east of the lake was reserved for Europeans. The land south of the lake is divided between the **Matusadona Game Reserve** and **Communal Lands**. District population in 1992 was 48,756.

KARIBA GORGE. A c.26 km stretch of the **Zambezi River** in which the river originally narrowed from a width of 640 m to less than 90 m at a point where it turns sharply to the north. Cutting through hard basement rocks, the gorge provided an ideal site for construction of **Kariba Dam**.

KAROI. Town serving as commercial center for **Hurungwe District**; located c.90 km northwest of **Chinhoyi,** on the main road to **Chirundu** (at 16°49'S, 29°41'E; alt. 1,310 m). The town was founded in 1945 as the center of a government resettlement scheme for European war veterans. Over the next two decades the region developed into one of the country's most profitable **tobacco** areas. During **UDI** local farmers diversified their crops and increased **cattle** production. Also important to the local economy are nearby **mica** mines. (N.B.: another, smaller Karoi village is located just south of the **Mavuradonha Mountains.**)

KAYA see KIA

KAZUNGULA. Botswana border post where the country touches **Zambia**, Namibia, and Zimbabwe.

KENNEDY, JOHN NOBLE (Aug. 31, 1893–June 1970). Sixth **governor** of Southern Rhodesia (1947–54). A Scot, Kennedy spent 30 years in the British army and navy before succeeding **W. E. C. Tait** as governor in 1947. He is regarded as one of the country's more open-minded governors and is noted for his attempts to mix socially with Africans. After Kennedy left office, **Edgar Whitehead** invited him to chair a national convention to discuss the country's future in 1960. Although the convention was unofficial, many of its proposals were developed in the subsequent constitutional conference. (See **Constitutions.**)

KGARI I (variant: Khari) (d. c.1828). **Ngwato** ruler credited with greatly expanding Ngwato power during the 1820s. Kgari was killed in the **Matopo Hills** while leading a raid against the **Kalanga**. His widow bore a son, **Macheng**, who was regarded as Kgari's rightful heir because he had been sired by an official "ghost husband." One of Kgari's natural sons, **Sekgoma I,** succeeded first, however. (See also **Khama III.**)

KHAMA III (variant: Kgama) (c.1837–1923). **Ngwato** ruler. Khama was the son of **Sekgoma I** (c.1810s–1883), who ruled the Ngwato from the mid-1830s until 1857, and then intermittently until 1875 (see **Macheng**).

Khama early fell under the influence of LMS agents, including **John Mackenzie**, and was later regarded as a model Christian ruler in Africa. A capable military leader, he led a successful defense against the **Ndebele** during an attack on Shoshong in 1863. Over the next 30 years he was regarded as an Ndebele nemesis, whose strategic importance was enhanced by the location of the Ngwato state astride the **Hunters' Road** to **Matabeleland**. After he became Ngwato ruler in 1875, he conciliated the Ndebele king **Lobengula** by renouncing the Ndebele pretender **"Nkulumane,"** whom his predecessors had supported. Thereafter he and Lobengula made protestations of friendship, but the two rulers never met and Ndebele-Ngwato relations were always touchy. In the mid-1880s Khama was a leading **Botswana** spokesman for creation of the **Bechuanaland Protectorate** and in 1895 he helped to prevent the new protectorate from falling under the administration of the **BSAC**.

KHAMI CULTURE. Term for stone-building culture that displaced the earlier **Leopard's Kopje culture** in the southwestern part of the country. Khami culture went into a decline around the early 15th century. The most outstanding ruins of the Khami tradition are **Khami, Dhlo Dhlo,** and **Nalatale**.

KHAMI RIVER (former variant: Khumalo River). A minor tributary of the **Gwai River**, the Khami rises south of **Bulawayo** and flows northwest to meet the Gwai c.50 km above the latter's confluence with the **Umgusa**. Though small, the river fills three dams, including Khami Dam (built in 1928), which supplies water to Bulawayo. The lake formed by this dam reaches part of the **Khami Ruins**.

KHAMI RUINS. One of the most important complexes of **stone ruins** in the country; located by the upper **Khami River**, after which it is named, c.21 km west of **Bulawayo** (at 20°9'S, 28°25'E; alt. 1,300 m). The complex comprises ten distinct ruins spread over a large area, 40 hectares of which were declared a National Monument in 1938. The structures display a fine standard of workmanship, featuring extensive checker-pattern wall decorations. The main structure in the complex, known simply as the Hill Ruin, is atop a rise surrounded by tiered retaining walls. The nearby Cross Ruin contains a "Maltese" cross made of stones laid flat. This structure has long been popularly attributed to early **Portuguese** missionaries, but no historical evidence supports such theories (see **Bayao, S.**). Partly submerged by the waters of Khami Dam is the Precipice Ruin—the largest decorated retaining wall in the country.

The Khami Ruins are the largest and probably the oldest of the **Khami culture** buildings in the southwest. They have been dated to the 17th century, and their last occupants were clearly associated with the **Changamire** state. However, the site was apparently not an important Changamire administrative center. It is possible that Khami was originally the center of the **Torwa** state, which the Changamire state seems peacefully to have displaced. If so, building may have commenced at Khami in the 16th century. Khami was abandoned as a Changamire center after the **Ndebele** occupation of the region in 1837–39. The Ndebele kept outsiders away from the ruins during the 19th century, and it is said that King **Lobengula** used the site as a private rainmaking center.

After Europeans occupied **Matabeleland**, the ruins were ransacked for **gold** ornaments by **Rhodesia Ancient Ruins, Ltd. R. N. Hall** undertook some crude excavations there between 1900 and 1910, while **David Randall MacIver** conducted the first scientific excavations in 1905. More thorough professional excavations were begun by K. R. Robinson in 1947.

The original name of the ruins site is not known. The local Ndebele still call the ruins *Ntaba zi ka Madhladhla*, named after a **mambo** who is said to have ruled there. Nearby is **Leopard's Kopje**.

KHOI (variant: Khoikhoi). Name preferred by the **Khoisan** people known to Europeans by the pejorative term "Hottentots." Khoi are known to have migrated south through present Zimbabwe thousands of years ago (see, e.g., **Ruchero Cave**), but the length of their occupation in the country is uncertain.

KHOISAN. Collective term for the ancient and complex family of languages containing **Khoi** and **San** languages, all of which are characterized by **"click" sounds**. The name Khoisan properly applies only to cultural, not physical groupings of people, but most Khoisan peoples share certain distinct characteristics, including small stature, light-colored skin, and steatopygia. (See **Languages**.)

KHONZA (variant: *konza*). **Sindebele** verb meaning "to serve." Adapted into limited English usage to express tributary relationships, as in the expression, "The Kaa chief konza'd Lobengula."

KHUMALO (variant: Kumalo). Common **Ndebele** clan name (see **Isibongo**). Khumalo clan members constituted most of **Mzilikazi's** original following when he left Zululand in c.1821. The royal branch of the clan provided the Ndebele kings and many other leading officials in the kingdom. (see, e.g., **Mlugulu; Mncumbathe; Mtshani**.)

KILDONAN. Village serving as the terminus of the branch **railway** line built in 1930 to connect the Harare-to-Chinhoyi line with the **chrome** mines just west of the **Umvukwe Hills** at 17°21′S, 30°37′E.

KIMBERLEY REEFS. Former name of **Bindura**.

"KING SOLOMON'S MINES" see **GOLD; HAGGARD, H. R.; OPHIR**

"KITCHEN KAFFIR" see **FANAKALO**

KNIGHT-BRUCE, GEORGE WYNDHAM HAMILTON (March 23, 1852–Dec. 16, 1896). **Anglican** missionary. After beginning his career as a cleric in the London slums, Knight-Bruce accepted the unpopular post of bishop of Bloemfontein in the heart of Calvinist **Afrikaner** territory. Anxious to extend mission work to the **Shona** people, he visited **Lobengula** in 1888 and got his permission to travel widely in **Mashonaland.** Three years later he returned with **Bernard Mizeki** and two other African catechists to open mission stations in British-occupied Mashonaland. In January 1891 he was made bishop of the newly established diocese of Mashonaland. He opened his first station at **Penhalonga**, on land granted by **Mutasa**. He then attempted to extend Anglican influence throughout the country with African teachers. Ill health forced his resignation in late 1894, and he died two years later from **malaria**.

KNOBKERRIE (variant: *kierrie*). A stick with a heavy knob at the end; used as a bashing or throwing weapon by many southern African peoples.

KOLOLO (Makololo). Members of a **Sotho** kingdom founded by Sebitwane (d. 1851) in the southern **Transvaal** during the early 1820s. After clashing with the **Ndebele** and other peoples in the western Transvaal, Sebitwane led the Kololo through **Botswana** into southern **Zambia,** occupying the upper **Zambezi** flood plains of the **Lozi** people by the early 1840s. During the late 1840s the **Ndebele** launched several large campaigns against the Kololo there, but each met with disaster. During the 1850s **David Livingstone** became an ally of the Kololo and attempted to plant an LMS mission among them (see **Matabele Mission**). When the Kololo were overthrown by the Lozi in 1864, many Kololo men sought refuge among the Ndebele in **Matabeleland.**

KOPJE (variant: *koppie*). **Afrikaans** term for a small hill; used widely throughout Southern Africa to refer to granite outcroppings which assume various shapes and formations. Such outcroppings occur throughout much of Zimbabwe, where they have played many historical roles. Early **San** left many of their **rock paintings** in *kopje* caves. Later **Shona** communities frequently erected their dwellings atop rugged clusters of rocks for defensive purposes. This practice served them well during the late 19th century, when they used firearms effectively to ward off **Ndebele** and **Gaza** raiders. The *kopjes* also served as effective strongholds early in the 1896–97 **Shona Revolt**. Later, however, the British ruthlessly dislodged rebels from their *kopje* caves and crevices with dynamite. Some *kopjes* were also used for religious shrines and stone edifices. (See also **Dombo; Dwala; Matopo Hills.**)

KOREKORE (a.k.a. "Northern Shona"). Linguistic and ethnic classification for the northernmost cluster of **Shona-speaking peoples**. The Korekore dialect (or Chikorekore) is spoken south of the **Zambezi River** from, roughly, the middle of **Lake Kariba** in the west to the point where the **Mazoe River** exits the country in the east. To the south, Korekore country merges into **Zezuru** territory. About one-sixth of the country's Shona speak a dialect of Korekore. Among the main Korekore subgroups are **Tavara, Budjga, Shangwe, Gova,** Nyungwe, Pfungwe, and Tande.

KRAAL. Widely used southern African term for a cluster of African dwellings, usually incorporating a livestock enclosure. The term may refer either to the enclosure itself or to the social unit that occupies it. *Kraal* is the **Afrikaans** form of Portuguese *curral,* for "cattle pen." The latter is closely related to Spanish *corral,* as used in North America.

KUMALO, MTOMPE (variant: Khumalo) (c.1875–1949). Born into the **Ndebele** royal **Khumalo** family, Kumalo (as he spelled his name) was in line to become an adviser to the king, had the kingdom not fallen in the 1890s. After the **1896 Revolt** his family settled near the LMS **Hope Fountain** mission station, where he attended school. In 1914 he went to Tiger Kloof Institution in South Africa to train for the ministry, into which he was ordained in 1917. He worked closely with **Neville Jones** at **Hope Fountain** the remainder of his life. In the 1940s Jones recorded Kumalo's life story and his views on Ndebele society and history in *My Fried Kumalo.*

KUNZWI-NYANDORO see **NYANDORO**

KUTAMA. Village in the southern **Makonde District** (at 17°48'S, 30°23'E). Kutama mission school is a Roman Catholic institution founded at the beginning of the First World War. By the 1930s the school had been developed into a major African teacher-training and technical school, attracting students from all over the country and surrounding territories.

KWEKWE (Que Que until 1982). Kwekwe is one of the country's largest urban centers, with a 1992 population of 74,982. It is located midway between Bulawayo and Harare at the very center of the country (at 18°55'S, 29°49'E; alt. 1,205 m). The town takes its name from the nearby **Kwe Kwe River**. It was established by **European** settlers at the beginning of the century to serve the needs of the adjacent **Globe and Phoenix Mine**. Kwekwe has remained an important center for the ranches and mixed farms in **Kwekwe District**. Large-scale manufacturing industries spill over into nearby **Redcliff**. Largely because of its industries, Kwekwe is one of Zimbabwe's most significant electrical-power-consuming areas, with nearly one-quarter of all the country's electrical energy being consumed in the area.

KWEKWE DISTRICT (Que Que District until 1985). Covering 9,120 sq km in central **Midlands Province**, Kwekwe District formerly was the northern part of **Gweru District**. Other districts that Kwekwe borders are **Bubi** and **Nkayi** on the west, **Gokwe** on the northwest, **Kadoma** on the northeast, and **Chirumanzu** on the east. The district headquarters are at **Kwekwe**, while other important centers include **Empress Mine** and **Redcliff**. Prior to 1980, the eastern two-thirds of the district was reserved for Europeans, while Tribal Trust Lands and some **Purchase Areas** were scattered in the west. District population in 1992 was 221,711.

KWE KWE RIVER (variant: Hwe Hwe). Rises c.20 km east of **Gweru**, flowing northwest to join the **Sebakwe River** just northeast of the town of **Kwekwe**. The river's name is believed to be an onomatopoeic rendering of some animal sound.

KYLE, LAKE. Located between **Masvingo** and the **Zimbabwe Ruins**, manmade Lake Kyle is by far the largest body of water lying entirely within the country (at 20°12'S, 31°E). Kyle Dam, completed in 1961, traps the waters of the **Mtilikwe River** and some of its tributaries to irrigate **sugar** and citrus estates in the southeastern low veld region (see **Sabi-Limpopo Authority**). The 92-sq-km lake and a somewhat smaller game reserve on its northern shores together form Kyle National Park, a major recreational area and tourist center. (See **Lakes**.)

L

L- . The letter *l* is not used in standardized **Chishona**, which ignores the **Kalanga** dialect. Instead Chishona uses only the rolled alveolar consonant *r*. By contrast, **Sindebele** almost always uses *l* where Chishona would use *r*. Hence, Chishona *Mwari* becomes Sindebele *Mwali,* etc.

LAAGER. Afrikaans term for fortified camp; usually formed by lashing **ox wagons** together in a tight circle, reinforcing gaps with thorny branches. The technique was developed by **Afrikaners** during their wars with the Ndebele and other African peoples in South Africa in 1830s. The same technique was later employed by the **Pioneer Column** and other British forces in present Zimbabwe during the 1890s. The term *laager* was also used in the broader sense of any fortified position, such as the towns besieged during the **Revolt** of 1896-97.

LABOUR PARTY. European political party that became the official opposition in the **Legislative Assembly** in 1934 when it won five of 30 seats against the **United Party.** Its representation achieved some success in widening its political base beyond the labor movement. The party later split into "Rhodesian" and "Southern Rhodesian" Labour parties, which won a total of five seats in 1946. Thereafter both parties greatly declined in support. (See **Mzingeli, C.**)

LABOUR RELATIONS ACT (1984). This act repealed the harshly discriminatory **Industrial Conciliation Act**. It established a labor relations board and employment councils, and legalized the formation of African trade unions. The regulations that followed defined the functions of, and established the means of, certifying and registering those unions. The power to certify unions and to declare strikes illegal if they threatened the country's overall economic security was placed under the minister of labor.

LAKES. Although the country has many **rivers**, it has virtually no natural lakes. Construction of **dams** has, however, created many artificial lakes used for water conservation and recreation. The largest lakes, in order of surface areas, are: **Kariba** (510,000 hectares [ha.]); **Kyle** (9,105 ha.); MacDougall, on the **Chiredzi River** (2,025 ha.); Chivero, on the **Hunyani River** (2,630 ha.); **Sebakwe** (1,520 ha.); and Bangala, on the **Mtilikwe River** (1.135 ha.). (See also **Fishing; National Parks.**)

LAMONT, DONAL RAYMOND (b. July 27, 1911). An Irish-born Roman Catholic cleric, Lamont came to Southern Rhodesia as a missionary in 1946. In 1957 he was made bishop of **Umtali**. Long noted as an outspoken critic of the white government's racial policies, Lamont became the center of international attention in 1976 as the first European convicted under the **Law and Order (Maintenance) Act** for failure to report the presence of nationalist guerrillas in his diocese. On October 1, 1976, he was sentenced to ten years at labor. An enormous international protest, including an appeal by Pope Paul VI, led to a significant reduction of the sentence the following February. The government then decided to unburden itself of a potential martyr, so it stripped him of his local citizenship and deported him in March 1977.

LANCASTER HOUSE CONFERENCE. Convened on September 10, 1979, in London, the Lancaster House Conference was the first all-parties conference held since the failed **Geneva Conference** of 1976. The convening of the conference by the recently elected government of British Prime Minister Margaret Thatcher was a direct result of negotiations held at the Commonwealth Conference in Lusaka in August (see **Lusaka Accord**). Within a week of the end of that conference, the British foreign secretary, Lord Peter Carrington, had issued invitations to all parties concerned with the resolution of the war and the future independence of the country. The **Zimbabwe Rhodesia** government delegation was led by the prime minister, **Abel Muzorewa**, and **Ian Smith**, who in effect represented the country's European community. The **Patriotic Front** delegation was led by **Joshua Nkomo** of **ZAPU** and **Robert Mugabe** of **ZANU**. Lord Carrington represented the British government and was the chairman of the conference.

Carrington prepared for the conference with the belief that it was imperative to avoid another failure like the Geneva Conference. He believed this could be accomplished by utilizing a "step-by-step" approach during the conference, with each step being completed before moving on to the next. Carrington then organized the conference agenda into three primary areas for negotiation: a new constitution, a transition period, and a cease-fire. Carrington began the conference by tabling for discussion a draft constitution written by British officials, which contained plans for a parliamentary system of government, guarantees for representation of the European minority following independence, and acceptance by the new government of existing government debts and obligations—particularly those to civil servants. The PF leaders initially opposed the British plan; they issued counterproposals calling for a presidential form of government, rejecting specific guarantees protecting minority rights, and rejecting promises to honor Rhodesian government debts and other financial commitments. The PF also wanted a constitutional clause guaranteeing land redistribution. The Muzorewa government agreed to the British proposals but stipulated that **sanctions** should be lifted and that the British government agree to maintain security during any transition period. Following private negotiations with British officials, the PF leaders agreed to compromise their positions. On September 24, they accepted a parliamentary form of government and reserved 20 percent representation for the European community for a period of seven years. They also agreed that these clauses could only be legally amended by a two-thirds vote of **Parliament**.

Talks then stalled when the PF refused to compromise further on the issue of land redistribution and walked out of the conference. On October 3, Carrington tabled what he called the final version of the constitutional settlement and demanded a formal PF decision on the document by October 11. This document agreed that the new independent government would acknowledge all existing financial debts and obligations, would pay full compensation for all land acquired by the government for redistribution, and would guarantee minority rights. The deadline passed without an announcement from the PF, and Carrington began bilateral negotiations with the Muzorewa delegation. However, two sets of meetings also occurred in private. In the first, discussions with representatives of the **Frontline States**—particularly **Mozambique**—strongly stressed that their principal supporters did not want the conference to fail because of PF intransigence. The second set of private meetings was held between PF leaders and Carrington. He committed British financial assistance to pay for the compensation required in acquiring land for redistribution. The U.S. ambassador to England also agreed that the United States would provide funds for land acquisition. Following these private meetings, Mugabe and Nkomo agreed to return to the conference, and on October 18 they agreed to the new **constitution**.

Negotiations on the second item on the conference agenda, the transition period, began immediately. Carrington again tabled a draft proposal for discussion. It called for a short transition period of three to four months and for the appointment of a British governor who would exercise full executive and legislative authority (see **Soames**). During the transition period, free elections, which would implement the new constitution, would be held. The PF again countered with its own proposals, calling for an international monitoring force for the **elections,** greater participation in the transitional government, and a longer period of time leading up to the elections. Muzorewa initially balked at the idea of new elections, but eventually agreed. Although the British government was hesitant to commit more men to a military monitoring force, it agreed to contribute troops to a Commonwealth force on the condition that the transition period be kept short. The PF leadership compromised on this last point, and on November 15, a final agreement regarding the transition period was signed.

The last item on the conference agenda, a cease-fire, was perhaps the most difficult to reach agreement on, largely because of the high degree of mutual distrust between the **Rhodesian Security Forces** and the military forces of the Patriotic Front. The Muzorewa delegation demanded that the continued infiltration of new guerrilla forces cease, while the PF distrusted the integrity of the security forces, which had continued to raid **ZIPRA** and **ZANLA** camps in **Zambia** and Mozambique, respectively, while the conference took place. The PF also demanded that all South African troops had to be removed from the country prior to a cease-fire. The Muzorewa government's acceptance of this stipulation was the first public acknowledgment that South African troops had continued to operate inside the country following their reported pullout in 1975. An additional problem area was the number of assembly points and their location for ZIPRA and ZANLA forces. The initial British proposal called for 15 camps to be located in the rural areas of the country. The PF political leadership believed that was insufficient and would make its forces appear small—and therefore politically weak—when compared to the more than 90 regular bases the Rhodesian security forces would be confined to following a cease-fire agreement. It was at this juncture of the negotiations that **Josiah Tongogara**, the ZANLA commander and member of the PF delegation, played a major role in the outcome of the conference. He argued that having fewer camps, and locating them in the rural border regions of the country was good in case the cease-fire broke down and his forces had to run for the relative safety of the neighboring states. He also reported to Mugabe that reports from ZANLA field commanders indicated than ZANU could expect a political victory in the upcoming elections, and that they should therefore not be delayed. Tongogara's strong support for a cease-fire and British acceptance of an additional assembly point for guerrilla forces convinced the PF political leadership to agree to a cease-fire. The resulting agreement made the military commanders of both sides responsible to the governor for the actions of their forces, called for a Commonwealth peacekeeping force of 1,350 men, separated the former combatants to their respective bases or assembly points, and prohibited any additional crossborder movements following the signing of the final Lancaster House Agreement on December 21.

LAND ACQUISITION ACT. Legislation unanimously approved in **Parliament** in March 1992. The explicitly stated goal of the act was to nationalize five million hectares of primarily European-owned commercial farmlands for redistribution to one million African subsistence farmers. The act declared that prices for the seized lands were to be established by government officials and paid for in government bonds, which were nearly worthless according to European farmers. In addition, land owners whose farms were seized were barred from suing the government over disputed compensation values. Local critics of the legislation claimed that its implicit purpose was to appease the common people of Zimbabwe who had been promised land through resettlement schemes since independence. By the early 1990s they were reported by all accounts to be highly disenchanted with the government of President **Robert Mugabe** for its failure to provide land. Internationally, the act was criticized for being anathema to the Economic Structural Adjustment Program **(ESAP)** which the Zimbabwean government had agreed to in 1991. In an attempt to blunt international criticism and the threatened diminution of foreign investments and aid, Mugabe introduced additional legislation which provided for fair market value compensation for seized lands and re-enstated those farmers' rights to appeal compensation decisions through the country's legal courts.

LAND APPORTIONMENT ACT (1930). Introduced into the **Legislative Assembly** in 1929, passed in 1930, and put into effect in April 1931, the Land Apportionment Act adopted the recommendations of the **Morris Carter Commission** by introducing the principle of racial segregation into land allocation throughout the country. Prior to this act the only racial element of official land allocation had been the creation of "Native Reserves" (see **Communal Lands**) restricted to communal African occupation. Outside the reserves there were no restrictions on land ownership. In practice, however, few Africans could afford to buy land, and by 1925 Africans had acquired only 18,210 hectares of nonreserve land. By contrast, **Europeans** had acquired c.12.5 million hectares of land, including virtually all high-veld land surrounding the **railway** lines and all major urban centers (see **Urbanization**). The Morris Carter Commission was set up in 1925 to investigate the question of allocating land outside the reserves, partly because of concern that Africans would be virtually excluded from further private land acquisitions, and partly because of European pressure to separate European and African farmlands.

The Land Apportionment Act defined six separate categories of land, of which the most important were Native Reserves (accounting for 22.4 percent of the whole country); Native **Purchase Areas** (7.7 percent); European areas (50.8 percent); and "unassigned areas" (18.4 percent). With minor exceptions, Africans could buy or lease individual plots only in the Purchase Areas, while Europeans could buy land anywhere within the much larger and generally superior European areas. Over the next three decades the act was frequently amended and revised to adjust the proportions of land and to designate new categories.

The revised Land Apportionment Act of 1941 extended the act to urban areas by acknowledging the existence of African townships in the midst of European areas. The act allowed Africans to live in, but not to own land in, the towns. (See also **Native [Urban Areas] Accommodation Act**.) After the Second World War major amendments to the act recognized the increasing inadequacy of the amount of reserve land by creating "Special Native Areas" to increase communal African holdings. Later these areas were consolidated with the reserves in newly designated "Tribal Trust Lands." By 1964 TTL accounted for 41.6 percent of total land; Purchase Areas, 4.4 percent; European area, 37 percent; "unreserved area" (which both Africans and Europeans could buy), 6.1 percent; and "national land" (including **game reserves** and **national parks**), 10.9 percent.

In the early 1960s the **United (Federal) Party** was moving toward repeal of the Land Apportionment Act by breaking down segregated categories of land, but this trend was reversed by the **Rhodesian Front** after it came to power. The RF simply halted the trend during the mid-1960s, so as not to imperil its attempts to reach a constitutional settlement with Britain. However, when the Republican **constitution** was promulgated in 1969, the Land Apportionment Act was superseded by the more rigidly segregationist **Land Tenure Act**.

Although the Land Apportionment Act was clearly the most significant element of the country's many discriminatory laws, it had the ironic effect of making impossible the kind of total racial segregation envisioned in South Africa's policy of "separate development" (see **"Two Pyramid" Policy**). The act formalized the haphazard allocation of European and African areas that had arisen before 1925, thereby fragmenting the country into sections mostly too small to provide economically or politically autonomous units. Nevertheless, the act and its successor have been the focus of most African rural protest since the 1930s, as they limited the rapidly growing African rural **population** to the agriculturally poorer and more isolated parts of the country, while causing considerable human suffering through periodic forced resettlement schemes. (See also **Agriculture**.)

LAND HUSBANDRY ACT see NATIVE LAND HUSBANDRY ACT

LAND TENURE ACT (1969). Land allocation law that replaced the **Land Apportionment Act** when the **Constitution** of 1969 was promulgated. By the mid-1960s virtually all land already reserved for Europeans was privately owned or controlled, thereby limiting the expansion of European commercial **agriculture**. Despite the fact that most European farms were clearly underutilized, the **Rhodesian Front** government sought a solution to the European agricultural problem by expanding the amount of land available to white farmers while more rigidly segregating African and European areas. The resulting Land Tenure Act converted most existing "unreserved land" into European areas, but otherwise made only minor changes in designated boundaries. The act divided the country into three basic categories of land: European, African, and "national"—the last comprising most of the **national parks** and **game reserves**. European and African areas were equalized, each with 46.6 percent of the total country. **Forest,** park, and game reserve lands were also included in parts of the European and African areas, leaving 40 percent of the country available to European farms and settlements; 41.4 percent to **Tribal Trust Lands**; and 3.8 percent to **Purchase Areas**.

Promulgation of the law was followed by more vigorous government efforts to evict African "squatters" from European areas, and by tightened controls over European entry into African areas. In March 1977 the **House of Assembly** amended the Land Tenure Act to allow Africans some access to formerly reserved European areas. The move was initiated by Prime Minister Ian Smith as a step toward an internal constitutional settlement after the failure of the **Geneva Conference**. (See also **"Protected Villages."**)

LANGUAGES. With the exception of a few tiny **San-speaking** bands in the west, the African peoples of the country all speak **Bantu languages**. **Chishona** is the first language of c.75 percent of the population and is an important second language among most of the rest. The most important minority languages are **Sindebele** and English. The latter is also an important second language among most Africans, as well as the only official government language. **Afrikaans** is the most widely spoken minority European language. **Fanakalo,** or "Kitchen Kaffir," serves as a *lingua franca* throughout the country.

LAW, AUGUSTUS HENRY (Oct. 21, 1833–Nov. 25, 1880). An English Jesuit priest, Law came to the country in 1879 as a member of the **Zambezi Mission**. Aided by **Ndebele** guides, he and **F. De Sadeleer** walked from **Bulawayo** to **Gazaland** in mid-1880. Shortly after being received by King **Mzila** in Gazaland, Law died from fever and dysentery.

LAW AND ORDER (MAINTENANCE) ACT (1960). Exceptionally tough security law introduced by **Edgar Whitehead**'s government in October 1960, shortly after government arrests of **National Democratic Party** leaders for provoking bloody urban riots. The act enabled the police (see **BSAP**) to declare any group of three or more people an unlawful assembly. It imposed heavy prison sentences for participation in proscribed gatherings, and it generally provided for the suppression of political dissent. The **Dominion Party** also supported the act in 1960, and its successor, the **Rhodesian Front**, repeatedly amended and toughened the law after coming to power, making it the primary instrument for suppressing African nationalist political activity. Citing the danger of **dissident** political activity, the government of **Robert Mugabe** did not repeal the act after independence, and it remained in affect into the 1990s. In 1994, the Supreme Court of Zimbabwe ruled that public demonstrations could no longer be banned under the act.

LAWLEY, ARTHUR (later Baron Wenlock) (Nov. 12, 1860–June 14, 1932). Early **BSAC** official. He served as secretary to **A. H. G. Grey** in 1896 and was unofficially left in charge of **Matabeleland** just as the **Ndebele Revolt** was ending. His status remained unclear until 1898, when he was designated **administrator** of Matabeleland. He later served as governor of Western Australia (1901), lieut. governor of the Transvaal, and governor of Madras (1905–11).

LEE, JOHN (b.July 10, 1827). The first European other than missionaries to settle in present Zimbabwe. **Mzilikazi** granted Lee a large tract of land west of the upper Shabani River in 1866. He later served both Mzilikazi and **Lobengula** as an adviser in dealings with other Europeans. He retired to the Transvaal in 1891, and two years later his **Matabeleland** farm was confiscated by the **BSAC** when he refused to fight against the Ndebele in the **Ndebele War**.

LEGION MINE. Village named after a group of local **gold** mines located on the lower **Shashani River** c.135 km south of Bulawayo in the **Matobo District** (at 21°55′S, 28°32′E). The mines were all opened over precolonial African workings.

LEGISLATIVE ASSEMBLY. Formal name for the country's main governing body from 1924 to 1965, when it was redesignated "Parliament." The 1969 **Constitution** reconstituted the body as the **House of Assembly**, the lower chamber of a new bicameral **Parliament**.

The **"Responsible Government"** Constitution of 1923 modeled the Assembly after the British House of Commons but placed sharp limitations on its power of legislation. The British Crown recognized the Assembly as Southern Rhodesia's primary lawmaking body but reserved the right to block any legislation it disapproved (see **Governors**). It further limited the Assembly's competence to purely internal matters, while excluding certain reserved constitutional clauses pertaining to African affairs. In practice, however, the Assembly and its **prime ministers** gradually broadened their range of competence and never had any legislation vetoed by the British government. When faced with local legislation such as the **Land Apportionment** and **Industrial Conciliation** acts, Britain tended to amend the Letters Patent upon which its reserve powers were based, thereby legitimizing the Assembly's actions.

From 1924 to 1961 the Assembly comprised 30 seats. Creation of the **federation** in 1953 headed off a planned expansion, but the constitution of 1961 anticipated the dismantling of the federation by increasing the number of Assembly seats to 65. Throughout this whole period the Assembly held at least one session each year and was reformed by general **elections** an average of about every fourth year.

Assembly members were elected by a technically color-blind franchise, but high property qualifications for voters left the settler community with an overwhelming majority through 1957. In that year new franchise qualifications created a special voters' roll for Africans. This dualism was refined by the 1961 constitution, which instituted a complex voting system with "A" and "B" rolls. "A" roll voters had higher educational, property, and income qualifications than "B" roll voters. The "A" roll elected 50 European Assembly members from 50 "electoral districts." By mid-1965 Europeans constituted 95 percent of the 97,284 "A" roll voters, while Africans constituted 92 percent of the 11,577 "B" roll voters. The impact of African voters was further diluted by an effective nationalist boycott of the general elections in 1962 and 1965.

LEGISLATIVE COUNCIL (Legco). By the Southern Rhodesia Order-in-Council of October 20, 1898, the British government introduced representative government into the territory with the creation of a Legislative Council similar to those introduced in other British colonies. The council had its first session in May of the next year, with four elected "unofficial" members and five "official" members nominated by the **BSAC**. As with the **Executive Council**, the BSAC **administrator** presided. A British resident commissioner sat on the council as a nonvoting member and was responsible for reporting on Legco decisions to the high commissioner for Southern Africa. The BSAC responded to persistent settler demands for increased representation by periodically adding new unofficial seats to Legco. By 1908 elected members held a majority, and by 1920 there were 13 such members. Over time Legco played an increasingly important role in lawmaking, but the elected members' majority was held in check by built-in restrictions on Legco's range of powers and by the administrator's power to veto legislation relating to revenue generation or to BSAC land and rights. Nevertheless, Legco became the first formal arena of settler politics, particularly after **Charles Coghlan** was elected in 1908. By the late 1910s the dominant issues the Council faced pertained to the constitutional status of the country following the planned termination of BSAC rule (see **Amalgamation; Responsible Government; Unionist Movements**). When Responsible Government was achieved in 1923, Legco was replaced by the **Legislative Assembly**.

LEMBA (Valemba; variants: Remba; Baremba; etc.). Small but historically prominent community living mainly in the **Mberengwa** area. The Lemba are descended from **Shona-speaking peoples** who converted to Islam prior to the early 18th century. They continue to preserve some **Muslim** terminology and greetings. By the 19th century they were noted as traders, metalworkers, potters, and weavers, and tended to live as endogamous groups within other societies. Many Lemba fell under the **Ndebele** tributary state during the 19th century and fought with the Ndebele in the **Revolt** of 1896.

LENGWE see **HLENGWE**

LEOPARD'S KOPJE CULTURE. Term for a late **Iron Age** culture, or industry, which extended over the southwestern parts of the country and into neighboring **Botswana** and the **Transvaal** from the end of the first millennium A.D. to about the 15th century, when it was displaced by the intrusive **Khami culture**. The culture is named after a site less than one km north of the **Khami Ruins**. The Leopard's Kopje culture complex featured mixed farming and limited **cattle** raising, and is archaeologically identified by characteristic shouldered pottery.

LEPROSY (a.k.a. Hansen's Disease). Infectious bacterial disease found throughout the country, particularly in the **Sabi** and **Zambezi** valleys. Leprosariums were established near **Masvingo** in 1926 and **Mutoko** in 1932. Willingness of sufferers to accept medical treatment has gradually improved, giving hope of eradicating the disease from the country. (See **Health.**)

LESSING, DORIS [nee Taylor] (b.Oct. 22, 1919). The best known and most distinguished **European** writer associated with the country, Lessing was born to British parents in Kermanshah, Persia (now Iran), where her father was a bank manager. In the mid-1920s her family immigrated to Southern Rhodesia, taking up maize farming near **Banket**. Around 1937 Lessing went to Salisbury to work as a secretary and telephone operator. In the early 1940s she helped to organize a local Communist Party, but it had little impact on the country's politics. She left the country for England in 1949 after two unsuccessful marriages, retaining the name of her second husband, Gottfried Lessing. Although Lessing started writing early, she published nothing of importance until she settled in England. Her first published novel, *The Grass Is Singing* (1950), had an implicitly Southern Rhodesian setting and depicted the psychological deterioration of a settler couple struggling on an isolated farm. A volume of short stories, *This Was the Old Chief's Country*, followed in 1951. Some of these and other short stories were later published in a major collection, *African Stories* (1965). With the exception of her "Children of Violence" pentalogy (1952–69), most of her later fiction is set outside Africa.

Her African fiction contains strong condemnations of settler society and colonialism, but she is most noted for her intensely personal treatment of the more general themes of individual alienation, madness, paranormal psychology, aging, and the fate of mankind. Her work is said to have had a particularly strong influence on feminists writers, and she has been mentioned as a prospective candidate for a Nobel Prize in literature. Besides fiction, she has also written poetry, essays, reviews, and dramatic scripts. (See **Literature.**)

Before 1980, Lessing returned to central Africa only once, in 1956. After traveling extensively throughout the region, she was declared a proscribed immigrant by the government of Southern Rhodesia because of her earlier political beliefs. She described that trip in *Going Home* (1957). Since 1980, Lessing has visited the country several times. In *African Laughter: Four Visits to Zimbabwe* (1992) she discusses memories of her childhood in the country and describes her impressions of independent Zimbabwe.

LEWANIKA see under **LOZI**

LIBERAL PARTY. European political party formed in 1943 by a former Huggins cabinet minister, Jacob Hendrik Smith (1881–1959), who attempted to combine **non-Labour Party** opposition against the ruling **United Party**. Despite its name, the Liberal Party represented strongly conservative interests that opposed government economic regulation and African political advancement. The party won 12 of 30 **Legislative Assembly** seats in 1946 but declined rapidly after 1948, when it won only five seats.

LILFORD, D. C. "Boss" (July 30, 1908–Nov. 3, 1985). Born in South Africa, Lilford built a prosperous 13,350-hectare farm near Harare. Once described as the wealthiest farmer in the country, he acted as a power broker in Rhodesian colonial politics. He helped Ian Smith oust **Winston Field** as premier in 1964 and consistently opposed any constitutional settlement proposal that would have transferred political power to Africans. In 1980, Lilford retired to his farm but remained vice-president of the **Rhodesian Front** until January 1982. He was murdered by unknown assailants on his farm in 1985.

LIMBO. Term used by European traders in the 19th century for a kind of coarse calico that is an important African trade item in the country. Derives from the **Nguni** word *ubulembu*, for "web."

LIMPOPO RIVER. Although it is the second-largest river on the African continent to empty into the Indian Ocean, the Limpopo carries only a fraction of the volume of water of the **Zambezi River.** During the dry season the Limpopo is usually little more than a stream and, as such, has never impeded human movements. The river rises in South Africa near Pretoria, whence it cuts about a 1,400 km curve, first to the northwest and then east and southeast to the sea. Its upper reaches are known as the Crocodile, or Oori, River, a name sometimes applied to its entire length. After forming a stretch of the **Botswana/South Africa** border, the Limpopo is fed by the **Shashi River.** From that point it flows east c.220 km, defining the **Zimbabwe/South Africa border** before entering Mozambique. Beitbridge is the main crossing point into Zimbabwe. Along with the **Sabi River** system, the Limpopo system drains the eastern side of the **Central Plateau.** The Shashi is its major Zimbabwean affluent. Others include—from west to east—the **Umzingwane, Bubye,** and **Nuanetsi.** J. F. Elton was the first person to map the central Limpopo in 1870. (See **Rivers.**)

LIPPERT CONCESSION (a.k.a. "Humbug Concession"). After the **BSAC** had used the **Rudd Concession** to legitimize its occupation of **Mashonaland** in 1890, the **Ndebele** king **Lobengula** still hoped to improve his position by playing off European powers against each other. To this end he granted sole rights to issue European land titles within BSAC-claimed territory to the German speculator Edward Amendes Lippert (1853–1925)—a cousin of **Alfred Beit**—and his agent Edward R. Renny-Tailyour (1851–1894). This document, which he signed at **Umvutsha** on November 17, 1891, became known as the "Lippert Concession." BSAC officials reportedly called the concession a "humbug," but they nevertheless bought it from Lippert a few months later for company shares and a large sum of money (some authorities argue that Lippert arranged in advance to sell the concession to the BSAC). Lobengula was outraged to learn the concession had fallen into BSAC hands. **L. S. Jameson** nevertheless argued that through the document Lobengula acknowledged European law in Mashonaland, thereby strengthening his company's pretexts for starting the **Ndebele War** in 1893. Thereafter the Lippert Concession was regarded by Europeans as a mainstay of BSAC land rights in the country.

LITERATURE. There is no pre-20th-century tradition of writing in the country, but most African societies have rich traditions of oral literature in the forms of myths, tales, poems, songs, and histories. Many of these have been translated and published, notably in the antiquarian journal **Nada**. Publication of modern forms of written literature is a relatively recent development, owing a great deal to the government's creation of the African Literature Bureau in 1953. This bureau was established to encourage vernacular writing for use in schools. The year 1957 saw publication of the first "novel" in **Chishona:** *Feso*, by **S. M. Mutswairo**. One of the most popular vernacular writers has been **Patrick Chakaipa**, who is credited with helping to bridge the gap between traditional oral literature and modern Western prose forms. **Ndabaningi Sithole** and **Stanlake Samkange** were two of the first African writers to publish in English. More recently, **Charles Mungoshi, Dambudzo Marechera, Shimmer Chinodya, Tsitsi Dangarembbga, Chenjerai Hove**, and **Yvonne Vera** have gained recognition for their novels. In common with African literature elsewhere, African writers in Zimbabwe have tended to focus on two dominant themes: the reaction to colonial political and social domination and the alienation of an increasingly industrial society. In addition, since the late 1970s writers like Chinodya and Hove have set story lines within the context of the war for national liberation. European literature relating to Zimbabwe is diverse. **H. Rider Haggard** may have been the first novelist to use Zimbabwean characters and vaguely Zimbabwean settings in *King Solomon's Mines* (1885). Ernest Glanville's *The Fossicker: A Romance of Mashonaland* (1891) is a fantasy very similar to *King Solomon's Mines*, but with more explicit Zimbabwean settings. **Bertram Mitford** wrote several novels with early **Ndebele** characters. **Olive Schreiner** followed with *Trooper Peter Halket of Mashonaland* (1897). **Gertrude Page** was the first settler novelist to use local settings. **Kingsley Fairbridge** and **Cullen Gouldsbury** were poets highly regarded within the settler community, but **A. S. Cripps** was the only poet writing on local themes to achieve much attention outside the country. The most distinguished writer associated with the country to date is **Doris Lessing**, a former settler, but she published all her major work after emigrating to England in 1949. (See **Bibliography**.)

LITHIUM. The country has some of the richest lithium ore deposits in the world. Production of this light metal was of little economic importance before the Second World War, but new technologies relating to jet aircraft, rocketry, and atomic power have since transformed lithium into one of the country's major **minerals**. World demand for lithium boomed during the 1950s. Major production was undertaken at **Bikita**, with minor mines in northeastern **Mashonaland**. After prices dropped in the early 1960s, only the Bikita mine remained open, producing an average annual output valued at £349,000 between 1961 and 1964. Total value of lithium ore production through 1964 was more than £4 million.

LIVINGSTONE, DAVID (March 19, 1813–c. May 1, 1873). Livingstone's name is strongly associated with Zimbabwean history, but his direct ties to the country were limited. He began his career as an LMS missionary in former **Ndebele** territory in the western **Transvaal** in 1841, but he soon grew restless to travel farther north. By 1851 he had reached the upper Zambezi headquarters of the **Kololo people**, with whom he explored the **Zambezi River** between 1853 and 1856. During his journey he visited and named the **Victoria Falls**. In 1858 he returned to the Zambezi in charge of an expedition concerned primarily with exploring the river's northern affluents. Through this whole period he was also encouraging the LMS to establish missions among the Kololo and Ndebele. His father-in-law, **Robert Moffat**, helped to plant such a mission among the Ndebele in 1859, but the Kololo mission was a disaster. One of the "**Matabele Mission's**" pioneer agents was Livingstone's brother-in-law, **John Smith Moffat**, whose work Livingstone personally financed for several years from the royalties from his successful book, *Travels and Reaches in South Africa.* Although Livingstone himself barely penetrated what is now Zimbabwe, his voluminous books and posthumously published letters and diaries contain valuable chronological details and allusions to events inside the country during the 1840s and 1850s—an otherwise poorly documented period.

LLEWELLIN, JOHN JESTYN (Baron Llewellin from 1945) (Feb. 6, 1893–Jan. 1957). After a long political career in England, Llewellin became the first governor-general of the **Federation of Rhodesia and Nyasaland** in 1953. He died in office and was succeeded by **S. R. Dalhousie.**

LOBENGULA KHUMALO (variants: Lo Bengula; Nombengula; Ulopen gula; Upengula; etc.) (c.1836-early 1894). **Ndebele** king (1870–94). Born in the western **Transvaal**, Lobengula was the son of **Mzilikazi** by a wife described as a "**Swazi.**" Little is known about his early life, but he appears to have narrowly escaped execution in the political crisis which occurred on his father's arrival in **Matabeleland** in c.1839. By the 1850s he was a member of the Mahlokohloko *ibutho.*

When Mzilikazi died in 1868, his older son, **Nkulumane**, was universally recognized as rightful heir to the kingship, but Nkulumane's whereabouts were unknown. Many Ndebele believed Nkulumane had been killed in the 1839 political crisis. An embassy to Natal failed to turn up the missing heir, so **Mncumbathe, Mhlaba, Lotshe, Gampu**, and other leading *izinduna* designated Lobengula as successor.

Lobengula's candidacy for the kingship caught resident European observers by surprise. Until then he had enjoyed no special status and was known for his adoption of European clothes and his close associations with European residents. Many Ndebele dismissed Lobengula's candidacy because of his mother's allegedly inferior social rank. Lobengula himself appears to have been unwilling to become king until the question of Nkulumane's fate was resolved. Further attempts to find Nkulumane in Natal produced no new information, so Lobengula was formally installed as king during the January 1870 *Inxwala.* Lobengula's authority as king was immediately challenged by pro-Nkulumane *amabutho.* In June, Lobengula personally led a successful assault against the rebels at the **Zwangendaba** *ibutho* town. Several hundred opponents, including their leader **Mbigo**, were killed. Many survivors fled to the Transvaal, where they schemed against Lobengula through the remainder of his reign. Lobengula was lenient to the rebels who remained within the kingdom, but these people continued to oppose him and he never gained complete control of the kingdom. One known attempt to overthrow him by force occurred in January 1872, when an "Nkulumane" pretender and another half-brother, **Mangwane**, tried to invade the country. In 1878 a semi-official British delegation led by **R. R. Patterson** was wiped out, apparently after Patterson tactlessly hinted that the British might support "Nkulumane's" claims to the Ndebele kingship.

Shortly after becoming king, Lobengula made the new **Gibixhegu** town his headquarters. About a year later he either relocated this town and changed its name or created a totally new **Bulawayo** as his headquarters. Thereafter Bulawayo, which was again moved in 1881, served as Lobengula's headquarters, but the king also spent much of his time in private villages such as **Umvutsha**. Like his father, Lobengula traveled about the kingdom frequently while living out of an **ox wagon**.

The local LMS missionaries had hoped that Lobengula would support their work, but he soon disappointed them. He stopped wearing European clothes and maintained a policy of merely tolerating the missionaries' presence. Nevertheless, he allowed Jesuits of the **Zambezi Mission** to open a Bulawayo station in 1879. The general failure of missionaries to win converts made them outspoken critics of both Lobengula and the Ndebele way of life. They increasingly lobbied for European conquest of the kingdom.

Although Lobengula allowed missionaries and many European traders to work inside the Ndebele kingdom, he strictly forbade them to enter **Mashonaland** (see **Coillard, F.**). He also exercised a near monopoly over the movements of **explorers** and **hunters**. He personally conducted most Ndebele trade with outsiders, from whom he obtained a considerable volume of such goods as firearms, **horses**, tools, and luxury items. These he used mostly to reward his supporters.

Mzilikazi had died just as Europeans were discovering **gold** at **Tati** and **Northern Gold Fields**. An influx of prospectors was thus one of the first problems with which Lobengula had to deal as king. European pressure for **mineral concessions** grew intense after he awarded his first formal concession to **Thomas Baines** in 1871. During the mid-1880s European imperial powers began competing for influence north of the Limpopo in an effort to head off **Afrikaner** expansion from the Transvaal. Lobengula signed a treaty with the Transvaal agent **P. Grobler** in 1887 and a similar treaty with Britain's agent **J. S. Moffat** the next year.

In October 1888 Lobengula awarded the **Rudd Concession** to agents of **Cecil Rhodes,** thinking he had signed a limited mineral concession. Rivals of Rhodes pointed out to Lobengula that the document had been seriously misrepresented, so he attempted publicly to repudiate it the next year. Rhodes sent his associate **L. S. Jameson** to Bulawayo to renegotiate the concession, while at the same time he obtained a **royal charter** for his newly formed **BSAC**. As Lobengula made fresh, minor concessions to Jameson, Rhodes and the BSAC assembled an occupation force known as the **Pioneer Column**. In mid-1890 the Column advanced into Mashonaland, establishing a beachhead for further British expansion. Whether Lobengula willingly permitted the Column to enter Mashonaland remains controversial, but he clearly made no serious attempt to stop it. Through all these proceedings he also tried to deal directly with the British government through **Mshete** and other emissaries. In 1891 he awarded the **Lippert Concession** to men he thought were rivals of Rhodes and the BSAC, but Rhodes himself acquired the document and used it further to validate BSAC occupation of Mashonaland.

Throughout his reign Lobengula oversaw frequent Ndebele military campaigns against neighbors. By the 1880s his relations with his neighbors were largely stabilized. Most campaigns by then were little more than tribute-collecting expeditions or "police actions" against recalcitrant subordinates. There were, however, notable military reverses against the distant **Tawana** and some peoples north of the **Zambezi River**. British occupation of Mashonaland provided Shona rulers with a new ally against resented Ndebele exactions, thereby increasing Lobengula's need to mount punitive expeditions. In mid-1893 Jameson—by then **administrator** of Mashonaland—used an Ndebele foray into the **Masvingo** area as an excuse for declaring war on Lobengula.

Lobengula attempted to negotiate a peaceful settlement through the ensuing **Ndebele War**, but the British were intent on outright conquest. Ndebele resistance was halfhearted, and the British quickly advanced on Bulawayo. In early November 1893 Lobengula had the town burned as he fled north with a large entourage. It is believed that he sought asylum with the **Ngoni** ruler **Mpezeni** in what is now eastern **Zambia.** What actually happened to him has been the subject of considerable mythmaking, but it is clear that he died of some illness without even reaching the Zambezi River—probably around February 1894. The location of his grave remained generally secret until its rediscovery near **Kamativi** in 1943, when it was declared a National Monument. Another myth, that Lobengula hid a vast "treasure," inspired fortune hunters well into the 20th century.

Like his father, Lobengula died without leaving a clear successor. He had many wives, but his "royal wife," **Xwalile,** bore him no children, and his favorite wife, **Lizigeyi,** produced no sons. When the British occupied Matabeleland, they did everything they could to abolish the Ndebele kingdom. At Rhodes' instigation three of Lobengula's sons, **Mpezeni, Njube,** and **Nguboyenja,** were sent to South Africa to be educated and kept out of the way. Meanwhile, another son, **Nyamanda,** asserted his own claim to the kingship, and restoration of the kingship became one of the major issues during the ensuing **Revolt**.

LOBOLO (Sindebele; *ilobolo*; **Chishona:** *rovora*; *ro'ora*). **Bantu** term widely used in southern Africa for payments made by husbands to the families of their brides. In what is now Zimbabwe the precolonial *lobolo* systems of different peoples were broadly similar, and have since been codified and elaborated in African law by the government. *Lobolo* has never been a system whereby husbands "bought" wives, but rather one in which the husbands made payments to their in-laws for guarantees that their wives would prove both fertile and faithful. In the 20th century, laws respecting *lobolo* have been increasingly concerned with defining parents' rights to children. Traditionally, *lobolo* payments were made in livestock—**cattle** when available; otherwise, sheep or goats—or **iron** hoes. Cattle are still used for *lobolo* payments, but cash payments have also become common. (For an example of royal *lobolo*, see **Xwalile.**)

LOCUSTS. Though the country contains no "outbreak areas" of these orthopteric insects, it has historically suffered periodic plagues of invading swarms. Red locusts (*Nomadacris septemfasciata*) are widespread throughout eastern and southern Africa and have usually entered the country from the north. Brown locusts (*Locustana pardalina*) are restricted to southern Africa and have entered the country mainly from outbreak areas in **Botswana.** A particularly devastating locust invasion hit the country in the early 1890s, adding to the suffering that contributed to the **1896 Revolts.** Other major invasions occurred in 1910, 1924, and 1934. Increasingly efficient retaliatory measures have lessened the amounts of crop damage, and international cooperative organizations have worked to destroy breeding grounds.

LOMAGUNDI (Shona chief) see **NEMAKONDE**

LOMAGUNDI DISTRICT (former variant: Lo Magundi) see **MAKONDE DISTRICT**

LONDON AND LIMPOPO MINING COMPANY (LLMC). Prospecting company formed in London in 1868 to exploit the **gold** fields found by Henry Hartley. In 1869 **John Swinburne** led a well-equipped expedition to the **Tati River,** where a small European settlement was founded. The LLMC's real objective, however, was the **Northern Goldfields,** so Swinburne went to **Inyati,** where he obtained **T. M. Thomas's** aid in persuading the **Ndebele** regent **Mncumbathe** to permit his party to prospect in **Mashonaland.** In return the LLMC provided an escort for the Ndebele embassy sent to Natal to interview the royal pretender **"Nkulumane."** Swinburne and **S. H. Edwards** prospected around the **Hartley Hills** in Mashonaland, but the next year the new Ndebele king awarded the northern concession to the rival **South African Gold Fields Exploration Co.** The LLMC men then retreated to the Tati area, where they began crushing quartz with the first mechanical crushing machines ever used in southern Africa. In 1870 the LLMC hired J. F. Elton to explore the **Limpopo River** in search of a route to the sea. Late the next month **Lobengula** awarded the LLMC an exclusive mining concession to Tati, where the LLMC outlasted all its smaller competitors. By 1871 the company was the sole proprietor of the Tati fields, but it was taking out little gold. By 1875 the company had abandoned the district. (See **Tati Concession.**)

LONDON MISSIONARY SOCIETY (LMS). Founded as a nondenominational evangelical society in 1795, the LMS soon fell under the aegis of the Congregational churches. It began opening missions in South Africa before the turn of the century and thereafter made the region one of its most intense foreign mission fields. Agents such as **Robert Moffat** and **David Livingstone** helped to make the LMS a pioneer in advancing Christianity into the interior regions. During the 1830s the LMS encouraged its Boston counterpart, the **American Board of Commissioners,** to open a mission among the **Ndebele,** then living in the Transvaal. In 1859 Moffat himself led a LMS party into the new Ndebele home in **Matabeleland,** where the **Matabele Mission** was permanently established. The LMS enjoyed little success in proselytizing among the Ndebele until after the **Ndebele Revolt** of 1896, but its agents played a crucial role in Ndebele affairs as the forerunners of European occupation. After the Revolt the **BSAC** confirmed the LMS in possession of its stations and granted it additional sites in Matabeleland. During the early 20th century the LMS enjoyed considerably more progress than it had seen in the country during the previous century, but its work was still limited by lack of staff and funds. By the time the LMS celebrated its centenary in 1959, it could claim 2,915 African church members, but this figure ranked only twelfth among the country's **missions** and accounted for less than 1 percent of the country's total avowed African Christians. In 1966 the LMS amalgamated with another body to become the Congregational Council for World Missions. (See **Missions.**)

LONELY MINE. Mining community located c.85 km north of **Bulawayo,** near the headwaters of the **Bubi River** in central **Bubi District** (at 19°30′S, 28°45′E). Lonely Mine began operations in 1906, exploiting a rich **gold** vein previously untouched by earlier **Shona** miners. **Nickel** and tungsten are also mined locally.

LOTSHE HLABANGANA (variant: Lotje) (d.Sept. 1889). A **Ndebele** *in-duna* of considerable seniority by the mid-1860s, Lotshe was leader of the Induba *ibutho.* After the death of **Mzilikazi,** Lotshe supported the candidacy of **Lobengula** and participated in an embassy to Natal in 1869 to investigate the disappearance of the preferred heir, **Nkulumane.** After Lobengula's installation as king, Lotshe's influence increased further. In 1879 he and **Xukutwayo** led the Ndebele delegation to **Gazaland** to fetch the royal bride, **Xwalile.** His prestige dipped badly after 1885, however, when he commanded a disastrous *impi* against the **Tawana** in central **Botswana.** Over the next several years he emerged as the most outspoken Ndebele advocate of peaceful accommodation with the Europeans, then pressing in on the Ndebele kingdom. He favored Lobengula's signing of the **Rudd Concession** in 1888, but then became the national scapegoat when Lobengula realized that the concession had been badly misrepresented. In early September 1889 Lotshe and many of his relatives were killed on Lobengula's authority.

LOUW, A. A. see under **MORGENSTER**

LOW VELD see **ALTITUDINAL ZONES; SABI-LIMPOPO AUTHORITY**

LOZI (Balozi; variant: Barotse). Large **Bantu**-speaking society living in the Zambezi floodplains of western **Zambia**—a region known as Barotse-land. The Lozi kingdom was occupied by the **Kololo** from the early 1840s to 1864. After the expulsion of the Kololo rulers, the Lozi themselves were unsettled by political strife until Lewanika (c.1845–1916) settled into power firmly in 1885. Lewanika's assumption of power coincided with renewed **Ndebele** military activity north of the **Zambezi River,** and the two states fought several times until 1893. The Lozi were the most formidable Ndebele enemy north of the Zambezi and competed with the latter for control of such riverine peoples as the **Nanzwa** and **Tonga**. (See also **Coillard, F.**)

LOZIGEYI DHLODHLO (d.Feb. 23, 1919). One of **Lobengula's** first wives, Lozigeyi lacked the official status of Lobengula's "great wife" (or "royal wife"), **Xwalile,** but she was unusually outspoken and was regarded as the king's most influential wife. In view of Xwalile's barrenness,

Lozigeyi might have produced a royal heir herself, but she bore the king only daughters. Lacking a son of her own, she championed the kingship claims of a cowife's son, **Nyamanda**, with whom she worked closely during the **1896 Revolt**. Afterwards she retired to **"Queens' Location"** on the middle **Bembezi River**, where she became wealthy. She subsequently broke with Nyamanda. In 1906 she wrote her will to leave everything she owned to another of Lobengula's sons, **Njube**. (See **Inkosikazi.**)

LUANZE (variant: Ruhanje). **Portuguese** trading **fair** located just south of the **Mazoe River** and west of the Mozambique border (at 16°55'S, 32°30'E). The fair operated from c.1580 to c.1680. Its ruins, now a national monument, are among the most extensive of early Portuguese sites.

LUNDI RIVER. A major internal river, the Lundi rises just south of **Gweru**, whose water it supplies from the Gwenoro Dam, built 30 km from the town in 1958. The Lundi flows generally southeast before joining the **Sabi** where the latter enters Mozambique. The Lundi's own major tributaries are the **Tokwe, Mtilikwe,** and **Chiredzi**.

LUNGSICKNESS (pleuropneumonia). Nonindigenous, contagious bovine disease. Long known in Europe, lungsickness was introduced into both South Africa and the United States in 1854. Seven years later South African traders brought oxen infected with the disease into **Matabeleland**. The **Ndebele** then lost thousands of **cattle** to the disease, though the local LMS agents helped to reduce the losses by inoculating uninfected animals and assisting in quarantining others. The last local outbreaks of the disease occurred between 1902 and 1904. (See **Health.**)

LUPANE. Administrative center of the district of the same name; located on the main road between **Bulawayo** and **Victoria Falls**, at a point near the confluences of the **Gwai, Bembezi, Bubi,** Gwampu, and Lupane rivers (at 18°56'S, 27°46'E). The Lupane River itself originates about 125 km due east.

LUPANE DISTRICT. Covering 8,670 sq km in the center of **Matabeleland North Province**, Lupane was created from the western part of the former **Shangani District**. Lupane borders the districts of **Binga** and **Gokwe** on the north, **Nkayi** on the east, **Bubi** and **Nyamandhlovu** on the south, and **Hwange** on the west. Prior to 1980 the northwestern corner of the district was reserved for Europeans, while the remaining territory was demarcated as Tribal Trust Land (now **Communal Land**) and some national **forest** land in the south. Population in 1992 was 94,469.

LUSAKA ACCORD. Name given to proposals accepted by leaders of Commonwealth countries at the Commonwealth Conference held in Lusaka, **Zambia,** in August 1979. British Conservative Prime Minister Margaret Thatcher had been elected in May, and at that time personally believed that Britain should accept the results of the Rhodesian elections held in April and recognize the government of **Abel Muzorewa**. However, after consultation with political and foreign-office advisers, Thatcher recognized that by officially accepting the election results, and thereby the **Internal Settlement Agreement**, Britain would be politically isolated and could be threatened with the dissolution of the Commonwealth. These dangers for Britain were strongly underscored when U.S. President Jimmy Carter announced that, despite congressional pressures, he was not willing to lift **sanctions** or recognize the legitimacy of the Muzorewa government until an all-parties agreement had been reached and internationally supervised **elections** had been held in Rhodesia. In addition, the United Nations and most Commonwealth members had already condemned the internal settlement agreement and stated that they would not recognize Muzorewa's government. Thatcher therefore decided not to immediately recognize Muzorewa but rather to attend the Commonwealth Conference and rely on her Foreign Secretary, Lord Peter Carrington, to actively work for agreement among Commonwealth leaders on new proposals for a quick solution to the "Rhodesian problem."

Thatcher, traveling with Queen Elizabeth II, arrived in Lusaka and was met by President Kenneth Kaunda, a strong supporter of the **Patriotic Front** and a leader of those Commonwealth members opposed to the internal settlement and the Muzorewa government. On the first day of the conference, Nigerian Foreign Affairs Minister Henry Adefope announced that Nigeria was nationalizing British Petroleum's production and marketing facilities, partly to encourage Britain to reevaluate its policies toward Rhodesia. Carrington was infuriated by the timing of the Nigerian announcement, fearing that it would cause Thatcher to end any new negotiations and recognize Muzorewa. However, Thatcher—who had been warned by the Queen not to let the conference fall apart over the Rhodesian problem—continued private discussions with several of the African Commonwealth leaders, who had impressed her with their commitment to finding a reasonable diplomatic solution. A small working group was then organized to draft a new set of proposals for ending the war in Rhodesia. The group included Thatcher, Kaunda, Adefope, President Julius Nyerere of Tanzania, Commonwealth Secretary General Sir Sridath Ramphal, and Prime Ministers Michael Manley of Jamaica and Malcolm Fraser of Australia. Following several meetings, the group produced a set of proposals that included Britain's acceptance of its "constitutional responsibility" to grant legal independence to Zimbabwe on the basis of majority rule; a call for a new democratic **constitution** that included safeguards for minority groups in the country; the recognition that a new independent government could only be chosen through free and fair **elections** supervised under British government authority, with additional Commonwealth observers; and the call for a British-sponsored all-parties constitutional conference. The draft of the proposals was unanimously accepted by the conference.

Within a week of the end of the Commonwealth conference, Carrington issued invitations to a new all-parties conference to be held in early September at **Lancaster House** in London.

M

MA-. Chishona prefix (class 6) for plural forms of unprefixed Class 5 nouns, e.g., *shave/mashave*. The *ma-* prefix is also used for things or people usually thought of as numerous or as a group, e.g., *Mashona*, "the Shona people." In the case of proper names, such prefixes are dropped in the dictionary. (See also **VA-**.)

Note that the **Sindebele** prefix *ama-* is frequently shortened to *ma-*, as in *madoda* (see **Indoda**).

MacDOUGALL, THOMAS MURRAY see under **TRIANGLE**

MACEQUECE INCIDENT (variant: Massi Kessi). After an abortive attempt by Britain and Portugal to delimit their spheres of influence in 1890, the village of Macequece (just east of present **Mutare**) became the arena of physical rivalry. **Major P.W. Forbes** secured the nearby town of **Mutasa** in November 1890 and the **BSAC** then occupied Macequece. The following April the British abandoned their fort there and camped a few km to the west. A larger **Portuguese** force then occupied the fort. On May 11, the Portuguese advanced on the British and a brief skirmish took place. The Portuguese withdrew, allowing the British to retake the fort. Meanwhile, negotiations in Europe resulted in the **Anglo-Portuguese Convention** the next month. This agreement placed Macequece (now known as Villa de Mancia) in Portuguese territory. (See **Mozambique**.)

MACHEKE. Town c.35 km east of **Marondera** on the main **road** and **railway** line to **Mutare** (at 18°9'S, 31°51'E; alt. 1,535 m). Nearby are the headwaters of the Macheke River, which flows south to feed the **Sabi River**. Founded in 1906, Macheke developed into a center for a major **tobacco** producing area.

MACHENG (variant: Matsheng) (c. 1892–1873?). **Ngwato** ruler. Captured as a child by the **Ndebele,** Macheng was taken to **Matabeleland** in 1842 and raised as a Ndebele. In 1857 **Robert Moffat** interceded in his behalf, obtaining his release from King **Mzilikazi.** With the aid of the Kwena ruler Sechele, Macheng made good his claim to the Ngwato chiefship, based upon his status as the official—though not physical—offspring of **Kgari**. After Mzilikazi's death in 1869, Macheng gave material support to the Ndebele royal pretender **"Nkulumane"** in order to improve the Ngwato position in the boundary dispute with the Ndebele over the **Tati gold fields**. Macheng himself had meanwhile been in and out of power among the Ngwato, and was finally ousted by **Khama III** in 1872.

McILWAINE, LAKE. Former name of Lake Chivero.

MADEIRA, DIOGO SIMÕES (fl. 1590–1620s). A **Portuguese** trader, Madeira was granted land in the Zambezi Valley by the governor of **Mozambique** town in 1590. By the early 1600s he was the most powerful military leader in the region of **Tete**. In 1607 he responded to **Munhumutapa Gatsi Rusere**'s appeal for Portuguese help by raising an army for the **Shona** king. On August 1, 1607, he met Gatsi Rusere by the **Mazoe River** and obtained the latter's mark on a treaty ceding all the country's mines in return for military protection. (See **Rudd Concession** of 1888.) Over the next several years Madeira waged successful campaigns in the Munhumutapa's behalf, but the locations of the ceded mines were not revealed. Madeira later lost and regained his Portuguese offices in purely European intrigues.

MAFUNGABUSI PLATEAU (variant: Mapfungavutsi). Isolated high veld area in the southern **Gokwe District** by the **Gwelo River** valley (at 18°25′S, 29°E). Infested with **tsetse flies** in the 19th century and only sparsely inhabited, the area is now designated a national forest reserve. The village of **Gokwe** is on the Plateau's northern slopes.

MAGOSIAN CULTURE (a.k.a. Shangula Culture). **Stone Age** culture period taking its name from a site in Uganda. The Magosian is associated with the last phase of the Middle Stone Age, or the Second Intermediate Period. It maintains features reminiscent of earlier Middle Stone Age tool complexes but shows trends that are characteristic of Late Stone Age industries.

MAGUIRE, JAMES ROCHFORT (Oct. 4, 1855–April 18, 1925). Born in Ireland and trained as a lawyer in England, Maguire came to the South African diamond fields in the 1880s and met **Cecil Rhodes** there. In 1888 he was a member of the **Rudd Concession** party to **Matabeleland.** He later returned to Britain and was elected to Parliament from Ulster. In London he represented Rhodes before the **BSAC** board of directors, on which he himself obtained a seat in 1898. He served as vice-president of the BSAC from 1906 to 1913 and was president from 1923 until his death. During the whole of this period he was one of the leading forces behind the expansion of Southern Rhodesia's **railways**.

MAHLOKOHLOKO (variants: Amahlokohloko; Amahlogohlogo; Matlokotloko). **Ndebele *ibutho*** raised by **Mzilikazi** in c.1850. The *ibutho*'s town stood on the watershed between the **Bembezi** and **Umgusa rivers**, near the latter's confluence with the Koce. Mzilikazi lived mostly in this town until the late 1850s, when he moved to **Inyati.** His successor **Lobengula** also lived with the Mahlokohloko until becoming king in 1870.

MAHUKU (a.k.a. Makobe; Nopelume) (d.1863). **Talowta** chief whose people lived by the upper Inkwezi (Inkwesi) River, where it was intersected by the **Hunters' Road**. Mahuku switched his allegiance from the **Ngwato** to the **Ndebele** after the latter settled in **Matabeleland** in the early 1840s, but it is unknown whether he did so voluntarily or by force. In any case, by 1854 his own town was being used as the southern port of entry into the Ndebele kingdom, and Mahuku was under the direct supervision of the Ndebele *induna* **Manyami**. When the Ndebele attacked the Ngwato town Shoshong in 1863 (see **Khama III; Mangwane**), Mahuku and his brother Kirelkiwe were accused of aiding the Ngwato and were killed by the Ndebele.

MAI CHAZA CHURCH see **CHAZA, MAI**

MAIZE (American Indian "corn"; a.k.a. *mealies*). The country's most important food crop among all farming communities, maize was introduced into the country some time before the 19th century. It is grown throughout the country but flourishes best only in the well-watered districts of the northeast. By the 20th century maize seemed to have displaced **millet** and sorghums as the primary African food crop. It ranked as the country's most valuable agricultural crop until the Second World War, when it was overtaken by **tobacco**. However, following the passage of the Maize Control Act of 1931, African farmers were virtually eliminated from the country's commercial maize production.

Since 1945 improved strains and expanded acreage have resulted in increased yields, growing from 350,000 tons in 1956 to over 2 million tons in 1982. Maize production particularly increased following **UDI** , when **sanctions** forced European tobacco farmers to diversify their crop production. While the government encouraged several crops, most tobacco farmers turned to maize, which could be easily exported. Production spurted again after 1980, when the newly independent government of Zimbabwe increased material and financial assistance to African farmers. In the five-year period spanning the 1976–77 to 1980–81 crops, African farmers produced about 71,000 tons annually, for approximately 11 percent of the total annual crop. By the end of the 1981–81 harvest, they had increased production to 363,000 tons, about 33 percent of total production; and in 1982–83 their maize production rose again to 369,000 tons or 55 percent of the total estimated crop. Throughout the 1980s African farmers continued to produce about 50 percent of the annual maize crop. Maize production in the early 1990s was adversely affected by severe drought conditions, and production in 1992 slipped to about 362,000 tons, but, with the end of the droughts in the mid-1990s production recovered, reaching 2.2 million tons in 1997. (See **Agriculture.**)

MAKGATHO, MOSES D. see under **AFRICAN METHODIST EPISCOPAL CHURCH**

MAKOLOLO see **KOLOLO**; and see under **MATABELE MISSION**

MAKOMBE (variant: Macombe). Dynastic title of the rulers of the **Barwe** kingdom of the Honde Valley. The dynasty was established by **Korekore** from the **Munhumutapa** state in about the 15th century and first documented by the **Portuguese** in 1506. Although their realm lay chiefly within what is now **Mozambique**, the Makombes played an important role in present Zimbabwe's history as intermediaries between the **Shona** states and the Portuguese in 1902 (see **Mapondera**).

MAKOMBWE. Plural of *gombwe*.

MAKONDE DISTRICT (Lomagundi District until 1985). Originally a huge district covering the northernmost wedge of the country, Makonde District lost its western section to form **Hurungwe District** in the 1940s, and later lost its remaining northern border section to create the **Guruve District**. The district now covers 13,170 sq km in **Mashonaland West Province**. Except for the southern fringe, the entire district was reserved for Europeans prior to 1980. The administrative center for the district is

Chinhoyi, with other important centers including **Banket, Mangula, Alaska Mine, Darwendale,** and **Mtoroshanga.** The economy of the district is based on mixed **agriculture** and diverse **mineral** production. District population in 1992 was 159,845.

Makonde is separated from Hurungwe District by the **Angwa River.** It also borders the districts of **Guruve** on the north, **Mazowe** and **Harare** on the east, and **Chegutu** and **Kadoma** on the south.

MAKONI. Dynastic title of the rulers of the **Maungwe,** whose **Manyika-speaking** people are known as Hungwe, or Maungwe. The extent of Maungwe territory over the past several centuries has roughly coincided with the area of the present **Makoni District,** which is named after the dynasty. The Makoni dynasty appears to have been established by a man named Muswere early in the 17th century. The name "Maungwe" first appeared in a **Portuguese** document of 1635. The paramountcy was originally tributary to the **Munhumutapa** state but became independent after the latter's late 17th-century disintegration.

Makoni IX Muswati died just as **Zwangendaba's Ngoni** invaded the country in the 1830s. Maungwe was hit hard by both the **Ngoni** invasion and the *shangwa* drought, as well as by internal political disputes. Under the reign of Makoni XI Nyamanhindi (c.1840–65), comparative peace and prosperity were restored, but disorder returned just before his death, when the **Gaza** invaded Maungwe. The next Makoni, Muruko, reigned through an area of intermittent warfare with the neighboring **Mutasa** paramountcy (c.1865–89). In the mid-1880s the Makoni obtained military aid from the Portuguese adventurer **Manuel de Sousa.** Soon after Mutota (a.k.a. Chingaira) became the next Makoni, peace was restored with the Mutasa, but then the **BSAC** occupied the country in 1890 (see **Pioneer Column**).

In 1894 the British established an administrative post at **Rusape.** Two years later Makoni Mutota became one of the most active leaders of the **Shona Revolt.** In August 1896 the British retaliated especially hard against his headquarters, dynamiting his people out of **Gwindingwi Hill.** Mutota surrendered, only to be tried and shot on September 4, 1896. One of his sons, Ndapfunya (d.1921), who had not participated in the Revolt, was made the first government-appointed Makoni.

MAKONI DISTRICT. Covering 8,020 sq km of the northern part of **Manicaland Province,** Makoni District is divided by the main road and railway line between **Harare** and **Mutare. Rusape** is the district's administrative center. Other major centers include **Nyazura** and **Headlands.** Makoni borders the districts of **Mutoko** on the north, **Nyanga** and **Mutasa** on the east, **Mutare** on the south, and **Wedza, Marondera,** and **Murewa** on the west. Prior to 1980 the well-watered central section of the district was reserved for Europeans. **Agriculture** is the main industry, with **tobacco** and **maize** being the main crops grown in the district. District population in 1992 was 242,611.

MAKUMBE CAVE (variants: Mkumbe; Nkumbe). A large cave north of **Domboshawa** in the Mwanga Hills (at 17°38′S, 31°22′E), Makumbe contains naturalistic polychrome **rock paintings** representing an exceptionally wide variety of animals, as well as "matchstick" human figures.

MALARIA. Infectious parasitic disease transmitted by several varieties of anopheline mosquitoes. The most widespread disease in the country (see **Health**), malaria is endemic to the low veld areas (see **Altitudinal Zones**). The disease is most active around April, after mosquitoes have bred through the long rainy season. In its most serious forms malaria can damage the brain (cerebral malaria) or the kidneys (blackwater fever). The Shona and other long-standing residents of the country are largely immune to the worst effects of the disease. Immigrant peoples and visitors are most susceptible to serious attacks. The **Ndebele,** for example, coming from a largely malaria-free area in the late 1830s, suffered many malarial deaths during their first decades in the country. A local doctor, **A. M. Fleming,** made a major contribution to worldwide malarial research.

MALINDIDZIMU. African name for **World's View** in the **Matopo Hills**.

MALTA TALKS. Held in secrecy on the island of Malta at the end of January 1978. **Robert Mugabe** and **Joshua Nkomo,** as leaders of the **Patriotic Front,** met with British Foreign Secretary Dr. David Owen and United States UN Representative Andrew Young. At the conclusion of the meetings, Owen announced that the talks had resulted in the two PF leaders' acceptance of the idea of independently observed and supervised elections to end the liberation war in Zimbabwe, but that they demanded the PF play a substantial role in any transitional governing body during the period leading up to those elections. They had also accepted the idea of a limited amnesty for Rhodesian state officials and bureaucrats, including politicians and members of the **security forces**.

Ian Smith and "moderate" nationalist leaders inside the country, who were at that time engaged in negotiations that led to the **Internal Settlement** agreement, rejected the points as described by Owen. However, the leaders of the **Frontline States** were greatly encouraged by Owen's announcement and insisted that discussions be continued. Although new talks were not scheduled immediately, the Malta talks helped to clear the way for further negotiations at the **Lancaster House Conference** in late 1979.

MALVERN, LORD. Title of **Godfrey Huggins** from 1955.

MAMA. Common **Bantu** word for mother; often used as a term of respect in addressing a woman. (See **Baba.**)

MAMBO (pl., *vamambo,* or *vadzimambo*). Generic **Shona** term for king or paramount chief. The title is associated with the rulers of the **Changamire** state but was also used by the **Munhumutapas** and other Shona-speaking states. "Mambo" is now often used as a polite form of address. (See **Inkosi.**)

MAMBO HILLS see **NTABAZIKAMAMBO**

MANA POOLS. A 2,810-sq-km **game reserve** covering the mopane **savanna** land between the **Zambezi River** and the **Zambezi Escarpment**, 50 km east of **Chirundu**. The riverine plain is dotted with deep holes that trap the flood waters, attracting numerous large animals. Mana

Pools is one of the few game reserves in the country easily accessible to tourists.

MANCHESTER GARDENS. Former name of **Vumba National Park**.

MANGULA see **MHANGURA**

MANGWANE KHUMALO (c.1825–c.1890s). Born in the **Transvaal**, Mangwane was the eldest son of the **Ndebele** king **Mzilikazi**. During the 1850s he was regarded as his father's heir apparent, but he did not get along well with his father. His political position deteriorated rapidly after 1862, when his confidant **Manxeba Khumalo** was executed. In March 1863 Mangwane commanded an unsuccessful *impi* against the **Ngwato** capital, Shoshong, in eastern **Botswana**. By the late 1860s it appeared that **Lobengula** was destined to become Ndebele king. Mangwane and other dissidents therefore fled the country when Mzilikazi died in 1868. In 1870 he and a contingent of the dispersed Zwangendaba *ibutho* met the pretender **"Nkulumane"** in Natal, where they planned a coup d'état against Lobengula. By late 1871 both men were in Shoshong, where the Ngwato ruler **Macheng** joined in their plot. The following January Mangwane directed an invasion of **Matabeleland** under "Nkulumane's" banner, but he seems to have sought the Ndebele kingship for himself. The invasion was easily repelled by Lobengula. Afterwards Mangwane and a few followers settled at Rustenburg in the Transvaal, where he was reported still to be living in 1890. A largely Sotho-ized community of his descendants still reside there.

MANGWE. Mangwe Pass is a defile in the **Matopo Hills** through which the old **Hunters' Road** ran in the 19th century (at 20°41′S, 28°4′E). South from the pass, the small Mangwe River flows into the **Shashi River**. John Lee established the first nonmissionary European settlement in the country near the pass in 1866, when entrance to the **Ndebele** kingdom was guarded nearby under the direction of **Manyami**. In 1893 the **BSAC** built Mangwe Fort there to protect British supply movements. The fort was made into a *laager* during the **Ndebele Revolt** of 1896, but it was never assaulted. Mangwe village is now a small center in a mainly **cattle**-producing region.

MANGWENDE. Dynastic title of the **Nhowe** rulers in the **Murehwa District**. The Mangwende dynasty was founded around 1710 by Mangwende Sakuvunza. The chiefdom was briefly occupied by the **Ngoni** during the 1830s and was attacked by the **Gaza**, but was relatively free of **Ndebele** raids during the 19th century. Mungati (or Mgati) became the last independent Mangwende in c.1880. He was shortly thereafter visited by **Manuel de Sousa**, who tried to bring the Nhowe into the **Portuguese** sphere, while getting the Mangwende to support him in a war against the **Budjga** in 1887. The Mangwende signed a treaty with Sousa afterwards, but then renounced the Portuguese when the **BSAC** occupied the country in 1890 (see **Pioneer Column**). Over the next several years the Nhowe grew increasingly resentful of British occupation, but the Mangwende reluctantly tolerated their presence. In March 1892 a headman named Gomwe was killed in a dispute with a British official. The Mangwende's son, **Mchemwa**, then became the most outspoken opponent of the

British. In June 1896 Mchemwa led the Nhowe into the **Revolt**, while the Mangwende himself played a passively supportive role. The Mangwende surrendered on September 3, 1897, and soon found that his prestige among the Nhowe was largely lost. The Nhowe were forced to resettle near **Murehwa,** in what is now the Mangwende **Communal Lands.** Mangwende Mungati died in May 1924. Two years later the government appointed Chibanda, a member of another family, as Mangwende.

MANGWENDE, WITNESS PASICHIGARE MAGUNDA (b.Oct. 15, 1946). One of Zimbabwe's most able and experienced younger political leaders, Mangwende was born in **Chivhu** but grew up in the nearby **Buhera.** Mangwende received a primary education at Zimuto Mission and then went on to the government-sponsored **Goromonzi** School and the School of Social Work. In 1970 he enrolled at the University of Rhodesia (now **University of Zimbabwe**) where he became involved in university political activities and was elected president of the Student Union. In 1973 he was expelled after being accused of involvement in anti-government politics. He left the country and attended the University of Southampton, England, where he earned a B.A. in international relations. He continued his education at The London School of Economics, where he received a Ph.D. in international relations. While in graduate school he continued to participate in politics. He joined the Zimbabwe African National Union (**ZANU**) sometime in the mid-1970s, becoming first the president of the Zimbabwe Students Union in Britain and later the general-secretary of the London branch of ZANU. In 1979 he left England after being appointed ZANU's representative in **Mozambique.**

Mangwende returned to the country immediately before the 1980 **elections.** He won a seat in **Parliament** and was appointed deputy defense minister by Prime Minister **Robert Mugabe.** In 1981, in a reshuffle of the cabinet following the dismissal of **Edgar Tekere,** Mangwende was promoted to the office of minister of foreign affairs. During his tenure as minister of foreign affairs he was very active in international diplomatic activities surrounding the issue of independence for Namibia. Following the **Unity Pact** and merger of ZANU and the Zimbabwe African People's Union (**ZAPU**), he was appointed minister of information, posts and telecommunications—effectively swapping cabinet positions with **Nathan Shamuyarira.** Following the 1990 elections he became minister of agriculture, and later was moved by President Mugabe to the post of minister of education and culture.

MANHLAGAZI. Chief town of the **Gaza kingdom** in the late 19th century; originally located just west of the **Mozambique** border near the slopes of **Mount Silinda.** Some authorities state that the town was founded by King **Soshangane** in the late 1830s, but he appears actually to have resided by the middle **Sabi River** only briefly before settling near the **Limpopo River** to the south. **Mzila** re-established Gaza headquarters by Mount Silinda in the early 1860s. The town was known as Manhlagazi at least by the time **Gungunyane** became king in 1884. Five years later Gungunyane shifted the town c. 475 km south to a location in Mozambique near the mouth of the Limpopo River. There the town was known to the **Portuguese** as Manjacaze.

MANICALAND PROVINCE. "Manica" is a variant form of **Manyika**, the name of a major cluster of **Shona-speaking peoples** who live in the **Eastern Highlands**. In its broadest sense, "Manicaland" encompasses Manyika territory in both the easternmost parts of the country and **Mozambique**. Officially, however, Manicaland is the name of the easternmost province, covering 35,219 sq km, stretching along the border with Mozambique. It includes the districts of **Buhera, Chimanimani, Chipinge, Makoni, Mutare, Mutasa,** and **Nyanga**. (See **Gazaland**.) The province is one of Zimbabwe's most important agricultural areas, producing nearly all of the country's **timber** and **coffee**, all of its **tea**, and much of its deciduous fruit. Dairy and beef **cattle**, as well as **maize, cotton, tobacco, sugar**, and many other crops are also produced. Tourism also plays a large role in the economy of the province.

MANIKUSA. Alternative name of the Gaza King **Soshangane**.

MANXEBA KHUMALO (variant: Monyebe) (d. Aug. 1862). An **Ndebele induna**, Manxeba was said to have been one of Mzilikazi's most influential advisers and confidants. (See also **Mangwane**.)

MANYAMI (fl. 1850s–70s). The **Ndebele** *induna* who oversaw the southwestern gateway to the kingdom, Manyami detained travelers along the **Hunters' Road** until the kings conveyed permission for them to proceed. By 1854 Manyami was stationed at the town of **Mahuku** by the upper Inkwezi River, which flows between the Ramaquabane and **Mangwe Pass**. In 1873 he was restationed at the first site. He seems to have retired or died in 1874.

MANYAMI RIVER (variant: Mhanyami). Original **Shona** name for the **Hunyani River**.

MANYANGA. Original **Rozvi** name for **Ntabazikambo**.

MANYANO see **RUWADZANO**

MANYIKA (variant: **Manica**). One of the main ethnic and linguistic clusters of the **Shona-speaking peoples**. The Manyika dialect (or Chimanyika) of Shona is spoken east of the **Zezuru** region and north of the **Ndau** region, mainly in the districts of **Makoni, Nyanga,** and **Mutare**, and in **Mozambique** south of the **Pungwe River**. About 75 percent of the Manyika people (the Vamanyika) live in the present Zimbabwe; the rest are in Mozambique. The Zimbabwean Manyika constitute about one-ninth of the country's total Shona-speaking population.

Among the local dialects of Manyika are Manyika proper, spoken by the people of the **Mutasa** kingdom, and Maungwe (or Hungwe), spoken in the **Makoni** kingdom.

MANYIKA, ROBSON DAYFORD (April 12, 1934–June 24, 1985). **ZANLA** commander and nationalist leader. Born at **Goromonzi**, Manyika was the son of a **Msingesi Purchase Area** farmer. He attended Chikwaka Primary School and was a boarder at Chiwiza Secondary School near **Marondera**. He completed his secondary education through a series of correspondence courses. He began political activities by joining the **Youth League** in 1957. In 1959 he was a committee member of the

African National Congress. He joined the **National Democratic Party** in 1960 and was elected organizing secretary for youth. By 1961 he had been appointed publicity and organizing secretary of the NDP. Following the banning of the NDP, he kept the same post in the newly formed ZAPU. When ZAPU was banned in September 1961, Manyika was arrested and sent to Hartley Prison until 1963. Following his release, he left the country, joining ZAPU forces in **Zambia.** He was sent to the Soviet Union for military training, and upon his return in 1965 was appointed chief of staff and charged with organizing **ZIPRA.** He was considered one of the important strategists of the initial stages of the armed struggle. In 1970 he joined ZANU, and two years later was appointed chief military commissar in charge of training and personnel in the **ZANLA** high command. During the 1971–1972 period, he helped to command ZANLA's offensive into the northeast region of the country. In 1976, Manyika went to the **Geneva Conference** as a military expert for ZANU. In 1977 he was elected to the ZANU Central Committee and became the deputy secretary for manpower planning and labor. He also attended both Malta conferences and the **Lancaster House Conference** as one of ZANU's military advisers. In 1980 he was elected to **Parliament,** representing **Mashonaland West,** and was appointed deputy minister of labor and social welfare in the newly independent government. At the time of his death he was contesting the Kariba Constituency in the 1985 general election. Following his death, he was buried at **Heroes' Acre** outside Harare.

MANZAMNYAMA RIVER. Variant name of the **Nata River.**

MAPFUMO, THOMAS (b. July 2, 1945). Born in **Marondera,** Mapfumo is arguably Zimbabwe's best-known vocalist, both domestically and internationally. He began singing in the late 1960s, and in 1973 formed a group called "The Hallelujah Chicken Run Band." In the early 1970s he came under the influence of radio broadcasts from the Voice of Zimbabwe, which featured liberation music broadcast from outside the country. He began to write and perform "Chimurenga songs," which supported the liberation struggle through innuendo, deliberate ambiguities, and linguistic camouflage. In 1976 he joined a group called the "Acid Band" as lead vocalist and writer, and in the next year released the band's first album, "Hokoyo" ("Watch Out"). With this album Mapfumo gained the attention of government authorities, who banned his music from the radio. He was then arrested and held for 90 days. In 1978 he formed the "Blacks Unlimited" band, and has continued his success and popularity. His music deals with the themes of liberation—not only from European political domination but also from racism and poverty—and pride in a free Zimbabwe and Africa. (See **Music.**)

MAPONDERA (a.k.a. Kadungure Mapondera) (1840s–1904). **Shona** chief and independent revolt leader. By the late 1880s Mapondera was a contender for a **Rozvi** chiefship near the **Umvukwe Hills** and the **Mazoe River.** Noted for his military leadership, he is said to have repelled several **Ndebele** raiding parties. In 1889 Mapondera and his brother Temaringa granted a mineral **concession** to **F. C. Selous,** but Mapondera was bitterly opposed to the subsequent **BSAC** occupation of the region (see **Pioneer Column**). When the BSAC administration attempted to impose a hut tax in 1894, Mapondera took his immediate family with him to the **Makombe** state in **Mozambique.**

Mapondera did not personally participate in the 1896–97 **Shona Revolt** in Southern Rhodesia, but was instead busy helping the Makombe to fight the **Portuguese.** Meanwhile, his old chiefdom fared badly in the Mashonaland Revolt. When he learned that his son had been killed and his cattle had been looted by the British, he returned home in early 1900 in a futile attempt to raise a new rebellion among the **Korekore.** After his followers were dispersed, he went north and allied with the last **Munhumutapa, Chioko.** With the aid of Chioko's soldiers Mapondera re-entered Mashonaland in early 1901 and attacked the administrative post at **Mount Darwin.** Again defeated, he returned to Mozambique to help the Makobe against the Portuguese again. The death of Chioko and the defeat of the Makombe the following year seem to have broken Mapondera's spirit to resist further. In August 1903 he returned to Mashonaland and surrendered to British authorities. Early the next year he was convicted of sedition and sentenced to seven years at hard labor. He died in prison during a hunger strike. (See **Mchemwa.**)

MARAMUCA (variant: Murimuka). **Portuguese** name for a trading **fair** and its surrounding district located just southwest of the **Umfuli River,** near present **Chegutu.** This fair seems to have been the southwesternmost Portuguese settlement in the country and was under the jurisdiction of the **Changamire** state during the 17th century. Maramuca was the center of a still-productive **gold** mining region and was unique in that it was inhabited by an isolated Zambezi **Tonga** community. The fair appears to have closed down around 1680.

MARANDELLAS see **MARONDERA**

MARANKE, JOHANE MOMBERUME (1912–1963). Founder of the largest independent church in the country: the African Apostolic Church of Johane Maranke. Maranke was born in the southwestern part of **Mutare District.** There he was partly educated and baptized by the American-based Methodist Episcopal Church (now **United Methodist Church**). He forsook a possible career in the Methodist clergy to become an ordinary laborer in **Mutare.**

Maranke had many visions from an early age. While in Mutare he claimed to have been told by God that he was the African John the Baptist and that he should form a church. That was 1932, when he returned to his homeland to begin his religious work. He quickly became nationally famous as a healer, exorcist, prophet, and teacher. He formed his own church, with his relatives filling most leadership posts, and he and his apostles began itinerating about the country. By 1940 there were more than 100 branches of his church. The church spread over an even wider area in the 1940s and 1950s as Maranke visited South Africa and countries north of the Zambezi. A leadership schism split his church on his death in 1963, but the main branch has continued to grow. By the mid-1960s an estimated 50,000 people within the country were members, with tens of thousands of other members in South Africa, **Botswana, Mozambique, Zambia,** Malawi, and Zaire. (See also **Chaza, Mai; Zwimba, M.**)

MARECHERA, DAMBUDZO (1952–August 18, 1987). Born in Vengere Township near **Rusape,** Marechera was one of the country's most highly acclaimed young writers in the 1980s. He attended St. Augustine's in **Penhalonga** and the University of Rhodesia (now UZ) in the early 1970s. He was expelled in 1973 for demonstrating against government policies. He continued his studies at New College, Oxford, but left in 1976 and became a free-lance writer in London. He published several poems and short stories and three novels: *The House of Hunger* (1978), *Black Sunlight* (1980), and *Mindblast* (1984). Similar to the work of many of Zimbabwe's African authors (see **Literature**), Marechera's novels deal with the themes of racial and individual alienation and deprivation caused by living in a society in which Africans possessed no authority of any kind.

MARI (Vamari; variant: Mhari). Branch of the **Karanga** cluster of **Shona,** part of whom were under the **Chivi** dynasty.

MARIMBA PARK. Suburb of **Harare** located c.16 km west-southwest of city center (at 17°53′S, 30°57′E). It was originally established by the government in 1961 to provide low-density housing for wealthy Africans, who were proscribed from buying homes in European areas. (See **Native [Urban Areas] Accommodation and Registration Act [1946]**.)

MARONDA MASHANU ("Five Wounds"). Independent mission founded by **A. S. Cripps**; located c.9 km northeast of **Chivhu** (at 18°55′S, 30°58′E). Between 1916 and 1926 Cripps operated the station as a branch of the nearby Anglican Wreningham Mission to the northeast. From 1930 till his death in 1952 he ran the mission independently of any organized body. The mission has since been sustained by its African members.

MARONDERA (Marandellas until 1982). A town located 71 km east of Harare on the main **railway** and **road** routes to **Mutare** and **Mozambique** (at 18°11′S, 31°33′E; alt. 1,660 m). The town takes its name from a local **Zezuru** chief's town. It serves as the administrative headquarters for both the **Marondera District** and **Mashonaland East Province.** Marondera is an important beef, dairy, **tobacco,** and wine producing center, and in 1992 had a population of 39,601, ranking it as one of the dozen largest towns in the country.

MARONDERA DISTRICT (Marandellas District until 1985). In the central part of **Mashonaland East Province,** the district was created in 1899, a year after the Harare-to-Mutare **railway** line was built through the area. The district was originally about 50 percent larger, but lost its southeastern wedge to create **Wedza District.** In addition to Wedza, the district borders the districts of **Goromonzi** and **Murehwa** on the north, **Makoni** on the east, **Chikomba** on the southeast, and **Harare** on the west. Prior to 1980, most of the district was reserved for Europeans, with the exception of some Tribal Trust Land (see **Communal Lands**) and **Purchase Area** land in the west. District population in 1992 was 144,487.

MASAPA (variant: Massapa). **Portuguese** trading **fair** located at the base of Mount Pfura (16°52′S, 31°37′E; see **Mukumbura District**). Established around 1575, Masapa quickly became the most important Portuguese center in the country because of its proximity to the headquarters of the

Munhumutapa. The resident Portuguese elected a leader to serve as *Capitão das portas* ("Captain of the gates")—a post confirmed by the reigning Munhumutapa and formalized by the Portuguese government. All traders entering or leaving the country had to pass through Masapa, where the *Capitão das portas* exacted taxes for the Munhumutapa and acted as local magistrate. Masapa lost its preeminent position to **Dambarare** in the early 17th century and was destroyed by a **Changamire** invasion in 1693.

MASEKO NGONI. First *Mfecane* band to enter the country in the early 19th century. Originally under the leadership of a man named Ngwane Maseko, this band appears to have migrated out of South Africa in the 1820s, passing through **Venda** territory, the present **Masvingo** area, and finally the **Harare** region. There they appear to have been joined by the **Ngoni** of **Nxaba**, with whom they defeated **Zwangendaba's** Ngoni. After c.1835 the Maseko Ngoni left the country through the **Mazowe** Valley. They traveled as far north as southern Tanzania, eventually turning south and settling in southern Malawi, where their state became known as the Gomani kingdom.

MASHABA The Mashaba Mountains form a range running along the western edge of the Central Plateau between the **Umfuli** and **Sebakwe** rivers. These mountains reach heights of over 1,400 m. Important dams have been built on the Sebadkwe and **Ngezi** rivers in gaps in the Mashabas.

MASHAVA. (Mashaba until 1982). Village located c.37 km west of **Masvingo** (at 20°3'S, 30°29'E). It has been an important **asbestos** mining center.

MASHAYAMOMBE CHINENGUNDU (variant: Mashiangombi) (d. July 23, 1897). **Shona** ruler and **Revolt** leader in 1896–97. During the mid-19th century Chinemgundu—whose dynastic title was Mashayamombe—led his branch of the **Zezuru** out of the present **Marondera District** to an area by the upper **Umfuli River** in the eastern **Chegutu District**. There he managed to maintain his independence despite **Ndebele** attacks in the 1860s. After the **BSAC** occupied the country in the early 1890s, his town was made a British administrative center. Despite the proximity of a British official, his town became one of the main planning centers for the Revolt that began in early 1896. There is some controversy about the degree to which Mashayamombe was influenced by religious leaders during the Revolt, but he clearly paid a visit to **Mkwati** in April and then was frequently visited by the **Kaguvi** medium, **Bonda**, and other religious officials during the following months. On June 14, 1896, Mashayamombe's people killed the local district commissioner, opening the **Shona Revolt.** Thereafter his fortified hill was one of the most active Revolt centers and was the Kaguvi medium's headquarters. The British made a special effort to defeat Mashayamombe, but he survived three major assaults in 1896 and then was left alone until early 1897. After **E. A. Alderson's** final assault in October 1896, Mashayamombe and "Kaguvi" were joined by Mkwati from

Matabeleland. On July 23, 1897, Mashayamombe was killed when British forces overwhelmed his hill and dynamited his cave refuges.

MASHOBANE (variants: Machobane; Matshobana) (fl. 1810s). Father of the future **Ndebele** king **Mzilikazi** and ruler of a small branch of **Khumalo** people in Zululand. In c.1816 Mashobane was executed by his father-in-law, Zwide, on suspicion of having aided the Zulu against the latter's Ndwandwe people. Mashobane's name later took a prominent place in the pantheon of Ndebele ancestors (see **Dlozi; Inxwala**). His name was also given to one of Bulawayo's African townships, Matshobana, during the 20th century.

MASHONALAND. During the mid-19th century, **Europeans** gave this name to the **Shona** territories east of **Matabeleland**, although many Shona did, and still do, live in both regions. Furthermore, many non-Shona peoples, including the **Tonga, Hlengwe,** and **Venda,** also live in parts of what has been called "Mashonaland." In 1890 the **BSAC** occupied Mashonaland and formalized use of the name as a territorial designation. Later in the 1890s the company divided all of what is now Zimbabwe into two roughly equal-size provinces. The somewhat larger eastern province was designated "Mashonaland," even though it included parts known as **Manicaland** and **Gazaland.** Later Manicaland and **Midlands** were made into separate provinces and Mashonaland was divided into northern and southern provinces. Still later, **Masvingo Province** was separated. In 1979, the two Mashonaland provinces were realigned to form the present three Mashonaland provinces (see **Provinces**). In colloquial usage the name "Mashonaland" is still frequently used in the same sense as it was in the 19th century.

Mashonaland Central Province covers 29,482 sq km and composes the districts of **Bindura, Guruve, Mazowe, Mukumbura, Muzarabani, Rushinga,** and **Shamva**.

Mashonaland East Province covers 26,813 sq km and includes the districts of **Goromonzi, Harare, Marondera, Mudzi, Murewa, Mutoko, Seke,** and **Wedza**.

Mashonaland West Province includes **Chegutu, Hurungwe, Kadoma, Kariba,** and **Makonde,** and covers an area of 55,737 sq km.

MASHONALAND FIELD FORCE (MFF). Name for the collection of British military units that fought against the **Shona** in the 1896 Revolt. The MFF was formed in August 1896, when Lt. Col. **E. A. H. Alderson** arrived in Salisbury with four companies of Imperial Mounted Infantry, which he combined with local **BSAC** and volunteer forces. The combined MFF force contained c.1,500 Europeans. The MFF operated successfully around Salisbury until the BSAC complained about paying its bills. By December 1896 it was out of the country and disbanded. Its place was taken by BSAC police (see **BSAP**).

MASS MEDIA TRUST. In January 1981 the government purchased the 42 percent interest of the **"Argus Group"** in the Rhodesian Printing and Publishing Company, thereby taking control of the country's five largest newspapers (see **Press**). The Mass Media Trust was then established to create editorial policy and make senior editorial appointments. In general, it has increased the number of African staff members on the papers and increased news coverage of Zimbabwe's majority African population.

MASUKU, LOOKOUT (d. April 5, 1986). Zimbabwe People's Revolutionary Army **(ZIPRA)** commander. Very little is known about Lookout Masuku's early life. He left school in the mid-1960s and went to **Zambia,** where he joined ZIPRA. Masuku apparently received advanced military and political training in the Soviet Union sometime in the late 1960s. In 1972 he was appointed commissar of ZIPRA. He held that post until 1978, when he was promoted to army commander. Masuku returned to Zimbabwe in late 1979 to help coordinate ZIPRA's participation in the **Lancaster House Conference** agreement which called for a cease-fire and the establishment of "assembly points" where ZIPRA and **ZANLA** combatants would gather. Following independence, he was appointed deputy commander of the **Zimbabwe National Army** and served in that post until 1982, at which time he was arrested on charges of conspiring against the government of Prime Minister **Robert Mugabe.** Masuku was tried in 1983 and acquitted, but continued to be held under a government detention order until early 1986, when he was released shortly before his death.

MASVINGO (Fort Victoria until 1982). Masvingo is the administrative and commercial center for both the **Masvingo District** and **Masvingo Province.** Masvingo is located just north of the **Zimbabwe Ruins** on the **Mtilikwe River** (at 20°5'S, 30°50'E; alt. 1,065 m). The site was chosen by the **Pioneer Column** in 1890, and a fort was built the following year to guard the main transport route to the north. European settlement grew, encouraged by local **mining** and by the town's favorable position in the transportation network. Conditions for Europeans remained unsettled, however, as the **Ndebele** continued to wage punitive military raids in the area. In July 1893 Ndebele *impi* raided particularly near the town, arousing European residents to demand **BSAC** retaliation (this was the "Victoria Incident"). The result was the **Ndebele War,** which had the ironic effect of initiating European settlement at **Bulawayo** and causing the town's own development to suffer as most northern commerce passed through **Matabeleland.** Construction in 1961 of the **Kyle Dam,** just southeast of the town, gave the area's tourist industry a boost by adding major recreational facilities to the already important attractions of Zimbabwe National Park. At the time of the 1992 census the population was 57,746.

MASVINGO DISTRICT (Victoria District until 1985). Covering 4,635 sq km of the west-central part of **Masvingo Province,** the district once extended south into what is now the **Chiredzi District.** Located on a transitional zone between the Central Plateau and the southeastern low veld, Masvingo is bordered by **Chivi** on the southwest, **Shurugwi** on the northwest, **Chirumanzu** and **Gutu** on the north, and **Zaka** on the east. District headquarters are at **Masvingo.** Other district centers and places of interest include **Mashaba, Zimbabwe Ruins,** and **Lake Kyle.** Prior to 1980, the central belt that encompasses these centers and the southern tip of the district were reserved for Europeans. The remaining parts of the district are now made up of mostly **Communal Lands**. District population in 1992 was 238,562.

MASVINGO PROVINCE (Victoria Province until 1985). One of eight administrative provinces in the country, Masvingo separates **Matabeleland South** on the west from **Manicaland** on the east and also borders **Midlands** on the north. On the southeast, Masvingo borders **Mozambique** between the **Sabi** and **Limpopo** rivers. The province covers 515,777 sq km and encompasses the districts **Bikita, Chiredzi, Chivi, Gutu, Masvingo, Mwenezi**, and **Zaka**.

MATABELE (variants: Matebele; Tebele). Name given to **Mzilikazi's** followers by South African **Sotho** peoples during the 1820s. Many meanings of the name have been suggested, but it is clear only that the Sotho had been calling **Nguni** immigrants from the east coast *Matabele* for centuries before Mzilikazi arrived in their country (see **Transvaal Ndebele**). Mzilikazi's following was but one of many *Mfecane* era bands called *Matabele* by the Sotho, but the name soon became primarily associated with his own people. Eventually, they adopted the name, giving it the **Nguni** form, *Amandebele*, which modern English renders as "**Ndebele.**"

Even after the Ndebele had left Sotho territory in 1838, most outsiders continued to call them "Matabele." This was largely because most visitors approached Ndebele country from the south, passing through Sotho territory and adopting Sotho forms of names. "Ndebele" is now the preferred name for the people, but "**Matabeleland**" has become fixed as a place name, and many people continue to use the name "Matabele."

MATABELE [National] HOME SOCIETY. Ndebele irredentist movement originally begun during the First World War by **Nyamanda**. The movement sought a national homeland for the Ndebele people, as well as restoration of the Ndebele kingship (see **Revolt**). The movement almost died out in the early 1920s but was revived in the late 1920s, when a formal "Matabele Home Society" constitution was drawn up and officers were elected. The society drew some Ndebele supporters away from the **RBVA** and **ICU**, but its appeal was narrowly ethnic and backward-looking, and the organization failed to have any impact on government policy during the 1930s.

MATABELE MISSION. LMS name for the mission it sent under **Robert Moffat** to **Matabeleland** in 1859. The LMS simultaneously sent a "Makololo Mission" to the **Kololo** of western **Zambia** in the hope that establishment of the two missions would help to mitigate hostilities between the Kololo and Ndebele. The Makololo Mission party was, however, devastated by fever, and that effort was abandoned. (See also **Hope Fountain; Inyati; Livingstone, David; LMS**.)

MATABELE WAR (1893) see **NDEBELE WAR**

MATABELELAND. During the mid-19th century, **Europeans** gave this name to the region around **Bulawayo** in which **Ndebele** settlements were concentrated (see **Matabele**). Gradually the name was applied to a much larger area, including many non-Ndebele territories. In 1893, **L. S.**

Jameson arbitrarily designated a border that separated Matabeleland from **Mashonaland.** This border started at the **Zambezi River,** followed the **Umniati River** to the **Central Plateau,** then continued down the **Shashe, Tokwe,** and **Lundi Rivers.** Once the entire country was under **BSAC** administration, the two regions were designated as separate administrative provinces. Matabeleland covered 47 percent of the country, Mashonaland the rest. Matabeleland was later divided into northern and southern provinces, which were fixed in 1962, while part of the original region helped to form **Midlands Province.**

Matabeleland North Province covers 76,813 sq km and borders **Botswana** to the west, while the **Zambezi River** and **Lake Kariba** separate it from **Zambia** to the north. The province encompasses the districts of **Binga, Bubi, Bulawayo, Hwange, Lupane, Nkayi,** and **Nyamandhlovu.**

Matabeleland South Province is in the southwestern part of the country and stretches along the borders with **Botswana** and **South Africa.** The province covers 54,941 sq km and comprises the districts of **Beitbridge, Bulilimamangwe, Gwanda, Insiza, Matobo,** and **Umzingwane.**

MATABELELAND RELIEF FORCE (MRF). First unit of British Imperial troops to fight against the **Ndebele** during the **1896 Revolt. H. C. O. Plumer** raised the MRF mainly among the mining communities between Kimberley and Mafeking in South Africa. About half of the MRF's c.800 men were former soldiers, including many who had served in the BBP and in the **Jameson Raid.** Under Plumer's command the MRF reached **Bulawayo** on May 14, 1896, clearing away the rebels around the town by the end of the month. MRF operations played a major role in turning the tide of the war against the Ndebele north of the **Matopo Hills.** (See also **Bulawayo Field Force; Carrington, F.**)

MATENDERE RUINS. Zimbabwe-type stone ruin in the **Buhera District** (at 19°32′S, 31°48′E). The main structure is an open-ended elliptical enclosure with a large decorated wall 168 m in length. The ruins have not been definitely dated, but were estimated by **G. Caton-Thompson** to have been contemporary with **Dhlo Dhlo.**

MATETSI. Village standing at the intersection of the Matetsi River and the **Bulawayo-**to-**Victoria Falls railway** line (at 18°5′S, 26°7′E; alt. 910 m). The Matetsi River rises in **Botswana** near **Pandamatenga,** flowing northeast till it meets the Zambezi below the **Batoka Gorge.**

MATIBI. Title of a chief of the Pfumbi branch of **Karanga** people living by the middle **Nuanetsi River.** By 1871 the Matibi was paying tribute to the **Ndebele.** He attempted to throw off Ndebele influence in the 1880s and was consequently attacked by them as late as 1892. The next year his people assisted the British in the **Ndebele War.** In the **1896 Revolt,** the Pfumbi also fought with the British against the Ndebele and their allies.

MATLOKOTLOKO (variant: Amatlokotloko) see **MAHLOKOHLOKO**

MATOBO DISTRICT. Matobo covers a narrow 7,230-sq-km area running directly south from **Bulawayo** to the **Botswana** border. The district borders the districts of **Bulilimamangwe** on the west, **Bulawayo** on the north, and **Umzingwane** and **Gwanda** on the east. **Matopos** is the administrative center. The southern part of the district is bisected by the **Shashani River** and is **Communal Land**. The northern part of the district is made up of commercial farms and ranches, except for the area of the Matopos National Park, part of the **Matopo Hills**. District population in 1992 was 89,281.

MATOJENI (a.k.a. Wirirani). Oracular shrine of the **Mwari cult**; located c.40 km southeast of **Bulawayo** on the northern fringe of the **Matopo Hills**. The shrine was founded at least as early as the mid-19th century, when it was one of four main Mwari cult centers. It still operates as the most influential and famous Mwari center in the country. Local priests send messengers (*vanyai*) over the southeastern parts of the country and the extreme northern part of the **Transvaal**, and they receive supplicants from the same region. (See also **Njelele**.)

MATOPE NYANHEHWE (a.k.a. Ndebedza; Mutavara) (fl. c.mid-15th century). Second ruler of the **Munhumutapa** state. After the death of his father **Mutota Nyatsimba** sometime before c. 1450, Matope acceded to the Munhumutapaship by engaging in an act of ritual intercourse with his half-sister, **Nehanda**, who became his consort. He then proceeded to extend his father's military conquests, subjugating the **Barwe, Manyika**, and other peoples as far east as the Indian Ocean. Matope's successors could not, however, hold his "empire" together. On his death in c.1480, he was succeeded by a son, Mavura Maombwe. Mavura was killed in a campaign within about a month. Another of Matope's sons, **Mukombero Nyahuma**, then became ruler.

MATOPO HILLS (variant: the Matopos). One of the country's most notable scenic and historic regions, the Matopos cover more than 3,000 sq km just below the **Figtree**-to-**Bulawayo road**. The hills are a spectacular assortment of granite **kopjes**, including large **dwalas** and bizarrely fractured "castle kopjes." Golati Mountain, at 1,550 m, is the highest point in the hills (at 20°29'S, 28°26'E).

Human occupation of the Matopos is estimated to go back 40,000 years. Among the innumerable **Stone Age** sites that pervade the hills, the most visually impressive are caves with **rock paintings** (see, e.g., **Bambatai; Nswatugi; Pomongwe;** etc.). By the mid-19th century the hills became the center of **Matojerri** and several other major **Mwari cult** shrines. In 1847 the Matopos were the focus of the first modern European foray into the country when **A. H. Potgieter** attacked the **Ndebele** there. In 1896 the Matopos became a major theater of war in the **Ndebele Revolt**.

In 1953 the Southern Rhodesian government set aside a 457 sq km section of the hills in northern **Matobo District** as the Rhodes Matopos National Park, which includes a 100 sq km game reserve. A popular tourist attraction in the park is **World's View dwala**, in which **Cecil Rhodes** and other European figures are interred. Less accessible is the grave of **Mzilikazi** in **Nthumbame Hill**, c.15 km to the northeast of the Word's View, just outside of the park.

MATOPOS. Village on the northern fringe of Matopos National Park serving as administrative center of **Matobo District** (at 20°25'S, 28°29'E).

MAUCH, KARL (May 1, 1837–April 1875). A German geologist and explorer, Mauch came to South Africa in 1864. In 1866 and 1867 he traveled in **Matabeleland** and **Mashonaland** and confirmed the presence of **gold** at both **Tati** and the **Hartey Hills.** Publication of his discoveries set off the first minor gold rush into the country and brought the first wave of **concession** hunters to the **Ndebele** court. In 1871 Mauch learned about the **Zimbabwe Ruins** from the Transvaal missionary Alex Merensky and set off in search of them. With the aid of **Adam Render**, he reached the ruins, but became stranded there for almost a year. During this time he compiled the first maps and descriptions of the ruins. Publications of his reports further stimulated European prospectors, also giving rise to the romantic myth that the Great Zimbabwe was the center of "King Solomon's Mines" (see **Ophir**). **R. N. Hall** later named the "Mauch Ruin" at Zimbabwe after him.

MAUND, EDWARD ARTHUR (1851–March 17, 1932). A British army officer, Maund served on **Charles Warren's** expedition in 1885. Afterwards he was delegated to announce the creation of the **Bechuanaland Protectorate** to **Lobengula** in neighboring **Matabeleland.** In late 1888 he returned to Matabeleland as a civilian, hoping to gain a mining **concession** for the company he had formed with George Cawston. He arrived at **Bulawayo** after the signing of the **Rudd Concession**, which he then tried to discredit with Lobengula. Partly on his initiative, he accompanied Lobengula's emissaries **Babayane** and **Mshete** to London. He returned to Matabeleland armed with arguments against **Cecil Rhodes'** party, but before he arrived there, he learned that his partner had joined Rhodes' group—a move he quickly emulated.

Although Maund had never traveled east of Bulawayo, **R. N. Hall** named one of the ruins groups at **Zimbabwe** after him.

MAUNGWE. Name of the country and of the people ruled by the **Makoni** dynasty.

MAVURA II MHANDE (a.k.a. Felipe) (c.1580s–May 25, 1652). The first **Munhumutapa** said to have been a "puppet" of the **Portuguese**, Mavura II acceded to the kingship in May 1629 after a combined African-Portuguese army helped him to oust **Nyambo Kapararidze**, a member of a rival ruling house. On May 24, 1629, Mavura signed a major treaty with the Portuguese that virtually made him a vassal of the Portuguese crown. Portuguese residents in the country became exempt from local law, and final authority and powers of taxation were given over to the "Captain of the Gates" at **Masapa**. More Portuguese entered the country and many were granted landed estates (*prazos*). Meanwhile, Mavura had to contend with Nyambo's continued resistance. Mavura died from an accidental gunshot wound in 1692 and was succeeded as Munhumutapa by his son **Siti Kazurukumusapa**. (For Mavura I, see under **Matope**.)

MAVURADONHA MOUNTAINS. A 1,200- to 1,500-m-high range forming the northern edge of the **Zambezi Escarpment** in the **Mukumbura District**.

MAWEMA, MICHAEL ANDREW (b.July 13, 1928). Active in the Railway African Workers' Union in the early 1950s, Mawema later became a leader in the **African National Congress**. He was abroad in early 1959 when many of the ANC leaders were arrested. After his return in 1960, he was for a short time president of the new **National Democratic Party**, being replaced by **Joshua Nkomo**. The following year he helped to form the **Zimbabwe National Party** to oppose the NDP. He joined the newly formed Zimbabwe African National Union (**ZANU**) in August 1963, and was almost immediately arrested. He was released in 1968 but restricted to the **Gutu** area for two years. In 1971 he was chosen by **Edson Sithole** as a second ZANU delegate to a meeting with Sir Alec Douglas Home in Harare, and thereby became a founder member of the **African National Council**. He mysteriously left the country in July 1972, going to the United States, where he attended Clark College and Teachers' College, Columbia University. In 1980 he first joined, then resigned from, the United African National Council, and then once again joined ZANU.

MAZOE see **MAZOWE**

"MAZOE PATROL." Incident in the **Shona Revolt** when a relief party from Harare rescued several Europeans besieged at Alice Mine, near **Mazowe**, on June 20, 1896.

MAZOE RIVER (variant: Mazowe). Rises just north of Harare, whence it flows north and then northeast, forming a brief stretch of the **border** with **Mozambique**, in which it enters the **Zambezi River**. Mazowe Dam, built in 1920, plugs a gap in the Iron Mask Hills c.40 km north of Harare. The dam serves to irrigate citrus farms in one of the country's most prosperous agricultural regions.

MAZORODZE, SIMON CHARLES (November 29, 1933–November 5, 1981). Born in **Mhondoro**, the son of a postman father and a mother who was chairperson of the Methodist Sangaro rural area. He attended several primary schools, graduating from **Waddilove**. After completing **Goromonzi** Secondary School, where he was a member of the **Capricorn Africa Society**, he studied medicine at the University of Natal in Durban, South Africa. He qualified in 1962, then returned to the country and took a government position as a medical officer at Harare Hospital, where he later specialized in obstetrics and gynecology (1967). In 1963 Mazorodze was a founding member of the **Zimbabwe African National Union**, but because he was a civil servant he was forced to work underground, giving financial support to the party. In 1967 he was transferred to Ndanga Hospital, southeast of Masvingo. In 1974 he left the government service and began to be more openly involved in political activities. He became heavily involved in the clandestine collection of financial support for **ZANLA**, and at night often treated wounded guerrilla fighters in the bush. In 1980 he was elected a member of **Parliament** from the **Masvingo Province** and was subsequently appointed deputy minister of health, and later minister of health. Following his death, he was buried at **Heroes' Acre** on November 8, 1981.

MAZOWE (Mazoe until 1982). Administrative headquarters for **Mazowe District**, located at the southern boundary of the district (at 11°31′S, 30°58′E).

MAZOWE DISTRICT (Mazoe District until 1985). Located northwest of Harare, Mazowe District covers 3,980 sq km in **Mashonaland Central Province**. It was originally almost twice as large, but lost its eastern area to form the **Bindura** and **Shamva** districts. The district borders the districts of **Harare** on the south, **Makonde** and **Guruve** on the west, **Mukumbura** on the north, and Bindura and **Goromonzi** on the east. Towns in the district include **Concession, Jumbo Mine, Amandas,** and Mvurwi. Prior to 1980, most of the district was reserved for Europeans, except for Tribal Trust Land (see **Communal Lands**) in the northeast. District population in 1992 was 198,319.

MBALABALA (Balla Balla until 1982). Located c.55 km due southeast of Bulawayo on the **West Nicholson railway** line (at 20°27'S, 29°3'E; alt. 1,098 m). The village serves as the railhead for the **Filabusi** mining region.

MBERENGWA (Belingwe until 1982). The administrative center for **Mberengwa District** in **Matabeleland South Province** (20°29'S, 29°55'E; alt. 1,065 m). Founded as a mining town in the 1890s, Mberengwa is now the center of a varied **mineral** industry, including important **asbestos, gemstone,** and **chrome** mines.

MBERENGWA DISTRICT (Belingwe District until 1985). Now covering 6,020 sq km in **Midlands Province**, it formerly included parts of the present **Zvishavane District,** which borders it on the north. The district also borders the districts of **Insiza** on the west, **Gwanda** and **Mwenezi** on the south, and a small section of **Chivi** on the east. Prior to 1980, the northern part of the district was reserved for Europeans, with most of the remainder being Tribal Trust Lands (see **Land Tenure Act**).

MBIGO MASUKU (c.1800s–June 1870). An **Ndebele** *induna,* Mbigo was apparently one of **Mzilikazi's** original followers out of Zululand. He achieved immense prestige in 1847, when his Zwangendaba *ibutho* rebuffed **A. H. Potgieter's** Afrikaner raiding party into the **Matopo Hills**. By the 1860s Mbigo was connected to Mzilikazi's family by marriage and was the head of an elite group of *amabutho.* After Mzilikazi died in 1868, Mbigo steadfastly supported the **Nkulumane** faction in the succession dispute. When **Lobengula** was installed as king in early 1870, Mbigo and his men refused to recognize him. Troops loyal to Lobengula crushed the rebels in a single battle at the Zwangendaba town in June 1870. Mbigo himself was killed. Lobengula pardoned the rebel survivors, but many fled the country and later joined another dissident, **Mangwane**.

MBIRA. Shona musical instrument of a type popularly known throughout southern Africa as "African pianos" or "thumb pianos." *Mbiras* contain 25 to 30 iron rods fixed to resonant wooden bases of various shapes. The instruments are held between the hands so that the player's thumbs can pluck the rods, which cover several octaves. The *mbira* is one of the most melodious Shona instruments, and has long been played by professional performers at social and ritual gatherings. (See **Music.**)

MBIRE. Traditional **Shona** name for a region between the **Dande** and **Guruhuswa,** which apparently encompassed the area around the present

Chegutu and **Marondera** districts. The name Mbire was also applied to a section of the **Zezuru** people ruled by the **Svosve** dynasty.

MBULALE (variants: Bulali; Umbulali) see **MZIZI, WILLIAM**

MCHELA CAVE (a.k.a. Cave of Hands). Located near **West Nicholson** in the **Gwanda District** (at 21°8'S, 29°2'E), Mchela Cave contains very fine polychrome **rock paintings** of elephants and giraffes. It is most noted, however, for its unique collection of hundreds of human handprints painted on the walls. Human remains have rarely been found in such cave sites, but Mchela contained a walled-up female mummy devoid of artifacts.

MCHEMWA (d.Aug. 1909). **Shona Revolt** leader. A son of the **Nhowe** ruler **Mangwende**, Mchemwa was a vociferous opponent of British occupation during the early 1890s. In June 1896 he led the Nhowe into rebellion, starting with the killing of the missionary **Bernard Mizeki**. After a few months of active fighting, he and his father retreated to the Bogoto Hills (17°18'S, 31°52'E). In September 1897 he reluctantly joined his father in surrender, but only after having failed to persuade the Nhowe to migrate with him to **Barwe** country. A year later he assembled other recalcitrant rebels, collected previously cached arms, and went east. For four and a half years his band roamed the eastern part of **Mashonaland** in a rare demonstration of residual violent resistance (see **Mapondera**). He surrendered in April 1903 and was killed six years later by a fellow Nhowe in revenge for a murder he had allegedly committed during his roaming period.

MEALIE. Widely used southern African term for **maize**. The word derives from Portuguese *milho* for a European variety of millet and has sometimes been loosely applied to other kinds of grain.

MELSETTER see **CHIMANIMANI**

MERENSKY, ALEX see under **BERLIN MISSIONARY SOCIETY**

METHODIST MISSIONS. The first Methodist missionaries to work in the country were agents of the London-based **Wesleyan Methodist Missionary Society**, who started at Salisbury in 1891. The Wesleyan Church is now known as the Methodist Church in Zimbabwe. The American Methodist Episcopal Church followed in 1897, starting its work at Umtali (now **Mutare**; see **United Methodist Church**). Black South African missionaries of the American-based **African Methodist Episcopal Church** started at Bulawayo in 1900. Another American-based society, the Free Methodist Church, began work in the southeastern low veld in 1939. (See **Missions**.)

METRICATION. In 1972 the government officially switched the country from the Imperial System of Weights and Measurements to the International System of Metric Weights and Measures. (On decimation, see **Currency**.)

MFECANE. Twentieth-century **Nguni** neologism equivalent to the term *Difaqane* ("the crushing") in **Sotho** languages. Widely used in modern historiography, *Mfecane* refers to the era of Zulu expansion in South

Africa during the 1820s and 1830s, when escalating northern Nguni warfare drove marauding bands onto the high veld. More broadly, *Mfecane* refers to the diaspora of new South African conquest states north of the **Limpopo River** during the same era. Most of these states, which included the **Ndebele, Kololo, Ngoni,** and **Gaza** peoples, passed through present Zimbabwe, disrupting the **Changamire** empire and unsettling the entire country.

MFENGU (variant: Fingo). Somewhat amorphous **Nguni-speaking** society living in the eastern Cape Province of South Africa. The first Mfengu were refugees from Natal, driven south in the 1820s by the Zulu wars of the *Mfecane.* Nicknamed Mfengu, "beggars," these refugees became alienated from their new Xhosa and other southern Nguni neighbors and sought to ally with the British colonial government by adopting Christianity and Western education rapidly. Individual Mfengu and families, such as **William Mzizi,** began entering **Matabeleland** in the mid-19th century. Others entered with the British as employees and soldiers during the 1890s. **Cecil Rhodes** thought the Mfengu would make useful African allies in Southern Rhodesia, so he sent **F. R. Thompson** to the Transkei in 1898 to recruit settlers. Hundreds of Mfengu responded to the scheme, and most became farmers around **Fingo Location.**

At first the Mfengu identified their interests with those of the **BSAC** government who sought exemption from discriminatory laws affecting Africans (see, e.g., **Pass Laws**). Gradually, however, they became disillusioned as the BSAC reneged on promises to allocate more land and generally treated the Mfengu indifferently. Many Mfengu, such as the Hlazo and Sojini families, then allied with local Africans and played leading roles in such movements as the **Matabele [National] Home Society** and the **RBVA.** One of the most outstanding of these leaders was **Martha Ngano.**

MFUNDISI (pl., *abafundisi*). **Sindebele** term for teacher or minister, usually synonymous with "the reverend." In **Chishona** the term is rendered *mufundisi.*

MGAGAO DECLARATION. In late 1975, the Zimbabwe African National Union (**ZANU**) and its military wing **ZANLA** (Zimbabwe African National Liberation Army) faced what many observers consider their greatest crisis of leadership. In December 1974, political leaders, including **Robert Mugabe** and **Ndabaningi Sithole,** had been released from prison. Mugabe had replaced Sithole as leader of ZANU while in prison in the early 1970s, but this change was not generally known or accepted outside of ZANU's central committee. Once out of prison, Sithole tried to reassert his leadership over the party and was opposed by Mugabe. The ensuing leadership struggle created general confusion among both ZANU cadres and ZANLA combatants, as few knew whose orders or policies to follow.

The factionalism was compounded by the assassination of **Herbert Chitepo** in March 1975. The Zambian government arrested a number of high-ranking ZANLA leaders, including its overall commander and chairman of the **DARE, Josiah Tongogara.** They were charged with Chitepo's death, which according to Zambian authorities was the result of "tribalist" factions within ZANU and ZANLA. As a result of the struggle for leadership and the detention of ZANLA's top commanders, the armed struggle against the Rhodesian government virtually came to a halt.

In the midst of these problems, in October 1975, a meeting between the detained ZANLA leaders and a number of lower-level commanders (who were forced to disguise themselves and present false credentials in order to see Tongogara and the others) was held in the Mpima prison in Lusaka, **Zambia**. The detained leaders wrote a letter stating their support for Mugabe in the leadership struggle and strongly denounced Sithole for his actions in downplaying the necessity for armed struggle and holding talks with **Ian Smith** earlier in 1975 and for not supporting the imprisoned ZANLA leaders in their claims of innocence. They instructed that the letter be taken to the ZANLA training camp at Mgagao, Tanzania. The letter was generally accepted, and 43 ZANLA field commanders signed what has become known as the Mgagao Declaration. They reaffirmed their belief that armed struggle inside the country was the only way to liberate Zimbabwe from white rule, declared continued support for the imprisoned leaders and requested that they be allowed to continue the war. The declaration also condemned Sithole for his participation in the African National Council (**ANC**), as well as its other leaders, **James Chikerema, Abel Muzorewa**, and **Joshua Nkomo**. It did not go as far as the earlier letter in proclaiming Mugabe's leadership of ZANU and ZANLA, but it did state that the commanders considered him the one leader most in line with their goals and that in the future they would speak only through Mugabe to the ANC or the leaders of the **Frontline States**. The declaration was then circulated to ZANLA camps throughout **Mozambique** and shortly won the endorsement of the majority of ZANLA's field commanders and combatants.

The Mgagao Declaration has been noted as a turning point for both Mugabe and Sithole. Acceptance by a majority of field commanders ended any chance Sithole had of asserting control over ZANLA, and thereby effectively ended his claim to lead ZANU. While he later took part in the **Internal Settlement** negotiations, Sithole never again held political power at any level. For Mugabe, on the other hand, it marked his emergence as the recognized leader of ZANU. Once he had been accepted by ZANLA, in short order the Organization of African Unity and the leaders of the Frontline States also recognized him as a major political figure in the liberation movement and as spokesman for ZANU and ZANLA. Mugabe then solidified his position as leader of ZANU, and has not been seriously challenged in that post since the Mgagao Declaration.

MHANGURA (Mangula until 1982). Town located 45 km north of **Zave** in the **Makonde District** (at 16°54'S, 30°9'E; alt. 1,370 m). The town developed rapidly after 1959, when the Mhangura **copper** mine opened. Since the late 1970s, the mine has been the country's leading copper producer, and is one of the few major modern copper mines not established over precolonial African workings. By 1985 the mine was producing one-half of all copper mined in the country.

MHLABA KHUMALO (variant: Umhlaba) (d.June 1892). **Ndebele** *induna*. During the interregnum following **Mzilikazi**'s death, Mhlaba's father **Mncumbathe** served as regent and Mhlaba himself participated in one of the embassies to Natal that searched for the missing heir

Nkulumane. When his father died a few years later, Mhlaba inherited his office as hereditary regent. By the late 1870s he was regarded as one of the four most influential *izinduna* in the kingdom. During the troubled period leading up to the **1893 Ndebele War**, Mhlaba's political enemies accused him of having supported Nkulumane's claims to the kingship against those of **Lobengula**. In June 1892 he and most of his family were wiped out by the Imbizo *ibutho*. However, his brother Mnyenyezi and his son Ntenende escaped the purge. The next year they acted as guides for **P. W. Forbes**' northern invasion column, which occupied **Bulawayo**.

MHLAHLANDLELA. Ndebele *ibutho* first raised by **Mzilikazi** in the **Transvaal** in the 1820s. **Gwabalanda** appears to have been the *ibutho's* first *induna*. By 1813 Mhlahlandlela was posted by the upper **Khami River** in **Matabeleland**. From that date Mzilikazi made the *ibutho's* town his chief residence. In 1941 European residents of the country erected the "Mzilikazi Memorial" at the spot where the town had stood at the time of Mzilikazi's death (at 20°20'S, 28°34'E).

MHONDORO (variant: *mondoro*). **Chishona** word for "lion" and tutelary spirits popularly called "lion spirits." *Mhondoro* spirits typically communicate through living mediums whom they possess after residing in the bodies of young lions. Such mediums, or *svikiro*, assume the personalities of their spirits and are themselves often called *mhondoro*. Most *mhondoro* are believed to be spirits of important ancestors—typically political rulers—and are closely associated with the welfare of whole communities, in contrast to the spirits of ordinary **midzimu**, who look after only individual or family interests (see also **Gombwe**). *Mhondoro* are attributed with powers of rainmaking, prophecy, divination, and healing, and they also function as intermediaries with the high god **Mwari**. In contrast to other healers, such as *nganga*, the *mhondoro* eschew the use of medicines in their work. *Mhondoro* mediums collect followings of acolytes, maintain shrines, and receive propitiary gifts. These organized activities have been described as "cults."

Mhondoro cults have been a major part of **Shona religion** since at least the 16th century. The mediums have also played an important role in the processes of political succession. Succession disputes were, and are, generally turned over to *mhondoro* for resolution, but the mediums rarely made recommendations that ran counter to popular sentiment. Their political role can thus be seen as the articulation of consensus within communities.

During the 19th century a famous *mhondoro*, **Chaminuka**, became a center of central **Shona** resistance to **Ndebele** domination. In the **1896–97 Revolt**, a number of *mhondoro* played key roles in organizing resistance to British occupation. The most notable of these, **Kaguvi** and **Nehanda**, have been described as instigators of the **Shona Revolt** and as representatives of a new kind of millennarian leadership that anticipated modern African nationalism. This view, developed mainly by T. O. Ranger, has been challenged by historians who argue that while the *mhondoro* clearly played an important part in the Revolt, they did so merely in their traditional role as articulators of majority opinion. (See also **Dzivaguru**.)

Despite the failure of the 1896–97 Revolt, the influence of *mhondoro* has remained great in the eastern parts of Zimbabwe, where their mediums have carried on their traditional functions. During the war for independence, many *mhondoro* became closely associated with the nationalist movements. Unlike secular political leaders, these *mhondoro* mediums were rarely suppressed by the white government, and many actively supported the **ZANLA** freedom fighters. According to one recent study, ZANLA combatants actively sought mediums' advice on dealing with the rural population in many districts. By showing veneration toward the ancestors and defining the war as a struggle to regain control of access to land, combatants were largely able to win the local support necessary to operate successfully against the **Rhodesian security forces**. Since independence, the government has continued to claim that it represents the will of the ancestors and has kept the allegiance of most mediums.

MI-. Chishona prefix (Class 4), normally used for plural forms of nouns starting with **mu-** . Thus for a term such as *midzimu,* see **Mudzimu.**

MIAMI see **MWAMI**

MICA. One of the most important nonmetallic **minerals** produced in the country, with the notable exception of **coal**. Significant mica production began at **Mwami** in 1919. A second major production center opened at **Rusape** in 1927. Through the 1920s production was valued at around £20,000 per year, reaching a peak of £52,000 in 1930. Production almost ceased during the 1930s but was revived by the Second World War's new demands. Between 1944 and 1948, production varied between £106,000 and £153,000 per year. Afterwards, production tapered off to £22,000 in 1964. Total production between 1919 and 1964 was valued at £1,697,000.

MIDLANDS PROVINCE. Covering 55,977 sq km in the center of the country, Midlands is the only one of the country's eight provinces not to touch an international border. Midlands is the country's major beef-producing province and presently includes the districts of **Chikomba, Chirumanzu, Gokwe, Gweru, Kwekwe, Mberengwa, Shurungwi,** and **Zvishavane.** The province's administrative center is located at **Gweru.**

MIGUEL, DOM (fl. 1600–1670). The first black southern African ordained a Christian minister, Dom Miguel's original African name is not known. He is known only to have been a son of **Munhumutapa Gatsi Rusere**. It appears that Dom Miguel joined an order of **Portuguese** Dominicans when his father signed a treaty with **Diogo Simoes Madeira** in 1607. He was then taken to Goa in India, where he is said to have later been made a doctor of divinity and the vicar of a Goanese church. He never returned to Shona country and appears to have died by 1670.

MILLET. Important African cereal crop, several varieties of which have been grown throughout southern Africa for many centuries. In the last hundred years or so, millet has tended to give way to **maize** as the primary African grain. (See **Agriculture.**)

MILTON, WILLIAM HENRY (Dec. 3, 1854–March 6, 1930). Early **BSAC** official. An Englishman, Milton came to South Africa in 1878 and entered the Cape civil service. By 1891 he had risen to the post of private secretary to Prime Minister **Cecil Rhodes,** whose confidence and friendship he won. In August 1896 Milton was transferred to Southern Rhodesia to assist in reorganizing the administration after the **Jameson Raid** and **Revolts** had revealed how chaotically the BSAC government was being run. Milton was soon also made chief secretary for native affairs. In July 1897 he became acting **administrator,** replacing **A. H. Grey.** In December 1898 his position was formalized when he was designated administrator of **Mashonaland** and senior administrator of Southern Rhodesia. In the latter capacity Milton oversaw **Arthur Lawley**'s administration of **Matabeleland** until 1901, when he himself became sole administrator for all of Southern Rhodesia. During his tenure of office Milton rebuilt the administration, following South African colonial precedents, and brought in many experienced South African civil servants, such as **P. D. L. Fynn.** On his retirement in 1914 he was succeeded by **F. P. D. Chaplin.**

MINERALS/MINING. Zimbabwe is said to have been the only British colony occupied solely because of its mineral wealth. True or not, it is clear that the **BSAC** and its supporters were lured to the country by the prospect of finding goldfields as rich as those discovered in the Transvaal's Rand in the 1880s. Although the country's **gold** reserves proved ultimately disappointing, mineral production long dominated the country's economic development and remains very important today. Diversity is now the most outstanding characteristic of the mining sector, with more than 50 kinds of minerals in commercial production.

 Iron is perhaps the most widespread commercial mineral in the country, and has been mined since at least A.D. 200. Production now meets local industrial needs, but its total value does not place the ore among the top mineral products.

 Copper has also long been mined in the country. Its exploitation in the 20th century was initially slow, but production increased rapidly after 1954.

 Gold has also been mined since the first millennium. Its role in international trade and **Shona** state formation was especially great from about the 12th to the 18th centuries. Production virtually ceased during the 19th century, until old workings were discovered by **Europeans**. Exaggerated estimates of the country's gold reserves helped the **BSAC** to obtain capital investors in Europe, and promises of mining rights lured early settlers. Although production fell short of expectations, gold ranked as the leading mineral produced and exported until the Second World War. In the late 1970s, as a result of a major rise in the international price, gold production increased and once again became the most valuable mineral produced in the country—a position it has maintained.

 Asbestos displaced gold as the most valuable mineral product between the early 1950s and the late 1970s. It now ranks third in value of production. **Coal** production has also been important throughout this century, although relatively little has been exported. **Nickel** has been mined in the country since 1928, and by the early 1990s became the second most valuable mineral produced. Other important minerals include **chrome, gemstones, lithium, mica, silver,** and **tin.** Sufficient limestone is quarried at **Colleen Bawn** to meet national cement needs. Mineral production in the 20th century was initially characterized by a vast number of small-scale European producers known as **"small-workers,"** but the historical trend has been towards concentration of production among large mines. Emphasis on mineral development during the early 20th century greatly influenced the patterns of urbanization and largely dictated the routes of the country's main **railway** lines. The diversity of minerals available facilitated local industrialization by meeting almost every major need with the notable exception of petroleum, which the country lacks completely.

MISSIONS, CHRISTIAN. Missionaries have played an important role in the history of the country. The first missionary to enter the country was **Gonçalo da Silveira,** a **Portuguese** Jesuit who succeeded in baptizing the reigning **Munhumutapa** in 1561. Silveira's murder at the hands of the **Shona** produced a Portuguese reaction that brought more intense European penetration of the country in the late 16th century. Over the next century, Dominicans established missions throughout the northeastern part of the country (see **Fairs**). Their success in proselytizing is unknown, however, and by the 1690s they were all out of the country.

The next missionaries to work among the country's peoples were Congregationalists. Agents of the **American Board of Commissioners for Foreign Missions** spent a fruitless year among the **Ndebele** when the latter were living in the western **Transvaal** in the 1830s. ABC agents later worked among the southeastern Shona in the 1890s. Meanwhile, their British counterparts of the LMS established the first permanent mission among the Ndebele in **Matabeleland** in 1859. Jesuits of the **Zambezi Mission** followed there in 1879. The Ndebele rulers discouraged European contact with Shona peoples, but agents of the **Dutch Reformed Church, Berlin Missionary Society,** and **Anglican** bodies made tentative efforts in **Mashonaland** in the 1880s. (See also **Coillard, F.**) None of these missions had any real success in gaining converts through this period, and the missionaries relentlessly criticized Ndebele society and called for British conquest. After the **BSAC** occupied Mashonaland in 1890, **Cecil Rhodes** personally encouraged missionary work by allocating generous tracts of land to 13 different societies during the 1890s. The already established bodies expanded their fields of operation, while **Methodist** and many other missionary societies entered the country. The BSAC government did not want the bother and expense of establishing an educational system for Africans, so they encouraged the missions to assume this responsibility by providing financial subsidies. (See **Education.**) By the 1920s there were 15 recognized mission bodies in the country, and these had formed a powerful lobbying organization, the **Southern Rhodesian Missionary Conference.**

In the years before independence the role of foreign missionaries became increasingly anomalous. Many missionaries persistently criticized the government's policies affecting Africans (see, e.g., **Lamont, D.**), but they nevertheless became increasingly alienated from African peoples. After the 1950s there was a strong African drift away from established mission churches into independent, African-run churches (see, e.g., **Chaza, M.; Maranke, J.; Zwimba, M.**). Some African clerics in the established churches became prominent leaders in the nationalist movement, but in very recent times European missionaries themselves frequently were the victims of violent attacks.

MITCHELL, GEORGE (April 1, 1867–July 4, 1937). Third **prime minister** of Southern Rhodesia (1933). Mitchell came to the country as a bank manager in 1895 and eventually rose to a prominent position in the **mining** industry. He meanwhile entered electoral politics. In 1930 he joined **H. U. Moffat**'s cabinet, and then replaced the latter as prime minister after **Rhodesian Party** leaders asked Moffat to resign in 1933. Already 66 years old when he assumed the office, Mitchell overburdened himself by taking on three additional ministerial portfolios. After less than three months in office, he lost his **Assembly** seat in the September 1933 general election and was replaced as prime minister by **Godfrey Huggins**.

MITFORD, BERTRAM (June 13, 1855–Oct. 4, 1914). English writer and traveler whose more than 40 popular novels included a series of romances based on **Ndebele history**. Mitford came to South Africa in 1814 to raise livestock but soon joined the Cape civil service, and by the late 1880s was proprietor of the *East London Advertiser*. From that period to the end of his life, he wrote popular novels, set mostly in southern Africa.

Mitford's *The King's Assegai* (1894) and *The White Shield* (1895), the first novels in a four-part series narrated by a character named "Untuswa," trace Ndebele history from **Mzilikazi**'s break with Shaka through the Ndebele-Zulu wars of the mid-1830s. These stories, which have thematic and structural similarities to *Mlimo: The Rise and Fall of the Matabele*, written later by **A. A. Campbell**, are among the earliest fictional works dealing with Zimbabweans. Only recently has it been discovered that the books contain information on Ndebele history that found its way into the presumably historical works of A. T. Bryant and others.

Mitford's later Zimbabwe-related novels treat Europeans caught up in struggles to conquer African societies. *The Triumph of Hilary Blackland* (1901) is set in the **1893 Ndebele War**; *John Ames, Native Commissioner* (1900), *In the Whirl of the Rising* (1904), and *A Legacy of the Granite Hills* (1909) are set in the **1896 Revolt** era. Despite Mitford's evident interest in the Ndebele and Zimbabwe, it is not clear what, if any, experience he personally had in the country. It is possible he got some of his ideas about the country from **Johannes Colenbrander**, a close friend to whom he dedicated *John Ames*. He also wrote a biography of Colenbrander, but the manuscript was lost around 1910.

MIZEKI, BERNARD (a.k.a. Mamiyeri Mizeka Gwambe) (c.1860–June 18, 1896). Famed Christian martyr. Born in **Mozambique** near Inhambane—apparently of **Tsonga** parents—Mizeki went to Cape Town with other boys to look for work in the early 1870s. There he attended a small mission school and was baptized an Anglican in 1886. He trained at a divinity college until 1891, when he accompanied Bishop **Knight-Bruce** to **Mashonaland.** Mizeki himself opened a small mission station near **Mangwende**'s town in central Mashonaland. He soon became fluent in **Chishona** and established a good rapport with the local people. Early in

1896 he married one of the Mangwende's granddaughters. When the **Shona Revolt** broke out the following June, Mizeki ignored advice to leave the country. On June 18th he was one of the first people killed by rebels led by **Mchemwa**.

MJAAN see **MTSHANI**

MKALIPHI see **KALIPHI**

MKUMBE CAVE see **MAKUMBE CAVE**

MLIMO (variants: *Umlimo; Molimo; Modimo; Morimo*). Generic **Sindebele** term for "god." In traditional **Sotho** religion, Modimo is the name of a remote high god regarded as the creator and controller of natural phenomena. These concepts are similar to **Ndebele** beliefs about the **Nguni** god **Nkulunkulu**. When the Ndebele kingdom started absorbing Sotho-speaking peoples during the 1820s, the Ndebele fused the concepts of Nkulunkulu and *Modimo*, naturalizing the latter name to *Molimo* or *Mlimo*. Christian missionaries have adopted "Mlimo" for "Jehovah," thereby further widening usage of the term to encompass almost any high god. Europeans have also frequently interchanged "Mlimo" with **Mwari**, the name of the central **Shona** high god. It should be noted that, in former times at least, Africans made a clear distinction between the concepts of Mlimo and Mwari and that the two names are not properly interchangeable. (See **Religion**.)

MLUGULU KHUMALO (variant: Umluguru) (fl. 1870s–1900s). An important **Ndebele** *induna,* Mlugulu was accused by Europeans of having killed **R. R. Patterson** in 1878. At about the same time, he succeeded his father Mlota as head of the Eyengo cluster of towns situated just northeast of the **Matopo Hills**. As a member of the royal **Khumalo** family, Mlugulu, his brother Nungu, and another relative, Bozongwana (d.1894) were officiating as "dance doctors" at the annual *inxwala* festivals by the late 1880s. These duties gave rise to the mistaken notion that Mlugulu was the "high priest" of the Ndebele nation—a misconception reinforced by recent religiously oriented interpretations of the **1896 Ndebele Revolt**, in which he played a major part. (See **Mkwati; Mwari**.) After King **Lobengula**'s death in 1894 Mlugulu became a leading advocate of restoration of the kingship. After the Revolt began, **Mlugulu, Sikombo,** and **Dhliso** were the main leaders in the eastern Matopos fighting, and they helped to install **Nyamanda** as king. In August 1896 Mlugulu was one of the *izinduna* who negotiated a truce with **Cecil Rhodes** in the famous "*indabas.*" Though he narrowly escaped execution by the British afterwards, he was made a salaried chief. Mlugulu continued to agitate for restoration of the Ndebele monarchy, calling for Lobengula's son **Njube** to return from South Africa in 1898.

MNANGAGWA, EMMERSON DAMBUDZO. (b. 1946). Considered one of the more radical of Zimbabwe's young politicians, Mnangagwa was born at **Zvishavane**. He attended Lundi School for a time, but concluded his secondary education at Kafue School in **Zambia**. As a student he was a member of both the Zambian United National Independence Party and the Zimbabwe African Peoples Union (**ZAPU**). Shortly after **Ndabaningi**

Sithole, Leopold Takawira, Robert Mugabe, and others broke away from ZAPU and formed the Zimbabwe African National Union **(ZANU)** in August, 1963, Mnangagwa left ZAPU and joined the new party in Zambia. He was sent to the People's Republic of China for military training and then returned to the country in mid-1963 when he led a group of Chinese trained **guerrillas** on a mission to blow up a train near **Masvingo.** He was arrested inside the country two years later and convicted of sabotage. Because he was still legally a minor, he escaped the death penalty but was sentenced to ten years in prison. He served nine years at the Khami Maximum Security Prison before being released as part of a general amnesty in 1974. He left the country and returned to Zambia, where he studied law and was admitted to the Zambian bar in 1976. He was then sent to **Mozambique** by ZANU and in 1977 was elected to the party's Central Committee. During this period in Mozambique, Mnangagwa became Mugabe's primary adviser on matters pertaining to security.He returned to the country in early 1980 and participated in the elections in March of that year. Following the elections, Mugabe named him minister of state in the **prime minister's** office, with responsibilities for state security. In that position, Mnangagwa was responsible for integrating the two liberation armies, the Zimbabwe People's Revolutionary Army **(ZIPRA)** and the Zimbabwe African National Liberation Army **(ZANLA),** with the remnants of the former **Rhodesian security forces,** into the Zimbabwe National Army **(ZNA).** He also helped to forge a mutual defense and security agreement with Mozambique which committed ZNA forces to duty inside Mozambique in an attempt to protect Zimbabwean **railway** traffic from attacks by the **Mozambique National Resistance.** In the mid-1980s he gained a reputation as a hardline supporter of ZANU and Prime Minister Mugabe and alienated many ZAPU supporters when he directed the government's heavy-handed crackdown on **dissidents** in **Matabeleland.** In 1988, following the promulgation of the **Unity Pact** between ZANU and ZAPU, President Mugabe appointed Mnangagwa minister of justice, legal, and parliamentary affairs. He retained that position throughout the 1990s,

MNCENGENE KHUMALO (variants: Mncene; Ningi; Nini; etc.) (d. April 1880). Sister of **Lobengula.** During the first decade of her brother's reign as **Ndebele** king, Mncengence was probably the most powerful woman in the kingdom. Lobengula then had no "royal wife" (see **Inkosikazi**) so he allowed the unmarried Mncengence to exercise considerable influence in his court. Unfortunately, her privileged position and close friendships with European traders earned her many enemies. Her position was directly challenged when Lobengula married the Gaza princess **Xwalile** in 1879. When Xwalie failed to become pregnant within a suitable period of time, Mncengence was accused by enemies of having bewitched the new royal wife. The following year Lobengula reluctantly assented to Mncengence's execution on these charges.

MNCUMBATHE KHUMALO (variants: Ncombate; Nombati; Umkumbaze; Uncombata; etc.) (c.1780s–c.1872/3). Hereditary regent and top adviser in the **Ndebele** kingdom. One of **Mzilikazi's** original followers out of Zululand, Mncumbathe inherited his rank as Ndebele regent from his **Khumalo** forebears. In 1829 he went to **Kuruman** to invite **Robert Moffat**

to visit Mzilikazi in the central Transvaal. Six years later he went to Cape Town as Mzilikazi's ambassador and signed a treaty of friendship with the British governor, Benjamin D'Urban. Through apparently somewhat older than Mzilikazi, Mncumbathe assumed active rule over the Ndebele kingdom after the latter's death in 1868. For 18 months he maintained firm control over the kingdom while working to have **Lobengula** recognized as the legitimate successor. He opposed the **Nkulumane** faction by insisting that he had personally supervised the young prince's execution 30 years before. He was succeeded in his offices by his son **Mhlaba**.

MNYANDA, BRADFIELD JACOB MABHASO (1906–July 29, 1970). Born and raised in South Africa's eastern Cape Province, Mnyanda came to what is now Zimbabwe to work as a **Methodist** teacher and lay evangelist in 1925. During his long residence there he also worked as a government interpreter and translator and as a journalist, editing *African Weekly*. In 1952 he returned to Port Elizabeth, where he worked in local government. Two years later he published *In Search of Truth*, a book describing African life in Southern Rhodesia. Probably because the book was published in Bombay it is little known; however, it is significant both as an insightful account and as perhaps the first book on the country written by an African.

MOFFAT, HOWARD UNWIN (Jan. 13, 1869–Jan. 19, 1951). Second **prime minister** of Southern Rhodesia (1927–33). The son of **John Smith Moffat**, H. U. Moffat was born at Kuruman. Through most of his early adult life he worked for the Bechuanaland Exploration Company, which had extensive mining interests in central Africa. He settled in the country after having served as a member of the BBP in the **1893 Ndebele War**. He also served in the **1896 Revolts** and in the **South African War**.

In 1920 Moffat was elected to the **Legislative Council**. Though he thought union with South Africa inevitable (see **Unionist Movement**), he joined **Charles Coghlan**'s **Responsible Government Party**. He later became the latter's first minister of mines and works on the achievement of Responsible Government in October 1923. On Coghlan's death in 1927, Moffat was made "premier"—a title he later had changed to "prime minister." Within two weeks he confronted an African miners' strike at **Shamva**.

Moffat inherited the increasingly pressing problem of territorial segregation, which had been articulated by the **Morris Carter Commission**. A liberal by the standards of his time, he resisted the calls for total segregation made by extremists such as **Godfrey Huggins** but nevertheless personally introduced the bill that led to the **Land Apportionment Act** in October 1930. Moffat then faced an economic crisis as the world depression hit the country's export trade hard. Moffat's handling of the economic situation provoked strong political opposition. Particularly unpopular was his purchase of the **BSAC**'s mineral rights for £2 million in June 1933. Leaders of his own **Rhodesian Party** called for his resignation to strengthen their position in the 1933 general election. Citing ill health, Moffat stepped down in favor of **George Mitchell** on July 6, 1933. He later reentered the **Legislative Assembly** in an attempt to revive the Rhodesian Party, but was badly defeated in the 1939 election.

MOFFAT, JOHN SMITH (March 10, 1835–Dec. 25, 1918). Born at Kuruman, Moffat was the son of **Robert Moffat**. The younger Moffat trained for a mission career, but when the LMS dallied over his appointment in 1859, his brother-in-law **David Livingstone** paid his expenses to work as an independent agent. In this capacity he joined **T. M. Thomas** and **William Sykes** in founding the **Inyati** mission in **Matabeleland**. In 1864 Moffat obtained a regular appointment within the LMS, but his wife Emily's health forced him to leave the country the next year.

Moffat returned south to work among the **Tswana** until 1879, when he resigned from the LMS because of friction with other missionaries. Thereafter he held a variety of government positions in South Africa. In 1887 he returned to Matabeleland as a British agent. The following year he obtained **Lobengula**'s signature on a treaty of friendship known as the **"Moffat Treaty,"** paving the way for British occupation of the entire country. He served as British resident in Matabeleland from 1890 to 1892 and then returned south for the last time. One of his sons, **H. U. Moffat**, later became prime minister of Southern Rhodesia.

MOFFAT, ROBERT (Sindebele form: Mshete) (Dec. 21, 1795–Aug. 9, 1883). A Scottish-born agent of the LMS, Moffat founded and managed the mission at Kuruman in South Africa for 45 years (1824-70). During this period he made five extended visits to the **Ndebele** and became **Mzilikazi**'s most intimate European friend. His first visit was in 1829, when the Ndebele king was living near the site of present Pretoria in the Transvaal. He revisited Mzilikazi in the western Transvaal in 1835. Mzilitazi developed a great trust in Moffat and tried to use him as his main intermediary in Ndebele dealings with Europeans. After the Ndebele migrated to **Matabeleland,** Moffat visited Mzilikazi there in 1854 in the company of the trader **S. H. Edwards**. This visit reopened Ndebele communication with Europeans and made Moffat the only literate observer to document Ndebele society both south and north of the **Limpopo River.**

Moffat returned to Matabeleland in 1857 to negotiate with Mzilikazi for the opening of a mission station. During this visit he obtained the release of the **Ngwato** captive **Macheng**. Two years later he led the first permanent mission party into what is now Zimbabwe, helping the LMS to found a station at **Inyati** early in 1860. Moffat's son, **J. S. Moffat**, was among the pioneer missionaries.

Moffat's influence on Mzilikazi is heavily stressed in most accounts written about the Ndebele king. One would suspect that this is due to the one-sided perspective of Moffat's own writings upon which historians of the Ndebele have had largely to rely. However, Ndebele traditions corroborate Moffat's role in their history.

MOFFAT TREATY. On February 11, 1888, **J. S. Moffat** obtained from the **Ndebele** king **Lobengula** signature to a document reaffirming the terms of **Mzilikazi**'s 1836 treaty of friendship with the British government (see **Mncumbathe**). Lobengula thereby pledged eternal Ndebele amity with the British and promised not to sign treaties or land grants with any foreign power without first obtaining permission of the British high commissioner for South Africa. Lobengula's most likely motive for signing this one-sided document was the hope of staving off the mounting pressure different Europeans were placing on his kingdom. The British government used the treaty to declare the territory north of the Limpopo to be within its "sphere of influence," paving the way for **Cecil Rhodes'** agents to obtain the **Rudd Concession**. (See also **Grobler, P.**)

MOLIMO (variants: *Modimo; Morimo*) see **MLIMO**

MONCKTON COMMISSION (1959–60). Investigatory body formed by the British government to assess attitudes toward the **federation** and to advise on constitutional changes. The commission contained 26 members from various Commonwealth territories and was headed by Lord Monckton. After hearing evidence from hundreds of witnesses throughout central Africa, the commission released its report in October 1960. The report emphasized the strong opposition of Africans north of the Zambezi to federation, while pointing out that many Southern Rhodesian Africans saw continued federation as preferable to purely territorial government by Europeans. The commission called for a general loosening of the federal structure to allow for greater African political power at the territorial level, and for wholesale reform of Southern Rhodesia's discriminatory racial laws and industrial hiring practices if the federation, in any form, were to continue. Southern Rhodesia's **pass laws** were cited as particularly unacceptable. These recommendations had little effect in Southern Rhodesia, whose territorial and federal leaders rejected the commission's findings, but a more important commission proposal was beyond their control. The commission's recommendation that individual territories be permitted to secede from the federation was adopted by the British government, resulting in the dissolution of the federation when Nyasaland and Northern Rhodesia (now Malawi and **Zambia**) exercised the new option.

MONDORO see **MHONDORO**

MONK'S KOP. Hill in the southern **Guruve District** (at 17°2′45″S, 30°35′15″E) containing a large cave ossuary filled with human skeletons and artifacts. Excavation of the site in the mid-1960s showed the artifacts to have cultural affinities with non-Shona peoples to the north—possibly riverine **Tonga** (see **Maramuca**). Radiocarbon dates indicate that the site was used during the late 13th or early 14th centuries. The finds therefore represent a much later manifestation of an indigenous non-Shona **Iron Age** culture than had previously been recognized in the region. The site falls within the "Ancient Park" National Monument, which also includes a number of **rock paintings**.

MONOMOTAPA. Popular English variant of **Munhumutapa**.

MONUMENTS, NATIONAL see **HISTORICAL MONUMENTS COMMISSION**

MONYEBE see **MANXEBA KHUMALO**

MOODIE TREK. First European effort to settle in **Gazaland**. In 1892 Dunbar Moodie (1861–1897), a South African of Scottish descent, got **Cecil Rhodes'** permission to settle Orange Free State families in the fertile southern reaches of the **Eastern Highlands** section of Gazaland. His cousin Thomas Moodie (1839–1894) organized and led about 30 Free State families on a grueling "trek" that lasted from May 1892 until January 1893. Twenty people completed the trip, establishing present **Chimanimani**.

MOODIE'S PASS. Pass blasted and cut through granite in the Mukuriro Hills (at 19°57'S, 31°44'E) by members of the **Moodie Trek** in 1892. The main road between **Masvingo** and **Birchenough Bridge** now goes through the pass.

MOPANE TREE (a.k.a. balsam; Rhodesian ironwood; turpentine tree). Characteristic tree of the dry low veld regions, particularly around the Limpopo and Zambezi valleys. The mopane grows as high as 13 m, but its wood has no commercial value. The tree is leguminous and produces edible seeds. (See **Forests**.)

MORGEN. Unit of land area introduced into southern African usage by early Dutch settlers. One *morgen* equals 8.85655 hectares or 2.11654 acres. One sq km equals 116.75 morgen. One sq mile equals 302,38 morgen.

MORGENSTER. Dutch Reformed Church mission station now serving as DRC headquarters in the country; located 6.5 km south of the **Zimbabwe Ruins**. The South African missionary A. A. Louw (1862–1956) founded Morgenster in September 1891, working there until his retirement in 1937.

MORRIS CARTER COMMISSION (1925–26). British Imperial commission headed by Morris Carter, a former Tanganyika chief justice, to investigate the question of allocating the nearly 45 percent of Southern Rhodesian land that was unassigned up to 1925. The commission collected evidence from more than 200 Europeans and more than 1,700 Africans. It found European farmers to be anxious for the introduction of segregation laws that would separate them from African farmers. Africans were found to be universally eager to get more land, and many were willing to accept the principle of segregation to get it. (See **Rbva**.) The commission's report, issued in 1926, proved a bitter disappointment to Africans. It recommended segregation of land on racial lines but proposed only slight additions to African lands. These recommendations formed the basis of the **Land Apportionment Act** introduced by **H. U. Moffat** into the **Legislative Assembly** in 1929.

MOSELEKATSE see **MZILIKAZI**

MOTO. News magazine originally published as a newspaper by the Roman Catholic Mambo Press in **Gweru**. Founded as a monthly in 1959, *Moto* was printed in **Sindebele, Chishona**, and English for African readers. During **UDI**, *Moto* attempted to avoid politically sensitive issues, but nevertheless was harassed by government **censorship**. In 1974 the government banned *Moto* for publishing allegedly subversive articles. *Moto* reappeared as a weekly publication in 1982.

MOUNT PLEASANT (a.k.a. Mutekedzi). Residential suburb of north **Harare**, in which the **University of Zimbabwe** is located.

MOUNTAINS. For most place names beginning with "Mount," see under proper names, e.g., **Hampden, Darwin, Silinda.** For general description of topographical regions, see **Altitudinal Zones.** See also **Dombo; Dwala; Kopje; Ntaba.**

MOVEMENT FOR DEMOCRATIC CHANGE (MDC). The first effective opposition party to emerge since independence in 1980. Launched in late 1999, the MDC's roots are in the country's labor movement. Most of its leadership, which includes **Morgan Tsvangirai,** Gift Chimanikire, Gibson Sibanda, and Welshman Ncube, were previously active in the Zimbabwe Congress of Trade Unions, which represents 90 percent of the country's organized labor groups.

The MDC was formed to contest what its leaders saw as **ZANU-PF**'s near monopoly on political power, as well as the autocratic rule and failed economic policies of **President Robert Mugabe.** The party's general-secretary, Tsvangirai, announced in February 2000 that the MDC would challenge ZANU-PF candidates in every constituency in the country in the June **elections** of that year. The MDC won fifty-seven seats, becoming the first major parliamentary opposition in the country since independence. Following the elections, the party leadership announced that it had named fifteen shadow cabinet ministers, and that Tsvangirai would challenge Mugabe in the 2002 presidential elections.

MOYO, JASON ZIYAPHAPHA ("JZ") (c.1924–Jan. 22, 1977). Trained as a builder and carpenter, Moyo became active in the trade union movement in **Bulawayo** in the early 1950s. In 1957 he helped to form the new **African National Congress,** becoming its chairman. He became a close ally of **Joshua Nkomo** and held leadership posts in **ZAPU** from its founding. In late 1964 he went to Lusaka, **Zambia,** as a member of ZAPU's external wing and began to organize **ZIPRA.** In 1976 he became second vice-president of ZAPU and was a delegate to the **Geneva Conference.** Moyo strongly advocated unity between ZAPU and ZANU and was a moving force behind the setting up of the **Patriotic Front** organization. In January 1977 he was assassinated in Lusaka by a parcel bomb. He was buried in Zimbabwe, at **Heroes' Acre,** in August 1980.

MOZAMBIQUE (variant: Mocambique). Zimbabwe shares its longest and most irregular **border** with this former **Portuguese** colony. Southern Mozambique, particularly the region between the **Zambezi** and **Sabi** (or **Save**) rivers, has long had close ties with the peoples of present Zimbabwe. The **Eastern Highlands** are a natural, but far from formidable, barrier between the two countries, and the Zambezi Valley has historically served as a corridor from the Indian Ocean to the interior. Most of the eastern **Shona peoples** live in this region which comprises territory from both countries. The entire area between the **Pungwe** and Sabi rivers is a Shona-speaking area containing the majority of the **Ndau.** Other peoples who live in regions comprising both countries include the **Chikunda, Barwe, Tonga,** and **Hlengwe.** The early **Munhumutapa** state extended into what is now Mozambique, and an important trade in **ivory** and **gold** through that country connected the Shona states with the coast.

Portuguese occupation of **Sofala** and other coastal towns began early in the 16th century, disrupting the existing trade patterns and beginning a gradual extension of Portuguese influence inland, particularly up the Zambezi Valley (see also **Sena; Tete; Zumbo**). Although the Portuguese claimed to control vast areas from an early date, their occupation of the interior region was not effective until the end of the 19th century. As late as the 1870s Portuguese posts paid tribute to the **Gaza** kings. Around that time, however, the Portuguese began to assert more effective control of the interior. In the 1880s Portuguese and Afro-Portuguese forces pushed the Gaza out of the Zambezi region and began conquering northeastern Shona chiefdoms (see **M. de Soisa**). British occupation of **Mashonaland** in 1890 made present eastern Zimbabwe and southern Mozambique the arena for Portuguese-British rivalry, nearly bringing the two European countries to war (see **Macequece Incident**). The **BSAC** sought a seaport and made a nearly successful effort to acquire Delagoa Bay from the Gaza king **Gungyane**. Meanwhile, the rivalry was settled through European diplomacy, and the present borders were tentatively laid down by the **Anglo-Portuguese Convention** of 1891.

Thereafter Portuguese relations with the British in colonial Zimbabwe were increasingly harmonious. In 1892 a **railway** was commenced at **Beira**, reaching **Mutare** in 1898. During much of the 20th century ties between the two countries have been based largely on mutually profitable rail transport connections. In 1955 a second major railway line connected Harare to Maputo (formerly Lourenzo Marques) by way of **Sango**.

As European colonies north of the Zambezi became independent under African majority rule in the 1960s, white Rhodesian- Portuguese relations were strengthened by the mutual interest in preserving white rule in southern Africa. After the declaration of **UDI** in 1965, Portugal largely ignored UN **sanctions**, thereby increasing the level of Rhodesian trade through Mozambique. Meanwhile, in 1964 a Mozambique nationalist movement known as **Frelimo** began extending its control over northern Mozambique. The fall of the Portuguese right-wing government in Libson in 1974 accelerated the liberation of Mozambique, which became independent on June 25, 1875, under President Samora Machel (see **Frontline States**).

Rhodesia's rail connections through Mozambique were initially uninterrupted, but in March 1876 Machel closed the border. Mozambique's losses in transport revenues from that time until Zimbabwe's independence in 1980 have been estimated at approximately $57 million a year. The cost to the **Ian Smith** regime is harder to estimate because it was able to divert much of its trade through **South Africa**, using a direct rail link through **Beitbridge**.

During the early 1970s **ZANU** and its military wing **ZANLA** began establishing both training centers and refugee camps in those areas of Mozambique controlled by Frelimo. Following Mozambique's independence, ZANLA forces were allowed to establish more camps throughout Mozambique and increasingly used them as staging areas from which to infiltrate freedom fighters back into the country. Historians now generally argue that until this time the Smith government was largely able to contain ZANLA activities inside the country, but from June 1975, the liberation forces were able to gain the upper hand. Although the Mozambican government of President Machel could never guarantee their continuation, military support and political guidance were freely given to

Zimbabwe's liberation forces whenever possible. The result of this support was the creation of a strong bond of solidarity between both the leadership and the peoples of the two countries. This bond continued past Zimbabwe's independence in April 1980. According to statements by Presidential **Mugabe** and other Zimbabwean governmental officials, Mozambican support for the Zimbabwean military forces assisted that government in its struggle with the **Mozambique National Resistance**. Beginning in July 1990, Zimbabwe continued to repay Mozambique's earlier assistance by mediating, along with Kenya, talks between the government of Mozambique and the MNR. Those talks culminated in the 1992 Rome Accords which ended the war between Frelimo and the MNR. In internationally monitored elections in October 1994, President Joaquim Chissano and Frelimo won the country's first multiparty elections with 53.3 percent of the vote; the MNR, and its political leader Afonso Dhlakama won c. 30 percent of the vote.

MOZAMBIQUE NATIONAL RESISTANCE (variants: MNR; RNM; Renamo). Initially an insurgent group opposing the **Frelimo** government in Mozambique, this organization was supported militarily and financially by South Africa in order to destabilize both the Mozambican and Zimbabwean governments. Following a 1974 agreement between the **Portuguese** secret service and the Rhodesian Central Intelligence Organization, the MNR was founded in 1975. It was believed that a force should be organized which would operate inside Mozambique, attacking **ZANLA** forces, as well as disrupting Mozambican support for those forces. By weakening Mozambique, it was hoped that ZANLA's ability to cross the border and wage war inside the country would also be weakened.

After Zimbabwe's independence, South Africa assumed responsibility for the continued operation of the MNR, which during the 1980s was used to terrorize the people of Mozambique and destabilized that country's economy. The MNR consistently threatened Zimbabwe's economy through its attacks on the rail and oil pipeline links to the ports of **Beira** and Maputo. In January 1981, Prime Minister **Robert Mugabe** and President Samora Machel of Mozambique signed a defense and security agreement to protect those links, partly through the use of Zimbabwean troops to guard the oil pipeline from Beira. In response, the MNR increased its incursions into the eastern districts of Zimbabwe.

In the late 1980s South Africa, increasingly affected by international opinion and a desire to end economic sanctions, declared that it was stopping its military support of the MNR and began to pressure MNR leaders to develop a political agenda. Afonso Dhlakama then emerged as the public leader of the MNR. In July 1990, Dhlakama and the MNR, and Frelimo and its new leader, Joaquim Chissano, entered into peace talks monitored by Zimbabwe and Kenya. Those talks culminated in the 1992 Rome Accords that ended fighting and called for open, internationally monitored multiparty elections. In October 1994, in Mozambique's first open election, Chissano and Frelimo won 53.3 percent of the presidential vote, while Dhlakama and the MNR won c. 30 percent of the vote.

MPEZENI JERE (c. 1832–1900). A son of **Zwangendaba** who was born in **Mashonaland** during the **Ngoni** migration, Mpezeni ruled the group that settled at Chipata in eastern Zambia. The Mpenzi Hills, just north-east of **Macheke**, are said to be named after him.

MPEZENI KHUMALO (c. 1880–1898). Son of the **Ndebele** king **Lobengula**. After his father's death in 1894, Mpezeni and his half-brothers **Njube** and **Nguboyenja** were sent to South Africa for education by the **BSAC**. Mpezeni died at Zonnebloem College in Cape Town.

MPHOENGS (variants: M'phoengs). A village of the southern **Bulimiamangwe District** near the **Botswana** border where the **Ingwezi River** enters the **Ramaquabane** (at 21°12′S, 27°51′E). Since a dam was built on the Ingwezi in 1967, an irrigation scheme has brought relief to this normally arid region of the country.

MPOTSHWANA NDIWENI (d. Oct. 1897). **Ndebele** *induna.* Mpotshwana and his brother Manyeu were leaders of the Nyamandhlovu *ibutho,* which was situated on the middle **Khami River**. Both men were noted supporters of **Lobengula** and were among the main military leaders in the **1896 Revolt**. They operated in the northern theater of the war in close association with **Nyamanda**, whose candidacy for kingship they supported. After the Ndebele suffered some major setbacks in July 1896, Mpotshwana was said to have made an abortive attempt to lead his own followers across the **Zambezi River**—an effort halted by illness among his troops. He then vigorously opposed efforts at negotiated settlement and became the last major rebel in the field after all other major leaders had surrendered. He was finally captured near the Zambezi in July 1897. He died several months later in jail.

MREWA see **MUREWA**

MSHETE. (1) (variants: Moshete; Umshete) (c. 1820s-1893?). Senior **Ndebele** *induna* and emissary. In 1889 King **Lobengula** sent Mshete and **Babyane** to London, along with **J. M. Colenbrander** and **E. A. Maund**, to get Queen Victoria's advice on the **Rudd Concession**. They returned to Lobengula with a note from the colonial secretary advising him to beware of signing away sweeping rights to a single concessionaire. Mshete later met twice with the British high commissioner in Cape Town—once in 1890 to attempt to head off the **Pioneer Column**, and again in 1893 to try to avert the impending **Ndebele War**.
    (2) Ndebele form of **Moffat**.

MTARAZI FALLS. At 162 m the highest waterfall in the country, Mtarazi deposits its water into the **Honde River Valley** in the southern **Inyanga Mountains**. Mtarazi National Park is a wild scenic area of 6,000 hectares that abuts the southern tip of Rhodes Inyanga National Park.

MTILIKWE RIVER (variant: Mutirikwi). Rises just northeast of **Gutu**, flowing south through **Lake Kyle**, then southeast to join the **Lundi River** between its confluences with the **Tokwe** and **Chiredzi** rivers. In 1963 Bangala Dam was built on the Mtilikwe, about halfway between Lake Kyle and the Lundi River. The Mtilikwe's waters make a major contribution to the irrigation schemes of the **Sabi-Limpopo Authority** in the southeastern low veld.

MTJAAN see **MTSHANI**

MTOA RUIN. Iron Age site in the **Bunbuzi ruins group.**

MTOKO see **MUTOKO**

MTOROLITE. A previously unknown **gemstone** first discovered in the **Great Dyke** in the 1960s, mtorolite is a green crypto-crystalline quartz.

MTOROSHANGA see **MUTORASHANGA**

MTSHANI KHUMALO (variants: Mjaan; Mtjaan) (c.1830s–1907). High ranking Ndebele *induna.* A cousin of King **Lobengula,** Mtshani was made commander of the elite Imbizo *ibutho* during the 1870s. The prestige of this *ibutho* grew enormously, but by 1890 Mtshani's authority over it was threatened. He supported Lobengula's policy of military nonaggression against the **BSAC,** while many Imbizo members agitated for action. Nevertheless, Mtshani played a leading role as a military commander in the **1893 Ndebele War.** He commanded Ndebele troops at the Battle of Shangani, assisted at the Battle of Bembezi, and then accompanied Lobengula on his flight north. After the war Mtshani appears to have retired from active leadership because of his advancing age. He collaborated with the Europeans during the **1896 Revolt,** but apparently did not actively fight against the rebels. (See **Faku; Gampu.**) Afterwards he was among the first *izinduna* to be made a salaried chief by the BSAC.

MTSHWELO, Z. C. see under **AFRICAN METHODIST EPISCOPAL CHURCH**

MU-. Chishona prefix for the singular forms of two classes of nouns. As a Class 1 prefix it is used with nouns for individual persons, such as a member of an ethnic or national group, e.g., *Mushona.* The normal plural for such nouns is *va-.* In the case of proper names, such prefixes are dropped in this dictionary.

As a Class 3 prefix *mu-* is used with names of trees and other objects, and its normal plural is *mi-.*

MUDZI DISTRICT. Originally demarcated in 1973, Mudzi is located in the northeastern section of **Mashonaland East Province.** The district is bisected by the main road from Harare to Nyamapanda, at the border with **Mozambique. Rushinga District** borders the district to the north, while **Nyanga** is to the southeast, and **Mutoko** to the southwest. Mozambique borders to the east. With the exception of the southern tip, the district is exclusively **Communal Lands.** District population in 1992 was 109,423.

MUDZIMU (variant plural forms: *midzimu; vadzimu*). Shona term for ancestor spirit. *Midzimu* are the most important kinds of spirits in everyday Shona life. In contrast to the "lion spirits," **mhondoro** and **gombwe,** which look after public welfare, the *midzimu* are primarily concerned with individual or family matters. They cannot harm their own families, but if they are offended, they can withdraw their protection. (See **Religion—Shona; Ndebele Dlozi.**)

MUFAKOSE. Second largest of **Harare's** "high-density suburbs," this former African township is located 12 km west southwest of the city center.

MUGABE, ROBERT GABRIEL (b. February 21, 1924). Tenth **prime minister** of the country, the first of the independent Republic of Zimbabwe and first **executive president**. Mugabe was born at **Kutama Mission** in **Makonde District**. He began his early education there and qualified as a primary school teacher in 1941. He taught at Kutama until 1943, and later at several places including **Empandeni** and **Hope Fountain** missions until 1950. He studied privately for his matriculation certificate before going to South Africa, where he graduated from Ft. Hare University with a B.A. degree in 1951. He returned to the country and continued his teaching career in local mission schools in 1952, and then taught in Northern Rhodesia in 1955, and in Ghana from mid-1958 to 1960.

Mugabe returned to Southern Rhodesia in May 1960 on leave and resigned his Ghanian teaching post in order to enter fulltime politics at home. He joined the **National Democratic Party** as secretary for publicity. After the NDP was banned, he served as **Joshua Nkomo's** deputy secretary in **ZAPU.** Mugabe was arrested several times in 1962 and 1963, and while released on bail managed to leave the country and travel to Dar es Salaam, Tanzania, where ZAPU had established operational headquarters in exile. He then broke with Nkomo and joined **Ndabaningi Sithole's** newly formed **ZANU** and became its secretary general. When Mugabe returned to the country in mid-1963 he was arrested by the government. He was released on bail but arrested again, along with other ZANU leaders, when the party was banned in 1964. He remained in prisons or detention camps for the next decade. While in detention he earned both Bachelor of Law and Bachelor of Administration degrees by correspondence from the University of London. He also spent considerable time tutoring other prisoners, and when he was eventually released in November 1974 he was studying for a Master of Law degree.

Sometime during late 1974 Sithole, while still in detention, was suspended from ZANU by a vote of the imprisoned executive committee and was replaced by Mugabe as the leading figure in the party. In December 1974 Mugabe was among the political prisoners released by **Ian Smith's** general amnesty. It was not generally known that Mugabe had replaced Sithole as ZANU's leader, and he was not then regarded as a major nationalist leader by people outside the party executive. Following the assassination of **Herbert Chitepo** in 1975, ZANU's executive committee voted to send Mugabe and **Edgar Tekere** into exile to **Mozambique.** They were charged with reorganizing the party structure and revitalizing the armed struggle through the reactivation of ZANU's military wing, the Zimbabwe African National Liberation Army (**ZANLA**). It was during this period that Mungabe was recognized as the uncontested leader of both ZANU and its ZANLA force (see **Mgagao Declaration**). By August 1976, he was regarded by the African leaders of the neighboring countries as a serious contender for top leadership within the divided liberation movements. On October 9, 1976, shortly before the opening of the **Geneva Conference**, Mugabe and Nkomo formed the **Patriotic Front** alliance. Mugabe then led the ZANU component of the PF delegation to the aborted conference, where he took a leading part in rejecting the Kissinger proposals.

At a 1977 ZANU Central Committee meeting held in Chimoio, Mozambique, Mugabe's position as a leader of the party and ZANLA was formalized with his election as a party president. Over the next three years, Mugabe was extensively involved in both the organization and operation of the party, as well as military strategies concerning ZANLA and the pursuit of the liberation war inside Zimbabwe. He traveled extensively, becoming one of the principal spokesmen in the international diplomatic campaign against the Smith, and then **Muzorewa** governments. In January 1978 Mugabe, along with Nkomo, held talks with British and American government representatives in Malta (see **Malta Talks**). The two PF leaders announced their support for the idea of independently observed and supervised elections within Zimbabwe, but demanded that they play a substantial part during any period leading up to those elections. When the **Internal Settlement** agreement was announced in early March, Mugabe condemned it as a sell-out to continued white minority rule. Later in the year, following a meeting of Commonwealth leaders in Lusaka in which a proposal for an all-party conference was approved, Mugabe agreed that ZANU would take part in the **Lancaster House Conference** in London. He then led the ZANU contingent of the PF delegation at the conference from September to December 1979.

Following the successful conclusion of the Lancaster House Conference, Mugabe returned to Zimbabwe on January 27, 1980, to contest the forthcoming **elections** as leader of ZANU (PF). He had earlier surprised Nkomo by announcing that ZANU would contest the elections independently, not as part of a united PF slate. Throughout the campaign Mugabe stressed the concept of reconciliation, that no vengeance would be sought against the white community, and that all sections of the **constitution** agreed to during the Lancaster House Conference would be adhered to completely. Mugabe personally won election to the **House of Assembly** from the **Highfield** electoral district in Harare, and ZANU secured 63 percent of the total black vote, winning a majority of 57 seats in the House of Assembly. On March 4, **Lord Soames,** the British **governor,** officially asked Mugabe to form the first independent government of the country. The following day he agreed to form a coalition government by naming members of ZAPU to his cabinet, but angered Nkomo when he appointed only four ZAPU members to relatively minor portfolios. On April 18, 1980, Mugabe took the oath of office and became the first prime minister of the independent Republic of Zimbabwe. He also kept the ministry of defense portfolio for himself.

Mugabe was faced with enormous tasks at independence. His image as a hardline Marxist and his calls for the necessities of land resettlement and the Africanization of the civil service, **health,** and **education** systems frightened many whites, yet did not go far enough for some of his own party members. He addressed these problems with calls for reconciliation between former enemies, and pragmatic solutions regarding the economy. He urged white commercial farmers to stay in the country and promised them security under the conditions established by the new constitution. He applied for membership in the Lome Convention which linked Africa and other developing areas with the European Economic Community (Zimbabwe was admitted in November).

In August he traveled to Britain and the United States to negotiate development loans for road, school, and hospital construction projects. In March of 1981 Mugabe chaired a major conference on reconstruction and development in Harare (see **Zimcord**) and asked delegates from 45 countries to contribute $1.2 billion towards the economic rehabilitation of Zimbabwe.

In August 1980 Mugabe was faced with a major political problem when **Edgar Tekere**, the minister of manpower planning and development and the man who had gone with him to Mozambique in the 1970s to reorganize the party, was arrested for the murder of a white farm manager. Tekere was considered by most observers to be one of the more radical members of ZANU. Mugabe's policy of reconciliation with the white community and the control over his own party were tested by this incident. Mugabe suspended Tekere pending trial in December (he was acquitted) and eventually dropped him from the cabinet in January 1981. The other major problem faced by Mugabe during his first year in office was that of internal security. In September he ordered **police** and **army** units to act against **dissidents** operating in **Matabeleland.** Nkomo, leader of the parliamentary opposition, strongly criticized the use and activities of the government security forces and in January 1981 was demoted by Mugabe.

In early 1982 Mugabe called for an increasingly socialist economy for the country and also stated that in the future all government policies would first be approved by ZANU. This was immediately denounced by Nkomo, which initiated a new political crisis between the two long-time rival leaders. In February, Mugabe proposed a plan to merge ZANU and ZAPU, which was also rejected by Nkomo. Later that month, following the discovery of large arms caches on farms reportedly owned by ZAPU, Mugabe dismissed Nkomo from government entirely. In June, Mugabe's official residence in Harare was attacked by armed men and he accused Nkomo of being linked to the attackers. Tensions between the two lessened to some extent following this incident, though they remained critical of one another for the next several years.

In August 1984 ZANU held its second party congress and Mugabe again pledged to create a one-party state in Zimbabwe. Mugabe was reelected president and first general secretary of the party. While campaigning for the country's general elections held in mid-1985, Mugabe stressed that the time was right to abolish the parliamentary seats reserved for whites and establish a one-party government. ZANU won an overwhelming victory, increasing its majority in Parliament to 63 seats, enough legally to amend the **constitution**. However, in the election for the white reserved seats, Ian Smith's party won 15 of the 20 reserved seats. This so angered Mugabe that he fired the one white member of his cabinet, Minister of Agriculture Denis Norman.

Following his party's victory, Mugabe began talks with Nkomo aimed at the eventual unification of ZANU and ZAPU and the creation of a one-party state. The talks continued for almost two years, although in April 1987 Mugabe announced that the negotiations were being called off because they served no useful purpose. After being upbraided by

President **Canaan Banana**, Mugabe reinstated the negotiations and on December 22, he and Nkomo signed the **Unity Pact**, amalgamating the two parties. In the meantime the government had introduced legislation in August to abolish the reserved white seats, and it had met unanimous approval in both houses of **Parliament**. This was followed by the introduction of a constitutional amendment to abolish the office of prime minister and create an "Executive Presidency," which would combine the roles of head of state, head of government, and commander-in-chief. This legislation also passed, and by a vote of Parliament Mugabe was declared Zimbabwe's first executive president. He was inaugurated on December 21, 1987.

Early the following year, the **Willowdale** corruption scandal shook Mugabe personally and public confidence in his government in general. He appointed a commission of inquiry headed by Wilson Sandura, the judge president of Zimbabwe. He chastised government officials for accusations of corruption and fired several ministers. However, he later granted presidential pardons to most of those involved. This action caused strong public criticism of Mugabe for the first time. He decided to make the upcoming elections a test of his handling of Willowdale. He easily won the 1990 presidential elections, receiving 2.03 million votes to 413,840 for his principal rival, Edgar Tekere. The victory seemed to reenforce his political authority and dominance.

However, challenges to that authority, lacking during the previous two decades, emerged. In August 1990, ZANU's politburo voted against Mugabe's long-standing call for the formal creation of a one-party state. Mugabe, facing his first major political defeat, announced that he was willing to accede to majority opinion. Six months later, in January 1991, he went further and announced that he was prepared to accept a multiparty democratic system. In June, he declared that his government and ZANU were dropping Marxism and socialism as their guiding principles. His greatest political challenge throughout the 1990s was been the question of the nationalization of European-owned farmlands and the resettlement of African peasant farmers on that land. In 1990 and 1991 he lobbied for legislation that would accomplish those two goals. He backed off when a continuing drought resulted in extremely low levels of agricultural production. With the alleviation of drought conditions in the following year, however, he reintroduced legislation and the Assembly passed the **Land Acquisition Act** in March 1992.

In May 1994, Mugabe made his first state visit to Britain since independence, partly in an attempt to assuage British concerns regarding his government's new land policy. In August 1994, after years of supporting South Africa's African National Congress and its struggle for majority rule, he made a state visit to South Africa and became the first leader of an African country to address the newly elected South African Parliament. In his speech, he congratulated South Africa on its recent all-race elections but warned the country about problems of what he termed "rising expectations." In August, he seemed to abandon his message of racial toleration in Zimbabwe when he announced that the government would no longer follow a policy of reconciliation between Africans and **Europeans**.

Even with this international recognition, by the mid-1990s Mugabe was beginning to face increased criticism within the country. For the first time, some of the opposition to his rule came from the ranks of ZANU-PF. In 1996 some local party activists openly suggested that Mugabe's powers as president be limited. While these particular suggestions were rejected by the party's leadership, similar calls for either limiting his power, and even for his retirement, continued to come from inside the party. By the late 1990s, general criticisms of Mugabe's govenment had begun to proffer that the roots of the nation's problems were grounded in his personal corruption. The growing acceptance of this view was seen as one of the reasons for the rejection of a Mugabe-endorsed national referendum on a new constitution in February 2000, as well as the sucess of the **Movement for Democratic Change** in parliamentary elections later that year.

MUJIBAS. Youths, both male and female, who actively supported the guerrilla forces of **ZANLA** and **ZIPRA** during the war. Usually described as the "eyes and ears" of the freedom fighters, these youths supplied information on whereabouts of **Rhodesian security forces**, acted as messengers, provided clothing and supplies, and often on "sell-outs" and "collaborators." No organization was ever formalized, and it has been estimated that about 50,000 such youths were active for the period 1972–79.

MUJURU, JOYCE (b. February 2, 1955). Mujuru, perhaps better known by her **Chimurenga** name, Teurai Ropa Nhongo, was born at Chahwanda village near **Mount Darwin**. She attended Howard Institute in **Mazowe District** until she passed Form 2 in 1973, at which time she joined the **ZANLA** liberation forces. She received some training inside the country and carried out several field operation assignments before being sent to **Zambia** in 1974 for further military training. That same year she joined ZANLA's general staff as overall commander of the Women's Detachment—which had been formed earlier in the year. The following year she moved to **Mozambique** as a political instructor. In 1976 she was appointed commander of the Chimoio refugee camp, the largest such camp in the country. It was at this time that she met and married **Solomon Mutuswa**. In 1977 she was appointed to **ZANU**'s central committee, the first woman ever appointed to so high a position in the party. The next year she became the party's secretary for women's affairs and was appointed to the national executive. After returning to Zimbabwe in 1980 she was elected to represent **Mashonaland Central** in the **House of Assembly**. In 1985 she was returned to **Parliament** representing the **Bindura/Shamva** area and was appointed minister of cooperatives, community development, and women's affairs, making her the country's youngest cabinet minister. She was later named minister of rural resources and water development, a post she held throughout the late 1990s. She officially changed her name back to Joyce Mujuru in 1987.

MUKOMBERO NYAHUMA (fl. late 15th century). Early **Munhumutapa** ruler. The son of Munhumutapa **Matope Nyanhehwe**, Mukombero is said to have become Munhumutapa after having abandoned his brother Mavura I to die in a battle in c. 1480. Over the next decade he struggled to put down the rebellion of another relative, **Changra**, who killed him and usurped the kingship in c. 1490. His son **Chikuyo Chisamarengu** later regained the kingship.

MUKOMBE see **KAMHARAPASU MUKOMBWE**

MUKUMBURA DISTRICT (Darwin District until 1985). A northeastern **border** district, Mukumbura borders the districts of **Muzarabani** on the west, **Bindura** and **Shamva** on the south, and **Rushinga** on the west. The district administrative center is at the village of **Mount Darwin** (at 16°47′S, 31°35′E), which is just northwest of Mount Pfura (renamed "Mount Darwin" by **F. C. Selous**). Prior to 1980, the southwestern part of the district was reserved for Europeans, while most of the remainder was Tribal Trust Land (see **Communal Lands**). District population in 1992 was 164,362.

MULUNGWANE HILLS. Small mountain ranges running north-south along the 29th line of east longitude, just southeast of **Bulawayo.**

MUNGOSHI, CHARLES (b. 1947). Born at Manyene, **Chivu,** Mungoshi attended St. Augustine's in **Penhalonga.** He writes novels, poems, plays, and short stories in both **Chishona** and English. He has published one novel in English, *Waiting for the Rain* (1976), and two in Chishona, *Ndiko Kupindana Kwamazuva* (1971) and *Kunyarara Hakusi Kutaura?* (1981). In addition, he published a collection of short stories in English, *The Setting Sun and the Rolling World* (1972). His work largely deals with the alienation and isolation from **Shona** culture that resulted when Africans were subjected to the cultural and political domination of Europeans.

MUNHUMUTAPA (variants: Monomotapa; Mwanamutapa; Mwene Mutapa; etc.). Dynastic title of the rulers of a **Shona** state now known by the same name. Long known to outsiders as "Monomotapa," the Munhumutapa state is one of the most famous African kingdoms in southern African history. Though the kingdom played a major role in the country's history, its importance has probably been somewhat exaggerated because it was much better documented than other early state systems (see **Shona History**). The **Portuguese** arrived in the region just after the Munhumutapa state had reached its peak power in the late 15th century. Portuguese traders and missionaries dealt mostly with the Munhumutapa people during the 16th and 17th centuries. They tended to exaggerate the state's importance with respect to other Shona states, about which they knew less.

The origins of the Munhumutapa state are not fully understood. It was established in the **Dande** region of the northern part of the present Zimbabwe in the early 15th century by **Mutota Nyatsimba**, the son of a Shona ruler from the southern **Guruhuswa** region. It remains unclear whether Mutota simply shifted his father's already established kingdom from the south or created an entirely new state in the north. It is also unclear what connections, if any, the Munhumutapa state had with the rulers of **Great Zimbabwe**. It is possible that the shift of Mutota's court to the north occasioned the decline of Great Zimbabwe as a political center. Whatever, Mutota's conquests in the north earned him the praise name *munhu mutapa*, "one who explores" or "one who pillages," and this name was adopted as a dynastic title by his successors. Mutota's son **Matope Nyanhehwe** extended the kingdom's influence as far east as the Indian Ocean, thus earning the state the modern description of "empire."

Munhumutapa control over outlying provinces was never complete. Matope's successors quickly lost territories to rebellious local rulers, giving rise to new dynasties in **Manyika, Maungwe, Barwe**, and elsewhere. Two of Matope's provincial administrators, **Torwa** and **Changa**, threw off Munhumutapa control in the south, laying the basis for the state's most powerful rivals.

During the 17th century, Portuguese intervention became a paramount problem. **Gatsi Rusere** and **Mavura II** made major concessions to the Portuguese, leaving their successors to struggle to regain Munhumutapa autonomy. In the 1680s the **Changamire** state to the south began an era of rapid expansion. **Munhwnutapa Kambarapasu**'s attempts to ally with **Changamire Dombo** against the Portuguese backfired. Changamire armies were turned against the Munhumutapa state, apparently reducing it to tributary status. Thereafter the state ranked as merely one of many unexceptional Shona polities. Some 18th-century rulers attempted to reassert the state's former power, but their successes were short-lived. The last titular Munhumutapa was **Chioko Dambamupute**, who died in 1902.

The following list of Munhumutapa rulers stops in the early 18th century for several reasons. After 1695 the state was only a minor power, and its center was shifting into what is now Mozambique. Furthermore, genealogical evidence on 18th and 19th-century rulers is poorly worked out at present.

Munhumutapa rulers: early 15th century Mutota Nyatsimba; mid-15th century Matope Nyanhehwe; c.1480 Mavura I Maombwe; c.1480–c.90 Mukombero Nyahuma; c.1490–c.94 Changa; c.1494–c.1530 Chikuyo Chisamarengu; c.1530–c.50 Neshangwe Munembire; c.1550–c.60 Chivere Nyasoro; c.1560–c.89 Negomo Chirisamhuru; c.1589–1623 Gatsi Rusere; 1623–29 Nyambo Kaparidzce; 1629–52 Mavura II Mhande; 1652–63 Siti Kazurukumusapa; 1663–c.92 Kambarapasu Mukombwe; c.1692–c.99 Chirimba (?); c.1699–c.1702 Nyadenga(?); c.1702–c.07 Dehwe Samutumbu; c.1707–c.11 Nyenyedzi Zenda; c.1711–c.19 Buruma Dangwarangwa; c.1719–c.40 Samatambira Nyamhandu.

MURENGA (pl. *mirenga*; variant: *mulenga*.) **Chishona** word for warlike spirit or for rebellion (see **Chimurenga**); also a war cry. The **Sindebele** equivalent is *umvuleka* (pl. *imivuleka*). The Shona form appears also to have been used to describe a manifestation of the high god **Mwari**; as such it was a title taken by the Revolt leader **"Kaguvi."**

MUREWA (Mrewa until 1982). The administrative center for both the **Mangwende Communal Lands** and the **Murewa District**, located on the northeastern edge of the Central Plateau (at 17°39'S, 31°47'E). The nearby Mrewa Cave contains **rock paintings** noted for their depiction of an unusually wide variety of subjects and styles. The name derives from Murehwa, a local **Zezuru** ruler.

MUREWA DISTRICT (Mrewa District until 1985). Covers 5,730 sq km in the eastern part of the **Mashonaland East Province**. It borders the districts of **Mutoko** on the east, **Makoni** on the southeast, **Marondera** on the south, **Goromonzi** and **Shamva** on the west, and **Mukumbura** on the north. Before 1980, with the exception of some European **tobacco** farms in the southern high-veld region, most of the district was comprised of Tribal Trust Land (see **Communal Lands**). District population in 1992 was 151,808.

MURUNGU (pl. *varungu*). **Chishona** term for European. Synonyms include *murumbi* and *mukiwa* (plurals, both *va-*). **Sindebele** equivalents are *ikhiwa* (pl. *amakhiwa*) and *umlungu* (pl. *abelungu*).

MUSENGEZI RIVER. Rises in the **Umvukwe Mountains**, flowing generally north. It is joined by the Kadsi and Mkumvura rivers by the **Mozambique** border, and it enters the **Zambezi River** at 31°15′E Long. (See **Dande**.)

MUSHANDIKE DAM (former variant: Umshandige). Built in 1938 on the Mushandike River, a short tributary of the **Tokwe**, just west of **Masvingo**. The dam's lake supplies irrigation water and offers **fishing** and recreational facilities for the 13,000-hectare Mushandike Dam and Lake National Park, which surrounds it.

MUSI O TUNYA (variant: Mosi- Oa-Tunya). **Tonga** name for **Victoria Falls**; variously translated as "smoke that rises" or "smoke that thunders," in reference to the smokelike appearance of the falls' mist. This name was heard by Europeans in South Africa at least as early as 1840. **David Livingstone** himself recorded the name before he coined the name "Victoria Falls" in 1855.

MUSIC. Dances and songs of many varieties have long played an important role in **Shona** life. Most songs are accompanied by instrumental music, produced mostly by **drums** and the *mbira*, a melodious plucking instrument. Other Shona instruments include flutes (sing., *chigufe*; pl., *zvigufe*); mouthbows (sing., *chipendani*; pl., *zvipendani*); and reed instruments known as panpipes (sing. and pl., *nyere*). Songs and instruments were less important in 19th-century **Ndebele** culture, and dances were mostly related to martial ceremonies, notably the *inxwala*.

Music in Zimbabwe's contemporary popular culture is both important and successful. During the liberation war, so-called "**Chimurenga** songs" and liberation music played a subtle but important part in informing the general African population about the nationalist struggle. This type of music, by musicians like **Thomas Mapfumo** and others, was considered enough of a threat by the government that much of it was banned from the radio. The government even attempted to ban live performances by Mapfumo several times. Popular music is very successful, and several of Zimbabwe's bands have, since the 1980s, become known in Europe and the United States. Among these are Mapfumo's Blacks Unlimited, the Bundu Boys, the Pied Pipers, Super Sounds, and James Chimombe and the O.K. Success.

MUSLIMS (variants: Moslems; Mohammedans; Moors). Although the country is landlocked, its commercial contacts with the eastern coast go back at least 1,000 years. In A.D. 947 the Arab geographer al-Masudi wrote about the **gold** trade through **Sofala**. This trade likely originated in what is now Zimbabwe, and it is possible that Muslim traders were visiting the country by the 10th century. These traders are often described as "Arabs," but they included Muslim Arabs, Persians, east Africans (mostly Swahili), and perhaps some Indians.

By the 15th century the Muslims had established a network of trading **fairs** in the country, and used these to funnel trade goods through Sofala. While their commercial influence was clearly great, their political and cultural impact was apparently small. (See **"Changamire"; Lemba**.) A figure of 10,000+ Muslims resident in the country by 1500 is frequently quoted, but a more realistic figure is around 200 people, including family members. Muslim commercial dominance ended during the 16th century, after the **Portuguese** occupied Sofala and began establishing their own trade centers in the interior. The few Muslims in the country today are mainly Indian immigrants (see **Asians**).

MUSSAMBAZES. Professional African traders who operated in **Shona** territory for **Portuguese** based on the **Zambezi River**. The word is actually derived from the Portuguese spelling of the **Chishona** term *mushambadzi* (see **Fairs**).

MUTAPA. Short form of **Munhumutapa**.

MUTARE (Umtali until 1982). Mutare is the fifth-largest urban center in the country, with a 1992 population of 131,808. It is an important industrial center, as well as the commercial and administrative center of both **Mutare District** and **Manicaland Province**. It is situated on the **Mozambique** border (at 18°57′S; alt. 1,190 m), across from **Villa de Manica** (formerly Macequece.)

Mutare is entirely a colonial creation. Soon after **Harare** was founded in 1890, a small party of Europeans entered Manicaland, where they obtained a treaty from the **Manyika** ruler **Mutasa**. They established Ft. Umtali near the Mutari River (which **Nguni** speakers rendered Mtali). A year later the settlement was shifted to a higher and healthier site, now known as **"Old Umtali."** This location also proved unsuitable when it was realized that the projected **railway** between **Beira** and Salisbury could pass only through a gap in the **Eastern Highlands** 15 km to the south. The settlement was again moved in 1896, this time to its present site. The several hundred European settlers forced to move were paid £50,000 by the **BSAC**.

During the 20th century Mutare has grown steadily as a center for **tobacco, maize, tea,** and other agricultural production, as well as **gold** mining and mixed manufacturing.

MUTARE DISTRICT (Umtali District until 1985). Eastern border district covering 7,160 sq km in the center of **Manicaland Province**. Mutare borders the districts of **Chimanimani** on the south, **Buhera** on the southwest, **Makoni** on the northwest, and **Mutasa** on the north. Administrative headquarters are the city of **Mutare**. Other important district centers include **Penhalonga** and **Old Umtali**. Prior to 1980, most of the well-watered and mountainous district was reserved for Europeans, with the southwestern corner mostly Tribal Trust Land (see **Communal**

Lands) and scattered pockets of **Purchase Areas**. District population in 1992 was 336,775.

MUTASA (variant: Umtasa). Dynastic title of the rulers of an important **Manyika** kingdom centered at **Bingaguru**, near present **Mutare**. The dynasty was established in the early 16th century as an offshoot of the **Makombe** dynasty of the **Barwe**. In 1575 Mutasa Chikanga signed a treaty of friendship with the explorer **V. F. Homem**. Manyika territory subsequently became an important area of local **Portuguese** trading activity.

During the 16th century the Mutasas struggled to maintain their independence against the **Gaza**, only to see their kingdom become the focus of Portuguese-British rivalry. Mutasa Chifambausiku (or Tendayi) was pressured to accept Portuguese sovereignty during the 1870s. In the late 1880s British prospectors entered the country, establishing mines at **Penhalonga** in 1889. In September 1890 the Mutasa signed a treaty with the **BSAC** official **Archibald Colquhoun**. Portuguese agents then moved in to reassert their influence, but were arrested by **P. W. Forbes** at Bingaguru in November. The **Anglo-Portuguese Convention** of 1891 resolved these European differences, and Manyika was partitioned between Southern Rhodesia and **Mozambique**, with the center of the kingdom lying in the British side. Mutasa Chifambausiku died in 1902 and was succeeded by Chakanyuka.

MUTASA, DIDYMUS EDWIN (July 27, 1935). Speaker of the **House of Assembly** of the first **Parliament** of independent Zimbabwe. Mutasa was born at Saint Faith's Mission in **Rusape**, the son of a village headman. He finished primary school in 1951. In 1957, as a delegate from the Makoni Students' Association, he attended the first **African National Congress**. In 1960 he established the Nyafaro Development Company in Nyanga, a collective farm, and later in that year joined the ministry of agriculture as an administrative officer. In 1961 he co-founded the Southern Region of the Federal Public Services Association. This organization acted to serve the interests of black civil servants, who were effectively excluded from the white-dominated civil servants' trade union. The new association was able to gain equity in pay based on qualifications.

Following the break-up of the **Federation**, Mutasa resigned from the civil service and joined with Guy Clutton-Brock to establish the Cold Comfort Society, a collective farming enterprise west of Harare. In the mid-1960s he became involved in the question of the **Tangwena Land Dispute**, raising money and becoming more openly defiant of government authorities. In November 1970, he was arrested as a result of this defiance and spent the next two years in prison. Released on the condition that he leave the country, he went to Britain, where he studied at Faircroft College and the University of Birmingham. He established the Birmingham Branch of the **Zimbabwe African National Union**, and in 1975 was elected ZANU (UK) district chairman. In 1976 he was a delegate to the **Geneva Conference**, and a year later moved to Maputo, **Mozambique**, to work full-time for ZANU. He was appointed to the Central Committee of the party in 1978 as deputy secretary of finance. Following the **Lancaster House Conference**, he returned to Zimbabwe and stood successfully as a ZANU (PF) candidate for **Manicaland Province.** On May 13, 1980, he was elected speaker of the assembly. In August 1984, at the Second Congress of ZANU (PF), he was elected a member of the Politburo and Central Committee, and he later served as the party's secretary for foreign affairs. Following the 1990 elections, Mugabe appointed him senior minister for political affairs in the office of the **president.** In a later cabinet reshuffling, Mutasa was appointed senior minister for national affairs, employment creation, and co-operatives. Following the 1995 elections, he left government to become the head of ZANU and its day-to-day organizational activities.

MUTASA DISTRICT. Demarcated in December 1973, Mutasa is a small, narrow-shaped district in the western part of **Manicaland Province.** **Nyanga District** is to the north, with **Makoni** to the west and **Mutare** on the south. The eastern border is shared with **Mozambique.** The district is made up exclusively of **Communal Lands.** The population in 1992 was 163,812.

MUTEKEDZA. Dynastic title of the rulers of a **Hera** chiefdom in present **Buhera District.**

MUTOKO (Mtoko until 1982). Mutoko is the administrative center of both **Mutoko District** and Mutoko **Communal Land** and is located on the middle-veld area just northeast of the Central Plateau (at 17°24'S, 32°13'E), The name is taken from the title of the ruler of the local **Budjga** people. Nearby is **Ruchero Cave.**

MUTOKO DISTRICT (Mtoko District until 1985). Roughly in the center of **Mashonaland East Province,** the district is bordered by **Rushinga District** at its northern tip, **Mudzi** to the northeast, **Makoni** to the southeast, and **Murewa** on the west, The **Ruenya River** separates it from **Nyanga District** on the east. Before 1980, most of the district was Tribal Trust Land (see **Communal Lands**), with land in the south reserved for Europeans and **Purchase Area** farmers. District population in 1992 was 122,941.

MUTORASHANGA (Mtoroshanga until 1982). Mutorashanga (at 17°9'S, 30°40'E) is at the center of an important **chrome** producing region in the **Makonde District.**

MUTORWA (pl. *vatorwa*). **Chishona** term for stranger, or foreigner, living within a community. Such a person might later give rise to a **shave** spirit medium.

MUTOTA NYATSIMBA (fl. early 15th century). Founder of the **Munhumutapa** state. According to tradition, Mutota was the son of a **Karanga** ruler in **Guruhuswa.** On the death of his father, he acceded to the chiefship and then shifted his court to the **Dande** region in the north, leaving Guruhuswa under a relative named **Torwa.** Mutota established his first headquarters just north of present **Guruve,** then moved to Chitako Hill, by the **Musengezi River.** His conquests of the local **Tavara** people earned him the nickname *Munhumutapa,* "the pillager"—a name his successors adopted as a dynastic title. Establishment of the new state near the **Zambezi River** led to greatly increased trade with coastal-based **Muslims**. On his death, some time before c.1450, Mutota was succeeded by his son, **Matope Nyanhehwe**.

MUTOPO (pl., *mitupo*). **Chishona** term for "totem" or clan name. Shona clans are patrilineal. They are divided into subclans known as *zvidao* (sing., *chidao* or *chidawo*). Rules of exogamy permit marriage between holders of the same *mutopo*, but not of the same *chidao*.

Mutopo and *chidao* are also sometimes translated as "praise name." *Mitupo* are typically named after animals with which certain taboos are associated. For example, members of the Soko clan are not allowed to harm vervet monkeys (*soko*). (See **Isibongo**.)

MUTSWAIRO, SOLOMON MANGWIRO (b. April 26, 1924). Born in **Mazowe District** to Christian missionary parents, Mutswairo was the author of the first novel published in **Chishona**. After graduating from the University College of Ft. Hare in South Africa in 1953, he returned to the country to teach in mission schools. In 1959 he was among a group of teachers who left Howard Institute and established the Mazowe Secondary School. In 1960 he left for the United States to study at the University of Minnesota. He eventually received a Ph.D. degree in African literature from Howard University of Washington, D.C., in 1978. He returned to Zimbabwe in 1981 and became a lecturer in Shona traditional literature and thought at the **University of Zimbabwe**.

In 1956 Mutswairo published *Feso* (trans. into English in 1974), a short novel set sometime before the European occupation of Zimbabwe. *Feso*—the name of a character—gave an account of Shona traditional life, administration, and welfare. Although the story was ostensibly a simple historical romance, it became regarded by African nationalists as an allegorical protest against European rule. This interpretation enhanced the book's popularity but caused it to be banned by the government in 1968. In 1978 he published *Mapondera: Soldier of Zimbabwe*, a novel in English about the 19th century Shona hero, Mapondera, and his resistance to the European occupation of Zimbabwe. He has also published several other novels and collections of poetry, both in Chishona and English.

MUTUSWA, SOLOMON TAPFUMANEY (b. May, 1945). Mutuswa is probably better known by his **Chimurenga** name, Rex Nhongo. Born in the Charter Tribal Trust Lands (see **Communal Lands**), he received his primary education at mission schools and attended Zimuto Secondary School. It was during his time at secondary school that he became involved in **ZAPU** youth politics and was arrested for leading a demonstration at the school. In 1962 he was expelled because of his political activities and went to **Zambia**, where he enrolled in a secondary school but was once again expelled for political activity. Mutuswa returned to Rhodesia in 1963 after learning of his father's illness. He worked for Dunlap from 1963 to December 1967, when he fled to **Botswana** to escape arrest on charges of bribing African policemen to allow the escape of three ZAPU members who were under guard at a hospital in Bulawayo. He immediately contacted ZAPU representatives and was sent to Zambia in March 1968. From 1968 to 1970 he received military training in Moscow and Bulgaria. Following his return to Tanzania in May 1970 he became disenchanted with ZAPU because he thought that it was not actively pursuing the armed struggle inside **Rhodesia**. He joined **ZANU** and **ZANLA** in March 1971, and a year later crossed into Rhodesia with a group of 60 guerrillas. He quickly rose through the ranks of ZANLA, and when **Josiah Tongogara** was held in detention in Zambia (1975–76), Mutuswa acted as commander of ZANLA. In 1977 he was elected to the Central Committee of ZANU and appointed deputy minister for defense. He became acting commander of ZANLA forces following the death of Tongogara in December 1979. In August 1981 he was appointed commander of the **Zimbabwe National Army** and promoted to the rank of lieutenant-general. In January 1987 he officially changed his name back to Solomon Tapfumaney Mutuswa.

MUZARABANI DISTRICT (Centenary District until 1985). Northern border district in **Mashonaland Central Province,** Muzarabani is bisected east to west by the **Zambezi Escarpment**. In addition to **Mozambique** to the north, the district is bordered by **Mukurnbura District** on the east, **Mazowe** to the south, and **Guruve** to the west. The administrative center for the district is located at the village of **Centenary**. The northern half of the district is **Communal Land**, while the southern half is an area of commercial farms and a rich **tobacco** growing region. Prior to 1980, the southern half of the district was reserved for Europeans. District population in 1992 was 69,851.

MUZENDA, SIMON VENGAI (b. October 20, 1922). Nationalist and ZANU vice president. Born at **Gutu** in **Masvingo District**, Muzenda was educated at **Gokomere** mission and at **Domboshawa** industrial school. He trained in South Africa as a carpenter at Marianhill College, where following his graduation he taught from 1948 to 1950. He then returned home and first worked in a furniture factory in Bulawayo before opening his own workshop in Barbourfields township in 1953. In that same year he was elected secretary general of the (British) African National Voice Association, an organization established by **Benjamin Burombo**. He was later a provincial organizing secretary for the **National Democratic Party** until it was banned in late 1961. He then joined the newly constituted **Zimbabwe African People's Union** as **Midlands** administrative secretary. In 1962 he was arrested by the government on charges of sedition and sentenced to 12 years in prison, but served only two years before being released.

Following **Ndabaningi Sithole**'s split with **Joshua Nkomo**, Muzenda joined the **Zimbabwe African National Union** and was appointed deputy organizing secretary. When ZANU was banned in mid-1964 he was again arrested and spent the next several years in prison and detention camps. He was released in early 1972 and immediately joined the **African National Council** and began working for the rejection of the **Pearce Commission** proposals. In 1975 he was sent to Lusaka as the ANC's deputy organizing sercretary. It was at this time that he became the main link between **Josiah Tongogara** and other **ZANLA** leaders detained by the Zambian government for the assassination of **Herbert Chitepo**, and ZANU's leadership not in prison. He was sent by these detained leaders to **Mozambique** to inform **Robert Mugabe** of their support. Although he apparently did not meet Mugabe at that specific time, he stayed in Mozambique and joined ZANU's executive. He eventually became vice-president and second secretary of ZANU, making him the number two person in the party.

Muzenda returned to Zimbabwe following the **Lancaster House Conference** and was elected to the **House of Assembly** from **Gweru**. In March 1980 he was appointed deputy prime minister and minister for foreign affairs by Mugabe. In January of the following year, he gave up the foreign affairs position and moved to the office of the prime minister as chief adviser on national defense. At the 1984 ZANU Party Congress Muzenda was reelected vice president and second secretary of the party. He was returned to **Parliament** in the 1985 elections and continued as deputy prime minister. Following the promulgation of the **Unity Pact** and restructuring of the government in late 1987, Mugabe appointed him one of two senior vice presidents, along with Joshua Nkomo. He retained that appointment throughout the 1990s.

MUZOREWA, ABEL TENDEKAYI (b. April 14, 1925). Prime minister of the short-lived **Republic of Zimbabwe Rhodesia** from June to December 1979. Born at **Old Umtali** Mission, he attended primary and secondary school at the mission and became an evangelist before going on to study at Hartzell Theological Seminary, Old Umtali, where he was ordained a minister of the **United Methodist Church** in August 1953. He worked as a pastor in the **Rusape** area until 1958 when he left the country to study at colleges in Missouri and Tennessee, earning B.A. and Master's degrees. He returned to the country in 1963 to become pastor at Old Umtali Mission, and a year later was appointed national director of the church's Christian Youth Movement. On August 28, 1968, he was made Bishop of Rhodesia—the top post of the UMC.

Muzorewa first came to public notice in 1971 when he was banned by the government from entering Tribal Trust Lands (see **Communal Lands**), an act which greatly restricted his work as bishop. Although having no prior nationalistic political experience, he was approached in November 1971 by a delegation representing both **ZAPU** and **ZANU** and asked to head a new organization being formed to oppose the Anglo-Rhodesian Settlement proposals. In December, he was made chairman of the **African National Council** and helped to convince the **Pearce Commission** that the proposals were unacceptable to the African majority. Muzorewa's leadership of the ANC made him a national political figure with an international reputation. His rejection of violence made the Rhodesian government willing to talk to him, and in July 1973 he was invited by **Ian Smith** to talks regarding constitutional change. The two men met 14 times in ten months, discussing issues based on proposals very similar to the Anglo-Rhodesian proposals. When the final draft of these was presented to the ANC executive, they were totally rejected.

In April 1974, the military coup d'etat in Portugal altered the political situation in Southern Africa, greatly affecting Muzorewa's political career. South Africa's Prime Minister John Vorster, wanting to put an end to warfare in the region before it could spread into his country, began to place increased pressure on Smith to find a peaceful solution to the war. At the same time, the presidents of the **Frontline States**, also wanting to put an end to the regional wars which were very harmful to their own economies, began to press the different Zimbabwean nationalist organizations to work together. In a meeting in Lusaka, **Zambia,** in December 1974, the nationalist leaders agreed to a Declaration of Unity, placing their organizations under the "umbrella" of the ANC, and headed by Muzorewa. The unity, however, was short-lived. In August 1975, Muzorewa was acknowledged as head of the African delegation, which included **Joshua Nkomo** and **Ndabaningi Sithole,** at the abortive **Victoria Falls Conference,** but soon afterwards the ANC began to fragment into its original components. Nkomo returned to Harare to head the "internal wing" of the ANC, while Muzorewa attempted to organize an "external wing" and guerrilla army, first in Lusaka and then Dar es Salaam and **Mozambique.** He failed to raise a fighting force and returned to the country just prior to the 1976 **Geneva Conference.**

Following the failure of that conference and Nkomo and **Robert Mugabe's** announcement of the **Patriotic Front,** which gained the support of both the **Organization of Africa Unity** and the Frontline presidents, Muzorewa was left without any real external support. He denounced the Patriotic Front as not representing the majority of Africans in the country. He was also angered by the British when they excluded him from cease-fire negotiations. Under these conditions Muzorewa, along with Sithole and **Chief Chirau,** was then willing to negotiate an **"internal settlement"** with Smith, provided he committed to the concept of majority rule and one-man one-vote. Smith made a statement apparently accepting these two points, and talks started in November 1977.

An agreement was reached in March 1978 calling for majority rule. A transitional government under an executive board was to be established to oversee the country until **elections** could be held. Muzorewa, along with the other three signatories, was a member of that executive board. In April 1979, elections where held and Muzorewa's United African National Council (see **ANC**) won 68 percent of the vote. He was asked to form a government and became prime minister of Zimbabwe Rhodesia in June 1979. He was also minister of defense, and in this role vigorously prosecuted the war, approving cross border raids into Zambia and Mozambique. However, he was unable to gain the hoped-for international recognition of his government. Following a Commonwealth Heads of Government meeting in Lukasa in August, the British government called for an all parties constitutional conference to be held at **Lancaster House** in London in September. Muzorewa led the Rhodesian delegation to that conference, which concluded in December with agreements having been reached on a new **constitution** and a cease-fire to the war. On December 12, the Zimbabwe Rhodesia House of Assembly voted to cease being an independent state, and Muzorewa's tenure as prime minister came to an end.

In the February 1980 elections the UANC won only three seats in **Parliament,** Muzorewa being elected from the **Mashonaland East Province.** In October 1983, he was arrested and held in detention following a trip to Israel, with a stop on his return in South Africa. He was released in September 1984. He lost his seat in Parliament in the elections of July 1985. In November of that year Muzorewa announced his retirement from public politics. However, he continued to be a vocal critic of both Mugabe personally and government policy in general. He reemerged into public political activities in the early 1990s when the UANC, which he still led, briefly joined with **Edgar Tekere's Zimbabwe Unity Movement**. In September 1994 he and Tekere announced the formation of the **United Party of Zimbabwe**, in association with the **Forum Party**, to contest the 1995 elections. Muzorewa and Tekere were named co-leaders. One month later, this opposition coalition split apart and Muzorewa publicly stated that he was the sole leader of the UP. Two weeks prior to the April 1995 elections, he criticized Mugabe, the government, and ZANU for creating "an uneven playing field" and declared that the UP was withdrawing from the campaign and elections.

MUZUNGU (pl., *vazungu*). Early **Chishona** term for **Portuguese**. (See also **Murungu**.)

MVUMA (variant: Mumvumi; Umvuma until 1982). Administrative center of the **Chirumanzu District**, Mvuma is located about halfway between **Masvingo** and **Gweru** on the former's branch **railway** line (at 19°17′S, 30°32′E; alt. 1,395 m). The town was founded in 1902 to serve the Falcon Mine, which was the country's leading **gold** and **copper** producer between 1912 and 1924. The mine was started over minor precolonial African workings, and it has retained its position as one of the country's leading copper producers.

MWAMI (Miami until 1982). Mwami village is located c.190 km northwest of Harare, which serves as the administrative center for **Hurungwe District** (at 16°40′S, 29°46′E). The village is surrounded by **tobacco** farms, **cattle** ranches, and various mines, the most important of which produce **mica**.

MWARI. Name of the **Shona** high god. There is considerable controversy and confusion over the origins and meaning of the name "Mwari," Mwari's role in different varieties of **Shona religion**, and the nature of Mwari belief. The name "Mwari" is used in at least three distinct contexts: (1) Mwari is universally used among the Shona for the concept of high god, or god of the sky, although various subgroups also use such other names as **Dzivaguru** and **Wedenga**. (2) A highly organized and influential cult system based in the **Matopo Hills** worships Mwari and communicates with him directly through oracular shrines maintained by a hierarchy of consecrated priests and messengers (see, e.g., **Matonjeni; Njelele**). This cult system is recognized mainly in the southern half of the country among the **Venda** and southern Shona—mainly the **Kalanga** and **Karanga**. According to some authorities, this cult system (sometimes called "Mwarism") has nothing to do with Mwari belief among the northern Shona—the **Zezuru** and **Korekore**. (3) Many Christian missionaries have translated "God" as "Mwari," thereby giving the name a loose, generic meaning. Further confusion has been caused by Europeans who frequently treat "Mwari" and the Sotho-Ndebele term *Mlimo* as synonyms in all three contexts.

Although there are numerous studies of Shona religion, there are significant disagreements about the role of Mwari. On some influential points, however, there seems to be general agreement. All Shona regard

Mwari as a remote high god. To many he is the creator of mankind, the provider of both good and evil, and the bringer of rain. Mwari stands above the ancestral spirits (see **Mhondoro; Mudzimu)** and unlike them, he never had an earthly existence. Mwari is not interested in personal affairs of mankind, but only in community or national matters.

There are two ways people approach Mwari: directly, through the oracular shrines in the Matopos; or indirectly, through intermediary ancestor spirits. The latter manifest themselves in such mediums as the *mhondoro*. These two modes of approach represent a basic split between southern and northern Shona religious systems; however, the two systems are not mutually exclusive, as some communities worship Mwari both ways.

Many theories about the origin of Mwari belief have been advanced, but a more immediate historical problem is the question of connections between the southern cult system and local political systems. Historians have formerly argued that the cult originated at **Great Zimbabwe** in the southeast, moving west to the Matopos with the **Rozvi Changamire** state. The notion that Great Zimbabwe was connected with either the Mwari cult or the Rozvi is now increasingly discredited. It appears instead that the cult originated among the Kalanga in the southwest, where the Rozvi found it in full operation on their own arrival. The relationship between the Rozvi rulers and the Mwari priests is also controversial. It has even been argued that the Rozvi had nothing to do with the cult, which may have been introduced to the region by Venda priests from the northern Transvaal after the breakup of the Changamire state in the early 19th century.

Yet another controversy surrounds the relationship between the 19th century **Ndebele** rulers and the Matopos Mwari shrines. The Ndebele are known to have consulted the oracles. From this bare evidence it has been argued that the Ndebele assimilated Shona Mwari belief into their own system of beliefs, truly merging their concepts of *Mlimo* with those of Mwari. It has further been argued that Mwari cult officials, notably **Mkwati**, inspired, organized, and directed the **1896 Ndebele Revolt** until a split developed between Mwari and Ndebele leaders. More recently it has been demonstrated that the Mwari cult had little influence on Ndebele life in the 19th century and that its priests played a limited role in the Ndebele Revolt. (See also the role of *mhondoro* in the **Shona Revolt**.)

Both the Mwari cult and more generalized Mwari belief have continued to flourish in the 20th century and must still be regarded as the country's dominant religion.

"MWENE MUTAPA" (variant: Mwanamutapa). Popular variant of **Munhumutapa**. "Mwene Mutapa" is usually translated by historians as "Master Pillager" but the **Chishona** word *Mwene*, meaning "owner," has incorrectly been substituted for *munhu*, "person."

MWENEZI (Nuanetsi until 1982). This village (at 21°25′S, 30°44′E) is the administrative headquarters for **Mwenezi District** and is located on the main road between **Masvingo** and **Beitbridge**.

MWENEZI DISTRICT (Nuanetsi District until 1985). A little-developed region in the **Masvingo Province**, covering 20,765 sq km between the

Bubye and **Lundi** Rivers. The district was originally part of the once huge **Chivi District**, which now touches Mwenezi only at the latter's northern boundary. Mwenezi also borders **Chiredzi** along the northeast and southeast, **Beitbridge** on the southwest, and **Gwanda** and **Mberengwa** on the west. District headquarters are at **Mwenezi**, with an additional important location being the village of **Rutenga**. Prior to 1980, except for the northwest sector, the district was reserved for Europeans. District population in 1992 was 101,354.

MWENYE (pl., *vamwenye*). **Chishona** term for **Muslim**; also used by other **Bantu**-speaking peoples in the Zambezi Valley. The term is apparently a variation of Chishona *mweni*, "stranger." The term *Mwenye* is also occasionally applied to the **Lemba** people.

MZILA (variants: Umzila; Muzila) (d.1884). The eldest son of **Soshangane**, Mzila became ruler of the **Gaza** kingdom in 1862 after ousting his brother Mawewe, who had usurped power on Soshangane's death. Mzila obtained his rightful kingship with the help of the **Portuguese**, who afterwards plagued him with claims of sovereignty over the Gaza. Mzila then shifted Gaza headquarters from the lower **Limpopo River** to **Mt. Silinda**, just west of the present **Mozambique** border (see **Manhlagazi**). There he continued his predecessor's policy of raiding surrounding **Shona** communities, but he failed in his attempts to conquer the **Manyika** of **Mutasa**. Portuguese pressure on his kingdom mounted, and the Portuguese ally **Manuel de Sousa** pushed the Gaza back from their outposts in the Zambezi Valley. In 1870 Mzila began a fruitless quest to seek British assistance against the Portuguese. He meanwhile established cordial relations with the **Ndebele** kingdom to the west, culminating in an exchange of royal wives with **Lobengula** (see **Xwalile**). After his death, Mzila was succeeded by his son **Gungunyane** (see also **Law, A.**).

MZILIKAZI KHUMALO (variants: Moselekatse; Silkaats; Umziligazi; etc.) (c.1790s–Sept. 1868). Founder and first ruler of the **Ndebele** kingdom. Mzilikazi was born in Zululand, the son of **Mashobane**, a minor **Khumalo** clan chief. He was raised at the court of his maternal grandfather Zwide, the ruler of the Ndwandwe, during an era of rapid northern **Nguni** political expansion and militarization. A year or so after Mzilikazi succeeded his father as Khumalo chief, he and his people shifted allegiance to the new Zulu king Shaka in c.1819. After serving Shaka as an apparently unexceptional frontier administrator, Mzilikazi defied the Zulu king's authority and led perhaps 500 people—mostly men—into the eastern **Transvaal** in c.1821. There he founded the Ndebele kingdom and began a two-decade career as a migratory military leader.

Mzilikazi entertained his first European visitors in 1829, while he was living near the site of present Pretoria. One of these visitors was the missionary **Robert Moffat**, for whom Mzilikazi developed a lifelong affection. Moffat and other Europeans also visited Mzilikazi in the western Transvaal in 1835, by which time Mzilikazi was living mainly in an **ox wagon**, in which he moved about his kingdom almost constantly. Another 1835 visitor was Dr. Andrew Smith, who was head of a scientific exploration expedition. When Smith returned to Cape Town, Mzilikazi sent along his adviser **Mncumbathe**, who signed a treaty in his name with the British governor Benjamin D'Urban in March 1836.

When the Ndebele left the Transvaal for present **Matabeleland** in 1838, they separated into two main migratory parties in eastern **Botswana.** One party followed **Kaliphi** (a.k.a. Gundwane) almost directly to the new homeland. Mzilikazi himself led the second party deeper into Botswana. He appears to have traveled no farther north than the Makarikari Pan, where he turned east, following the **Nata River** into Matabeleland in c.mid-1839. When he rejoined the rest of his people, he found they had installed his son **Nkulumane** as acting king in his place. In what became famous as the **Ntabazinduna** affair, Mzilikazi eliminated the dissident *izinduna* (chiefs) and thereafter experienced no further serious challenges to his authority. The fate of Nkulumane during this affair remained a mystery during the rest of Mzilikazi's lifetime, creating serious problems for his successor **Lobengula**, another son. Over the next 14 years Mzilikazi appears to have played a less active role in Ndebele warfare than previously. His communications with the European world were reopened in 1854 when Robert Moffat paid him a visit. Moffat found him badly overweight and suffering from various ailments of the joints which left him immobile, and the missionary administered some medicinal relief. Mzilikazi accompanied Moffat on a leisurely wagon journey to the north, and then returned to central Matabeleland to trade **ivory** with **S. H. Edwards**. Many more European traders and hunters soon entered the country, but Mzilikazi retained a monopoly over Ndebele commerce. Moffat visited again in 1857, obtaining permission to bring Christian missionaries into the country. Two years later Moffat brought in an LMS party which established a permanent, but long unsuccessful, mission station at **Inyati.** Mzilikazi's health continued to deteriorate badly during his last years. Meanwhile, European interest in the country increased greatly because of **gold** discoveries. After his death in early September 1868, Mzilikazi was interred at **Nthumbane**. Mncumbathe acted as regent until the installation of Lobengula in early 1870.

MZILIKAZI MEMORIAL. National Monument on the 1860s site of the **Ndebele** *ibutho* town **Mhlahlandlela.** (See also **Nthumbane.**)

MZINGELI, CHARLES (1905–1981). Perhaps the country's single most powerful African protest leader before the rise of mass nationalism in the late 1950s, Mzingeli was born into an **Ndebele** family near **Plumtree**. He was raised a Roman Catholic and received some education at **Empandeni** before leaving home to become a railway worker at age 14. He worked in **Bulawayo,** Northern Rhodesia and, apparently, South Africa before returning to Bulawayo in the late 1920s. There he joined the newly formed **ICU**. In late 1929 he was made ICU's organizing secretary and was sent to Salisbury, which he then made his permanent home. He gave speeches before large crowds, denouncing the white establishment and calling for an end to interethnic African rivalries. As an Ndebele in a **Shona** region, he was notably successful in enrolling members in the ICU. His radicalism brought down constant government harassment—resulting in his brief imprisonment—and forced his reluctant break from the Roman Catholic Church. After the collapse of the ICU in the mid-1930s he made his living by working as a musician in dance bands.

In 1941 Mzingeli turned away from purely African trade unionism by joining the once exclusively **European Labour Party**, for which he formed an African branch in Harare. The expulsion of African members from the Labour Party in 1944 dispelled his hopes of working with progressive Europeans. In early 1946 he joined with other African labor leaders to form the **RICU** and was made its leader. During the late 1940s he led the African fight agrainst the **Native (Urban Areas) Accommodation Act** and other discriminatory laws and was a leading spokesman before the government during the general strike of 1948. He was also elected to the advisory board in Harare, dominating this body for ten years as the township's "unofficial mayor." He meanwhile maintained himself by running a small grocery store.

Mzingeli's continuing prestige was recognized in 1952 when he was named acting president of the **All-African Convention**. However, this organization was short-lived, and Mzingeli was accused by his fellow officers of being too difficult a person to work with. The **Youth League**, which formed in 1955, made Mzingeli its first target, denouncing him as an outmoded reformist. By 1957 he had lost his advisory board seat and his days as a radical were over. Now disillusioned with African nationalists, he turned to multiracial organizations and joined the ruling **UFP**. During the 1961 constitutional conference he personally presented the UFP's proposals for the double roll "A" and "B" franchise (see **Constitution of 1961**).

MZIZI, WILLIAM (a.k.a. Mbulale) (fl.1830s–1890s). **Mfengu** "war doctor" among the **Ndebele**. Mzizi appears to have been born in Zululand around 1830 and to have fled with his family to the eastern Cape during Dingane's reign. He lived near Peddie until c.1859, and then went to Lesotho to work for King Moshweshwe, finally settling among Waterboer's Griqua near Kimberley. In the late 1860s his son—also named William Mzizi (or Hlegizana)—went to **Matabeleland** as a **hunter**. There he told **Mncumbathe** and other *izinduna* of his father's skill as a war doctor. Ndebele officials then sent for the elder Mzizi to assist in resolving the current succession dispute—apparently because Mzizi claimed a connection with the ancestral **Khumalo**. Mzizi is said to have "consecrated" the new King **Lobengula** after his arrival in Matabeleland.

Mzizi's family and other Mfengu were given land to live on near **Bulawayo,** where they were known as the Amazizi. During Lobengula's reign Mzizi became famous as a "war doctor," administering medicines to *impis* before and after raids (his son may have shared in this work). He married a daughter of Lobengula and was granted many special privileges, such as owning **horses** and an **ox wagon**. By the late 1880s he was blind. He later blamed his handicap for his failure to confer success on Ndebele forces during the **1893 Ndebele War**.

N

NADA (Native Affairs Department Annual). Published continuously from 1923 to 1980, this annual journal served as a forum for the writings of African administration officers and other amateur researchers into African affairs. Its articles dealt mostly with African history, contemporary life, and customs. Though many of *Nada*'s contributions suffered from poor scholarship or narrow antiquarian perspectives, the journal also published many others of seminal importance—notably those pertaining to regional histories. These have proved to be invaluable sources for Africanist scholars. In 1964 the journal was officially retitled *The Ministry of Internal Affairs Annual*, but the familiar acronym "*Nada*" was retained as the lead title.

NAGANA (Animal *trypanosomiasis*). Endemic parasitic disease transmitted among animals by the **tsetse fly**. The name "nagana," now used widely in Africa, derives from the Zulu word *nakane*. Feral animals are largely immune to nagana, but the disease is usually fatal to the larger domestic animals. The role of nagana in African history can hardly be exaggerated. It has determined human migration routes, influenced settlement patterns, and prevented some peoples from breeding livestock. During the **Ndebele** migration from Zululand to **Matabeleland** during the 1820s and 1830s, the threat of nagana to **cattle** may have altered the direction of their route as many as three different times. After the Ndebele settled in Matabeleland, the presence of the tsetse fly restricted their settlements to the region south of the **Samabula Forest**. Other peoples in the country—mostly the **Shona**—lived in more dangerous nagana areas and consequently kept fewer cattle than they otherwise might have. The reduction of the disease during the 20th century has been due mainly to the reclamation of tsetse-infested areas. (See also **Sleeping Sickness; see Health.**)

NALATALE RUINS (variants: Naletali; Nanatali; N'natali). Small but famous stone ruin complex of the **Khami culture** period built on a large granite dome in the southern **Gweru District** (at 19°53'S, 29°32'E). The ruins comprise a single, isolated building complex noted for its long and complexly decorated wall and for its commanding view of the surrounding countryside. The building, which may not have been completed by the 19th century, is believed to have been intended as only a temporary dwelling—perhaps for the **Changamire** rulers. The only recorded excavation of the site was a brief one undertaken by **D. Randall-MacIver** in 1905.

NAMABYZYA see **NANZWA**

NANATALI (variant: N'natali) see **NALATALE RUINS**

NANDI. Village on the **Chiredzi River** serving as the terminus of a branch southeastern **railway** line completed in 1964–65 (at 20°58'S, 31°44'E).

N'ANGA. Varient of **nganga.**

NANZWA (Abananzwa; variants: Nambya; Nambzya; etc.). Cluster of peoples living mostly in the **Hwange District** which takes its name from **Zank**e (or **Hwange**), the title of the most important Nanzwa rulers. The origin of these peoples is controversial. They are often classified as a branch of the **Kalanga** cluster of **Shona**-speakers, but many now speak **Sindebele.** It is generally believed that the first Zanke was a **Rozvi** immigrant from the **Changamire** state who imposed his rule over local **Tonga.** It is not clear, however, whether this conquest took place before or just after the Changamire state itself was broken up by the **Ngoni** invasions of the early 1830s. The early Zankes are also said to have built and resided in the **Bumbuzi Ruins.**

From the 1840s to the 1890s the Nanwza were heavily pressured by the **Ndebele** in the southwest, the **Kololo,** and then the **Lozi** north of the **Zambezi River.** In 1853 the Ndebele raided the Nanzwa, killing Zanke Lusumbami (or Rusumbami), and making Silisa the new Zanke. Silisa proved a reluctant vassal, however, and was driven across the Zambezi by the Ndebele in 1862. By the 1870s the Nanzwa were paying tribute to both the Ndebele and the Lozi and were living on both sides of the Zambezi. The Ndebele helped to make Nekatembe the next Zanke in the 1880s, but their raids continued into the 1890s. In 1893 Nanzwa chiefs brought the Wankie coal fields to the attention of Europeans at **Tati,** and Wankiewas subsequently developed into one of Africa's major producing centers. The Zankes are now government-paid chiefs.

NATA RIVER (a.k.a. Manzamnyama). Draining one of the country's driest regions, the Nata is the largest stream to flow from Zimbabwe to **Botswana.** It rises near **Figtree,** whence it flows northwest and then west into Botswana, where it enters the Makarikari Pan. Part of the river separates the districts of **Nyamandhlovu** and **Bululmamangwe.**

NATIONAL ARCHIVES OF ZIMBABWE (NAZ). During the period of **BSAC** administration, public records were not centrally housed; storage was left to individual government departments. After 1923 interest in preserving records grew, culminating in the **Legislative Assembly's** creation of the national archives in 1935. Under the direction of Chief Archivist V. W. Hiller, the new archives surveyed and collected surviving public records and sought to acquire privately held documents. As these records were assembled in Salisbury (now Harare), Hiller attempted to retrieve the large body of records stored in the BSAC's long-closed London offices. Unfortunately, those records were destroyed during a German air raid in 1941. After the war Northern Rhodesia and Nyasaland (now **Zambia** and Malawi) added their official records to the repository, which became known as the Central African Archives (see **Central African Council**). In 1956 the **federation** government established the National Archives Trust to coordinate planning for the creation of an official national archives. In 1958 the Federal Archives Act designated the institution of the CAA as the National Archives of Rhodesia and Nyasaland. A new archives building was opened in 1961, and it quickly ranked as one of the largest, best-housed and organized historical archives in tropical Africa—a reputation it has maintained. When the federation broke up two years later,

Zambia and Malawi withdrew their territorial records while retaining access to the purely federal records left in Harare.

Through a vigorous acquisitions policy which has included extensive photocopying and microfilming of overseas documents and the active collection of oral histories within the country, the NAZ has developed into an unrivaled center for local historical research. The main divisions of the NAZ are (1) *Public Archives*, housing official government records, most of which are protected by a 30-year rule. (2) *Historical Manuscripts Collection*, containing private papers of individuals, families, churches, and other nonofficial bodies. Notable are papers of **David Livingstone** and the **Moffat** family. (3) *Library*, which houses more than 39,000 volumes of Africana. The NAZ library also is the official depository for all books and periodicals published in the country. (4) *Records Management*, which is responsible for the storage of government documents less than 30 years old, not open to public inspection. About 10 percent of these are eventually placed in Public Archives. (5) *Federal Records*, government documents from the period of federation. (6) *Pictoral Collection*, notably the paintings of **Thomas Baines**. (7) *Oral History Programs*, which collects oral materials on **Chishona, Sindebele**, and the English to supplement the documentary materials of NAZ. Materials collected cover a wide range of topics, from interviews with spirit mediums to popular songs from the period of the war for national liberation. (8) *Photographic Collection*, comprising several thousand photographs that document the history of the country from the European occupation to the present. (9) *Map Collection*. (See **Bibliography** for published archival guides and other NAZ publications.)

NATIONAL CONSTITUTIONAL ASSEMBLY (NCA). Founded in late 1997 following an eighteen-month political crisis in the country. That crisis first developed when **President Robert Mugabe** announced that he was appointing a constitutional reform commission. The stated goal of the commission was to draft a new constitution that would do away with sections of the 1980 constitution deemed no longer acceptable by the government. (See **Constitutions.**)

Opposition parties, on the other hand, viewed the commission as an attempt by Mugabe to entrench both **ZANU-PF**'s near monopoly control of **Parliament,** and Mugabe's own powers as president. At a meeting in **Gweru,** representatives of fourteen opposition parties agreed to form an alliance between themselves, as well as with civic groups and the country's labor movement, in an attempt to defeat the imposition of a new constitution. In September 1999, as an off-shoot of NCA activities, the **Movement for Democratic Change** was launched following the government's announcement that it would hold a nationwide initiative to approve the new draft constitution. In the February 2000 initiative vote, that draft constitution was rejected by almost 55 percent of the voters.

NATIONAL DEMOCRATIC PARTY (NDP). Predominately African political party founded on January 1, 1960, as the successor to the banned **African National Congress**. With most of the ANC leadership under government arrest, the NDP introduced such new leaders as **J. M. Chinamano, Herbert Chitepo, Michael Mawema, Robert Mugabe, S. T. Parirenyatwa, Leopold Takawira**, and Reuben Jamela, a trade union leader. In April, Mawema, the acting president, led a NDP delegation to the London conference on federal constitutional review and managed to head off **Edgar Whitehead**'s efforts to secure greater independence for Southern Rhodesia's white electorate. In July Mawema and other NDP leaders were arrested under the terms of the **Unlawful Organizations Act** for their supposed membership in the banned ANC. The NDP mounted large-scale demonstrations in the main urban centers to protest these arrests, and violence erupted when the government responded with police repression. The government then passed the **Law and Order (Maintenance) Act**.

A leadership dispute in the NDP was resolved later that year in favor of a compromise candidate, **Joshua Nkomo**, who was recalled from his voluntary exile in November to become president. In February 1961 Nkomo headed an NDP delegation at the constitutional conference, where the party eventually rejected proposals for the 1961 **constitution**. The party later called for an African boycott of the **elections** (see **"Build a Nation"**). On December 9, 1961, Whitehead's government banned the NDP. Shortly thereafter the party's leaders formed the **Zimbabwe African People's Union**.

The NDP differed from its predecessor, the ANC, in making a more direct attack on the constitutional basis of minority rule. Although it succeeded in having the **Native Land Husbandry Act** abolished, it concentrated more on demanding majority rule than on seeking reforms for specific grievances. The largely intellectual leadership of the party is said to have been less in touch with the rural areas. Nevertheless, the NDP is generally regarded as the country's first effective mass African political movement.

NATIONAL MONUMENTS see **HISTORICAL MONUMENTS COMMISSION**

NATIONAL PARKS. There are 15 national parks in the country, ranging in size from tiny **Ewanrigg** to Connecticut-size **Hwange**. The parks, and a similar number of **game reserves**, cover almost one-eighth of the country. Since the **Legislative Assembly** passed the National Parks Act in 1949, parks have been developed to meet three needs. Like the game reserves, some parks protect wildlife resources; unlike the reserves however, the parks are designed for public access. Other parks have been developed primarily to protect naturally scenic or historic attractions (see also **Historical Monuments Commission**). Foremost in this category are **Victoria Falls, Matopos, Chinhoyi Caves, Inyanga**, and **Zimbabwe**. The third category comprises a number of small parks developed mostly around artificial lakes for recreational **fishing** and camping. Many of these parks are near urban centers. **Lake Chivero** and **Ewanrigg** are close to Harare; **Ngezi** and **Sebakwe** are near Kwekwe and Kadoma; **Mushandike** and **Kyle** are near Masvingo; and **Vumba** is near Mutare.

NATIONAL PEOPLE'S UNION (NPU). Successor political party to the **United People's Party**, formed in June 1969. The NPU started with most of the African members of **Parliament**, but only Josiah Gondo (d. Oct. 1972) retained his seat after the 1970 election. In March 1972 NPU leaders dissolved the party and encouraged its members to support the **African National Council**. (See also **Centre Party**.)

NATIONAL RAILWAYS OF ZIMBABWE (NRZ) (formerly Rhodesia Railways Company). Autonomous state-owned corporation created in 1949 as the Rhodesia Railways Company after purchase from the **BSAC** in 1947. The company was originally created as a subsidiary of the BSAC in 1893, under the name Bechuanaland Railway Company. In 1899 the name was changed to Rhodesia Railways Ltd. The company built and operated **railway** lines in present **Zimbabwe**, **Zambia**, and **Mozambique**. The name was changed to NRZ following independence in 1980. (See **Railways**.)

NATIVE ACCOMMODATION AND REGISTRATION ACT see **NATIVE (URBAN AREAS) ACCOMMODATION AND REGISTRATION ACT**

NATIVE AFFAIRS DEPARTMENT ANNUAL see *NADA*

NATIVE CHRISTIAN CONFERENCE see under **SOUTHERN RHODE-SIAN MISSIONARY CONFERENCE**

NATIVE LAND HUSBANDRY ACT (LHA; a.k.a. African LHA) (1951). One of the white Southern Rhodesian government's most ambitious schemes to transform African life, the LHA was passed in mid-1951, three years after it had been published as the "Native Reserves Land Utilization and Good Husbandry Bill." The goal of the law was to improve conservation measures, to regulate the size of livestock herds, and, most importantly, to divide communal land holdings within the Native Reserves into individual family plots in order to make cash-earning peasants out of traditional farmers. The law combined the earlier Natural Resources Act of 1941 with many of **E. D. Alvord**'s agricultural programs, with the intention of making individual African farmers responsible to the government for the efficient operation of their holdings.

A key element of the LHA was transference of authority to allocate land from the government chiefs to the Native Commissioners (see **Districts**). The sheer magnitude of the task of surveying, dividing, and allocating plots was ultimately beyond the means of the government. Most of the reserve lands (see **Communal Lands**) were left unaffected by the time the scheme was abandoned in the early 1960s. More important was the widespread African resistance to the law. Destocking schemes were always unpopular, as were any schemes for massive change imposed from above. Further, while the law was naturally resisted by the traditional African authorities whom it undermined, it was also attacked by educated and urban Africans. An assumption of the law was that increased industrialization of the towns would absorb the reserves' surplus populations, obviating the need to provide rural land to all the country's Africans—a principle theoretically enshrined in the **Constitution of 1923** . The passage of time proved the invalidity of this assumption, while giving urbanized Africans opportunity to voice their fears of being left without security in either the reserves or in the towns, where they could not own land (see **ANC; Burombo, B; NDP; Ricu**). In practice the Africans affected by the LHA in the reserves tended to ignore its provisions, carrying on much as before, and the government finally let the law lapse because of its unenforcibility.

In 1965 the **Rhodesian Front** government passed the Tribal Trust Land Act, reversing objectives of the LHA. The TTL Act reinstated the authority of the chiefs to allocate land on communal principles, and it expressed the goal of having the TTLs absorb surplus African urban populations. (See **Agriculture; Land Apportionment and Tenure Acts; Urbanization.**)

NATIVE MIRROR. Early name of the *Bantu Mirror.*

NATIVE REGISTRATION ACT (1936) see under **PASS LAWS**

NATIVE RESERVES see **COMMUNAL LANDS**

NATIVE (URBAN AREAS) ACCOMMODATION AND REGISTRATION ACT (1946). Law introduced by **Godfrey Huggins** to enforce provisions of the **Land Apportionment Act** pertaining to segregation of towns. The law compelled municipal authorities to set aside land for African residences away from white residential and business areas and to provide housing units whose rents were to be paid by employers. An innovative feature of the law stipulated that rents for bachelors and married couples were to be the same, thereby promoting the stabilization of families in the towns in anticipation of a gradual shift of Africans away from the rural areas (see **Native Land Husbandry Act**). Although implementation of the law led to improved housing conditions, particularly in the capital, Africans vigorously protested the discriminatory principles upon which it was based, as well as the law's failure to provide security of tenure to Africans. (See **Urbanization.**)

NDANGA DISTRICT see **ZAKA DISTRICT**

NDAU. Ethnic and linguistic term for one of the main clusters of **Shona-speaking peoples**. The Ndau (or Vandau) live mainly in the southeastern part of the country and in **Mozambique**, from just west of the **Sabi River** to the Indian Ocean, and between the Sabi (or Save) River in the south, to c. 19°30′S lat. in the north. Nearly two-thirds of the Ndau live in Mozambique. Those who live in Zimbabwe constitute about 6 percent of the country's Shona population. During the 19th century Ndau territory was occupied by the **Nguni**-speaking **Gaza**, who left a strong Nguni cultural imprint on the local people. For this reason the Ndau are also known as **"shangane"**—a variant name of the Gaza—and the area they occupy in Mozambique is still called **"Gazaland."**

Since the independence of Zimbabwe in 1980, the area of the country inhabited by the Ndau—principally **Chipinge District**—has consistently opposed the **ZANU** dominated government of President **Robert Mugabe**. The area has voted for opposition candidates in every general **election** since independence—electing **Ndababningi Sithole** in the 1995 elections.

NDEBELE KINGDOM. (1) *History.* The Ndebele state was founded in South Africa in c.1821, when **Mzilikazi** left Zululand with c.500 kinsmen. During the state's first few years it was highly mobile, moving north from base to base in the eastern part of the **Transvaal**. By combining comparatively well-developed fighting techniques, efficient discipline, and a strong impulse for collective survival, the Ndebele conquered and absorbed many of the mainly **Sotho**-speaking communities they encountered during their migrations. Their numbers were further augmented by voluntary submissions of other *Mfecane*-derived **Nguni** bands. The Ndebele occupied Pedi territory for about one year and then turned southwest, settling along the middle Vaal River between c.1823 and c.1827. Their attempts to establish permanent settlements there were hindered by frequent raids by Sotho, Griqua, and other peoples. The Ndebele then sought greater security along the northern slopes of the Magaliesberg Mountains, in the area around present Pretoria (c.1827–32). Through these years the Ndebele continued to mount their own raids, reaching into eastern **Botswana** and, on one occasion, even into present Zimbabwe (see **Kaliphi**). Both the Ndebele population (see **Ndebele People**) and **cattle** herds continued to grow.

Although the Ndebele repelled most major attacks on their own cattle posts, continued harassment by enemies threatened their long-term security. After a large-scale assault by the Zulu of Dingane in 1832, the Ndebele moved farther west. From 1832 to 1837 they lived along the upper Marico River in the western Transvaal. By then the military strength of the kingdom was unrivaled by its African neighbors. The situation changed after 1835, when **Afrikaner** families began migrating inland from the British-ruled Cape Colony in the exodus known as the "Great Trek." Clashes with advance Afrikaner parties in 1836 led to very effective Afrikaner retaliation against Ndebele towns early the next year (see **Potgieter, A. H.**). Independent Griqua campaigns and a second major Zulu attack made the Ndebele situation critical by the end of 1837. The Ndebele then moved into eastern Botswana, where they subsequently divided into two migrant parties. Under the leadership of Kaliphi, one party advanced almost directly into present **Matabeleland** where they established the permanent Ndebele base. Mzilikazi's party continued north, finally rejoining the other Ndebele in Matabeleland in about mid-1839. There Mzilikazi had to deal with a political crisis which ultimately left permanent scars in the kingdom's fabric (see **Nkulumane; Ntabazinduna**).

Ndebele occupation of the new, mainly **Shona**-speaking region was made easier by the political disruption of the **Changamire** state in the wake of **Ngoni** invasions. During the 1840s raiding parties extended Ndebele influence over neighboring Shona communities, cattle were retrieved from former Sotho tributaries in the south, and several abortive campaigns were waged against the **Kololo** north of the **Zambezi River**. The next decade was a period of relative tranquility, marked by the reestablishment of contacts with European missionaries (see **London Missionary Society; Moffat, R.**), traders (see **Edwards, S. H.**), and **hunters**. By the early 1860s the main challenge to the Ndebele dominance of the region came from the **Ngwato** to the southwest. The Ndebele never completely subdued all the neighboring Shona peoples, but these never seriously threatened the security of the kingdom itself. (See **Tohwechipi**.)

A third phase in the kingdom's history began in 1868. Mzilikazi's death inaugurated a divisive interregnum (see **Mncumbathe**), and rediscovery of Shona **gold** workings initiated an era of increasingly intense European pressure for **concessions** (see **Mauch, K.; northern Goldfields; Tati**). **Lobengula** was made king early in 1870, but he soon had to put down a rebellion (see **Mbigo; Zwangendaba**). Afterwards his reign was never free of internal challenges. By the late 1880s the expansion of European imperial pressure—then affecting all of tropical Africa—clearly threatened the kingdom's independence. One of the last major states in southern Africa to retain its independence, the Ndebele kingdom became the focus of British, **Portuguese**, and the Afrikaner diplomatic rivalries north of the **Limpopo River**, even though the kingdom effectively controlled less than half of what became Zimbabwe. (See **Gaza Kingdom**.)

British interests prevailed through the vehicle of **Cecil Rhodes' BSAC**. By exaggerating the extent of Ndebele dominance north of the Limpopo while misrepresenting rights granted by Lobengula (see **Lippert Concession; Moffat Treaty; Rudd Concession**), the BSAC occupied **Mashonaland** in 1890. It then used that territory as a base for invading the Ndebele in 1893 (see **Ndebele War**). It has long been argued that Lobengula's death in early 1894 brought the kingdom to an end, but this view has been challenged by J. R. Cobbing, who has demonstrated that the nonmonarchical institutions of the state were only slightly disrupted, that the Ndebele were far from "demilitarized," and that British occupation of Matabeleland was slight up to 1896. According to this view, the **Revolt of 1896** was the last gasp of the kingdom itself, and restoration of the monarchy was a main objective of the rebels (see **Nyamanda**). After the revolt, BSAC occupation of the Ndebele became effective for the first time. Communities were relocated into reserves (see **Communal Lands**), and the kingdom became only a memory, despite continued Ndebele efforts to restore the monarchy (see **Matabele Home Society**).

(2) *Description*. In contrast to the earlier, large **Munhumutapa** and **Changamire** state systems, the Ndebele kingdom was highly centralized and capable of rapid and efficient military mobilization. However, these characteristics have probably been exaggerated in the comparatively large literature on the 19th century Ndebele kingdom. Family clans (see **Isibongo**) played a small part in Ndebele political organization, but the kingdom was effectively a collection of hereditary chieftaincies (*izigaba*), whose members owed a common allegiance to the kings (see **Inkosi**). Cutting across these chieftaincies were a large number of male age-sets, or *amabutho* (see **Ibutho**), which the kings periodically raised to be trained as military police units. The kings also appointed chiefs (see **Induna**) over the *amabutho*, but over time the units tended to evolve into chieftaincies whose leadership became effectively hereditary. Tension between the kings and the chieftaincies increased over time, particularly as outlying chiefs sought greater autonomy. This was a problem experienced particularly by Lobengula, and it partly explains Ndebele disunity in the 1893 Ndebele War and the 1896 Revolt. (For examples of important chiefs, see **Faku; Gampu; Mhlaba; Mlugulu; Mpotshwana; Mtshani; Xukutwayo;** et al.)

Throughout the history of the kingdom, raids were regularly mounted against other African communities. One purpose of raids, particularly in the early decades, was to capture new people to incorporate into the society, and cattle. The kings maintained their power partly by overseeing the distribution of booty. They also tended to monopolize the conduct of foreign trade (see, e.g., **Horses; Ivory; Ostriches**). The 19th-century Ndebele kingdom has typically been characterized as economically parasitic, but the mainstays of the Ndebele diet were grains that the Ndebele themselves grew (see **Agriculture**). Cattle were important as symbols of wealth and prestige and as currency in social transactions such as marriage (see **Lobolo**), but beef played a small role in diet.

A second purpose of raids was to reduce neighboring communities to tributary status. Tributaries provided goods and services, which the kings redistributed among the Ndebele, and tributary communities stood as "buffers" against potential foreign enemies. The notion that the Ndebele laid waste a wide band of surrounding territory is a popular but unfounded myth, as the Ndebele actually were surrounded by tributary communities.

A third purpose of raids was to punish tributaries whose loyalty wavered. It was raids of this nature into **Mashonaland** in the early 1890s that gave **L. S. Jameson** his immediate pretext for waging war on the Ndebele in 1893.

The core of the Ndebele kingdom was a c.10,000 sq km area surrounding **Bulawayo** between the **Matopo Hills** on the south and the **Somabula Forest** on the north. The area of effective Ndebele domination over tributaries was considerably larger, but still only a large part of the territory later designated as the province of Matabeleland. People lived in villages and towns of various sizes, up to several hundred people each. Some of these towns were associated with the *amabutho,* but few approached the enormous sizes popularly ascribed to "regimental towns." Many adult males participated in military campaigns for a few weeks during the dry seasons (see **Climate**). Otherwise, the day-to-day lives of the bulk of the people were very similar to those of other, non-Ndebele peoples in the country.

NDEBELE PEOPLE (Amandebele; on origin of name, see "MATABELE"). The largest group of non-Shona-speaking people in the country, the Ndebele live mostly in the southwestern districts, particularly around **Bulawayo**. Creation of a "Ndebele" ethnic identity coincided with the formation of the **Ndebele kingdom** in the early 19th century. Along with the kingdom, this sense of ethnic identity developed as increasing numbers of **Nguni, Sotho, Shona**, and other peoples were incorporated into the society. However, while the kingdom ended in the 1890s, concepts of Ndebele identity have continued to develop.

During the 19th century Ndebeleness was primarily a political concept, measured by allegiance to the kings. An individual might therefore have been regarded as a Ndebele before adopting all aspects of the dominantly Nguni Ndebele culture. The sudden abolition of the kingdom by the Europeans made such former political allegiances largely irrelevant (though many chieftaincies survived). Unlike the case of the **Gaza**, whose kingdom was abolished in southern **Mozambique,** the identity of the Ndebele remained strong into the 20th century. The inchoate kingdom impressed its **Sindebele** language on most of its subjects permanently. Ndebele society subsequently grew larger through both natural population growth and voluntary acculturation by individuals eager to share the historical identity. This latter phenomenon has compounded the problem of defining who is a "Ndebele." Language has become the most important modern criterion. Another is family name (see **Isibongo**). Nineteenth-century Ndebele society was broadly inclusive (see, e.g., **Mzizi, W.; William the Griqua**), but today only family names brought to the country by the original immigrants from South Africa guarantee recognition as a Ndebele to any individual. This situation implies a certain contradiction, as the majority of the people regarded as Ndebele by the late 19th century were of local origin.

During the mid-19th century, Europeans began to propound the notion that Ndebele society was rigidly divided into three "castes." The aristocratic *zansi* were said to be at the top politically and socially. The *enhla* were in the middle, and the majority *holi* were at the bottom, in an allegedly servile capacity. Intermarriage between these "castes" was said to be forbidden, and is said still to be rare. It should be stressed that there is no evidence that the Ndebele ever practiced a caste system comparable to that found in Indian Hindu society. The terms *zansi* and *enhla* served mainly to identify people on the basis of their geographical origins—a system more analogous to eastern American "high society." It remains to be demonstrated to what extend these distinctions helped or hindered Ndebele individuals' actual social and political opportunities.

Historically, estimates of the size of the Ndebele population have been crude because of primitive census-taking techniques and the problem of identifying who are Ndebele. With these limitations in mind, the following figures may be taken as indicative of the orders of magnitude of the numbers of Ndebele since the 1820s: c.1821: 500 people; the 1830s: 20,000; c.1840s: 10,000; the 1890s: 100,000; in 1948: 300,000+; and in 1976: 1,000,000+. (See also **Population; Religion—Ndebele**.)

NDEBELE REVOLT see **REVOLTS OF 1896/97**

NDEBELE RULERS. Historians have generally recognized only two Ndebele monarchs, but other leaders also played roles. C.1821–68 **Mzilikazi**, 1868–69 **Mncumbathe** (regent), 1870–94 **Lobengula**, 1894–96 (interregnum), 1896 **Nyamanda**.

NDEBELE WAR (1893) (a.k.a. Matabele or Anglo-Ndebele War). Popular descriptions of the British occupation of the **Ndebele kingdom** as a "war" are misleading. There were few military engagements, and most Ndebele were left largely unaffected by the occupation until the much larger-scale hostilities of the **1896 Revolt**.

Historians have recently argued that the Ndebele War was planned by **Cecil Rhodes** and the **BSAC** as early as 1889 because of Lobengula's repudiation of the **Rudd Concession**, with which the company had hoped to gain control of the country peacefully. The Ndebele themselves anticipated a direct British invasion of their country the next year, when the company's **Pioneer Column** occupied neighboring **Mashonaland**. The Mashonaland occupation was carried out without violence, but it left the Ndebele surrounded by hostile neighbors (see **Borders**). As British settlement of Mashonaland became more extensive, tensions in the frontier zone increased. Ndebele intentions to avert war with the British were manifested by **Lobengula**'s repeated efforts to negotiate with the British government (see **Mshete**), but the company built up an anti-Ndebele propaganda campaign by cataloguing Ndebele raids on the **Shona** and other "incidents."

On July 18, 1893, a Ndebele punitive raid against Shona tributaries near Masvingo was blown into a major incident by the British administrator **L. S. Jameson**, whose attitude toward the Ndebele was particularly bellicose. Jameson instructed **P. W. Forbes**, then magistrate at Salisbury (now Harare), to prepare company forces for war. As late as October Lobengula sent three peace emissaries south with **J. Dawson**. Two of these men were killed by the **Bechuanaland Border Police** at **Tati** in a misunderstanding. Meanwhile, the British launched three separate columns against the Ndebele. Those setting out from Harare and Masvingo converged at Iron Mine Hill on October 15. From there they marched southwest toward **Bulawayo**. A third column of BBP troops marched northeast from Tati.

On October 25, Forbes' northern column engaged **Mtshani**'s Ndebele forces at the headwaters of the **Shangani River** in a *laager* action. The Ndebele recaptured **cattle** collected by the column but retreated in the face of machine-gun fire. On November 1, the column engaged the Ndebele in a somewhat briefer action by the headwaters of the **Bembezi River**. The Battles of Shangani and Bembezi, as they came to be called, were the largest actions of the "war." Ndebele casualties in these battles are usually said to have been enormous, but contemporary evidence suggests that only a few hundred Ndebele men were actually killed.

After Lobengula learned of these setbacks, he burned Bulawayo and fled north with a large retinue. He continued attempts to negotiate a truce, but his lines of communication with British authorities were defective. Forbes' column occupied Bulawayo on November 4. The BBP column under **Goold-Adams** arrived a week later, after a brief skirmish with **Gampu**'s forces by the **Mangwe Pass**.

The British saw the war as won when they occupied Bulawayo. Ndebele resistance continued in the west and south, but the British soon abandoned attempts to deal with this opposition and instead concentrated on capturing Lobengula. A column under Forbes went north, but a detachment now known as the **"Shangani Patrol,"** under **Allan Wilson**, was annihilated, and the effort to capture Lobengula was abandoned. The remainder of Forbes' column encountered heavy Ndebele pressure during its retreat, and no further attempt was made to pacify the northern Ndebele. Reports of Lobengula's death were later received, and the British declared the Ndebele kingdom at an end.

Most literature on the Ndebele War suggests that the main British achievements were simply occupation of Bulawayo and confiscation of large numbers of cattle. Except for the looting of their cattle, most Ndebele settlements were little affected by the British occupation over the next two-and-a-half years. Some Ndebele supported the British presence (see **Faku; Gampu; Mtshani**), but few were disarmed. The institutions of the kingdom continued, but without a monarch. Restoration of the monarchy then became a central issue in the Revolt of 1896.

NDLOVU, MASOTSHA (c.1890–July 2, 1982). A member of **ZAPU**'s Central Committee, Ndlovu was active in nationalist political movements for more than 50 years. He first became active in political struggle as a member of the South African Communist Party and the Trade Union Movement in the 1920s. He returned to Zimbabwe and helped to organize the **Industrial and Commercial Union**, becoming its secretary in 1929. Following his death, the government declared him a National Hero, and he was buried in **Heroes' Acre**.

NEGOMO CHIRISAMHURU MUPUNZAGUTU (a.k.a. Sebastiao) (c.1543–c.1589). First Christian **Munhumutapa**. Still a youth when he succeeded his father **Chivere Nyasoro** as king in c.1560, Negomo soon got himself into international difficulties. Late in 1560 a **Portuguese** priest, **Gonçalo da Silveira**, arrived at Negomo's court in the **Dande**. Silveira's selflessness contrasted sharply with the avarice of the Portuguese traders, making a deep impression on the young king. Within a month Negomo accepted baptism, taking the name "Dom Sebastiao" in honor of the Portuguese king. His mother was also baptized. Soon hundreds of other **Shona** sought similar sanctification. Local *nganga* and **Muslims** apparently convinced Negomo that Silveira was a dangerous spy, so he allowed Silveira to be killed in March 1561. He quickly regretted this murder, however, and had many of those responsible for it executed. Later the Portuguese government organized the **Francisco Barreto** expedition to avenge Silveira's death and to seize the country's **gold** and silver mines.

When the Barreto expedition finally arrived at the lower **Zambezi River** in 1572, Negomo was having difficulties with rebellious **Tonga** tributaries in the area around **Sena**. Through intermediaries Negomo negotiated an agreement with Barreto and the latter's successor, **Vasco Homem,** whereby the Portuguese put down the Tonga revolt in return for rights to mines in **Manicaland** and **Guruhuswa**—regions Negomo did not even control. The Portuguese thus secured Negomo's eastern districts for him without gaining anything tangible in return. Trade also increased in the Munhumutapa state as new **fairs** were opened throughout the country. Negomo died in c.1589 and was succeeded by **Gatsi Rusere**, a member of a collateral ruling family. Negomo's own son **Mavura II** also later became Munhumutapa. (For Changamire Negomo, see under **Dombo.**)

NEHANDA (variant: Nyanda). Name of a **Shona** "lion spirit," or *mhondoro,* which possessed female mediums in the **Zezuru** region around the Mazoe Valley. (N.B.: the Korekore have a *mhondoro* of the same name, said to be the spirit of the consort-sister of the early Munhumutapa **Matope**.) By the 19th century the Zezuru Nehanda mediums were among the most influential in central Shona territory and were regarded as equivalent in status to the famous **Chaminuka**. During the **1896–97 Revolt** "Nehanda" played a leading role in instigating the first killings of white settlers in the **Mazowe** area and in organizing resistance among the central Shona paramount chiefs. She was popularly—but incorrectly—described by Europeans as a "witch." During the Revolt she allied with **Kaguvi**, another *mhondoro* leader. In contrast to Kaguvi, she urged her own followers to repudiate European material goods and to fight with traditional weapons. She was captured in December 1897 and was tried along with Kaguvi the following March. On April 27, 1898, she and Kaguvi were hanged. A new Nehanda medium emerged in 1906 and quickly reestablished the reputation enjoyed by her predecessor before the Revolt.

NEMAKONDE (variants: Lomagundi; Maconde). Dynastic title of the rulers of a small but important **Korekore** chiefdom in the south of the present **Makonde District**. During the 19th century the Nemakondes became tributaries of the **Ndebele** kingdom. The Nemakondes themselves were said to have made annual trips to Bulawayo to deliver tribute payments. In 1889 Nemakonde Hodza sought to escape Ndebele domination by accepting **Portuguese** "protection" from **Manuel de Sousa** and **J. C. P. d'Andrada**. When the **BSAC** occupied **Mashonaland** the next year, Hodza shifted his allegiance to the British. In 1891 the Ndebele king **Lobengula** sent him an ultimatum to resume his former obligations. Hodza ignored the warning. In November 1891 he was killed by Ndebele soldiers, who apparently had the support of his local political rivals. The British protested the killing in what has been regarded as the first "incident" leading to the **Ndebele War** of 1893.

The new Nemakonde, Mazimbaguba, acknowledged British sovereignty but soon came to resent forced labor levies on his people. In late 1894 violent clashes over tax collection led to deaths on both sides. The Nemakonde joined in the **Revolt** of 1896–97, but his territory lay outside the main theaters of war throughout the conflict. The chiefdom is now in the Magondi Communal Area (at 17°45′S, 29°50′E).

NESHANGWE MUNEMBIRE (d. c.1550). Early **Munhumutapa**. The son of a leper ineligible to rule (Munyore Karembera), Neshangwe succeeded his uncle **Chikuyo Chisamarengu** as the Munhumutapa in c.1530. He established his headquarters west of the lower **Hunyani River** in the **Dande**. His reign was most notable for his success in expelling the **Changamire** from the **Mbire** region in c.1547. This feat earned him the praise-name "Munumbire," "owner of Mbire." On his death in c.1550, the kingship was assumed by Chikuyo's son, **Chivere Nyasoro**.

NEWSPAPERS see **PRESS**

NGANGA (variant: N'anga). **Shona** professional healers and diviners; sometimes described as "medicine men." *Nganga* have long played an important role in Shona everyday life. They treat mental and physical ailments, exorcise malevolent spirits such as *ngozi* from unwilling hosts, divine causes of misfortune, and offer medicines and other forms of protection for all kinds of enterprises. Individual *nganga* may claim to be proficient in all skills, but most specialize. Many are, for example, proficient herbalists (see **Chiremba**). Though they have demonstrated considerable skill in treating illness, they do not necessarily compete with Western-type physicians, as patients often consult both. Some *nganga* are also practicing Christians. Most *nganga* are men, but many are women of equal reputation.

Nganga either learn their techniques as apprentices or obtain their skills through possession by spirits—typically *shave.* Spirit-possession is usually regarded as a necessary condition for treating cases involving witchcraft or malevolent spirits. Diagnoses in such cases are often made by entranced *nganga* while throwing "divining dice" (see **Hakata**). *Nganga* share many characteristics and functions of other spirit mediums, such as the *mhondoro,* but differ in that they treat mainly individual or family cases, they work for fees, and they make great use of medicines and material devices. (See **Health; Religion—Shona.**)

NGANO, MARTHA (fl. 1890s–1920s). An *Mfengu* immigrant from South Africa, Ngano came to Southern Rhodesia in 1897 and became an Apostolic Faith Mission teacher in **Bulawayo.** Perhaps one of the best-educated local African women of her era, she was recruited into the **RBVA** as it was being formed in 1922-23. In 1924 she became secretary of the organization, remaining its leading spokesperson through the 1920s. She pushed hard for increased government registration of African voters. She particularly criticized the government for making English literacy a voter qualification while teaching only vernacular languages in African schools, and she demanded that communally held property be counted in voter qualification requirements. A dynamic public speaker, she successfully established many rural branches of the RBVA throughout **Matabeleland.**

NGEZI (variants: Ingezi; Ngesi). The country has three rivers with this name, all of which rise near the crest of the **Central Plateau.** The southwestern-most Ngezi River rises near the source of the **Shangani River,** flowing southeast c.135 km before meeting the **Lundi River** by the village of Ingezi (at 20°34′S, 30°24′E). The central Ngezi rises between the towns of Lalpanzi and **Umvuma,** flowing almost directly south c.75 km to feed the **Tokwe River.** Just above this confluence it is joined by the **Shashe River.** The northeastern-most Ngezi rises near the source of the **Sabi River,** flowing c.100 km west to feed the **Umniati River** just west of the **Mashaba Mountains.** Ngezi Dam was built in a gap in these mountains in 1945. The dam provides local irrigation water and is surrounded by a small **national park.**

NGONI (variants: Abangoni; Angoni; Mangoni; Wangoni). Itself a variation of the name **"Nguni,"** "Ngoni" has been loosely applied to all the various Nguni-speaking migrant bands of the *Mfecane* era. In its narrower and more proper sense, however, the name applies only to migrant bands led by **Zwangendaba, Nyamazana, Maseko,** and **Nxaba**—all of whom passed through present Zimbabwe during the 1830s. These same peoples are also frequently called **"Swazi,"** the name of a northern Nguni branch to which the original Ngoni leaders were closely related. Other names by which the Ngoni were known in central Africa during the 19th century include **Landeen** and **Dzviti.** Modern Ngoni communities—like their **Ndebele** counterparts—contain descendants of numerous southern and central African societies. Distinct Ngoni communities still exist in **Zambia,** Malawi, and Tanzania, but there are no longer any in Zimbabwe.

NGOZI. A class of **Shona** ancestor spirits characterized by their malevolent or vengeful behavior. Victims of accidents, illness, or other misfortune frequently blame *ngozi* for their troubles and seek means of appeasing or retaliating against them. The word *ngozi* is nearly synonymous with "danger" or "harm" in both **Chishona** and **Sindebele.** When used to describe a Shona spirit, *ngozi* refers more to the spirit's malevolent behavior than to the type of spirit itself.

NGUBOYENJA LOBENGULA (b. c.1880/81–c. 1950). Fifth son of **Lobengula**, by a wife named Sitshwapa Ndiweni. After his father's death in 1894, Nguboyenja and his half-brothers **Njube** and **Mpezeni** were sent to the Cape Colony for European education. Nguboyenja proved an excellent student, so he was sent to England for further studies in 1907. Had he been allowed to pursue his own interests, he might have become the country's first African lawyer (see **Chipeto, H.**); however, the **BSAC** wanted to keep him out of politics and instead encouraged him to study veterinary medicine. The company regarded him and Njube as the only possible successors to King Lobengula, but they had no intention of restoring the **Ndebele** monarchy, thus adding to Nguboyenja's frustrations. He was permitted to visit Bulawayo in 1908, but found his activities there so severely circumscribed by the government that he soon voluntarily returned to South Africa. There he appears to have suffered a complete nervous breakdown, for he soon became an uncommunicative recluse. Nevertheless, as late as 1931 members of the **Matabele Home Society** were collecting money to get him medical treatment in the hope of returning him to **Matabeleland. F. W. T. Posselt** reported that Nguboyenja was still "a cripple" in 1945.

NGUNGUNYANA see **GUNGUNYANE**

NGUNI. Term for a cluster of southeast **Bantu** languages originally spoken along the eastern coast of **South Africa**. The Nguni cluster is comparable to the **Sotho** cluster spoken mainly in the highland areas north of the Orange River. Nguni languages are further divided into southern and northern branches. The former are spoken by the Pondo, Thembu, Xhosa, and other peoples of southern Natal, the Transkei, and the eastern Cape Province. The northern branch includes **Swazi** and Zulu, spoken by peoples in northern Natal, Zululand, and Swaziland. In contrast to Sotho, most Nguni languages contain many **"click" sounds** borrowed from **Khoisan** languages.

NGWATO (BAMANGWATO). Sotho speaking people of the western, or **Tswana**, branch. In the late 18th century the Ngwato broke away from the Kwena and moved north to settle around Shoshong (at 22°57′S, 26°29′E) in what is now eastern **Botswana**. Another split occurred almost immediately, as the **Tawana** separated and moved farther north. Under the rule of Khama I and his successors, **Kgari** and Sekgoma, the Ngwato became the dominant people of eastern Botswana. Their settlements extended into the southwestern part of present Zimbabwe, where some Ngwato still live.

During the late 1820s the **Ndebele** began occupying the western **Transvaal.** The Ndebele then started raiding Ngwato cattle and collecting tribute, but they never completely subdued the Ngwato. In 1838 the Ndebele occupied Ngwato territory briefly during their own migration to present **Matabeleland.** Ndebele **cattle** raids against the Ngwato resumed in the early 1840s, when the Ndebele captured the future Ngwato ruler **Macheng**. Through the rest of the 19th century the Ngwato were perhaps the most formidable threat to Ndebele security. The Ndebele and Ngwato raided each other's cattle frequently, and both societies claimed overlapping territory around the **Tati River**. However, their conflicts never developed into a major war. In early 1863 **Mailikazi's** son **Mangwane** led the last major attack on the Ngwato at Shoshong. Under the leadership of the future Ngwato ruler **Khama III**, Ngwato horsemen armed with guns repelled the assault easily.

From the 1860s Ngwato territory assumed increasing importance in Zimbabwean affairs as the entry route to Matabeleland (see **Hunters' Road**). The Ngwato gave refuge to many Ndebele political dissidents, including Mangwane and the pretender **"Nkulumane."** In January 1872 Macheng lent these men a military force to invade Matabeleland in the hope of overthrowing King **Lobengula,** but the Ngwato troops retreated before reaching Matabeleland. After Khama III became Mgwato ruler in 1875, he renounced "Nkulumane's" claims, and relations with the Ndebele eased.

Declaration of the **Bechuanaland Protectorate** in 1885 created a new strain in Ngwato-Ndebele relations, but the Ngwato now had the British as allies. In 1890 Khama provided Ngwato men to help the **BSAC's Pioneer Column** cut a road into **Mashonaland.** Ngwato mercenaries were recruited by the British for the 1893 **Ndebele War,** but Khama withdrew them before they saw any military action.

NHONGO, REX see **MUTUSWA, SOLOMON TAPFUMANEY**

NHONGO, TEURAI ROPA see **MUJURU, JOYCE**

NHOWE (Vanhowe; variants: Wanoe; Nhohwe). A branch of the **Zezuri** cluster of **Shona**-speaking peoples now living mainly in the **Murehwa District.** Since the early 18th century they have been ruled by the **Mangwende** dynasty.

"NIBMAR." Acronymic slogan meaning "No Independence Before Majority African Rule." British Prime Minister Harold Wilson coined the expression in a declaration of British policy towards Rhodesian constitutional negotiations in December 1966. (See **Five Principles.**)

NICKEL. Minor production of this mineral began at the Noel Mine (at 21°18'S, 28°34'E) in the **Gwanda District** in 1928, remaining small through the 1950s. In the late 1950s major new discoveries were made at the Empress Mine near **Kadoma,** the Trojan Mine near **Bindura,** and near **Shamva.** Thereafter production gradually increased until nickel ranked as the third most important mineral produced in the country by 1983. Although it slipped to fourth by 1987, nickel production in that year was in the amount of Z$73.4 million. Production value radically increased through the late 1980s and early 1990s, rising to become the country's second most valuable mineral in 1991, when nickel's value reached Z$354 million. Production of that level was maintained throughout the 1990s.

NIEKERK RUINS see **VAN NIEKERK RUINS**

NINI see **MNCENGENCE**

NJANJA (Vanjanja). A branch of the **Zezuru** cluster of **Shona**-speaking peoples now living mainly in the **Chikomba District.** During the 18th and 19th centuries the Njanja mined **iron** at nearby **Mount Wedza** and became famous as smiths. They maintained a widespread trade network in iron tools and implements, such as the *mbira*. (See also **Hera.**)

NJELELE. Mwari cult oracular shrine in the **Matopo Hills**; located c.50 km south-southwest of **Bulawayo.** Its origins remain controversial, but it is believed to have been the most senior and influential Mwari shrine during the 19th century—at least within the southwestern part of **Matabeleland.** (See **Matojeni.**)

NJUBE LOBENGULA (c.1879/80–June 10, 1910). Fourth son of the **Ndebele** king **Lobengula,** by a wife named Mpoliana Ndiweni. After the **Ndebele War of 1893** the **BSAC** sent Njube and his half-brothers **Nguboyenja** and **Mpezeni** to the Cape Colony to be educated. After the **1896 Revolt,** Ndebele interest in restoring the monarchy centered on Njube and Nguboyenja because they were the only sons of Lobengula whom the company considered eligible successors to the defunct kingship (see **Nyamanda**). However, company officials had no intention of restoring the monarchy. They frustrated Njube's attempts to regain a foothold in **Matabeleland,** where **Mlugulu** and other senior *izinduna* agitated for his return. Njube was allowed to visit **Bulawayo** in late 1900, but his arrival there created such a commotion among the Ndebele that the company soon returned him to the Cape. Thereafter he managed to extract increasingly large sums of money from the company. He is said to have lived "riotously" until dying of tuberculosis in Grahamstown, where he is buried. He left two sons, Albert and Rhodes Lobengula.

NKAI DISTRICT see **NKAYI DISTRICT**

NKALIPI see **KALIPHI**

NKAYI DISTRICT (Nkai District until 1985). Covering 4,565 sq km of the east-central part of **Matabeleland North Province,** Nkayi was formed from the northeastern section of **Bubi District.** The district is bordered by the districts of **Lupane** on the west, **Gokwe** on the north, **Kwekwe** on the east, and **Bubi** on the south. Nkayi village (at 19°S, 28°54′E) is the administrative center. Nkayi is a little-developed region made up almost entirely of **Communal Lands.** District population in 1992 was 113,302.

NKOMO, JOSHUA MQABUKO NYONGOLO (June 19, 1917–July 2, 1999). Nationalist. Born in the **Mataba District** near **Bulawayo,** Nkomo attended local mission schools and worked as a truck driver before going to South Africa in 1941. He eventually trained as a social worker in Johannesburg. He returned to Southern Rhodesia in 1947 and became the first African social worker employed by **Rhodesia Railways.** From this position he moved into trade unionism and became the general secretary of the Rhodesia Railways African Employees Association. Meanwhile, he completed a bachelor's degree by correspondence from the University of South Africa.

Nkomo began his political career as an officer in the **All-African Convention** in 1952. The same year he accompanied **Godfrey Huggins** to London in order to represent African opinions concerning **Federation.** He denounced the Federation plans on his return home, but a year later contested the **Matabeleland** seat in the Federal Assembly, losing to **M.**

M. Hove. He then became president of the Bulawayo branch of the old **African National Congress**. When the ANC was reorganized in 1957, Nkomo was elected president. He was out of the country when the government made sweeping arrests of ANC leaders in 1959. The following year he was elected president *in absentia* of the new **National Democratic Party**.

Nkomo participated in the 1960–61 constitutional conference in London (see **Constitutions**). He initially accepted the **United (Federal) Party**'s proposals, but withdrew his endorsement under pressure from fellow NDP officers. When the NDP was banned in December 1961 Nkomo was again out of the country. This time he was in Tanganyika (present Tanzania), where he immediately formed **ZAPU** with the support of **Ndabaningi Sithole**. The following year Nkomo traveled widely and got the United Nations to recognize Southern Rhodesia as an international problem. After his return to Southern Rhodesia the government banned ZAPU in September 1962, arresting Nkomo in October.

Nkomo was repeatedly arrested and released by the government through 1963. Meanwhile, he and Sithole split over nationalist strategy. Sithole formed **ZANU**, and Nkomo formed the **People's Caretaker Council** to hold together the remaining ZAPU leadership. Immediately after **Ian Smith** came to power in April 1964, Nkomo was again arrested. He then spent most of the next decade in prisons and detention camps, emerging occasionally to participate in talks with visiting British emissaries.

Smith finally released Nkomo in December 1974 in order for him to participate in Lusaka talks leading to a new constitutional conference. Nkomo was not rearrested on his return to Salisbury (now Harare) on December 12, when he made his first public appearance in the country since 1964. Through most of 1975 he stayed out of the country, even while participating in the August **Victoria Falls Conference**. Nkomo had joined other nationalist leaders under the "umbrella" of the **African National Council** in December 1974, but after the Victoria Falls Conference collapsed, he denounced Sithole and **James Chikerema**, thereby reestablishing the old party rifts.

At the end of 1975 Nkomo returned to the country as head of the "internal" ANC. He was then recognized as a political moderate, in contrast to **Abel Muzorewa** and **Robert Mugabe**. From mid-December to mid-March 1976 Nkomo and Ian Smith held a series of informal weekly talks, but these produced no tangible results and Nkomo was increasingly criticized by other nationalist leaders. In May 1976 he again left the country to consult with leaders abroad. He returned to Salisbury in late September 1976, announcing his willingness to participate in a new round of constitutional talks based upon the proposals made by U.S. Secretary of State Henry Kissinger. Shortly before the ensuing **Geneva Conference**, Nkomo made a surprise move by announcing formation of a **"Patriotic Front"** with Robert Mugabe. Nkomo and Mugabe jointly led the PF delegation to the Geneva Conference and most forcibly argued for the transfer of power to the African majority.

After the conference ended in failure, Nkomo remained outside the country and used his authority to help expand the recruitment activities and increase the military operations of **ZIPRA**. This gave Nkomo something he had previously lacked, command of a strong military force in the liberation war. In December 1977, Smith met with Muzorewa, Sithole, and Chief **Jeremiah Chirau** for talks aimed at creating an **internal settlement** in which the white minority would have veto powers over a black-dominated **Parliament**. At the end of January 1978, Nkomo and Mugabe held talks with British and American representatives in Malta (see **Malta Talks**). They declared their support for the idea of independently observed and supervised elections as long as the PF played a substantial role during any transition period leading up to elections. When the Internal Settlement agreement was announced in early March, Nkomo and Mugabe denounced it and declared that the liberation war would continue. In August 1978 Nkomo held secret talks with Smith in Lusaka which were immediately denounced by Mugabe and almost split the PF alliance. However, the PF remained united and after an August meeting of Commonwealth leaders in Lusaka in which a proposal for a new all-party conference in London was passed, the two leaders agreed to attend as joint heads of the PF delegation. On September 10 Nkomo and Mugabe for the PF, Muzorewa and Smith representing the government of **Zimbabwe Rhodesia**, and Lord Carrington of Britain as chairman, met in London for the **Lancaster House Conference**.

Following the successful conclusion of the Lancaster House Conference Mugabe surprised Nkomo by announcing that ZANU candidates would stand independently during the upcoming elections, not as members of the PF. Nkomo returned to the country on January 13, 1980, to contest the elections as head of PF-ZAPU. In the February elections Nkomo's party finished second to Mugabe's ZANU (PF), with 24 percent of the vote. Mugabe was asked by British Governor **Lord Soames** to form the government for the new Republic of Zimbabwe. In March Mugabe agreed to a coalition government with ZAPU members and offered Nkomo the home affairs portfolio. Nkomo accepted but was visibly disappointed and angered that only three other ZAPU members were included in the new cabinet. In January 1981 he was demoted by Mugabe to minister without portfolio.

In early 1982 conflicts between ZANU and ZAPU surfaced when Mugabe announced that in the future only ZANU-approved policies would be adopted by the government. Nkomo objected on the grounds that this would violate the Lancaster House agreement and supersede the authority of Parliament. In February Nkomo rejected a call by Mugabe to merge the two parties. Later that month, following the discovery of large caches of arms on farms reportedly owned by ZAPU supporters, Nkomo was dismissed from government on charges that he was involved in plotting a coup. Nkomo continued to criticize Mugabe's calls for the creation of a one-party state and complained that the government was persecuting ZAPU members and supporters. In March 1983 Nkomo fled to **Botswana** and then to Britain, claiming that government soldiers had tried to kill him during an illegal search of his home in Bulawayo. He returned to Harare in August after he was threatened with the loss of his seat in Parliament. In October 1984, ZAPU held its first party congress in a decade, and Nkomo again rejected the idea of a one-party state for Zimbabwe. He also criticized the government for failing to restore the economy and for the actions of government troops in Matabeleland. He was then reelected as president of ZAPU. Throughout the mid-1980s, the government consistently linked reports of **dissident** activity with Nkomo and ZAPU. While Nkomo repeatedly denied the alleged connections with dissidents and condemned their violence, he strongly criticized the Mugabe government for not addressing the economic problems in Matabeleland which he said were the actual cause for the dissidents' activities.

Sometime after the 1985 election, in which ZANU increased its parliamentary majority over ZAPU, Nkomo and Mugabe began a series of talks aimed at the unification of the two parties and the creation of a one-party state in Zimbabwe. The on-again-off-again negotiations covered almost two years and culminated in a December 1987 announcement that Nkomo and Mugabe would sign a **Unity Pact** amalgamating the two former rival parties. In April 1988 Nkomo was appointed "interim" second vice president, essentially making him the third most powerful person in the government; later in the year the "interim" was dropped. At the same time he was named senior minister of local government, rural and urban development by Mugabe. He retained those appointments following the 1990 **elections,** but kept only the position of vice president after the 1995 election. A year later he was diagnosed with prostate cancer and, while retaining the vice presidency, largely withdrew from public life for the last three years of his life.

NKOSI see **INKOSI**

NKULUMANE KHUMALO (variants: Unkulumane; Kuruman; a.k.a. "Kanda") (c.1825–1839?). An important but enigmatic figure in **Ndebele** history, Nkulumane was the son of **Mzilikazi** by the latter's "royal" wife (see **Inkosikazi**), who is said to have been the daughter of the Ndwandwe king Zwide. Whatever was Nkulumane's mother's exact identity, Nkulumane himself was clearly heir apparent to the Ndebele kingship. He is said to have been named "Nkulumane" in honor of **Robert Moffat's** mission station at **Kuruman**, but he must have been born well before Mzilikazi met Moffat in 1829.

When the Ndebele migrated from the western **Transvaal** to present **Matabeleland** in 1838–39, Nkulumane traveled with **Kaliphi's** division, arriving there about a year before Mzilikazi himself did. This first group of migrants seems to have made Nkulumane king in order to celebrate the *inxwala* in Mzilikazi's absence. When Mzilikazi finally arrived in Matabeleland, he interpreted this action as treasonous and had many of the responsible *izinduna* executed (see **Ntabazinduna**). Some traditions hold that Nkulumane escaped or was sent to Natal. Others say that he was executed—a fate for which **Mncumbathe** later assumed personal responsibility. His fate remained a public secret for three decades.

When Mzilikazi died in 1868 Ndebele leaders still agreed that Nkulumane was rightful heir to the kingship, but they disagreed as to what had become of him. Nkulumane was rumored to be living in Natal, so the first of three delegations went there to investigate in December. Meanwhile, **Lobengula** was put forth as a candidate for the kingship by Mncumbathe. The embassy to Natal found an Ndebele man named Kanda in the employ of Theophilus Shepstone, a colonial official. Kanda initially denied he was the missing heir, but later changed his story. Shepstone evidently encouraged Kanda to claim that he was Nkulumane in order to inject Natal's influence into Ndebele politics. By the end of 1869 most Ndebele leaders concluded that Kanda was not Nkulumane. Lobengula then became king.

Die-hard Nkulumane supporters, led by **Mbigo**, resisted Lobengula but were suppressed in the battle at **Zwangendaba** in June 1870. Nevertheless, Shepstone provided Kanda with a wagon and some men a year later and sent him to **Ngwato** country to organize a coup. Kanda was joined by **Mangwane**—another disgruntled contender for the kingship— who took up the cause of "Nkulumane" to attract support. In Shoshong the two men obtained military support from **Macheng**, whose own political career contained striking parallels to that of Kanda. In January 1872 Kanda and Mangwane's invasion force approached Matabeleland, but the Mgwato pulled out at the last minute. Mangwane led a handful of Ndebele dissidents into Ndebele territory, sending out messengers to raise the cry of revolt in the name of "Nkulumane." A few people responded, but Lobengula's loyalists easily routed the invaders.

Kanda afterwards retired to Rustenburg in the **Transvaal**. There he continued to attract anti-Lobengula followers until his own death in 1883. While it is almost certain that he was not the true Nkulumane, it is possible that he was in fact one of Mzilikazi's many sons. Whoever he was, his attempt to become Ndebele king evidently inspired **H. R. Haggard**'s character "Umbopa" in *King Solomon's Mines*.

NKULUNKULU (variant; Unkulunkulu). **Nguni** name for their high god, meaning "greatest of the great." Nkulunkulu has stood at the top of traditional **Ndebele** religious beliefs since **Mzilikazi** left Zululand. He is a partly anthropomorphic sky god, regarded as the creator and as the master of nature. Though he is omnipresent, he has otiose characteristics that make it necessary for people to approach him through intermediary ancestor spirits (see **Idlozi**). To a great extent, Ndebele concepts of Nkulunkulu have fused with **Sotho** concepts of **Mlimo**, for the two names are now freely interchanged. (See **Religion—Ndebele**.)

NOE (WANOE; variant: NOHWE) see **NHOWE**

NOGOMO see **NEGOMO**

NOMBATI see **MNCUMBATHE**

NORTHERN GOLDFIELDS. A 19th-century European nickname for the region between the **Gwelo** and **Hunyani** rivers; now known as the Hartly Goldfields (see **Gold**). The name distinguished the region from the Southern Goldfields around **Tati** after old **Shona** goldworkings were identified in both areas by **Henry Hartley** and **Karl Mauch** in 1866–67. (See **South African Goldfields Exploration Co.**)

NORTHERN LIGHT GOLD AND EXPLORING COMPANY see **TATI CONCESSION**

NORTHERN OPTIMIST. Original name of the *Gwelo Times.*

NORTHERN RHODESIA. Name by which **Zambia** was known as a British colony from 1911 to 1964. From the early 1890s to 1911 the **BSAC** administered the territory as two separate units, Northwestern and

Northeastern Rhodesia. When written with a capital "N" neither of these terms properly applies to areas within present Zimbabwe.

NORTON. Small industrial town just west of Harare on the main road to Bulawayo (at 17°53′S, 30°42′E; alt. 1,370 m). Norton's development has accelerated since the 1950s, when nearby Lake Chivero was created on the **Hunyani River.** After **Kariba Dam** was built, Norton became one of the main intake points for the country's **electrical power** network.

NQABA see **NXABA**

NSWATUGI CAVE. Considered one of the finest **rock painting** sites in the country, Nswatugi is located in **Matopos National Park** about six km southwest of **World's View.** The paintings feature particularly fine polychrome pictures of giraffes. Archaeological digs at the site by **Neville Jones** and others have also turned up important late **Stone Age** evidence.

NTABAZIKAMAMBO (variants: Taba Zika Mambo; Thabas-Zi-Ka-Mambo; etc.; a.k.a. Manyanga). **Ndebele** name for the **Changamire** center known to the **Rozvi** as Manyanga; located in the Mambo Hills (19°32′S, 29°4′E), c.40 km northeast of **Inyati,** near the **Shangani River.** The site is a large, massive granite outcropping with a natural citadel. It now contains some stone walls and the remains of huts and is a National Monument on a private farm.

Manyanga was one of several main Changamire centers (see **Dhlo Dhlo; Nalatale**) until the 1830s, when **Zwangendaba's Ngoni** sacked it and killed the reigning Changamire, **Chirisamhuru.** According to one tradition, Chirisamhuru hurled himself into the Ngoni throng from the citadel when his defeat appeared inevitable. During the **1896 Ndebele Revolt** the Mambo Hills served as an important refugee hiding place until it was overwhelmed by British forces in July. It has been argued that Mkwati established a **Mwari** cult shrine there just before the Revolt, but this view had been recently challenged.

NTABAZINDUNA (variants: Thabas Induna; Intaba Yezinduna; etc.). The "Hill of the Induras," Ntabazinduna is a prominent, flat-topped *kopje* near the source of the **Bembezi River,** northeast of modern **Bulawayo** (at 20°2′S, 28°51′E). It has apparently long been used as a lookout point and was known to the **Rozvi** as *Dombo ro Mambo* ("Mambo's Rock"). Since the mid-19th century the hill has held an important but unclear place in **Ndebele** tradition. It is known that when **Mzilikazi** belatedly rejoined his people in **Matabeleland** after migrating from the Transvaal, he found his son **Nkulumane** installed as acting king in his place (c.1839). He responded to this situation by having many dissident *izinduna* (see **Induna**) executed. According to some traditions the *izinduna* were hurled off the hill that thus bears their name; however, the sides of the hill are insufficiently precipitous for such a method of execution. Other traditions hold merely that the *izinduna* were tried atop the hill and that they were executed elsewhere.

NTHUMBANE (variant: Entumbani). *Kopje* on the northern fringe of the **Matopo Hills** (at 20°23′S, 28°36′E) in which the body of **Mzilikazi** was interred in November 1868, several months after his death. During the midst of the **1868 Revolt** Mzilikazi's grandson **Nyamanda** was made king there by fellow rebels. Later during the Revolt British soldiers desecrated the tomb, angering **Cecil Rhodes,** who had the site repaired and resanctified with oxen sacrifices. Nthumbane is now a National Monument (see **Mzilikazi Memorial).** Rhodes himself is said to have selected **World's View** for his own grave partly because of its nearness to Mzilikazi's tomb.

NUANETSI see **MWENEZI**

NUANETSI RIVER (Shona variant: Munetsi). Rising on the **Central Plateau** near Lancaster (20°13'S, 29°18'E), the Nuanetsi flows generally southeast through the **Mwenezi District,** joining the Limpopo in **Mozambique.** Mwenezi village stands where the river is crossed by the main road between Beitbridge and Masvingo.

NXABA MSANE (variants: Nqaba; Ngabe; a.k.a. Mpakana; Mpanka; Nyaba; Sikwanda) (fl.1820s-c.1840). **Ngoni** migration leader. Originally a hereditary clan chief in northern Natal, Nxaba became one of the many **Nguni** leaders to leave South Africa during the *Mfecane* wars. His career is imperfectly known. He appears to have led his followers through the eastern Transvaal into southern **Mozambique** in c.1822. He possibly clashed with **Mzilikazi's Ndebele** along the way. He later allied with the **Maseko Ngoni** while raiding **Portuguese** posts along the coast. In the early 1830s he seems to have been defeated by the **Gaza** king **Soshangane** just before entering **Mashonaland.** There he operated as a roving predator among the Shona until 1835, when he clashed with Zwangendaba's **Ngoni,** who then crossed the **Zambezi River.** Nxaba appears then to have separated from the Maseko and to have returned to the east coast, where he attacked **Sofala.** By about 1840 he had again moved inland, this time as far north as Barotseland in western **Zambia.** He arrived there about the same time as Sebitwane's **Kololo.** His following was broken up by the Kololo, and he himself seems to have been drowned by the **Lozi.**

NXWALA. Spelling variant of *inxwala*, whose proper radical is -*xwala*, not -*nxwala*.

NYAGUMBO, TAPFUMANEYI MAURICE (December 12, 1924–April 20, 1989). Nationalist, **ZANU** party official, and government minister. Born in **Rusape** in the **Makoni District,** Nyagumbo was educated at St. Faith's Mission and St. Augustine's in **Penhalonga.** After completing his primary education in 1940, he went to South Africa in search of work. There he joined the South African Communist Party and was an active member until it was banned in 1948. He then joined with **James Chikerema** and helped form the Central African Social Club, becoming its secretary in 1953. The goal of the club was to increase the political awareness of fellow countrymen working in South Africa. In 1955 he was deported for allegedly being in contact with supporters of the Kenyan Mau Mau movement.

After returning home Nyagumbo rejoined Chikerema and was one of the founders of the **Youth League.** He later became secretary of the Rusape branch of the **African National Congress.** When the ANC was banned in 1959, he was detained and restricted to **Gokwe District** for a short time but disagreed with the leadership of **Joshua Nkomo,** and when

ZANU was formed in 1963, became its organizing secretary. In 1964 he was again detained by government authorities when ZANU was banned and spent the next decade in prison. He was released along with Nkomo, **Ndabaningi Sithole, Robert Mugabe,** and other nationalist leaders in 1974 but within months was rearrested, convicted, and sentenced to 15 years in prison on charges of recruiting for **ZANLA.** He was released in December 1979.

Following his release he actively participated in the forthcoming **elections** as ZANU-PF's national organizing secretary. He was elected to the **House of Assembly** and appointed minister of mines in the new government. In 1984, at the second ZANU Party Congress, Nyagumbo was elected to the party's politburo and central committee. In the 1985 **general elections** he was returned to the House of Assembly from Dzivarasekwa electoral district and became minister of state for political affairs in the **prime minister**'s office. In early 1988, following a cabinet reshuffle by President Mugabe, he was appointed senior minister for political affairs. On April 20, 1989, following accusations that he was involved in the **Willowdale** scandal, Nyagumbo committed suicide by reportedly swallowing poison.

NYAI (variant plurals: Banyai; Manyai; Vanyai). A **Chishona** term meaning "messenger." Historically it referred to subjects of the **Changamire** state and soldiers of the **Munhumutapa** state after the 1690s. One more specific application is, however, important. Shona chiefdoms of the **Karanga** dialect clustered in the southeastern part of the country came to be known as the Vanyai ("Banyai" to Europeans) by the late 19th century. Their region thus came to be known as "Banyailand" (see **Adendorff Trek**).

NYAMANDA LOBENGULA KHUMALO (c. 1873–1925). Son of the **Ndebele** king **Lobengula** by the latter's wife Mbida Mkwanansi. Apparently Lobengula's favorite son, Nyamanda was by the early 1890s the strongest candidate for succession to the kingship in the absence of any sons by Lobengula's "great wife" **Xwalile.** Nyamanda's cause was championed by another, and influential, wife of Lobengula, **Lozigeyi.**

During the **1896 Ndebele Revolt** Nyamanda, his younger brother Shakalisa, and Lozigeyi became the main leaders of the northern rebels, establishing their headquarters by the middle **Bembezi River.** On June 15, 1896, Nyamanda was installed as Ndebele king at **Nthumbane** by a group of powerful *izinduna* including **Babayane, Sikombo, Dhliso, Mlugulu,** and others. After the Revolt collapsed, Nyamanda surrendered to the British in December and was made a government chief in January 1897. Later, however, the **BSAC** government deposed him, leaving him with neither a position nor land. His presumptive status as Ndebele king was ignored by the government, and other Ndebele leaders turned away from him in favor of **Njube** and **Nguboyenja** in the hope of finding a more acceptable candidate for the kingship. Nyamanda nevertheless started the **Matabele (National) Home Movement** during the First World War to push for a Ndebele national homeland for the restoration of the kingship. He was aided by South African political activists, including members of **AMEC,** the South African **ANC,** and local *Mfengu.*

From 1919 to 1921 Nyamanda spearheaded an aggressive campaign to secure British government recognition of Ndebele grievances, but his efforts were futile in the face of local and British concern with the larger questions of the constitutional status of Southern Rhodesia after the demise of BSAC rule in 1923 (see **Responsible Government**). In his last years Nyamanda became an active member of **RBVA**.

NYAMANDHLOVU DISTRICT. Western district covering 12,590 sq km in **Matabeleland North Province.** The **Nata River** separates the district from **Bulilimamangwe District**, from which it was divided in 1910, on the south. **Bulawayo** and **Bubi Districts** border it on the east, **Lupane** and **Hwange** on the north. The district is little developed, with **agriculture,** livestock, and timber its main industries. Its administrative center is the village of Nyamandhlova (at 19°52′S, 28°16′E; alt. 1,220 m). **Sawmills** is another important center for the district. Prior to 1980, the eastern part of the district was reserved for Europeans, with the remainder being Tribal Trust Land (see **Communal Lands**). District population in 1982 was 90,780. The name of the district is taken from an Ndebele *ibutho* (see **Mpotshwana**).

NYAMAZANA (variant: Nyamabezana) (fl.1830s–1890s). **Ngoni** migration leader and wife of **Mzilikazi.** According to tradition, Nyamazana was the niece of the Ngoni king **Zwangendaba**, from whom she separated with a small band of followers when most of the Ngoni crossed the **Zambezi River** into **Zambia** in 1835. She led her band from place to place in **Shona** territory until encountering an *impi* of the recently arrived **Ndebele** in c.1840. Nyamazana's people then were absorbed into the Ndebele and she became one of Mzilikazi's wives.

Little is known about Nyamazana's subsequent life. During the **1896 Revolt**, an unrelated woman with a similar name, Nyambezana, met **C. J. Rhodes** and helped to rearrange his peace negotiations with the Matopos rebels (see also **Grootboom, J.; "indaba"**). Rhodes is said to have so greatly admired this woman that he afterwards kept her photograph mounted in his bedroom.

(N.B.: An unrelated man named Nyamazana was a prominent vassal of **Sikombo** until he was killed by his master around April 1896.)

NYAMBO KAPARARIDZE (c.1580s?–1652). The son of **Gatsi Rusere**, Nyambo was the last member of the house of **Neshangwe** to hold the **Munhumutapa** kingship. He became the Munhumutapa in 1623, devoting his brief reign to holding onto his own position. A year later he had to put down a revolt of his own brothers. He then had to deal with rival claimants supported by the **Portuguese**, who were dissatisfied with Gatsi Rusere's cession of mines in 1607. In 1628 a general war with the Portuguese broke out. In May 1629 a combined Portuguese-African army ousted Nyambo from power and replaced him with **Mavura II**. Nyambo spent the remainder of his life trying to regain power.

NYANDA see **NEHANDA** and under **NYAMANZANA**

NYANDORO (a.k.a. Kunzwi, or Kunzwi-Nyandoro) (fl.c.1860s–1915). It is not clear whether Nyandoro was the first ruler of his chiefdom or if "Nyandoro" was a dynastic title shared by a predecessor. In any case,

Nyandoro was a member of the Pfumbe branch of the **Korekore** cluster of **Shona** from northern **Murehwa District** who moved into central **Zezuru** territory and established a strong independent chiefdom in the mid-19th century. His people became known as Tsunga. During the 1860s he was repeatedly attacked by the **Ndebele** and forced to move about frequently. By the 1870s his people were living just west of the **Mangwende**'s country in the southern Murehwa District. There he established a stronghold on a naturally fortified hill and armed his men well with guns obtained from dealings with **Manuel de Sousa** in the 1880s.

When the British occupied **Mashonaland** in the 1890s, Nyandoro maintained cordial relations with individual Europeans but refused to acknowledge British sovereignty. From October 1895 until the outbreak of the **1896 Revolt** he successfully resisted British efforts to collect hut tax payments. His defiance is regarded as the first signal of the impending Revolt, in which he played a prominent part. During the Revolt he held his position for an entire year until a massive British assault on June 19, 1897, drove him into flight. He then lived as a refugee, finally surrendering at the end of August. Afterwards he retained both his chiefship and his prestige among neighboring Shona. The British watched him suspiciously. Around 1907 his people were moved to the **Marondera District,** where his successors are still called Nyandoro.

NYANDORO, GEORGE BODZO (b. Oct. 8, 1926). Nationalist and **UANC** member. Born in **Marondera Distict**, Nyandoro is the grandson of the famous 1896 Revolt leader, Chief **Nyandoro**. His father was deposed as government chief in 1946 for criticizing the government. Nyandoro himself taught briefly in the mid-1940s and then became active in both **Charles Mzingeli**'s and **Benjamin Burombo**'s quasipolitical movements. In 1952 he became provisional secretary of the **All-African Convention**, and he helped to found the **Youth League** three years later. He played a leading role in organizing African farmers for both the Youth League and **African National Congress** until he was imprisoned during the government sweep of ANC leaders in February 1959. After his release in 1963 he joined **Joshua Nkomo** in the **PCC** and then based himself in Lusaka, **Zambia,** as a ZAPU official. He left ZAPU in 1970 and helped **James Chikerema** to form **FROLIZI** the following year. In 1975 he became closely identified with **Abel Muzorewa** and the **ANC**. He served first as secretary for external affairs in the reconstitutioned UANC and then as minister of lands, natural resources, and rural development under Muzorewa's UANC government. He retired from political life in 1979 and following independence became a successful businessman.

NYANGA (Inyanga until 1982). This town is located on the western edge of the **Inyanga Mountains** (at 18°13′S, 32°45′E; alt. 1,860 m). It serves as administrative center for the region's stock- and fruit-producing industries.

NYANGA DISTRICT (Inyanga District until 1985). Eastern border district in the extreme north of **Manicaland Province**, covering 6,635 sq km. The **Ruenya River** separates it from the **Mutoko District** on the northwest and from **Mudzi** on the north. It also borders the districts of **Makoni** on the west and **Mutasa** on the south. The **Gairezi River** forms the northern part of the boundary with **Mozambique**. Before 1980, the northern part of the district was Tribal Trust Land (see **Communal Lands**), while most of the southern part was national land and land reserved for Europeans. District population in 1992 was 128,439.

NYANGWE FORT. Most famous example of a class of massively built stone enclosures characteristic of the **Inyanga Ruins**. The structure stands atop Nyangwe Hill, beside the Mare River in the center of Nyanga National Park (at 18°17'S, 32°47'E; alt. 2,025 m). The ruin features crude but massive stone work, many linteled entrances, "loopholes," and parapets. In common with other such "forts," Nyanwange is believed to have been used as a lookout point and refuge from about the late 16th century.

NYASHANU. Dynastic title of the rulers of an important **Hera** chiefdom in the present **Buhera District.**

NYATSIME COLLEGE. African secondary school and technical college stressing business education; founded in 1960. Located at Seki, just south of Harare.

NYAZURA (Inyazura until 1982). Village in the southern **Makoni District**, located c.73 km northwest of **Mutare** on the **railway** line to Harare (at 18°43' S, 32°10'E; alt. 1,220 m).

NYIKA. Chishona term for "country" or "territory"; used particularly for the territory of a chiefdom or for the chiefdom itself. (For Nyika people, see **Msnyika.**)

NYORA. Cicatrization marks or "tattoos" once commonly made on **Shona** youths.

O

OCCUPATION (BRITISH) OF MASHONALAND see **PIONEER COLUMN**

OCCUPATION (BRITISH) OF MATABELELAND see **NDEBELE WAR**

ODZANI RIVER. Rises in the hills north of **Mutare,** whence it flows west into the Odzi River. A dam on the Odzani forms Lake Alexander (alt. 1,615m), which supplies Mutare's municipal water. The lake is the largest stretch of **bilharzia**-free water in the country. Below the lake are the Odzani Falls (18°46'S, 32°42'E).

ODZI. Town located 32 km west of **Mutare** on the Harare road; the center of a **tobacco** and mixed agriculture region (at 18°58′S, 32°23′E; alt. 960 m).

ODZI RIVER. One of the main tributaries of the **Sabi River**, the Odzi flows south from the **Inyanga Mountains**.

OFFICER ADMINISTERING THE GOVERNMENT (OAG). Office created by the **Rhodesian Front** government shortly after **UDI** in 1965. In the revised 1965 **Constitution** the OAG was given virtually the same functions as the British **governor** had held under the 1961 Constitution. The OAG theoretically represented the British Crown but was not so acknowledged by the British government. In 1970 the OAG became the **president** under a republican constitution. **Clifford Dupont** was the only person to hold the office.

OLD UMTALI. Located just northwest of present **Mutare**, to which its original European settlers were removed in 1896 when the Beira **railway** line opened. In 1898 the **BSAC** administration granted the site of "Old Umtali" and its buildings to American missionaries of the Methodist Episcopal Church (see **UNITED METHODIST CHURCH**). The Methodists made the town their headquarters and established a lay theological training center there. In the 1980s the site became the home of Africa University, one of the country's two privately funded universities.

OMAY RIVER (variant: Ume) see **BUMI RIVER**

OPEN FORUM see **FORUM PARTY OF ZIMBABWE**

"OPERATION NOAH." Project undertaken to rescue animals from the Zambezi Valley when the waters of **Lake Kariba** began to rise in 1959. Thousands of animals were boated or forced to swim from newly created islands to the mainland.

"OPERATION SUNRISE." Government code name for the arrest of about 500 **African National Congress** leaders on the morning of February 26, 1959.

OPHIR. Ancient biblical country said to be rich in gold and connected with Solomon and Sheba. Though Ophir is now thought to have been located in southwestern Arabia, its whereabouts were long the subject of intense speculation. Incredibly, the notion that Ophir lay within present Zimbabwe has played a role in the country's history since the 16th century, when **Muslim** traders introduced the idea to the **Portuguese**. The idea gained currency as more was learned about Shona **stone ruins** and the **gold** trade through **Sofala**, which itself has been equated with "Ophir." When John Milton wrote *Paradise Lost* in the 1660s, he included a passage linking Sofala with Ophir. The idea was revived in the 1860s when the German missionary **Alexander Merensky** began circulating the first European reports of the **Zimbabwe Ruins**. Merensky popularized the expression "King Solomon's Mines," which was picked up by **H. R. Haggard**. Early European investigations of Great Zimbabwe led to further speculations about the ruins having ancient Near Eastern origins (see **Zimbabwe Controversy**). **Cecil Rhodes** accepted these interpretations,

248

and his **BSAC** promoted the idea that **Mashonaland** was indeed "Ophir," in order to attract prospectors and settlers. All subsequent scientific archaeological investigations discredited such ideas, however.

OSTRICHES. These giant flightless birds are now rarely seen outside of the country's **national parks** and **game reserves**, but they once pervaded the country's semi-arid **savanna** regions. Early **San** inhabitants used ostrich egg shells as water containers and as painting surfaces (see **Rock Paintings**). They also made necklace beads from shell fragments—a practice adopted by later **Bantu**-speaking inhabitants. Early **Shona** states traded both ostrich shell fragments and ostrich feathers. In the 19th century the **Ndebele** made extensive use of ostrich plumes in their headdresses and robes. An export trade developed when ostrich plumes became fashionable in Europe. This trade peaked in the early 1880s, when European prices were at their highest.

OTTO BEIT BRIDGE. Spans the **Zambezi River** just above the Kafue confluence at the village of **Chirundu**. Named after Otto Beit (1865–1930), a younger brother of **Alfred Beit**, the bridge was opened in mid-1939. (See **Beitbridge**.)

OX-WAGONS (a.k.a. trek wagons). Principle transport vehicles used by European and Griqua traders, missionaries, and immigrants in the 19th century. These heavily built wagons were developed in South Africa by **Afrikaner** farmers, and they cost from £80 to £300 new. Essentially tented boxes on wheels—similar to American "covered wagons"—ox-wagons were typically pulled by spans of 23 oxen requiring three-man crews. Carrying capacities were limited; locomotion was slow; routes were circumscribed by terrain, seasonal conditions, and availability of fodder; and oxen were highly vulnerable to local diseases (see **Health**). Nevertheless, the wagons served as the main means of carriage in the country from the 1860s until the development of **railways** in the 1890s. The **Ndebele** kings owned some wagons from the 1830s, but these were mainly for their own personal use, and wheeled transportation played an insignificant role in African transportation generally. (See also **Hunters' Road; Transport**.)

P

PAGE, GERTRUDE (Mrs. Alexander Dobbin) (1873–April 1, 1922). English-born writer. Page came to the country with her Irish husband around the turn of the century. There she wrote a series of popular novels dealing with local rural life, which made the country better known in England. Her books included *Love in the Wilderness* (1907), *Paddy-the-Next-Best-*

Thing (1908), *Edge o' Beyond* (1908), *Jill's Rhodesian Philosophy* (1910), and *The Rhodesian* (1912). In 1911 she was officially honored as the colony's best publicist in England, where her books sold well. In other writings she condemned forced recruitment of African labor and supported women's suffrage. (see also **Literature; Women's Franchise Ordinance.**)

PAGET, EDWARD FRANCIS (July 8, 1886–April 21, 1971). **Anglican** cleric. Bishop of the Church of England's Diocese of Southern Rhodesia (1925), and archbishop of the Province of Central Africa (1955).

PAINTINGS see **ROCK PAINTINGS**

PARIRENYATWA, TICHAFA SAMUEL ("Pari") (1927–Aug. 14, 1962). Trained in medicine in Johannesburg, Parirenyatwa became the country's first African doctor in 1957. After working briefly as a government medical officer at Antelope Mine, he entered private practice in **Harare** township. There he became politically active. He was a close associate of **Joshua Nkomo**, serving as the latter's deputy after the formation of **ZAPU** in 1962. A vastly popular leader, he was considered a prime contender for top political leadership in the nationalist movement until he was killed in a car accident while driving from Salisbury to Bulawayo to meet with Nkomo. An official government commission of inquiry ruled his death accidental, but many of his followers and fellow nationalists believed he had been murdered by whites. His funeral drew enormous crowds. In death he became a figure of legendary stature and was honored after independence when the country's largest hospital, in Harare, was renamed in his memory.

PARLIAMENT. The country's **Legislative Assembly** was formally designated "Parliament" after **UDI** in 1965. Prior to UDI the term "parliament" applied properly only in the generic sense of a legislative session, although members of the Assembly styled themselves "Members of Parliament" as early as 1933. The **Constitution of 1969** made Parliament bicameral. The main body became the **House of Assembly,** and the **Senate** was created as an **upper chamber,** following the South African system.

"PARTNERSHIP." Concept articulated by European politicians—especially **Godfrey Huggins**—during the 1950s as the goal of **federation**. The term "partnership" was meant to imply an equality of African and European responsibilities and benefits, but to Africans it came to symbolize European hypocrisy because real political and economic power lay almost entirely in European hands.

PASIPAMIRE. Most famous of the **Chaminuka** mediums.

PASS LAWS. The **BSAC** administration issued the first pass law in 1892 to control African entry into Salisbury (now **Harare**). Over the next decade similar laws were refined and extended throughout the country. Initially, the pass system was used to facilitate labor recruitment and to provide a means of checking on individual tax payments. With the passage of time, however, the system was used increasingly as a means of maintaining racial segregation, particularly in the towns. African adult males were required to carry an assortment of documents, of which the most important was the registration certificate, or book, known as the "*situpa*." African men were required to show these documents to any policeman on demand. Failure to carry up-to-date documents was a criminal offense, punishable by fines or imprisonment. Reform or abolition of the pass laws was a primary goal of the earliest African nationalist movements. In 1936 **Godfrey Huggins** personally introduced the Native Registration Act, which required African men in towns to obtain additional documentation certifying that they were employed or seeking employment. Later legislation modified many rules, but the basic requirement that all adult African males carry registration certificates at all times was not abolished until independence.

PATRICK, MOTHER see **COSGRAVE, MARY ANN**

PATRIOTIC FRONT (PF). Political alliance between **Robert Mugabe's** **ZANU** and **Joshua Nkomo's ZAPU**, announced in mid-October 1976. The alliance came into being as a result of the strong urging of leaders of the **Frontline States**, who felt that leaders of the armed struggle had to be represented at the forthcoming **Geneva Conference**. They also believed that the war could continue indefinitely if the two liberation movements did not join forces and present a united front. Both Mugabe and Nkomo represented the PF at the conference, and in January 1977 the Liberation Committee of the Organization of African Unity (OAU), following the recommendation of the Frontline Presidents, recognized the PF as the sole legitimate liberation organization representing the people of Zimbabwe. In July the general conference of the OAU endorsed that recognition, primarily because between them, the two leaders controlled virtually all the liberation forces fighting inside the country (although the alliance never extended to their separate military operations). Following the failure of the Geneva conference, the PF's military forces continued to press the war, while the political leaders continued to call for the resignation of the **Ian Smith** government, the disarming of the **Rhodesian security forces**, and the creation of a transition government under British and PF leadership.

In 1978 the PF leadership rejected invitations to join negotiations with the Smith government, negotiations that eventually resulted in the signing of the **Internal Settlement** agreement between Smith and conservative nationalist leaders **Abel Muzorewa, Ndabaningi Sithole,** and **Jeremiah Chirau**. The PF condemned the Internal Settlement as a sell-out to the Smith regime, as it in effect left military and police powers, as well as substantive political control of the country, in the hands of the white minority. They also refused to enter into any cease-fire agreement. With the support and backing of the OAU, PF leaders talked to the governments of Britain and the United States and to the General Assembly of the United Nations, urging that international **sanctions** not be removed and that the new government of **Zimbabwe Rhodesia** be denied recognition. Partly as a result of this display of unity by the PF, the extreme right wing of the **Rhodesian Front** finally recognized the necessity of agreeing to talks in which the liberation forces' leadership would represent the African majority. In September 1979 Mugabe and Nkomo led the PF delegation to the **Lancaster House Conference**. Following the successful conclusion of that conference, Mugabe announced in late December that ZANU would contest the upcoming **elections** as an independent party, not in alliance with ZAPU. In the campaign that followed, both ZANU and ZAPU claimed to be the legitimate representative of the now defunct Patriotic Front; each party believed the stature of that recognition would benefit it during the elections. British officials in charge of monitoring the elections insisted that the two parties be recognized as ZANU-PF and PF-ZAPU, giving equal credit to each for its part in the liberation struggle, while denying a favored status to either.

PATTERSON INCIDENT (1878). In 1878, Captain R. Robert Patterson led a semiofficial embassy to **Bulawayo** to investigate charges of **Ndebele** mistreatment of British travelers in **Matabeleland**. Patterson alarmed the Ndebele king **Lobengula** by hinting that the British might support the cause of the royal pretender "Nkulumane." Lobengula nevertheless permitted Patterson to continue north to hunt by the **Victoria Falls**, providing him with a 20-man escort.

About a month later Patterson, two European companions, two African employees, and five of the Ndebele guides perished at the lower **Gwai River**. British Transvaal authorities later claimed that Patterson's party had been murdered on Lobengula's orders. Lobengula denied any personal responsibility in the affair, claiming that the men had died after drinking from a waterhole poisoned by **San** hunters. **H. R. Haggard** and others agitated for British retribution against the Ndebele, but the dispute was eventually ignored by British officials.

PAULING, GEORGE (Sept. 1854–Feb. 10, 1919). British railroad contractor. Pauling came to South Africa in 1875 and worked on government railroads there until becoming an independent contractor. After meeting **Cecil Rhodes** in 1891 he directed the construction of most of present Zimbabwe's early **railway** lines. In the late 1890s he held several major posts in the **BSAC** administration in the country.

PAVER BROTHERS see under **AFRICAN NEWSPAPERS, LTD.**

PEARCE COMMISSION (1972). British government body commissioned to investigate the acceptability of the Anglo-Rhodesian settlement proposals in early 1972. After the failed **"Fearless Talks"** of October 1968, the governments of Britain and Rhodesia did not attempt formally to resolve their constitutional dispute over **UDI** until early 1971, when British officials began holding secret talks with Rhodesian officials in Salisbury. By September news of these talks was public, and Lord Goodman was openly visiting Rhodesia as a special emissary. In mid-November Alec Douglas Home, British foreign secretary and former prime minister, met with **Ian Smith** in Salisbury. On November 24 these two men signed an agreement which came to be known as the Anglo-Rhodesian Settlement Proposals.

These new proposals were widely seen as a significant British retreat from the **"Five Principles"** articulated six years earlier. The proposals called for immediately increased African representation in **Parliament**, and they contained complex formulae which would theoretically bring majority rule to the country. Skeptics noted that even under the best of circumstances this transformation could not occur until well into the 21st century. In the meantime the UDI government was to be recognized. In contrast to earlier British settlement proposals, the 1971 agreement was based upon modification of the **Constitution** of 1969, not that of 1961. The Rhodesian government promised to work to end racial discrimination, to review the cases of political prisoners, and to promote certain advances in African economic welfare, but it was required neither to abrogate existing discriminatory laws nor to make guarantees against future retrogressive constitutional amendments. Britain did hold firm on one crucial principle—that the proposals undergo a "test of acceptability" by the people of the country as a whole before they would be implemented. The prevailing British mood was that the proposals represented the last chance for a graceful withdrawal from the country's responsibility for Rhodesia. The House of Commons approved the proposals by a 297-to-269 vote on December 1, 1971, and a commission was created to investigate the question of the proposals' acceptability within Rhodesia. Lord Edward Pearce, a former high court judge with no African experience, was named to head the 24-man commission. His deputies were Sir Maurice Dorman, ex-governor of Sierra Leone; Sir Glyn Jones, ex-governor of Nyasaland (Malawi); and Lord Harlech, former ambassador to the United States (a fourth deputy, Sir Frederick Pedler, withdrew before the commission began its work). The other commissioners were all Europeans with former African colonial backgrounds.

The Pearce Commission arrived in Rhodesia in the third week of January 1972. Since the Rhodesian government refused to allow a public referendum on the proposals, the commission sampled public opinion through public and private meetings and by correspondence. It canvassed the country for two months, completing its work on March 10 and issuing its formal report in late May. The commission reported wide acceptance of the proposals among European Rhodesians, mixed reactions among Asians and Coloureds, and 97 percent negative responses from the more than 100,000 Africans polled. Because of the overall numerical preponderance of Africans in the country's **population**, the commission concluded that the people of the country as a whole rejected the proposals, which were then officially abandoned by Britain.

Creation of the commission set off a dramatic mobilization of African political activity. The **African National Council** was formed in December 1971 in order to organize opposition to the proposals. Although growth of the ANC was largely spontaneous, the ANC itself was generally credited with eliciting the successful African opposition. Spontaneous mass demonstrations occurred frequently in urban centers. These occasionally grew unruly, bringing down severe police reprisals. The police killed a few dozen demonstrators—mainly in **Gweru**—and arrested more than a thousand political leaders, including the **Chinamanos** and **Judith** and **Garfield Todd**. The Rhodesian government charged that subversive elements were coercing Africans into rejecting the proposals, but African opposition appeared both natural and universal. Most African members of Parliament and almost half of all government chiefs openly voiced opposition to the proposals, though both groups were noted for their support of the white government.

Charges and countercharges continued long after the commission published its report, but the unmistakable finding of the commission was that almost all Africans deeply distrusted the existing Rhodesian government. The whole episode brought Rhodesia back to the center of world attention, and it started a new era in African nationalist political activity within the country. The ANC evolved into a permanent political body. Some of its leaders continued to conduct private consultations with Smith's government in order to bring about a constitutional change, but external bodies such as **ZANU** and **ZAPU** instead committed themselves to the violent overthrow of the regime. Late 1972 thus saw the launching of the liberation struggle.

PENHALONGA. Town near the Mozambique border (at 18°53'S, 32°41'E), about 10 km north of **Mutare.** The town arose by the Penhalonga **gold** mine, which was named after a **Portuguese** count when it was started by British prospectors in 1889. The nearby Rezende Mine was also started at the same time. In mid-1891 Bishop **Knight-Bruce** founded the St. Augustine Mission in Penhalonga, thereby starting **Anglican mission** work in the country. The local gold mines were largely worked out early in the 20th century, and the area is now a diverse agricultural region.

PENNEFATHER, EDWARD GRAHAM (Feb. 12, 1850–April 29, 1928). First commander of the **British South African Police** and overall commander of the **Pioneer Column.** After the BSAP's manpower was sharply curtailed in late 1891, Pennefather resigned his command and returned to South Africa.

PEOPLE'S CARETAKER COUNCIL (PCC). Interim African political party formed by **Joshua Nkomo**'s loyal **ZAPU** supporters in August 1963, soon after the formation of the rival **ZANU.** Nkomo was imprisoned in April 1964 and the PCC was banned by the government on August 26, 1964. PCC leaders then regrouped in Lusaka, **Zambia,** where they later reconstituted the council as ZAPU.

PETROGLYPHS. Although there are vast numbers of **rock paintings** throughout the country, only about 10 petroglyph, or rock engraving, sites have been found. The most sophisticated of these is a finely carved representation of a giraffe, located just off the Bulawayo road about 32 km north of **Beitbridge.** Crudely engraved representations of **animal spoor** have been found at **Bumbuzi** in **Hwange District.** All of these petroglyphs are ascribed to **Stone Age** peoples of undetermined antiquity. In addition, pecked etchings, apparently of village plans, have been found near **Chimanimani,** but these are attributed to **Iron Age** peoples.

PFUMBI see **MATIBI**

PHILLIPS, GEORGE ARTHUR (c.1837–1896). English **hunter** and trader. Phillips lived in **Matabeleland** from 1864 to 1890 and became an intimate friend of the Ndebele king **Lobengula.** He is regarded as one of the latter's strongest Westernizing influences.

"PIONEER." This term is used in two distinct senses. (1) European traders, **hunters,** missionaries, and explorers who entered the country before 1880. (2) Europeans who settled in the country during the 1890s.

PIONEER COLUMN (1890). Collective name for the British forces that occupied **Mashonaland** in late 1890. The column was assembled in mid-1890, after **L. S. Jameson** persuaded the **Ndebele** king **Lobengula** to modify his repudiation of the **Rudd Concession**. The column comprised three main components: (1) The "Pioneer Corps" of 212 men (mainly South African whites), recruited and organized by **Frank Johnson**, who acted as a private contractor for **Cecil Rhodes**. Most of these men were given military ranks and assigned to three "troops." **F. C. Selous** served as chief scout. Other civilians included L. S. Jameson and **Archibald Colquhoun**; (2) Five hundred members of the **British South African Police** commanded by Lt.-Col. **E. G. Pennefather,** who was also overall commander of the column. This group was heavily armed in anticipation of attack by the Ndebele; (3) About 200 **Ngwato** mercenaries led by the brother of **Kamah III.**

The column entered present-day Zimbabwe from eastern **Botswana** at the end of June 1890. It followed a gently curving route to the northeast, skirting the southeastern fringes of the Ndebele kingdom's domain. Along the way it built and garrisoned forts at **Tuli, Chikomba, Masvingo,** and **Harare**, where it halted on September 12, 1890. The column was disbanded on September 30th, after a fort was completed at present Harare. Most of its members dispersed to prospect for **gold.** In addition to daily wages, the members of the "Pioneer Corps" were rewarded with 1,210-hectare (3,000-acre) farms and 15 gold claims each; the police got 1,640-hectare (4,500-acre) farms.

So as not to compromise British claims of Ndebele sovereignty over Mashonaland—upon which the British right of occupation was allegedly based through the Rudd Concession—the occupation was carried out without reference to the rights of the **Shona,** with the exception of the **Manyika** ruler **Mutasa**. While the column was advancing into Mashonaland, the Ndebele prepared for war, but no armed conflict developed. The Shona, apparently unaware of the British intention to occupy their country permanently, did not forcibly resist until the **Revolt** of 1896.

PIT STRUCTURES (a.k.a. pit circles; pit dwellings; etc.) see **STONE-LINED PITS**

PLUMER, HERBERT CHARLES ONSLOW (March 13, 1857–July 16, 1932). British army officer of 20 years' experience and the rank of colonel when he was asked to recruit and to train the **Matabeleland Relief Force** in 1896. Under his command the MRF arrived at **Bulawayo** on May 14, 1896, becoming the first unit of British Imperial troops to fight in the **Ndebele Revolt**. Plumer's arrival ended the first phase of the Revolt, shifting the Ndebele mainly to the defensive. Under **F. Carrington**'s overall command Plumer engaged in considerable action during the war. Four years later he commanded the **Rhodesia Regiment**, which relieved **Baden-Powell** at Mafeking in the **South African War**. In 1919 Plumer was made viscount in recognition of his services as general of the British Second Army in France during the First World War.

PLUMTREE. Southwestern border town, established on the main **railway** line and road from **Francistown** in **Botswana** (at 20°29′S, 27°49′E; alt. 1,385 m). The town is the administrative center for the **Bulilimamangwe**

District as well as commercial center for an extensive **cattle**-raising region.

POLICE see **BRITISH SOUTH AFRICA POLICE**

POLITICAL PARTIES see under names of individual organizations

POMONGWE CAVE. An important **Stone Age** site, Pomongwe Cave once contained the most easily accessible **rock paintings** in the **Matopo Hills** (at 20°33′S, 28°31′E). During the early 1970s the paintings were mostly destroyed in an unsuccessful attempt at permanent preservation.

POPULATION/CENSUSES. The first government census was taken in 1901, but only the settler population was counted. The African population was merely estimated, at c. 500,000. Formal censuses of the European population were thereafter periodically taken, and increasingly precise estimates of the African population were made. A sample formal census of Africans was undertaken in 1948, but the first full African census was not taken until 1962. The last full national census was taken in 1992.

According to government estimates and censuses, the African population first exceeded 1 million in 1930; 2 million in 1950; and 3 million in the late 1950s. The 1969 census enumerated 4,818,000 Africans, 228,044 Europeans, and 23,525 Asians and Coloured people in a total population of 5,069,570. The 1982 census gave a total population count of 7,546,071, while the 1992 census placed the country's population at 10.4 million people. In 1998 it was estimated that the population had grown to c. 11 million—showing a growth rate of about 3.5 percent annually since 1985. In 1999 the government estimated that the population would reach 13.1 million by the beginning of 2000, and 15.5 million in 2005. According to 1992 census materials, 76 percent of the population belong to the various **Shona** groups, 18 percent are classified as **Ndebele,** with the remainder divided between the **Tonga** (2 percent), **Hlengwe** (1 percent), **Venda** (1 percent), and **Europeans, Asians,** and mixed-race or **Coloured** (2 percent).

In addition, the 1992 census returns indicate the number of people living in urban centers (defined as cities or towns with a minimum population of 2,500) is approximately 29 percent of the population, while 71 percent live in the rural areas—down from approximately 80 percent in 1969. Approximately 50 percent of the population is under the age of 15.

PORTUGUESE. The goldfields of present Zimbabwe attracted Portuguese interest before Vasco Da Gama even reached southeast Africa or the Portuguese knew where the goldfields were. Through Arab writings the Portuguese knew about the rich **gold** trade conducted through the **Muslim** port of **Sofala,** and they were quick to believe that the region was the biblical land of **"Ophir."** They occupied Sofala in 1505, hoping simply to tap the existing trade, but soon found themselves drawn deeper and deeper into the interior in search of the actual goldfields.

Antonio Fernandez became the first known European to enter present Zimbabwe in c.1511. He was soon followed by *sertanejo* traders, who communicated news of the **Munhumutapa** state to the coast. Portuguese officialdom then followed the traders up the **Zambezi River,**

occupying Muslim trading **fairs** at **Sena** and **Tete** in the 1530s. In late 1560 the Jesuit priest **Goncalo da Silveira** entered **Mashonaland**, thus becoming the first missionary in the country (see **Missions**). Silveira also became the country's first Christian martyr when he was murdered by the **Shona**. A decade later the Portuguese crown launched a major military expedition to avenge Silveira's death and to seize whatever goldfields could be found. Neither **Francisco Barreto** nor his successor **Vasco Homem** successfully penetrated the country, but they obtained Munhumutapa **Negomo**'s concession of trading privileges. The Portuguese then tried to sweep the Muslims out of the Zambezi Valley.

Union of the Portuguese and Spanish crowns in 1580 retarded official Portuguese involvement in the southeast African interior, and it introduced new problems of competition with the Dutch and British on the Indian Ocean. Private trading and military ventures nevertheless increased. Trading fairs were opened in **Manicaland** and northeastern Mashonaland, and Dominican missionaries opened numerous stations among the Shona. Traders like **D. S. Madeira** meddled in Shona politics and were meddling in Munhumutapa political successions by the early 17th century.

It is uncertain to what extent the Portuguese penetrated the vast southwestern section of the country during the early period. **S. D. Bayao** intervened in a **Changamire** succession dispute in the 1640s, but the military posts he established were soon withdrawn. Archaeologists have turned up Portuguese relics in present **Matabeleland** sites. These have often been interpreted as indications of direct Dominican mission activity at **Dhlo Dhlo** and **Khami**. More likely, such relics were simply trade items or booty from Changamire wars in the northeast. The Changamire state began expanding into the northeast in the 1680s, wiping out most Portuguese centers by the early 1690s. Thereafter the Portuguese conducted trade with the Shona from peripheral bases in Manicaland and a new fair opened at **Zumbo** in c.1714. Dominican and Jesuit missionary efforts left no lasting mark on the country, and Portuguese influence generally gradually diminished in the country through the 1830s. The **Gaza** invasion of the **Eastern Highlands** at that time drove the Portuguese back even farther from the interior and reduced many surviving Portuguese outposts to tributaries.

Portuguese imperial influence in the interior underwent a resurgence in the late 1880s, when it became clear that British and **Afrikaners** would compete with Portugal for political mastery of Mashonaland. **J. C. P. d'Andrada** and **Manuel de Sousa** moved through northern Shona territory, trading firearms and obtaining treaties from minor rulers. By then it was too late, however. The **BSAC** occupied Mashonaland proper in 1890, resulting in direct clashes between British and Portuguese agents. Incidents at **Macequece** and Delagoa Bay nearly led to a British-Portuguese war, but an amicable settlement was reached in the **Anglo-Portuguese Convention** of 1891. Thereafter small-scale Portuguese immigration into Zimbabwe continued through the 20th century. This increased greatly after the Portuguese revolution of 1974, when it became clear that Portugal's neighboring colony, **Mozambique**, was soon to become independent.

PORTUGUESE EAST AFRICA (PEA). English name for colonial **Mozambique.** In a broader historical sense, the name has also been applied to most of the eastern African coast, whose port towns Portugal dominated during the 16th and 17th centuries.

POSSELT, FRIEDRICH WILHELM TRAUGOTT (d.1950). Officer of wide experience in the Southern Rhodesian Native Affairs Department from 1908 to 1941. An amateur ethnographer and historian, Posselt published numerous articles and books on both the **Ndebele** and **Shona** peoples. (See **Bibliography.**)

Note that the "Posselt Ruin" at **Zimbabwe** was named after an apparently unrelated hunter, Willie Posselt, who discovered the **"Zimbabwe Birds."**

POSTAL SYSTEM AND STAMPS. Mail services of sorts from **Matabeleland** to South Africa began in 1859, when newly arrived **LMS** agents began using African runners to carry letters. This informal system of runners continued through the 19th century, though runners were increasingly replaced by European riders and wagon drivers. In 1892 the **BSAC** administration established the first formal post office in Salisbury (present-day **Harare**), and it began issuing postage stamps carrying its own name. In 1900 the territory entered the Universal Postal Union. The name **"Rhodesia"** first appeared as an overprint on BSAC stamps in 1909, fully displacing the BSAC imprint the next year. The name "Southern Rhodesia" appeared on stamps from 1924 to 1965—except during the years of **federation.** Franking machines were first used in 1928, and air services began in 1932. The first locally printed stamps were not produced until 1961. In 1966 the name "Rhodesia" reappeared on stamps and the traditional portrait of the British monarch was dropped. Following independence in 1980, the name **"Zimbabwe"** appeared on stamp issues, which often depict the country's natural resources—both animal and mineral.

By the late 1980s, there were about 170 full post offices in the country, 47 postal telegraph offices, and 86 postal agencies.

POTGIETER, ANDRIES HENDRIK (a.k.a. Ndaleka) (Dec. 19, 1792–March 1853). **Afrikaner** leader during South Africa's "Great Trek" of the 1830s. In mid-1836 Potgieter led a Voortrekker scouting party from the present Orange Free State across the **Limpopo River,** reaching the upper **Bubye River** in what is believed to have been the first European penetration of present Zimbabwe since the early **Portuguese** days. The following year he commanded two major Voortrekker assaults on **Ndebele** settlements—then in the western **Transvaal**—thereby contributing to the pressure that drove the Ndebele into what became **Matabeleland.** As Voortrekkers settled in the Transvaal during the 1840s, Potgieter strove to organize commando raids against the Ndebele in their new home. He finally led a commando against Ndebele towns in the **Matopo Hills** in 1847. This raid was repelled by the *induna* **Mbigo.** Potgieter afterwards ceased to trouble the Ndebele, and he is believed to have signed a peace treaty with Ndebele emissaries shortly before his death.

PRESIDENTS. The office of president was created under the republican **Constitution of 1969.** The office superseded that of the British **governor,** and the president was empowered to appoint **prime ministers** and judges, sign legislative bills, and proclaim general **elections.** During the **UDI** period, there were three presidents: **Clifford Dupont** (1970–1975), **J. J. Wrathall** (1975–1978), and **Josiah Gumede** (May–Dec. 1979).

The **Lancaster House Constitution** kept the office of the president as head of state and commander-in-chief of the armed forces, but the office continued to be largely ceremonial. The first president of the independent Republic of Zimbabwe was **Canaan Banana,** who served from April 1980 until his retirement in December 1987. Following an act of **Parliament** in October 1987, the office of prime minister was abolished and its duties as head of government were amalgamated with those of the president, as head of state, to form what has been termed an "executive presidency." According to that act, the president will be elected to a six-year term of office—although **Robert Mugabe,** the first president in the new system, was appointed by Parliament. On December 31, 1987, Mugabe was inaugurated as Zimbabwe's first executive president. He easily won election to the office in the 1995 elections. Under the system in place since 1987, the president has much greater political authority than prime ministers exercised, including the ability to veto acts of Parliament—subject to an override by a two-thirds vote of Parliament.

PRESS. Newspaper publication began almost immediately after the British occupation of **Mashonaland** in the early 1890s when numerous small papers sprang up, but most of these were short-lived, and all catered strictly to the interests of the **European** settler communities being established throughout the country. Of the commercial papers which survived into the 20th century, the most important were absorbed by the South African-based **Argus Group.** Argus controlled the *Rhodesia Herald, Sunday Mail, Bulawayo Chronicle, Sunday News, Umtali Post,* and many other publications through its subsidiary, the Rhodesian Printing and Publishing Company. Small independent papers included the *Gwelo Times, Fort Victoria News, Gatooma Mail,* and *Midlands Observer.* The Argus Group papers generally supported the Southern Rhodesian and **federation** governments until 1964 when it refused to support **Ian Smith**'s government in calling for **UDI.** The newspapers then came under increasing attack, including harassment of reporters and staff by the **Rhodesian security forces,** loss of advertising from supporters of Smith's government, and under the regime's emergency regulations, the imposition of **censorship.** In January 1981, the newly independent government announced that it had purchased the Argus group's controlling interest in the country's five major newspapers (the *Herald, Sunday Mail, Chronicle, Sunday News,* and *Post*) and that in the future they would be controlled by the newly created Zimbabwe **Mass Media Trust.** The Mass Media Trust then organized Zimbabwe Newspapers, Ltd., which officially publishes the newspapers.

In theory, the restrictions and censorship placed on the press during the period of UDI were removed following independence. However, despite charges from opposition politicians such as **Joshua Nkomo, Edgar Tekere, Abel Muzorewa,** and **Ndabaningi Sithole** (see **Forum Party;**

Zimbabwe African People's Union; Zimbabwe Unity Movement) that the country's major newspapers often act as propaganda agents for the government, particularly during periods leading up to national **elections**, individual reporters and editors have repeatedly been harrassed, and even arrested and imprisoned, for being critical of government programs and for reporting allegations of corruption. Some of the most blatant instances of the government's heavy-handed attempts to control the press occurred during the **Zimbabwe National Army**'s crackdown on dissidents in **Matabeleland** in 1984; during the **Willowdale** scandal; and in April 1995 when senior editors of the *Financial Gazette* were arrested on charges of defaming the character of President **Robert Mugabe**. After publishing reports that he had secretly married a former secretary whom he had been involved with prior to the death of his wife, they were arrested, held for forty-eight hours and later heavily fined.

Beginning in the 1930s there have been many newspapers published primarily for an African readership, although these have been mostly controlled by whites and have been largely politically impotent. African newspaper publication began with the weekly *Bantu Mirror*. It was most prolific during the 1950s when **African Newspapers, Ltd.** was at its peak. The *African Daily News* (**ADN**), founded in 1956 by African Newspapers, was the first daily aimed specifically at an African readership. The group died after the *ADN* was banned by the government in 1964 for supporting African nationalism and opposing the government's call for UDI. The few attempts at independent African newspaper publication, such as *Chapupu* and the *Zimbabwe Sun,* were also suppressed by the Smith government. In their place, beginning in 1965 the government's Ministry of Information published a free propaganda paper, the **African Times.** The African readership daily *Zimbabwe Times* operated for sixteen months until it was also banned in 1978, apparently at the request of Bishop **Abel Muzorewa**, for opposing the **internal settlement** and advocating a conference which would include the **Patriotic Front**. In 1985, Zimbabwe Newspapers began publishing *Kwayedza/Umthunywa,* in both the **Chishona** and **Ndebele** languages, specifically for the African readership of the country.

PRESTAGE, PETER (Feb. 27, 1842–April 11, 1907). English Jesuit missionary. Prestage came to South Africa in 1877 to serve in the Jesuit college at Grahamstown. In 1882 he joined the **Zambezi Mission** and spent two years at **Tati** before moving on to **Bulawayo**. In 1887 he persuaded **Lobengula** to grant the Jesuits land for a station at **Empandeni**, where he was joined by **Andrew Hartmann** a year later. The two Jesuits closed this station down in 1889 and joined the **BSAC**'s **Pioneer Column** as chaplains the next year. Prestage then helped **Mary Cosgrave** establish a hospital, the country's first, in Salisbury in 1891. The following year he joined Hartmann in founding the **Chishawasha Mission** nearby. After the 1896–97 **Revolts** Prestage returned to work at Empandeni. In 1902 he attempted to start yet another station in Northern Rhodesia, but he abandoned the effort because of poor health.

PRIME MINISTERS. From the achievement of **Responsible Government** in 1923 until December 1987, the head of government was the prime minister ("premier" until 1933). In theory, from 1923 until the

Constitution of 1969, British **governors** held discretionary power over appointments of the prime ministers, but in practice the office always went to the recognized heads of the ruling parties in the **Legislative Assembly.** The governors also consistently followed the advice of the prime ministers in designating cabinet members (see **Executive Council**). Following the republican Constitution of 1969, the **president** of the country officially appointed the prime minster, but other than that the system remained the same as before 1969. This system was retained in the Constitutions of both the short-lived **Zimbabwe Rhodesia** and the independent Republic of Zimbabwe. The post was abolished by act of **Parliament** in October 1987, when the offices of head of government and head of state were combined under an "executive" president.

The prime ministers were: 1923–27 **Charles Coghlan;** 1927–33 **H. U. Moffat;** 1933 **George Mitchell;** 1933–53 **Godfrey Huggins;** 1953–58 **Garfield Todd;** 1958–62 **Edgar Whitehead;** 1962–64 **Winston Field;** 1964–78 **Ian Smith;** 1979 **Abel Muzorewa;** and 1980–87 **Robert Mugabe.** (For federal prime ministers, see under **Federation.**)

PRINCE EDWARD DAM see under **HUNYANI RIVER**

"PROTECTED VILLAGES." In 1974 the Rhodesian government responded to increasing infiltration of nationalist guerrillas—particularly in the northeast—by concentrating isolated African farming communities in "protected villages." The program was designed to sever communications between guerrillas and uncommitted Africans. By mid-1977 an estimated 300,000 people were living in such villages, with government plans for creation of many more. The villages averaged about 2,500 residents, living within chain-link fence enclosures (unfenced settlements were apparently known as "consolidated villages") illuminated by electric lights at night. Soldiers stationed at the villages had orders to shoot dusk-to-dawn curfew violators without challenging them. The government provided no food or supplies for the residents, who typically had to walk long distances to work their farms. Malnutrition became a serious problem in the villages, as farms fell prey to neglect, untended livestock, and vermin.

PROVIDENTIAL PASS. Defile in the Devuli Hills, just west of **Kyle Lake,** through which the **Pioneer Column** ascended from low to high veld in early August 1890 (at 20°11'S, 30°47'E). So named because its discovery was thought to have delivered the column from the last serious threat of **Ndebele** attack during its advance into **Mashonaland.**

PROVINCES, ADMINISTRATIVE. Between the 1890s and 1962 the country was administratively divided into two provinces of roughly equal size: **Mashonaland** and **Matabeleland.** In 1962 the country was redivided into seven provinces, encompassing a total of 50 **African administrative districts.** In March 1979, the country was again reorganized into eight provinces, by that time encompassing 55 administrative districts. The eight provinces are **Manicaland, Mashonaland Central, Mashonaland East, Mashonaland West, Matabeleland South, Matabeleland North, Midlands,** and **Masvingo.**

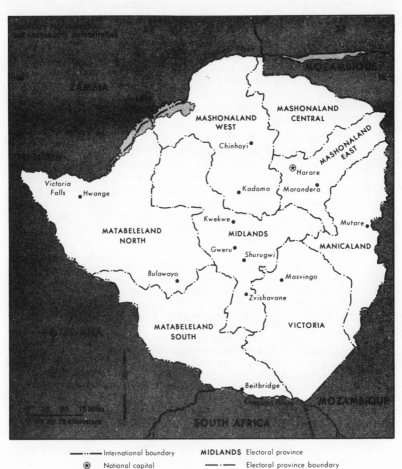

Figure 5: Administrative Provinces

The provinces are administered by provincial administrators—the most senior officials of the Ministry of Local Government and Urban Development in each province. Closely related to this structure is that of the Provincial Council, which is composed of the mayors and chairmen of the cities, towns, rural and district councils within each province. The Provincial Council is chaired by the provincial governor, who is a political appointee and whose functions are defined as being political, consultative, developmental, and coordinative. The provincial administrator acts as the chief executive officer to the Provincial Council. The basic function of the Provincial Councils is to bring together the district-level representatives to set development goals and coordinate development projects within each province. They are assisted in this function by Provincial Development Committees, made up of the heads of ministries and departments at the provincial levels, chaired by the provincial administrator.

PUNGWE. Term used during the 1970s period of the war of liberation to refer to meetings held after sunset, often lasting all night, between Zimbabwe African National Liberation Army (**ZANLA**) freedom fighters and rural villagers. During these meetings, the freedom fighters would explain in political terms questions affecting the African population of the country. These included discussions on land distribution and ownership, taxes, local cattle-dipping regulations and fees, education, and other topics of concern to the local people. Political and more traditional songs were also sung. Freedom fighters would request, if not demand, support from the villagers. This support could include food, clothing, money, or information concerning the movements of government forces in the areas. In addition, local "sell-outs" or "collaborators" were often denounced and sometimes killed, and young men and women were recruited at these meetings (see **Mujibas**). This technique for rural politicization has been described as a major contributor to **ZANLA's** and **ZANU's** successes.

PUNGWE RIVER. Rises in the **Inyanga Mountains**, whence it flows east, through **Mozambique** to the Indian Ocean, between **Beira** and **Sofala**. The Pungwe is fed by the **Honde River**, and it forms a short stretch of the **border** between Zimbabwe and Mozambique. In 1891 **L. S. Jameson** and **Frank Johnson** made an adventurous trip down the Pungwe in a futile attempt to demonstrate its potential as a passageway into the country.

PURCHASE AREAS (PAs). In 1930 the **Land Apportionment Act** created "Native Purchase Areas" (later redesignated "African Purchase Areas"), in response to African demands for more land expressed before the **Morris Carter Commission** five years earlier. Land equal to 7.7 percent of the country was originally set aside for Purchase Areas, in which individual Africans were to be able to buy or lease farms—but the designated areas were scattered, isolated, unsurveyed, and mostly semi-arid. Due to the fact that it was virtually impossible for local Africans to accumulate the capital necessary to purchase or lease these farms, the response to the scheme was limited during the 1930s, with mostly *Mfengu* and other foreign Africans acquiring the available farms. In the 1940s, with the expansion of the country's economy as a result of the Second World War, some local Africans were finally able to accumulate enough capital to purchase farms in the PAs. By 1968 there were about 7,000 PA farms in operation, providing for about 2.7 percent of the country's resident African population.

Most PA farmers employed the same farming techniques as used in the Tribal Trust Lands (now **Communal Lands**) and few received government technical or financial assistance commonly provided to settler farmers. Relatively few PA farmers ever achieved any degree of commercial success. By the late 1970s there were approximately 85 blocks of PA land, located mostly around the fringes of lands then reserved for European occupation. The largest PA lands were located in central **Chikomba District, northeastern Gokwe, northwestern Kadoma,** and southwest **Mutoko Districts**. The Purchase Areas were officially dissolved under the 1977 Tenure Amendment Act, however, they retained their separate territorial boundaries and identities.

Q

Q- . In languages such as **Sindebele,** which contain **click sounds,** the letter *q* represents the palatal click, as in *ukuqwaqwaza,* "to make a clicking noise." The letter *q* is not used in **Chishona** orthography.

QUE QUE see **KWEKWE**

QUEENS' LOCATION (a.k.a. Queens' Kraal). Site by the **Bembezi River** where **Lozigeyi** and others of **Lobengula**'s widows settled after the **Ndebele War of 1893**. Queen's Mine and Queen's Mountain (both at 19°48′S, 28°45′E) are nearby. Queen's Mine takes its name from an abandoned **gold** mine pegged just before the 1896 Revolt.

R

R-. See under **L**

RADIO AND TELEVISION see **ZIMBABWE BROADCASTING CORPO-RATION**

RAILWAYS. When the **British South Africa Company** occupied the country in the early 1890s, it had several reasons for rapid railway development. Its 1889 **charter** required it to extend rail services to the **Zambezi River**; the 1891 **Anglo-Portuguese Convention** required that the BSAC connect **Beira** with **Mashonaland**; development of the new colony's **mineral** resources depended upon good transport facilities; and **Cecil Rhodes**, the BSAC leader, was personally motivated to connect Cape Town with Cairo by rail. Only this last goal was unachieved.

The first two rail lines were started almost simultaneously from Beira to Salisbury (now **Harare**) through Umtali (now **Mutare**), and from Vryburg, South Africa, to Salisbury, through **Bulawayo**. Most of the early construction was contracted by **George Pauling**. In contrast to government-sponsored transport projects elsewhere in southern Africa, these construction projects were financed by a private company, Rhodesia Railways, a BSAC subsidiary.

The Beira line was begun in 1892, reaching Umtali in 1898 and Salisbury a year later. To overcome engineering problems the line east of Umtali was built with narrow-gauge track, but this was later replaced with 3'6" (1.067 mi) gauge, which became standard throughout southern Africa and Congo (formerly Zaire). **Malaria** and dysentery killed more than 900 Indians and Europeans who worked on the line in **Mozambique.**

The line originating in South Africa was begun in 1893. It ran through Francistown, **Botswana**, reaching Bulawayo in 1897. The Harare link was completed only in 1897, because of the disruption of the **South African War**. The present-day sites of **Gweru, Kwekwe,** and **Kadoma** later developed into major urban centers along this line.

Rhodes' plan to extend a line north from Salisbury through present **Zambia** received little support for economic reasons. The idea was permanently dropped after the discovery of **coal** at **Hwange**. A line between Bulawayo and Hwange was then completed in 1903, and extended to **Victoria Falls** the next year. After a bridge was built across the Zambezi by the Falls, the line was extended into Zambia, reaching the Copperbelt and connecting to southern Congo's mines a few years later.

Branch lines, mainly to major mining centers, have been added continuously since the main lines were finished. Important lines were opened to **Chinhoyi** in 1902, **West Nicholson** in 1905, **Masvingo** in 1911, and **Shamva** in 1918. In 1955 a major new connection with Mozambique was made by way of **Sango**, linking the country to the port of Maputo (formerly Lourenzo Marques). An additional, and direct, link with South Africa was extended off **Rutenga** to **Beitbridge** in 1974. In 1991, 2,759 km of track were in use throughout the country, and by 1999 there were c.3,000km of track in use.

Throughout the 20th century the country's railway network has greatly facilitated economic development by transporting bulky export goods, moving coal for thermal **electrical power** generation, and earning revenues from the transshipment of Zambian exports (mainly copper). By the mid-1980s the country's trains were devoting more than 90 percent of their carrying capacity to freight, which amounted to more than 13 million metric tons annually. In 1991 the railways carried nearly 15 million metric tons of freight, and 2.9 million passengers.

From early 1976, when the lines to Beira and Maputo were closed by the newly independent Mozambican government in support of Zimbabwe's national liberation forces, all rail traffic had to pass through South Africa. The increased pressure this put on the country's economy may have helped to accelerate its independence. The Maputo line was reopened in 1980, and the Beira line in the following year. The Maputo line was once again lost to Zimbabwe in the mid-1980s when it came under constant disruption by forces of the **Mozambique National Resistance.**

Since independence, the country's railways have been operated by the National Railways of Zimbabwe (NRZ), an autonomous state corporation. In 1981 the NRZ initiated the first phase of the proposed electrification of the system, converting c.811 km of track on the Harare to Gwera line to electricity and ordering 80 electric locomotives. That first stage of electrification was completed in October 1983. In October 1998, the government announced that it was seeking private operators for the NRZ.

RAMAQUABANE RIVER. Flows south from **Plumtree** for 130 km before joining the **Shashi River.** The whole length of the Ramaquabane forms part of the **border** with **Botswana.**

RANA. Acronym for Rhodesia and Nyasaland Airways, a predecessor of **Air Zimbabwe** during the 1930s. Since *rana* is also the Latin word for "frog," the name came to symbolize the airline's puddle-jumping reputation.

RANCHE HOUSE COLLEGE. Private adult-education college, founded in **Harare** in the early 1960s with money from the **Beit Trust** and other nongovernment funds. As a nonracial institution it has served a uniquely diverse variety of southern African communities. (see **Education.**)

RANDALL-MacIVER, DAVID (1873–1945). British archaeologist. From April to August 1905 Randall-MacIver investigated **Iron Age** ruins with the support of the Rhodes Trust and the British Association. The first professionally trained archaeologist to work in the country, he was invited specifically to investigate the claims of ancient and exotic origin of the **stone ruins** made by **J. T. Bent, R. N. Hall,** and others. After working briefly at several different sites, he made a major dig in the main enclosure of the **Zimbabwe Ruins.** His findings, published in *Mediaeval Rhodesia* (London, 1906) contained two startling conclusions: that the ruins were of purely local African origin and that Great Zimbabwe itself was constructed only after about the A.D. 1300s—not in ancient times. Professional archaeologists immediately accepted his findings, but local settlers were outraged. Hall published a tendentious rebuttal a few years later, and the **Zimbabwe Controversy** was started. Although Randall-MacIver's findings are still regarded as essentially sound, his main error was in ascribing somewhat too late a date to Zimbabwe's construction. In 1929 **Gertrude Caton-Thompson** was called in to investigate this question.

THE RANGE. Village just east of **Chivhu** in the **Chikomba District** (at 19°S, 31°2′E) serving as the local African administrative center. Chikomba District was formerly called the Range-Charter District. The Range Dam on the upper **Sebakwe River**, built in 1968, provides water for Chivhu.

RANGER, TERENCE OSBORN (b. Nov. 19, 1929). A British historian, Ranger came to the country in 1957 to teach in the newly created **University College**. There he became interested in African history and began researching and writing about African resistance to colonial rule. Ranger has written profusely and is regarded as perhaps the leading British authority on central African history. (See **Bibliography**.)

REDCLIFF. Industrial town just south of **Kwekwe** at the heart of the country (19°2′S, 29°47′E; alt. 1,220 m). Named after a mountain of **iron** ore in the area, Redcliff is virtually an adjunct of the Zimbabwe Iron and Steel Company (ZISCO), which administers the town and employs most of its adult residents. ZISCO (formerly RISCO—Rhodesian Iron and Steel Company) was established as a government-owned commission in 1942 in order to mine and process local iron ore deposits to meet the country's internal needs. Although production increased steadily, limited national markets and other problems caused the government to sell the company to a consortium of British industrialists in 1957. Since 1961 the company has maintained an annual production of more than 360,000 metric tons of heavy and light steel products. Redcliff's 1992 population was 29,959.

REFORM PARTY. Short-lived European political party formed by supporters of **Godfrey Huggins** in 1931. Its members were mostly dissidents from the ruling **Rhodesian Party**, from which it differed mainly in its fervor for territorial racial segregation. The Reform Party won the 1933 general election, bringing Huggins to power as **prime minister.** A party revolt against Huggins's leadership soon caused him to dissolve **Parliament** in order to call a new election as the head of the newly formed **United Party.** Only one member of the Reform Party retained his legislative seat, and the party faded into insignificance.

REFORMED INDUSTRIAL AND COMMERCIAL UNION (RICU). Essentially an African protest organization, the RICU was formed early in 1946 by **Charles Mzingeli** and other African labor leaders in Salisbury. The RICU revived the name of the defunct **Industrial and Commercial Union**, but failed to reestablish the earlier body's national impact. Nevertheless, under Mzingeli's presidency the RICU became the dominant voice of African political and economic dissent in the Salisbury area, while **Benjamin Burumbo** inherited the ICU tradition in Bulawayo. The RICU led local protests against the **Native (Urban Areas) Accommodation Act**, and it became the local center of the 1948 general strike. In the mid-1950s, however, both Mzingeli's leadership and the RICU itself were eclipsed by the new **Youth League** and the **African National Congress**.

"REGIMENTS," NDEBELE see **IBUTHO**

RELIGION, NDEBELE. Traditional **Ndebele** beliefs have changed little since the 19th century. In common with other **Nguni** peoples, the Ndebele believe in the remote high god, **Nkulunkulu**, who must be approached indirectly, through ancestor spirits (see **Idlozi**). These beliefs were modified somewhat by absorption of **Sotho** concepts of *mlimo* adopted during the formative years of the Ndebele kingdom. When the Ndebele arrived in **Matabeleland** in c.1839, they found a local cult system worshipping **Mwari** in the **Matopo Hills**. Previously it had been thought that the Ndebele adopted Mwari worship so thoroughly that the Mwari cult leaders were influential in Ndebele politics by the end of the 19th century (see **Revolt**). It now appears, however, that the Mwari cult system had only a small influence on Ndebele beliefs. (See also **Missions**.)

RELIGION, SHONA. A large and complex body of beliefs have been described as making up "Shona religion," but not all **Shona** groups accept all aspects of these beliefs, nor is belief in many important features confined to the Shona people. Nevertheless, it is possible to make some generalizations about Shona religion. In simplified terms, the Shona venerate a complex hierarchy of spirits and a high god, **Mwari**, who stands above the spirit hierarchy. The spirits are either personal (see **Mudzimu; Ngozi; Shave**), or communal (see **Mhondoro; Gombwe**). These spirits typically communicate with the living through mediums known as *svikiro*. The high god Mwari can be approached in either two ways—a distinction which represents an apparently basic split between northern Shona and southern Shona and **Venda** religious observances. In the north spirit mediums act as intermediaries in dealings with Mwari. In the south and southwest Mwari can be approached directly through oracular shrines centered in the **Matopo Hills**. The Mwari cult is an elaborate and highly organized religious system with few indigenous parallels in southern Africa.

Other aspects of Shona belief less directly concerned with the spirit world are the arts of healing and divination. There are many male and female professional *nganga* (see also **Chiremba**) who offer individuals cures and protection from everyday maladies and accidents, which are frequently attributed to witchcraft. While many such practitioners have readily accommodated to Christianity, Mwari priests and spirit mediums have remained antagonistic to Christianity in order to preserve the sacred veneration of ancestors. (See also **Missions**.)

REMBA see LEMBA

RENDER, ADAM (variant: Renders) (1822–1876?). An enigmatic figure, Render is credited with having been the first European to visit the **Zimbabwe Ruins**.

REPUBLIC OF SOUTH AFRICA see SOUTH AFRICA

REPUBLICAN FRONT see RHODESIAN FRONT

RESERVES, AFRICAN see COMMUNAL LANDS

RESPONSIBLE GOVERNMENT MOVEMENT. By the time of the First World War it was generally acknowledged that **BSAC** rule would end within a decade. Two alternatives were seen for the country's constitutional future: union with South Africa (see **Unionist Movement**) or local responsible government. The latter effectively meant full self-government by the tiny **European** minority. As early as 1908 settlers had held the majority of seats on the territory's **Legislative Council**, but their powers were severely limited, and the country's large capital interests doubted the economic feasibility of a fully responsible government regime. Despite such opposition, the majority of the European farmers, small workers, and wage earners supported the idea of responsible government as the only attractive alternative to either union with South Africa or continued BSAC rule.

In 1917 the Responsible Government Association (later known as the Rhodesian Responsible Government Party) was formed. The association received a major boost two years later when **Charles Coghlan** joined. As the leader of the elected members of Legco, Coghlan was made the association's president and leading spokesman (see **Tawse-Jollie, E.**). The movement placed increasing pressure on the British government to provide a responsible government **constitution**, and its goals were supported by the reports of the **Cave** and **Buxton** commissions in 1920–21. In the 1920 election the party won 12 of 13 legislative seats. There was virtually no organized African opposition to the movement—perhaps because the unionist alternative was even less attractive to Africans—and even missionaries such as **A. S. Cripps** and **John White** lent the movement tacit support.

On October 27, 1922, a referendum was held among the electorate. Responsible government was approved by 8,774 voters, while 5,989 people voted for union. At the most, about 60 Africans were eligible to vote. The referendum settled the issue, leaving only the constitutional and fiscal arrangements to be worked out. Southern Rhodesia was declared a British Crown Colony in September 1923 and Coghlan was sworn in as first premier on October 1. The **Legislative Assembly** replaced Legco, and a British **governor** replaced the office of BSAC **administrator**. The new responsible government was required to pay £2 million to the Crown for the public works and unalienated land, while the Crown in turn paid the BSAC £3.75 million for the same interests in both Southern and Northern Rhodesia together. The BSAC retained only its mineral rights (later sold to **H. U. Moffat**'s administration) and its interests in the **railways**. Day-to-day operation of the government changed little. Meanwhile, the Responsible Government Party was recognized as the **Rhodesian Party** in late 1923.

REVOLTS OF 1896–97 (a.k.a. *chimurenga* or *chindunduma*). Between late March 1896 and October 1897 a large part of the country's **population** rose in violent rebellion against white settlers and the **BSAC** administration. About 10 percent of the whites in the country were killed; all development stopped as the government mobilized military forces; and the BSAC was brought nearly to a point of collapse. No other tropical African colony experienced an early rebellion of comparable scale or impact.

The **Ndebele** and **Shona** peoples and their allies waged essentially separate revolts, but they rose for much the same reasons, and at roughly the same time. Their grievances against the BSAC and settlers were many: land encroachments, **cattle** seizures, forced labor recruitment, inept and bullying police and administrators, and a general BSAC failure to legitimize its presumed sovereignty. Further, in early 1896, the country was devastated by drought, **rinderpest**, and **locust** invasions. Africans tended to attribute these natural disasters to the European occupation. Africans still owned good supplies of firearms and ammunition, and the Europeans in the country were entirely unprepared for war.

(1) *The Ndebele Revolt* can be seen as a continuation of the 1893 **Ndebele War**. The BSAC had occupied central **Matabeleland**, seized many cattle, and seen the end of King **Lobengula**, but it had not effectively disarmed or broken up the quasimilitary *ibutho* organization. The Ndebele were aggrieved by their humiliation, by the company's refusal to recognize their *izinduna* (see **Induna**) or a new king, and by the company's continuing seizures of cattle. The **Jameson Raid** of late 1895, which took many troops out of the country, has been seen as a trigger to the Revolt. Whether or not this was true, it is evident that the rising was being planned at least as early as February 1896. On March 20, 1896, the Ndebele began to kill African policemen and Europeans around **Filabusi**. By the end of the month virtually the entire kingdom and its former tributaries were in open revolt. The BSAC's first response was to organize the **Bulawayo Field Force**.

Progress of the revolt was too complex to detail here, but general observations can be made. Ndebele leaders cooperated with each other until their lines of communication were severed around August, but they had no unitary command structure. One major group coalesced around the **Khumalo** royal family by the **Bembezi River** in the north. Leaders of this bloc included Lobengula's son **Nyamanda**, his wife **Lozigeyi**, and *mpotshwana* and many other *izinduna*. A second and more loosely united group operated in the **Matopo Hills** under the leadership of **Babayane, Dhliso Mathemu, Mlugulu, Sikombo** and others. A third group operated around the **Insiza River**, east of the Matopos. Among its leaders was **Somabulana**. Allied with these groups were such non-Ndebele tributaries as the **Lemba, Birwam Rozvi, Kalanga**, and **Dumbuseya**, which played a small role as well. Not all Ndebele rebelled. Some formerly powerful *izinduna*, notably **Mtshane**, remained neutral. Others, notably **Gampu** and **Faku**, actively collaborated with the British. These collaborators helped the British especially to keep southwestern supply routes open, and their fighting with the rebels had overtones of an Ndebele civil war.

By the end of April 1896 the Ndebele had driven Europeans out of the outlying areas and had most survivors under siege in *laagers* at **Bulawayo**, Belingwe (now **Mberengwa**), and elsewhere. This moment represented the height of Ndebele success. In mid-May **H. C. O. Plumer** arrived with the **Matabeleland Relief Force**, and the Ndebele war against the BSAC became a guerrilla war against British Imperial forces. On June 2, **Frederick Carrington** took command of British forces, and the Ndebele soon found themselves fighting a defensive war. Rebel forces got lifts when the Shona Revolt (see below) began in mid-June, and when Nyamanda was proclaimed Ndebele king on June 25, but by then many rebels were already surrendering. The situation progressively deteriorated as rebels were driven from their stores of grain and their ammunition ran short.

In August British forces began assaulting guerrilla positions in the Matopo Hills. This campaign proved so difficult that **Cecil Rhodes** and other company leaders decided to attempt a negotiated peace for fear that the expenses of the Matopos fighting would break the company. On August 21, Rhodes conducted the first "*indaba*" with southern rebel leaders. Northern leadership was ignored, but the general situations had gotten so bad for all rebels that virtually all major leaders surrendered by December. Many rebel leaders were then made government-salaried chiefs, but the Ndebele regained no lost land, and other reforms were minor.

(2) *Shona Revolt*. Both the origins and course of the revolt in **Mashonaland** were more complex than those of the Ndebele rising. It has been estimated that something under one-third of all Shona rebelled. Most of these were people in the **Chegutu, Chikomba, Harare, Marondera, Murehwa, Makoni, Mazowe,** and eastern **Makonde** districts. Most Shona had grievances against the BSAC, but the central and northern Shona were perhaps those most intensely pressured by British occupation. Further, the rebels included many of the paramount chiefs who had previously sought arms and alliances in the late 1880s in an effort to repel Ndebele raids and, occasionally, to fight each other. Their determination to rebel was encouraged by religious authorities, notably the mediums of **Kaguvi** and **Nehanda** and the **Mwari** cult figure **Boda**. The main rebel leaders were mostly paramount chiefs, or members of ruling families. These included **Mashayamombe, Mangwende** and son **Mchemwa, Makoni, Hwata, Nyandoro, Mutekedzi, Chinamora, Nemakonde**, and others.

Many Shona groups living in a belt running south from the **Chirumanzu District** collaborated with the British—either against other Shona, or against the Ndebele. All generalizations about the revolts are risky, but collaborators such as **Chirumanzu, Chivi,** and **Matibi** tended to represent those Shona who had borne grudges against the Ndebele but had not been influenced by **Portuguese** attempts at alliance. Shona groups in the extreme north, extreme east, and southeast mostly remained neutral throughout the revolt.

The Shona Revolt first erupted in the third week of June 1896, catching Europeans in **Zezuru** territory completely by surprise. Whereas doubts had previously existed about the endurance of Ndebele acquiescence to European rule, the Shona had been regarded as passive, cowardly, and unlikely to fight. After the revolt started, the ruthlessness, courage, and persistence of the Shona rebels soon dispelled all such notions.

The absence of Europeans troops in Mashonaland and problems of supply left the military initiative in the hands of the rebels until August, when **E. A. H. Alderson** arrived and organized the **Mashonaland Field Force.** Alderson directed a campaign of assaults against Shona strongholds, but these were heavily fortified and well-defended with firearms. Strong defensive positions gave the Shona an advantage lacked by most Ndebele rebels outside the Matopos. After the Ndebele revolt was effectively suppressed in October Carrington's Imperial troops arrived from Matabeleland. Little was accomplished before December, however, when all Imperial forces were removed from the country to save the BSAC money. **BSAC police** then took over.

Hostilities generally ceased through the rainy season that ensued, but attempts at negotiation in January 1897 proved fruitless. To an extent even greater than among the Ndebele rebels, the Shona lacked a central command structure. The British were thus hard pressed to know exactly whom to strike or with whom to deal, to achieve significant results. As hostilities again picked up around March, more effective assaults were mounted against Shona strongholds. Dynamite was used ruthlessly to blast defenders out of caves. By October virtually all major rebel leaders had either been killed or captured. Surrenders were taken unconditionally, and many defeated rebels were executed. Afterwards, Shona chiefdoms underwent profound changes as the government began installing its own nominees as chiefs.

RHINOCEROS. Both white (*Ceratotherium simum*) and black (*Diceros bicornis*) rhinos were fairly common in Zimbabwe until the mid-19th century. Both varieties, particularly the white, were easily killed by **hunters** armed with firearms after that time, and they were routinely shot for meat and hides (see **Sjambok**). From the 1860s rhinos were increasingly killed for their horns, which were then sold to the Near East or east Asia. By the end of the 19th century the white rhinos were virtually extinct in Zimbabwe, although in the early 1970s some were reintroduced to **national parks** from Natal. Black rhinos continued to inhabit the **Zambezi** Valley in the 20th century. In 1987 there were about 2,000 black rhinos in Zimbabwe, with nearly 500—the largest viable breeding herd in Africa—in the Zambezi Valley. However, beginning in the early 1980s Zimbabwe's black rhinos began to be threatened with extinction at the hands of poachers from **Zambia.** In 1984 the Zimbabwean government initiated an extensive rescue program—including shooting poachers on sight and capturing and moving as many rhinos as possible to safer sanctuary areas deeper inside the country—and an international diplomatic and media campaign to end the trade in rhino horns.

RHODES, CECIL JOHN (July 5, 1853–March 26, 1902). South African financier and politician. Born in Hertfordshire, England, Rhodes came to South Africa in 1870 to improve his health. Within a year he was at the Kimberley diamond fields, where he collected mining claims and began amassing a personal fortune. Later he invested successfully in the Rand goldfields. By 1888 he and his personal ally, **Alfred Beit**, had either bought out or co-opted all their competitors on the diamond fields, so they formed De Beers Consolidated Mining, Ltd. As company chairman, Rhodes was able to marshal De Beers' financial power to help forward his developing imperial schemes.

Rhodes' first venture in imperialism came in the early 1880s, when he assisted the maneuverings leading to the creation of the **Bechuanaland Protectorate.** He favored British/Afrikaner cooperation in South Africa, but was opposed to further expansion of the existing **Afrikaner** republics. The British government was reluctant to compete directly with the Afrikaner republics in northward expansion, so Rhodes personally took the initiative. In 1888, he, **C. D. Rudd,** and **F. R. Thompson** formed a syndicate to seek a **mineral** concession from the **Ndebele** King **Lobengula**. The result was the **Rudd Concession**. This in turn led to formation of the **British South Africa Company**, of which

Rhodes became a director. Thereafter Rhodes used the BSAC as his primary tool to extend British authority north of the **Limpopo River.** In late 1889 the BSAC was granted a royal **charter** that gave it rights to govern central African territory. The company organized the **Pioneer Column** the next year to exercise its charter rights by occupying **Mashonaland.** Through these proceedings **L. S. Jameson** acted as Rhodes' personal agent in the interior. The following year, 1891, Rhodes himself finally visited Mashonaland, where he listened to settlers' complaints. In 1893 BSAC forces occupied neighboring **Matabeleland,** and the country to be called **"Rhodesia"** assumed nearly its present shape.

Meanwhile, Rhodes was active in the Cape Colony's Parliament, to which he had first been elected in 1880. On July 17, 1890—just after the Pioneer Column crossed into present Zimbabwean territory—Rhodes was sworn in as prime minister of the Cape. He pledged his government to the task of reconciling differences between Afrikaners and British settlers in South Africa, as he hoped to see the whole region united under the British flag. Unable to gain the cooperation of Paul Kruger's government in the **Transvaal,** Rhodes backed the disastrous **Jameson Raid** in late 1895. When his personal involvement was revealed, he had to resign both his premiership and his BSAC directorship. Several months later the **Revolts** began. Rhodes salvaged some of his prestige by personally negotiating a truce with Ndebele rebel leaders in August 1896 (see **"Indaba"**), but his days of real power were over. He devoted his remaining years mostly to personal projects. After a prolonged illness, he died near Cape Town. A large **railway** procession carried his body to the **Matopo Hills,** where it was interred at **World's View.**

RHODES MATOPOS NATIONAL PARK see **MATOPO HILLS**

RHODESIA. see also entries entitled **RHODESIAN**

"RHODESIA" [the name]. When the **BSAC** received its **charter** in 1889, the first name proposed for its prospective African territories was **"Zambezia."** Other names considered included "Charterland" and "Cecilia," the later in honor of **Cecil Rhodes.** As the BSAC extended its authority over territory on both sides of the **Zambezi River,** the names "Northern" and "Southern Zambesia" came to refer to those regions of present-day **Zambia** and Zimbabwe, respectively. Meanwhile, it was apparently Rhodes' associate **L. S. Jameson** who proposed "Rhodesia" as an alternative name in 1890. This new name became popular after the BSAC added **Matabeleland** to its domain in 1894, thereby rendering **"Mashonaland"** an inadequate designation for the company's entire southern Zambezia sphere. In May 1895 an administrator's proclamation made "Rhodesia" the official name for the company's northern and southern territories. Two years later "Southern" and "Northern Rhodesia" were designated separate entities, and the name "Rhodesia" was formally recognized by the British secretary of state.

When Northern Rhodesia became independent Zambia in 1964, Southern Rhodesia dropped the "Southern" in its own name. The 1965 **Constitution** formally accepted the name "Rhodesia" for the country. In February 1979, as a result of the **Internal Settlement** agreement, the names "Rhodesia" and "Zimbabwe" were combined to form **"Zimbabwe**

Rhodesia," the name chosen by **Parliament** to designate the new government created by that agreement. Neither "Rhodesia" nor "Zimbabwe Rhodesia" were ever officially recognized by either the British government or the United Nations.

RHODESIA ANCIENT RUINS, LTD. (a.k.a. Ancient Ruins Company). Organization granted exclusive concession by the British South Africa Company administration in September 1895 to prospect for treasure in the **stone ruins** of **Matabeleland.** The Ancient Ruins Company was organized by members of the Bechuanaland Exploration Company and by W. G. Neal (d.1906/7), a South African prospector. The company's prospectors soon started work at the **Dhlo Dhlo** ruins, where they extracted nearly 20 kg of **gold** beads and other objects. Their work was interrupted by the **rinderpest** epidemic and the **Revolts** until September 1897. From then until May 1900 an additional 50 sites were pillaged (not including the **Zimbabwe Ruins**), but these failed to yield sufficient gold to make the operation profitable. After **Hans Saur** called attention to the terrible damage to the company's men were inflicting on historic sites, the company's work was halted by court order in May 1900. The following year the **Legislative Council** passed the country's first ordinance protecting ruins from treasure hunters. The Ancient Ruins Company was then disbanded in 1903. Meanwhile, Neal tried to salvage the company's reputation by turning over its written records to **R. N. Hall,** who published a massive descriptive account of the country's ruins. (See also **Historical Monuments Commission.**)

RHODESIA FIELD FORCE (RFF). British Imperial military unit raised during the **South African War** to defend the country from **Afrikaners** and to invade the **Transvaal** from the north. In 1900 the RFF advanced from **Beira** to the Transvaal under the command of General **Frederick Carrington.**

RHODESIA HERALD (RH) see *HERALD*

RHODESIA PRINTING AND PUBLISHING COMPANY see **"ARGUS GROUP"; ZIMBABWE NEWSPAPERS, LTD.**

RHODESIA REGIMENT. The first unit with this name was raised by Col. **H. C. O. Plumer** on the eve of the **South African War** in 1899. This regiment helped to relieve the siege of Mafeking the next year and then was disbanded. During the First World War the 1st Rhodesia Regiment was raised among European volunteers. This unit saw limited military action against **Afrikaner** rebels within South Africa and against Germans in South West Africa (Namibia) before disbandment in 1915. The same year the 2nd Rhodesia Regiment was raised for the East African campaign. After rigorous actions against German forces in present Tanzania, this unit was disbanded in April 1917. In 1929 the Rhodesia Regiment was reconstituted, and it was later expanded for service in the Second World War.

RHODESIA UNIONIST ASSOCIATION. Party formed in 1919 to support the movement for union with South Africa, in opposition to the **Responsible Government Movement.** The association was headed by Herbert

T. Longden, a Bulawayo lawyer. It received much of its support from the local mining industry. (See **Unionist Movement**.)

RHODESIAN see also entries beginning **RHODESIA**

RHODESIAN ACTION PARTY (RAP). Right-wing political party formed in July 1977 by 12 European members of **Parliament** expelled from the **Rhodesian Front** by **Ian Smith** after they failed to support his proposed legislation easing racial discrimination. Under the interim leadership of Ian Sandeman, the party called for a slower timetable in the move toward majority rule and for guarantees in any settlement achieved. The party won no parliamentary seats in the election of August 31, 1977.

RHODESIAN AFRICAN RIFLES (RAR). Until the late 1970s, an all-black army unit, under white officers. The unit's origins go back to 1898, when an African reserve company was incorporated into **British South African Police** as a standing unit. This unit served against the Germans in South West Africa (Namibia) in 1914, and then became the nucleus of the Rhodesian Native Regiment raised in 1916 to fight in the East African campaign. This regiment was disbanded after the war, but many of its members reentered the police *askari* (African) division. The RAR itself was first raised in June 1940, when veteran *askaris* served as its first noncommissioned officers. During the Second World War the RAR served with distinction in Burma. Afterwards the RAR was nearly disbanded, but was kept together to serve along the Suez Canal. The RAR was maintained as a unit in the new **federation** army during the 1950s and played an active role in antiguerrilla campaigns in Malaya in 1956–58.

After **UDI** in 1965 the RAR's strength was maintained at battalion size—a little more than 1,000 men. With the intensification of the liberation war in the early 1970s, the government reluctantly responded to white manpower shortages by increasing the number of RAR battalions. In 1973 a second RAR battalion was raised, and by 1978 a third RAR battalion had been formed. The exact number of Africans who served in these units is not known. Following independence in 1980, the three former RAR battalions joined the newly created **Zimbabwe National Army**, but were not integrated with forces from **ZIPRA** or **ZANLA**. In early 1981 Prime Minister **Robert Mugabe** turned to these units, still officered by whites, to suppress a series of clashes within ZIPRA-ZANLA integrated battalions stationed outside **Bulawayo.**

RHODESIAN BANTU VOTERS' ASSOCIATION (RBVA). Now regarded as the first association to focus African attention on the national political center, the RBVA was essentially an elitist organization dominated by **Ndebele, Mfengu**, and other immigrant African leaders. The movement was started in 1922 by Abraham Twala, a **Zulu Anglican** teacher from South Africa. Twala rejected violent protest movements, seeking instead to draw Africans into active participation in territorial electoral politics. His followers held their first meeting at **Gweru** on January 20, 1923, when they formally launched the RBVA. Twala himself held no post in the organization. Leadership posts went instead to Ernest Dube, an Ndebele teacher; Thomas Mazinyane, a **Sotho** immigrant; and Garner Sojini, a prosperous Mfengu farmer. **Martha Ngano** became secretary the following year and was the RBVA's leading spokesperson through the balance of the decade.

A general meeting of the RBVA was held in July 1923 and a constitution was drafted. This document asserted the organization's respectful intentions to cooperate with the government in a peaceful effort to uplift the condition of the country's African peoples. Fewer than 30 Africans were then registered voters, so the RBVA sought a wider membership to demonstrate broader African support. Nevertheless, the government dismissed the organization as an unrepresentative body dominated by foreigners bent on agitating local Africans. When the **Morris Carter Commission** collected evidence on land allocation in 1925, RBVA leaders strove to be heard. The commission's report and the ensuing **Land Apportionment Act** were bitter disappointments.

Despite the RBVA's goal of becoming a territory-wide organization, its effective branches were limited to **Matabeleland,** and **Mashonaland** was never penetrated. In 1929 Ngano participated in a meeting with leaders of the **ICU** and other African organizations, but efforts to create a unified congress movement failed. The **Bantu Congress,** which arose five years later, was completely unrelated to the organizations of the 1920s.

RHODESIAN BROADCASTING CORPORATION (RBC) see **ZIMBABWE BROADCASTING CORPORATION (ZBC)**

RHODESIAN COMMENTARY see under *AFRICAN TIMES*

RHODESIAN FRONT (RF). European political party founded in March 1962 to succeed the **Dominion Party** and such rightist allies as the Southern Rhodesian Association and the United group. The RF campaigned against the country's membership in the **federation** with a policy of "Rhodesia First," outlining a set of principles stressing the primacy of European interests. Under the leadership of party president **Winston Field,** chairman **Clifford Dupont,** and deputy chairman **Ian Smith,** the RF defeated the **United (Federal) Party** in the following December's general elections.

The RF consistently stood for the exclusion of external control over settler interests. Field's failure to get Britain to pledge Rhodesian independence during the dissolution of federation talks was a chief cause of the RF's ousting him from the premiership in favor of Ian Smith in April 1964. Under Smith's leadership the party made independence its chief cause, and intensified government harassment of African nationalist organizations. The party proved its strength in August 1964, when Dupont defeated **Roy Welensky** in a parliamentary by-election. In May 1965 it won all 50 reserved European seats in the **Legislative Assembly.** On the strength of this election and a general referendum of the previous November, the RF government issued its **Unilateral Declaration of Independence** on November 11, 1965.

The RF was the first European political party to develop a broad-based organization among Europeans. Earlier European political parties were little more than transient bodies mobilized by top leadership before each election. During UDI a large percentage of the country's European electorate were dues-paying RF members, and regular party members played a role in the decision-making process through the party organization, direct personal influence on MPs, and annual conventions. The party's organization also gave a disproportionate influence to its rural membership, thereby sidestepping what it considered the more moderate electorate in the urban centers. It also made a strong appeal to more recent immigrants who appeared to be more recalcitrant to change in the lifestyle which had originally attracted them to the country. Because of this broad-based support, the RF won all 50 European parliamentary seats in the general **elections** of 1965, 1970, 1971, and 1977. They were also able to win all seats reserved for whites in the 1979 and 1980 general elections, and 15 of 20 reserved seats in the 1985 elections.

Following the visit of the **Pearce Commission** in early 1972, the party began gradually to accept the principle of greatly increased African participation in government. In April 1977 a party convention voted to support a resolution acknowledging the inevitability of African majority rule but called for guarantees that whites would retain a major share of power in any future African government. A second resolution authorized the government to continue negotiations which would bring about such a political transformation. Several months later twelve MPs bolted the RF to form the **Rhodesia Action Party** to resist the RF's apparent liberalization. However, the party was not weakened as in the August 1977 general election it once again won all 50 reserved European parliamentary seats.

In early 1973, Smith used the authority given him in the earlier party resolutions to initiated negotiations with the more conservative internal nationalist leaders **Abel Muzorewa, Ndabaningi Sithole,** and **Jeremiah Chirau**. The RF hoped to sidestep the externally based militant liberation forces' leadership and sign an agreement with the three internal nationalist leaders. On March 3, 1978 an **Internal Settlement** agreement was signed by Smith and the three African leaders. The agreement embodied what the earlier RF resolutions had called for in any negotiations, the retention of substantive political and security powers in the hands of the white minority. However, the RF failed to achieve the hoped for recognition of the newly named **Zimbabwe Rhodesia** and subsequent lifting of international **sanctions**. The liberation forces controlled by the **Patriotic Front** refused a cease-fire and the war continued. The more conservative elements of the RF finally accepted that they would have to negotiate directly with the leadership of the liberation movements. In the ensuing **Lancaster House Conference**, a new **constitution** was agreed to which, when implemented in early 1980, ended the RF's 16-year control of the government of the country.

Under the new constitution, twenty seats in the **House of Assembly** were reserved for the white electorate for a seven-year period, and minority rights guaranteed. In the general elections of early 1980 the RF won all 20 of these seats. In June 1981 the RF changed its name to the "Republican Front," saying that the name "Rhodesian Front" would be an anachronism. Smith, who was retained as the leader of the party, stated that though the name had been changed, the basic principles and policies were still considered to be sound and correct. In March of the following year, nine RF members of Parliament resigned from the party citing Smith's failure to respond in a positive manner to acts of conciliation by the new government. These nine eventually formed the Independent Zimbabwe Group, staying in Parliament and generally voting with the government.

In July 1984, the party once again changed its name, this time to "Conservative Alliance of Zimbabwe." The CAZ contested the mid-1985 elections for the 20 white reserved seats against opponents from the Independent Zimbabwe Group. The CAZ won 15 of these seats. In August 1987, the remnants of the CAZ still in **parliament** voted with the majority in the House of Assembly to amend the Lancaster House constitution and abolished the seats reserved for whites.

RHODESIAN IRONWOOD see **MOPANE**

"RHODESIAN MAN." Popular name for an early human subspecies (*Homo sapiens rhodesiensis*) that occupied eastern and central Africa during the early middle **Stone Age**. Some authorities describe this subspecies as an African equivalent of its European contemporary, the Neanderthal Man (*Homo sapiens neanderthalensis*). The name "Rhodesian Man" was coined in 1921 when the first Rhodesioid skull fragments were discovered at Broken Hill, Northern Rhodesia (now Kabwe, **Zambia**).

RHODESIAN PARTY (a.k.a. Rhodesia Party). Name given to Southern Rhodesia's ruling **Responsible Government Party** by **Charles Coghlan** in late 1923. The party held power until 1933, when **Godfrey Huggins** led his breakaway **Reform Party** to victory. Two years later most of the Rhodesian Party members joined with Huggins' supporters to form the **United (Rhodesian) Party**. Some conservative Rhodesian Party members under **H. U. Moffat** later attempted to revive the party, but they were decisively defeated in the 1939 election. By 1946 no party members still held **Legislative Assembly** seats.

RHODESIAN RIDGEBACK DOG (a.k.a. Rhodesian lion dog). The only internationally recognized dog breed developed in southern Africa, ridgebacks are large dogs with short, light hair, distinguished by a forward-pointing ridge atop their backs. The breed originated in South Africa, where Europeans interbred European hunting dogs with indigenous ridgebacked varieties. The missionary **Charles Helm** brought a pair of the dogs to **Matabeleland** in 1875. There the breed was standardized and given its name, which was officially registered in 1922.

RHODESIAN SECURITY FORCES. The Southern Rhodesian government had no standing army, as such, before 1951. The forces used during the 1890s in the **Pioneer Column, Ndebele War,** and **Revolts** were a combination of British Imperial troops, **BSAP**, and local volunteer forces. In 1898 the various volunteer bodies were combined into a reserve unit known as the **Southern Rhodesian Volunteers**. This unit formed the nucleus for such wartime units as the **Rhodesian Regiments** organized during the **South African War** and the First World War. The Second World War saw a great enlargement and reorganization of the security forces for foreign campaigns, but the **Rhodesian African Rifles** was the only unit to survive postwar disbandments. In 1951 the government began organizing a standing army, while making its air force an autonomous service. Two years later these forces were absorbed into the new

federation army and air force, which were dominated by Southern Rhodesian officers.

After the breakup of federation in 1963, federal forces in southern Rhodesia reverted to the territorial government, with Southern Rhodesia obtaining most military equipment. In 1964 the army had only 3,400 men on active duty, and this number remained nearly constant for the next decade. Dramatic expansion began only after 1973, by which time the liberation of central **Mozambique** regions by **FRELIMO** had opened a major new front in the previously relatively small-scale guerrilla war for national liberation (see **ZANLA; ZIPRA**). In 1974 the government began allocating increasingly larger shares of its budget to security and began increasing manpower rapidly by broadening the age groups subject to the military draft, tightening deferments, lengthening tours of duty for regular army personnel, and more frequently calling up reservists in the Territorial Force, the reserve contingent of the army. By 1979 there were 8,500 men in the regular army, about 1,200 in the air force, 8,000 in the BSAP, and an additional 15,000 army and 35,000 BSAP reservists. At full strength, the security forces totaled around 60,000 men; however, only about 16,000 were operational at any given time.

With the escalation of the liberation war in the early 1970s the security forces expanded rapidly. There were three basic components: the regular army, the BSAP, and the air force. The army had two main elements, the Rhodesian Light Infantry (RLI) and the Rhodesian African Rifles (RAR). Both units operated with basic patrols called "sticks," made up of five to seven men each, and were generally involved in day-to-day "search and destroy" operations. The RLI was a single battalion of 1,000 white soldiers in three commando units, while the RAR were black soldiers (with white officers) in three battalions. The army also had three special forces: the Special Air Service (SAS), the Grey Scouts (GS), and the Selous Scouts (**SS**). The SAS was all white, while the GS and SS had both African and European soldiers. The SAS had 250 highly trained commandos and specialized in ambushes and cross-border raids into neighboring countries. The GS, a mounted infantry battalion, was involved in silent-pursuit operations and also took part in cross-border raids. The SS was considered the army's elite tracking and clandestine operations unit.

The BSAP during the period of the war became a paramilitary organization and worked closely with the regular army, particularly in intelligence gathering. The air force was made up of three strike squadrons and two helicopter squadrons. Most of its equipment was in operation at the time of **UDI**.

Operationally, the Rhodesian security forces utilized two basic tactics during the 1970s. Inside the country they depended on "search and destroy" operations to combat nationalist guerrillas. Their helicopters gave them superior mobility, and the government instituted a program of **"protected villages"** to isolate guerrilla units in rural areas. Externally, the government again had two elements to its strategy of conducting the war. In 1975 the Rhodesian Central Intelligence Organization, with the cooperation of **Portuguese** military authorities, established the Mozambique National Resistance (**MNR**) to attack ZANLA forces inside Mozambique and destabilize the Mozambican economy so that FRELIMO would lessen its support for ZANLA. In addition, beginning in the mid-1970s the army carried out a number of what it called "preemptive strikes" against both ZANLA and ZIPRA training bases in neighboring countries. Between 1976 and 1979, more than 30 air strikes and commando raids were made into Mozambique, **Zambia,** and **Botswana.** The idea was to disrupt the forward bases nearest the borders, which would lengthen the supply lines of the guerrilla forces already inside the country, thereby making it more difficult for them to continue fighting.

The greatest problems faced by the Rhodesian security forces were increasing shortages of European manpower and equipment, in conjunction with the escalating cost of the war on the economy. Although South Africa provided much of the security forces' needs, **sanctions** curtailed most armaments imports. The resulting equipment shortages meant that the security forces were using artillery, aircraft, and other heavy equipment that had been in use at the time of UDI. In addition, acquisition of replacement parts was always a critical problem.

Manpower shortages became an increasing problem after 1975 and the independence of Mozambique. Constantly greater numbers of men were required to combat the escalating numbers of ZANLA forces infiltrating the country after that time. In 1972 all European males aged 18–25 were subject to conscription and 12 months' active duty in the security forces. In 1974 the age limit was raised to 38, and in 1976 military service was extended to 18 months. In 1977 all white reservists aged 18-38 were required to serve six months each year on security duties, and the age limit for service was raised to age 50. In 1979 the conscription of white males aged 50–59 was announced for "anti-terrorism" duties in the country's major urban centers. In addition to calls for increased European manpower, between 1974 and 1977 the government raised two battalions of RAR (making the army about 80 percent African volunteers). These increasing call-ups, particularly of Europeans, placed greater and greater strains on the country's economy. The escalating cost of maintaining larger numbers of men in the security forces also had a major effect on the economy. Between 1972 and 1978, the government increased defense spending approximately 610 percent, to a cost of about $Rh750,000 a day. Without the assistance of South Africa, which paid over half the Rhodesian defense budget, the government could not have continued fighting through the late 1970s.

RHODESIANA. Journal of the Rhodesiana Society, an antiquarian organization. Started as an annual in 1956, it became semiannual in 1963. *Rhodesiana* articles dealt mostly with early European activities in the country. The journal was superseded by *Heritage* in 1981.

RHODESIOIDS see "RHODESIAN MAN"

RINDERPEST EPIDEMIC (1896–98). Rinderpest, or "cattle plague," is a virulent, highly infectious disease affecting ruminant animals, especially **cattle.** It causes fever, dysentery, inflammation of the mucous membranes, and speedy death. The disease was unknown to southern Africa before the late 19th century, though it had long been epidemic in Asia and had even reached Western Europe as early as 1,500 years ago. The virus spreads both directly and indirectly among ruminants and can be carried for periods up to several months in hay, cloth, and other articles, and in other animals and vermin.

Rinderpest first appeared in sub-Saharan Africa after being introduced into Somalia in 1889. From there it spread quickly through eastern Africa, reaching **Zambia** by late 1892. The **Zambezi River** appears to have halted the epidemic temporarily, for it was not reported in present Zimbabwe until it reached **Bulawayo** in February 1896. There it quickly devastated game, cattle, and draft oxen. The **Ndebele** people, who had recently lost most of their cattle to the **British South African Company**, were hit the hardest. To add to their consternation, the company administration began shooting cattle to halt the spread of the disease. These calamities apparently contributed to the outbreak of the ensuing **Revolt**. Meanwhile, the disease spread rapidly into **South Africa**, reaching Cape Town by late 1897.

The impact of the rinderpest epidemic on the country was great. It was estimated that up to 95 percent of the country's cattle succumbed to the disease. The devastation of oxen severely impaired **transportation**, hindering European defenses against the revolt, driving up import prices for some time, and accelerating the building of the first **railways**. The loss of cattle also forced Africans to turn increasingly to **agriculture** and to wage labor.

Although rinderpest had hit Western Europe only two decades earlier, the first medical advances against it were made in southern Africa after 1896. With new immunizing techniques developed in South Africa, inoculation of cattle began in late 1897 in **Matabeleland**. By late 1898 the disease was virtually eradicated, and no further major outbreaks have occurred since in the country. (See **Health**.)

"RING KOPS." Nineteenth-century European nickname for **Ndebele** men who wore **headrings**. From **Afrikaans** word *kop* for "head."

RIVERS. The most uniformly high altitude of the country relative to surrounding regions makes it a single great watershed, laced with an immense number of rivers (see **Altitudinal Zones**). However, the country's **climate** delivers too little rainfall to keep all these rivers flowing year round, and there are few natural catchments to collect the water (see **Lakes; Vleis**). Much of the rainfall drains off quickly in seasonal floods, leaving most rivers either dry or mere trickles during the winter months. None of the rivers—except parts of the **Zambezi**—are navigable. Water conservation is a crucial problem, resulting in the building of weirs and **dams** throughout the country.

The **Central Plateau**, which runs from southwest to northeast, forms the main watershed. Its rivers are grouped into four separate drainage systems: (1) Between **Plumtree** and **Shabani** a number of important rivers flow south or southeast into the **Limpopo**, which defines the border with South Africa. (2) From Shabani to **Marondera** a somewhat larger number of rivers flow southeast into the **Sabi**, which is also fed by rivers rising in the **Eastern Highlands**. More than half the country's water runoff drains through these two river systems, which are now being exploited by the **Sabi-Limpopo Authority**. (3) Across the entire width of the northern part of the country a large number of rivers flow generally north into the Zambezi. The Limpopo, Sabi, and Zambezi all empty into the Indian Ocean through **Mozambique.** (4) Of minor significance are the **Nata** and a few other small rivers that flow west into **Botswana's** Markikari Basin. Yet another group of rivers—unconnected with the Central Plateau—rise in the Eastern Highlands, flowing east directly into the sea. The **Pungwe** is the most notable of these. Their contribution to the country's water resources is slight, as they enter Mozambique almost immediately after they rise.

ROADS. Before the arrival of Europeans in the country in the mid-19th century, there were neither wheeled vehicles nor true roads. The advent of **ox-wagon** traffic led to the development of the **"Hunters' Road"** through **Matabeleland,** but this was little more than a wagon track. The basis for the first true road was the route cut by the 1890 **Pioneer Column** between **Tati** and **Harare.** European occupation of the entire country during the 1890s promoted the building of a road network, with the best roads linking the main European centers. Problems created by heavy seasonal rains (see **Climate**) were tackled with a major bridge building program after 1924, and with the **strip road** program of the early 1930s. Full-width asphalt roads were not started until the late 1940s. By the mid-1970s the country contained c.8,000 km of major paved roads, c.25,000 km of unpaved roads, and c.10,000 km of municipal roads. By the early 1990s, the total length of roads in the country had increased to c.12,000 km of paved roads, c.27,000 km of unpaved roads, and c.10,000 km of municipal roads.

ROCK PAINTINGS. It is said that southern Africa contains more specimens of ancient rock art than does the entire rest of the world. Most sites are found in South Africa, but Zimbabwe itself has more than 1,500 known rock art sites. A handful of these sites contain **petroglyphs.** The rest have only paintings. Rock art is therefore virtually synonymous with rock paintings in Zimbabwe.

The ancient artists painted almost exclusively on granite surfaces. Exfoliation and other natural processes of decay make granite surfaces impermanent. The oldest extant paintings therefore cannot be more than about 7,000 years old. If any paintings were executed earlier, they have probably left no trace. The surviving paintings thus are associated with late **Stone Age** cultures. This association is further supported by the depiction of such late Stone Age culture features as bow-and-arrow-carrying humans in most hunting paintings.

Since the paintings appear on granite surface, it is not surprising that the rocky **Matopo Hills** contain one of the largest concentrations of paintings in Africa (see, e.g., **Bambata; Bulubahwe; Nswatugi; Pomongwe;** and **Silozwane Caves;** and **White Rhino Shelter**). There are also many sites in the highland areas of **Mashonaland** (see, e.g., **Diana's Vow; Domboshawa; Epworth; Makumbe; Mrewa; Ruchero;** and **Zombepata**). Isolated but important sites are also scattered elsewhere, e.g., **Mchela.**

No technique has yet been devised to date the paintings. Many occur in or near former occupation sites, notably caves, which provide datable artifacts and bones, but these materials cannot always be confidently associated with the paintings themselves. It is generally agreed that **San** people executed the best paintings of at least the most recent centuries, but it is not certain that San were also the earliest artists. Attempts have been made to link southern African rock art with similar forms elsewhere, but diffusionist theories are, by their nature, highly speculative and unrewarding.

The variety of subjects depicted in the paintings is vast. While certain animals, such as antelope, **elephants,** and giraffes, appear frequently, a bewildering array of other animals, including birds, reptiles, and even insects, also appear. Human figures are typically depicted as hunters. Herders also occasionally appear, as do people in domestic and ceremonial scenes. A difficulty in interpreting the paintings arises from the fundamental distinction in stylistic treatment. Animal figures are typically naturalistic, while human figures are highly stylized, and therefore not amenable to positive ethnic identification. Frequently depicted steatopygic hunters were likely **Khoisan** peoples. Other human figures are believed to have been **Bantu-speakers**. In contrast to paintings in South Africa, Zimbabwe has no known examples of European figures in rock paintings.

C. K. Cooke offers a useful typology of painting styles with these numbers: (1) Simple monochrome silhouettes without movement. (2) Similar paintings depicting movement. (3) More realistic outline drawings, which are rare. (4) Realistic polychromes depicting complex interactions among humans and animals. This style is most common. (5 and 6) Crude copies of presumably earlier styles, believed to have been painted recently by Bantu-speakers. Cooke suggests a chronological framework corresponding to these numbered styles; however, any such chronology remains speculative for the reasons suggested above. Further difficulties arise from the universal problem of attempting to assign subjective art forms to precise categories. This difficulty is manifest in the fact that paintings assigned to "early" styles are occasionally found superimposed over "late" styles. If such problems can ever be resolved, the country's rock paintings may yet prove to be as valuable a historical record as they are an esthetic resource.

RODWELL, CECIL HUNTER (Dec. 29, 1874–Feb. 1953). Second **governor** of Southern Rhodesia (1928–34). After serving in the **South African War**, Rodwell joined the staff of British high commissioner Lord Milner (1901–03), and served as Imperial secretary in South Africa. He then became governor of Fiji (1918–24) and of British Guiana (1925–28) before replacing **J. R. Chancellor** in Southern Rhodesia. In contrast to his predecessor, Rodwell was reluctant to advise **Godfrey Huggins** on ministerial appointments. He later returned to South Africa to work in the mining industry. He was succeeded in Southern Rhodesia by **H. J. Stanley**.

ROLI (variant: ROLE) see **HOLI**

ROTSE (BAROTSE) see **LOZI**

ROWORO (variant: ROORA). **Chishona** form of **lobolo.**

ROZVI (variant: Rozwi; Barcozwi; Varozvi; etc.). Name of an important but enigmatic section of the **Shona people**. Although the name "Rozvi" pervades the literature on Shona History, authorities differ greatly on who these people were and are, and on where they came from. The Rozvi have been variously described as an intrusive alien group; an indigenous and ancient Shona "tribe"; a clan; a dynasty; and a dialect group (usually affiliated with **Kalanga**). Today people calling themselves Rozvi are spread throughout the country. Rozvi identification is prestigious, and the claims of some Rozvi are disputed by others. The only universally recognized Rozvi are those people whose *mutupo* is Moyo Ndizvo (or Mhondizvo). Other Rozvi base their identification on historical political connections with what were once Rozvi-ruled states.

According to the most convincing interpretations of Rozvi identity, the original Rozvi were purely indigenous Shona associated with the rise of the **Changamire** state initiated by **Dombo** in the late 17th century. Dombo's destructive conquests earned his followers the nickname *varozvi*, or "destroyers" (see **Dzviti**). There is no uncontestable evidence that the name Rozvi was applied to any Shona group before the time of Dombo, though the Changamire state itself clearly had ties with the **Torwa, Munhumutapa**, and other Shona states (see **Shona History**). The rulers of the Changamire state apparently adopted the name "Rozvi" during the 18th century. The name later conveyed considerable political prestige because of this association.

The **Nguni** invasions of the early 19th century **Mfecane** broke up the Changamire state, causing rapid dispersal of Rozvi people throughout the rest of the country, particularly to the southeast. Since then many small chieftaincies have claimed Rozvi connections, but it is likely that some such claims are spurious. Confusion over Rozvi identity has been magnified by alterations in traditional histories, which project Rozvi population movements and conquests deep into the pre-Dombo past.

Rozvi identity has also been perpetuated in the name *Abelozwi* for Shona incorporated into the **Ndebele** state (see **Holi**). It should also be noted that while attempts have been made to link the Rozvi with the **Lozi**, or "Rotse," of western Zambia, there is no evidence to connect these two peoples. (See also **Urozvi**.)

RUCHERO CAVE (a.k.a. Mtoko Cave). Important **rock painting** site located near **Mutoko** village. The cave's main frieze features figures interpreted as **Khoi** men herding sheep.

RUDD, CHARLES DUNELL (Oct. 22, 1844–Nov. 1916). British businessman. Rudd came to South Africa in 1865 and later became a partner of **Cecil Rhodes** in the Kimberley diamond fields. With Rhodes he helped to found DeBeers Consolidated Mining Company, of which he became a director, and he obtained a major interest in the Rand goldmines in the 1880s. From 1883 to 1888 he represented Kimberley in the Cape Parliament. In late 1888 he replaced **Ivon Fry** as Rhodes' agent at **Bulawayo**, where he got **Lobengula** to sign the "**Rudd Concession**." He retired to England in 1902.

RUDD CONCESSION (1888). Popular name for agreement signed on October 30, 1888, by the **Ndebele** king **Lobengula** and **C. D. Rudd, F. R. Thompson**, and **J. R. Maguire** as agents for **Cecil Rhodes**. Acquisition of the concession by a syndicate comprising Rhodes, Rudd, and

Thompson led directly to formation of the **British South Africa Company** and its royal **charter** the next year.

There were two versions of the concession: one written in English and fully accepted by the BSAC and the British government; the other an oral version communicated to the Ndebele by the interpreter **C. D. Helm**, who also signed the written version as a witness. As the Ndebele soon learned to their distress, the two versions differed greatly. This mattered little to Rhodes and his associates, however, as their main purpose in obtaining the concession was not so much formation of an agreement with the Ndebele kingdom, as the securing of a signed document that could be used to exclude European imperial competitors from the territory north of the **Limpopo River.**

The Ndebele understood the agreement as a limited **concession** for a small number of Europeans to prospect near the **Ramaquabane River**. By contrast, the written document granted Rhodes' group "exclusive charge over all metals and minerals" in all of Lobengula's domain—the extent of which the BSAC exaggerated in its representation to outsiders. Only the **Tati Concession** area was specifically excluded. The document also gave the grantees power to exclude—with Ndebele assistance if necessary—other prospectors and concessionaires from the region, and the right of veto over any future Ndebele concessions.

The oral and written versions of the concession seem to have coincided only on the form of payment to the Ndebele. Lobengula was to receive £100 each lunar month; 1,000 rifles and 100,000 rounds of ammunition; and an armed steamboat placed on the **Zambezi River**, or £500 cash. The BSAC honored all but the last of these provisions.

Rhodes' rivals in Bulawayo soon alerted the Ndebele to the discrepancies between the oral and written versions of the concession. These revelations brought about a political crisis in which the *induna* **Lotshe** was killed. King Lobengula meanwhile sent **Babayane** and **Mshete** to London to seek advice, and then publicly repudiated the concession in January 1889. In March Helm admitted to the Ndebele his deceptive interpretation of the concession, spurring further Ndebele renunciations and refusals to accept shipments of the concession rifles. Although the BSAC continued to regard the concession as a valid agreement, Rhodes sent **L. S. Jameson** to Bulawayo several times to renegotiate the agreement. Alarmed at the prospect of armed British invasion, Lobengula modified his previous oral agreement on a few points to gain time. Jameson then distorted Lobengula's position in order to convince the British government that Lobengula had in fact confirmed the original written concession. After the BSAC occupied **Mashonaland** with its **Pioneer Column** in 1890, the validity of the Rudd Concession became less important, as British occupation was an accomplished fact. Nevertheless, Lobengula was persuaded to sign the **Lippert Concession** in 1891, thinking he was dealing with a rival European party. He in fact was dealing with agents of the BSAC, which used his various concessions to build a legal justification for the **Ndebele War of 1893**. Thereafter the BSAC claimed territorial authority over **Matabeleland** by right of conquest.

RUENYA RIVER. One of the most important rivers in the northeast, the Ruenya itself flows northeast, separating the **Mutoko** and **Nyanga** districts. It is joined by the **Gairezi River** as it enters **Mozambique**, where it is known as the Luenha, finally feeding the **Zambezi**.

RUINS. Although the country's **borders** were artificially created by Europeans during the 1890s, they have since been found to encompass a nearly congruent region of stone ruins unparalleled in tropical Africa. More than 400 stone building sites are known within the country. Almost all of these represent purely indigenous building traditions. Two independent traditions have been identified; both share techniques of mortarless granite block construction. Ruins are most common in, but by no means exclusive to, the belt of granite outcroppings that coincides roughly with the **Central Plateau** and central **Eastern Highlands**.

Rudimentary stone walling was initiated by the late **Leopard's Kopje culture** people, but substantial building in stone is believed to have originated at the site of the **Zimbabwe Ruins** only in about the 12th century. There techniques were developed that spread to more than 150 other sites by the mid-15th century, when Zimbabwe itself was abandoned. The early **Munhumutapa** rulers, who are believed to have migrated into the northern **Dande** region from Zimbabwe around this time, continued the building tradition there, but only briefly. The Dande is outside the granite area, so stone building was apparently given up to make use of more accessible construction materials. The **Torwa** and **Changamire** states continued the stone-building tradition in the south, shifting the center west to southern **Matabeleland**. There the **Khami Culture** arose as a Zimbabwe derivative. The Khami-type builders made great use of retaining walls, in contrast to the Zimbabwe-type emphasis on freestanding walls. This tradition, too, was largely abandoned in the early 19th century, after the *Mfecane* invasions disrupted Shona life.

The second independent building tradition is found in the **Inyanga Ruins** in the northeast. Stonework there was cruder, with more emphasis on massive structures, and considerable work on retaining walls for cultivation terraces. The Inyanga tradition started somewhat later than its southern counterparts, but also appears to have ended in the early 19th century.

Many theories have been advanced for non-African origins of the country's stone ruins, but none stand up against scientific archaeological research. **Portuguese** traders and missionaries did, however, leave many ruins in the northeastern part of the country during the 16th and 17th centuries (see **Fairs**). There are no similarities between their ruins and those of the purely indigenous traditions. (See also **Iron Age**.)

RUKWADZANO RWE WADZIMAYI see RUWADZANO

RUSAPE (Variant: Rusapi). Commercial and administrative center established in the **Makoni District** in 1894. Rusape stands on the main road between **Mutare** and **Harare** (at 18°32'S, 32°7'E; alt. 1,405 m). Population by the mid-1980s exceeded 10,000 and in 1992 was 14,401. Nearby is **Diana's Vow Cave**.

RUSHINGA DISTRICT. Located in the northeastern sector of **Mashonaland Central Province,** Rushinga is made up entirely of **Communal Lands** and is bisected by the **Masowe River.** The district is bordered on the north by **Mozambique; Mukumbura District** is to the west, **Mudzi** to the east, and **Mutoko** and **Murehwa** to the south. District population in 1992 was 75,332.

RUTENGA. Village in southeastern low veld, at the junction of the main road from **Beitbridge** to **Masvingo,** and the Somabula-to-Sango **railway** line (at 21°15′S, 30°44′E). In the mid-1970s the railway was extended from Rutenga to Beitbridge, giving the country its first direct rail link to **South Africa.**

RUWADZANO (variant: Rukwadzano). **Chishona** term for "fellowship," popularly applied to a **Methodist** women's movement introduced to the country in 1919 from the **Transvaal,** where the movement was called **Manyano.** Ruwadzano organizations have historically mobilized African women to support Methodist evangelism and to maintain high family spiritual and moral principles. Since the 1960s these organizations have become more directly concerned with community and national problems, and have occasionally been mobilized in political protests.

Although the first *ruwadzano* arose among members of the **Wesleyan Methodist** churches, the largest organization is that affiliated with the **United Methodist Church**—the *Rukwadzano rwe Wadzimayi* (literally, "Women's Fellowship"). This organization was founded in 1929 at the **Old Umtali** Mission and has since developed into both the largest lay organization in the UMC and the largest African women's voluntary organization in the country. By 1971 it claimed nearly 8,700 dues-paying member—43 percent of the UMC's total membership. As is the case with other *ruwadzano,* the members of the *Rukwadzano rwe Wadzimayi* wear distinctive uniforms and emblems at gatherings, and they assemble for annual revivals during the Easter week. A major contribution of such organizations has been their raising of women's self-esteem and social assertiveness.

S

SABI-LIMPOPO AUTHORITY (SLA). Major government irrigation project established in 1965 to develop the southeastern low veld region, covering a 65,000-sq-km sector east of **Beitbridge** and **Zvishavane,** and south of **Masvingo** and **Chimanimani.** An initial goal of the project was to encourage European settlement in the low veld (see **Altitudinal Zones**). This met with little success, apparently due to a lack of private investment funding as a result of the imposition of international **sanctions** following the declaration of **UDI**.

The SLA was empowered to coordinate all aspects of governmental economic and social planning in the region, but in practice it has concentrated on building **dams** and developing irrigation for both private and SLA-operated estates. The region has fertile soils, well suited for **sugar**, citrus, and other crops, but its rainfall is drained by the **Sabi, Lundi,** and **Limpopo** river systems, which empty through the low veld. The SLA started with a 25-year plan to bring under cultivation more than 300,000 hectares (750,000 acres) of land, but by 1975 it was estimated that only 40,500 hectares were under cultivation. The administrative and commercial center for the SLA is at **Chiredzi**.

SABI RIVER. The largest river inside the country, the Sabi rises at a point midway between **Chivhu** and **Marondera** on the **Central Plateau,** flowing southeast more than 200 km to its junction with the **Odzi River** west of **Chimanimani**. From there it flows south a somewhat greater distance, and then is joined by the **Lundi River** at the country's lowest point, where as the Save River it enters **Mozambique** and then empties into the Indian Ocean by Mambone. (See **Rivers**.)

SADZA. A thick **millet** porridge, which has traditionally been the staple dish of the **Shona** people. The equivalent **Ndebele** dish is *isitshwala,* a porridge made from **maize**.

SALISBURY see **HARARE**

"SALTED HORSES." Nineteenth-century term for **horses** thought to be immune from **horsesickness** by virtue of their having survived a bout with the disease. Such animals commanded from five to 10 times as much money as "unsalted" horses, with prices ranging from £40 to £100 a head during the late 19th century. Fraud was common among horse traders, although guarantees of survival were a part of most deals.

SALUGAZANA see **TENKELA**

SAMKANGE, STANLAKE JOHN WILLIAM (March 11, 1922–March 8, 1988). The second son of **T. D. Samkange**, Stanlake Samkange was born in the Zwimba Reserve of **Makonde District.** He was educated at **Waddilove Institution**—which provided the setting for his novel *The Mourned One* (1975)—and at Adams College and Ft. Hare University College in South Africa. After returning to the country in 1946, he briefly taught at a government school before organizing one of the country's first independent African schools at **Nyatsime,** just south of **Harare.** In 1951 he entered nationalist politics as secretary-general of the old **African National Convention.** The next year, he helped to organize the **All-African Convention** and served as secretary-general. In January 1954, he stood unsuccessfully for an African seat in the first federal Parliament.

From 1952 to 1957, Samkange worked as a freelance journalist. In 1957 he went to the United States, and one year later earned a master's degree from Syracuse University. After returning home in 1959, he joined the United Rhodesian Party; he was elected junior deputy president in June, when that party evolved into the **Central African Party.** In 1966 he returned to the United States and earned a Ph.D. in history from Indiana University in 1968. He remained in the United States until 1976, teaching at several universities, including Northwestern and Harvard. In October of that year, he was appointed a political advisor to the **African National Council** delegation to the **Geneva Conference**. After returning home, he continued to advise **Abel Muzorewa**, becoming secretary for education in the UANC. In 1979 he was elected to the **Zimbabwe Rhodesia Parliament**, but in June he resigned from the UANC and joined **James Chikerema** in the Zimbabwe Democratic Party. He resigned from ZDP in 1980, retired from political life, and founded the Harare Publishing House.

Samkange wrote a number of books, including *The Mourned One, On Trial for My Country* (1966), and *Origins of Rhodesia* (1968).

SAMKANGE, THOMPSON DOUGLAS (1887–Aug. 27, 1956). **Methodist** minister and nationalist leader. Samkange was born in the **Makonde District**'s Zwimba reserve, where he later declined a government chiefship. He was educated at **Waddilove Institution** and afterwards was ordained a Methodist minister. During his long and varied career he served as president of the African division of the **Southern Rhodesian Missionary Conference** and as president of the old **African National Congress** from the mid-1940s. During his last years he developed Pakame Mission, 30 km southeast of **Shurugwi**. His children included **Stanlake Samkange** and Sketchley Samkange, the latter an active **ANC** and NDP leader who accidentally drowned in Lake Nyasa in 1961.

SAN (a.k.a. "Bushmen"; Twa; **Sarwa;** etc.). "San" is a **Khoi** word preferred as the collective name for the **Khoisan** people, once commonly called "Bushmen." Once widespread in eastern and southern Africa, there are now only a few tens of thousands of San in southern Africa. Most live in Namibia and **Botswana**; others reside in southern Angola. A few bands also still live on the western fringes of present Zimbabwe, but it is difficult to determine the exact number, as the remaining bands move freely across the Botswana border. Nevertheless, it is clear that the numbers are small.

The San are descendants of the **Stone Age** peoples who predominated in the country prior to the arrival of **Bantu-speakers** in the early first millennium A.D. The early San were mostly hunter-gatherers who lived in small, nomadic bands. They are generally credited with production of most of southern Africa's **rock paintings**. The often-stated assumption that the San were either "exterminated" or driven out of the country by invading Bantu-speakers is insupportable. Current research indicated that there may not have been more than a relative handful of San inhabiting the region of present Zimbabwe when the first **Shona-speaking peoples** arrived in the area. T. N. Huffman argues that the few San words present in **Chishona** derive from earlier contact south of the **Limpopo River,** prior to the Shona entering the region of present Zimbabwe.

SANCTIONS. (1) *Imposition.* Immediately after **Ian Smith's Rhodesian Front** government issued its **Unilateral Declaration of Independence** in November 1965, the British government made it clear it would not attempt to use military force to bring down the rebel regime. Britain instead quickly imposed various economic sanctions against Rhodesia, which Prime Minister Harold Wilson predicted would cause Smith's speedy collapse. Britain moved to block Rhodesian access to capital markets and export credits in Britain and banned British import of Rhodesian **sugar** and **tobacco**—soon adding **chrome, iron, copper,** and **asbestos** to the list. The United Nations Security council meanwhile resolved that no member nation should aid or recognize the Rhodesian regime, and it instituted what has been called "Phase One" of international economic sanctions. These called for voluntary bans on imports of key Rhodesian products, as well as an embargo on sales of petroleum to the country. In March 1966 Britain began a naval blockade of ships carrying Rhodesian-bound petroleum through the Mozambique Channel of the Indian Ocean. The next month the UN Security Council ruled that Britain could use force, if necessary, to stop petroleum deliveries. Because of Rhodesia's total dependence on imported petroleum, the effort to stop its delivery to the country was regarded as the key element of sanctions policies.

The apparent failure of voluntary sanctions to weaken the Rhodesian regime caused the UN General Assembly to urge the Security Council to take tougher action. On December 16, 1966, the Security Council initiated "Phase Two" by passing a resolution calling for mandatory sanctions against importation of selected Rhodesian goods. This phase lasted until May 1968, when the Security Council established a "Phase Three" policy of comprehensive mandatory sanctions. Rhodesia's evident success in combating sanctions caused the Security Council periodically to pass more refined resolutions, closing loopholes and broadening applications; but proposed resolutions against Rhodesia's trade collaborators, **South Africa** and Portugal, failed to pass on several occasions. By 1977 it was generally recognized that no sanctions policy against Rhodesia would work without the cooperation of South Africa, which had steadfastly ignored sanctions. As a consequence there was increased international pressure to invoke economic sanctions against South Africa itself. The strength of this threat lay largely in South Africa's own dependence upon foreign suppliers of petroleum. South Africa responded to the threat by intensifying its own efforts to persuade the Rhodesian regime to find a constitutional settlement with African nationalists.

(2) *Responses to Sanctions.* Efforts of the Rhodesian regime to combat sanctions began at least a year before UDI, and UDI itself was timed so as not to interfere with advance sales of such products as tobacco and sugar to foreign markets. In anticipation of sanctions, the Rhodesian government had earlier instituted import controls, cultivated trade relations with countries least likely to honor international sanctions, arranged for long-term trade agreements wherever possible, and repudiated foreign debts for which Britain could be held responsible. South Africa and Portugal then allowed transshipment of Rhodesian exports through South Africa, **Mozambique**, and Angola under the pretext that Rhodesian goods were originating in those countries, so as to fool buyers otherwise honoring sanctions. Some nonmembers of the UN, such as Switzerland and West Germany (which joined the UN in 1973), continued to trade legally with Rhodesia, while many other countries, notably Japan, traded

covertly with Rhodesia. By 1972 Rhodesia's total foreign trade, much altered in composition, had reached its pre-UDI levels in value, and the UN reported that from one-third to one-half of all Rhodesian exports were reaching member nations that nominally adhered to sanctions polices. The subsequent independence of Angola and Mozambique soon added new restrictions to Rhodesia's trade channels, but the main effect of this political transformation was merely to make Rhodesia more reliant on South Africa. Meanwhile, the United States, through its **Byrd Amendment**, was the only other UN member openly to flout UN sanctions, but the U.S. reversed its policy in 1977. Nevertheless, by then goods that clearly originated in Rhodesia were still reaching many nations, including nominally hostile black African countries, and the UN was revealing extensive sanctions violations by the Soviet Union and some of its east European allies. Neighboring **Zambia** remained the most consistently rigorous adherent to sanctions policies, but even that country was importing South African goods through Rhodesia, despite the official closure of its borders and the latent state of war.

(3) *Impact of Sanctions.* Sanctions were not debilitating to the Rhodesian economy as a whole, with some industries being adversely affected, while others apparently benefited from the imposed isolation. The tobacco industry in particular suffered losses in both scale of production and share of export markets during the sanctions period. Tobacco was easily identified by international traders and had a low value-to-bulk ratio. However, with the benefit of government assistance programs and subsidies aimed at making the country self-sufficient in agricultural production, European commercial farmers were able to diversify production and create markets for crops such as wheat, barley, and **cotton**. Mineral production and exports, while being negatively impacted by sanctions at first, fairly rapidly regained a strong standing in Rhodesia's export trade. In general, mineral exports were not hit hard by sanctions because of their ratio of value to bulk, and they could be relatively easily "disguised" by transshipping. Some manufacturing industries appeared to benefit from the lack of competition that sanctions provided. From the late 1960s to the early 1970s, cotton spinning and weaving, iron and steel productions, and other intermediate and capital goods industries in the country rapidly expanded their domestic markets. These industries benefited from loopholes in sanctions legislation that allowed Rhodesian companies to acquire franchises for domestic production from foreign companies that could not legally export their products to Rhodesia.

By the late 1970s, the cumulative effect of international sanctions was strongly being felt inside the country. As activities by **ZANLA** and **ZIPRA** guerrillas intensified, agricultural production began to fall. In addition, the cost of securing sufficient oil supplies necessary to maintain the war effort greatly increased in the mid-1970s, as international oil prices rose rapidly. Recent studies demonstrate that Rhodesia's real gross domestic product declined after 1974, while its military spending greatly increased, thereby forcing the government to go into debt. In late 1978, in direct response to the continuing threat to both the economy and the war effort, the Smith government began to investigate ways of having sanctions lifted. One of the major reasons was the hope that a peace agreement would lead directly to the lifting of sanctions. When the **Internal Settle-**

ment Agreement failed to gain international recognition and sanctions were therefore kept in force, the government of **Zimbabwe Rhodesia** was virtually forced to agree to participate in the **Lancaster House Conference.**

SANGO (Vila Salazar until 1982). Established as a **railway** station rear the **Mozambique border** when the railway line to Maputo (formerly Lourenzo Marques) was opened (at 22°3′S, 31°42′E). Originally, the village was named after the Portuguese dictator Antonio de Oliveira Salazar. The Mozambique post on the opposite side of the border was named Malvernia (now **Chicualacuala**), after the **federation**'s prime minister, Lord Malvern (**Godfrey Huggins**). After Mozambique gained independence from Portugal in 1975, it closed its borders to **Rhodesia** in March 1976. At that time the village became a frequent target of **ZANLA** forces operating from within Mozambique. In late May 1977, Rhodesian forces used the post as a staging site to launch a foray deep into Mozambican territory.

SANYATI RIVER. Name once more commonly used for the stretch of the **Umniati River** below its confluence with the **Umfuli.**

SARWA (Masarwa; variants: Maisiri; Amasili). **Bantu** name for **San people** living in Zimbabwe and Botswana.

SAUER, HANS. (June 11, 1857–Aug. 28, 1939). An **Afrikaner** medical doctor and lawyer, Sauer made a fortune on the diamond and goldfields of South Africa. He came to present Zimbabwe to assist **Cecil Rhodes** in a mining venture in **Matabeleland.** He later participated in Rhodes's "**indaba**" with rebel **Ndebele** during the 1896–97 **Revolts.** Sauer was elected to the **Legislative Council** in 1899, but moved to England the following year. He published *Ex Africa* in 1937, a colorful but not thoroughly reliable autobiography.

SAVANHU, JASPER ZENGEZA (b. 1917). Journalist and politician. Born in the **Goromonzi District** and educated at **Waddilove** and **Domboshawa** Technical School, Savanhu emerged as a radical labor organizer in **Bulawayo** during the Second World War. He was a vigorous critic of the government and was an active leader of the old **African National Congress.** Forced by illness to turn to less physically demanding activities, he joined the staff of the **African Newspapers, Ltd.**, group, becoming its editor-in-chief by the early 1950s.

In 1952 Savanhu accompanied **Joshua Nkomo** and **Godfrey Huggins** to the London conference on **federation.** Though he opposed creation of the federation, he accepted its inevitability and defeated **Stanlake Samkange** and others in the first election for one of the two federal assembly seats reserved for Africans (the other African elected was **M. M. Hove**). He was reelected twice, becoming the only Southern Rhodesian African to serve in the federal assembly for its entire duration. Throughout his tenure of office he generally supported the polices of the ruling **United (Federal) Party** to which he belonged, and he became popularly regarded as a government "stooge" by Africans. In 1958 Prime Minister **Roy Welensky** appointed Savanhu parliamentary secretary to the minister of home affairs—a post that made him the highest-ranking African member of government to that date in Rhodesia. In August 1962, however, he embarrassed UFP leadership by resigning his ministerial post to protest the failure of the government to make "partnership" meaningful. After dissolution of the federation the next year he was treated as a pariah by African nationalists.

SAVANNA. An internationally used term for grassy plains with scattered, scrubby trees, such as characterize most of Zimbabwe and the rest of the great African plateau. This type of vegetation is the product of limited rainfall (see **Climate**), which inhibits larger tree growth (see **Forests**), while allowing tall grasses to predominate. It is well-suited for extensive livestock raising. The Zimbabwean savanna differs somewhat from that of other African countries in that it is frequently broken up by granite *kopjes,* moist *vleis,* and other kinds of terrain. (See **Altitudinal Zones.**)

SAWMILLS. Village on the **railway** line in the central **Nyamandhlovu District** (at 19°35′S, 28°2′E). Appropriately named, the village is the center of the local hardwood industry (see **Forests**).

SCHREINER, OLIVE (March 25, 1855–Dec. 12, 1970). South African author. A former governess in the Cape Colony who gained fame with the novel *The Story of an African Farm* (London, 1883), Schreiner married Cape politician Samuel Cronwright in 1894 and then campaigned and pamphleteered with her husband for liberal causes. Both were especially suspicious of **BSAC** activities in the present Zimbabwe. During the **Ndebele/Shona Revolt of 1896–97,** Schreiner wrote a novel *Trooper Peter Halket of Mashonaland* (London 1897), which presented a scathing indictment of BSAC mistreatment of Africans and of **Cecil Rhodes'** policies. In her later life, she turned her pen to support radical feminist causes.

"SEA COWS" see **HIPPOPOTAMUSES**

SEASONS see **CLIMATE**

SEBAKWE RIVER. Rising on Mount Mtoro (18°54′S, 31°5′E), just northeast of **Chivhu,** the Sebakwe River flows generally west in a sweeping curve below the **Umniati River,** which it joins just west of the **Kwekwe**-to-**Kadoma** road. The Sebakwe Dam, built in the **Mashaba Mountains** in 1957, is one of the country's largest internal **dams**. Its lake covers 60 percent of the 2,510-hectare Sebakwe National Park, which surrounds it. This dam, and the smaller Dutchman's Pool Dam built north of Kwekwe in 1954, supply Kwekwe and the surrounding farms with water.

SEBITWANE (d.1851). Founder-king of the **Kololo**.

SEBUNGWE DISTRICT. Former **administrative district** covering 32,845 sq km in the northwest, between the **Zambezi, Umniati, Kana** and **Gwaai** rivers. Sebungwe's successor districts are **Gokwe** in the east, **Binga** in the west, and part of **Kariba** in the northeast.

SEKE DISTRICT (Seki District until 1985). Seke is located in the south-central part of **Mashonaland East Province**. Established in 1978 from sections of the three districts that now border the district, it is the smallest district in the country. The **Hunyani River** separates the district from **Goromonzi District** to the north; **Harare District** is to the west; and **Marondera** is to the southeast and east. Except for the westernmost tip, Seke is exclusively **Communal Lands**. The district population in 1992 was 75,080.

SEKGOMA (variant: Skehome) (c.1815–1883). Ruler of the **Ngwato** and father of **Khama III**.

SELOUS, FEDERICK COURTENEY (Dec. 31, 1851–Jan.4, 1917). Hunter and author. Born in London, Selous came to southern Africa in 1871 to hunt elephants. Over the next two decades, he traveled and hunted widely in **Matabeleland** and **Mashonaland,** collecting animal specimens for British museums and writing numerous magazine articles about his exploits. he achieved some renown with the publication of two popular books, *A Hunter's Wanderings in Africa* (1883) and *Travel and Adventure in South-East Africa* (1893), and his career is believed to have inspired **H. R. Haggard**'s fictional character "Allen Quartermain." Selous's writings extolled **Shona** culture, but he used his unique knowledge of the Shona to help **Cecil Rhodes** and the **BSAC** to lay claim to Mashonaland. In 1890 he served as guide to the **Pioneer Column**, which occupied Mashonaland. After the BSAC occupied Matabeleland three years later, Selous settled there with his family. During the **Ndebele Revolt of 1896**, he fought with the **Bulawayo Field Force** and then wrote *Sunshine and Storm in Rhodesia* (1896), describing the early stage of the revolt. Afterwards he hunted big game throughout the world until the First World War, in which he was killed by German forces in the East African campaign. (See **Hunters; Ivory.**)

SELOUS SCOUTS (SS). Former elite Rhodesian army unit, which specialized in counterinsurgency operations during the war for national liberation in the 1970s. While responsible for many counterinsurgency operations during the war, the SS is most noted for three actions: (1) the January 1973 founding and use of so-called "pseudo gangs"—Africans (often former guerrillas) recruited and trained to operate in rural areas to gather intelligence information on activities of **ZANLA** and **ZIPRA** forces. Pseudo gangs also attempted to ambush such forces, disrupted rural agricultural productions, and often terrorized local people. The government would then commonly claim that these acts of sabotage and terror had been committed by ZANLA or ZIPRA forces. The government thereby hoped to forestall rural support and assistance to liberation forces. (2) The August 1976 raid on refugee camps located at Nyadzonia, **Mozambique,** in which more than 1,000 Zimbabweans where either killed or wounded. While ZANLA later admitted there were armed combatants guarding the camps, the great majority of casualties were civilian refugees. (3) The infamous raids in November 1977 on refugee camps located at Chimoio and Tembwe, both inside Mozambique. The Chimoio raid lasted for three days and more than 1,000 Zimbabweans, again mostly civilian refugees, were killed.

Following independence, the SS was officially disbanded, but a number of SS veterans, both African and European, formed the core of the new **Zimbabwe National Army**'s One Parachute Battalion. (See **Rhodesian Security Forces.**)

SELUKWE see **SHURUGWI**

SENA. Mozambique town on the right bank of the **Zambezi River,** about 260 km up from the coast. Established as a **Muslim** trading post perhaps as early as the 10th century, Sena was occupied by the **Portuguese** in 1531. Thereafter it became a major base for trade routes to **Shona** country. The name "Sena" has also been applied to a local branch of **Bantu** languages.

SENATE. Established in 1970 by the 1969 **Constitution,** this body formed the upper chamber of **Parliament.** During the **UDI** period, the Senate's main function was to approve bills amending the entrenched clauses of the constitution, in effect assuming the reserved powers once held by the British Crown. It was composed of a total of 23 members, ten elected by the European member of the **House of Assembly**; ten African chiefs selected by the **Council of Chiefs**; and three members appointed by the **president**.

In 1980, following agreements made at the **Lancaster House Conference**, the Senate membership was restructured. Total membership was raised to 40 seats, with ten seats reserved for seven years for members elected by Europeans members of Parliament. Of the remaining 30 seats, ten were to be elected by the Council of Chiefs, based on separate polls of **Ndebele** and **Shona** chiefs; 14 seats were to be elected by the 80 members of the House of Assembly; and the remaining six seats were to be appointed by the president, based on the advice of the **prime minister**. It continued to be essentially a rubber stamp for bills passed by the lower chamber. The governments was dissatisfied with the idea of the Senate because half of its membership were reserved for members of two groups which it saw as representing traditional and conservative elements in the society, Europeans and chiefs.

In 1987, in accordance with the guidelines set down by the Lancaster House Constitution, the government introduced legislation to abolish seats in Parliament reserved for Europeans. In October, this legislation received unanimous approval, and the ten reserved seats in the Senate were abolished. They were then filled by a vote of the House of Assembly, with all ten seats going to members of **ZANU,** including four European members. In 1990 the government introduced legislation to do away with the Senate entirely, and created a unicameral Parliament with a total membership of 150.

SENGWA RIVER. Rises on the **Mafungabusi Plateau,** whence it flows west, then north, entering Lake **Kariba** at the latter's midpoint—a location which was once the Kansala Rapids on the **Zambezi River.**

SERTANEJO. Portuguese term for backwoodsman, applied to early traders and adventurers operating in the inland areas of the Zambezi Valley. (See, e.g., **Bayao; Madeira.**)

SHABANI see **ZVISHAVANE**

SHAMUYARIRA, NATHAN MARWIRAKUWA (b. September 29, 1929), Nationalist, journalist, and government minister. Born in **Mhondoro** into a family of a Methodist evangelist, Shamuyarira received his preliminary education at the **Waddilove Institute**, qualifying as a teacher. He then taught at various schools around the country, including Tegwani and **Domboshawa**. In 1953 he turned to journalism and became a reporter for **African Newspapers, Ltd.**, becoming editor of the *African Daily News* in 1956 and the group's editor-in-chief in 1959. In September 1962 he resigned from his position following policy and political disputes with the publishers and joined **ZAPU**. The next year he quit ZAPU and became a founding member of **ZANU**, as well as a member of its National Executive.

In 1964 he fled the country and studied at Princeton University. During this period, he wrote *Crisis in Rhodesia* (1965), a personal memoir with a historical survey of African nationalism in Rhodesia. After graduating in 1967, he spent some time at Nuffield College, Oxford University, before lecturing in political science at the University of Dar es Salaam in Tanzania. He also served as ZANU's secretary for external affairs until late in 1974, when he became treasurer of the newly formed **FROLIZI** after he resigned his post at the university. Following disagreements with the FROLIZI leadership in 1973, he resigned and returned to the University of Dar es Salaam and to ZANU. In 1977, he once again left the university and went to **Mozambique**, where he was appointed director of ZANU's education department and later administrative secretary.

In the 1980 election campaign, he served as the administrative secretary of the party's election directorate, and also won election to **Parliament** from **Mashonaland West**. He was appointed minister of information and tourism in independent Zimbabwe's first cabinet, and in a 1982 cabinet reshuffle became minister of information, posts, and telecommunications. In 1984, at ZANU's Second Party Congress, he was elected to the party's Politburo and Central Committee and appointed secretary for publicity and information. In 1985, he was reelected to Parliament, representing **Makonde** West. In an early 1988 cabinet reshuffle, President **Mugabe** appointed Shamuyarira minister of foreign affairs, a post he retained after the 1990 **elections**. In a cabinet reshuffle following the 1995 elections, Shamuyarira was appointed minister of public service, labor, and social protection. In May 1996 he was appointed minister of industry and commerce.

SHAMVA. Administrative and commercial center of the district of the same name. The town of Shamva, originally called **Abercorn**, was formerly an important **gold**-mining center. Shamva Gold Mine operated between 1908 and 1930, and was reopened in the late 1970s. In the third week of September 1927, the mine was the site of a major African labor strike. About 3,500 mine and contractor employees—almost all from eastern **Zambia** and Malawi—struck for better wages and improved accident compensation. Heavy government pressure caused the strike to collapse, but it nevertheless demonstrated to the country the ability of African workers to organize effectively on a large scale. Subsequent closure of the mine halted the town's development, and in 1969 its population was less than 1,000. The town stands at the terminus of a branch **railway** line from **Harare** (at 17°19′S, 31°34′E; alt. 970 m).

SHAMVA DISTRICT. Shamva was carved out of **Mazowe** and **Mukumbura** districts. The **Nyagui** and **Mazowe** rivers separate Shamva from the **Murehwa District** on the east. Shamva also borders on the district of

Mukumbura on the north and **Bindura** on the west, and touches **Goromonzi** on the south. Except for some Tribal Trust Land (see **Communal Lands**) in its center and northwest corner, the district before 1980 was reserved for Europeans. District population in 1992 was 94,047.

SHANGANE (Amashangane; variants: Shangaan; Changana). After **Soshangane** founded the **Gaza kingdom** in the early 19th century, his followers became known as *Amashangane*, "the people of Soshangane." In this narrow sense, "Shangane" is synonymous with "Gaza." Since the mid-19th century, however, the name *Shangane* has acquired a looser meaning. It is now frequently applied to **Ndau, Hlengwe**, and other peoples formerly associated with the Gaza. Most of the people now called "Shangane" do not speak the **Nguni** language of the original Gaza. In contemporary usage the name is best regarded as a regional, rather than ethnic, identification.

SHANGANI DISTRICT. Former 10,485-sq-km district surrounding the **Shangani River** in the west. Originally the northern part of **Bubi District**, Shangani itself was divided into the present **Lupane** and **Nkai** districts. Its former administrative center was at the village of **Lupane**. The village of Shangani is a small trading center of the main railway line (at 19°47′S, 29°22′E; alt. 1,375 m).

"SHANGANI PATROL" (a.k.a. "Wilson Patrol") (1893). The "Shangani Patrol" traditionally symbolized to many European settlers the blood sacrifice made in occupying the country during the early 1890s. After the **BSAC** had occupied the **Ndebele** capital, **Bulawayo**, during the **Ndebele War**, **L. S. Jameson** dispatched Major **P. W. Forbes** with a column to pursue King **Lobengula**, who was fleeing north in November 1893. Heavy rains allowed Forbes's column to advance only c.27 km in 14 days, so Forbes sent back the wagons and most of his men on November 28. On December 3, the force camped on the south bank of the **Shangani River**. Forbes then sent Major **Allan Wilson** and a few dozen men across the river to reconnoiter. That evening Wilson reported he had found Lobengula and asked for reinforcements. Forbes was reluctant to move at night, so he sent only a few more men. The next day the river rose so high it was almost unfordable. **F. R. Burnham** reported that Wilson's patrol was trapped by the Ndebele, who then killed all 34 of its members. Months later the bodies were recovered below the river's confluence with the **Gwelo**. The bones were temporarily buried at the **Zimbabwe Ruins** and later reinterred with a shrine at **World's View** in the **Matopo Hills**.

Only recently has it been pointed out that this last action of the Ndebele War was an Ndebele victory and that the event itself demonstrated the incompleteness of the British "conquest."

SHANGANI RIVER. The main tributary of the **Gwai River**, the Shangani rises near **Dhlo Dhlo**, whence it flows generally northwest before meeting the Gwai near Lubimbi Hot Springs. Along the way the Shangani is fed by the Vungu and **Gwelo** rivers from the east.

SHANGWA. Chishona term for misery or famine; associated particularly with a widespread drought and famine that occurred just before the *Mfecane* invasions of the 1830s.

SHANGWE (Vashangwe; variants: Shankwe, Bashngwe). Small **Shona** community speaking a subdialect of **Korekore**. Since at least the early 19th century the Shangwe have lived in the **tsetse**-infested region around the **Bumi River** just southeast of central **Lake Kariba**. During the 19th century the Shangwe avoided **Ndebele** raids by paying tribute in salt obtained from the Bari Pan (at 17°34'S, 28°35'E).

SHASHANI RIVER. Rising near the midpoint of the **Plumtree**-to-**Bulawayo** road, the Shashani flows south by southeast for c.160 km before joining the **Shashi River** at the **Botswana** border.

SHASHE RIVER (not to be confused with Shashi). Rises on the **Central Plateau** near Felixburg (at 19°26'S, 30°50'E). The Shashe initially flows north, but quickly turns west and then south to feed the **Ngezi River** just above the latter's confluence with the **Tokwe**. The Shashe defined part of the "boundary" between **Mashonaland** and **Matabeleland** declared by **L. S. Jameson** in 1893.

SHASHI RIVER (not to be confused with Shashe). One of the main tributaries of the **Limpopo**, the Shashi rises in **Botswana** about 50 km west of **Plumtree**. It flows south, curving below **Francistown**, then is joined by the **Ramaquabane River** at the Zimbabwe **border**, except at the **"Tuli Circle."** During the 19th century the Shashi was regarded as the boundary line between the **Ndebele** and **Ngwato** spheres of influence.

SHAVASHA (Vashavasha; variant: Shawasha). Branch of the **Zezuru** cluster of **Shona-speaking peoples**, living mainly in the present **Harare District**, northeast of the capital city. The most important of the Shavasha royal dynasties was that of the **Chinamoras**.

SHAVE (variants: shabe; shawe; shavi; pl., mashave). A variety of **Shona** spirits. In contract to personal ancestor spirits (see **Mudzimu**), and tutelary community spirits (see **Mhondoro** and **Gombwe**), the mashave are nontutelary spirits of strangers. These strangers are usually people who die locally and are not buried properly. They may include neighboring Shona individuals, Europeans, animals—especially baboons—or even airplanes. The mashave are said to select the hosts whom they possess rather arbitrarily. They are usually benevolent, but they may be malevolent, in which case they are also classed as *ngozi,* whom the unwilling mediums try to have exorcised. Mashave are often credited with giving their hosts special skills, such as hunting, ironworking, *mbira* playing, or healing and divining skills from mashave. Many mashave are thought to be very fond of dancing. They possess their hosts, particularly women, in lively dancing séances that frequently develop into popular social events. (See **Religion—Shona.**)

SHIMMIN, ISAAC (1860–Feb. 26, 1933). British missionary. An agent of the **Wesleyan Methodist Missionary Society**, Shimmin helped to establish **Epworth Mission**. He directed Wesleyan work in **Mashonaland** from 1891 to 1907.

SHONA HISTORY. The problem of dating the earliest arrival of **Shona-speaking peoples** in the country has long perplexed historians. On the basis of oral traditions, dates as late as the 11th through 15th centuries have been variously assigned to this event. In view of the early first millennium dates that archaeologists have established for the beginnings of the local **Iron Age**, a second millennium date for the Shona arrival leaves the problem of identifying their immediate Iron Age predecessors. The introduction of the Iron Age is generally attributed to the arrival of the first **Bantu-speakers**. The modern dominance of the country by Shona suggests that they must have been among the first Bantu-speakers to arrive. Indeed, linguistic research indicates that this was the case. The widespread distribution and diversification of Shona dialects (see **Chishona**) point to an early first millennium Shona presence in the country. Linguistic research further suggests that Chishona developed as a distinct language *within* the country, where it separated from a parent language that also gave rise to other southeast Bantu languages that developed differently after other early migrants moved farther south.

The history of the country since the early first millennium is, then, essentially the history of its Shona-speaking peoples, who absorbed the original **Khoisan** and, possibly, Central Sudanic (a branch of Chari-Nile) speakers. Most later arrivals to the country became Shona-speakers as they too were absorbed by the dominant group.

Little is known about the political systems of the Shona before about the 14th century. By then the first large-scale state system had arisen among the **Karanga** branch of Shona. This state was centered in the southeast at the site now known as the **Zimbabwe ruins**. The Zimbabwe state declined suddenly in the 15th century. At the same time an apparently related state was established by the **Munhumutapa** dynasty in the northern **Dande** region. This state briefly developed into an empire along the southern banks of the **Zambezi River**. It then went into a gradual decline as tributary provinces broke away, forming autonomous states, and as other competing Shona states rose to prominence. The most important to these were the **Torwa** and **Changamire** states in the south, and the **Mutasa** or originally Chikanga dynasty in the east. Shona-derived dynasties were also established over such non-Shona peoples as the **Barwe** in the northeast.

In the late 17th century the Changamire state rapidly developed into an empire that dominated more of the country than did any other precolonial state system. The Changamire rulers became known as "**Rozvi**," a name that has caused considerable confusion in reconstructing Shona history generally. The Rozvi empire, like its predecessor states, was really more a confederation than a centralized polity. It comprised a collection of tribute-paying chiefdoms with their own dynasties. The tendency toward local autonomy was persistent, and by the late 18th century the "empire" was disintegrating. The *Mfecane* invasions of the 1830s accelerated this process. Afterwards there were more than 100 independent Shona chiefdoms, many of which had to struggle for autonomy against the raids and tribute exactions of the newly arrived **Ndebele** and **Gaza** kingdoms. Shona independence came to its decisive end only in 1897, however, after the failure of a large-scale **Revolt** against British occupation of the country. Since then Shona chiefdoms have survived merely as government-sanctioned administrative units in **Communal Lands**, formerly called "reserves" or "Tribal Trust Lands."

Even during the peak periods of the large-scale Shona states, Shona societies remained rooted in subsistence **agriculture** and limited animal husbandry. State systems emerged partly as a response to competition for control of **ivory** and **gold** trades with the east coast, but these pursuits were essentially limited, part-time economic activities within the total Shona economic systems. Generalizations about Shona political structures are difficult to make, but their lack of uniform systems of political succession stands out clearly. Shona social structure is patrilineal, and family power blocs often developed quickly. Competition for political succession among rival families was—and still is—a major feature of Shona politics. Fission occurred frequently within dynasties and was a major cause of the proliferation of autonomous states. Rivalries among neighboring states were often intense, accounting for the relative ease with which the **Ndebele** dominated the western part of the country in the 19th century, as well as contributing to the failure of the Shona to mount an effective resistance against the British in the 1890s.

SHONA LANGUAGES see **CHISHONA**

SHONA PEOPLES (Mashona, or Vashona). Roughly three-quarters of the country's people are known as "Shona." Not all of these people recognize the name, however. Historically, Shona have tended to identify themselves as members of either dialect clusters, such as **Karanga**, or smaller groupings, such as **Shavasha**. The origin of the name "Shona" itself is obscure. The name was almost certainly coined by outsiders in the early 19th century (see **Swina; Nyai**). Its invention is usually attributed to the **Ndebele**, who are said to have used it as a term of abuse, but a European traveler, Andre Smith, recorded the name "Mashoona" in 1835—three years before the Ndebele settled in the country. The country's later European rulers applied the name "Shona" to all peoples belonging to the large cultural grouping now generally called Shona. The Shona themselves began accepting the name as increasing external pressures gave them a greater sense of commonality. Government-sponsored standardization of the Shona language, or **Chishona**, in the 1930s, and the spread of literacy enhanced the trend toward unification of Shona identity.

The country's **borders** correspond fairly closely to the perimeters of Shona distribution, except in the east, where Shona communities extend across part of **Mozambique**. The term **"Mashonaland"** was applied by Europeans to the eastern parts of the country, where few non-Shona peoples lived in the 19th century, but Shona-speakers also pervade **Matabeleland** in the west, and some spill over into **Botswana**. The Ndebele are the most numerous single non-Shona people in the country, but most present Ndebele are physically descended, at least in part, from 19th century Shona incorporated into the Ndebele state (see **Holi**).

Despite many attempts to classify the Shona into component "ethnic groups" or "tribes," no satisfactory classification has been achieved. There are few simple correlations between dialect groups, ethnic groups, and historical political units. Individuals, families, ruling dynasties, and even whole communities have historically moved about the country frequently. Almost every modern Shona community is a complex ethnic amalgam. Nevertheless, a number of distinct dialect clusters are generally recognized as meaningful divisions. These correspond, at least broadly, to recognized ethnic divisions. **Korekore**-speakers live in the north; **Zezuru** live around **Harare; Manyika** are in the east; **Ndau** in the southeast; **Karanga** in the south; and **Kalanga** in the far west. A seventh recognized branch, the **Rozvi**, are found throughout the country, confounding attempts at neat regional classifications.

SHONA RELIGION see **RELIGION—SHONA**

SHONA REVOLT (1896–97) see **REVOLTS OF 1896–97**

SHONA SCULPTURE. While carving in stone dates back at least one thousand years in the area that is present-day Zimbabwe (see **Zimbabwe "Birds"; Zimbabwe Ruins**), the modern art form that is internationally referred to as "Shona Sculpture" began in the late 1950s when the first curator of the national Museum, Frank McKewan, began to actively support young sculptors and display their art at the museum. Shona Sculpture is so named because it is almost exclusively done by Shona artists (see **Shona Peoples**). By the early 1990s, it had gained widespread international recognition for its originality and beauty and is considered the country's leading art form.

The first generation of sculptors were self-taught, while younger artists have often apprenticed under one of the older artists. Many of the sculptors consider the process of carving a spiritual act and generally claim that "the image is inspired by the stone itself or by ancestral family spirits" (see **Religion, Shona**). Some of the most famous of these artists include Henry Munyaradzi, Nicholas Mukomberanwa, Lazarus Takawira, Damian Manuhwa, and Richard Mteki.

SHURUGWI (Selukwe until 1982). Important **mining** town and administrative center of **Shurugwi District** (at 19°30′S, 30°′E; alt. 1,445 m). The town was established in 1899 on goldfields, and has since become one of the country's major **chrome** producing centers. It is just southeast of **Gweru**, to which it is connected by a branch **railway** line. Population in 1992 was 6,029.

SHURUGWI DISTRICT (Selukwe District unit 1985). Covers 3,550 sq km at the southern bend of **Midlands Province**. It borders the districts of **Chirumanzu** on the east, **Masvingo** and **Chivi** on the southeast, **Zvishavane** on the south, **Insiza** on the southwest, and **Gweru** on the west and north. Shurugwi is a well-wooded and well-watered district. Prior to 1980 the western and northeastern sections were reserved for Europeans, with the remainder being Tribal Trust Land (see **Communal Lands**). District population in 1992 was 86,617.

SIKOMBO MGUNI (fl. 1860s–1890s). **Ndebele** *induna,* closely associated with **Xukutwayo**, under whom he served in the northeastern part of the kingdom. From at least the early 1860s Sikombo accompanied Xukutwayo on many military campaigns. he later married a daughter of **Lobengula** and became influential at **Bulawayo.** In 1889 he was associated with **Lotshe** in the group accused of selling out the kingdom to Europeans, but he emerged unscathed to become one of Lobengula's main advisers. In early 1895 Sikombo was one of the major planners of the **Revolt** that began the next year. During the Revolt he was a top leader in the eastern **Matopo Hills.** Afterwards he participated in the peace negotiations with **Cecil Rhodes** and was made a salaried chief in the **Umzingwane District.**

SILINDA, MOUNT (variant: Selinda). Located near the **Mozambique** border at 20°25′S latitude, where a post leads to Espungabera. The hill rises to 1,065m, with the **Chirinda Forest** covering its slopes. During the 19th century the **Gaza** kingdom maintained its **Manhlagazi** headquarters nearby. In 1893 the **BSAC** granted the land around the hill to the **American Board of Commissioners for Foreign Missions** which established its Mount Silinda Mission there (see also **Alvord, E. D.**).

SILOZWANE CAVE. Important **rock painting** site located on the southern edge of the **Matopo Hills** (at 20°38′S, 288°35′E). Its paintings feature unusually large representations of animals and humans, the latter evidently depicting **Bantu**-speaking agriculturalists.

SILUNDIKA, TARCISSIUS MALAN GEORGE ("TG") (March 1929–April 9, 1981). Nationalist, **ZAPU** central committee member and government minister. Born near **Plumtree,** Silundika received his primary education at **Empandeni Mission,** then went on to St. Francis College in Natal in 1945. In 1951 he enrolled at Fort Hare College in South Africa, but was expelled the following year for political activism. In 1954 he studied at Pius XII University College in Lesotho, but was forced to withdraw for lack of funds. He returned home and taught at Empandeni Secondary School for two years, then joined the Federal Broadcasting Corporation (see **Zimbabwe Broadcasting Corporation**) for a short time, before becoming a research assistant in African Studies at the University College of Rhodesia and Nyasaland (see **University of Zimbabwe**). Silundika became involved in nationalist politics in 1959 when he was a founding member of the **National Democratic Party,** being elected its secretary-general in November 1960. In December he was a delegate to the constitutional review conferences in London, and in February 1961 a delegate to the Constitutional Conference in Salisbury. He was a loyal supporter of **Joshua Nkomo,** and in 1963 was appointed publicity secretary of the **People's Caretaker Council.** He then moved to Lusaka as an external representative of that organization. In 1976 he was a ZAPU delegate to the **Geneva Conference** and in 1979 was an adviser to Nkomo at the **Lancaster House Conference.** After the agreement at Lancaster House, he returned to Zimbabwe and was elected a ZAPU member of **Parliament** for **Matabeleland South.** Prime Minister **Robert Mugabe** appointed him minister of posts and telecommunications, and in 1981 minister of roads, road traffic, posts, and telecommunications. At the time of his death from a stroke, Silundika was a member of the ZAPU Central Committee. He was buried at **Heroes' Acre** on April 11, 1981.

SILVEIRA, GONÇALO DA (Feb. 26, 1526–March 16, 1561). First Christian missionary in the country. Born into a **Portuguese** noble family, Silveira joined the Society of Jesus in 1543 and was sent to the Jesuit mission in Goa in 1556. After hearing of the interest of the **Shona Munhumutapa** in Christianity, he hurried off to **Mozambique** in 1560, and then went up the **Zambezi River** to the court of Munhumutapa **Negomo Chrisamhuru**. He arrived there around Christmas. Silveira apparently impressed Negomo with his piety, for he baptized the Munhumutapa and his mother within a month. Over the next several months he baptized another 300 or so Shona. It is usually said that **Muslim** traders in the country conspired against Silveira, telling Negomo that the priest was a spy. It appears, however, that it was actually Shona *nganga* who recommended his murder after they had cast *hakata* divining bones to determine his intentions. In any case, Negomo had Silveira strangled on the night of 15–16 March. His body was thrown into the **Musengedzi River**. A decade later the Portuguese government used Silveira's martyrdom as a justification for launching **Francisco Barreto**'s punitive expedition against Negomo. (On Jesuits, see also **Zambezi Mission**.)

SILVER. Significant extraction of this metal in the country began only with modern European **gold** mining, which separates silver as a byproduct. Through 1964, total production value of silver was £1,462,267. With the significant rise of international silver prices in the late 1970s, production was increased, with c.$(Z)51,726,000 being produced from 1980 to 1985.

SINDEBELE (variant: Isindebele). The language of the **Ndebele people**. Sindebele is closely related to Zulu, an **Nguni** language from which it separated when **Mzilikazi** began his migrations in c.1821. Sindebele differs from Zulu largely in its accretion of foreign **Bantu** words, drawn mostly from **Sotho** and **Shona** languages. Until recently, schools used mostly Zulu for texts for Ndebele pupils, but these have caused confusion because of somewhat different orthographies. Sindebele, for example, makes less use of the aspirative -*h*- after consonants, as in *dlozi/dhlozi*. Like other Nguni languages, Sindebele contains many **click consonants**. In common with all Bantu languages, Sindebele nouns employ a complex system of noun prefixes, such as **aba-, ama-, i-, isi-,** and **izi-**. Since the fall of the Ndebele kingdom in the 1890s, speaking Sindebele has become the single most important criterion for individuals claiming "Ndebele" identity.

SINOIA see **CHINHOYI**

SIPOLILO DISTRICT see **GURUVE DISTRICT**

SIRI CHENA CHURCH (a.k.a. Church of the White Bird) see under **ZWIMBA, MATTHEW**

SITHOLE, EDSON FURATIDZAYI CHISINGAITWI (June 5, 1935–declared legally dead, June 1, 1988). Politically active from 1951, Sithole helped to found the **Youth League** in 1955, the reorganized **African National Congress** in 1957, and the **Zimbabwe National Party** in 1961. After the collapse of the ZNP, he became a leader in **ZANU**, but spent most of the 1960s in prisons and detention camps. Through this period he continued his education by correspondence and became the country's second African attorney in 1963. After one of his releases from detention in late 1971 he became publicity chairman of the new **African National Council**, which he helped to found. He was again imprisoned in 1972.

He was released in December 1974 and went to **Zambia.** He participated in the **Victoria Falls Conference** the following year as an ANC representative and then mysteriously disappeared from the streets of Salisbury (now **Harare**) on October 15, 1975. It is generally accepted that he was a victim of a government kidnapping. The government of Zimbabwe officially declared Sithole dead on June 1, 1988.

SITHOLE, NDABANINGI (July 21, 1920–Dec. 12, 2000). Born at **Nyamandhlovu,** Sithole was educated at **Garfield Todd's** Dadaya mission school and at **Waddilove** during the late 1930s. During the 1940s and early 1950s he taught at mission schools and obtained a degree by correspondence from the University of South Africa. He then studied divinity in New Hampshire from 1955 to 1958, returning home to be ordained a minister at the ABC's **Mount Silinda Mission.** During this period he also published some fiction in both **Sindebele** and English and attracted international attention with the publication of *African Nationalism* (1959), a political treatise calling for an end to racialism in Africa. In early 1960 he abandoned his teaching career and joined the newly formed **National Democratic Party,** in which he was elected treasurer later in the year.

After the government banned the NDP, Sithole joined **Joshua Nkomo** in **ZAPU.** ZAPU was banned in 1962, and Sithole and Nkomo found themselves disagreeing increasingly about what strategy the nationalist movement should employ. Sithole, with the backing of several African leaders, advocated working within the country, while Nkomo proposed forming a government in exile. In July 1963 the two leaders split permanently. The following month Sithole formed **ZANU,** while Nkomo formed the **PCC.** When ZANU was banned by the government a year later, Sithole was arrested. He was in and out of prison until early 1969, when he was sentenced to six years in prison on a charge of plotting to kill Prime Minister **Ian Smith.** After being sentenced, Sithole took the opportunity to publicly disavow "terrorist activities" and "violence" as a means of ending minority rule in the country.

While in prison in the mid-1970s, Sithole was involved in a struggle for the leadership of ZANU. A group of ZANU leaders, including **Robert Mugabe, Edgar Tekere,** and **Maurice Nyagumbo** believed that Sithole's 1969 disavowal of violence was a rejection of ZANU's commitment to the armed struggle against white minority rule. This struggle for leadership of ZANU came to a head at Que Que Prison in 1974 when the party's leaders imprisoned there decided that the leadership of the party should be put to a vote. It was impossible to call a party congress, so six leaders agreed they would vote among themselves. The vote resulted in Sithole being replaced by Robert Mugabe as leader of the party. However, Sithole retained his title as president of ZANU, and as a result the struggle between Sithole and Mugabe to be recognized as legitimate leader of ZANU persisted for several years.

In late 1974 Sithole was released from detention in order to attend constitutional talks in Lusaka. He was accepted by several African leaders, including Julius Zyerere of Tanzania and Kenneth Kaunda of **Zambia,** as the leader of ZANU on the condition that he agree to the unity of the various Zimbabwe liberation movements under the umbrella

African National Council. After signing the Lusaka Declaration which proclaimed this unity, Sithole returned to the country and in March 1975 was arrested on charges of plotting to kill several rival nationalist leaders. However, following the urging of South Africa's Prime Minister John Vorster, the government soon released him. Later in 1975 Sithole participated in the **Victoria Falls Conference**, during which time he was loosely allied with **Abel Muzorewa**. During this period it became increasingly clear that Sithole had lost any claim to the leadership of ZANU. African student organizations in England rejected him, and more importantly the military leaders of the military wing of ZANU, operating out of camps in Tanzania and **Mozambique,** issued the **Mgagao Declaration**, proclaiming that they had lost all belief in Sithole and Muzorewa. Both groups stated that they recognized Robert Mugabe as the leader of ZANU. Following this rebuff, Sithole began to work more closely with Muzorewa, although he continued to claim publicly that he maintained the leadership of ZANU. Sithole broke with Muzorewa in early 1977. Sithole then formed a group which he called the "African National Council (Sithole)."

In late 1977 Sithole joined Muzorewa and Chief **Jeremiah Chirau** in talks with Ian Smith, and the resulting **Internal Settlement** agreement was signed in March of the following year. A transitional government was established under the leadership of an executive council, in which Sithole joined the three other signatories in sharing the rotating chairmanship. In April 1979 parliamentary **elections** for the newly proclaimed **Zimbabwe Rhodesia** were held, and Sithole's party (renamed ZANU [Sithole]) finished a distant second behind Muzorewa's **UANC**.

The Muzorewa government was not recognized by the international community, and following the **Lancaster House Conference** in late 1979, new elections for an independent Zimbabwe were called. Sithole contested this election under the banner ZANU (Sithole), but failed to win a single seat in the new **Parliament**. In 1984 Sithole went into self-proclaimed exile in the United States where he began to proclaim private enterprise as the cure for Africa's development problems and was a strong critic of the Mugabe government's commitment to the socialist development of Zimbabwe.

On August 15, 1991, Sithole announced that he would return to Zimbabwe. He returned in 1992 and quickly formed a political party, **ZANU-Ndonga**, in opposition to Mugabe's government and ZANU. He contested the 1995 election and won a seat in the **House of Assembly** representing the **Chipinge** South constituency in the province of **Manicaland.** In October 1995 he was arrested by police officials investigating reports of a conspiracy to assassinate President Mugabe. Released on bail a few days later, he was eventually convicted on treason charges in December 1997 and sentenced to two years in prison. His party, ZANU-Ndonga, won one seat in the 2000 parliamentary elections.He appealed and while out on bail his health deteriorated. In September 2000, he was allowed to travel to the United States for medical treatment. He died there on December 12, 2000.

SITI KAZURUKUMUSAPA (d.1663). In May 1652 Siti succeeded his father, **Mavura II**, as **Munhumutapa**. Usually described as weak and vacillating, Siti was beset by an ambitious younger brother and by unruly

Portuguese residents in the kingdom. In 1663 an army of Portuguese landowners (*prazeros*) organized against him, but he was suddenly assassinated by his own noblemen. His brother then became Munhumutapa.

SITUPA. Widely used African term for registration certificates, from the **Nguni** term for thumb, or thumbprint. The **Chishona** form is *chitupa*. (See **Pass Laws**.)

SJAMBOK. Whip, about two meters long, made of tough animal hides and used for driving livestock. Not to be confused with the much longer cracking whips used on teams of oxen. From a Malay word introduced into South Africa.

SKERM. Temporary fence of thorn trees and branches made to protect travelers at night; derives from the Dutch work *scherm* for "fence" or "screen." Frequently used in 19th-century travel accounts.

SKOKIAAN. Alcoholic beverage made from fermented cereals spiked with typically toxic ingredients such at tobacco, methylated spirits, or carbonates. Though illegal and often physically harmful or even fatal to drinkers, *skokiaan* has been a popular drink in African townships, particularly during the late 1940s. Prostitutes and other women, known as "Skokiaan Queens," have made small fortunes from its sale. It was introduced to the country from Johannesburg. The term apparently derives from the **Afrikaans** word *skok*, for "shock" or "jolt."

"SLAVE PITS" see **STONE-LINED PITS**

SLEEPING SICKNESS (trypanosomiasis). Human variety of a parasitic disease transmitted by certain varieties of **tsetse flies**. Though less severe than the equivalent animal disease, **nagana**, sleeping sickness can cause death. The first case recorded in the country occurred in 1912, after the disease had entered the country from the north. Since then the disease has been combated mainly by eliminating tsetse-fly breeding grounds. The disease now occurs only along the northern borders, especially in and around the lower **Hunyani River**. (See **Health**.)

SMALLPOX. This serious infectious viral disease is now eliminated from the country, and it has not been a major health threat since 1909, when an epidemic occurred in the northern **districts**. The first recorded epidemic occurred in 1862, when the disease entered **Matabeleland** from South Africa. Accompanied by measles, smallpox killed many **Ndebele** people. In 1893 members of an Ndebele *impi* contracted the disease during a campaign into the Zambezi Valley. The Ndebele soldiers remained in quarantine through the ensuing **Ndebele War**. King **Lobengula** is believed to have died from smallpox during his northward flight early the next year. (See **Health**.)

SMALL-WORKERS. Term for European miners—particularly **gold** miners—running small-scale operations, typically those producing less than 28 kg (1,000 oz) of gold per year. The number of such miners increased rapidly after 1904, when the **BSAC** administration began allowing individual prospectors and small syndicates to work claims without having to float capitalized companies. In 1933, 755 "small" mines produced 127,459 oz of gold. By contrast, the country's ten "big" mines (more than 10,000 oz a year) produced 333,243 oz; and 71 "medium" mines produced 154,566 oz. In more recent times small-workers have taken over most of the country's **gemstone** production.

SMITH, IAN DOUGLAS (b. April 8, 1919). Eighth **prime minister** of Rhodesia (1964–1978). Smith was born in the **Shurugwi District**—making him the country's first native-born prime minister. He joined the British Royal Air Force in 1939 and became a fighter pilot. After the war he attended Rhodes University in Grahamson, South Africa, graduating with a commerce degree.

When Smith returned to Southern Rhodesia he acquired a large cattle ranch. In 1948 he was elected to the **Legislative Assembly** as a member of the **Liberal Party**. Five years later he switched to the **United (Federal) Party** and was elected to the new federal assembly. In that body he rose to the post of chief government whip under Prime Minister **Roy Welensky**. Smith broke with the UFP in 1961 to help form a party less amenable to political concession to Africans. As a member of the new **Rhodesian Front** he was elected to the territorial assembly in December 1962. He then served as a deputy prime minister under **Winston Field** until 1964, when he joined a right-wing revolt within the party, which ousted Field and made Smith himself prime minister.

Smith took office on April 13, 1964, pledging to secure Rhodesia's independence under white rule. Within a few days he ordered the arrests of **Joshua Nkomo** and other nationalist leaders. In September he went to London for constitutional talks with British Prime Minister Alec Douglas-Home. In order to impress Britain with Rhodesia's support for independence, he organized the **"Domboshawa Indaba"** of African chiefs in October, and held a referendum on the issue among the European electorate in November. To strengthen his hand in the government, he ordered a new general election for May 7, 1965, in which the RF swept the 50 reserved European seats. Further negotiations with Britain broke down in October, so on November 11, 1965, he led the signing of the **Unilateral Declaration of Independence**.

Smith entered office vowing never to allow majority African rule during his lifetime. After the **Pearce Commission** visit of early 1972 he increasingly softened his stance on the maintenance of European political monopoly. His first major shift came in March 1976, when he announced he was willing to reconsider the issue of Rhodesian independence. Increased fighting with **ZANLA** and **ZIPRA** forces, as well as mounting pressure from the government of **South Africa**, clearly helped alter Smith's position. In September 1976 he met with U.S. Secretary of State Henry Kissinger and South African Prime Minister John Vorster, who apparently persuaded him that Rhodesia could no longer count on Western support in any all-out war with African liberation movements. On September 24 he stunned the world by announcing his willingness to negotiate a transition to African majority rule within two years. He quickly withdrew from the ensuing **Geneva Conference** because of fundamental disagreements with nationalist representatives over the form of the necessary transition-period government, but he continued to assert his intention to negotiate a transition to African rule with nationalist leaders based within the country.

In 1977 he met with American UN Ambassador Andrew Young and British Foreign Secretary David Owen to hear a new Anglo-American plan for bringing about majority rule. In September he went to **Zambia** to confer with President Kenneth Kaunda, despite the long hostile relations between the two countries. Following this series of meetings, Smith announced on November 24 that he had finally accepted the principle of universal adult suffrage for Rhodesia. The following month he began negotiations with **Abel Muzorewa, Ndabaningi Sithole**, and **Jeremiah Chirau** to bring about a purely internal settlement. It became apparent that by refusing to recognize and negotiate with the externally based liberation movements that were conducting the armed struggle within the country, Smith aspired to an agreement with the more conservative nationalist leaders inside the country, in the hope that he could preserve as much European privilege and power as possible.

The **Internal Settlement** agreement was signed by Smith and the three internal nationalists in March 1978. The transition government created by the agreement was headed by an executive council. Smith shared the rotating chairmanship of this council with the other three signatories to the agreement. In April 1979 parliamentary elections were held and the RD, led by Smith, won all 20 **House of Assembly** seats and ten seats in the **Senate** reserved for the European electorate. Abel Muzorewa's **UANC** won the majority of nonreserved seats in the House of Assembly, and all those in the Senate. Muzorewa became prime minister of the newly renamed **Zimbabwe Rhodesia.** Smith was appointed minister without portfolio, but was generally recognized as maintaining the real power in the government. The Muzorewa government was never recognized by the international community and was thereby forced to accept the convening of the **Lancaster House Conference** in September. Smith was a member of the Zimbabwe Rhodesia delegation to those talks, which reached an agreement for a new **constitution** for an independent Zimbabwe. According to the agreement, 20 seats in the House of Assembly and ten seats in the Senate were reserved for Europeans. In the **elections** held in February 1980, the RF, still led by Smith, captured all the reserved seats. Smith then became perhaps the harshest critic of the newly elected government of **Robert Mugabe.** In 1983 Smith was confronted with defections by a number of RF MPs, who withdrew from the party but kept their seats as members of the newly formed Independent Zimbabwe Group. In 1985, the RF renamed itself the Conservative Alliance of Zimbabwe. Smith remained leader of the party, and in June led the CAZ to a surprising election victory, capturing 15 of the 20 reserved seats.

In April 1987, following a trip to South Africa in which he delivered a series of speeches calling on the South African government to continue its efforts at breaking economic sanctions and maintaining minority rule, Smith was suspended by the House of Assembly for a period of one year. On May 13 he resigned his leadership of the CAZ, a post he had held for more than 23 years, and retired from politics.

SOAMES, ARTHUR CHRISTOPHER JOHN (Oct. 12, 1920–Sept. 16, 1987). Ninth and last **governor** of Southern Rhodesia (1979–80). Born in Buckinghamshire, England, Soames was educated at Eton and Sandhurst and served in the military before winning election as a Conservative MP from Bedford in 1950. In 1960, he was appointed minister of agriculture by Harold Macmillan. Soames later served as ambassador to France (1968–72), and played a main part in gaining Britain's entrance into the European Economic Community. From 1973 to 1977 he served as vice-president of the EEC Commission. In 1978, Margaret Thatcher appointed him lord president of the council and he served as leader of the House of Lords.

In December 1979, after he was nominated by Thatcher, Queen Elizabeth appointed Soames to be governor of Southern Rhodesia, with the responsibility of implementing the cease-fire and transfer of sovereignty that had been agreed to at the **Lancaster House Conference**. While Soames had experience in African affairs, he was considered qualified because of his diplomatic skills and experience in Europe.

Soames arrived in **Harare** on Dec. 12, 1979, officially marking the return of British sovereignty over the country. During his short tenure as governor, he was in charge of a five-nation, 1,300-man peacekeeping force, and charged with overseeing **elections,** which were successfully held in February 1980. Following the official transfer of power in April 1980, Soames returned to England. In a Cabinet reorganization in 1981, he was replaced as leader of the House of Lords.

SOCIETY FOR THE PROPAGATION OF GOSPEL (SPG) see **ANGLICANS**

SOFALA. Former **Mozambique** coastal port, once located just south of the **Pungwe River.** Sofala was the southernmost **Muslim** town on the eastern coast at least as early as the 10th century, when it was noted by the Arab writer al-Masudi. By 1300 it was the main outlet for Shona **gold** exports, which were then funneled through Kilwa in present Tanzania. The **Portuguese** occupied Sofala in September 1505, severing this trade link. Thereafter, the town declined into insignificance. (See also **Yufi; Ophir.**)

SOMABULA FOREST. Region just northwest of **Gweru** now the center of the country's **gemstone** production. During the early 19th century the forest was considerably more extensive than it now is. The region was infested with **tsetse flies,** which limited the northern extent of **Ndebele cattle** grazing, but by the end of the century the Ndebele had cut the forest back considerably for fuel and building materials.

Somabula River is a minor tributary of the **Gwelo River.** The village of Somabula is located 27 km southwest of Gweru, on the main road to **Bulawayo** (at 19°42′S, 29°40′E; alt. 1,415 m).

SOMABULANA DHLODHLO (fl 1880s–1890s). **Ndebele** *induna.* By the 1890s Somabulana was serving as regent of the Insinga chieftaincy, whose head town was located about 50 km east of **Bulawayo.** During the 1896 **Revolt** he became one of the main military leaders in the region between the **Insiza River** and the **Matopo Hills.** In the first *indaba* with **Cecil Rhodes,** he emerged as a leading Ndebele spokesman. After the revolt he was made a salaried chief, but was deposed by the Native Department within a year.

SOSHANGANE NXUMALO (variants: Shoshangane; Sotshangane; a.k.a. Manikusa) (c.1790s–c.1859). Founder-king of the **Gaza** state. Born in what is now Zululand, Soshangane became a leading military commander in Zwide's Ndwandwe confederation during the 1810s. After Shaka's Zulu broke up the Ndwandwe in c. 1819, Soshangane led a group of kinsmen north into southern **Mozambique.** There he began building up a kingdom through conquests and voluntary submissions. His subsequent migrations are complex and are intertwined with those of other major *Mfecane* leaders, including **Zwangendaba, Nxaba,** and **Maseko.** By the 1830s Soshangane was operating within present Zimbabwe, near **Mount Silinda.** There he defeated **Nxaba** and established his headquarters. Within a few years he returned to the lower **Limpopo** basin in Mozambique. His successors later reestablished Gaza headquarters inside Zimbabwe.

SOSWE see **SVOSVE**

SOTHO (Basotho; variant: Basutu). Sotho languages constitute one of the most important divisions of southern **Bantu.** Sotho-speakers have long been numerically dominant in **Botswana,** Lesotho, and South Africa north of the Orange River. These peoples are linguistically divided into three clusters, each containing distinct ethnic and political groups. The peoples of the western cluster are commonly known as **Tswana.** Scattered small Sotho communities have long been established in the southwestern parts of present Zimbabwe. Many additional Sotho entered the country in 1838–39 as part of the **Ndebele** migrations into **Matabeleland** from the **Transvaal.** These Sotho, who had become attached to the Ndebele kingdom during its formative decades, were eventually absorbed into the kingdom's predominantly **Nguni** culture, in which they were known as *enhla.*

SOUSA, MANUEL ANTONIO de (a.k.a. Gouveia; variants: Guveya; Kuvheya) (Nov. 10, 1835–Jan. 1892). **Portuguese** warlord of Goanese extraction (whence his nickname, "Gouveia"); first came to **Mozambique** to administer family estates in the early 1850s. Based south of the lower Zambezi River, he built up his power by assembling a private army and by marrying into many African royal families, while simultaneously gaining Portuguese recognition as *Capitão-Mor* over **Manicaland.** In the mid-1870s Sousa allied with the **Manyika** ruler **Mutasa** against the **Makoni** and **Makombe** chiefdoms, and then sought to claim the Makombe title for himself. By the 1880s he was the most powerful ruler between the **Zambezi** and **Pungwe** rivers.

In 1886 Sousa occupied the northeastern part of **Mashonaland.** The next year he achieved a temporary military success against the **Mutoko** chiefdom. Anxious to buttress its own territorial claims against the northward surge of the British, the Portuguese government brought Sousa to Lisbon in 1888 with **J. C. P. d'Andrada.** There Sousa was feted and made a "colonel" in the Portuguese army. In 1889 he and Andrada secured treaties for Portugal from northern **Shona** rulers. After the **BSAC** occupied Mashonaland in 1890, Sousa and Andrada went to Manicaland to secure the Mutasa's cooperation. In November a small force of British troops under **P. W. Forbes** "arrested" the two Portuguese representatives, who were sent to the Cape. Both were released the next year, and Sousa returned to his own territory in May. He found that during his absence his personal empire had begun to disintegrate. While fighting to restore his authority the following year, he was badly wounded. Unable to walk, he was killed by a child.

SOUTH AFRICA, REPUBLIC OF (formerly Union of South Africa). Zimbabwe is separated from South Africa by a stretch of the **Limpopo River**. Historical connections between the two regions began deep in the past, when Zimbabwe served as a corridor for southward population movements into South Africa. After **Khoisan** peoples had passed through, Zimbabwe appears to have been the area in which the early south **Bantu-speaking** peoples broke into separate groups, giving rise to South Africa's **Sotho** and **Nguni** peoples and others.

The long period of mainly southward population movements was reversed in the early 19th century when South Africa's *Mfecane* wars sent powerful Nguni states north into the regions of present Zimbabwe and its neighbors. The Nguni were soon followed by an influx of South African **hunters, missionaries**, and traders. In the late 19th century, competition for regional dominance between the British empire and the newly formed **Afrikaner** republics made present **Botswana** and Zimbabwe the potential prizes of expansionism. One of the consequences of this competition was the formation of the **British South Africa Company**, which occupied the region of present Zimbabwe as a private operation in the 1800s.

When the administration of Southern Rhodesia, as it was then called, was firmly organized, it was modeled after that of the Cape Colony, in whose administration the first governor, **W. H. Milton**, had served. Southern Rhodesia adopted the Cape's **currency**, and after the **South African War** joined the South African Customs Union. Although the new colony was strongly tied to South Africa through the transportation and **communications** network, trade, civil services, settlers, and other links, its leaders rejected incorporation into the Union of South Africa when it was being formed in 1808–10. As the BSAC administration was about to end in the early 1920s, the issues of union with South Africa again arose. South African Prime Minister Jan Smuts, South Rhodesia's powerful mining interests, and its local **Unionist Movement** favored union, but most settlers wanted autonomy. The settlers voted for **Responsible Government** over union in a 1922 referendum.

Thereafter Southern Rhodesia's interests in expanding its external ties were directed toward **amalgamation** with Northern Rhodesia (now **Zambia**). Creation of the **Federation of Rhodesia and Nyasaland** in 1953 heralded a further major shift of the country's orientation from the south to the north. The country's African population generally opposed the federation, supporting it only to the extent that it helped to shift Southern Rhodesia away from the forms of racial oppression being developed in South Africa. Collapse of the federation in 1963 and the subsequent independence of Malawi and Zambia reversed Rhodesia's northward orientation, driving its white government back into an informal but strong alliance with South Africa. When the government of **Ian Smith** declared its independence (see **UDI**) in late 1965, it effectively declared its intention to continue building the country on South African lines.

Rhodesia's ties with South Africa extended into many different fields. The top military leaders of South Africa, Rhodesia, and Portugal conferred regularly as the prelude to an unofficial military alliance in the growing struggle against African liberation movements in southern Africa. In August 1967 South African troops began entering the country to help guard the Zambezi Valley against incursions by freedom fighters based in Zambia (see **ZANLA**). By 1970 South African troops accounted for about half—three to four thousand—of the government military forces deployed inside Rhodesia. South Africa claimed these troops were merely "paramilitary police," but they were clearly operating as combat soldiers. Under mounting international criticism, and in order to improve its own relations with black-ruled African nations, South Africa withdrew these troops by August 1975, but continued to assist the Smith regime with locally produced and imported weaponry.

The world's attempt to cripple Rhodesia with economic **sanctions** following the declaration of UDI virtually made the country into a South African colony. Even before UDI, South Africa ranked behind only Britain as a trading partner. In 1965 it supplied 23 percent of Rhodesia's imports and bought 9 percent of its exports. During the period of UDI, the two countries made a number of secret trade agreements, and if South Africa had not assisted the Smith government in sanctions busting, it is questionable whether Rhodesia could have held out against the **ZANU** and **ZAPU** liberation movements throughout the 1970s.

By the mid-1970s it was becoming apparent even to South Africa that Rhodesia's ability to survive much longer was doubtful. As a result of this growing awareness, the South African government decided to pursue a two-sided policy. On the surface, the South African government appeared to resign itself to accepting an African-ruled, independent Zimbabwe and began to call for an orderly transition to a "nonracial" government. To this end Prime Minister John Vorster participated in the **Victoria Falls Conference** and put increasing pressure on Smith to accept a settlement with African nationalist leaders. However, at the same time the South African government initiated a secret, two-headed policy of attempting to undermine, or "destabilize," the African-ruled nations of southern Africa and continued clandestinely to support Rhodesia (and eventually **Zimbabwe Rhodesia**). This policy of destabilization towards its north neighbors included the funding and military support for dissident groups in southwest Zambia and **Mozambique** (see **Mozambique National Resistance**), as well as the outright miliary invasion of Angola in 1975.

In 1980, with the independence of Zimbabwe, this later policy of destabilization was also directed against Zimbabwe. In a variety of ways, ranging from delaying of **railway** transit of Zimbabwe-bound imports, the use of sabotage and support for the MNR, to at least two South African Defense Force commando raids into the suburbs of Harare, South Africa continued throughout the 1980s to attempt to intimidate the government and meddle in the economy of Zimbabwe.

Despite these attempts at intimidation, Zimbabwe remained a strong critic of South Africa's minority white government and political supporter of that government's principle African opposition party, South Africa's African National Congress. Throughout the 1980s Zimbabwe continued to call for the imposition and maintaining of international sanctions against South Africa. Partly in response to those sanctions, by late 1989 the South African government, under the leadership of newly elected State President F. W. DeKlerk, began to end its policy of minority rule (known as apartheid). DeKlerk announced his commitment to political change and initiated the repeal of "petty apartheid" laws and released seven African nationalist leaders from prison. He then began direct talks with Nelson Mandela, the imprisoned leader of South Africa's ANC. In February 1990, Mandela was released from prison and restrictions on all African opposition parties were lifted. By February 1991, all discriminatory legislation had been repealed and the government, in conjunction with Mandela and the ANC, announced that open, all-race elections would be held in the near future. In elections of April 1994, Mandela was elected president of South Africa. Later that month, Zimbabwe established diplomatic relations with South Africa, officially ending years of political animosity between the two countries. In August of that year, President Mugabe made an official state visit to South Africa. During that visit he became the first African leader to address the newly elected all-race South African Parliament.

SOUTH AFRICAN GOLD FIELDS EXPLORATION COMPANY. Prospecting company formed as a subsidiary of the Natal Land and Colonization Company to seek **gold mining concessions** in **Matabeleland.** The company hired **Thomas Braines** to lead its first expedition. Baines enlisted the aid of **Henry Hartley** and **J. L. Lee,** and then obtained the support of the Ndebele regent **Mncumbathe** in mid-1869. This company competed for the rights to prospect in the **"Northern Goldfields"** with the **London and Limpopo Mining Company** which was supported by the missionary **T. M. Thomas** and the *induna* **Mbigo.** In July 1869 Baines led a party of prospectors to the Hartley Hills, which he named, but then all Europeans had to leave the country because of the Ndebele succession dispute. The following April Baines obtained a verbal concession to the Northern Goldfield from the new King **Lobengula.** Lobengula reconfirmed the "Baines Concession" in writing on August 29, 1871, but the company was meanwhile collapsing. After Baines's death the concession passed through several parties' hands until it was bought by the **British South Africa Company** around 1890. (See also **Tati Concession.**)

SOUTH AFRICAN REPUBLIC (19th century) see **TRANSVAAL**

SOUTH AFRICAN WAR (a.k.a. Boer War; Second Boer War; Anglo-Boer War) (Oct. 1899–May 1902). The largest military conflict ever fought in southern Africa, it was waged between **Afrikaners** of the **Transvaal** and Orange Free State Republics and the British Imperial Government. The war was the climax of British and Afrikaner competition for mastery of southern Africa. It was, in part, aggravated by tensions arising from the **British South Africa Company**'s efforts to block Afrikaner expansion north of the **Limpopo River** (see **Adendorff Trek**). By 1896 any hopes for a peaceful reconciliation of British and Afrikaner differences were shattered when **Cecil Rhodes** supported the abortive **Jameson Raid** on Paul Kruger's government. Although the Afrikaners eventually lost the war, they obtained a settlement that paved the way for their later political domination of South Africa.

Except for brief Afrikaner raids north of the Limpopo at the onset of hostilities, the South African War did not affect Southern Rhodesia directly. Its indirect impact was, however, great. During the first few months of the war Afrikaners besieged Kimberly, Mafeking, and other South African centers, effectively cutting off **railway** transport into Southern Rhodesia and driving up prices of the colony's imported goods. British settlers there enthusiastically supported the war. It is estimated that about 1,700 men—from a total white population of only 11,000—saw military service in South Africa. The interruption of supplies and the severe drain on settler manpower closed down the colony's mines and halted construction of the railways. Existing railway lines in the colony were clogged with British troops and supplies brought in through **Beira**. The colony's limited manufacturing capacity contributed to British armament production, and the BSAC administration was once again nearly broken by increased wartime expenses.

The colony's African population was not militarily involved in the war, but it too suffered from higher prices and from the temporary halt in labor migration to South Africa. With the exception of **Mapondera**, Africans did not take advantage of the general disruption to rebel.

After the war ended Southern Rhodesia recovered fairly quickly. It had escaped the devastation experienced within South Africa, and it received a new influx of Europeans from the south for this reason. Railway construction, especially, was accelerated. (See also **Rhodesia Field Force; Rhodesia Regiment; BSAP; Southern Rhodesian Volunteers.**)

"SOUTHERN AFRICA." Application of this geographical term has varied. Some authorities apply it to the great bulge of the continent south of the equator—an area roughly congruent with the distribution of **Bantu**-speaking peoples. More commonly the term is restricted to the area south of the **Zambezi River**. That usage is employed in this dictionary. It should be noted that "southern Africa" and **"central Africa"** overlap in Zimbabwe.

SOUTHERN AFRICAN DEVELOPMENT COORDINATION CONFERENCE (SADCC). Regional economic organization begun in April 1980 and headquartered in **Harare**. Its members—Angola, **Botswana**, Lesotho, Malawi, **Mozambique**, Swaziland, Tanzania, **Zambia**, and Zimbabwe—joined together with the primary goal of reducing their overall economic dependence on **South Africa**. Member countries believe this can be accomplished only through coordinated regional development planning. By coordinating development projects, member states reduce duplication of effort, avoid conflicts, and maximize their use of limited resources. SADCC was also seen as a central agency to facilitate and control foreign economic participation and assistance in the region. In theory, each member state has primary responsibility for at least one regional development program, with that state's minister acting as head of that SADCC program. Zimbabwe is charged with developing programs aimed at securing the region's food supplies.

By the mid-1980s SADCC members had concentrated their efforts on developing regional programs to improve transport, telecommunications, energy, and regional trade. SADCC members created the Beira Corridor Authority to oversee the redevelopment of Beira harbor, as well as the **railway** and road networks that link Beira to SADCC members through Zimbabwe. It has also coordinated the development of a regional telecommunications system in which all member states are linked by satellite, connected electricity grids, and coordinated postal services. These programs all reduced dependence on South Africa in those areas.

However, by 1987 SADCC had not developed as many regional programs as its members had initially projected. Most observers agree that SADCC's slow progress has been the result of a combination of a strong response by the South African government—including the holding up of transit goods, commando raids on Beira, and support for the **Mozambique National Resistance**—and minimal financial support from major western states. In addition, because SADCC was established as a decentralized, nonbureaucratic organization, coordinating policy between its nine members has proved more difficult than expected. While it has the power to set policy and select individual projects, the SADCC secretariat has found continued emphasis on national priorities by member states a hindrance to regional planning.

"SOUTHERN RHODESIA." Name given to the country in 1897 to differentiate it from Northern Rhodesia. The white government changed the name to **"Rhodesia"** in 1964 when Northern Rhodesia became independent as **Zambia**, but Britain, the United Nations, and other governments never officially recognized this change.

SOUTHERN RHODESIAN AFRICAN NATIONAL CONGRESS see **AFRICAN NATIONAL CONGRESS.**

SOUTHERN RHODESIAN MISSIONARY CONFERENCE (SRMC). Interdenominational body formed in 1906 to coordinate the work of **missions** and to represent their interests before the government. Initially founded as a Protestant organization, by the 1920s, the SRMC represented all the major missions in the country, including those of the Roman Catholics. By this time the SRMC was one of the most powerful lobbying bodies in the country. The government regarded it as a valid representative of African interests, and government officials regularly attended the SRMC's biennial meetings. Under the leadership of **John White**, SRMC chairman from 1924 to 1928, the SRMC particularly championed the improvement of African **education**, stimulating the government to form the Department of Native Education in 1927. A subordinate body comprising African clerics, the Native Christian Conference, was formed in 1926. This body's resolutions were communicated to the government through the SRMC, making it the only African organization to have anything like an official voice in the government.

After reaching its peak influence in the early 1930s, the SRMC swiftly declined as a lobbying body. The missionaries lost **H. U. Moffat** and other allies in the government, and the balance of influence in African affairs passed back to the native Affairs Department, which favored preservation of traditional African life. Interdenominational squabbles disrupted the SRMC, and the Roman Catholics and other denominations began dropping out.

SOUTHERN RHODESIAN VOLUNTEERS (SRV). Reserve territorial military force, formed in 1898 out of the heterogeneous white volunteer forces that had served in the **Revolts of 1896-97.** The SRV provided the nucleus of the **Rhodesia Regiments** formed during the **South African War** and the First World War, and it has been described as the nucleus of the modern army.

SPRUIT. Small stream, or dry watercourse; from the **Afrikaans** word for "sprout" or "stream."

"SQUATTERS." Term popularized in the late 1990s to identify persons participating in the illegal occupation of white-owned commercial farms. The great majority of squatters identified themselves as **ZANLA** war veterans. The head of a Zimbabwe war veterans' association claimed that its members were tired of waiting for the government to legally acquire and redistribute white-owned lands and had decided to occupy those lands in defiance of the law. However, white farmers' groups, opposition political leaders, and several foreign governments criticized both President **Robert Mugabe** and **ZANU-PF** for encouraging, if not organizing, the farm occupations as a way to divert the general public's attention away from government corruption. This view gained greater support when Mugabe refused to condemn the squatters' actions.

STANLEY, HERBERT JAMES (July 25, 1872–June 5, 1955). Third governor of Southern Rhodesia (1935–42). A career British civil servant, Stanley was resident commissioner in Northern and Southern Rhodesia (1915–18) and governor of Northern Rhodesia (1924–27) before replacing **C. H. Rodwell** as governor of Southern Rhodesia in 1935. He was strongly committed to the idea of central African **amalgamation** and is credited with helping to formulate **Godfrey Huggins**'s ideas on this goal. He was succeeded by **Evelyn Baring** in 1942.

STILLBAY CULTURE. Stone Age culture of the middle period; also known as **Bambata** culture within Zimbabwe. It is characterized by pressure-flaked stone implements and is associated with the period of **"Rhodesian Man."**

STONE AGE. Modern man (*Homo sapiens*) has occupied the country for at least 100,000 years, and his hominid antecedents there go back perhaps a further million years. The country is rich in Stone Age sites of early man, and these have been investigated more intensively than in most tropical African countries. The country's Stone Age culture sequence corresponds with that developed for the rest of eastern and southern Africa. Authorities generally divide the Stone Age into Early, Middle, and Late periods, with two intermediate periods, each representing a major shift in tool-making techniques. Many "cultures" or "industries," are assigned to each period. The terminology for these is complex, changing constantly as archaeologists make new finds and reclassify old ones. Dates are based upon carbon-14 and other tests, but it should be understood that different cultures often overlapped in both time and space.

The *Early Stone Age* (ESA) extended from the very earliest pebble and flaked-stone tool users of the pre-*Homo sapiens* era to the first fire users in about 40,000 or 30,000 B.C. The last thirty millennia of the ESA are also known as the First Intermediate Stone Age.

The *Middle Stone Age* (MSA) heralded the mastery of fire and refinements in pressure-flaked stone implements. The MSA ended in roughly 9000 B.C., with the previous ten millennia also known as the Second Intermediate Stone Age. The most important local MSA industries are **Stillbay** and **Magosian**.

The *Late Stone Age* (LSA) extended from the end of the MSA into the first millennium A.D., when it was displaced by intrusive **Iron Age** cultures. There was no "Bronze Age." The LSA saw the refinement of small stone implements, or microliths, bored stones, polished axes, and hollow scrapers. It is believed that the bow and arrow were introduced early in the LSA. The dominant LSA industry within present Zimbabwe is generally known as **Wilton**, the culture associated with the country's prolific **rock paintings**. **Khoisan** peoples are generally regarded as the modern descendants of LSA peoples. Isolated pockets of **San** have maintained an advanced from of LSA culture into modern times.

STONE-LINED PITS (a.k.a. pit structure; "slave pits"; etc.). General term for a class of **ruins** characteristic of the **Eastern Highlands,** particularly within the **Inyanga Ruins** complex, where thousands of such structures have been found. Remarkably uniform in their dimensions, the pits are typically circular, with stone-lined floors about 6m in diameter, and stone walls 2 to 3m in height. They are partly dug into hillsides, with narrow entrances on their upper sides, and small drain holes on their lower sides. They are usually surrounded by platforms that once supported dwelling structures. Most pit sites were abandoned by the 19th century. Many odd theories have since been advanced to account for their functions. It is said, for example, that **Cecil Rhodes** coined the term "slave pits" on the assumption that the pits were used to imprison slave laborers. The most widely accepted theory—supported by local traditions—holds that the pits were used to house small livestock, probably pigs and goats.

STONE RUINS see **RUINS; IRON AGE**; and names of individual sites.

STRIP ROADS. Single-lane roads comprising parallel strips of asphalt pavement. Government engineers invented the strip-road technique in 1930 as a means of building durable all-weather **roads** cheaply. During the world Depression a major strip-road building program was begun, partly to provide employment for European workers. The program ended in 1945, by which time about 3,000 km of strip roads crisscrossed the country. Thereafter only full-width paved roads were built.

SUGAR. Commercial production of this crop began at the **Triangle Estate** in the southeastern low veld during the 1920s. Successful irrigation schemes led to greatly increased production during the mid-1950s, when the **Hippo Valley Estate** was started nearby. Steady growth in production continued for the next decade, but the industry was hit hard by post-UDI **sanctions**. Production began to increase again in the late 1970s and since 1980 has rapidly expanded. In 1981 a third major sugar-producing estate, Mkwasine, delivered 100,000 tons of cane to the Hippo Valley Estates for processing. Mkwasine is the result of a government settlement scheme and was designed to accommodate 196 smallholders on units of 10 hectares each.

In 1991 nearly 3 percent of the country's total exports were from raw and refined sugar. In addition to the production of sugar for export, Zimbabwe also produces several sugar products, including molasses, which is used as a supplement in **cattle** feed, and cane spirits, used in the distilling of gin, vodka, and brandy. However, the most important by-product produced is ethanol, which is mixed with gasoline and has helped decrease Zimbabwe's reliance on external sources of fuel. Ethanol is produced at a Triangle Estates' plant which has been operational since 1980. (See **Sabi-Limpopo Authority; Agriculture.**)

SUMMERS, ROGER F. H. (b. 1907). British-born archaeologist. Summers came to the country in 1947 to serve as Keeper of Antiquities in the National Museum of **Bulawayo.** He also served on the **Historical Monuments Commission** from 1950 to 1967 (as chairman, 1954-59). During the 1950s he conducted major archaeological digs at **Inyanga, Zimbabwe, Dhlo Dhlo** and other **Iron Age** sites. He has published extensively on the Iron Age sequence, and has written on **Ndebele history**, stressing a militaristic interpretation of the Ndebele state. In 1970 he left the National Museum for the South African Museum in Cape Town. (See **Bibliography.**)

SUNDAY MAIL. Harare-based affiliate of the daily *Herald.* It was founded as the *Weekly Review* and later renamed *Sunday Mail* when it was acquired by the **Argus Group** newspapers in the mid-1930s. In January 1981 the government of Zimbabwe bought the Argus Group's holding in the Rhodesian Printing and Publishing Company and established the **Mass Media Trust,** effectively bringing the *Sunday Mail* and other major newspapers under government ownership.

SVIKIRO (variant: *tswikiro*). Mediums possessed by Shona spirits, such as the *Mhondoro.* Not to be confused with the spirits themselves. (See **Religion—Shona.**)

SVOSVE (variants: Soswe; Swoswe). Dynastic title of the rulers of an **Mbire** chiefdom of the **Zezuru** cluster of **Shona.** The chiefdom was established around the early 18th century in the southeastern part of the present **Marondera** and **Wedza** districts. The Mbire suffered greatly during the 1830s, when the region was occupied by **Zwangendaba's Ngoni.** Sometime later Svosve Gusha was killed during a **Gaza** raid. In 1896–97 Svosve Chikosha participated in the **revolt** against the British. He was captured by the British and died soon afterwards. Since then the Svosves have been government chiefs, and the Mbire have lived mostly in the Wedza **Communal Lands.**

SW-. Many **Chishona** words spelled with *sw-* should properly have *sv-*, which consonant cluster is an unvoiced alveolar labialized sibilant fricative.

SWAZI (Amaswazi). The Swazi constitute one of the major branches of **Nguni-speaking peoples** in southern Africa. The modern country of Swaziland, which lies about 360 km south of Zimbabwe, derives from the Swazi kingdom, which arose in the early 19th century, at the same time the neighboring Zulu kingdom was developing. When the *Mfecane* wars affected Swaziland, many Swazi clans and individuals joined the various Nguni bands that migrated north. There were so many Swazi among the **Ngoni** that the name "Swazi" has frequently been used as a synonym for "Ngoni" in central Africa. Other Swazi were absorbed by the **Ndebele,** but still retained their Swazi identity. The Ngoni of **Nyamazana**, who joined the Ndebele around 1840, are perhaps the best known "Swazi" in Zimbabwean history.

SWINA (variant: Svina; pl., Amaswina, or Maswina). Alternative name for the **Shona**, usually regarded as derogatory. It is often suggested that the **Ndebele** were the first to call the Shona "Swina," but the word itself appears to derive from **Chishona** *svina* (or *tsvina*) for "dirt."

SWINBURNE, JOHN (1831–July 15, 1914). First chairman of the **London and Limpopo Mining Company**. Between 1868 and 1870, Swinburne led an expedition to **Matabeleland** to seek a **gold**-mining **concession.**

SYKES, WILLIAM (March 13, 1820–July 22, 1887). English agent of the **London Missionary Society**. Together with **J. S. Moffat** and **T. M. Thomas**, Sykes opened the first permanent mission station in the country at **Inyati** in 1860, where he remained until his death. In nearly 27 years of proselytizing, he failed to obtain a single **Ndebele** convert.

T

TABA. Variant of Sindebele word *intaba*, for "hill"; usually rendered *ntaba* in place names.

TAIT, W. E. CAMPBELL (Aug. 12, 1886–July 17, 1946). Fifth **governor** of Southern Rhodesia (1945–46). Career naval officer, Tait resigned from his post as commander-in-chief of British southern Atlantic forces at Simonstown, South Africa, to become governor of Southern Rhodesia in 1945. He died in office and was succeeded by **J. N. Kennedy**.

TAKAWIRA, LEOPOLD (c. 1916–June 15, 1970). Nationalist leader. Born at **Chirumanzu** and educated at **Kutama** and in Natal, Takawira became a government schoolmaster in **Highfield** in the late 1930s. By the early 1950s he was a leader member of the African Teachers' Association. Attracted by the ideals of the federal **"partnership"** policy, he left teaching to join the **Capricorn Africa Society**, in which he became an executive officer. He became disillusioned with "partnership" and turned to nationalist politics, joining the new **African National Congress** and then helping to found the **National Democratic Party** in the late 1950s. In September 1960 he was acting president of the NDP after **Michael Mawema** was forced to resign, but lost this post to **Joshua Nkomo** in a party election. He then was appointed external representative in London. In 1961 he sent a cable back home denouncing the 1961 constitutional conference, for which Nkomo flew to London to reprimand him. Following the banning of the NDP, **ZAPU** was formed and Takawira was appointed secretary for external affairs. He soon broke with Nkomo and joined **Ndabaningi Sithole** in **ZANU**, becoming the party's first vice-president. He was arrested in late 1964 and spent the remainder of his life in prison. Suffering from diabetes and denied medical attention by officials of the Smith government, he collapsed and went into a coma. Following a postmortem, a court inquiry ruled that he had died as a result of negligence. He was first buried at his home area in Chirumanzu, then reburied at **Heroes' Acre** on August 11, 1982.

"TAKING THE GAP." Expression popularized in the late 1970s and early 1980s to refer to Europeans who emigrated to avoid living in an independent Zimbabwe under African majority rule.

TALOWTA (Batalowta; variant: Talaota). Small branch of **Sotho-speaking people** who apparently broke away from the **Ngwato** in the early 19th century, when they settled in the region just west of the **Matopo Hills** in southwestern Zimbabwe. After the arrival of the **Ndebele** in the country, a Talowta chief named **Mahuku** submitted to **Mzilikazi**'s rule.

TANGWENA, REKAYI (c. 1910–June 10, 1984). Born in the Gaeresi area of **Nyanga,** Tangwena had no formal education. He first went to work in a **Penhalonga** mine when he was nine years old. He later worked as a waiter in both **Bulawayo** and **Harare** before becoming a **railway** engineer's assistant. In 1963 he returned to his home permanently. Although never officially recognized by the Smith government, he became chief of the Tangwena people in the late 1960s. He gained international recognition in the early 1970s through his leadership efforts to keep the lands his people were living on from being taken over by the government (see **Tangwena Land Dispute**). In 1972, when tractors and bulldozers, supported by government troops, were sent to demolish his villages, he escaped to the bush and mountainous area of Nyanga and continued to resist. In 1975, he helped **Robert Mugabe** and **Edgar Tekere** cross the border into **Mozambique**. Under his leadership, the Tangwena people also provided guides and trackers, as well as shelter, clothing, and general assistance to refugees and **ZANLA** forces in the Nyanga region for the remainder of the armed struggle. In March 1980 he became a senator in the first independent **Parliament** of Zimbabwe. After he died in June 1984, be was buried at **Heroes' Acre** outside Harare.

TANGWENA LAND DISPUTE. The Tangwena people are a small branch of the **Shona** who have lived in what is now the border region of the **Inyanga Mountains** for at least eight generations. In 1902, their chief, Dzeka Chigumira (d. 1928), got government permission to move about 70 Tangwena families to the Southern Rhodesian side of the border in order to avoid the conflict between Makombe and the **Portuguese** in **Mozambique.** Unbeknownst to the Tangwena, their ancestral land was sold to a private company by the **BSAC** in 1905, and it was later declared European land by the 1930 **Land Apportionment Act.** Most Tangwena land was later sold to the Gaeresi Ranch Company (centered at 18°48'S, 32°52'E), which left them alone until the **Rhodesian Front** came to power. Under government pressure the Ranch Company tried to evict the Tangwena in 1963. This effort began a decade-long struggle between the government and the Tangwena, who steadfastly refused to move to the nearby Holdenby Tribal Trust land (18°25'S, 32°55'S). The government lost a legal battle in the courts with the Tangwena in 1968 and then issued a special proclamation in order to evict them legally. From 1969 to 1972 the government attracted international indignation by burning and bull-dozing Tangwena homes and impounding their **cattle** in efforts to drive them out of Gaeresi Ranch. Under their new and officially unrecognized chief, **Rekayi Tangwena**, the son of Dzeka, the Tangwena persistently resisted, while enduring many sacrifices and hardships.

TATI CONCESSION. District of 5,355 sq km in eastern **Botswana** that surrounds the Tati River and contains **Francistown.** During the 19th century the **Ndebele** regarded the area as part of their domain, but this claim was disputed by the **Ngwato.** European interest in the region grew rapidly after **gold** was discovered there in 1866. The first serious effort to mine in the area was made by the **London and Limpopo Mining Company**, which obtained an Ndebele **concession** in 1870. Work was soon abandoned, however. In 1880, **S. H. Edwards** and several other men formed a new syndicate, the Northern Light Gold and Exploring Company, which obtained a fresh Ndebele concession in return for an annual rent. Over the next seven years King **Lobengula** reconfirmed and elaborated on this company's exclusive mining rights at Tati. In 1888 the company was effectively transformed into the Tati Concession Mining and Exploration Company, Ltd., in which **Alfred Beit** was a major shareholder, and Lobengula granted it further monopolies over grazing, timber, and settlement. Later that year the Tati Concession was specifically excluded from the **Rudd Concession** granted to **Cecil Rhodes'** group. In 1892 British High Commissioner Henry Loch brought the area under the administration of the new **Bechuanaland Protectorate**, but the British government later recognized the company's ownership of the land.

When Bechuanaland was about to become independent as **Botswana** during the 1960s, white settlers in the Tati district petitioned either to become independent or to be affiliated with South Africa or Rhodesia, but the district's land was eventually incorporated into Botswana.

TAVARA (variant: Tawara). **Shona** group occupying the area between northern **Mukumbura District** and the **Zambezi River,** mostly within **Mozambique**. The Tavara language, or Chitavara, is usually classified as a subdialect of **Korekore**, but Tavara culture is so distinct from that of the Korekore that the Tavara are often described as a separate ethnic group.

TAWANA (Batawana). Branch of western **Sotho-** or **Tswana-speaking** people in central **Botswana**. During the 19th century the **Ndebele** launched several long-distance raids against the Tawana. The April 1885 raid proved a major disaster for the Ndebele, and has often been cited as evidence of their military decline in the late 19th century.

TAWSE-JOLLIE, ETHEL MAUDE (nee Cookson) (March 8, 1878–Sept. 21, 1950). Politician. Born in England, Ethel Cookson married **A. R. Colquhoun** in 1900 and visited Southern Rhodesia with him in 1904. After his death 10 years later, she returned to the colony and soon married John Tawse-Jollie, a local farmer. She quickly got involved in politics as a leader in the **Responsible Government** movement and as an advocate of women's suffrage (see **Women's Franchise Ordinance**). In 1920 she was elected to the **Legislative Council**. After Responsible Government was attained, she represented **Umtali** in the **Legislative Assembly** (1923–27), thereby becoming the first female parliamentarian in the British Empire. A strong supporter of the empire, she opposed union with South Africa and the local movement to make **Afrikaans** a second official language. She presented these views and an account of the Responsible Government movement in her book, *The Real Rhodesia* (1924). During the Second World War she served as the country's women's employment officer.

TEA. Zimbabwe is self-sufficient in tea production, which began in the 1920s. Approximately 10,000 tons a year are produced in the eastern districts to the north and south of **Mutare.** The country consumes about 40 percent of the total crop, with the remainder being exported to Europe. Since the 1980s the tea industry has been undermined by the general weakness of the international tea market. The country has nine tea-processing factories, including Ratelskoek, one of the largest such factories in Africa.

TEKERE, EDGAR ZAGANAI (b. April 1, 1937). Born near **Rusape,** Tekere was the second son of a teacher who later became an Anglican priest. He was educated at various primary schools in the eastern districts region, and St. Augustine's secondary school near Mutare. During the time he was at St. Augustine's, he joined the **Youth League.** In 1958, after graduating, he moved to Salisbury and worked for a short time in a religious bookstore. He also continued his political activities by joining the old **African National Congress,** and in early 1959 was briefly detained for his activities. In January 1960, he joined the **National Democratic Party** and following its banning in December, joined the newly constituted **ZAPU** and was elected secretary of the Salisbury District council. Following the split of the ZAPU leadership in 1963, Tekere joined **ZANU,** and by May 1964 had been appointed deputy secretary for Youth and Culture. He was detained in December of that year and remained in detention for the next ten years.

Tekere was released in December 1974 to enable him to travel to Lusaka, **Zambia,** as part of the ZANU delegation for talks designed to unite the different nationalist parties under the **African National Council.** Upon returning to the country, he was assigned the **Midlands** and southern provinces regions in which to recruit new volunteers to ZANU and **ZANLA.** In March 1975, ZANU's central committee decided to send Tekere with **Robert Mugabe** to **Mozambique** in order to provide political leadership to their external forces. In 1980, he won election from **Manicaland Province** to **Parliament** and was appointed minister of manpower training and development. He was considered by many observers to be a member of the more radical wing of ZANU, in that he argued there was little, if any, room for whites in an independent Zimbabwe.

On August 6, 1980, he was arrested and detained after being accused of the murder of a white farm manager near **Harare.** Although acquitted in December, he was dropped from the cabinet in January 1981, and in August lost his post as secretary general of ZANU after criticizing the party leadership for losing touch with the country's black majority and for contributing to the decay of the social and economic goals of the liberation struggle. Despite his criticisms of Mugabe and ZANU he remained a member of the party and was even elected ZANU (PF) chairman of Manicaland Province in 1983, a post which automatically gave him membership in the Central Committee. However, following a number of disagreements with Mugabe, he was removed from that post in May 1987. On October 21, 1988 he was expelled from the party on the grounds that he had breached party discipline.

On April 30, 1989, Tekere launched the Zimbabwe Unity Movement **(ZUM)** as an opposition party to ZANU. He declared that this party was open to all racial and ethnic groups in the country and was formed to oppose Mugabe's call for a one-party state. In the **elections** of 1990, he ran for the presidency against Mugabe, but was soundly defeated, gaining only 413,840 votes out of nearly 2.1 million. In June 1991, the executive leaders of ZUM announced that Tekere had been "retired" from the party after he refused to agree to a new party constitution and leadership structure. Tekere resisted his "retirement," and other members broke away from ZUM and formed the **Democratic Party of Zimbabwe.** He then maintained control of ZUM and continued to be perhaps the most vocal critic of President Mugabe, the government, and ZANU in the early 1990s.

TELEGRAPHS. In June 1889 the **BSAC** built the country's first telegraph line from Mafeking, South Africa, to **Tati.** The line was extended to **Masvingo** in October 1891, and to **Harare** in 1892. Shortly after the 1893 **Ndebele War,** the South African connection reached **Bulawayo,** from which it too was extended to Harare. In 1895 Harare was connected with **Beira,** through **Mutare.** The **South African War** interrupted communications with the south, requiring that messages be conveyed by sea from Beira. After the war most of the rest of the country was gradually brought into the telegraphic network. (See **Transport and Communications; Postal System.**)

TELEPHONES. During the 1896 **Ndebele Revolt,** jerry-built telephones were introduced at **Bulawayo** in order to connect the British military command with outlying forts. A formal telephone exchange was first established in present-day **Harare** in 1898, with other major urban centers soon following. By 1930 there were 4,200 telephone sets in operation throughout the country. This number increased to 21,000 in 1950, and to about 56,000 in 1975, by which time fully automatic equipment linked the major urban centers. In 1984, as a part of a **SADCC** sponsored project, Zimbabwe became part of a regional satellite-dish telephone system, greatly improving its telephone connections to other southern African urban centers, as well as to Europe.

TELEVISION see **ZIMBABWE BROADCASTING CORPORATION**

TENKELA (a.k.a. Salugazana; Wamponga) (fl.1870s–1900s). Either a *Mhondoro* or a **Mwari** cult figure, Tenkela worked closely with Mkwati during the 1896-97 **Revolts**. After Mkwati's death in **Mashonaland** in September or October 1897, Tenkela withdrew into the northern part of the country, where she was captured by the British the next year. She was taken to **Bulawayo** and tried for insurrection but was freed because of insufficient evidence.

TETE. Mozambique town on the south bank of the **Zambezi River** (at 16°11′S, 33°34′E). Originally a **Muslim** trading **fair**, Tete was occupied by the **Portuguese** in the 1530s. It continued to serve as an important inland base for coastal trade with **Mashonaland**, and it developed into the largest inland Portuguese town. The name "Tete" was later also given to the Mozambican province between Zimbabwe and Malawi.

THABA. Variant of **Sindebele** *intaba* for "hill"; usually rendered *ntaba* in place names.

THOMAS, THOMAS MORGAN (March 13, 1828–Jan. 8, 1884). Pioneer missionary. A Welshman, Thomas came to **Matabeleland** with the first **London Missionary Society** party in 1859. He soon mastered the **Sindebele** language and became one of King **Mzilikazi's** European confidants. Thomas's fellow missionaries resented his intimacy with the **Ndebele** and his trading activities, and they quibbled with him over spelling rules for Sindebele, into which they were translating religious texts. After Mzilikazi's death in 1868, Thomas meddled in the Ndebele succession dispute (see **Nkulumane**) and attempted to control European miners seeking **concessions.** His colleagues charged him with improper political and commercial conduct, so he was recalled to England and expelled from the LMS. While in Britain Thomas hastily wrote Welsh and English versions of a long book, *Eleven Years in Central South Africa.* This book proved a small popular success, particularly in Wales, where Thomas also collected contributions to start a new mission. The book, despite many flaws, still stands as the single most valuable description of Ndebele life in the mid-19th century.

In 1875 Thomas returned to Matabeleland as an independent missionary, founding a new station at Shiloh. There he later baptized the first handful of Ndebele converts to Christianity (see **Sykes, William**).

THOMPSON, FRANCIS ROBERT (a.k.a. "Matabele Thompson") (1857– May 5, 1927). South African concessionaire. While working as an African labor organizer at the Kimberley diamond mines, Thompson met **Cecil Rhodes**. Because of his presumed knowledge of Africans and their languages, he was asked to accompany **C. H. Rudd** to **Bulawayo** in 1888. He participated in the negotiations leading to the **Rudd Concession** and then remained in the country briefly after Rudd had left. Fearful for his personal safety, he suddenly bolted from the country, thereby increasing **Ndebele** anxieties about the concession. He later served in the Cape Parliament (1895–1903) and lived briefly in Southern Rhodesia. His daughter published his "autobiography" posthumously.

THOMSON, JOHN BODEN (1841–Sept. 1878). Scottish **London Missionary Society** agent. Thomson founded the **Hope Fountain** Mission near **Bulawayo** in the early 1870s.

THONGA. Variant of Tsonga. See **HLENGWE**.

"TIGER TALKS" (1966). About five months after **UDI**, British officials began visiting Salisbury to discuss a reopening of formal constitutional negotiations. On December 2–4, 1966, Prime Minister **Ian Smith** and British Prime Minister Harold Wilson negotiated an agreement aboard the British cruiser *HMS Tiger* just off Gibraltar. Their agreement called for a temporary suspension of Rhodesian independence while the 1961 **Constitution** was modified to conform to Britain's **"Five Principles."** Although Wilson was widely criticized for having virtually conceded independence to Smith's government, his own cabinet quickly approved his agreement with Smith. Smith's cabinet, however, rejected the plan on December 5, citing the dangers posed by allowing reestablishment of a British presence in the country, and what they regarded as an offensive call to return to "legality." Wilson then immediately called upon the UN to impose mandatory economic **sanctions** against the country. The next official round of negotiations was called the **"Fearless Talks."**

TILCOR see **TRIBAL TRUST LAND DEVELOPMENT CORPORATION**

TIME. The country is bisected by its standard meridian at 30° east longitude. Along with the rest of southern Africa, it lies entirely within a time zone two hours ahead of Greenwich Mean Time and seven hours ahead of Eastern Standard Time in the United States.

TIN. This metal has been found at sites scattered throughout the country. Alluvial tin occurs, but the metal is extracted mostly from cassiterite (SnO_2), the most common tin ore. There is no direct archaeological evidence of pre-20th-century tin-mining in the country, but bronze objects containing 8–12 percent tin have been found at **Khami, Zimbabwe,** and elsewhere. It is possible that such bronze was made from local **copper** and tin imported from the **Transvaal,** where old workings have been found. Modern production of tin began in 1908 at mines mainly in eastern **Mashonaland.** Production increased greatly after 1936, when a major mine was started at **Kamativi,** near **Hwange.** Since the mid-1950s the country has been self-sufficient in tin production (see **Minerals/mining.**)

TOBACCO. The date of tobacco's introduction to the country is uncertain, but it appears to have been introduced by early **Portuguese**, since many

Chishona terms for tobacco are clearly borrowed from Portuguese. By at least the 19th century the Shona themselves were growing fine grades of tobacco in **Mashonaland**. Commercial production of the crop by European settlers began at **Mutare** in the 1890s. Production developed steadily over the next three decades, rising rapidly only in the late 1920s. However, the sudden spurt in production of 1927 and 1928 glutted the market, depressing prices and producing a slump. Production again rose quickly during the Second World War, when British dollar shortages turned British markets away from American sources of tobacco. By 1945 tobacco had become the country's top foreign-exchange earning export. Between 1945 and 1956 production tripled in quantity and quadrupled in value. Further expansion of export markets, improved strains of Virginia flue-cured leaf, and careful government regulation of the industry lead to more dramatic production increases over the next decade. By 1965 the country was producing nearly 112 million kg of tobacco annually, accounting for nearly half the value of the country's total agricultural production. The country then ranked as the world's second leading producer of tobacco, after the United States, and it supplied more than a quarter of the world trade in Virginia flue-cured leaf.

Post-UDI **sanctions** dealt the industry a heavy blow, with both production and the total number of growers decreasing. Compared to many other primary export goods, tobacco was easy to identify, making the enforcement of sanctions relatively efficient. Production thus fell off rapidly after 1965, with the government imposing limits of just over half the pre-UDI levels by 1968. Public tobacco auctions were terminated and export sales were conducted through more clandestine methods in attempts to break sanctions. By 1972 the country's growers began to expand the total acreage under tobacco production, but with the intensification of the war in the mid-1970s, production again fell.

With independence in 1980, tobacco production for an international market rapidly increased, with the 1982 crop greatly surpassing expected production levels and values. In both 1984 and 1985 record crops were produced, and from 1984 to 1986 record amounts of foreign exchange were earned by the industry as a result of increased production. Production continued to increase thereafter, and in 1992 a new record of 200 million kg was reached. That year's crop earned over £1.6 billion in foreign exchange, making tobacco the country's main export.

Three types of tobacco have traditionally been grown in Zimbabwe: Virginia flue-cured, Burley, and Turkish. Virginia flue-cured has always been the most important in acreage and export value, and has been grown on large-scale commercial farms, thereby restricting it to settler farmers. Since 1980, the government has encouraged the production of Virginia flue-cured tobacco by African smallholders and peasants in the **Communal Lands**. Most production is in the modern **Mashonaland provinces**, where soil and climatic conditions are ideal.

TODD, REGINALD STEPHEN GARFIELD (b. July 13, 1908). Fifth **prime minister** of Southern Rhodesia (1953–58). Born in New Zealand, Todd came to the country in 1934 and worked as a missionary at Dadaya Mission, c.15 km northwest of **Zvishavane**, until 1946. At that time he gave up mission work for politics and was elected to the **Legislative**

Assembly on the **United Party** ticket. When **Godfrey Huggins** assumed leadership of the new **federation** government in 1953, Todd replaced him as territorial premier. During his administration he helped to promote African **education** and African participation in electoral politics but also supported forceful measures to break up labor strikes. His most notably liberal action was appointment of **Robert Tredgold** as head of a commission to investigate widening the franchise in 1956.

In January 1958 Todd's cabinet resigned to protest his leadership. Instead of stepping down, he bucked tradition by attempting to form a new government, but was voted out of office by a special party congress in February. His liberal image and support of enfranchising more Africans are generally cited as the reasons for his ouster.

After his dismissal as prime minister, Todd briefly served in the cabinet of his successor, **Edgar Whitehead**. He broke with Whitehead in order to contest the general election of June 1958 as the head of the reconstituted United Rhodesian Party. Following the complete defeat of this party at the polls, he formed the short-lived **Central African Party**.

During the 1960s Todd became increasingly outspoken against the **Rhodesian Front** government of **Ian Smith**. In 1965-66 Smith had him restricted to his farm near Zvishavane. When the **Pearce Commission** arrived in early 1972, Todd, along with his daughter Judith Todd, strongly protested the proposed Anglo-Rhodesian settlement. They both were imprisoned, attracting considerable international attention. Released from prison after six weeks, he was placed under a strict detention order at this farm until May 1976. At the **Geneva Conference**, Todd served as a consultant to **Joshua Nkomo**, and in 1977 he toured the United States in an effort to persuade the U.S. government to strengthen its economic **sanctions** against Rhodesia.

At independence in 1980, President **Canaan Banana**, acting on the recommendation of Prime Minister **Robert Mugabe**, appointed Todd to a seat in the **Senate**. He served in that position until 1985 when, citing his age, he retired from active politics. In 1986, at the suggestion of the New Zealand government, Todd was knighted by Queen Elizabeth II of Great Britain.

TOGWA see **TORWA**

TOHWECHIPI (variant: Towechipi; a.k.a. Chibambamu, variant: Sibambamu)(d. c. 1873). **Changamire** ruler and leader of resistance against **Ndebele**. Tohwechipi was apparently installed as Changamire at **Dhlo Dhlo** after his father, **Changamire Chrisamhuru**, was killed by **Ngoni** invaders in the early 1830s. When **Mzilikazi's** Ndebele arrived in present **Matabeleland** in the late 1830s, Tohwechipi and many other **Rozvi** people fled east. Although a split had previously developed within the Changamire dynasty, Tohwechipi was recognized as *mambo,* or ruler, by the rival Mutinhima faction during the 1850s. By then he was living near the **Zimbabwe Ruins** and was leading Rozvi raids against Ndebele cattle posts. Around the early 1850s Tohwechipi used firearms to defeat the Ndebele in a battle, earning himself the onomatopoeic nickname "Chibambamu," after the sound of gunfire. Despite his use of firearms, Tohwechipi was soon driven even farther east by the Ndebele. In late 1866 the Ndebele captured him in the Mavange Hills of the upper **Sabi** Valley.

He was taken before Mzilikazi, but was soon released. Described as "old" in 1866, he died around 1873. His title of *mambo* passed to a son of his former rival, Mutinhima, but the Changamire dynasty was finished as a significant political entity.

TOKWE RIVER. Rises on the **Central Plateau** near Lalapanzi (at 19°20'S, 30°11'E), flowing south, then southeast, to join the **Lundi River** above its confluence with the **Mtilikwe.** West of **Masvingo,** the Tokwe is fed by the **Mushandike River.**

TONGA (BATONGA). Many **Bantu-speaking peoples** between Malawi and South Africa are known by this name. Two Tonga groups are part of the Tsonga cluster of peoples (see **Hlengwe**). Another Tonga group, associated with the **Barwe,** occupied part of the **Nyanga District** along the border with **Mozambique.** The westernmost branch of the **Shona**-speaking **Ndau** are also called Tonga.

The most important Tonga group in present Zimbabwe has long occupied both sides of the **Zambezi River,** between the **Victoria Falls** and **Kariba.** They are also known as Batonka, or Batoka (as in **"Batoka George"**). About 20,000 of these people were forcibly removed from the Zambezi Valley when **Lake Kariba** was filling in the late 1950s. These Zambezi, or "river," Tonga are related to the Ila and other Zambian peoples. **Tsetse flies** have prevented them from keeping significant numbers of livestock, so they have been mainly cultivators and fishermen (see **Fishing**). During the 19th century they were noted as great boatmen, playing a major role in ferrying combatants in the **Ndebele-Kololo** wars of the 1840s. During the late 19th century they were forced to pay tribute to both the Ndebele and the **Lozi** and were hard pressed by raids from both sides of the river, particularly during the 1880s. In 1893 the Tonga were hit by **smallpox,** which they transmitted to an Ndebele raiding party on the eve of the **Ndebele War.**

TONGOGARA, JOSIAH MAGAMA (c. 1938–December 26, 1979). **ZANLA** commander. Born in the Nhema Tribal Trust Lands (see **Communal Lands**) near **Selukwe,** Tongogara was educated through Standard VI at an **Anglican** mission school. In 1960 he went to Northern Rhodesia (now **Zambia**) and studied bookkeeping. He joined **ZANU** in the early 1960s while in Zambia, and was sent to China in 1966; there he underwent military training at the Nanking Academy in Beijing. He was appointed commander of ZANLA in 1972, and in the following year was elected to the **DARE** and thereafter was chairman of the Supreme Council. In 1975, Tongogara and other ZANU leaders were detained by the government of Zambia and charged with the death of **Herbert Chitepo.** He was held in a maximum security prison for more than a year before being brought to trial, at which time he was acquitted. He represented ZANLA at the **Lancaster House Conference** and was considered a key figure in reaching an agreement.

Tongogara was the most popular of the military leaders among the ZANLA combatants, and strongly maintained that the military struggle should continue until the main principles of one-man/one-vote, majority rule, and independence had been agreed to by the Rhodesian government. Once those goals had been agreed to, he believed that to continue fighting was wrong. Following the signing of the **Lancaster House Agreement** on December 21, 1979, Tongogara returned to **Mozambique** to brief his field commanders on the terms of the cease-fire agreed to in London. While traveling from Maputo to Chimoio, he was killed in a lorry accident. He was buried in Maputo until August 11, 1980, at which time his body was returned to Zimbabwe and was interred at **Heroes' Acre** national cemetery, outside Harare.

TORWA (variants: Togwa; Toloa). Name of a little-understood but possibly historically pivotal **Shona** dynasty. The eponymous Torwa is claimed, possibly speciously, by **Munhumutapa** tradition to have been a relative of **Munhumutapa Matope** and to have been appointed to administer a southern district of the Munhumutapa state in the late 15th century. During the early 1490s this Torwa and another ruler, **Changa**, are said by the same traditions to have rebelled against Matope's successor, with Changa briefly becoming Munhumutapa. When Changa was overthrown, Torwa appears to have retreated to the south, establishing an independent state in the **Guruhuswa region**. Little is known about Torwa's successors, except that they used "Torwa" either as their dynastic title or as the name of their kingdom. Recent research has indicated that the Torwa state may have been responsible for introducing **Khami culture** to the region now known as **Matabeleland,** and that **Khami** itself was built as a Torwa center. The **Changamire** dynasty appears to have displaced the Torwa dynasty in the late 16th century, after **Munhumutapa Neshangwe** expelled the Changamire people from the **Mbire** region in the northeast.

TRACHOMA. Viral eye infection, transmitted by ordinary flies and unhygienic wash towels. The disease inflames the eyes and can cause partial or full blindness. It is a major health problem in rural areas, particularly among children. (See **Health.**)

TRANSPORT AND COMMUNICATIONS. The country's transport and communications networks are among the best in tropical Africa. An impetus for rapid development of these networks lay in the **British South Africa Company's** early need to make the country economically profitable. **Telegraph** lines were built as fast as the company occupied the country. **Railway** lines and a formal **postal system** followed quickly. Bridge and **road** building programs have also been extensive. Newspapers began appearing immediately after British occupation. **Telephone** services began in the late 1890s. Radio broadcasting commenced in the 1930s, followed by television in the early 1960s (see **Zimbabwe Broadcasting Corp.**) Since July 1, 1970, all postal, telephone, and telegraph services have been in the hands of the government-owned Telecommunications Corporation.

TRANSPORT DRIVER. Term used for drivers of **ox-wagons** in the 19th century and for truck drivers in the 20th century.

TRANSVAAL. Now a province of the **Republic of South Africa**, the Transvaal covers a 286,070 sq km area between the Vaal and **Limpopo** rivers. It is the only part of South Africa that borders present-day Zimbabwe. Its people, mostly **Sotho** and **Venda**, have historically moved

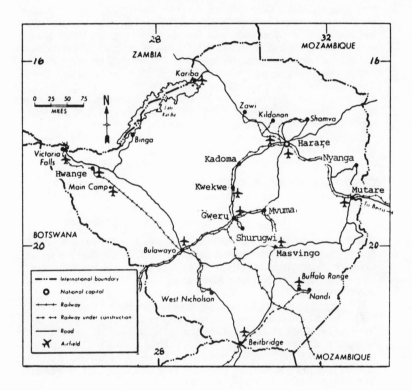

Figure 6: Transportation System

freely back and forth across the easily fordable Limpopo. During the 1820s and 1830s **Mzilikazi's Ndebele** kingdom occupied a series of settlements in the Transvaal before permanently settling in present **Matabeleland.** After the Ndebele left, **Afrikaner** emigrants from the Cape Colony (now Cape Province) began occupying the Transvaal, establishing the South African Republic in 1852. Thereafter the Limpopo was increasingly recognized as a boundary line.

The British government occupied the Transvaal from 1877 to 1881. The Afrikaners regained their independence after the First Boer War, and Paul Kruger became their president in 1883. During the 1880s Afrikaner interests in further northward expansion elicited British responses. The **Bechuanaland Protectorate** was declared over present **Botswana** in 1885, and the **British South Africa Company** occupied **Mashonaland** in 1890. In the mid-1880s, the discovery of vast goldfields in the central Transvaal's Rand region led to the influx of British prospectors, giving **Cecil Rhodes** cause to meddle in Transvaal politics. At Rhodes' instigation the abortive **Jameson Raid** was launched from present Zimbabwe in 1895. This affair helped to touch off the Ndebele and Shona **Revolts** and led directly to the **South African War of 1899–1902.**

Beitbridge was completed in 1929, and has since remained as the main link between Zimbabwe and the Transvaal. In 1974 the first **railway** link between the two regions was established through Beitbridge.

TRANSVAAL NDEBELE. Collective name for several remotely related African communities in the **Transvaal.** These communities are frequently said to have been created by stragglers from **Mzilikazi's Ndebele** 19th-century migrations, but they clearly existed long before his arrival.

TREDGOLD, ROBERT CLARKSON (b. June 2, 1899–April 8, 1977). Judge Tredgold's mother was a daughter of **J. S. Moffat**; his father, Clarkson Henry Tredgold (1865–1938), was an immigrant from South Africa who became a Southern Rhodesian justice. R. C. Tredgold himself was born in **Bulawayo.** He studied at Oxford on a Rhodes Scholarship and returned to central Africa to practice law. In 1934 he was elected to the **Legislative Assembly** as a **United Party** member. From 1936 to 1943 he served as **Godfrey Huggins'** minister of justice and defense. In 1943 he became a High Court justice, rising to chief justice in 1950. In 1955 he became chief justice of the **federation.** He resigned in 1960 to protest against Southern Rhodesia's proposed **Law and Order (Maintenance) Bill.** Highly regarded for his judicial integrity, Tredgold is generally regarded as having had a liberal but paternalistic attitude toward Africans. In 1956 he headed a commission to study franchise reform in Southern Rhodesia. His report, only partly adopted, advocated a double-roll system that would exclude most Africans from the top roll, while giving many more Africans a lower-roll vote that would count less. He published his autobiography, *The Rhodesia That Was My Life*, in 1968.

TREK. Term used for journey or migration, from Dutch/**Afrikaans.** Also used as a verb.

TRIANGLE. Center of a major **sugar** estate in the southeastern low veld, just north of the **Lundi/Mtilikwe** confluence (at 21°2′S, 32°27′E; alt. 420

m). During the 1920s Thomas Murray MacDougall (1881–1964), a Scottish immigrant, began a large-scale private irrigation scheme at the Triangle Estate, while pioneering the country's sugar industry. The government bought him out in 1944 but later allowed the estate to revert to private ownership, while assisting in irrigation development. By the early 1960s Triangle and neighboring **Hippo Valley** were the country's only major sugar producers. Post-**UDI sanctions** reduced sugar export markets sharply, so agricultural production was greatly diversified to serve local markets. (See also **Sabi-Limpopo Authority.**)

TRIBAL TRUST LAND DEVELOPMENT CORPORATION (Tilcor). Body established by the Rhodesian government in 1968 to promote industrial development of African rural areas. Despite ambitious plans, Tilcor had initiated only two manufacturing industries and a few irrigation schemes by the early 1970s.

TRIBAL TRUST LANDS (TTL) see **COMMUNAL LANDS**

TRUEY THE GRIQUA (Truey David) see under **WILLIAM THE GRIQUA**

TRYPANOSOMIASIS see **SLEEPING SICKNESS; NAGANA**

TSETSE FLY (*Diptera glossina*). Blood-feeding insect, several varieties of which transmit the trypanosome parasite that gives the disease trypanosomiasis to animals (see **Nagana**) and humans (see **Sleeping Sickness**). The insect is found only in tropical Africa. It thrives in shady, dry places near the game on which it feeds. It is rarely found above altitudes above 1,000 m, and tends to live by water, which attracts game. Since the insect tends not to migrate, destruction of its habitat is an effective means of combating the very serious diseases it carries.

Before the 19th century tsetse flies covered most of the country's lowland areas. **Ndebele** settlement in **Matabeleland** in the 1840s began a process of tsetse-fly retreat, as the Ndebele cut back the **Somabula Forest**. Increasingly intensive big-game **hunting** accelerated the retreat of tsetse by diminishing the flies' natural food supplies. The **rinderpest** epidemic of 1896 destroyed huge numbers of **cattle**, pushing the tsetse fly "belt" even farther north. After these setbacks the flies began recovering their former territories at a rate of about 2,500 sq km/year. During the present century the government has combated tsetse flies by clearing indigenous **forests** and shooting game. The intensification of guerrilla warfare in the mid-1970s inhibited tsetse-fly-abatement work, allowing the flies to begin a new recovery of territory.

TSH-. **Chishona** words starting with this digraph, which is sounded as *ch-* in "church," are now generally spelled with *ch-*. *Tsh-* also appears frequently as a variant of the *sh-* sound in **Sindebele** and other **Nguni** languages.

TSONGA (variant: Thonga) see **HLENGWE**

TSORO. **Chishona** name for the widespread African board game played with pebbles or pips in rows of holes. The game is played throughout the country, as well as much of Africa.

TSVANGIRAI, MORGAN (b. Mar. 10, 1952). Trade unionist and political leader. Born in **Gutu,** the eldest of nine children, Tsvangirai attended Munyira Primary School and Gokomere High School. Upon finishing his secondary education he began working to help support his family. In 1972 he began working at Mutare Clothing, where he was first exposed to trade unionism. Two years later he took a job at the Trojan Mine, near **Bindura.** While there he joined **ZANU** and was named a political commissar. Tsvangirai worked at the mine for ten years, eventually becoming a general foreman. While employed at the mine he devoted his time to union work rather than politics. He rose up through union ranks, becoming branch chairman of the Association of Mine Workers' Union. By the mid-1980s he had been elected to the executive of the National Mine Workers' Union and became its Secretary-General in 1988.

As Secretary-General of the NMWU, Tsvangirai began criticizing the government for failing to support the union in its disputes with mine owners over wages and working conditions. In 1989, he personally broke with ZANU-PF and also convinced the union's leadership to do the same. Shortly after, he was arrested, charged with spying for **South Africa,** and imprisoned for six weeks. For most of the early 1990s he focused on building the union and, again, generally stayed clear of politics. During that same period, however, the country's economy began to decline rapidly. In the mid-1990s Tsvangirai was elected to the executive of the Zimbabwe Congress of Trade Unions and began to publicly voice criticisms of the government, focusing much of the blame for the worsening conditions on President **Robert Mugabe.** In 1997, in response to the economic decline, he led the country's first general strike. Later that year he was nearly killed when unknown assailants broke into his office, beat him, and attempted to throw him out of a tenth-story wndow.

In 1999, Tsvangirai was a founding member of the **National Constitutional Assembly** and entered politics full-time. He was increasingly vocal in his criticisms of both government economic policy and ZANU-PF's monopoly of political authority in the country. In late 1999 he resigned from the executive of ZCTU and helped to launch an opposition party, the **Movement for Democratic Change,** and was immediately named its general-secretary. In Febuary 2000 he announced that the MDC would challenge ZANU-PF in every constituency in the country in that year's general **elections.** He contested the seat for Buhera North in **Manicaland Province.** Following the MDC's showing in that election, Tsvangirai announced that he would challenge Mugabe in the 2002 presidential elections.

TSWANA (Batswana; variants: Bechuana; Bechwana). Common name for the western branch of **Sotho-speaking** peoples. Tswana groups have long been the majority population in present **Botswana** and the western **Transvaal.** Some of these peoples, notably the **Ngwato** and **Talowta,** occupied parts of southwestern Zimbabwe as late as the 19th century. The arrival of the **Ndebele** in **Matabeleland** after 1838 led to a retreat of some Tswana communities towards the west and southwest. Other Tswana groups were absorbed into Ndebele culture, both in Matabeleland and during the kingdom's formation earlier in the Transvaal.

TULI. The Tuli River rises in the **Matopo Hills**, whence it flows south c. 160 km before joining the **Shashi River** at the **Botswana** border. Just below this confluence the boundary line leaves the Shashi, curving into **Botswana** in an arc known as the "Tuli Circle," a Zimbabwean region now designated a "Controlled Hunting Area." The small town of Tuli stands by the Shashi, at a point near the center of the Tuli Circle. The town was founded when the **Pioneer Column** established Fort Tuli (at 21°56'S, 29°11'E) just before it crossed the Shashi River in July 1890. The town appeared destined to develop into a major stop along the main road to Salisbury, but its development was arrested when British occupation of **Matabeleland** in early 1894 led to the opening of another route through **Bulawayo.**

TURK MINE. Village between **Inyati** and the **Bembezi River**, adjacent to the Turk Gold Mine (19°43'S, 28°47'E), long one of the country's major **gold** producers.

TWALA, ABRAHAM see under **RHODESIAN BANTU VOTERS' ASSO-CIATION**

"TWO PYRAMID POLICY." Concept articulated by **Godfrey Huggins**'s government in the late 1930s in order to express the goal of completely separate European and African development. The concept was largely abandoned by the late 1940s, when the fragmentation of land and the growing economic interdependence of Africans and Europeans were seen to point up to the impracticality of total territorial segregation. (See **Partnership.**)

TYPHOID FEVER (a.k.a. enteric fever). This infectious bacterial disease is widespread in the country and is one of the country's most serious **health** problems.

U

U- (1) In **Chishona** *U-* is a noun prefix (Class 14) for a wide variety of nouns, including those pertaining to states of being and places, as in **Urozvi**, "the country of the Rozvi." It is sometimes rendered as *hu-* or (or *hw-* before vowels) or as *bw-*.

(2) The initial *u-* of many **Ndebele** and other **Nguni** proper names is usually dropped in English usage. Thus, for Umzilikazi and Umzila, for example, see Mzilikazi and Mzila, etc. By contrast, the initial *u-* of many Nguni derived place names, such as Umzingwani River, is usually retained. Convention, rather than logic, dictates these usages, and consistency is difficult to attain.

ULOPENGULA see **LOBENGULA**

UME RIVER (variant: Omay) see **BUMI RIVER**

UMFULI RIVER (variants: Mupfure; Mumvuri). One of the **Umniati River**'s main tributaries, the Umfuli rises about 35 km southwest of **Marondera**, flowing c. 200 km northwest before it joins the Umniati's course to the **Zambezi**. Numerous small dams on the river supply regional water needs.

UMGUSA RIVER (variant: Umguza). Rises near **Ntabazinduna**, flowing northwest to feed the **Gwai River**. Several dams built on the Umgusa in 1936 and 1947 provide irrigation water to the region just north of **Bulawayo**.

UMNIATI RIVER (variant: Munyati). One of the country's most reliable **Zambezi** affluents, the Umniati rises north of **Chivhu** on the **Central Plateau**, whence it follows a long, winding course before entering the east end of **Lake Kariba**. Most important of its own tributaries are the **Sebakwe, Umsweswe,** and **Umfuli** rivers. The stretch of the Umniati below the Umfuli confluence was once more commonly called the Sanyati River.

UMTALI see **MUTARE**

UMTALI POST. Founded in December 1893 as the *Umtali Advertiser*, this newspaper was absorbed by the **"Argus Group"** in 1895. (See **Press**.)

UMTASA. Nguni form of **Mutasa**, the dynastic title of **Manyika** rulers.

UMVUKWE HILLS. Mountain range running astride the northern part of the **Great Dyke**, along the boundary between the **Makonde** and **Mazowe** districts, north from a point about 50 km northwest of **Harare**. Most of the range exceeds 1,500 m in elevation, with Mount Umvukwe (at 17°12′S, 30°41′E) being the highest point, at 1,748 m. The hills are rich in **chrome** ore, which is mined intensively. Mvurwi Village (at 17°2′S, 30°51′E) is the administrative and commercial center for an important **tobacco**-producing region.

UMVUMA see **MVUMA**

UMVUTSHA (variants: Umbutchwa; Umbutja). Small, later 19th-century **Ndebele** village, located just north of **Bulawayo** on the right bank of the **Umgusa River**. It was one of several private *kraals* in which **Lobengula** frequently resided and conducted Ndebele state business. It was here that he signed the **Rudd Concession** in 1888.

UMZINGWANE DISTRICT (former variants: Mzingwana; Mzingwane). District covering 2,760 sq km of **Matabeleland South Province**, just southeast of **Bulawayo**. The district was separated from Bulawayo District in 1897, but was later reabsorbed into Bulawayo and neighboring districts before being recreated in its present shape. It now borders the districts of Bulawayo on the northwest, **Bubi** on the north, **Insiza** on the east, **Gwanda** on the south, and **Matobo** on the southwest. Except for some Tribal Trust Land (see **Communal Lands**) in the southwestern corner, prior to 1980 the entire district was reserved for Europeans. Administrative headquarters are at **Esigodini**. District population in 1992 was 62,954.

UMZINGWANE RIVER (variants: Umzingwani; Mudzingwani). Rising in the **Matopo Hills,** just south of **Bulawayo,** the Umzingwane first flows east, then turns south, following a course roughly parallel to that of the **Tuli River,** located c. 50 km to its west. The Umzingwane meets the **Limpopo** just above **Beitbridge.** Its largest affluent is the **Insiza.** Umzingwane Dam was built just south of present **Esigodini** in 1958 to contribute to Bulawayo's water supply.

UMCOMBATA see **MNCUMBATHE**

UNILATERAL DECLARATION OF INDEPENDENCE (UDI) (1965). Colloquial name for proclamation issued by the Rhodesian government of November 11, 1965, declaring it to be independent but loyal to the monarchy under Queen Elizabeth II.

The proclamation was the culmination of British-Rhodesian constitutional negotiations begun during the creation of the **Southern Rhodesian Constitution** of 1961. The **Rhodesian Front Party** came to power in December 1962, pledged to the achievement of independence under white rule. When Prime Minister **Winston Field** failed to press Britain hard enough on this issue, he was replaced by **Ian Smith** in April 1964. Smith's government soon attempted to demonstrate popular support for independence by getting African chiefs to endorse the idea at the October **"Dombashawa Indaba,"** and by having the predominantly European electorate vote overwhelmingly for independence in a November referendum (58,091 "yes," 6,906 "no"). Negotiations with Britain continued through October 1965, when British Prime Minister Harold Wilson visited Salisbury (now **Harare**) for the last time. On November 11 Smith publicly proclaimed Rhodesia's independence from Britain, and the action has since been known almost universally as "UDI." The UDI proclamation was signed by Smith and all 15 members of his cabinet. Except for the proclamation's expression of loyalty to the British monarch, its wording deliberately recalled that of the American Declaration of Independence. It pointed out that the government had exercised self-rule for 42 years and that it had always been loyal to the British Crown. It then went on to claim that the country represented a rare bastion of civilized democracy in the region that the country's people enthusiastically endorsed independence, and that the British government had failed to negotiate the country's future in good faith.

International reaction to UDI was both swift and negative, and no country ever formally recognized Rhodesia's independence. Britain declared the regime "illegal," but had previously disavowed the use of military force. It instead instituted unilateral economic **sanctions**, which were soon internationalized by the United Nations.

The internationally recognized "illegal" status of the UDI government ended on December 12, 1979 when Lord **Arthur Soames** arrived in Salisbury to take up his post as **governor**, thereby officially marking the return of British sovereignty over the country.

UNION PARTY. Avowedly **Afrikaner** nationalist party that emerged briefly to field two unsuccessful candidates in the 1939 general election.

UNIONIST MOVEMENT. The idea of joining the country to **South Africa** first arose when the unification of South Africa's four colonies was being planned. In 1908 **Charles Coghlan** attended the national convention in South Africa as a nonvoting delegate with this possibility in mind. Coghlan and other Southern Rhodesian politicians thought that union with South Africa was probably inevitable, but they decided to wait until a more propitious moment because of the disadvantageous position Southern Rhodesia's small **European** community would give the country in the context of South Africa's emerging constitution.

The union idea was revived a decade later as an alternative for the country's future after the termination of **BSAC** rule. By then, however, Coghlan and most other settlers opposed union, instead favoring autonomous **Responsible Government**. The BSAC and local industrials favored union with South Africa, and the **Rhodesia Unionist Association** was formed by a faction of settlers. Major capitalist interests within the country feared bankruptcy under a responsible government, seeing the union as their salvation. Opponents of union feared South African—and particularly **Afrikaner**—domination, a loss of African laborers to the south, and an influx of poor South African whites (*bywoners*), higher taxes, and trouble with South African labor unions. In the absence of a realistic third alternative to union and responsible government, missionary and nonwhite opinion tended to favor the latter.

Prime Minister Jan Smuts of South Africa pushed hard for Southern Rhodesia's entry into the Union of South Africa. He is said to have bribed Coghlan with an offer of a cabinet post to this end. In 1922 Smuts published a definite offer to Southern Rhodesia, promising provincial status, a generous number of parliamentary seats, substantial local autonomy, development funds, expansion of the port of **Beira**, and preservation of existing civil servant jobs. The unionist movement was backed by the **Argus Group** newspapers, but unionist organization did not match that of Coghlan's Responsible Government movement. In October 1922 the settlers voted three to two in favor of responsible government, thereby killing the unionist movement. (See **Amalgamation Movement**.)

UNITED AFRICAN NATIONAL COUNCIL see **AFRICAN NATIONAL COUNCIL (ANC)**

UNITED FEDERAL PARTY see **UNITED PARTY**

UNITED METHODIST CHURCH (UMC) (formerly: Methodist Episcopal Church). Missionaries of the American-based Methodist Episcopal Church followed their British **Wesleyan** counterparts into the country in 1898. Under the leadership of Joseph Hartzell they established their headquarters at **Old Umtali**, which was granted to them by the **BSAC**. Throughout the early 20th century the Americans concentrated their work in the eastern and northeastern parts of the country, while the Wesleyans and other **Methodist** societies operated elsewhere. David Mandisodza was the first African ordained a minister in 1924. In 1968

Abel Muzorewa became bishop of the national church. The same year the worldwide church became known as the United Methodist Church after a series of mergers among various American Methodist bodies. By the early 1970s the UMC claimed over 20,000 African members in all parts of the country.

In 1959 the American and British Methodists began sharing theological training facilities, with the **Epworth** Theological College concentrating on ministerial training, and the Old Umtali Biblical Institute training lay workers. Women members have developed an influential lay organization known as **Ruwadzano**. (See **African Methodist Episcopal Church**.)

UNITED PARTY (UP) (a.k.a. United Federal Party). The country's governing party for three decades, the UP was formed by **Godfrey Huggins** in 1934 out of a merger of the main leaderships of the **Reform Party** and the originally ruling **Rhodesian Party**. The UP won majorities in every general election from 1934 to 1958, except that of 1946, when Huggins nevertheless retained control of the government. When the **federation** was being formed in 1953, the UP was reorganized as the United Rhodesia Party (URP), incorporating former supporters of the **Liberal** and **Labour** parties. Huggins also formed a separate Federal Party to become the United Federal Party (UFP). The party leadership's ouster of **Garfield Todd** from the territorial premiership early that year created a split, with Todd contesting the June election as head of a reconstituted URP. The new URP won no **Legislative Assembly** seats, while the UFP held off a strong challenge from the **Dominion Party** to retain control of the government. In late 1962 the UFP lost the general election to the DP's successor, the **Rhodesian Front**. Afterwards it was reorganized as the Rhodesian Party, which faded away when the FR swept the 1965 election.

UNITED PARTY OF ZIMBABWE (UPZ). Short-lived opposition political party founded in the early 1990s. (See **Zimbabwe Unity Movement**.)

UNITED PEOPLE'S PARTY (UPP). African political party announced on May 31, 1965, by 10 African members of **parliament** who had originally been elected to "B" roll seats as representatives of the **United (Federal) Party**'s successor, the Rhodesia Party. The UPP was recognized as the official opposition by the **Rhodesian Front** government, becoming the first African body so recognized. The UPP sought majority rule through constitutional change, but was wracked by leadership quarrels over the efficacious means to be employed. Tolerated by the RF because of their ultimate political impotence, the UPP leaders were regarded as government "stooges" by leaders of extra-parliamentary nationalist parties. A splinter group under Chad Chipunza (b. 1923), an uncle of **Abel Muzorewa**, formed a breakaway **Democratic Party** in August 1968, but the two bodies reunited as the **National People's Union** in June 1969.

UNITED RHODESIA PARTY see **UNITED PARTY**

UNITY PACT. Following the 1985 general **elections**, talks aimed at uniting the country's two main political parties—the Zimbabwe African National Union (**ZANU**) and Zimbabwe African People's Union (**ZAPU**)—began in Harare. **Robert Mugabe**, as president of ZANU, and ZAPU's leader **Joshua Nkomo** met several times over the next two years. Though rumors of a settlement between the feuding leaders and their supporters were rife, no agreement was reached. The main hurdles seemed to be the role ZAPU members would have in any future single-party government and the security and "equal" treatment of **Ndebele peoples** in **Matabeleland**. In April 1987 Mugabe abruptly announced an end to the negotiations, saying that they were deadlocked and that further talks would serve no purpose. President **Canaan Banana** entered the negotiations and strongly advised Mugabe that, in the best interests of the whole country, the talks should continue. Mugabe agreed to reenter negotiations, and in mid-December the two leaders announced an agreement to amalgamate ZANU and ZAPU. Under the terms of the agreement the "new" party would be called ZANU (Patriotic Front [PF]), and it would proclaim the acceptance of the principles of Marxism-Leninism and the desire to establish a socialist society in Zimbabwe. The ZANU Central Committee would be expanded by 30 percent to accommodate the addition of ZAPU leaders, and Nkomo would be appointed a senior minister in the new government (he became vice-president in the new "executive presidential" system in early 1988). The Unity Pact was then signed on December 22, 1987. In late April 1988, in keeping with the newfound optimism and air of unity in the country, President Mugabe proclaimed a general amnesty for all political offenses and invited all exiles to return to Zimbabwe.

UNIVERSITY OF ZIMBABWE (UZ). Moves to found a local university for **European** students began in 1945. The coming of the **federation** in 1953 transformed the original concept into a multiracial university college for all central Africans under the aegis of the new federal government. The Salisbury city government donated land in the suburb of **Mount Pleasant,** where Queen Elizabeth II laid the first foundation stone in July 1953. In September the British government capitalized the project with a one-time grant of £1.25 million and construction began in earnest. In February 1955 the University College of Rhodesia and Nyasaland (UCRN) was incorporated as an autonomous institution by royal charter. A special relationship was established with the University of London, which later awarded UCRN degrees. When a medical school was begun in 1963, a similar arrangement was established between UCRN and the University of Birmingham in England.

UCRN opened to its first 70 full-time students in March 1957. Enrollments rose to over 550 by 1964, when it was reconstituted as the University College of Rhodesia (UCR) and separate institutions were begun in **Zambia** and Malawi. After the breakup of the federation, the Rhodesian government assumed responsibility for the university college's financing. On January 1, 1961, the special ties with the University of London were terminated, and the UCR assumed full autonomy as the University of Rhodesia (UR), awarding its own degrees for the first time.

Originally established as an expression of the federation's stated policy of **"partnership,"** the university became a social and political anomaly within the country during the period of **UDI**. Despite its dependence upon the **Rhodesian Front** government for funding, the university as a whole maintained its academic autonomy, and became a unique enclave of racial integration in the center of an increasingly hostile political environment. Students and some faculty often presented the strongest criticism of the Smith government's policies during this period. In 1980, UR became the University of Zimbabwe (UZ), and the royal charter, as the basic constitutional instrument of the university, was replaced by an act of the Zimbabwe **Parliament** in 1982. The **president** of Zimbabwe also holds the title of chancellor of the university. The first black principal of the university was Dr. Walter J. Kamba. In 1990 there were c. 500 faculty members and a student enrollment of 9,255. By 1999, UZ enrollment had risen to 9,575.

The practice of criticizing government continued after independence, with students and some faculty members often being extremely vocal in their criticism of government policy. Conflicts between students and the government reached a climax in July 1989 when students rioted after police came on the campus to stop a rally by the **Zimbabwe Unity Movement.** The government of President **Robert Mugabe** responded by closing the university for a short time in October of that year. A second crisis, resulting in student riots in August 1995, occurred when the government pressured university officials to suspend several student leaders who had led protests in support of detained labor leaders. The university was closed again in 1998 following several days of demonstrations in which students strongly criticized the government.

UNLAWFUL ORGANISATIONS ACT (1959). Law passed by the government of **Edgar Whitehead** after the banning of the **African National Congress,** giving the police wide powers of search and seizure and enabling the government to arrest any person in any way associated with a banned organization. In July 1960 sections of the act were invoked to arrest leaders of the **National Democratic Party** for their presumed membership in the banned ANC. Subsequent amendments to the act further increased government controls over political organizations, and the act was later invoked to ban ZAPU, ZANU, PCC, and FROLIZI.

UROZVI (variant: Vurozvi). Literally, "the country of the **Rozvi**"; used mainly to refer to the traditional domain of the **Changamire** state.

URUNGWE DISTRICT see **HURUNGWE DISTRICT**

USHER, WILLIAM FILMER (1850–Sept. 22, 1916). A British trader, Usher came to **Bulawayo** in 1883 and became an advisor and letter-writer for King **Lobengula.** During the 1893 **Ndebele War** he and **J. Fairbairn** were left unharmed in Bulawayo when Lobengula fled the British invasion. Their treatment at the hands of the **Ndebele** is frequently cited as evidence of Lobengula's goodwill toward Europeans.

USHEWOKUNZE, HERBERT (b. 1934). Long considered one of Zimbabwe's more radical politicians, Ushewokunze was born in **Marondera** and received his early education at Madizma school before graduating from **Waddilove Institute**. He then attended the University of Natal, **South Africa,** where he studied medicine and qualified as a doctor. While in South Africa he became interested in politics and joined the Pan African Congress of South Africa. He joined the Zimbabwe African National Union (**ZANU**) after returning to the country in the mid-1960s. He left the country in 1968 to join ZANU forces in **Mozambique.** In 1976 he was a ZANU delegate at the **Geneva Conference** and in the same year was appointed ZANU's secretary of health and became a member of the party's politburo.

He returned to the country in early 1980 to contest the **elections** and won a seat in **Parliament** representing the **Chinamora** constituency, just north of **Harare.** Prime Minister **Robert Mugabe** appointed him minister of health in April 1980, but Ushewokunze was dismissed from the cabinet in late 1981 after clashing with Mugabe over policy regarding the Public Service Commission, which Mugabe chaired and was responsible for appointing executive posts in the country's civil service. However, he dramatically reappeared in government on February 17, 1982 when he was appointed to the powerful position of minister of home affairs. In that position he helped direct the suppression of **dissident** activities in **Matabeleland,** ordered the arrest and detention of several former members of the **Rhodesian security forces** on charges of subversion, and strongly supported the repeated extensions of the state of emergency— which had been in effect since the early 1960s and required renewing every six months. In January 1984, after being widely criticized by opposition politicians for his use of emergency powers, he was demoted to the post of minister of transport and roads. In August of that year, however, at ZANU's second Party Congress he was reelected to the party's politburo and placed in charge of ZANU's commissariat of cultural affairs. Following the **Unity Pact** Ushewokunze was again demoted, this time to the relatively minor position of minister of state without portfolio in the office of President Mugabe. After being reelected to Parliament in the 1990 elections, he was appointed minister of energy resources.

UXWITI see **ZWIDE**

V

VA- Chishona noun prefix (Class 2), normally used for plural forms of Class i *mu-* prefix nouns for people. In the cases of proper names, such prefixes are dropped in this dictionary; thus for "vakaranga," for example, see **Karanga.** For ordinary nouns, see under *mu-* e.g., *vadzimu,* see **Mudzimu.** (Cf. **MA-.**)

VAKOMAMA (f. Vasikana). Term used in rural areas during the war of liberation to refer to freedom fighters. From **Chishona** for "boys" and "girls." (See **Guerrillas; Mujibas.**)

VAMBE, LAWRENCE (b. 1917). Journalist and novelist. Born at **Chishawasha,** Vambe was educated at the mission station there and in

South Africa. He was a journalist for the **African Newspapers, Ltd.**, and in 1953 was appointed as editor-in-chief. In 1958 Vambe received a British MBE as a reward for his journalistic support of the **federation**. He left the country in 1959, following the banning of the **African National Congress**. He worked as an information attaché in London for three years. Vambe returned to the country in 1962 and became a public relations officer for the **Anglo-American Corporation**. In 1964 he transferred to Lusaka, and was later sent to the London office of Anglo-American, where he worked until 1970. He then stayed in England and began writing a series of books. His first, *An Ill-Fated People* (1972), recounts the history of the country up to the 1920s through the eyes of the **Shavasha** people. *From Rhodesia to Zimbabwe* (1976) carries the story through 1962, while injecting Vambe's own memoirs. Vambe returned to Zimbabwe in 1979 and established the Monomutapa Development Company, Ltd., and has since become a successful businessman.

VAN DER BYL, PIETER K. F. V. (b. Nov. 11, 1923). **Tobacco** farmer and politician. Born in South Africa, van der Byl came to the country following the Second World War. Elected to the **Legislative Assembly** in 1962, by 1969 he had become minister of information. He later served **Ian Smith** as minister of defense (1976), and foreign minister at the **Geneva Conference**. A noted hard-liner on the question of African majority rule, he left the country after independence.

VAN NIEKERK RUINS. Major lowland complex of **Inyanga Ruins** group, covering more than 50 sq km north of the Inyanga National Park (at 18°8′S, 32°41′E). The complex extends along about 9 km of the Nyangombe River; a 36 sq km section of the ruins east of the river was declared a National Monument in 1946. The ruins were first examined in 1905 by **David Randall-MacIver**, who named them after a local farmer who had found them some years earlier. The ruins include numerous examples of walled enclosures, "forts," stone-lined **pits**, and agricultural terraces. They appear to have been built and occupied during the 18th and early 19th centuries. **Mt. Ziwa** is located within the complex.

VELD. From the Dutch/**Afrikaans** word for "field"; a term for open grassland country, such as characterizes much of southern Africa. The terms "low veld," "middle veld," and "high veld" refer to the **altitudinal zones**.

VENDA (BAVENDA). Branch of **Bantu-speaking** people occupying an apparently distinct intermediate linguistic position between **Shona-** and **Sotho-speakers**. The Venda appear to have lived in the **Matabeleland** region until about the late 17th century, when most of them crossed the **Limpopo River** into northwestern **Transvaal**. Venda royal clans are connected to those of the southern Shona. During the 19th century many Venda recrossed the Limpopo into present Zimbabwe, where they became noted as **iron** workers and gunsmiths. They traded firearms to the Shona and occasionally served as mercenaries in Shona wars. The Venda also became closely associated with the **Mwari** cult centers in the **Matopo Hills**. One historian has recently argued that it was the Venda themselves who founded these cult centers, but his thesis has not yet been widely supported. (See also **Lemba.**)

VICTORIA DISTRICT see **MASVINGO DISTRICT**

VICTORIA FALLS (a.k.a. **Musi O Tunya**). One of the world's most spectacular natural scenic attractions, the Victoria Falls are easily the country's top tourist draw. They lower the mile-wide **Zambezi River** an average of 93 m at a point roughly in the middle of the river's long course. The relatively straight crest of the falls is divided into separately named individual falls, all of which are visible from the Zimbabwean bank, which lies across the first of a series of gorges formed by earlier recessions of the crest. Water flows across the falls at a mean annual rate of about 57 million liters (c. 15 million gallons) per minute. This rate increases by a factor of eight during the peak flood season (see **Climate**).

The falls were first brought to the attention of the outside world by **David Livingstone**, who named them during his first visit in November 1855. Seven years later **Thomas Baines** depicted them in the first oil paintings.

VICTORIA FALLS BRIDGE. Towering about 90 m over the **Zambezi River** just below the Victoria Falls, this 202-m bridge was opened in 1905. It was built to carry two **railway** tracks linking Southern and Northern Rhodesia at a site offering a spectacular view of the falls. In 1930 the structure was strengthened and modified to handle automobile traffic (see **Roads**). The bridge has always been a major link between present Zimbabwe and **Zambia,** but in early 1973 President Kaunda of Zambia closed the Zambian side in an act of support for the liberation forces against the **UDI** government of **Ian Smith**. Zambia reopened this border crossing in October 1978. The **border** between the two countries runs through the center of the bridge, and when the **Victoria Falls Conference** was held on the bridge in August 1975, delegates sat within a single railroad car, but on opposite sides of the border.

VICTORIA FALLS CONFERENCE (1975). In December 1974 Rhodesian government officials met with representatives of the **African National Council** in Lusaka, **Zambia,** to arrange for a constitutional conference. **Ian Smith**'s government abandoned its previously rigid position in regard to the recognition of African nationalist groups only after considerable joint pressure from the governments of **Zambia** and **South Africa**, and in the face of dangers posed by imminent **Mozambican** independence. On December 11, 1974, Smith announced his intention to release political prisoners in return for a cease-fire and agreement to participate in a constitutional conference at a then-undetermined site.

After prolonged disagreement over the site of the conference, Smith and his top aides met with **Abel Muzorewa, Ndabaningi Sithole, Joshua Nkomo, James Chikerema**, and other nationalist leaders in a railroad dining car atop the **Victoria Falls Bridge** on August 25, 1975. South Africa's Prime Minister John Vorster and Zambia's President Kenneth Kaunda attended the first session, in which both sides projected optimism. However, the talks ended the second day, after Smith refused to consider allowing nationalist leaders wanted for "terrorist" activities to participate freely in politics within the country, where, he insisted, the final constitutional settlement should be worked out.

VICTORIA FALLS NATIONAL PARK. Forming a 595-sq km triangle west of the **Victoria Falls–Bulawayo** road and south of the **Zambezi River,** this park is one of the country's most popular tourist centers. It encompasses the falls themselves and a large game reserve. In the mid-1970s tourism began dropping as **ZIPRA** forces stepped up their operations in the area. However, since independence in 1980 tourism to the region has steadily increased.

VICTORIA FALLS TOWNSHIP. Founded during the construction of **Victoria Falls Bridge,** this town (located at 17°56′S, 25°50′E; alt. 910 m) has served as a major tourist center, a **border** post, and the commercial and administrative center for the northwest corner of **Hwange District.** It is connected to **Bulawayo** by a 441-km **road** and **railway,** and it has an international airport. (See **Air Zimbabwe.**)

VICTORIA PROVINCE see MASVINGO PROVINCE

VIEW OF THE WORLD see WORLD'S VIEW

VILA SALAZAR see SANGO

VILJOEN, JAN WILLEM (1811–1891). **Transvaal** hunter, trader, and government agent. Viljoen hunted in **Matabeleland** from 1861 through the 1880s. In 1865 he was sent by the Transvaal government to persuade **Mzilikazi** and the Ngwato ruler **Macheng** to accept **Afrikaner** protectorates, but this mission failed.

VLEI. **Afrikaans**-derived term (from Dutch *vallei*) for a shallow depression in the earth that collects water just below the surface level. *Vleis* are found throughout the country, and they have often been important water sources for people during the dry winter months. (See **Donga.**)

VUMBA MOUNTAINS. Region just southeast of **Mutare,** along the **Mozambique** border. The minuscule Vumba National Park, covering only 200 hectares (494 acres), is essentially a botanical garden. It was known as "Manchester Gardens" until purchased by the **federation** government in 1957. A well-known feature of the region is Leopard Rock Hotel, an attractive stone edifice built by Italian prisoners during the Second World War. The park also includes **Bunga Forest.**

W

WA- Common **Bantu** noun prefix for plural forms of names of peoples; frequently written in place of **va-** in **Shona** names. Such prefixes are dropped for proper names in this dictionary. For example, for "Wanhowe" (or Wanoe), see **NHOWE**. (Cf. **AMA-, BA-, MA.**)

WADDILOVE INSTITUTION. One of the most important African educational facilities in the country, Waddilove was originally founded by **Wesleyan** missionaries as the Nenguwo Mission in the early 1890s. It became "Waddilove" in 1915. **John White** developed the station into a training center after 1910. The Wesleyans later shifted theological training to their **Epworth Mission**, making Waddilove a teacher-training center. It is located about 20 km southeast of **Marondera** (at 18°15′S, 31°32′E).

WANKIE see **HWANGE**

WATA see **HWATA**

WEDENGA (variant: *Nyadenga*). **Chishona** term for "supreme spirit," or "god of heaven"; variously used as a synonym for, or description of, the high god **Mwari**. Some early translations of Christian scriptures also used "Wedenga" for God.

WEDZA. The **Chishona** word *hwedza* means "tomorrow," or "the day after tomorrow." Spelled "Wedza," it appears in many place names, perhaps because non-Shona travelers were sometimes confused by **Shona** who answered "*Hwedza!*" when asked for directions. Wedza was also the name of a 19th-century **Dumbuseya** ruler. The best-known places called Wedza are in the present **Wedza District**. They include the Wedza Mountains (18°45′S, 2°35′E). Within this range Wedza Mountain (a.k.a. Dangamwire Mountain; alt. 1,800 m) has long been famous as a rich **iron**-bearing area, exploited by the **Njanja** and **Hera** peoples. Just north of this peak is Wedza village, the district headquarters. Another well-known Wedza Mountain is in the **Mberengwa District** (at 20°15′S, 29°32′E).

WEDZA DISTRICT. Once the southeastern section of **Marondera District**, Wedza now covers 2,570 sq km in **Mashonaland East Province**. It borders the districts of **Makoni** on the east, **Buhera** on the south, **Chikomba** on the west, and **Marondera** on the north. Prior to 1980, the northern part of the district was reserved for Europeans, the broad central belt was Tribal Trust Land (see **Communal Lands**), and the southern tip was **Purchase Area** land. District population in 1992 was 69,981.

WELENSKY, ROY RAPHAEL (Jan. 20, 1907–Dec. 5, 1991). Second and last prime minister of the Federation (1956–63). Born in Salisbury to poor immigrant parents, Welensky had little formal education before joining **Rhodesia Railways** in 1924. In 1933 he moved to Broken Hill, Northern Rhodesia (now Kabwe, **Zambia**), and soon became a powerful trade union leader. He was elected to the Northern Rhodesian Legislative Council in

1938, becoming leader of its unofficial members in 1947. Following the war he joined **Godfrey Huggins** in leading the fight for **federation**.

When federation was achieved in 1953, Welensky took a seat in the Federal Assembly and joined Huggins's government first as a cabinet minister, and later as deputy premier. He assumed the premiership when Huggins retired in November 1956. Under his tutelage the **United Federal Party** was formed.

Welensky began to grow alarmed with Britain's apparently increasing support of African majority rule, so he began to advocate dominion status for the federation as a means of maintaining white rule. He threatened to declare independence, thereby alienating his African supporters and establishing the European mood which later condoned **Ian Smith**'s **Unilateral Declaration of Independence**. Unable to prevent the federation's dissolution in 1963, he retired from politics after losing a byelection for a seat in the **Southern Rhodesian Legislative Council** in 1964, in which he opposed a **Rhodesian Front** candidate and that party's advocacy of independence from Britain. He emigrated to Britain in 1981.

WESLEYAN METHODIST MISSIONARY SOCIETY (WMMS). Agents of the London-based WMMS were among the first missionaries to work north of South Africa's Vaal River in the 1820s. In 1829 one of these missionaries, James Archbell, tried to start a mission among **Mzilikazi**'s **Ndebele,** who then lived near present Pretoria. In 1891 the WMMS entered **Mashonaland** and **Isaac Shimmin** founded **Epworth Mission** near present **Harare.** Early efforts were concentrated in northern Mashonaland, but stations also were established in **Matabeleland** after the 1893 **Ndebele War.** The Wesleyans produced one of the country's most influential European missionaries, **John White**, who founded the **Waddilove Institution.** They also had the distinction of training the first **Shona** teacher to break away from a mission church to form an independent Christian church—**Matthew Zwimba.** By 1959 the Wesleyans claimed more than 24,000 African members throughout the country. Their local church has since become known as the Methodist Church in Zimbabwe. (See also **United Methodist Church; Methodists.**)

WEST NICHOLSON. Town in the **Gwanda District** just south of the tip of the **Insiza District,** where the **Bulawayo**-to-**Beitbridge** road meets the **Umzingwane River** (at 21°4′S, 29°22′E; alt. 850 m). The town was founded in the late 1890s near the Nicholson Gold Mine and is now the center of an important beef-producing region. Since 1905 it has been the terminus of a branch **railway** line from Bulawayo, by way of **Heany Junction.**

WESTBEECH, GEORGE (d. July 1888). British trader. In the mid-1860s Westbeech came to **Matabeleland** to trade. There he formed a commercial partnership with **G. A. Phillips** in 1868. Operating from his own base at Pandamatenga in the north, he became an intimate friend of both the **Ndebele** King **Lobengula** and the **Lozi** rulers of western **Zambia**. He used his unique dual influence to help mitigate disputes between the two nations and to introduce British influence into the Lozi country.

"WESTBEECH ROAD." A 19th-century track that branched off from the **"Hunter's Road"** at **Tati**, extending north to the **Zambezi River** by way of Pandamatenga.

WHA WHA DETENTION CENTER. Located northeast of **Gweru** (at 19°22'S, 30°1'E), Wha Wha was the main detention center for political prisoners following the closure of **Gonakudzingwa** in 1974. At the height of the liberation struggle, more than 500 African political prisoners were thought to be held at Wha Wha.

WHITE, JOHN (Jan. 6, 1866–Aug. 7, 1933). English missionary. An agent of the **Wesleyan Methodist Missionary Society**, White came to the **Transvaal** in 1888, and transferred to **Mashonaland** in 1894. There he founded Nengubo Mission, which he later developed into **Waddilove Institution**, and he began a farm project at **Epworth**. From the time he started his work he was an outspoken critic of government treatment of Africans, and he was one of the first Europeans to point out the abuses that led to the **Shona Revolt of 1896–97**. In 1901 he was made chairman of the Methodist mission district, and he later became principal at Waddilove. Criticized by Europeans for his "negrophilia," he was a leading voice in the southern **Rhodesia Missionary Conference**, which he and his Anglican ally **A. S. Cripps** tried to transform into a strong lobbying body for African rights. Through the 1920s he fought relentlessly for extensions of African land rights. Frustrated in his attempts to win significant government concessions, he reluctantly advocated territorial segregation—on the condition that African areas first be enlarged. His advocacy of segregation lent support to the government's **Land Apportionment Act** of 1930. Ill health later forced White's return to England, where he died.

WHITE BIRD, CHURCH OF THE see under **ZWIMBA, MATTHEW**

WHITE RHINO SHELTER. Important **rock painting** site, located about one km east of **World's View** in the **Matopo Hills**. Its pictures include what are regarded as some of the country's fines monochrome outline drawings. The main figures are large wildebeests, but the cave takes its modern name from smaller representations of black and white **rhinoceroses**.

WHITE RHODESIA COUNCIL. Settler organization founded in 1949 to campaign for the principle of white supremacy in the country. Under the leadership of Charles Olley the council advocated dominion status, white job reservation, territorial segregation of the races, and exclusion of Africans from elected offices.

WHITEHEAD, EDGAR CUTHBERT FREMANTLE (Feb. 8, 1905–1971). Sixth **prime minister** of Southern Rhodesia (1958–62). Born in Berlin of British parents, Whitehead came to the country in 1928 to enter the civil service after an Oxford education. In 1939 he was elected to the **Legislative Assembly**. He resigned the next year to join the British army. After the war, he served as Southern Rhodesia's high commissioner in London (1945–53). Through this period he also served as **Godfrey Huggins'·**

minister of finance, posts, and telegraph, until retiring because of his poor health.

Whitehead came out of retirement in 1957 to become the **federation**'s minister in Washington, D.C. He returned home early in 1958 to head the government, after a special **United Federal Party** congress ousted **Garfield Todd** from the premiership. Whitehead stood for his own assembly seat in a **Bulawayo** byelection in April, but was surprisingly defeated by a **Dominion Party** candidate. He then dissolved the assembly, calling a general election for June, which was the last his party won. His government was a transitional period for both white and black political movements. Early in 1959 he declared a state of emergency and banned the **African National Congress**. Two years later he banned the ANC's successor, the **National Democratic Party**. Although Whitehead encouraged greater African participation in electoral politics under the terms of the **Constitution of 1961** (see also **"Build A Nation"**), he succeeded only in alienating Africans from established politics. In December 1962 his party lost the general election to the **Rhodesian Front**, and **Winston Field** became prime minister. Afterwards Whitehead retired to England, where he died.

WILLIAM THE GRIQUA (a.k.a. Willem; Velani) (c.1820s–1859). **Ndebele induna.** Born a Griqua in South Africa, William and his younger cousin Truey David were captured by the Ndebele during a raid on Griqua hunters by the Vaal River in 1834. William soon mastered the **Sindebele** language and Sesotho (the language of the **Sotho**), and became a personal interpreter for **Mzilikazi.** After the Ndebele moved to **Matabeleland,** William became a soldier and was eventually honored with the **headring** of an **indoda.** He served in at least one of the campaigns against the **Kololo**, during which he was badly wounded. By the 1850s he had an Ndebele family, he commanded at least 100 men as an *induna,* and he was said to be well-trusted by the king. His cousin Truey returned to South Africa with **Robert Moffat** in 1854, but William elected to remain with the Ndebele. Five years later, however, he was executed, apparently in connection with some kind of **cattle** dispute. Although his end was tragic, his career demonstrated the pan-ethnic inclusiveness of 19th-century Ndebele society.

WILLIAM-POWLETT, P. B. R. W. (March 5, 1898–Nov. 10, 1985). Seventh **governor** of Southern Rhodesia (1954–59). After a career in the British Navy, William-Powlett succeeded **J. N. Kennedy** as governor of Southern Rhodesia. He was in turn succeeded by **H. V. Gibbs.**

WILLOUGHBY, JOHN CHRISTOPHER (Feb. 10, 1859–April 16-1918). Military officer. Willoughby served as second-in-command of the **Pioneer Column, Cecil Rhodes'** agent to **Beira,** military adviser to **L. S. Jameson** during the **Ndebele War,** and commander of the **Jameson Raid**. He also later served in the **South African War** and in the East African campaign of the First World War.

WILLOWDALE. The name itself is derived from the company which operates Zimbabwe's only automobile assembly plant, Willowdale Motor Industries. The term was used to encompass the events surrounding the most famous case of political corruption, and the scandal which ensued, in the country following independence in 1980. In March 1989, the *Chronicle* (see **Press**) published articles accusing government ministers of corruption in their dealings with Willowdale Motor Industries. The law allowed anyone to purchase a new automobile and resell it, but only at government-mandated prices. Generally, people wanting a new automobile had to place their names on a long waiting list. The newspaper reports charged that ministers used their privileged positions to place their own names at the top of the waiting list. After obtaining the new automobiles, they then resold them at exorbitant prices, thereby making illegal profits. The government of President **Robert Mugabe** at first dismissed the reports of ministerial corruption as opposition politics. The government even went so far as to remove the *Chronicle*'s editor from his job. However, public criticism continued to grow and, in response to that criticism, Mugabe was forced to appoint a commission of investigation in January 1990.

Headed by the judge president of Zimbabwe, Wilson Sandura, the commission issued subpoenas to several high-ranking officials. Initially, witnesses denied any knowledge or involvement. However in early March Frederick Shava, minister of labor, resigned from office after admitting that he had perjured himself when testifying to the commission. This was followed on March 10 by the resignation of Defense Minister Enos Nkala, who also admitted to giving false evidence before Sandura's commission. On April 14, three additional high-ranking officials resigned—Minister for Higher Education Dzingai Mutumbuka, Minister for Industry and Technology Cllistus Ndlovu, and the governor of **Matabeleland North province,** Jacob Mudenda. Perhaps the greatest tragedy of the affair occurred on April 20 when, after denying receiving kickback payments from the directors of Willowdale, Senior Minister for Political Affairs **Maurice Nyagumbo** died after swallowing poison.

Frederick Shava was later charged with lying to the commission. He was convicted and sentenced to nine months in jail. President Mugabe was clearly shaken by the scandal and in particular by the suicide of Nyagumbo, a longtime political ally. And while Mugabe publically chastised all those involved, in July 1990 he pardoned Shava.

WILMOT, ALEXANDER (April 9, 1836–April 3, 1923). Scottish-born author and member of the Cape Colony Legislative Assembly (1889–1910), where he became an avid supporter of **Cecil Rhodes**. Rhodes commissioned Wilmot to study the origins of the **Zimbabwe Ruins** culture. He did most of his research in European archives, where he collected arcane evidence intended to support **J. T. Bent**'s theory that Zimbabwe was built by ancient Phoenicians. He published his findings in *Monomotopa (Rhodesia)* (London, 1896), a book that also served to debunk **Portuguese** claims to having had priority in the **Shona** territories claimed by Rhodes' **British South Africa Company**.

WILSON, ALLAN (1856–Dec. 4, 1893). Scottish-born soldier. Wilson came to South Africa in 1878 and served in several local British military units. After prospecting in **Mashonaland** during the early 1890s, he was commissioned a major in the army formed by **L. S. Jameson** to fight the **Ndebele** in July 1893. Wilson commanded the Victoria Column, which joined **P. W. Forbes'** column at Iron Hill Mine, whence the combined forces marched on **Bulawayo** to end the **Ndebele War**. After occupying Bulawayo, Wilson led the famous **"Shangani Patrol,"** which was wiped out.

WILTON CULTURE. Name, taken from a South African site, for a Late **Stone Age** industry found throughout eastern and southern Africa. It is the dominant LSA industry within present Zimbabwe, where it has also been known as Matopo Industry. It is characterized by small, finely crafted stone tools and weapons, polished axes, bored stones, and associations with **rock painting** sites. One major phase of the Wilton Culture is named after **Pomongwe Cave**. Wilton Culture contrasts with the large stone implements characteristic of the Smithfield Industry, which predominated south of the **Limpopo River**.

WOMEN'S FRANCHISE ORDINANCE (1919). When the **Legislative Council** was created in 1898, voting was open only to males over 21 years old who met certain income and property qualifications. In 1919 **C. P. Coghlan** put the Women's Franchise Ordinance through the **Legislative Council** at the last session before a general election. This was an apparent political maneuver, sanctioned by the enhanced respect European women in the country had garnered through their wartime services. The ordinance allowed women to qualify for the vote on the basis of their husbands' financial means, provided they were not married polygamously. This stipulation effectively barred the few African women who might otherwise have become eligible to vote. (American women got the vote a year later; South African white women, 11 years later.)

WOOD, JOSEPH GARBETT (Jan. 4, 1833–Sept. 25, 1894). South African **concession** hunter. In late 1887 Wood was granted a mining concession near the **Shashi River** by the **Ndebele** king **Lobengula**. This region was also claimed by the **Ngwato**, who had given mining rights to another party. The dispute over land ownership that followed was settled in 1891 when Wood's group, the Ngwato concession party, and the **BSAC** amalgamated their different interests. Wood's account of his experiences, *Through Matabeleland,* was published shortly after he died.

WORLD'S VIEW. Two well-known lookout points in the country were given this name by **Cecil Rhodes**. One is on the western edge of the **Inyanga Mountains**, overlooking scenic plains. The second, more properly known as "View of the World," is a prominent granite *kopje* in the middle of the spectacular **Matopo Hills**. This latter site contains the graves of **Rhodes, L. S. Jameson, Charles Coghlan,** and the members of the **"Shangani Patrol."** It was previously known to the **Ndebele** as *Malindidzimu,* "the dwelling place of spirits." (See **Nthumbane**.)

WRATHALL, JOHN JAMES (Aug. 28, 1913–Aug. 31, 1978). Second **president** of Rhodesia (1975-78). Born and educated in England, Wrathall emigrated to Southern Rhodesia in 1936. He worked there in the government tax department until becoming a chartered accountant in 1946, and he was later elected to the **Legislative Assembly**. When the **Rhodesian Front** took power in December 1962, he entered **Winston Field**'s cabinet. After **Ian Smith** became prime minister in April 1964,

Wrathall became minister of finance. In this capacity he has been credited with much of the country's success in overcoming the effects of economic **sanctions** during **UDI**. He was rewarded with the additional post of deputy prime minister in September 1966. On December 10, 1975, he left the cabinet to succeed **Clifford Dupont** as president of the country until his sudden death in mid-1978.

X

X-. In languages such as **Sindebele**, which contain **click sounds**, the letter *x* represents a consonant made with a lateral click, as in Xukut-wayo. This sound can be modified, as in *inxwala*, wherein the *nx* represents a nasalized lateral click.

XUKUTWAYO MLOTSHA (d. Nov. 1890). **Ndebele** *induna*, described as one of the most powerful men in the kingdom during the 1860s. Xukut-wayo was chief of the cluster of towns around the Intemba and Izinkondo *amabutho* (see **Ibutho**), located by the upper **Bubi River**. **Sikombo Mguni** was his head subchief and successor as chief. Xukutwayo commanded an *impi* against **Chibi** in 1861, and directed the capture of **Tohwechipi** in 1866. In 1870 he moved his towns south to an area about 25 km east of present **Bulawayo**. In 1879 he and **Lotshe** went to **Gazaland** to fetch **Lobengula**'s royal bride, **Xwalile**. During the 1880s he returned to Gazaland to deliver the balance of **cattle** owed for *lobolo*, but was refused entry to the country.

XWALILE (variant: Cwalili) (fl.1870s–1900s). **Lobengula**'s "royal wife" (or "great wife") (see **Inkosikazi**). In 1871 Lobengula sent oxen to the **Gaza** king **Mzila** to open negotiations for an exchange of royal wives. Lobengula preferred Mzila's eldest daughter, Dombole, but Mzila thought her too old to be suitable. Instead he offered a younger daughter, Xwalile. In August 1879 the **Ndebele** *izinduna* **Lotshe** and **Xukutwayo** fetched Xwalile and her large retinue from **Gazaland** to **Bulawayo**. The next month Lobengula married Xwalile and seven of her "sisters" in a three-week ceremony. These wives became popularly known as the "Gaza Queens." The mar-riage got off to a poor start, with the new wives insulting Lobengula publicly. There was also a dispute with the Gaza kingdom over the *lobolo* payment that was never fully resolved, and Lobengula never sent any Ndebele wives to the Gaza king. Worse, Xwalile was expected to bear Lobengula's heir in her capacity as royal wife, but she proved infertile. Lobengula's sister **Mncengence** was accused of bewitching her. Xwalile's childlessness left open the question of Lobengula's successor. Xwalile herself was soon banished to the town of the Mzinyathi *ibutho*, where she became the subject of many adultery rumors during the 1880s. After the 1896 **Revolt** the **British South Africa Company** provided Xwalile and the other "Gaza Queens" with small pensions, but she and her kinswomen were unhappy among the Ndebele, so they returned to Gazaland.

Y

YOUNG, HILTON see **HILTON YOUNG COMMISSION**

YOUTH LEAGUE (YL) (a.k.a. City Youth League; Southern Rhodesian African National Youth League). Now regarded as the country's first truly modern nationalist movement, the YL was founded as a civic organization, the **Harare** Youth Club, in August 1955. Under the leadership of **James Chikerema, George Nyandoro**, and Dunduzu Chisiza (1930–62)—a Nyasaland immigrant who was later deported—the YL quickly developed into a mass political movement active in both towns and rural areas. The YL successfully contested the political influence of **Charles Mzingeli**, ignoring purely trade union issues while challenging the very authority of the government to rule over Africans. In August 1956 the YL organized a successful bus boycott in Harare. A year later the league merged with the **Bulawayo** branch of the old **African National Congress** to launch a revitalized and more aggressive ANC.

YUFI. When the famous Arab traveler Ibn Battuta (1304–1377) visited Kilwa Kisiwani on Tanzania's costs in 1331, he described the source of **Sofala**'s **gold** as "Yufi, in the country of Limiin," a month's march inland from Sofala. Assuming that his "Sofala" was then at its later-known location, it is likely that Ibn Battuta's "Yufi" referred to the kingdom that built the **Zimbabwe Ruins**. If so, this may be the earliest explicit documentary reference to a place within present-day Zimbabwe.

Z

ZAKA. Village located on the **Chiredzi River** (at 20°21'S, 31°27'E; alt. 760 m). Established in 1923, it is the administrative center of the **Zaka District.**

ZAKA DISTRICT (Ndanga District until 1985). After having had its boundaries completely redrawn several times, Zaka District now covers 8,754 sq km in the center of **Masvingo Province.** On the west, the **Mtilikwe River** separates it from **Masvingo District,** out of which it was carved in 1899. On the east, Zaka borders **Bikita District,** which was separated from it in 1920. On the south Zaka borders **Chiredzi District,** the central part of which was formerly part of Zaka. The village of **Zaka** is the district administrative center. The only other significant center is the village of Ndanga (at 20°11'S, 31°20'E). Zaka is now all **Communal Land.** In 1992 the district population was 191,631.

ZAMBEZI ESCARPMENT. Steep ridge running from east to west along approximately 16°30' south latitude. The escarpment separates the Zambezi Valley from the **Central Plateau.** The scarp drops as much as 1,500 m in the **Mavuradonha Mountains.** (see also **Dande; Mana Pools.**)

ZAMBEZI MISSION. In the late 1870s the Roman Catholic Society of Jesus began to organize a major missionary thrust into central Africa. This effort was known as the Zambezi Mission. Under the leadership of Henri Depelchin the first party of Jesuits reached **Tati** in August 1879. Several men remained there while the rest advanced to **Bulawayo,** where they were hospitably received by King **Lobengula.** The Jesuits performed many small services for the **Ndebele,** but like their Protestant predecessors of the **London Missionary Society,** they had almost no success in attracting converts. Their attempts to build a substantial station were ruined when Lobengula removed the town of Bulawayo to a new location in mid-1881. Six years later the Jesuits relocated their own station at **Empandeni.** Meanwhile, the Zambezi Mission segmented in an ambitious effort to open new stations elsewhere. In 1880 Augustus Law and Frans DeSadeleer made a disastrous trip to **Gazaland.** Other Jesuits traveled north in several unsuccessful attempts to start missions at Pandamatenga and in **Lozi** country. It was only after the 1896–97 **Revolts** that the Jesuits put their work within present Zimbabwe on a sound footing. (See **Prestage, P.; Hartman, A.**)

ZAMBEZI RIVER (variant: Zambesi). The fourth largest river in Africa, the Zambezi is also the continent's only major river to empty into the Indian Ocean. It rises in the extreme northwest corner of **Zambia,** near the sources of the Congo River, whence it turns south, flowing through eastern Angola and western Zambia before meeting Zimbabwe at **Kazungula.** From there the river flows in a generally northeasterly direction, defining the entire 715-km **border** between Zimbabwe and Zambia. It enters **Mozambique** just west of **Zumbo** where it is fed by the large

Luangwa River from the north. About 65 km east of Kazungula, the Zambezi dramatically plunges over **Victoria Falls**. From there it enters the **Batoka Gorge**, which now meets the calm waters of artificially made **Lake Kariba**, whose great dam taps the river's enormous hydroelectric potential.

The Zambezi draws most of its waters from its northern affluents. Zimbabwe contributes a smaller share through rivers that drain the **Central Plateau**. The most important of these affluents are—from west to east—the **Gwai, Sengwa, Bumi, Umniati, Hunyani**, and **Mazoe** rivers. The last two of these rivers meet the Zambezi inside Mozambique. The broad, flat Zambezi Valley is a hot, sultry region, containing some of the country's wildest and least-populated terrain. (See **Altitudinal Zones; Climate.**)

Stretches of the Zambezi are navigable, but the river has never afforded a practical transportation link to the sea. Between Victoria Falls and the coast, the river drops more than 900 m, thereby creating impassable falls and rapids along the way. Further, the mouth of the river is a shallow, muddy system of deltas, navigable only by small boats. Early **Portuguese** explorers attempted to penetrate the interior by way of the Zambezi Valley, but they never transformed it into a significant avenue of commerce. Since the 1890s the country's main access route has been overland, from **Mutare** to **Beira**.

Historically, the Zambezi has tended to separate cultural regions; however, its many stretches of comparatively shallow and sluggish water have been far from unfordable. In 1835, for example, **Zwangendaba** led his entire **Ngoni** nation across the river at a point near Zumbo. Later in the 19th century the **Ndebele** met with disaster on at least one occasion while campaigning against **Kololo**, but they later waged many successful campaigns against other peoples on the northern side. During the present century major crossing points have been established at **Kazungula, Victoria Falls, Kariba**, and **Chirundu**. (See **Rivers.**)

"ZAMBEZIA." Long a popular European term for the region around the **Zambezi River**, "Zambezia" was unofficially adopted as the name of the **British South Africa Company's** central African territories until the name **"Rhodesia"** was adopted in 1895. Zimbabwe was, until then, called "Southern Zambezia," and **Zambia**, "Northern Zambezia." When Northern Rhodesia became independent 1964, "Zambezia" was contracted to form the country's new name, "Zambia." Zambezia has also been the name of a province in Mozambique.

ZAMBIA. With a smaller population and almost twice the land of Zimbabwe, Zambia is separated from the latter by about 715 km of the **Zambezi River** between **Kazungula** and **Zumbo**. From very early times Zambia was a corridor for population movements into present Zimbabwe and beyond, but more recent movements across the Zambezi have generally been less fluid than has been the case along Zimbabwe's other **borders**. The only major African peoples living in both Zambia and Zimbabwe are the **Tonga**. During the early 19th century *Mfecane,* such migrant groups as the **Kololo** and **Ngoni** crossed the Zambezi into Zambia, but the river appears to have been one of the obstacles to further northward migration by the **Ndebele**.

During the late 19th century the same northward imperialist thrust that took the **British South Africa Company** into present Zimbabwe took the company into Zambia, where it established two colonies, North-Eastern and North-Western Rhodesia, in the 1890s. In 1911 the BSAC brought these two territories under a single administration as Northern Rhodesia. When Southern Rhodesia gained **Responsible Government** as a British Crown Colony in 1923, the BSAC also quit Northern Rhodesia, which became a British protectorate.

From the early 20th century Northern Rhodesia's economy, built around copper mining, was tied into that of Southern Rhodesia. A **railway** link between the two countries was established through **Victoria Falls** in 1904–05. Thereafter most of Northern Rhodesia's export trade was carried through Southern Rhodesia. As Southern Rhodesia itself turned away from closer ties with **South Africa**, increased attention was given to **amalgamation** of Southern and Northern Rhodesia. This was achieved in 1953, when the two countries, along with Nyasaland (now Malawi), were joined in the **Federation of Rhodesia and Nyasaland**. From the start of federation, however, African opinion in the northern territories strongly opposed Southern Rhodesian settler domination. African political activities in the northern territories focused upon opposition to the federation, from which both territories were allowed to secede at the end of 1963. On October 24, 1964, Northern Rhodesia became independent as "Zambia" (a contraction of **"Zambezia"**) with Kenneth Kaunda as first prime minister (later, first president).

Thirteen months after Zambia's independence, the white minority government of **Rhodesia** declared its **unilateral declaration of independence**. President Kaunda moved quickly to have Zambia implement partial **sanctions** against the illegal regime. In 1972 **Zambia** closed its **borders** with Rhodesia, an act of economic self-sacrifice and an important political act against the Rhodesia regime. With the imposition of sanctions, the majority of Zambia's trade goods had to be rerouted at a substantial increase in cost. Some trade went by truck through **Botswana** and **Mozambique**, but much of it was redirected through Tanzania. After the border closure in 1972 Zambia diverted most of its rail traffic though Angola, but that route was lost when civil war in that country closed the railway line in August 1975. This caused great economic hardship for Zambia as the Tanzam railway through Tanzania, being built by the People's Republic of China, was not scheduled for completion until the following year. When it opened Zambia had a direct link with the port at Dar es Salaam. By 1978, 90 percent of Zambia's trade went through Dar es Salaam. The monetary cost of imposing and maintaining sanctions was staggering to Zambia. The United Nations has estimated that in the 1973–79 period alone, the cost to Zambia was $1.25 billion annually in lost revenues and higher transportation costs. The cost in delayed development and human suffering is impossible to estimate. Zambia's economy was also hurt during this period by the constant fall in the international price of copper. The combination of falling copper prices and increased transport cost created a crisis in the Zambian economy in the mid-1970s. This economic crisis and the resulting domestic political pressure—particularly from commercial farmers—caused the Zambian government to open its borders to railway transport through Rhodesia in 1978.

Throughout the late 1960s and 1970s Zambia allowed Zimbabwean liberation forces to operate from within its borders. As early as 1966, sporadic military raids into Rhodesia were launched from Zambian territory. President Kaunda also played an active role in trying to unite the different liberation organizations. After efforts at unity between the Zimbabwe African Nation Union (**ZANU**) and the Zimbabwe African People's Union (**ZAPU**) in the late 1960s failed, Kaunda supported the creation of a new organization, the Front for the Liberation of Zimbabwe (**FROLIZI**). Although FROLIZI failed, Kaunda continued his efforts to bring about unity of the liberation movements. He believed that only through unity would a negotiated settlement with the Smith regime be obtained, and it was in Zambia's interests to see an end to the war as quickly as possible. In 1975 he was a principle force behind the **Victoria Falls Conference**. From the mid-1970s Kaunda worked within the format of the **Frontline States** to exert pressure on both the Smith government and liberation movements to find an acceptable negotiated solution to the war. His efforts saw some success with the formation of the **Patriotic Front** in October 1976. Also in that year, ZANU's military wing ceased operating from within Zambia, shifting operations to newly independent Mozambique. From that time Zambia more openly supported ZAPU and its military wing. (See **Zimbabwe African National Liberation Army; Zimbabwe People's Revolutionary Army**.)

Zambia's continued support of the Zimbabwean liberation movements resulted in frequent incursions by **Rhodesian security forces**. In addition to Zimbabwean refugees and military forces, several thousand Zambian civilians were killed in these raids. Zambia also had the additional cost of maintaining large refugee camps throughout the liberation war. In 1978, the refugee population reached a high of 70,000.

At the time of Zimbabwean independence, and for many years thereafter, Kaunda and Zambians in general were considered heroes by the people and government of Zimbabwe. However, the end of the liberation war in Zimbabwe, the lifting of international sanctions and the general revitalization of Zimbabwe's economy was not accompanied by a revival of Zambia's economy. Largely as a result of the continuance of depressed prices in the world copper market, Kaunda's government was faced with a deteriorating economy throughout the 1980s. By the end of the 1980s the government was facing a political crisis as rising unemployment and increasing economic hardship eroded popular support for Kaunda and his government.

In 1990, the government reluctantly accepted the imposition of an International Monetary Fund Structural Adjustment Program in order to receive foreign loans it hoped would reverse the country's economic crisis. One condition of the program was that the government discontinue subsidizing production of cornmeal, the country's staple food. Upon implementing this condition, the government was faced with urban rioting and a popular call for the reintroduction of multiparty democratic elections—so that people had a say in policies that affected them so directly. In March 1990, however, the country's ruling party, the United National Independence Party (UNIP) rejected proposals to create a multiparty political system. By May, following mounting resentment toward the UNIP, the government and Kaunda himself, Kaunda announced plans for a referendum on the introduction of a multiparty democracy. In June the government doubled the price of cornmeal and was immediately confronted with the largest riots in the capital city, Lusaka, since the days prior to independence. The rioting and calls for the end of UNIP-rule then rapidly spread nationwide. By mid-September, an opposition party, the Movement for Multi-Party Democracy (MMD) had been formed and was attracting crowds in excess of 70,000 to prodemocracy rallies throughout the country. On September 27, the UNIP reversed itself and endorsed the referendum; and on December 7, Kaunda signed a bill which transformed Zambia into a multiparty democracy.

During early and mid-1991, the MMD campaigned for elections and increased its popular support, while the UNIP was shaken by the defection of several longtime members, including former and current cabinet ministers. Elections were held October 31 and November 1. The MMD, under the leadership of presidential candidate Frederick Chiluba, the former head of Zambia's Congress of Trade Unions, won 100 of 150 parliamentary seats. Chiluba was sworn in as the country's second president in November. In January 1992, Kaunda resigned as UNIP chairman, a position he had held for nearly 30 years, and a year later announced his retirement from politics.

Unfortunately, the end of the political crisis did not end the country's economic problems. After the election, Chiluba was unable to implement programs to revitalize the copper industry and the country's unemployment rate remained at nearly 18 percent of the workforce. In addition, his government was plagued by accusations of inefficiency and corruption.

ZANKE (variants: Hwange; Wankie). Dynastic title of the **Nanzwa** rulers.

ZANSI. Sindebele term for "south," applied to members of **Ndebele** society who came from the south, i.e., **Nguni** country in South Africa (properly, sing., *izansi;* pl., *abezansi*). These people are descendants mostly of **Mzilikazi's** original northern Nguni followers and of other Nguni who joined him in the **Transvaal.** The term was apparently first used in this context during the 1820s and 1830s. At that time Ndebele society was absorbing many **Sotho-speaking** peoples who became known as *enhla,* or "those from the north." The *zansi* were soon a minority within the growing society, and they constituted an even smaller part of the whole population after the *holi* were added north of the **Limpopo River.** Because the *zansi* occupied most hereditary offices within the Ndebele kingdom, they were a dominant and highly visible minority by the mid-19th century. Europeans described the *zansi* as a closed aristocracy, giving rise the to the exaggerated notion that the Ndebele were divided into a rigid, three-tier "caste" system.

ZAVE (Zawi until 1982). Located due northwest of **Harare,** this small village serves as the terminus of the branch **railway** line into the **Makonde District** (at 17°13'S, 30°2'E).

ZASWI see ZAVE

ZEEDERBERG COACHES. Mule-drawn carriages, similar to stage coaches of the United States, from which country many Zeederberg coaches were imported in the late 19th century. Mail and passenger services on such coaches were introduced into Zimbabwe during the 1890s by the South African Zeederberg family. During the early 20th century these coaches were soon displaced by expanding **railway** services.

ZEZURU (a.k.a. "Central Shona"). Linguistic and ethnic name for the central-most cluster of **Shona-speaking peoples**. The Zezuru (or Vazezuru) constitute about a quarter of the country's Shona peoples. They live mainly in the region between **Chinhoyi** in the northwest, **Mvurwi** in the north, **Mutoko** in the northeast, **Wedza** in the east, **Bikita** in the southeast, and **Kwekwe** in the southwest. As the central Shona dialect, Zezuru (or Chizezuru) contains the largest number of typically Shona language features. For this reason, and because Zezuru people surround the highly developed **Harare** region, Chizezuru forms the basis of standardized **Chishona**. Among the important ethnic subgroups of the Zezuru are the **Shavasha, Hera, Gova, Njanja,** and **Mbire.**

"ZHUWAWO." Symbolic name for mythical common man (analogous to, e.g., the German *Jedermann*) popularized by the **African National Congress** during the late 1950s to express the movement's non-elitist ideals. From **Chishona** word for ordinary laborer.

ZIMBA. (a.k.a. Zumba; Mumba). Famous, but historically poorly understood migrant bands that ravaged the entire eastern African coast during the late 16th century, while earning a reputation as cannibals. The Zimba people apparently derived from Marave, just north of the lower **Zambezi River**. In 1597 two groups of "Zimba" entered Zimbabwe during the reign of Munhumutapa **Gatsi Rusere**. One group was forcibly expelled, the other was apparently peacefully absorbed by the **Shona.**

ZIMBABWE [the name] (variants: dzimbabwe; dzimbahwe). (1) Generic **Chishona** term for stone dwelling (pl. *madzimbabwe*). Both the etymology of the word and its precise applications are controversial. It is usually interpreted as a contraction either of the phrase *dzimba* ("large house") *da* ("of") *mabwe* ("stones"), or of *dzimba woye* ("venerated house"). *Dzimbabwe* is also translated into "walled grave" or "royal court." Some authorities argue that these different translations actually derive from several similar, but distinct, Chishona words, but in practice the term "zimbabwe" is applied in English to different kinds of stone structures. It should be understood that "Great Zimbabwe" of the **Zimbabwe Ruins** is merely the largest and most famous of many **ruins** known as "zimbabwes."

(2) Since independence in April 1980, "Zimbabwe" has been the official name of the country. The use of "Zimbabwe" in a political context, as the name to replace **"Rhodesia"** once African majority rule and independence were achieved, apparently first occurred in 1961 with the formation of the **Zimbabwe National Party**.

ZIMBABWE AFRICAN NATIONAL LIBERATION ARMY (ZANLA). Name of the military wing of the Zimbabwe African National Union (**ZANU**)

ZANLA always had its main base of support in **Mashonaland,** and the majority of its combatants were **Shona.** However, it was always a command policy that combatants not operate in their home areas. It is difficult to pinpoint when ZANLA was formed. According to one recent study, ZANU opened a military training camp at Itumbi, Tanzania, in 1965; the nationalist combatants who engaged **Rhodesian security forces** at the **Battle of Chinhoyi** in April 1966 are generally referred to as ZANLA members. By early 1968 ZANU cadres inside the country were actively recruiting young men to leave the country for military training. It is also known that by early 1969 ZANU leadership felt it necessary to from a military high command to coordinate military operations. In April of that year eight ZANU leaders met in Lusaka, **Zambia,** and formed the *Dare re Chimurenga* (commonly referred to simply as DARE), literally meaning "Council of the Rebellion" (see **Chimurenga**), although it apparently had no members with actual military training until the early 1970s. From the mid-1960s until the early 1970s ZANLA operations were based in Zambia and directed by **Herbert Chitepo,** the exiled leader of ZANU. In 1972 **Josiah Tongogara** was appointed commander of ZANLA, and in 1973 he was elected to chair DARE; from that time DARE's members were all military commanders.

The exact command structure of ZANLA is also not clear, but apparently after 1973, with the appointment of Tongogara, the DARE chairman was also the overall commander of ZANLA forces, and theoretically directed all operations. Tongogara, who evoked great loyalty from his subordinates, held this position from 1972 until his death in 1979; **Rex Nhongo** was then appointed acting commander. Below the commander was a general staff, then, apparently, the military commanders of ZANLA's training camps in Zambia (only until the early 1970s), Tanzania, and **Mozambique.** They were followed by the field commanders, and then the leaders of groups of freedom fighters operating inside **Rhodesia.** Each group had five combatants, including a political commissar, and generally operated within five-group patrols. ZANLA went through two tactical stages. The first, beginning with the battle of Chinhoyi and lasting until about mid-1971, was based on the strategy of direct confrontation with Rhodesian security forces. This involved infiltration of combatants from Zambia, and proved to be highly unsuccessful; the much better equipped and trained Rhodesian security forces had little trouble in defeating ZANLA's forces in these early skirmishes. In 1972 ZANLA changed its operation tactics to those which have been generally credited with making it much more effective militarily, and eventually contributing to the political triumph of ZANU. Masterminded by Chitepo, ZANLA dropped its confrontational strategy and adopted tactics based on the examples of the People's Republic of China and **FRELIMO** in Mozambique. From mid-1971 emphasis was placed on politicizing the peasantry in rural areas, hit-and-run raids on government outposts (police camps, cattle-dipping tanks, etc.), ambushes of military patrols, and attacks on European-owned farms. Chitepo had two aims: to dispel the notion of the European community's military invincibility, with guerrilla forces that would be difficult to defeat decisively; and to escalate the cost of war for the Rhodesian government by forcing it to deploy military forces throughout the country to combat roaming bands of freedom fighters. The increased pressure on the government would eventually force it to agree to negotiations to end the war. Its strategy of politicizing the peasantry is often given as the main reason that ZANU was able to dominate the 1980 **elections**.

Beginning in mid-1971 ZANLA began to put the new strategy into effect by infiltrating forces into the northeast region of the country. For more than a year these forces concentrated on building contacts with the local African peoples in the Tribal Trust Lands (now **Communal Lands**) and establishing an infrastructural support system. In December 1972 a group attacked Altena farm in the **Centenary** area, an act that marked the beginning of a series of attacks on European-owned farms and the start of the new phase of the armed struggle. The success of this strategy was then followed with increased infiltration of ZANLA forces into the eastern and southern regions of the country over the next several years. It has been estimated that about 100 ZANLA combatants were inside the country in 1971. That number rose to c. 700 by 1976, 3,000 by mid-1977 and more than 10,000 (including 1,500 to 2,000 women) by late 1979. In addition, ZANLA reportedly had nearly 20,000 other combatants in camps in Mozambique and Tanzania undergoing military training at the time of the **Lancaster House Conference**.

ZANLA's successes after 1972 must to a large extent be credited to its association with FRELIMO in Mozambique. After a decade of armed struggle with the **Portuguese**, FRELIMO controlled **Tete** Province in northwest Mozambique. The FRELIMO leadership allowed ZANLA, which it had helped to train, to establish forward camps in the province. Those camps made it much easier to infiltrate combatants and to keep them supplied than it had been from ZANLA's previous camps in Zambia and Tanzania. With Mozambican independence in 1975, FRELIMO further assisted ZANLA by allowing it to open additional camps throughout Mozambique. This opened Rhodesia's entire eastern **border**, greatly taxing the Rhodesian security forces' abilities to curtail the infiltration of ZANLA forces into the country. The independence of Mozambique also greatly facilitated ZANLA recruitment inside Rhodesia. New recruits, primarily students who voluntarily left school, could more easily leave areas throughout Mashonaland and cross into Mozambique for military training than when the closest camps had been located in central Zambia. This helps to explain ZANLA's rapid troop buildup after 1975. The closeness of its camps in Mozambique also helps to explain why ZANLA is generally credited with carrying the greatest burden of the fighting against Rhodesian security forces during the period from 1972 to 1979.

At the Lancaster House Conference, ZANU leadership agreed that its ZANLA forces would collect at assembly points inside the country and that ZANLA would be integrated along with **ZIPRA** and former Rhodesian security forces into a new **Zimbabwe National Army**.

ZIMBABWE AFRICAN NATIONAL UNION (ZANU). ZANU was founded on August 6, 1963, under the leadership of **Ndabaningi Sithole** when dissident members of the Zimbabwe African People's Union (**ZAPU**) rejected **Joshua Nkomo**'s leadership. Sithole, and others including **Leopold Takawira** and **Robert Mugabe**, were critical of Nkomo's long absences from the country and his proposed establishment of a government in exile. The ZANU founders were more committed to a strategy of internal organization and political action within the country.

In May 1964 ZANU held its first general congress in **Gweru**, where Sithole was elected president and Mugabe secretary general. On August 26, 1964, ZANU was banned by the government, along with the People's Caretaker Council (**PCC**), a ZAPU front organization. Sithole, Mugabe, and most party leaders in the country were arrested and spent the next decade in prison. During the decade, ZANU leaders, though in prison, maintained a large degree of authority as the recognized political leadership of ZANU while an external ZANU organization based in Lusaka, **Zambia**, under the leadership of **Herbert Chitepo** as chairman of a Revolutionary Council, developed after late 1965. The external organization created the **Zimbabwe African National Liberation Army** as the party's armed wing in the mid-1960s, and established the military organization necessary to conduct an armed struggle against the government of **Rhodesia**.

While in prison Sithole's policies and attitudes began to be questioned by the imprisoned members of the party executive, including **Mugabe, Edgar Tekere,** and **Maurice Nyagumbo**. In 1970, a secret vote by six members of this group removed Sithole as party leader and replaced him with Mugabe. Because it was virtually impossible to inform the external element of ZANU of this change in leadership, a struggle for the recognized leadership of the party between Sithole and Mugabe developed openly after the two were released in late 1974. This struggle persisted until late 1975 when both ZANLA's military leadership and a large group of its field commanders rejected Sithole completely and began openly to support Mugabe (see **Mgagao Declaration**). Mugabe's ZANLA support generally won him the acceptance of the ZANU factions that had previously questioned his authority. However, his leadership of the party was not formalized until a ZANU Central Committee meeting, held in Chimoio, **Mozambique**, in 1977.

In 1975, following the assassination of Chitepo and the Zambian government's arrest of most of ZANLA's leadership for his murder, ZANU moved its headquarters to Mozambique. In early 1976 ZANU joined with ZAPU to form the **Patriotic Front**. It then participated in the **Geneva Conference** later in the year. After the failure of that conference, ZANU continued to operate as part of the PF in international diplomatic talks, but in actual practice remained a separate entity from ZAPU. It maintained its own party organization and recruitment, as well as conducting the war, through ZANLA, with its own political agenda and strategy. ZANU political commissars accompanied ZANLA combatants inside Rhodesia and explained ZANU's policies, particularly questions relating to the ownership of the land, to the local peasantry. They also established a loosely structured local party organization and gained a wide acceptance of ZANU in the areas in which ZANLA operated (see **Mashonaland**). It was the development of this political infrastructure during the 1972–79 period of the war for national liberation which is generally considered instrumental in explaining ZANU's political victories after 1979.

In 1979 ZANU took part in the **Lancaster House Conference** as part of the PF delegation. Following the successful completion of that conference, Mugabe surprised most observers by announcing that ZANU would contest the forthcoming elections as an independent party, not as a member of the PF. During the campaigning for the general election, ZAPU attempted to register the name "Patriotic Front" for itself, believing that that would help give it an electoral advantage. In addition, Sithole entered the elections under the "ZANU" banner—claiming the party name he had used when contesting the **Internal Settlement** elections the previous year. The British officials overseeing the election ruled that the party headed by Mugabe should officially be referred to as "ZANU (Patriotic Front)." In the 1980 general elections ZANU (PF) won 63 percent of the total vote, and 57 of 80 **House of Assembly** seats contested by black candidates (Europeans voted for 20 "reserved" seats). Mugabe was then asked to form the first government of the independent Republic of Zimbabwe. Following the elections, the party kept the official name "ZANU (PF)."

Since 1980 ZANU increased its control throughout the Mashonaland provinces. It established a tighter party organization and was virtually unopposed in local urban and rural council elections until the late 1990s. However, in the years immediately following independence, ZANU was not able to transfer that success to the areas of **Matabeleland**. There were hundreds of reported clashes between followers of the two parties, particularly around the time of the 1985 elections. The main source of rivalry seemed to be fears of the predominantly **Ndebele**-supported ZAPU that the government, dominated by the predominantly Shona-supported ZANU, would not extend equal political rights, and material resources for economic development to all regions of the country. These fears were to a great extent allayed following the 1985 elections, as leaders of the two parties initiated a series of talks which culminated in the December 1987 signing of the **Unity Pact** amalgamating ZAPU and ZANU. At a specially convened party congress on April 9, 1988, ZANU representatives unanimously approved the Unity Pact, and the party officially absorbed ZAPU.

In August 1984 ZANU held its Second Party Congress in Harare. The congress adopted a new party constitution which accepted "Marxism-Leninism" as the official party ideology, as well as the idea of a one-party state for Zimbabwe. The congress also elected Mugabe party president and first secretary, and **Simon Muzenda** vice president. Mugabe and Muzenda were re-elected to these posts within ZANU at party congresses in December 1989 and September 1994. In the 1985 general elections, ZANU increased its **parliamentary** majority to 63 seats, winning 76 percent of the total black vote (Europeans still voted for "reserved" seats).

Since the late-1980s, ZANU increased its political hold on government, while at the same time losing some of its popular support. In the 1990 general elections, ZANU won 116 **House of Assembly** seats, but only 54 percent of registered voters voted. In early 1995, for the first time in two decades, reports of factionalism in ZANU surfaced. Local membership, apparently resenting Mugabe's long-time control of the party, rejected many candidates proposed by the central committee of the party. Although the party won 118 House of Assembly seats (55 unopposed) in the elections held later that year, voter turnout remained at an estimated 54 percent. Although the party's politburo rejected formalizing a one-party state system for Zimbabwe in August 1990, and in June 1991, Mugabe announced that ZANU was abandoning Marxism and Leninism as party and state ideologies, it was not until September 1994 that ZANU convened its second National Congress since independence and officially renounced Marxism, Leninism, and scientific socialism as guiding principles and accepted the concepts of a market-based economy. Mugabe argued that this change in guiding political principles was brought on partly in response to Zimbabwe's pursuit of loans from the World Bank and International Monetary Fund and partly because socialism was being abandoned over much of the world following the end of the Cold War.

By the mid-1990s opposition to ZANU's near monopolistic hold on political power had greatly increased. Subject to mounting accusations of corruption at all levels of the party, ZANU faced its greatest challenge since independence in 2000. In February of that year, a ZANU-supported referendum to adopt a new constitution was defeated. In national elections held in June, ZANU was challenged by candidates of the **Movement for Democratic Change** in every constituency in the nation. When the results of the election were announced, it was clear that while the party had maintained its support in rural areas, it had suffered a major political defeat in the country's urban centers. The MDC had won 57 seats, making it the first effective opposition group to challenge ZANU's control of government. Moreover, the results were interpreted by many as a rejection of the party's control of government and, more specifically, as a repudiation of Mugabe's continued leadership of both ZANU and the government.

ZIMBABWE AFRICAN NATIONAL UNION-NDONGA (ZANU-NDONGA). Political party founded in early 1993 by **Ndabaningi Sithole** following his return to the country. ZANU-Ndonga was established as a platform for Sithole's outspoken criticism of government policy in general, **ZANU**'s political dominance in the country following the **Unity Pact**, and, in particular, the leadership of President **Robert Mugabe**. ZANU-Ndonga was one of five opposition parties to contest the 1995 **elections**, and the only one to win any seats in **Parliament**. It won 6.5 percent of the vote and captured two seats in **Chipinge** South constituency in the southeastern province of **Manicaland**. This area is the home region of the **Ndau** people and had been an area of opposition to ZANU since independence. In the June 2000 elections, ZANU-Ndonga retained only one of its seats in parliament.

ZIMBABWE AFRICAN PEOPLE'S UNION (ZAPU). African nationalist political party founded on December 18, 1961—nine days after the government banned the **National Democratic Party**. With **Joshua Nkomo** as president, ZAPU adopted virtually the entire NDP organization, leadership, and goals. In September 1962 the government banned ZAPU and arrested all its officers except Nkomo, who was out of the country. During the next year many nationalist leaders regrouped in Dar es Salaam, Tanganyika (now Tanzania). A split between these leaders began to develop, based on criticism of Nkomo's frequent absences from Southern Rhodesia and his proposed strategy of forming a government in exile. In a surprise move in mid-1963, Nkomo returned to Salisbury, where he denounced **Ndabaningi Sithole, Leopold Takawira, Robert Mugabe,** and others as "dissidents" and expelled them from the party. These men returned home and announced formation of the Zimbabwe African

National Union (**ZANU**) on August 8, 1963. Nkomo quickly countered by announcing the formation of the **People's Caretaker Council**, with himself as head. The PCC was merely a front organization for the banned ZAPU, whose name resurfaced after the banning of the PCC in August 1964. After **Ian Smith** came to power in April 1964, Nkomo and most of the ZAPU leadership were arrested and spent most of the next decade in prisons and detention camps. ZAPU then reorganized externally in Lusaka, **Zambia**, under the leadership of **Jason Moyo** and others. It was during this period that Moyo began to establish the military wing of ZAPU, the Zimbabwe People's Revolutionary Army (**ZIPRA**). Throughout the early 1970s there were several attempts by leaders of the **Frontline States** to reunite ZAPU and ZANU, but none succeeded (see **Front For The Liberation of Zimbabwe**). In December 1971 ZAPU leadership joined with other nationalist leaders to form the **African National Council**. ZAPU, however, continued to operate out of its Lusaka headquarters, even though Nkomo returned to **Rhodesia** and worked for nearly a year as head of the ANC (Nkomo) organization. He held a series of talks with Smith, and while he claimed to speak for the external ZAPU, it is not entirely clear that he officially represented ZAPU at those meeting. In early 1976 Nkomo left the country and regained control of ZAPU in Zambia.

Later in 1976 Nkomo and ZAPU joined Mugabe and ZANU to form the **Patriotic Front**, and participated in the **Geneva Conference.** After the failure of this conference, Nkomo returned to Zambia and directed an intensified recruiting campaign for ZIPRA. This was partly in response to increasing criticism of ZAPU by Kenneth Kaunda—the president of Zambia and ZAPU's primary supporter among the Frontline States. Kaunda had become concerned that ZAPU was not contributing an equal share to the war effort. As a result of this military buildup, ZAPU became more allied with the Soviet Union, its main supplier of military materials.

In late 1979, as part of the PF, Nkomo and ZAPU took part in the **Lancaster House Conference**. Many observers expected Nkomo to win the **elections** that followed that conference. However, in a surprise move, Mugabe announced that ZANU would contest the elections independently of the PF. This meant that ZAPU would have to do the same and put ZAPU at a disadvantage. Unlike ZANU and **ZANLA** in **Mashonaland,** ZAPU had not developed a program of politicizing the rural areas of **Matabeleland** in which ZIPRA primarily operated. The party appeared to lack the political infrastructure that ZANU had developed in the Mashonaland provinces. Although most observers at the time did not see it, ZAPU was also at a disadvantage because its support came largely from the **Ndebele** people in Matabeleland, and that group accounted for only about 15 percent of the total population. In the 1980 general elections ZAPU won only 24 percent of the black vote (whites voted for 20 "reserved" seats) and 20 seats in the **House of Assembly**. In the government formed by Mugabe, only four cabinet posts went to ZAPU members. Over the next several years ZAPU developed a more formal party organization in Matabeleland but was not able to expand into other areas of the country. From 1982 to 1985, ZAPU supporters were involved in hundreds of reported clashes with ZANU supporters. On a national level, Nkomo was almost constantly critical of both the government and ZANU. The primary cause of concern for ZAPU leadership was the calls by Mugabe and other ZANU leaders for the establishment of a one-party state in Zimbabwe. In 1982 ZAPU cabinet ministers were dismissed following the discovery of arms caches at farms reportedly owned by ZAPU supporters. The continuing conflict between the parties climaxed in 1983, when Nkomo fled the country, claiming that government troops had tried to kill him. After his return in August, ZAPU leadership continued to criticize the government, but tensions diminished somewhat. Tensions increased again during the period leading up to the 1985 general election, with supporters from both parties dying in political clashes. In the elections, ZAPU parliamentary members "crossed the aisle" and joined ZANU. Simultaneously, Nkomo and the ZAPU leadership joined in a series of talks with ZANU. These eventually culminated in the signing of a **Unity Pact** in December 1987 by Nkomo and Mugabe, and the amalgamation of ZANU and ZAPU. At a specially called party congress on April 2, 1988, more than 5,000 ZAPU delegates voted to officially approve the Unity Pact and merge with ZANU.

A grassroots organization calling itself "New ZAPU" attempted to revitalize the party in Matabeleland and contest the June 2000 House of Assembly elections. While it supported 23 candidates in those elections, it failed to win any seats.

ZIMBABWE "BIRDS." The only sizeable representational carvings yet found in a precolonial archaeological site are eight soapstone "bird" figures taken from the **Zimbabwe Ruins** between 1889 and the early 1900s. Though more reptilian than avian in overall appearance, these figures are called "birds" because they are winged (but without tails) and bipedal. Each specimen is about 36 cm in height, carved atop a meter-long monolith. Except for numerous monoliths with only geometric incisions, nothing similar has been found anywhere else in the country. Seven of the bird figures were taken from the Hill Ruin at Zimbabwe; the eighth was found in the valley Phillips Ruin. Since their original locations were not accurately recorded when they were collected, their placement and function have inspired considerable controversy. Some authorities speculate that each figure symbolized the ancestral spirit of a former ruler. During the 20th century the "birds" have come to symbolize the Zimbabwe Ruins themselves, and they are frequently depicted in illustrative materials, including stamps, the government's official coat of arms, and the Zimbabwean flag.

ZIMBABWE BROADCASTING CORPORATION (ZBC). Radio broadcasting began experimentally during the early 1930s, drawing heavily upon British Broadcasting Corporation (BBC) programs and recorded music. By 1941 a regular studio was established in Salisbury (now **Harare**), where a full-time professional broadcaster was employed. During the 1940s this studio concentrated on English-language programming, while African listeners were served by broadcasts originating in Lusaka, Northern Rhodesia (now **Zambia**). The **federation** government took over English broadcasts in the 1950s, formally establishing the Federal Broadcasting Corporation (FBC) in 1958. After the federation's breakup in late 1963, the headquarters of the FBC were transformed into the Southern Rhodesian Broadcasting Corporation (later called the Rhodesian Broadcasting Corporation [RBC]), which soon reached the entire country from seven medium-wave stations.

Television broadcasting began as a private commercial operation in 1960, initially serving only Salisbury. In 1964 the government-owned RBC bought out the Rhodesian Television Company, making television broadcasting a government monopoly. Additional stations were added in **Bulawayo** in 1961, **Gweru** in 1970, and **Mutare** in 1972. Each station transmitted over a radius of only 160 km, but it was estimated that by the early 1970s, 80 percent of the country's settler population was being reached, with a growing number of African viewers in the main urban centers.

After the **Rhodesian Front** assumed power in 1962, the RBC increasingly became an instrument for government propaganda. When the government acquired the RBC in 1964, it replaced the corporation's board members and news service personnel with RF supporters willing to practice self-**censorship**. **Ian Smith** openly stated his aim of using the broadcast media to counter unfavorable criticism leveled by the country's independent **press**. BBC programs, which previously dominated the airwaves, were largely eliminated, and their place was taken by South African Broadcasting Corporation and RBC-produced programs. Following independence, the RBC was renamed the Zimbabwe Broadcasting Corporation (ZBC), and new board members, including four Africans and the European former chairman of the RBC, were appointed. The radio component was reorganized into three branches: Radio 1—with general programming and news services in English; Radio 2—broadcast in the **Ndebele** and **Shona** languages; and Radio 3—which carried youth, music, and current-affairs programming. By the early 1990s, an additional branch, Radio 4, was transmitting educational programming. In 1993, there were c. 522,000 licensed radio receivers in the country. Zimbabwe television broadcasts on two channels, and in 1991, 137,090 television sets were licensed. While there is some locally produced programming on television, most entertainment programs come from either Britain or the United States. Both radio and television news and commentaries rely strongly on the government-controlled Zimbabwe Inter-Africa News Agency for versions of domestic and foreign events. At the end of 1996, the government announced that it was ending its monopoly control of the ZBC.

ZIMBABWE CONFERENCE ON RECONSTRUCTION AND DEVELOPMENT (ZIMCORD). A major fund-raising conference held in **Harare** in March 1981. Forty-five nations, mostly representing Western industrialized nations, the Middle East, and Asia, attended, along with 15 UN agencies and 10 international aid societies. Prime Minister **Robert Mugabe** asked for donations totaling $US 1.2 billion to be used to rehabilitate the economy. Pledges totaling c. $US 800 million were received, with the largest donors being British ($US 284 million), the European Community ($US 175 million), and the United States. However, many of those pledges never materialized.

ZIMBABWE CONTROVERSY. An expression generally applied to the debate over the origins of the **Zimbabwe Ruins**. The "controversy" had its roots in early Muslim and **Portuguese** myths about **Ophir** and "King

Solomon's Mines." The Solomonic myth of Zimbabwe's origins was adopted by **Karl Mauch,** the first European to describe Zimbabwe, and was later elaborated by **J. T. Bent, R. N. Hall, A. Wilmot,** and other antiquarian investigators of the ruins. On the basis of this myth, racialist assumptions of African creative incapacity, popular diffusionist theories, superficial similarities between features of the Zimbabwe Ruins and Near Eastern structures, and the apparent absence of local African traditions about the origins of the ruins, Bent and Hall published elaborate arguments that the ruins had been built by ancient Near Easterners, such as Phoenicians or Sabean Arabs. Such theories went unchallenged until scientific archaeological investigation was initiated by **David Randall-MacIver** in 1905.

Publication of Randall-MacIver's findings turned the theories of ancient and exotic Zimbabwe origins inside-out. Randall-MacIver demonstrated that the ruins were purely African in origin and of comparatively recent ("medieval") date. Randall-MacIver's strong attack on Hall's work embarrassed the latter, who—unlike Randall-MacIver—was a local settler with aspirations for further employment at the ruins sites. Hall responded with a vigorous rebuttal, thus keeping alive in the local public mind a debate which was, for all trained scholars, already closed.

ZIMBABWE NATIONAL ARMY (ZNA). Created in 1980 when elements from **ZANLA, ZIPRA,** and the **Rhodesian Security Forces** were integrated. Following the cease-fire agreed to at the **Lancaster House Conference**, ZANLA and ZIPRA guerrillas began gathering at assigned Assembly Points throughout the country, while units of the Rhodesian security forces assembled at their bases. Beginning in May 1980, former ZANLA and ZIPRA officers and NCOs began training under British advisors. The training was intended to create a battalion-level command structure. Initially the top graduate from each training class, regardless of former affiliation, was appointed to command one of the newly organized integrated battalions, with the second in command being a member of the other group. This procedure was changed in early 1981, when political considerations were made in appointing battalion commanders—the result being that more former ZANLA officers became battalion commanders.

The newly trained commanders took charge of integrated battalions—units made up of formers ZANLA and ZIPRA combatants. By the end of 1982, the ZNA had 29 integrated battalions, organized in four brigades. Each brigade also had artillery, engineering, signal and other support units assigned. These support units were generally made up of former Rhodesian security forces units. The ZNA also had three highly trained combat battalions, basically former **Rhodesian African Rifle** battalions, assigned to the 1st, 3rd, and 4th Brigades. The ZNA also had a unique element, the 5th Brigade. Although theoretically part of the ZNA, in reality it was outside of the Army's regular command structure. Formed in August 1981 from two unintegrated ZANLA battalions and perhaps another 3,000 former ZANLA combatants and trained by North Korean advisers, the operation of this unit was always shrouded in mystery. It was more heavily mechanized than other ZNA units and reportedly followed orders directly from Prime Minister **Robert Mugabe**'s office. Its most publicized operations in **Matabeleland** in 1982–83 were officially directed at the suppression of **dissident** activities. However, it came under very severe local and international criticism for its reportedly brutal treatment of the local **Ndebele** in that region. As a result of that criticism, it was reportedly disbanded in 1984, with its units being integrated into the ZNA's other four brigades and a newly formed 6th Brigade.

Beginning in the mid-1980s and lasting until September 1993, between 8,000 and 10,000 ZNA troops were annually stationed inside **Mozambique** in an attempt to protect **road** and **railway** transport from sabotage by units of the **Mozambique National Resistance**. While the exact numerical strength of the ZNA is hard to determine, in 1986 it reportedly had 41,000 trained men and women under arms. By 1994, that number had increased to approximately 47,000, consisting of 26 infantry battalions, supported by one armored, one field artillery, and one engineer regiment. The air force had an additional 2,000 personnel in eight squadrons. In July of that year, President Mugabe announced that in response to peace talks in Mozambique and improved political conditions in **South Africa**, the ZNA would be cut in strength to about 30,000. However, these cuts in ZNA strength did not immediately take place, with combined manpower reaching 40,000 in early 1997.

In mid-1998, the Zimbabwe government announced that it was sending ZNA troops to the Democratic Republic of the Congo to support the regime of Laurent Kabila. By September 1999, there were an estimated 11,000 ZNA troops in that country. Though very unpopular in Zimbabwe, those troops continued their service in the Congo through much of 2000.

ZIMBABWE NATIONAL PARK. A 723-hectare (1,786-acre) area surrounding the **Zimbabwe Ruins** was declared a **national park** in 1951. In addition to the ruins, the park includes a museum maintained by the **Historical Monuments Commission**, a golf course, and limited tourist lodgings. Just to the north is **Lake Kyle**.

ZIMBABWE NATIONAL PARTY (ZNP). Short-lived nationalist political party founded in June 1961 to oppose the **National Democratic Party**, which had initially endorsed the terms of the **Constitution of 1961**. Among the ZNP leaders were **Patrick Marimba, Michael Mawema**, and **Edison Sithole**. Never able to attract a significant following, the ZNP faded quickly after the emergence of the **Zimbabwe African People's Union** later that same year.

ZIMBABWE NEWSPAPERS, LTD. Formed in 1980 to supersede the Rhodesia Printing and Publishing Company (see **Press**). While the company is responsible for the day-to-day publishing of Zimbabwe's major newspapers, their general editorial policies are overseen by the **Mass Media Trust**.

ZIMBABWE PEOPLE'S ARMY (ZIPA). Short-lived military command organization established by commanders from both the Zimbabwe African National Liberation Army (**ZANLA**) and Zimbabwe People's Revolutionary Army (**ZIPRA**) on November 24, 1975. Following the collapse of the Zambian-supported Front for the Liberation of Zimbabwe (**FROLIZI**), 10 military commanders representing ZANLA and ZIPRA met in Maputo, **Mozambique**, to discuss the possibility of joining forces in order to more actively pursue the guerrilla war against the government of **Rhodesia**. The meeting apparently came about as a result of the growing dissatisfaction of those commanders with the fractionalization among the political leaders of **ZANU** and **ZAPU**. The commanders in the field advocated winning the armed struggle before determining the political leadership. As a result of the agreement reached in Maputo, early in 1976 ZANLA and ZIPRA units began to merge at military training camps at Morogoro, originally a ZIPRA camp, and Mgagao, a ZANLA camp, both in Tanzania. However, by May political conflicts developed between combatants at the Morogoro camp; in June these spread to Mgagao. The conflicts were apparently founded in different ideas regarding military tactics, as well as political education employed by the two forces. In early 1977, following the collapse of the **Geneva Conference** and the buildup of ZIPRA by **Joshua Nkomo**, the ZIPRA units were withdrawn from the dual command. The official end of ZIPA came at a Central Committee meeting of ZANU held at Chimoio, Mozambique, in September 1977. The ZIPA leadership was denounced by party leader **Robert Mugabe** as "counterrevolutionary."

Although purged from ZANLA and imprisoned by Mozambican authorities, the ZIPA commanders influenced future policy. The ZANLA high command came to support the idea that military commanders would be responsible for the actual conduct of the liberation war—not the political wing, which had had no military training. Unlike ZIPA, however, they accepted the idea that the two should work in unison.

ZIMBABWE PEOPLE'S DEMOCRATIC PARTY (ZPDP). Party founded in 1989 in opposition to the governmental policies of president **Robert Mugabe**, although it did not contest the 1990 elections and apparently disbanded sometime following those elections. The ZPDP is perhaps most notable for the fact that it was the first political party in the country's history to be headed by a woman, Isabel Pasalk.

ZIMBABWE PEOPLE'S REVOLUTIONARY ARMY (ZIPRA). The armed wing of the Zimbabwe African People's Union (**ZAPU**). Its areas of recruitment and operation were primarily in **Matabeleland,** and most of its combatants were **Ndebele**. Although its command structure formed during the mid-1960s in Lusaka, **Zambia**, under the direction of **Jason Moyo**, ZIPRA remained a small, relatively ineffectual fighting force until the mid-1970s. The main reason for the slow development of ZIPRA as a military organization was ZAPU's long-standing strategy of pursuing negotiations, rather than a commitment to armed struggle, to end white rule in Rhodesia. ZAPU's leader, **Joshua Nkomo**, apparently accepted the idea of total armed struggle only after the failure of the **Geneva Conference** and mounting pressure from his main supporter, President Kenneth Kaunda of Zambia. Kaunda's pressure was based on a growing belief that the government of **Ian Smith** would accept a negotiated peace only when the European community faced hardships resulting from escalation of the war being waged by the Zimbabwe African National Liberation Party (**ZANLA**) in the **Mashonaland** provinces of Rhodesia.

Nkomo returned to Zambia in early 1977 and, with increased material support from the Soviet Union, began to redirect ZAPU's strategy toward the rapid buildup of ZIPRA. ZIPRA troop strength in the early 1970s was estimated at about 1,000—very few, if any, operating inside present Zimbabwe—and by 1979 had grown to more than 20,000 trained combatants. However, only about 3,000 combatants operated at any given time inside the country. ZIPRA's main training camps were located in Zambia and Angola, and its combatants were recruited primarily from refugee camps located in **Botswana.** The recruits were then flown to the camps for training under Soviet military advisers. The command structure for ZIPRA passed though two distinct stages. Prior to the rapid buildup of the army in the early 1970s, ZIPRA was under the overall command of Jason Moyo. During that period the levels of organization below Moyo were relatively simple and informal. Beginning in the early 1970s, ZIPRA buildup necessitated the formation of a more formal command structure. In 1972 a "War Council," under the direction of Moyo and **Dumiso Dabengwa**, was formed to plan and direct ZIPRA's activities. At the same time Alfred Mangena was appointed overall field commander. In 1976, Joshua Nkomo, Samuel Munodawafa, and Akin Ndlovu joined the War Council, and in 1978, **Lookout Masuku** replaced Mangena as overall field commander. Subordinate to the field commander, ZIPRA had a commissar who directed the overall political training for combatants. From 1972 to 1978, Masuku was commissar, and from 1978 until ZIPRA's official disbanding in 1981, J. Z. Dube held the position. In addition, ZIPRA also had a chief of staff (1972–76, J. D. Dube; 1976–1980, J. Maseko) who directed the army's operations and support departments. Below this senior command level were training camp and local field commanders. Unlike ZANLA, ZAPU and ZIPRA leaders never developed a policy for the politicization of the rural areas. As a consequence, even though ZIPRA combatants operated in the Tribal Trust Lands (now **Communal Lands**) of Matabeleland, neither the party nor its army developed a strong local network of support involving local peoples. ZIPRA tactics emphasized quick incursions into the western regions of the country and then withdrawal back into Zambia. Also in contrast to ZANLA, which was organized and equipped as a guerrilla force, ZIPRA was equipped as a conventional force. In addition, ZIPRA leadership tended to hold forces at camps in Zambia and Angola in the apparent belief that they would be needed in a "decisive battle" with ZANLA following the collapse of the Smith regime.

ZIPRA is probably best known for two of the most publicized acts of the liberation war. On September 3, 1978, and on February 12, 1979, ZIPRA combatants shot down two civilian passenger planes, killing 102 passengers and crew.

Following agreements made at the **Lancaster House Conference** in December 1979, ZIPRA combatants assembled at point in Matabeleland in early 1980 and began to be integrated into the newly organized Zimbabwe National Army (**ZNA**). Shortly after independence, fighting broke out between former ZIPRA and ZANLA units billeted outside **Bulawayo**. These clashes were eventually brought under control by units of the newly organized ZNA.

ZIPRA ceased to exist as an official organization in early 1981, after its combatants had either been mustered out of active service or joined ZNA. However, with the number of open conflicts between ZANU and ZAPU escalating, and a widely held belief that the Ndebele were being discriminated against by the new, ZANU-dominated government, a large number of former ZIPRA members of the ZNA deserted in the early 1980s. The government called these ex-combatants "**dissidents**" who were attempting to destabilize the government. The government also charged that these former ZIPRA members were still under the direction of ZAPU, a charge flatly denied by Nkomo and other ZAPU leaders.

ZIMBABWE REPUBLIC POLICE see **BRITISH SOUTH AFRICA POLICE**

ZIMBABWE RHODESIA. Name applied to the country by the 1979 **Constitution,** which was the product of the **Internal Settlement** agreement of the previous year. Bishop **Abel Muzorewa** was sworn into office as **prime minister** on May 29, 1979, and the constitution and name "Zimbabwe Rhodesia" officially took effect the following day. In theory Zimbabwe Rhodesia was a multiracial state in which the African majority shared power with the European minority. In reality the government continued to be dominated by Europeans, as entrenched clauses in the constitution left control of the civil service, army, and police in their hands. The **Patriotic Front** and **Frontline States** accused Muzorewa of collaborating to conceal continued European rule, and vowed to intensify the armed struggle against Zimbabwe Rhodesia. On Muzorewa's orders, the **Rhodesian security forces** raided **ZANLA** and **ZIPRA** camps in Angola, **Zambia,** and **Mozambique.** No country recognized the legitimacy of Zimbabwe Rhodesia, and its government was forced to accept negotiations that would include the Patriotic Front. The Zimbabwe Rhodesia government was represented at the **Lancaster House Conference** by a delegation headed by Muzorewa and **Ian Smith**. Following agreements worked out at that conference, the Zimbabwe Rhodesia **House of Assembly** voted on December 12, 1979, to cease to exist as an independent state and return to colonial status under a British-appointed **governor**. Later that day, **Lord Soames** arrived in Salisbury and took over responsibility for governing the country, and Zimbabwe Rhodesia officially ceased to exist.

ZIMBABWE RUINS (a.k.a. Great Zimbabwe). Justly famous as the site of the largest stone edifice built in early sub-Saharan Africa, Zimbabwe played a seminal role in the country's history. It was the original center of monumental stone buildings (see **Ruins**); the center of the earliest known large-scale state system (see **Shona History**); and probably the earliest local center of international trade (see **Gold; Yufi; Muslims**).

Description. The ruins are located in the **Mtilikwe** basin, on the southern scarp of the **Central Plateau,** about 29 km southeast of **Masvingo** (at 29°17′S, 30°56′E; alt. 1,1000 m). Their surroundings are perennially moist, well-wooded, and filled with granite outcroppings, whose natural exfoliation provides easily dressed building stones. The ruins' complex comprises three main groups. On the north is the Hill Ruin (a.k.a. "**Acropolis**"), built atop a *kopje* that rises about 100 m above the rest of the complex. The hill contains a complicated network of enclosures separated by freestanding walls and natural rock formations. One enclosure contains a natural cave that occasionally resonates voices into the lower valley, giving rise to speculation that this cave was an early oracular shrine that may have provided an original religious basis for the whole complex (see **Religion—Shona**).

About 600 m due south of the Hills' "Western Enclosure" is the famous Elliptical Building on the valley floor. This structure has also been popularly called "the Temple," "the Great Enclosure," and other names that reflect modern confusion over the structure's original purpose. Though built later than the Hill Ruin, the Elliptical Building clearly became the complex's most important structure. The overall enclosure is shaped like an irregular ellipse more than 250 m in circumference. The great "outer wall" rises to nearly 10 m in height, and expands to more than 5 m in thickness in places. This wall alone is said to be the largest single precolonial African structure in sub-Saharan Africa. It contains a greater volume of stones than the entire rest of the complex. Inside the main enclosure are smaller enclosures, a smaller and older wall separated from the eastern outer wall by the narrow "parallel passage," and the famed **"conical tower"** at the southern end of the parallel passage.

Between the Hill Ruin and the Elliptical Building is the "Valley of Ruins." The valley contains 10 distinct ruins, half of which were named after 19th-century Europeans (**Karl Mauch, George Phillips, E. A. Maund, Adam Renders,** and **Willie Posselt**) by **R. N. Hall**. These ruins contain most of the architectural features of the Elliptical Building, but each is built on a much smaller scale.

Three wall styles have been discerned in the complex. The earliest (style "P") features undressed facing blocks arranged in uneven and undulating courses. Most of the Hill Ruin is built in this style. A later style ("Q") represents the finest stonework found in the complex and is that which was later employed in the best **Khami Culture** buildings in the west. This style features dressed and carefully matched stone blocks, arranged in closely fitting, even courses, as in the Elliptical Building's outer wall and conical tower. The third style ("R") is regarded as a degenerate form of the intermediate style. Its walls are built with ill-matched and loosely fitted stones in uncoursed rows. An even later period of building has left many walls that are little more than crude piles of stones.

Other notable feature of the complex include numerous sandstone monoliths, including the famous **Zimbabwe "birds,"** linteled doorways, stairways, turrets, and a particularly fine chevron frieze atop the Elliptical Building's southeastern outer wall. Most of the enclosures formerly contained *daga* huts, and it is believed that most interior stone wall and dirt floors were once thoroughly plastered with *daga*. Many walls—all of which are unmortared—have collapsed, and others have been badly damaged by overgrown vegetation and treasure hunters. Considerable rebuilding by late occupants of the site and by early 20th-century government workers, the disappearance of almost all *daga*-work, and damage done by untrained archaeologists have all greatly altered the original appearance of the ruins.

History. Attempts have been made to periodize the ruins' occupation sequences, but these have not yet achieved a consensus among archaeologists and historians. Such periodizations have been produced frequently, and sometimes greatly revised, adding to the bewildering terminology applied to the country's **Iron Age** culture history. The general trend in modern scholarship, however, has been to contract the length of the whole stone-building era to within the first half of the present millennium. It is now generally agreed that Zimbabwe was abandoned as a major cultural and political center during the 15th century. Nevertheless, the site still ranks both as the longest-occupied center in the country and as the original stone-building complex.

After a few centuries of very early Iron Age occupation, Zimbabwe seems to have been unpopulated until the late 11th century. Stone building began in about the 12th century, and the 13th century saw major refinements in metal working, spinning, weaving, and stone carving. An elite minority among the local **Karanga** people was emerging in the region. By the 14th century these people were clearly engaging in a profitable gold trade with the east coast, apparently through the port of **Sofala**. Little is known about the nature of this state system, but its rulers were almost certainly receiving tribute payments and laborers from a large area, as the immediate region had insufficient resources to support the estimated 2,000 people who resided at Zimbabwe during its peak period.

The Elliptical Building is now generally believed to have contained the chief ruler's residence and court. The valley ruins probably housed lesser officials and royal family members, while the bulk of the population lived in surrounding, nonstone dwellings. The "Zimbabwe Culture" was spread throughout the southern part of the country by the construction of more than a hundred similar, but smaller, stone complexes. These were probably residences of provincial administrators or local tributary chiefs.

The elaborate and permanent nature of Zimbabwe's buildings was incompatible with the essentially subsistence **agriculture** on which the society was based, making its rulers heavily dependent upon tribute and external trade. In the early or mid-15th century the site was suddenly abandoned, perhaps as a response to changing political or commercial circumstances. Furthermore, local forests appear to have been largely depleted as a result of heavy use of fire, burned to accelerate granite exfoliation for the collection of building stones. It appears possible that the establishment of the **Munhumutapa** state in the north around this time represented a shift of the Zimbabwe state's power center. A direct connection between these two state systems remains to be proven, however.

After the 15th century Zimbabwe was cut off from foreign trade and no new building was undertaken by its remaining inhabitants. It is unclear who occupied the site over the next several centuries, but by the early 19th century, the minor Mugabe chiefdom was centered near Zimbabwe. This chiefdom had nothing to do with the earlier Zimbabwe rulers, and its people's ignorance of the buildings' origins later contributed to European theories about ancient non-African builders. Zimbabwe is frequently said to have been sacked by **Mfecane** invaders during the 1830s, but there is no evidence that this really happened. By the time Europeans arrived in Zimbabwe in the 1870s, Zimbabwe's buildings were heavily overgrown with vegetation and in a state of advanced dereliction.

Archaeological investigations. **Karl Mauch** became the first European to study Zimbabwe in 1871. He produced the first drawings of the ruins and introduced the first explicit theories about their early non-African origins. After the **BSAC** occupied **Mashonaland** in 1890, Europeans recklessly pillaged the ruins, despite administrative efforts to protect them. **J. T. Bent** was commissioned to investigate the site in 1891, but his work was careless and destructive of the stratigraphical evidence. The next authorized excavator, **R. N. Hall**, did even more damage. The first professional archaeologists to excavate were **David Randall-MacIver** and **Gertrude Caton-Thompson**. The only other major excavations were undertaken in 1958 by **Roger Summers** and K. R. Robinson. When their work was completed, the government issued a 25-year moratorium on excavations at Zimbabwe. (See also **Zimbabwe Controversy,** above.)

ZIMBABWE SUN. Newspaper briefly published in Salisbury (now **Harare**) by the Zimbabwe African National Union (**ZANU**) and the **People's Caretaker Council** in 1964. Like *Chapupu* and other African nationalist publications, the *Sun* was quickly banned by the white government. After 1964 most nationalist papers, such as the **Zimbabwe African People's Union**'s *Zimbabwe Review* and ZANU's *Zimbabwe News*, were irregularly issued from external cities, especially Lusaka, **Zambia.**

ZIMBABWE UNITED PEOPLE'S ORGANIZATION (ZUPO). Conservative African political party formed on December 29, 1976, by progovernment chiefs following the failure of the **Geneva Conference.** Headed by **Jeremiah Chirau**, ZUPO was aligned with the government of **Ian Smith** on most substantive political issues, and never had much popular support. It did not win any seats in the **internal settlement** election of April 1979 and did not contest the 1980 elections. Chirau announced the dissolution of the party in March 1982.

ZIMBABWE UNITY MOVEMENT (ZUM). Political party launched by **Edgar Tekere** on April 30, 1989. ZUM was established following President **Robert Mugabe**'s announced plans to create a one-party state in Zimbabwe once the ten-year time limits of the **constitution** agreed to at the **Lancaster House Conference** expired in 1990. When announcing the founding of ZUM, Tekere stated that the party's goals included attracting support from the country's racial and ethnic groups not represented by the **Shona**-dominated **ZANU**, and restoring political power to traditional chiefs. He also claimed that ZUM had support from European-owned businesses, the country's trade unions, veterans' groups, and students at the **University of Zimbabwe.** ZUM's first test came in July 1989 when a candidate put forward by the party challenged a Mugabe-supported ZANU candidate in a byelection. The ZUM candidate lost, but Tekere and the party gained national exposure when he publicly charged that the police had prevented ZUM from holding rallies and the state-controlled **press** and **media** had refused to take ZUM advertising. ZUM then announced that it would challenge ZANU in the 1990 **elections,** including Tekere running against Mugabe. While ZUM gained 20 percent of the popular vote, it was only able to win two seats in **Parliament.** Tekere lost in the presidential vote by a margin of five to one. The party claimed that not only had its candidates been harassed by

ZANU supporters during the election campaign, but that the police had acted illegally during the election by denying ZUM party workers access to polling locations throughout the country.

In June 1991 Tekere and the ZUM executive had a falling out when Tekere rejected a new party constitution and leadership structure already passed by the executive. Tekere retained control of ZUM, but the majority of the executive resigned and formed the **Democratic Party**. ZUM later incorporated **Abel Muzorewa's United African Council** and together continued to publicly criticize Mugabe's plan for a one-party state. In September 1994 Tekere and Muzorewa announced that they had merged with members of the smaller **United** and **Forum** parties to form a new **United Party**. They declared that they were co-leaders, and that a third leader would be announced later. The stated goal of the new party was to unite those groups in opposition to ZANU and to contest the upcoming 1995 elections. However, the merger of the two opposition leaders was extremely short-lived. In October, Muzorewa announced that a disagreement among the leaders had occurred and had resulted in his appointment as the sole leader of the new party. Tekere responded by saying that ZUM had withdrawn from the merger and would continue to oppose the government as an independent political party. Two weeks prior to the elections ZUM pulled out, citing an "unlevel playing field" and contending that the current electoral laws made it virtually impossible for an opposition party to win.

ZIWA (variant: Zewa). Archaeological term for an early **Iron Age** culture, or industry, named after a site on the slopes of Mount Ziwa, a 1,745 m high mountain in the **Nyanga District** (at 18°8′S, 32°40′E). The Ziwa cultural complex covered the extreme northeastern part of the country and has been dated to as early as A.D. 300. Roughly contemporary with the **Gokomere** culture to the southwest, Ziwa is now regarded as a variant of the Gokomere and not an independent tradition. Within the Nyanga region there appears to have been a hiatus of several centuries between the end of Ziwa occupation and the beginning of the terrace-building culture of the **Inyanga Ruins** complex in about the 15th century.

ZIZI, WILLIAM see **MZIZI, WILLIAM**

ZOMBEPATA CAVE. Important **Stone Age** archaeological site in the **Guruve District** (at 16°51′S, 30°34′E). The cave also contains **rock paintings** that incorporate several features rarely observed elsewhere in the country. These include infrequently painted animal figures and geometric figures resembling active beehives.

ZUMBO. Mozambican town just northeast of the confluence of the Luangwa and **Zambezi** rivers, where the present **borders** of Zimbabwe, **Mozambique,** and **Zambia** meet. The town was founded around 1714 as a trading **fair**, situated so as to take advantage of the **gold** trade from the **Changamire** state, from which direct **Portuguese** trade was debarred. Through the 18th century Zumbo served as the most important **Shona** trading link with the outside world, while simultaneously connecting Portuguese trade with Zambian peoples to the north. The present Zambian town of Feira was established as a fair on the opposite side of the Luangwa River in c. 1788.

ZVI-. Chishona prefix (Class 8), normally used for plural forms of **chi-** prefix nouns.

ZVISHAVANE (Shabani until 1982). **Mining,** commercial, and administrative center of **Zvishavane District,** located just south of the country's center (at 20°20'S, 30°2'E; alt. 925 m). Shabani Mine began exploiting **asbestos** deposits just before the First World War and became the country's largest producer of this product by the mid-1970s. The town has grown along with the mine, and until 1982 had the same name. In 1992, Zvishavane was ranked eleventh among the country's urban centers, with a population of 16,071.

ZVISHAVANE DISTRICT (Shabani District until 1985). Covering 2,490 sq km in the northeastern corner of **Matabeleland South Province,** the district was formerly the northern part of **Mberengwa District,** the rest of which now borders Zvishavane on the south. The district also borders **Chivi** on the east, **Insiza** on the west, and **Shurugwi** on the north. Before 1980, the central part of the district was reserved for Europeans, the other parts being mostly Tribal Trust Lands (see **Communal Lands**). District population in 1992 was 98,710.

ZWANGEDABA. Ndebele *ibutho* raised by King **Mzilikazi** in the early 1840s. Its town was situated by the upper **Bembezi River** near the present site of the Turk Mine. Under the leadership of *induna* **Mbigo Masuku,** the men of Zwangendaba played a key role in turning back **A. H. Potgieter's** invasion of the **Matopo Hills** in 1847. The members of the *ibutho* were said to be pure *zansi.* Partly for this reason Zwangendaba led the opposition to **Lobengula's** accession to the kingship in 1870 in the belief that Lobengula's mother was of non-*zansi* origin. Mbigo was a leading advocate of locating the presumably missing royal heir, **Nkulumane,** even after Lobengula was made king in January 1870. By the middle of that year the Zwangendaba, Induba, Inqobo, and Nyamayendhlovu *amabutho* still refused to acknowledge Lobengula's authority. In June Lobengula assembled a force of around 5,000 to 6,000 loyal men to subordinate the dissidents. The other rebel *amabutho* fell into line, but the Zwangendaba refused even to negotiate. On June 5 the loyalists crushed the Zwangendaba at their town in a bloody battle in which Mbigo and about 300 to 400 of his men died. Their town was razed, and the name of Zwangendaba became anathema within the Ndebele kingdom. Lobengula treated Zwangendaba survivors leniently, but many fled south, joining **Mangwane** and the pretender "Nkulumane" in the **Transvaal.** The men who stayed in **Matabeleland** were dispersed through other *amabutho,* in which they kept alive the spirit of resistance to Lobengula through the rest of his reign.

ZWANGENDABA JERE (c. 1780s–c. 1845). Most important of the **Ngoni** migration leaders and father of **Mpezeni Jere.** Zwangendaba was hereditary chief of the Jere clan in South Africa's northern **Nguni** country. During the 1810s he became a leading military commander in Zwide's Ndwandwe state. After the Ndwandwe were defeated by Shaka's Zulu around 1819, Zwangendaba fled north with a band of followers. Through conquests and voluntary submissions, he built up his following in southern **Mozambique** during the 1820s. Late in that decade he appears to have allied with the Gaza king **Soshangane** at Delagoa Bay. The two leaders clashed around 1830, so Zwangendaba led his people into **Shona** country in Zimbabwe. There his Ngoni apparently disrupted the **Changamire** state, and perhaps killed the reigning king, **Chrisamhuru**. Early in 1835 Zwangendaba appears to have been defeated near the **Mazoe River** by the Ngoni of **Nxaba** and **Maseko**. Toward the end of the year Zwangendaba crossed the **Zambezi River** into present **Zambia** near **Zumbo**. According to tradition, the crossing took place the day of a solar eclipse, which must have been that of November 20, 1835.

Part of Zwangendaba's following remained in **Mashonaland** under the leadership of his kinswoman **Nyamazana**. Zwangendaba continued north with the bulk of his Ngoni, including many new Shona recruits who were eventually absorbed into Ngoni society. Zwangendaba himself traveled as far north as the Zambia/Tanzania border region, where he died in the mid-1840s. His kingdom then divided into five major groups that later settled in Tanzania, Zambia, and Malawi. The modern Songea District of southern Tanzania is named after Songea Mbano (c. 1836-1906), a Zambian-born Ngoni whose Shona parents were captured by Zwangendaba in Mashonaland.

ZWIMBA, MATTHEW (c. 1880s–1930). Independent church founder. Zwimba's father, Chigaga, was made a government-salaried chief in the Zwimba Reserve (now **Communal Land**) of the southern **Makonde District** after the **1896–97 Revolts**. Matthew Zwimba was thus raised in a family loyal to European rule. He converted to Christianity at a local **Wesleyan** mission and became a teacher and lay evangelist. After starting the first school in the Zwimba Reserve, he got into disciplinary conflicts with mission authorities, who transferred him to **Kadoma.** Outraged by this arbitrary action, Zwimba got into further difficulties with his superiors, until he was dismissed from all his positions in 1907. Now fiercely opposed to white authority, he returned to Zwimba Reserve, where he clashed with government authorities and was briefly imprisoned.

In 1915 Zwimba started his own church just outside the reserve at Kanyemba. He soon reentered the reserve and took over his former mission school. He called his new church *Siri Chena*, the "Original Church of the White Bird." Drawing upon Christian and **Shona** symbols he described the "white bird" as the dove of the Holy Ghost and the messenger of the Shona high god **Mwari**. He made "saints" of Shona killed by Europeans in the Revolts. Alarmed government officials suspected sedition and quickly moved to suppress his church by proscribing him and his brother from preaching or teaching. Persistent government harassment discouraged people from joining Zwimba's church, which languished from lack of support. Despite Zwimba's failure, his church— the first such independent body founded by a Shona—became an important symbol of African resistance to white rule, and Zwimba's personal prestige remained great. In 1925 he testified before the **Morris Carter Commission** in behalf of local chiefs.

ZWITI (Mazwiti) see **DZVITI**

THE BIBLIOGRAPHY

CONTENTS

6. POLITICS AND GOVERNMENT

7. RELIGION

8. SCIENCES

9. SOCIAL

10. SERIAL PUBLICATIONS

INTRODUCTION

Although modest in size, Zimbabwe—formerly Rhodesia—has attracted a great deal of attention since the mid-19th century. As a result, there is an abundance of published material on almost every aspect of Zimbabwean studies.

The present bibliography is only a carefully selected sampling of what is available in Zimbabwean studies. Additional sources can be found in Oliver and Karen Pollak's *Rhodesia/Zimbabwe: An International Bibliography* (1977). The Pollaks' bibliography covers works published through mid-1975, so the present bibliography gives special attention to works published since that date. In particular, this bibliography has added more than 200 new entries to that of the revised second edition, in an effort to provide the most current bibliography available to students of Zimbabwean studies.

In general, this bibliography gives priority to books over articles; recent publications over older publications; specialized studies of Zimbabwe over general studies of larger regions; and materials reasonably accessible to American and British students over more difficult-to-find materials. The bibliography includes a number of recent doctoral dissertations to help indicate current trends in scholarship and to call attention to new scholars who have not yet published extensively.

In order to conserve space, this bibliography omits all articles contained in cited books, such as Peel and Ranger, *Past and Present in Zimbabwe*, which are listed under their editors' names.

Government publications are a special problem, as always, because their bibliographical details are typically chaotic and they are generally difficult to obtain. For pre-1965 government publications, see Audrey A. Walker, *The Rhodesias and Nyasaland: A Guide to the Official Publications* (1965). American holdings of government publications from the UDI period are at best sporadic. For Zimbabwean government publications, see the annual *Zimbabwe National Bibliography*, which can be obtained by writing to the National Archives of Zimbabwe, Private Bag 7720, Causeway, Harare, Zimbabwe.

1. GENERAL WORKS

Compilation of this dictionary was made easier by the existence of a number of encyclopedias and handbooks on Zimbabwe and Southern Africa, but none of these treats African peoples and history in any depth. Mary Akers (ed.), *Encyclopedia Rhodesia* (1973), for example, is most useful for geography, natural history, and European history and government institutions.

2. BIOGRAPHY

Biographical data on Europeans in Zimbabwean history is relatively easy to find. Edward Tabler, *Pioneers of Rhodesia* (1966), contains detailed biographies of more than 400 people who visited the region of present Zimbabwe between 1836 and 1880. T. W. Baxter and E. E. Burke, *Guide to the Historical Manuscripts in the National Archives of Rhodesia* (1970), contains useful brief biographies of individuals (and institutions) whose papers are in the National Archives.

Several books are useful for information about modern African political leaders. Diana Mitchell, *Nationalist Leaders in Zimbabwe: Who's Who* (1982) and Alan Rake, *Who's Who in Africa: Leaders for the 1990s* (1992) have biographies of more than 50 figures, and briefer notes on several dozen others.

3. CULTURE

There is a significant body of literature on prehistoric rock paintings, but most of this is merely descriptive. C. K. Cooke, *Guide to the Rock Art of Rhodesia* (1974), and Roger Summers (ed.), *Prehistoric Rock Art of the Federation* (1959), are both well-illustrated and remain important reference works.

Literature is discussed within the dictionary. Here it need only be added that Colin and O-Lan Style, *Mambo Book of Zimbabwean Verse in English* (1986), is a useful anthology of poetry published in Ndebele, Shona, and English.

Among studies of the media, the books by former newspaper editors and publishers W. D. Gale, B. G. Paver, John Parker, Nathan Shamuyarira, and Lawrence Vambe are useful. In addition, books by Julie Frederikse, Elaine Windrich, and E. T. Rusike are very helpful in understanding the role of the media during the period of the liberation struggle and since independence.

4. ECONOMICS

Duncan Clarke's essay of economic bibliography (see 1. GENERAL—Bibliographies and Research Guides) remains the best introduction to works on economics published before 1973. The *Zimbabwe Journal of Economics* (1967+) also remains an important forum for a wide spectrum of economic views.

5. HISTORY

There is still no satisfactory one-volume history of the country. Most of the histories published before are apologiae for white rule, of varying degrees of sophistication. L. H. Gann, *A History of Southern Rhodesia* (1965), was the first professionally written history of the country, but has a strong Eurocentrism and carries the story only up to 1934. Useful regional histories are T. O. Ranger (ed.), *Aspects of Central African History* (1968), and David Birmingham and Phyllis M. Martin (eds.), *History of Central Africa* (1983).

Iron Age archaeology and history are very well served. Useful introductions to the subject can be found in the articles and books by P. S. Garlake, T. N. Huffman, K. R. Robinson, and Roger Summers. See also the dictionary entry **Zimbabwe Controversy.**

Early Shona history was pioneered by D. P. Abraham, but his articles are difficult for nonspecialists to interpret. One should therefore start with David Beach, *The Shona and Zimbabwe, 900–1850* (1980), H. H. K. Bhila, *Trade and Politics in a Shona Kingdom* (1982), and S. I. Mudenge, *A History of Munhumutapa* (1984). The antiquarian journal *Nada* is loaded with articles on Shona history, but these are of such mixed value that only the most important are listed here.

The books by Eric Axelson and M. D. D. Newitt remain among the best introductions to early Portuguese involvement in central Africa. Original Portuguese documents are available in English translation, thanks to G. M. Theal (ed.), *Records of South-Eastern Africa* (1898-1903), and the *Documentos Sobre os Portugueses* (1962+).

The 19th century is naturally the best-known precolonial era. There are numerous firsthand accounts written by travelers and missionaries, and most of these have been reprinted—sometimes more than once—by Books of Zimbabwe (Bulawayo; formerly Books of Rhodesia), Negro Universities Press (New York), and Frank Cass (London). Many previously unpublished documents are also available in book form in volumes edited by E. C. Tabler, J. P. R. Wallis, and others.

Ndebele history has long attracted considerable attention, but solid scholarship is a recent development. R. K. Rasmussen, *Migrant Kingdom* (1978), treats the early history of the Ndebele, while the works of Tendai Muntunhu and Julian Cobbing cover the later years of the Ndebele kingdom.

J. D. Omer-Cooper, *The Zulu Aftermath* (1966), is now somewhat outdated, but it remains an important starting point for the study of the *Mfecane* era as a whole. In addition to the Ndebele studies cited, Omer-Cooper is usefully supplemented with articles by Gerhard Liesegang and J. H. Bannerman.

In common with historical scholarship elsewhere in Africa, the late-19th-century era of European occupation and African resistance has inspired an immense body of literature. H. M. Hole's books are perhaps the most useful statements of a British participant in the occupation era. Philip Mason, *The Birth of a Dilemma* (1958), turned attention to the African perspective, which was continued by Stanlake Samkange, *Origins of Rhodesia* (1968). T. O. Ranger, *Revolt in Southern Rhodesia* (1967), inspired an important debate on African resistance to European occupation and rule.

The era of British South Africa Company rule is well covered in Gann's *History of Southern Rhodesia*, which is usefully supplemented by Ranger's *African Voice in Southern Rhodesia, 1898–1930* (1970), and James A. C. Mutambirwa, *The Rise of Settler Power in Southern Rhodesia* (1981). J. S. Galbraith, *Crown and Charter* (1974), is an analysis of the company's early days.

For the era of "Responsible Government," which started in 1923, one might start with Elaine Windrich, *The Rhodesian Problem, 1923–1972* (1975), a documentary history. Richard Gray, *The Two Nations* (1960), treats the country within the context of British central Africa, and remains the most thorough history of the country's African political and labor movements through 1953. Gray is richly supplemented by Lawrence Vambe, *From Rhodesia to Zimbabwe* (1976), which is at once a personal memoir and a history of African politics into the 1960s. Colin Leys, *European Politics in Southern Rhodesia* (1958), remains one of the best accounts of purely European politics through the late 1950s.

The federation era inspired an enormous contemporary body of commentaries and speculations, most of which are now completely outdated. Among the works listed here, the most accessible are Herbert Spiro's long article in *Five African States* (1963), and Patrick Keatley, *The Politics of Partnership* (1963). A comprehensive study of the UDI period in Zimbabwean history is yet to be written, but B. V. Mtshali, *Rhodesia: Background to Conflict* (1968), Paul L. Moorcraft, *A Short Thousand Years: The End of Rhodesia's Rebellion* (1979), and David Caute, *Under the Skin: The Death of White Rhodesia* (1983), are all useful.

Several works attempting to analyze the period of the war of liberation have emerged since independence. Andre Astrow, *Zimbabwe: A Revolution That Lost Its Way?* (1983), Patricia Chater, *Caught in the Crossfire* (1985), T. O. Ranger, *Peasant Consciousness and Guerrilla War in Zimbabwe* (1985), David Lan, *Guns and Rain* (1985), and Norma Kriger, *Zimbabwe's Guerrilla War: Peasant Voices* (1992), are extremely helpful in attempting to understand this complicated period in Zimbabwe's recent history.

6. POLITICS AND GOVERNMENT

Objective studies covering politics and government are rare, but D. J. Murray, *The Government System in Southern Rhodesia* (1970), J. D. Jordan, *Local Government in Zimbabwe* (1984), and Larry Bowman, *Politics in Rhodesia* (1973), provide solid starting points. More recent developments can be followed in such periodicals as *African Report* (New York), *Africa Today* (Denver), and *Africa Contemporary Record* (London).

Articulation of African nationalist viewpoints began with Ndabaningi Sithole, *African Nationalism* (2nd ed., 1968). Other important early contributions were made by Enoch Dumbutshena, Leonard Kapungu, Nathan Shamuyarira, and others. More recent studies include Masipula Sithole, *Zimbabwe: Struggles within the Struggle* (1979), and Stanlake Samkange, *The Origins of African Nationalism in Zimbabwe* (1985).

The works on African policy and administration prior to independence are quite a mixed bag, with useful articles going back to the early years of *Nada* (1923–79). Among the more recent overviews are the works of J. F. Holleman and A. K. H. Weinrich.

Claire Palley, *Constitutional History and Law of Southern Rhodesia* (1966), is a nearly definitive treatment of the country's legal history up to UDI. It is well supplemented by the works of Gloria Passmore, G. L. Chavunduka, Joan May, and others.

The studies published before independence regarding the country's military forces were generally standard military histories. This subject is still best approached through R. S. Roberts' review article in *Rhodesian History* (1974; now *Zimbabwean History*). A number of works dealing with the Rhodesian security forces' counterinsurgency operations have recently appeared, including J. K. Cilliers, *Counter-Insurgency in Rhodesia* (1985), and Ron Reed Daly, *Selous Scouts: Top Secret War* (1982). Studies dealing specifically with the liberation forces of ZANLA or ZIPRA have yet to appear.

7. RELIGION

Religious studies have attracted an unusual amount of attention in Zimbabwe, with many studies available on the history and practice of African traditional religions, mission churches, and African independent churches. Anthony Dachs (ed.), *Christianity South of the Zambezi* (1973), and T. O. Ranger and John Weller (eds.), *Themes in the Christian History of Central Africa* (1975), both deal with a broader range of religious topics than their titles imply, making each a useful introduction to religion in Zimbabwe. Michael Bourdillon and Michael Galfand have both published many studies of traditional religious beliefs. M. L. Daneel's monumental study of Shona independent churches set a high standard for the study of Christian independency in Africa.

The history of mission churches is well covered in both primary and secondary published sources. Paul King (ed.), *Missions in Southern Rhodesia* (1959), is a handy, though hard to find, overview of this subject. More recent studies include Ian Linden, *Church and State in Rhodesia, 1959–1979* (1979), and Edna McDonagh, *Church and Politics: From Theology to a Case History of Zimbabwe* (1980).

8. SCIENCES

George Kay, *Rhodesia: A Human Geography* (1970), remains a good, though somewhat outdated, introduction to Zimbabwean geography. His article in *Geographical Journal* (1981) is a good supplement to the earlier work. Specialized geological publications are numerous, as is attested by C. C. Smith and H. E. van der Heyde's large bibliography, but a more recent edition would be welcome. Medical studies are best approached through the books by Michael Gelfand and G. L. Chavunduka, and in the *Central African Journal of Medicine*. Since the traditional African arts of healing are also tied into religious beliefs, some attention should also be paid to the literature on religion.

9. SOCIAL

The starting point for any study of the African peoples of the country is still Hilda Kuper, A. J. B. Hughes, and J. van Velsen, *The Shona and Ndebele of Southern Rhodesia* (1954). Michael Bourdillon, *The Shona Peoples* (1976), remains a valuable general study, while Paul Chidyausiku, *Broken Roots: a Biographical Narrative on the Culture of the Shona People in Zimbabwe* (1984), is the most recently published. Many specialized studies have been published, including many articles in *Nada, Africa,* and elsewhere.

The literature on education is diverse. It is perhaps best approached through the works of Marshall Murphee, Fay Chung, and Emmanul Ngara, *Socialism, Education, and Development: A Challenge to Zimbabwe* (1985); and Roger Riddell, *Education for Employment* (1980).

The study of immigrant societies is introduced with the works by L. H. Gann and Peter Duignan, and through the more recent studies by B. A. Kosmin and Barry Schutz. Interethnic or "race" relations is obviously a well-covered field. Dickson Mungazi, *The Cross Between Rhodesia and Zimbabwe: Racial Conflict in Rhodesia 1962–1979* (1981) is a good r study.

Urban studies are best approached in Clive Kileff and W. C. Pendleton (eds.), *Urban Man in Southern Africa* (1975), I. R. N. Cormack, *Towards Self-Reliance: Urban Social Development in Zimbabwe* (1983), and articles in the *Journal of Social Development in Africa* (Harare; 1986+).

10. SERIAL PUBLICATIONS

This bibliography lists most past and present Zimbabwean newspapers, excluding political publications (which are generally short-lived, published sporadically, and difficult to acquire). The most important of these newspapers are discussed in the dictionary, and general discussions of newspapers can be found under the headings of PRESS, AFRICAN NEWSPAPERS LTD., ARGUS GROUP, and MASS MEDIA TRUST.

This bibliography also lists a selection of specialized serial publications published within Zimbabwe, as well as a few specialized journals on southern Africa published elsewhere.

ABBREVIATIONS USED IN BIBLIOGRAPHY

+	Indicates continuous publication since the date shown
Afr.	Africa(n)
Arch.	Archive(s); Archaeology
BOR	Books of Rhodesia
Bul.	bulletin
comp.	compiler
dev.	development
Econ.	Economics
ed.	editor; edited; edition
fed.	federation
Hist.	history; historical
Instit.	Institute
Internat.	International
Jnl.	Journal
Lib.	Library
Nat.	National
NUP	Negro Universities Press
OUP	Oxford University Press
Proc.	proceedings
pseud.	pseudonym
Pub.	published; Publishing
R.	Review
rep.	reprint edition
rev.	revised
rev. art.	review article
Rhod.	Rhodesia(n)
S.Afr.	South Africa(n)
So.Afr.	Southern Africa(n)
Soc.	Society
Stud.	Studies
Trans.	translated; Transactions
Univ.	University
UP	University Press
Zimb.	Zimbabwe

1. GENERAL

Bibliographies and Research Guides

Ansari, S. (ed.). *Liberation Struggle in Southern Africa: A Bibliography of source material.* Gurgaon, India: Indian Documentation Service, 1972. 118p.

Baxter, T. W. (ed.). *Guide to the Public Archives of Rhodesia.* Vol 1: *1890–1923.* Salisbury: Nat. Arch. Rhod., 1969.

_____, and E. E. Burke. *Guide to the Historical Manuscripts in the National Archives of Rhodesia.* Salisbury: Nat. Arch. Rhod., 1970. 527p.

Bennett, T. W., and Sally Phillips. *A Bibliography of African Law, with Special Reference to Rhodesia.* Salisbury: Univ. Rhod., 1975. 324p.

Burke, Eric Edward. *A Bibliography of Cecil John Rhodes (1853–1902).* Salisbury: Central Afr. Arch., 1952. Rep. in *The Story of Cecil Rhodes* (Salisbury: Central Afr. Arch., 1952), 115–92.

_____. "Rhodesia in books," *Rhodesiana,* 24 (1971), 11–20.

Clarke, Duncan G. "The economics of underdevelopment in Rhodesia: an essay on selected bibliography," *Current Bibliography on Afr. Affairs,* VI, 3 (1973), 293–332.

Coggin, C. "Rhodesian bibliography: a survey," *Rhod. Librarian,* II, 4 (1970), 81–98.

Cooke, Cranmer Kenrick. *A Bibliography of Rhodesian Archaeology from 1874.* Salisbury: Nat. Museums and Monuments of Rhod., *Arnoldia,* VI, 38 (1974), 56p.

Johnstone, I. J. *Zimbabwean political materials published in exile 1959–1980: a bibliography.* Harare: Nat. Arch. Rhod., 1987.

McNamara, E. *Women in Zimbabwe: An Annotated Bibliography.* Harare: University of Zimbabwe, 1989. 170p.

Pollak, Oliver Burt, and Karen Pollak. *An International Bibliography of Theses and Dissertations on Southern Africa.* Boston: G. K. Hall, 1976. 236p.

_____, and _____. *Rhodesia/Zimbabwe: An International Bibliography.* Boston: G. K. Hall, 1977. 621p.

Smith, Craig C., and H. E. van der Heyde. *Rhodesian Geology: A Bibliography and Brief Index to 1968.* Salisbury: Trustees of the Nat. Museums of Rhod., 1971. 252p.

Thompson, Leonard, Richard Elphick, and Inez Jarrick. *Southern African History Before 1900: A Select Bibliography of Articles.* Stanford, CA: Hoover Instit. Press, 1971. 102p.

Walker, Audrey A. (comp.). *The Rhodesians and Nyasaland: A Guide to the Official Publications.* Washington, DC: Lib. Congress, 1965. 285p.

Wilding, Norman W. (comp.). *Catalogue of the Parliamentary Papers of Southern Rhodesia and Rhodesia, 1954–1970 and the Federation of Rhodesia and Nyasaland, 1954–1963.* Salisbury: Univ. of Rhodesia, 1970. 161p.

Willson, Francis Michael Glenn, and Gloria C. Passmore (comps.). *Catalogue of the Parliamentary Papers of Southern Rhodesia, 1899–1953.* Salisbury: Univ. of Rhodesia, 1965. 484p.

Zhuwarara, R., and M. Zimunya. "Zimbabwean Literature in English, 1966–85: A Bibliography," *Research in African Literatures*, 18 (1987), 340–42.

Zimbabwe National Bibliography (formerly *Rhodesian National Bibliography*, 1967–79; *List of Publications Deposited in the Library of the National Archives*, 1960–66). Harare: Zimb. Nat. Arch., 1960+. Annual.

Zimmerman, Zea E. *Zimbabwe's First Decade of Independence, 1980–1990: A Select and Annotated Bibliography*. Johannesburg: South Africa Institute of International Affairs, 1991.

General Information: Encyclopedias, Handbooks, Guides

Akers, Mary (gen. ed.). *Encyclopaedia Rhodesia*. Salisbury: College Press, 1973. 454p.

Berens, Dennis (ed.). *Concise Encyclopaedia of Zimbabwe*. Mambo Press, 1987. 444p.

Brelsford, W. V. (ed.). *Handbook to the Federation of Rhodesia and Nyasaland*. London: Cassell; Salisbury: Govt. Printer, 1960. 803p.

Joelson, F. S. (ed.). *Rhodesia and East Africa*. London: East Africa and Rhodesia, 1958. 662p.

Levin, L. S. (ed.). *Rhodesia and Nyasaland*. Salisbury: Central Afr. Airways, 1961. 662p.

Macmillan, Allister. *Rhodesia and Eastern Africa: Historical Descriptive, Commercial and Industrial Facts, Figures, and Resources*. London: W. H. and L. Collingridge, 1931. 414p.

Nelson, Harold D. (ed.). *Zimbabwe: a country study*, 2nd ed. Washington, DC: American UP, 1983. 360p.

Official Yearbook of (the Colony of) Southern Rhodesia. Salisbury: Rhod. Printing and Pub. Co., 1924, 1930, 1932, 1952.

Rosenthal, Eric (comp.). *Encyclopedia of Southern Africa*. 6th ed. London: Frederick Warne, 1973. (First pub., 1961).

Southern Rhodesia Department of Statistics. *Statistical Yearbook of Southern Rhodesia*. Salisbury, 1924, 1938, 1947.

Standard Encyclopedia of Southern Africa. 12 vols. Cape Town: Nasou, Ltd., 1970–76. D. J. Potgieter, ed.-in-chief.

United States Board on Geograhic Names. *Southern Rhodesia: Official Standard Names* [Gazetteer]. Washington, DC: Defense Mapping Agency Topograhic Center, 1973. 363p.

Travel and Modern Description

Berlyn, Phillippa. *This Is Rhodesia*. Salisbury: College Press, 1969. 184p.

Cooke, Cranmer Kenrick. *A Guide to the Historic and Pre-Historic Monuments of Rhodesia*. Bulawayo: Hist. Monuments Commis., 1972. 84p.

Edwards, S. J. *Zambezi Odyssey*. Cape Town: T. V. Bulpin, 1974. 230p.

Fisher, Allan C., Jr. "Rhodesia, a house divided." *National Geographic* (May 1975), 641–71.

Hills, Denis. *Rebel People*. London: Allen and Unwin, 1978.

Hoare, Rawdon. *Rhodesian Mosaic*. London: J. Murray, 1934. 259p.

Jumbo Guide to Rhodesia. Salisbury: Wilrey Publications, 1972. 252p.

Murphy, Ian. *Zimbabwe: Africa's Paradise*. London: Corporate Brochure Co., 1994. 191p.

Ransford, Oliver, and Peter Steyn. *Historic Rhodesia.* Salisbury: Longman Rhodesia, 1975. 70p.

Tanser, George Henry (ed.). *The Guide to Rhodesia.* Salisbury: Winchester Press, 1975. 337p.

Tanser, Tony, and Philippa Berlyn. *Rhodesian Panorama.* Salisbury: Mardon, 1967. 242p.

Wadia, Ardaser Sorabjee N. *The Romance of Rhodesia: Being Impressions of a Sightseeing Tour of Southern and Northern Rhodesia.* London: J. M. Dent, 1947. 146p.

2. BIOGRAPHY

Collections of Biographies

Cary, Robert, and Dianna Mitchell. *African Nationalist Leaders in Rhodesia: Who's Who.* Johannesburg: Africana Book Soc.; London: Rex Collings; Bulawayo: BOR, 1977. 310p.

Dickie, John, and Alan Rake. *Who's Who in Africa.* London: African Development, 1973. 602p. (Rhodesians: pp.357–86.)

Dictionary of South African Biography. 5 vols. (projected). Cape Town and Johannesburg: Tafelberg-Uitgewers, Ltd., 1968+. Vol I: ed., W. J. de Kock; Vol. II: ed., D. W. Kruger.

Lipschutz, Mark R., and R. Rasmussen. *A Dictionary of African Historical Biography.* 2nd ed. Berkeley and Los Angeles: Univ. of California Press, 1986. 328p.

Lloyd, Jessie M. (comp.). *Rhodesia's Pioneer Women (1859–1896).* Rev. and enlarged by Constance Parry. Bulawayo: Rhodesian Pioneers and Early Settlers' Soc., 1974. (First pub., 1960). 105p.

Mitchell, Diana. *African Nationalist Leaders in Zimbabwe: Who's Who in 1980.* Salisbury: Diana Mitchell, 1980. 106p.

Profiles of Rhodesia's Women. Salisbury: Nat. Fed. of Business and Professional Women of Rhod., 1976. 176p.

Rake, Alan. *Who's Who in Africa: Leaders for the 1990s.* Metuchen, NJ: Scarecrow Press, 1992. 448p. (Zimbabweans: 421–440.)

Segal, Ronald. *Political Africa.* London: Stevens and Sons, 1961. 475p.

Tabler, Edward C. *Pioneers of Rhodesia.* Cape Town: C. Stuik, 1966. 185p.

Pre-20th-Century Figures

Beach, D. N. *Mapondera: Heroism and History in Northern Zimbabwe, 1840–1904.* Gweru: Mambo Press, 1989. 96p.

Becker, Peter. *Path of Blood: The Rise and Conquests of Mzilikanzi.* London: Longmans, 1962. 289p.

Bhebe, Ngwabi. *Lobengula of Zimbabwe.* London: Heinemann, 1977. 48p.

Blair, R. "Selous: a reassessment," *Rhodesiana,* 17 (1967), 1–26.

Bulpin, Thomas Victor. *The White Whirlwind* [J. W. Colenbrander].

Colquhoun, Archibald R. *Dan to Beersheba: Work and Travel in Four Continents.* London: W. Heinemann, 1908. 348p.

Colvin, Ian D. *The Life of Jameson.* 2 vols. London: E. Arnold, 1923. 314, 352p.

Cooke, Cranmer Kenrick. "Lobengula: second and last king of the Amandebele—his final resting place and treasure," *Rhodesiana,* 23 (1970), 3–53.

Farrant, Jean. *Mashonaland Martyr: Bernard Mizeki and the Pioneer Church.* Cape Town: OUP, 1966. 258p.

Flint, John. *Cecil Rhodes.* Boston: Little, Brown, 1974. 268p.

Hassing, Per. "Lobengula," in Norman R. Bennett (ed.), *Leadership in Eastern Africa* (Boston: Boston UP, 1968), 221–60.

Henderson, Ian. "Lobengula: achievement and tragedy," *Tarikh*, 2, 2 (1968), 53–68.

Johnson, Frank. *Great Days: The Autobiography of an Empire Builder.* London: G. Bell, 1940. 366p. (Rep., BOR, 1972.)

Langham-Carter, R. R. *Knight Bruce: First Bishop and Founder of the Anglican Church in Rhodesia.* Salisbury: Christ-Church, Borrowdale, 1975. 72p.

Lockhart, John Gilbert, and Alfred Beit. *The Will and the Way; Being an Account of Alfred Beit and the Trust Which He Founded, 1906—1956.* London: Longmans, Green, 1958. 106p.

———, and C. M. Woodhouse. *Rhodes.* London: Hodder and Stoughton, 1963. 511p.

Mauch, Karl. *Karl Mauch: African Explorer.* Ed. & trans. by F. O. Bernard. Cape Town: C. Struik, 1971. 247p.

Millais, J. G. *A Life of Frederick Courteney Selous, D.S.O.* London: Longmans, Green, 1919. 387p. (Rep., Salisbury: Pioneer Head, 1975.)

Moffat, Robert U. *John Smith Moffat, Missionary; A Memoir.* London: John Murray, 1921. 388p. (Rep., NUP.)

Newton, Gwenda. "The go-between—John Grootboom," *Rhodesiana*, 29 (1973), 68–75.

Northcott, Cecil. *Robert Moffat.* London: Lutterworth, 1961. 357p.

Preller, Gustav S. *Lobengula: The Tragedy of a Matabele King.* Johannesburg: Afrikaanse Pers-Boekhandel, 1963. 318p.

Ranger, Terence. "The last word on Rhodes?", *Past and Present*, 28 (July 1964), 116–27.

Rasmussen, R. Kent. "A lost man in southern African history: Saliphi/Gundwane of the Ndebele," *Internat. Jnl. Afr. Hist. Studies*, X, 1 (1977), 96–110.

———. *Mzilikazi of the Ndebele.* London: Heinemann, 1977. 48p.

Rea, W. F. ["The life of Gonçalo da Silveira, 1526–1560"], *Rhodesiana*, 6 (1961), 1–40.

———, "Livingstone's Rhodesian legacy," *History Today*, 23 (1973), 633–9.

Rotberg, Robert I. *The Founder: Cecil Rhodes and the Pursuit of Power.* Oxford: OUP, 1988. 800p.

Rouillard, Nancy (ed.). *Matabele Thompson: His Autobiography.* Rev. ed. South Africa: Central News Agency, Dassie Books, 1957. 160p. (First pub., London: Faber and Faber, 1936. 293p.)

Wallis, John Peter Richard. *Thomas Baines of King's Lynn.* London: J. Cape, 1941. 351p. (New ed., Cape Town, 1976.)

Woollacott, R. C. "Pasipamire—spirit medium of Chaminuka, the 'Wizard' of Chitungwiza," *Nada*, XI, 2 (1975), 154–67.

20th-Century Figures

Andrews, C. F. *John White of Mashonaland.* London, 1935. 316p. (Rep., NUP.)

Bhebe, N. *Benjamin Burombo; African Politics in Zimbabwe, 1947–1958.* Harare: College Press, 1989. 160p.

Gann, Lewis H., and Michael Gelfand. *Huggins of Rhodesia; The Man and His Country.* London: G. Allen and Unwin, 1964. 285p.

Gibbon, Geoffrey. *Paget of Rhodesia.* Bulawayo: BOR, 1973. 164p.

Godwin, Peter. *Mukiwa: A White Boy in Africa.* New York: Atlantic Monthly Press, 1996. 418 p.

Hotz, P. *Muzukuru, Guerilla's Story.* Johannesburg: Ravan, 1990.

Joyce, Peter. *Anatomy of a Rebel; Smith of Rhodesia.* Salisbury: Graham Pub. Co., 1974. 480p.

Lamont, Donal. *Speech from the Dock.* London: Kevin Mayhew, 1977. 143p.

Lessing, Doris. *Going Home.* New York: Popular Library, 1968. 253p. (First pub., London: M. Joseph, 1957.)

Long, B. K. *Drummond Chaplin: His Life and Times in Africa.* London: OUP, 1941. 373p.

Makambe, E. P. "The Limitations of a Patron/Client Relationship in Colonial Zimbabwe; the British South Africa Company versus Helese Ginya, 1902–1905," *Transafrican Journal of History,* 19 (1990), 43–60.

Megahey, Alan J. *Humphrey Gibbs, Beleaguered Governor: Southern Rhodesia, 1929–69.* New York: St. Martin's Press, 1998. 241 p.

Moyo, Temba. *The Organizer: Story of Temba Moyo.* Recorded and ed. by Ole Gjerstad. Richmond, Brit. Col.: Liberat. Support Movement Press, 1974. 85p.

Mungazi, D. *The Honoured Crusade: Ralph Dodge's Theology of Liberation and Initiatives for Social Change in Zimbabwe.* Gweru: Mambo Press, 1991. 142p.

_____. *The Last British Liberals in Africa: Michael Blundell and Garfield Todd.* Westport, CT: Praeger, 1999. 285 p.

_____. *The Last Defenders of the Laager: Ian Smith and W. W. de Klerk.* Westport, CT: Praeger, 1998. 226 p.

_____, and L. Kay Walker. *Colonial Agriculture for Africans: Emory Alford's Policy in Zimbabwe.* New York: Peter Lang, 1998. 228 p.

Muzorewa, Abel T. *Rise Up and Walk.* London: Evans Brothers, 1978. 289p.

Ndansi Kumalo. "The story of Ndansi Kumalo of the Matabele Tribe, Southern Rhodesia," recorded by J. W. Posselt and Margery Perham, in M. Perham (ed.), *Ten Africans* (London: Faber and Faber, 1936), 63–79.

Nkomo, Joshua. *Nkomo, the story of my life.* London: Methuen, 1984. 270p.

Nyagumbo, Maurice. *With the People: an autobiography from the Zimbabwean struggle.* London: Allison and Busby, 1980. 248p.

Ranger, Terence. "Thompson Samkange: Tambaram and Beyond," *Journal of Religion in Africa,* 23, 4 (1993), 318–46.

Sauer, Hans. *Ex Africa.* London: Geoffrey Bles, 1937. 336p.

Sithole, Ndabaningi. *Letters from Salisbury Prison.* Nairobi: Trans-africa, 1976. 186p.

_____. *Obed Mutezo: The Mudzimu Christian Nationalist.* Intro by T. O. Ranger. Nairobi: OUP, 1970. 210p.

Skelton, Kenneth. *Bishop in Smith's Rhodesia.* Gweru: Mambo Press, 1985. 152p.

Smith, David, and Colin Simpson. *Mugabe.* Salisbury: Pioneer Head, 1981. 217p.

Steere, D. V. *God's Irregular: Arthur Shearly Cripps.* London: Soc. for the Propagation of Christian Knowledge, 1973. 158p.

Taylor, Don. *The Rhodesian: Life of Sir Roy Welensky.* London: Museum Press, 1955. 191p.

Tredgold, Robert C. *The Rhodesia That Was My Life.* London: G. Allen and Unwin, 1968. 271p.

Wallis, John Peter Richard. *One Man's Hand: The Story of Sir Charles Coghlan.* London, 1950. (Rep., Bulawayo: BOR, 1972. 254p.)

Weiss, Ruth. *Sir Garfield Todd and the Making of Zimbabwe.* London: J. B. Tauris, 1999. 256 p.

Werbner, R. *Tears of the Dead: A Social Biography of an African Family.* Edinburgh: Edinburgh Univ. Press, 1991. 211p.

3. CULTURE

Art: Ancient and Modern

Cooke, Cranmer Kenrick. *A Guide to the Rock Art of Rhodesia.* Salisbury: Nat. Museums and Monuments, 1974. 64p. illus.

_____. *Rock Art of Southern Africa.* Cape Town: Books of Africa, 1969. 166p.

Garlake, Peter S. *The Hunter's Vision: The Prehistoric Art of Zimbabwe.* London: British Museum Press, 1995. 176p.

Jocabson-Widding, A. "Pits, Pots and Snakes: An Anthropological Approach To Ancient African Symbols," *Nordic Journal of African Studies,* 1, 1 (1992), 5–27.

Johnson, I. F. "New Shona sculpture," *African Arts,* VII, 1 (1973), 87–8.

McEwen, Frank. "Shona art today," *African Arts,* V, 4 (1972), 8–11.

Polakoff, C. "Contemporary Shona sculpture at the Musée Rodin, Paris," *African Arts,* V, 3 (1972), 57–9.

Summers, Roger F. H. (ed.). *Prehistoric Rock Art of the Federation of Rhodesia and Nyasaland.* Illus. by Elizabeth Goodall. Salisbury: Nat. Pub. Trust, 1959. 267p.

Woodhouse, H. C. "Rock paintings of southern Africa," *African Arts,* II, 3 (1969), 44–9.

Languages and Linguistics

Beeton, D. R., and Helen Dorner. *A Dictionary of English Usage in Southern Africa.* Cape Town: OUP, 1975. 196p.

Bhila, H. H. K. "Munhumutapa: the history and mis-spelling of a Shona term," *Rhod. Hist.,* 5 (1974), 79–80.

Cade, S. E. Altken. *Kitchen Kaffir Dictionary.* Salisbury: Central Afr. Press, n.d. 48p.

Dale, D. *A Basic English-Shona Dictionary.* Gwelo: Mambo, 1975. 212p.

_____. *Shona Companion.* Gwelo: Mambo, 1968. 192p.

Doke, Clement Martyn. *A Comparative Study in Shona Phonetics.* Johannesburg: Univ. of Witwatersrand Press, 1931. 298p.

_____. *Report on the Unification of the Shona Dialects*. Hertford, England: Stephen Austin, 1931. 156p.

Fivaz, Derek, and Jeannette Ratzlaff. *Shona Language Lessons*. Salisbury: Word of Life Pubs. and Rhod. Literature Bureau, 1969. 169p.

Fortune, George. *A Guide to Shona Spelling*. Salisbury: Longman Rhodesia, 1972. 64p.

_____. *Elements of Shona (Zezuru dialect)*. 2nd ed. Salisbury: Longmans, 1967. 286p. (First pub., 1957.)

Hannan, M. *Standard Shona Dictionary*. 2nd ed. Salisbury: Marden, 1972. 996p.

Magura, Benjamin. "Style and Meaning in African English; A Sociolinguisic Analysis of South African and Zimbabwean English." Ph.D. thesis, Univ. of Ill., Urbana-Champaign, 1984.

Pelling, James. *A Practical Ndebele Dictionary*. Bulawayo: Daystar Pubs., 1966. 148p.

_____ , and Pamela Pelling. *Lessons in Ndebele*. Salisbury: Longman Rhodesia, 1974. 210p.

Pongwent, A. J. C. *Studies in Shona Phonetics: An Analytical Review*. Harare: Univ. of Zimbabwe, 1989. 172p.

Rasmussen, R. Kent. "From Cillicaats to Zelkants: the orthographic odyssey of Mzilikazi," *Rhodesiana*, 33 (1975), 52–61.

Shenk, J. R. *A New Ndebele Grammar*. Bulawayo: Brethren in Christ Church, 1971. 229p.

Stevick, Earl W. *Shona: Basic Course*. Washington: Foreign Service Institute, 1965. 633p.

von Sicard, Harald. "The derivation of the name Mashona," *African Studies*, 9, 3 (1950), 138–43.

Literature: African Languages

Chitepo, Herbert W. *Soko Risina Musoro*. Trans. and ed. by Hazel Carter. London: OUP, 1958. 63p. (Rep. in S. M. Mutswairo, ed., below.)

Chiwome, E. "The Role of Oral Traditions in the War of National Liberation in Zimbabwe: Preliminary Observations," *Journal of Folklore research*, 27, 3 (1990), 241–47.

Fortune, George. "75 years of writing in Shona," *Zambezia*, 1, 2 (1969), 55–67.

_____. "Shona traditional poetry," *Zambezia*, 2, 1 (1971), 41–60.

_____. "Variety in Shona literature," *Nada*, X, 4 (1972), 69–76.

Hamutyinei, M. A., and A. B. Plangger (eds.). *Tsumo-Shumo: Shona Proverbial Lore and Wisdom*. Gwelo: Mambo, 1974. 500p.

Hodza, A. C. *Denhe renduri renhorimbo: Shona life and thought expressed in Shona traditional poetry*. Salisbury: Univ. of Rhod., 1977. 53p.

_____ , and George Fortune. *Shona Praise Poetry*. Oxford: Clarendon Press, 1979. 401p.

Jacobson-Widding, A. "Individual Identity in African Story Telling," *Nordic Journal of African Studies*, 2, 1 (1993), 5–33.

Kahari, G. P. *The Rise of the Shona Novel: A Study in Development*. Gweru: Mambo Press, 1990. 407p.

_____. *Aspects of the Shona novel*. Gweru: Mambo Press, 1986. 214p.

_____. *The Novels of Patrick Chakaipa*. Salisbury: Longman Rhodesia, 1972. 110p.

_____. "Tradition and innovation in Shona literature," *Zambezia,* 2, 2 (1971), 47–54.

_____. "Tradition and innovation in the Shona novel," *Nada,* XI, 3 (1976), 309–20.

Krog, E. W. *African Literature in Rhodesia.* Gwelo: Mambo, 1966. 236p.

Lamplough, R. W. *Matabele Folk Tales.* Cape Town: OUP, 1968. 48p.

Mutswairo, Solomon M. (ed.). *Zimbabwe Prose and Poetry.* Washington, DC: Three Continents Press, 1974. 276 p.

Literature: English Language

Afejuku, Tony E. "Autobiography or history? Lawrence Vambe's *An Ill-Fated People,*" *Research in African Literatures,* 19 (1988), 508–19.

Brewster, Dorothy. *Doris Lessing.* New York: Twayne, 1965. 173p.

Brown, G. R., et al. (comps.). *Arthur Shearly Cripps: A Selection of His Prose and Verse.* Gwelo: Mambo, 1976. 308p.

Fairbridge, Kingsley. *Kingsley Fairbridge: His Life and Verse.* Bulawayo: BOR, 1974. 246, 118p. (Includes *The Life of Kingsley Fairbridge,* first pub., London, 1927.)

Finn, D. E. *Poetry in Rhodesia: 75 Years.* Salisbury: College Press, 1968. 80p.

Gouldsbury, Cullen. *Rhodesian Rhymes.* Bulawayo: BOR, 1969. 264p. (First pub., 1932.)

Lessing, Doris. *African Stories.* New York: Ballantine, 1966.

Manion, Eileen C. "Transcendence Through Disorder: A Study of the Fiction of Doris Lessing." Ph.D. thesis, McGill Univ., 1980.

Schleuter, Paul. *The Novels of Doris Lessing.* London and Amsterdam: Feffer and Simons, 1973.

Snelling, John. *A New Anthology of Rhodesian Verse.* Oxford: Blackwell, 1950. 104p.

Steele, Murray C. *"Children of Violence" and Rhodesia: A Study of Doris Lessing as Historical Observer.* Salisbury: Cent. Afr. Hist. Assoc., 1974.

Style, Colin, and O-Lan Style. *Mambo Book of Zimbabwean Verse in English.* Gweru: Mambo Press, 1986. 417p.

Viet-Wild, Flora. *Teachers, Preachers and Non-Believers: A Social History of Zimbabwean Literature.* Oxford: Zell, 1992. 408p.

Zhuwarara, Rino. "The Growth of Zimbabwean Fiction in English 1950–80." Ph.D. thesis, Univ. of New Brunswick, 1984.

Zimunya, M. *Those Years of Drought and Hunger: The Birth of African Fiction in English in Zimbabwe.* Gweru: Mambo Press, 1982. 129p.

Literature: Novels in English

Chalmers, J. *Fighting the Matabele.* London: Blackie, 1898. 288p.

Chinodya, Shimmer. *Harvest of Thorns.* Harare: Baobab Books, 1989. 248p.

Cripps, Arthur Shearly. *Africans All.* London, 1928.

Dangarembga, Tsitsi. *Nervous Conditions.* Seattle: Seal Press, 1989. 204p.

Flockemann, M. "'Not-Quite Insiders and Not-Quite Outsiders': The 'Process of Womanhood' in *Beka Lamb, Nervous Conditions,* and

Daughters of the Twilight," *Journal of Commonwealth Literature,* 27, 1 (1992), 37–47.

Foster, K. "Soul-food for the Starving: Dambudzo Marechera's *House of Hunger,*" *Journal of Commonwealth Literature,* 27, 1 (1992), 58–70.

Fullerton, Alexander. *The White Men Sang.* London: Peter Davies, 1958. 216p.

Gale, William Daniel. *Black Sunset: A Novel of the Matabele War.* London: John Long, 1954. 224p.

Glanville, Ernest. *The Fossicker: A Romance of Mashonaland.* London: Chatto and Windus, 1891. 331p.

Griffiths, Reginald. *The Grey About the Flame.* Cape Town: Howard Timmins, n.d., [1947/8]. 191p.

Haggard, H. Rider. *Benita: An African Romance.* New York: Longmans, Green, 1906. 229p.

_____. *Doom of Zimbabwe.* London: Hodder and Stoughton, 1917. 320p.

_____. *King Solomon's Mines.* London: Cassell, 1885. 320p.

Hole, Hugh Marshall. *Lobengula.* London: Philip Allan, 1929. 211p.

Hove, Chenjerai. *Bones.* Harare: Baobab Books, 1988. 113p.

_____. *Shadows.* Harare: Baobab Books, 1991. 111p.

Ibrahim, Huma. "The Violated Universe: Neo-Colonial Sexual and Political Consciousness in Dambudzo Marechera," *Research in African Literatures,* 21 (1990), 79–90.

Kadhani, M., and M. Zimunya (eds.). *And Now the Poet Speaks (Poems Inspired by the Struggle for Zimbabwe).* Gweru: Mambo Press, 1981. 178p.

Katiyo, Wilson. *Going to Heaven.* London: Rex Collings, 1978? c.160p.

Lessing, Doris. *The Grass Is Singing.* New York: Ballantine, 1964. (First pub., London, 1950).

_____. *African Laughter: Four Visits to Zimbabwe.* London: Flamingo, 1993. 442p.

Marechera, Dambudzo. *Black Sunlight.* London: Heinemann, 1980. 117p.

_____. *House of Hunger.* New York: Pantheon Books, 1979. 167p.

_____. *Mindblast.* Harare: College Press, 1984. 159p.

Mitford, Bertram. *In the Whirl of the Rising.* London: Methuen, 1904. 311p.

_____. *John Ames Native Commissioner: A Romance of the Matabele Rising.* London: F. V. White, 1900. 312p.

_____. *The King's Assegai: A Matabili Story.* Longon: Chatto and Windus, 1894. 248p.

_____. *A Legacy of the Granite Hills.* London: John Long, 1909. 318p.

_____. *The Triumph of Hilary Blachland.* London: Chatto and Windus, 1901. 344p.

_____. *The White Shield.* New York and London: Frederick A. Stokes, 1895. 364p.

Mungoshi, Charles. *Coming of the Dry Season.* Nairobi: OUP, 1972. 60p.

_____. *Some Kind of Wounds and Other Short Stories.* Gweru: Mambo Press, 1980. 179p.

_____. *Waiting for the Rain.* London: Heinemann, 1975. 180p.

Page, Gertrude. *Jill's Rhodesian Philosophy.* London: Hurst and Blackett, 1910. 230p.

_____. *The Rhodesian*. London: Hurst and Blackett, 1912. 360p.

Partridge, Nan. *Not Alone: A Story for the Future of Rhodesia*. Gwelo: Mambo, 1972. 142p.

Rorke, Melina. *Melina Rorke—Told by Herself*. London: G. G. Harrap, 1939. 284p. (Rep., Bulawayo: BOR, 1971; South Africa: Dassie Books, n.d.)

Samkange, Stanlake. *The Chief's Daughter Who Would Not Laugh*. London: Longmans, Green, 1964.

_____. *The Mourned One*. London: Heinemann, 1975. 150p.

_____. *On Trial for My Country*. London: Heinemann, 1966. 160p.

_____. *The Year of the Uprising*. London: Heinemann, 1977. 144p.

Schreiner, Olive. *Trooper Peter Halket of Mashonaland*. London: T. Fisher Unwin, 1897. 264p.

Sithole, Ndabaningi. *The Polygamist*. London: Hodder and Stoughton, 1972. 178p.

_____. *Roots of a Revolution: Scenes from Zimbabwe's Struggle*. London: OUP, 1977?

Thomas, S. "Killing the Hysteric in the Colonised's House: Tsitsi Dangerembga's *Nervous Conditions*," *Journal of Commonwealth Literature*, 27, 1 (1992), 26–36.

Uwakweh, Pauline A. "Debunking Patriarchy: The Liberational Quality of Voicing in Tsitsi Dangarembga's *Nervous Conditions*," *Research in African Literatures*, 26 (1995), 75–84.

Vera, Yvonne. *Butterfly Burning*. New York: Farrar, Strauss and Giroux, 1998. 151 p.

Viet-Wild, Flora. *Dambudzo Marechera: A Sourcebook*. Oxford: Zell, 1992. 419p.

_____. "'Dances With Bones': Hove's Romanticized Africa," *Research in African Literatures*, 24, 3 (1993), 5–12.

_____. *Survey of Zimbabwean Writers: Educational and Literary Careers*. Bayreuth: Bayreuth Univ., 1992. 172p.

Walker, Ken. *The Barrier*. Salisbury: Galaxie, 1972. 399p.

Whishaw, Fred. *The White Witch of the Matabele*. London: Griffith Farran Browne, n.d. [1897]. 326p.

Media: Broadcasting, Publishing, and the Press

Couzens, T. (ed.). *Zimbabwe: The Search for Common Ground Since 1890: From the Pages of DRUM Magazine*. Lanseria: Bailey's African Photo Archives, 1992. 323p.

Dellar, Geoffrey. "The changing pattern of Rhodesian publishing," *Rhod. Librarian*, I, 3 (1969), 71–6.

Fraenkel, Peter. *Wayaleshi: Radio in Central Africa*. London: Weidenfeld and Nicholson, 1959. 224p.

Frederikse, Julie. *None But Ourselves: masses vs. media in the making of Zimbabwe*. Johannesburg: Raven Press, 1982. 368p.

Gale, W. D. *The Rhodesian Press: The History of the Rhodesian Printing and Publishing Company, Ltd*. Salisbury: Rhod. Printing and Pub. Co., 1962. 225p.

George, N. "Using Radio for Community Mobilisation: Experiences in Zimbabwe and Kenya," *Africa Media Review*, 7, 2 (1993), 52–68.

Harris, Phil. *Reporting Southern Africa.* Ghent (Belgium): UNESCO, 1981. 168p.

Kinloch, Graham C. *Flame or Lily: Rhodesian Values as Defined by the Press.* Durban: Alpha Graphic, 1970. 134p.

Parker, John. *Rhodesia: Little White Island.* London: Pitman, 1972. 166p.

Paver, B. G. *His Own Oppressor.* London: Peter Davies, 1958. 235p.

Pearce, C. "Civil Society and The State: An Analysis of Articles on Education in the Zimbabwean Press, January 1989–April 1990," *Compare,* 21, 1 (1991), 27–48.

Powell, Jon T. "South-central Africa," in Sydney Head (ed.), *Broadcasting in Africa* (Philadelphia: Temple UP, 1974), 125–33.

Rusike, E. T. *The Politics of the Mass Media.* Harare: Roblaw, 1990. 111p.

Smith, M. "Censorship in Rhodesia: the experience of a Salisbury editor," *Round Table,* 59 (London, 1969), 60–7.

Wason, E. *Banned: African Daily News, Southern Rhodesia 1964.* London: H. Hamilton, 1976. 161p.

Windrich, Elaine. *The Mass Media in the Struggle for Zimbabwe.* Gweru: Mambo Press, 1981. 112p.

———. "Rhodesian censorship: the role of the media in the making of a one-party state," *Afr. Affairs,* 78, 313 (1979), 523–534.

Zaffiro, James J. "Broadcasting and Political Change in Zimbabwe 1931–1984." Ph.D. thesis, Univ. Wisconsin-Madison, 1984.

Music and Drama

Axelsson, Olaf. "Notes on African musical instuments in Zimbabwe," *Arts of Zimbabwe,* 2 (1981/82), 55–62.

Berliner, Paul F. *The soul of Mbira.* Berkeley: Univ. of California Press, 1978. 312p.

Cary, Robert. *The Story of Reps: The History of the Salisbury Repertory Players.* Salisbury: Galaxie, 1975. 240p.

Jones, Claire. *Making Music: Musical Instruments of Zimbabwe Past and Present.* Harare: Academic Books, 1992. 183p.

Kaarsholm, P. "Mental Colonisation or Catharsis? Theatre, Democracy and Cultural Struggle from Rhodesia to Zimbabwe," *Journal of Southern African Studies,* 16, 2 (1990), 246–75.

Kahari, G. R. "The history of the Shona protest song: a preliminary study," *Zambezia,* 9, 2 (1981), 79–101.

Kavanagh, R. M. "Theatre for Development in Zimbabwe: An Urban Project," *Journal of Southern African Studies,* 16, 2 (1990), 340–51.

Maraire, Dumisani. *The Mbira Music of Rhodesia* (booklet with record). Seattle: Univ. of Washington Press, 1970.

Sherman, Jessica. "Songs of the Chimurenga," *Afr. Perspectives* (Johannesburg), 16 (1980), 80–88.

Taylor, C. T. C. *The History of Rhodesian Entertainment, 1890–1930.* Salisbury: M. O. Collins, 1968. 186p.

Tracey, Andrew. "The Matepe *mbira* music of Rhodesia," *African Music,* II, 4 (Johannesburg, 1961), 44–63.

Tracey, Hugh T. "The *mbira* class of African instruments in Rhodesia (1932)," *African Music,* IV, 3 (1969), 78–95.

Wortham, C. J. "The state of the theatre in Rhodesia," *Zambezia,* 1, 1 (1969), 47–53.

Philately: Postage Stamps

Drysdall, A., and D. Collis. *Mashonaland: A Postal History, 1890–1896.* London: Christie's Robson Lowe, 1990. 171p.

Mashonaland Philatelic Society. *A Guide to the Postage Stamps of The Rhodesias and Nyasaland, 1888–1963.* Salisbury: The Soc., 1965. 149p.

Smith, Robert C. *Rhodesia: A Postal History; Its Stamps, Posts, and Telegraphs.* Salisbury: Mardon, 1967. 454p.

_____. *A Supplement to Rhodesia: A Postal History.* Salisbury: Mardon, 1970. 62p.

4. ECONOMICS

General

Arrighi, Giovanni. *The Political Economy of Rhodesia.* The Hague: Mouton, 1967. 60p.

Auret, Diana. *A Decade of Development: Zimbabwe, 1980–1990.* Gweru: Mambo Press, 1990.

Barber, William J. *The Economy of British Central Africa: A Case Study of Economic Development in a Dualistic Society.* London: OUP; Stanford, CA: Stanford UP, 1961. 271p.

Baynham, Simon (ed.). *Zimbabwe in transition.* Stockholm: Almquist and Wiksell, 1992.

Bond, P. "Economic Origins of Black Townships in Zimbabwe: Contradictions of Industrial and Financial Capital in the 1950s and 1960s," *Economic Geography,* 69, 1 (1993), 72–89.

Bratton, Michael. "Settler state, guerrilla war and rural underdevelopment in Rhodesia," *Issue,* 9, 1/2 (1979), 56–62.

_____. *Uneven Zimbabwe: A Study of Finance, Development and Underdevelopment.* Trenton: Africa World Press, 1998. 515 p.

Chattopadhyay, Rupak. "Zimbabwe: Structural Adjustment, Destitution and Food Insecurity," *R. Afr. Pol. Econ.,* 27, 84 (2000), 307–316.

Clarke, Duncan G. *The Distribution of Income and Wealth in Rhodesia.* Gweru: Mambo Press, 1977. 125p.

_____. *The Economics of African Old Age Subsistence in Rhodesia.* Gweru: Mambo Press, 1977. 71p.

_____. *Foreign companies and international investment in Zimbabwe.* London: Catholic Inst. for Intl. Stud., 1980. 275p.

_____. "Public sector economics in Rhodesia: the growth and impact of the public sector," *Rhod. Jnl. Econ.,* VI (1972), 48–60.

Cole, R. L. "Commercial banking in Rhodesia," *Rhod. Jnl. Econ.,* VIII (1974), 55–65.

Davies, C. S. "Tribalism and economic development," *Nada,* X, 2 (1970), 78–83.

Helmsing, A. H. J. *Small-scale Rural Industries in Zimbabwe: An Overview.* Harare: Zimbabwe Environmental Research Organization, 1992. 27p.

Johnson, D. "Settler Farmers and coerced African labour in Southern Rhodesia, 1936–46," *Journal of African History,* 33, 1 (1992), 111–28.

Lehman, Howard P. "The Paradox of State Power in Africa: Debt Management Policies in Kenya and Zimbabwe," *African Studies Review*, 35 (1992), 1–34.

Makumbe, John. *Participatory Development: The Case of Zimbabwe.* Harare: Univ. of Zimbabwe, 1997. 142 p.

Mlambo, K., and S. Kayizzi-Muger. "The Macroeconomics of Transition: Zimbabwe in the 1980s," *African Development Review*, 3, 1 (1991), 47–67.

Moore, D. S. "Contesting Terrain in Zimbabwe's Eastern Highlands: Political Ecology, Ethnography and Peasant Resource Struggles," *Economic Geography*, 69, 4 (1993), 380–401.

Ncube, Mthuli. *Development Dynamics: Theories and Lessons from Zimbabwe.* Brookfield, CT: Avebury, 1991.

Ndlela, Daniel. *Dualism in the Rhodesian colonial economy.* Lund: Univ. of Lund, 1981. 241p.

Ndlovu, Lindani B. *The Systems of Protection and Industrial Development in Zimbabwe.* Brookfield, CT: Avebury, 1994.

Palmer, Robin, and Neil Parsons (eds.). *The Roots of Rural Poverty in Central and Southern Africa.* London: Heinemann, 1977. c.320p.

Ramsay, D. I. "Capital and productivity in Rhodesia," *Rhod. Jnl. Econ.,* VIII, 2 (1974), 67–82.

Riddell, Roger. *Alternatives to poverty.* London: Catholic Inst. for Intl. Relations, 1977. 22p.

Schatzberg, Michael G. (ed.). *The political economy of Zimbabwe.* New York: Praeger, 1984. 276p.

Seidman, Ann, Robert Seidman, D. Ndlela, and K. Makamura. *Transnationals in Southern Africa.* Harare: Zimb. Pub. House, 1986. 219p.

Skalnes, Tor. *The Politics of Economic Reform in Zimbabwe: Continuity and Change in Development.* New York: St. Martin's Press, 1995.

Stoneman, Colin. "Foreign capital and the reconstruction of Zimbabwe," *R. Afr. Pol. Econ.,* 11 (1978), 62–83.

Sylvester, Christine. *Zimbabwe: The Terrain of Contradictory Development.* Boulder, CO: Westview, 1991.

Thompson, Cecil H., and Harry W. Woodruff. *Economic Development in Rhodesia and Nyasaland.* London: D. Dobson, 1954. 205p.

Ushewokunze, Herbert. "Zimbabwe: problems and prospects of socialist development," *Race and class*, 23, 4 (1982), 275–285.

Utete, C. M. B. *The Road to Zimbabwe: the political economy of settler colonialism, national liberation and foreign intervention.* Washington, DC: UP of America, 1979. 170p.

West, Michael O. "Pan-Africanism, Capitalism and Racial Uplift: The Rhetoric of African Business Formation in Colonial Zimbabwe," *African Affairs*, 92 (1993), 263–83.

Agriculture and Animal Husbandry

Akwabi-Ameyaw, K. "The Political Economy of Agricultural Resettlement and Rural Development in Zimbabwe: Family Farms and Producer Cooperatives," *Human Organization*, 49, 4 (1990), 320–38.

_____. "Producer Cooperative Resettlement Projects in Zimbabwe: Lessons from a Failed Agricultural Development Strategy," *World Development*, 25, 3(1997), 437–456.

Alvord, Emory D. "Agricultural life of Rhodesian natives," *Nada*, 7 (1929), 9–16.

Bush, Ray, and L. Cliffe. "Agrarian policy in migrant labour societies: reform or transformation in Zimbabwe," *R. Afr. Pol. Econ.*, 29 (1984), 77–94.

Cheater, Angela. "Small-scale freehold as a model for commercial agriculture in Rhodesia-Zimbabwe," *Zambezia*, 6, 2 (1978), 117–127.

_____. "Women and their participation in community agricultural production: the case of medium-scale freehold in Zimbabwe," *Development and Change*, 12, 3 (1981), 349–377.

Clements, Frank, and Edward Harben. *Leaf of Gold: The Story of Rhodesian Tobacco.* London: Methuen, 1962.

Danckwerts, J. P. "Technology and economic development of African agriculture in Rhodesia," *Rhod. Jnl. Econ.*, IV, 4 (1970), 17–30.

Duncan, B. H. G. "The wages and supply position in European agriculture," *Rhod. Jnl. Econ.*, VII, 1 (1973), 1–13.

Dunlop, Harry. *The Development of European Agriculture in Rhodesia, 1945–1965.* Salisbury: Univ. of Rhod., 1971. 71p.

Le Roux, A. A. "African agriculture in Rhodesia," *Rhod. Agric. Jnl.*, LXVI (1969), 146–52.

Loewenson, Rene. *Modern Plantation Agriculture.* London: Zed Books, Ltd., 1992.

Massell, Benton F., and R. W. M. Johnson. *African Agriculture in Rhodesia: An Econometric Study.* Santa Monica, CA: Rand Corp, 1966. 138p.

Mbanga, Trish. *Tobacco, A Century of Gold.* Harare: ZIL Publications, 1991. 239p.

Mbiba, B. *Urban Agriculture in Zimbabwe.* Brookfield, CT: Avebury, 1995. 220p.

Metcalfe, C. B. *A Guide to Farming in Rhodesia.* Salisbury: Rhod. Farmer Pubs., 1971. 166p.

Mlambo, A. S., and E. S. Pangeti. *The Political Economy of the Sugar Industry in Zimbabwe, 1920–1990.* Harare: Univ. of Zimbabwe, 1996. 90 p.

Mosley, Paul. "Agricultural development and government policy in settler economies: the case of Kenya and Southern Rhodesia, 1900–60," *Econ. Hist. R.*, 35, 3 (1982), 390–408.

Mtisi, Joseph. "Relationship Between Government and Private Enterprise in the Forestry and Timber Industry: The Case of Zimbabwe," *Eastern African Social Science Research Review*, 6, 2 and 7, 1 (1990/91), 47–64.

Nobbs, E. A. "The native cattle of Southern Rhodesia," *S. Afr. Jnl. Science*, 24 (Dec. 1927), 328–42.

Nyambura, P. S. "The Origins and Development of the Cotton Industry in Colonial Zimbabwe, 1903–1935," *Eastern African Social Science Research Review*, 6, 2 & 7, 1 (1990/91), 141–56.

Oliver, J. *Introduction to Dairying in Rhodesia.* Salisbury: Univ. of Rhod., 1971. 152p.

Phillips, John, et al. *The Development of the Economic Resources of Southern Rhodesia with Particular Reference to the Role of African Agriculture.* Salisbury: Gov. Printer, 1962. 484p.

Phimister, Ian R. "Peasant production and underdevelopment in Southern Rhodesia, 1890–1914," *Afr. Affairs*, LXXIII (Apr. 1974), 217–28.

Pollak, Oliver B. "Black farmers and white politics in Rhodesia, 1930–1972," *Afr. Affairs*, LXXIV (1975), 263–77.

Shutt, Allison. "'We Are the Best Poor Farmers': Purchase Area Farmers and Economic Differentiation in Southern Rhodesia, ca. 1925–1980." Ph.D. thesis, U.C.L.A, 1995.

Stocking, M. A. "Aspects of the role of man in erosion in Rhodesia," *Zambezia*, 2, 2 (1972), 1–10.

Tracey, L. T. *Approach to Farming in Southern Rhodesia*. London: Univ. of London Press, 1953. 428p.

Weiner, C. "Agricultural Restructuring in Zimbabwe and South Africa," *Development and Change*, 20, 3 (1989), 401–28.

_____. "Socialist Transition in the Capitalist Periphery: A Case Study of Agriculture in Zimbabwe," *Political Geography Quarterly*, 10, 1, (1991), 54–75.

Weinmann, H. *Agricultural Research and Development in Rhodesia, 1924–1970*. Salisbury: Univ. of Rhod., 1975. 240p.

_____. *Agricultural Research and Development in Southern Rhodesia, 1890–1923*. Salisbury: Univ. of Rhod., 1972. 166p.

Weinrich, Anna Katherine Hildegaard. *African Farmers in Rhodesia: Old and New Peasant Communities in Karangaland*. London: OUP for Internat. Afr. Inst., 1975. 342p.

Yudelman, Montague. *Africans on the Land: Economic Problems of African Agricultural Development . . . with special Reference to Southern Rhodesia*. Cambridge, MA: Harvard UP, 1964. 288p.

Zinyama, L. M. "Agricultural Development Policies in the African Farming Areas of Zimbabwe," *Geography*, 71 (1986), 105–15.

Commerce and International Sanctions

Arnold, Guy. *Sanctions Against Rhodesia, 1965–1972*. London: Africa Bureau, 1972.

Cole, R. L. "The tariff policy of Rhodesia, 1899–1963," *Rhod. Jnl. Econ.*, II (1968), 28–47.

Davies, R. J. "Aspects of trade policy in the Federation of Rhodesia and Nyasaland," *Rhod. Jnl. Econ.*, VII, 3 (1973), 165–72.

Doxey, Margaret P. *Economic Sanctions and International Enforcement*. London: OUP, 1971. 162p.

Gibson, C. A. "Export development: the mining industry as an exporter," *Rhod. Jnl. Econ.*, VI (1972), 72–80.

Girdlestone, J. A. C. "The foreign exchange costs of Rhodesian economic development," *Rhod. Jnl. Econ.*, IV (1970), 31–45.

_____. "A policy for import control," *Rhod. Jnl. Econ.*, II (1968), 59/69.

Handford, John F. *Portrait of an Economy: Rhodesia Under Sanctions*. Salisbury: Mercury, 1976. 208p.

Hawkins, R. T. R. "Export development: transport for exports," *Rhod. Jnl. Econ.*, VI (1972), 49–57.

Irvine, Alexander G. *The Balance of Payments of Rhodesia and Nyasaland, 1945–1954*. London: OUP, 1959. 643p.

Kapungu, Leonard. *The United Nations and Economic Sanctions Against Rhodesia*. Lexington, MA: D. C. Heath, 1973. 155p.

Le Roux, A. A. "British sanctions legislation," *Rhod. Law Jnl.*, IX (1969), 40–81.

Margoles, W. "Export development: agriculture as an exporter," *Rhod. Jnl. Econ.*, VI (1972), 81–7.

Minter, William, and Elizabeth Schmidt. "When Sanctions Worked: The Case of Rhodesia Reexamined," *Afr. Affairs*, 87 (1988), 207–37.

Park, Stephen, and Anthony Lake. *Business as Usual; Transactions Violating Rhodesian Sanctions.* New York: Carnegie Endowment for Internat. Peace, 1973. 54p.

Schmidt, Elizabeth S. *United Nations Sanctions and South Africa: Lessons from the Case of Southern Rhodesia.* New York: UN Center Against Apartheid, 1987. 36p.

Strack, H. R. *Sanctions: The Case of Rhodesia.* Syracuse, NY: Syracuse UP, 1977. c256p.

Wild, Volker. *Profit Not for Profit's Sake: History and Business Culture of African Entrepreneurs in Zimbabwe.* Harare: Baobab Books, 1997. 324 p.

Industry

Abrahamson, A. E. "Industrialisation and employment in Rhodesia," *Rhod. Jnl. Econ.*, III (1969), 24–30.

Bennell, P. "Market Power and Mark-Ups: Manufacturing Industry in Zimbabwe," *Eastern African Economic Review*, 8, 2 (1992), 135–41.

Cameron, J. D. "Industrial growth and the subsistence economy," *Rhod. Jnl. Econ.*, III (1969), 16–23.

Federation of Rhodesian Industries. *Survey of Rhodesian Industry.* Salisbury, 1954. 139p.

Graylin, J. C. "Industrial development in Rhodesia," *Rhod. Jnl. Econ.*, III (1969), 38–43.

Harris, Peter S. "Industrial development in Rhodesia," *Rhod. Jnl. Econ.*, XLII (1974), 65–84.

Kaliyati, J. W. *The Iron and Steel Industry in Zimbabwe and Regional Cooperation in the SADCC Context.* Harare: Zimbabwe IDS, 1991. 42p.

Mair, S. "Agricultural Demand-Led Industrialisation: An Option for Zimbabwe?," *African Development Perspectives Yearbook*, 2, (1990/91), 556–76.

McCrystal, L. P. "Dispersal of economic activity and industrial development." *Rhod. Jnl. Econ.*, III (1969), 31–41.

Mussett, B. H. "Rhodesia's industrial policy," *Rhod. Jnl. Econ.*, III (1969), 7–14.

Stoneman, Colin. "The Industrialisation of Zimbabwe: Past, Present and Future," *Afrika Focus*, 6, 3–4 (1990), 245–67.

Stringer, Brian. "Trade and industry," *Rhod. Jnl. Econ.*, IV (1970), 23–8.

Tow, Leonard. *The Manufacturing Economy of Southern Rhodesia: Problems and Prospects.* Washington, DC: Nat. Acad. of Sciences, 1960. 141p.

Labor and Unions

Adams, J. "Female Wage Labour in Rural Zimbabwe," *World Development*, 19, 2/3 (1991), 163–77.

_____. "The Rural Labour Market in Zimbabwe," *World Development*, 22, 2 (1991), 297–321.

Arrighi, Giovanni. "Labour supplies in historical perspective: a study of the proletarianization of African peasantry in Rhodesia," *Jnl. of Development Studies*, 6 (1970), 197–234.

Brand, C. M. "Politics and African trade unionism in Rhodesia since Federation," *Rhod. Hist.*, 2 (1974), 88–109.

Brand, Veronica. "One Dollar Work Places: A Study of Informal Sector Activities in Magaba, Harare," *Jnl. Social Dev. in Afr.*, 1, 2 (1986), 53–74.

_____. "Women informal sector workers and structural adjustment in Zimbabwe," in *Social Change and Economic Reform in Africa*. Uppsala: Scandinavian Institute of African Studies, 1993.

Bratton, Michael. "Micro-democracy? The Merger of Farmer Unions in Zimbabwe," *African Studies Review*, 37 (1994), 9–37.

_____. "The public service in Zimbabwe," *Pol. Sci. Q.*, 95, 3 (1980), 441–464.

Chavunduka, G. L. "Farm labourers in Rhodesia," *Rhod. Jnl. Econ.*, VI, 4 (1972), 18–25.

Clarke, Duncan G. *Agricultural and Plantation Workers in Rhodesia*. Gweru: Mambo Press, 1977. 298p.

_____. *Domestic Workers in Rhodesia: The Economics of Masters and Servants*. Gwelo: Mambo, 1974. 88p.

_____. *Unemployment and Economic Structure in Rhodesia*. Gweru: Mambo Press, 1977. 81p.

_____. *The Unemployment Crisis*. London: Catholic Inst. for Intl. Stud., 1978. 36p.

Crookes, K. B. "Labour problems in Rhodesia: an employer's viewpoint," *Rhod. Jnl. Econ.*, VI (1972), 1–8.

Davies, Rob. *The informal sector: A solution to unemployment?* London: Catholic Inst. for Intl. Stud., 1978. 32p.

Dawson, R. "The Rhodesian employment problem: three views; towards a better understanding of manpower supply in Rhodesia," *Rhod. Jn. Econ.* VII (1972), 1–20.

Fulton, P. R., and R. Lucas. "Job Security Regulations and the Dynamic Demand for Industrial Labour in India and Zimbabwe," *Journal of Development Economics*, 40 (1993), 241–74.

Gelfand, Michael. "Migration of African labourers in Rhodesia and Nyasaland, 1890–1914," *Cent. Afr. Jnl. Medicine*, VII (Aug. 1961), 233–300.

Gussman, B. "Industrial efficiency and the urban African: a study of conditions in Southern Rhodesia," *Africa*, XXIII, 2 (1953), 135–44.

Harris, Peter S. *Black Industrial Workers in Rhodesia*. Gwelo: Mambo, 1974. 71p.

_____. "Government policy and African wages in Rhodesia," *Zambezia*, 2, 2 (1972), 39–45.

_____. "Industrial workers in Rhodesia, 1946–1972," *Jnl. So. Afr. Studies*, I, 2 (Apr. 1975), 139–61.

_____. "Ten popular myths concerning the employment of labour in Rhodesia," *Rhod. Jnl. Econ.*, VIII (1974), 38–48.

Hooker, J. R. "The African worker in Southern Rhodesia: black aspirations in a white economy, 1927–36," *Race*, VI, 2 (1964), 142–51.

Loewenson, Renee. "Child Labour in Zimbabwe and the Rights of the Child," *Jnl. Social Dev. in Afr.*, 6, 1 (1991), 19–31.

Mackenzie, J. M. "African labour in the Chartered Company period," *Rhod. Hist.*, 1 (1970), 43–58.

Malaba, Luke. "Supply, continuity and organization of African labour in Rhodesia," *R. Afr. Pol. Econ.*, 18 (1980), 7–28.

Mitchell, J. C. "Structural plurality, urbanisation and labour circulation in Rhodesia," in J. A. Jackson (ed.), *Migrations* (Cambridge, England: Cambridge UP, 1960), 156–80.

Mswaka, T. E. "African unemployment and the rural areas of Rhodesia," *Rural Africana*, 24 (East Lansing, MI, 1974), 59–73.

Mupedziswa, Rodreck. *The Social Sector and Employment in Zimbabwe: A Study of Small Scale Production Enterprises in the Greater Harare Area.* Harare: School of Social Work, 1990. 53p.

Murphree, Marshall W. *Employment Opportunities and Race in Rhodesia.* Denver: Univ. of Denver, Center on Internat. Race Relations, 1973. 39p.

Pape, J. "Still Serving the Tea: Domestic Workers in Zimbabwe, 1980–1990," *Jnl. So. Afr. Studies*, 19, 3 (1993), 387–406.

Pettman, B. O. *Manpower Inventory Study of Zimbabwe.* Harare: Whitson Foundation, 1982. 167p.

Phimister, Ian R. "The Shamva mine strike of 1927: an emerging African proletariat," *Rhod. Hist.*, 2 (1971), 65–88.

_____. "Origins and aspects of African worker consciousness in Rhodesia," in E. Webster (ed.), *Essays in Southern African Labour History* (Johannesburg: Ravan Press, 1978).

Phimister, Ian R., and Charles van Onselen. *Studies in the history of African mine labour in colonial Zimbabwe.* Gweru: Mambo Prress, 1978. 150p.

_____ , and _____. "The political economy of tribal animosity: a case study of the 1929 Bulawayo Location 'faction fight,'" *Jnl. So. Afr. Studies*, 6, 1 (1979), 1–43.

Pollak, Oliver B. "The impact of the Second World War on African labour organisation in Rhodesia," *Rhod. Jnl. Econ.*, VII, 3 (1973), 121–38.

Ranger, Terence O. "The mobilization of labour and the production of knowledge: the antiquarian tradition in Rhodesia," *Jnl. of Afr. Hist.*, 20, 4 (1979), 507–524.

Ranney, Susan I. "The Labour Market in a Dual Economy: Another Look at Colonial Rhodesia," *Journal of Development Studies*, 21 (1985), 505–24.

Reynolds, P. *Dance Civet Cat: Child Labour in the Zambezi Valley.* London: Zel, 1994. 176p.

Riddell, Roger C. "The Salisbury Municipal Worker's Union—a case study," *Rhod. Jnl. Econ.*, VII, 1 (1973), 25–40.

Scott, Peter. "Migrant labour in Southern Rhodesia," *Geog. Review*, 44, 1 (New York, 1954), 29–48.

Sithole, Edson. "The African worker in Southern Rhodesia," *World Trade Union Movement*, X (Paris, Oct. 1958), 17–20.

Steele, Murray C. "White working-class disunity: the Southern Rhodesia Labour Party," *Rhod. Hist.*, 1 (1970), 59–81.

Stoneman, Colin. *Skilled labour and future needs.* London: Catholic Inst. for Intl. Relations, 1978. 53p.

van Onselen, Charles. *Chibaro: African Mine Labour in Southern Rhodesia, 1900–1933.* London: Pluto Press, 1976. 326p.

_____. "The 1912 Wankie colliery strike," *Jnl. Afr. Hist.*, XV, 2 (1974), 275–89.

_____. "Worker consciousness in black mines: Southern Rhodesia, 1900–1920," *Jnl. Afr. Hist.*, XIV, 2 (1973), 237–55.

Vickery, Kenneth. "The Second World War Revival of Forced Labor in the Rhodesias," *Internat. Jnl. Afr. Hist. Studies*, 22, 3 (1989), 423–37.

Warhurst, Philip R. "The Tete Agreement," *Rhod. Hist.*, 1 (1970), 31–41.

Weinrich, A. K. H. "Changes in the political and economical roles of women in Zimbabwe since independence," *Cultures* (Paris), 8, 4 (1982), 43–62.

Zimbabwe Women's Bureau. *Black Women in Zimbabwe.* Harare: Zimb. Women's Bureau, 1981. 47p.

_____. *We Carry a Heavy Load: Women in Zimbabwe speak out.* Harare: Zimb. Women's Bureau, 1981. 51p.

Land and Land Policy

Alexander, J. "The Unsettled Land: The Politics of Land Redistribution in Matebeleland, 1980–1990," *Jnl. So. Afr. Studies*, 17, 4 (1991), 581–610.

Bulman, Mary Elizabeth. *The Native Land Husbandry Act of Southern Rhodesia: A Failure in Land Reform.* Salisbury: Tribal Areas of Rhod. Research Foundation, 1973. 45p.

Cheater, Angela. "Formal and informal rights to land in Zimbabwe's black freehold areas: a case study of Msengezi," *Africa*, 52, 3 (1982), 77–91.

_____. *Idioms of Accumulation: rural development and class formation among freeholders in Zimbabwe.* Gweru: Mambo Press, 1984. 199p.

Chiviya, Esau M. "Land Reform in Zimbabwe: Policy and Implementation." Ph.D. thesis, Indiana Univ., 1982.

Christopher, A. J. "Land tenure in Rhodesia," *S. Afr. Geog. Jnl.*, 13 (1971), 39–52.

Clutton-Brock, Guy. *Rekayi Tangwena: Let Tangwena Be.* Gwelo: Mambo, 1969. 25p.

Cripps, Arthur Shearly. *An African for Africans: A Plea on Behalf of Territorial Segregation Areas and of Their Freedom in a South African Colony.* London: Longmans, Green, 1927. 203p.

Duggan, William R. "The Native Land Husbandry Act of 1951 and the rural African middle class of Southern Rhodesia," *Afr. Affairs*, 79, 315 (1980), 227–239.

Dunlop, Harry. "Land and economic opportunity in Rhodesia," *Rhod. Jnl. Econ.*, VI, 1 (1972), 1–19.

Fleming, C. J. W. "Systems of land tenure," *Nada*, XI, 1 (1974), 53–63.

Floyd, B. N. "Changing patterns of African land use in Southern Rhodesia," *Rhodes-Livingstone Jnl.*, 25 (1959), 20–39.

_____. "Land apportionment in Southern Rhodesia," *Geog. Review*, 12 (New York: Oct. 1962), 566–88.

Garbett, G. K. "The Land Husbandry Act of Southern Rhodesia," in Daniel Biebuyck (ed.), *African Agrarian Systems* (London: OUP, 1961), 185–202.

Hamilton, P. "The changing pattern of African land use in Rhodesia," in J. B. Whitton and P. D. Wood (eds.), *Essays in Geography for Austin Miller* (Reading, England: Reading UP, 1965), 247–71.

International Defence and Aid Fund. *Rhodesia: The Ousting of the Tangwena.* London: Christian Action, 1972. 51p.

Jacobs, Susie. "Gender and Land Reform: Zimbabwe and Some Comparisons," *International Sociology*, 7, 1 (1992), 5–34.

_____. "Women and land resettlement in Zimbabwe," *R. Afr. Pol. Econ.*, 27/28 (1984), 33–50.

Johnson, R. W. M. "Human problems in Central Africa. Four papers on the social and economic problems of the reserves of Southern Rhodesia," *Rhodes-Livingstone Jnl.*, 36 (1965), 1–108.

Kinsey, B. H. "Emerging policy issues in Zimbabwe's land resettlement programs," *Dev. Policy R.* (London), 1, 2 (1983), 163–196.

_____. "Forever gained: resettlement and land policy in the context of national development in Zimbabwe," *Africa* (London), 52, 3 (1982), 92–113.

Machingaidze, V. E. M. "Land Reform in Colonial Zimbabwe: The Southern Rhodesia Land Husbandry Act and African Response," *Eastern African Social Science Research Review*, 6, 2 and 7, 1 (1990/91), 14–46.

Mackenzie, J. M. "Red soils in Mashonaland: a re-assessment," *Rhod. Hist.*, 5 (1974), 81–8.

Moyana, Henry. *The Political Economy of Land in Zimbabwe.* Gweru: Mambo Press, 1984. 194p.

Moyo, Sam. *The Land Question in Zimbabwe.* Harare: SAPES Books, 1995. 333p.

_____. *Land and Democracy in Zimbabwe.* Harare: SAPES Books, 1999. 27p.

Moyo, Sam, et al. "Land Reform and Changing Social Relations for Farm Workers in Zimbabwe," *R. Afr. Pol. Econ.*, 27, 84 (2000), 181–202.

Myers, Edgar, and Glenn C. W. Ames. "Land tenure and agricultural development in Zimbabwe," *Jnl. of Afr. Stud.*, 11, 2 (1984), 83–91.

Nkiwane, Solomon M. *Zimbabwe's International Borders: A Study in National and Regional Development in Southern Africa.* Harare: Univ. of Zimbabwe, 1997. 107 p.

Palmer, Robin H. *Land and Racial Domination in Rhodesia.* London: Heinemann, 1977. c.352p.

_____. "Land Reform in Zimbabwe, 1980–1990," *Afr. Affairs*, 89, 335 (1990), 163–81.

Phimister, Ian. "Rethinking the Reserves: Southern Rhodesia's Land Husbandry Act Reviewed," *Jn. So. Afr. Studies*, 19, 2 (1993), 225–39.

Riddell, Roger. *The Land Question.* London: Catholic Inst. for Intl. Relations, 1977. 38p.

_____. "Prospects for land reform in Zimbabwe," *Rural Africana*, 4/5 (1979), 17–31.

_____. "Zimbabwe's land problem; the central issue," *Jnl. Commonwealth and comp. pol.*, 18, 1 (1980), 1–13.

Rifkind, M. L. "Land apportionment in perspective," *Rhod. Hist.*, 3 (1972), 53–62.

Roder, Wolf. "The division of land resources in Southern Rhodesia," *Annals of Assoc. of American Geog.*, 54, 1 (1964), 41–58.

Sibanda, Concern J. *The Tribal Trust Lands of Rhodesia.* Swansea: Univ. College of Swansea, 1979. 60p.

Sibanda, H. M. "Problems of Land Use Planning in the Communal Areas of Zimbabwe: A Case Study of Gutu District, Masvingo Province," *Applied Geography*, 10, 2 (1990), 135–46.

Venturas, D. A. E. "Land settlement in Rhodesia, 1890–1940," *So. Afr. Outlook* (Cape Town), 109, 1302 (1979), 183–185.

Weinrich, Anna K. H. *Black and White Elites in Rural Rhodesia.* Manchester, England: Manchester UP; Totowa, NJ: Rowman and Littlefield, 1973. 244p.

Wrathall, J. J. "The Tribal Trust Lands: their need for development," *Nada*, X (1969), 92–9.

Mining

Baines, Thomas. *The Gold Regions of South Eastern Africa.* London: E. Stanford, 1968. 187p. (Rep., Bulawayo: BOR, 1968.)

Bradbury, John, and Eric Worby. *The Mining Industry in Zimbabwe: Labour, Capital and the State.* Toronto: Centre for Dev. Area Stud., McGill Univ. Press, 1984. 36p.

Carlylle-Gall, C. *Mines of Rhodesia.* London: Afr. and Rhod. Mines Publ. Co., 1937. 735p.

Hedley, R. J. "Industrial growth and the mining industry," *Rhod. Jnl. Econ.*, III (1969), 29–37.

Huffman, T. N. "Ancient mining and Zimbabwe," *Jnl. S. Afr. Instit. Mining and Metallurgy*, LXXIV, 6 (1974), 238–42.

Johnson, James Paul. *The Mineral Industry of Rhodesia.* London: Longmans, Green, 1911. 90p.

Nicoll, I. M. *Mining and Industry.* Salisbury: M. O. Collins, 1973. 35p.

Phimister, Ian R. "Alluvial gold mining and trade in nineteenth century south central Africa," *Jnl. Afr. Hist.*, XV, 3 (1974), 445–56.

_____. "Ancient mining near Great Zimbabwe," *Jnl. S. Afr. Instit. Mining and Metallurgy*, LXXIV, 6 (1974), 233–7.

_____. "The reconstruction of the Southern Rhodesian gold mining industry, 1903–19," *Econ. Hist. Review*, XXIX, 3 (1976), 465–81.

_____. "White mines in historical perspective: Southern Rhodesia, 1890–1953," *Jn. So. Afr. Studies*, III, 2 (1977), 187–206.

Summers, Roger. *Ancient Mining in Rhodesia.* Salisbury: Nat. Museums of Rhod., 1969. 236p.

van Onselen, Charles. "The role of collaborators in the Rhodesian mining industry, 1900–1935," *Afr. Affairs*, 72 (1973), 401–18.

Wilson, N. D. (comp.). *Notes on the Mining Industry of Southern Rhodesia.* Salisbury: Gov. Printer, c1933. 94p.

Transport and Communications

Barnes, J. C. "The Beira–Mashonaland Railway," *Rhodesiana*, 37 (1977), 1–16.

Croxton, Anthony H. *Railways of Rhodesia: The Story of the Beira, Mashonaland and Rhodesia Railways.* Newton Abbot, England: David and Charles, 1973. 315p.

Hyatt, Stanley Portal. *The Old Transport Road.* London: A. Melrose, 1914. 301p. (Rep., Bulawayo: BOR, 1969.)

Letcher, Owen. *When Life Was Rusted Through.* New ed. Bulawayo: BOR, 1973. 54p. (First pub., 1934.)

McAdam, J. "The birth of an airline: the establishment of Rhodesia and Nyasaland Airways," *Rhodesiana,* 21 (1969), 36–50.

Pauling, George. *The Chronicles of a Contractor.* Rep. ed., Bulawayo: BOR, 1969. 264p. (First pub., 1926.)

Smith, R. Cherer. "The Africa trans-continental telegraph line," *Rhodesiana,* 33 (Sept. 1976), 1–18.

Varian, H. F. *Some African Milestones.* Oxford: Ronald, 1953. 272p. (Rep., Bulawayo: BOR, 1973.)

West, John H. "Railway economics in Rhodesia," *Rhod. Jnl. Econ.,* II (1968), 48–57.

5. HISTORY

General Histories and Historiography

Alexander, Jocelyn. "State, peasantry and resettlement in Zimbabwe," *R. Afr. Pol. Econ.,* 21, 61 (1994), 325–45.

———, et al. *Violence and Memory: One Hundred Years in the 'Dark Forests' of Matabeleland.* Portsmouth, NH: Heinemann, 2000. 288 p.

Baxter, T. W., and R. W. S. Turner. *Rhodesian Epic.* 3rd ed. Cape Town: H. Timmins, 1973. c.240p. (First pub., 1966.)

Beach, D. N. "Documents and African society on the Zimbabwean plateau before 1890," in Beatrix Heintze and Adam Jones (eds.), *European Sources for Sub-Saharan Africa Before 1900: Use and Abuse.* Paideuma Mitteilungen zur Kultukunde, no. 33 (Stuttgart: Franz Steiner Verlag Wiesbaden, 1987), 129–45.

———. "*NADA* and Mafohla: antiquarianism in Rhodesia and Zimbabwe with special reference to the work of F. W. T. Posselt," *History in Africa,* XIII (1986), 1–11.

Berens, Dennis (ed.). *Concise Encyclopedia of Zimbabwe.* Gweru: Mambo Press, 1987. 444p.

Birmingham, David, and Phyllis M. Martin (eds.). *History of Central Africa,* 2 vols. London: Longman, 1983. Vol 1, 315p.; Vol. 2, 432p.

Blake, Robert. *A History of Rhodesia.* New York: Knopf, 1977.

Bulpin, Thomas Victor. *To the Banks of the Zambezi.* London: Nelson, 1965. 441p.

Chigwedere, Aeneas. *From Mutapa to Rhodes, 1000 to 1890.* London: Macmillan, 1980. 168p.

Cooke, Cranmer Kenrick. "The Commission for the Preservation of Natural and Historical Monuments and Relics: a history," *Rhodesiana,* 24 (1971), 32–54.

Denoon, Donald, with Balam Nyeko. *Southern Africa Since 1800.* London: Longman; New York: Praeger, 1972. 242p.

Gann, Lewis H. *Central Africa: The Former British States.* Englewood Cliffs, NJ: Prentice-Hall, 1971. 180p.

_____. *A History of Southern Rhodesia: Early Days to 1934*. London: Chatto and Windus, 1965. 354p.

_____, and Peter Duignan. *Burden of Empire: An Appraisal of Western Colonialism in Africa South of the Sahara*. New York: Praeger, 1967. 435p. (Special ref. to Rhodesia.)

Hanna, Alexander John. *The Story of the Rhodesias and Nyasaland*. 2nd ed. London: Faber and Faber, 1965. (First pub., 1960.) 331p.

Historians in Tropical Africa: Proceedings of the Leverhulme Inter-Collegiate History Conference Held at the University College of Rhodesia and Nyasaland, September 1960. Salisbury: Univ. Coll. of Rhod. & Nyasa., 1962. (Chapters are individually paginated.)

Illustrated Life Rhodesia. *All Our Yesterdays, 1890–1970: A Pictorial Review of Rhodesia's Story from the Best of "Illustrated Life Rhodesia.Review of African Political Economy,"* Salisbury: Graham Pub. Co., 1970. 201p.

Kaarsholm, Preben. *Cultural Struggle and Development in Southern Africa*. Portsmouth, NH: Heinemann, 1992. 258 p.

Kane, Nora S. *The World's View: The Story of Southern Rhodesia*. London: Cassell, 1954. 294p.

Meredith, Martin. *The Past is another country: Rhodesia 1890–1979*. London: Andre Deutsch, 1979. 383p.

Molgard Jensen, S. *Our Forefathers' Blood: Interviews From Zimbabwe*. Copenhagen: Mellomfolkelight Samvirke, 1992. 109p.

Mosley, Paul. *The settler economies: studies in the economic history of Kenya and Southern Rhodesia, 1900–1963*. Cambridge: Cambridge U.P., 1983. 183p.

Mothibe, Tefetso Henry. "Organized African Labor and Nationalism in Colonial Zimbabwe, 1945–1971." Ph.D. thesis, Univ. of Wisconsin-Madison, 1993. 307p.

Munenge, S. *A Political History of Munhumutapa, c1400–1902*. London: James Currey, 1988. 420p.

Mungazi, Dickson A. *Colonial Policy and Conflict in Zimbabwe: A Study of Cultures in Collision, 1890–1979*. Bristol, PA: Crane Russak and Company, 1992. 200p.

Nyangoni, Wellington Winter. *Underdevelopment, Imperialism and Neocolonialism in Zimbabwe*. Marlborough, MA: Msasa Publications, 1992. 593p.

Phimister, Ian R. "Accommodating imperialism: the compromise of the settler state in Southern Rhodesia, 1923–1979," *Jnl. Afr. Hist.*, 25, 3 (1984), 279–294.

_____. *Wangi Kolia: Coal, Capital and Labour in Colonial Zimbabwe, 1894–1954*. Harare: Baobab Books, 1994. 194p.

Potts, D. *Zimbabwe*. Oxford: Clio, 1993. 402p.

Ranger, Terence O. *Are We Not Also Men? The Samkange Family and African Politics in Zimbabwe, 1920–64*. Portsmouth, NH: Heinemann, 1995.

_____. "The historiography of Southern Rhodesia," *Trans-Afr. Jnl. Hist.*, I, 2 (1971), 63–76.

_____. *Voices from the Rocks: Nature, Culture and History in the Matopos Hills of Zimbabwe*. Oxford: James Curry, 1999. 305 p.

_____. (ed.). *Aspects of Central African History.* London: Heinemann, 1968. 291p.

Ransford, Oliver. *The Rulers of Rhodesia: From Earliest Times to the Referendum.* London: J. Murray, 1968. 345p.

Rayner, William. *The Tribe and Its Successors; An Account of African Traditional Life and European Settlement in Southern Rhodesia.* London: Faber and Faber; New York: Praeger, 1962. 239p.

Rhodesiana Society. "Bulawayo lectures on aspects of Rhodesian history," *Rhodesiana,* 29 (Dec. 1973), 1–87.

_____. *Occasional Paper I: A Record of the Proceedings at a Series of 5 Lectures on Rhodesia, 1896 to 1923.* Salisbury: Mashonaland Branch, Rhod. Soc., 1976. 95p.

Schmidt, Elizabeth. *Peasants, Traders and Wives: Shona Women in the History of Zimbabwe, 1870–1939.* Portsmouth, NH: Heineman, 1992.

Seidman, G. *Zimbabwe: A New History.* Harare: Zimb. Pub. House, 1982. 140p.

Shepperson, George. "British Central Africa," in Robin Winks (ed.), *The Historiography of the British Empire-Commonwealth* (Durham, NC: Duke UP, 1966), 237–47.

Shutt, Allison K. "'We Are The Best Poor Farmers': Purchase Area Farmers and Economic Differentiation in Southern Rhodesia, 1925–1980." Ph.D. thesis, Univ. of California, Los Angeles, 1995. 456p.

Standing, T. G. *A Short History of Rhodesia and Her Neighbors.* London: Longmans, 1935. 210p.

Stokes, Eric, and Richard Brown (eds.). *The Zimbesian Past: Studies in Central African History.* Manchester, England: Manchester UP, 1966. 427p.

Thompson, Leonard M. (ed.). *African Societies in Southern Africa: Historical Studies.* London: Heinemann, 1969. 336p.

Tindall, P. E. N. *A History of Central Africa.* New York: Praeger, 1968. 348p.

Vambe, Lawrence. *From Rhodesia to Zimbabwe.* London: Heinemann, 1976. 290p.

_____. *An Ill-Fated People: Zimbabwe Before and After Rhodes.* London: Heinemann, 1972. 254p.

Verrier, Anthony. *The road to Zimbabwe, 1890–1980.* London: J. Cape, 1986. 364p.

Walker, Eric A. *A History of Southern Africa.* 3rd ed. London: Longmans, 1957. 973p. (First pub., 1928.)

Weitzer, Ronald J. *Transforming Settler States: Communal Conflict and Internal Security in Northern Ireland and Zimbabwe.* Los Angeles: Univ. of California Press, 1990.

Wills, A. J. *An Introduction to the History of Central Africa.* 3rd ed. London: OUP, 1973. 450p. (First pub., 1964.)

Wright, Harrison M. *The Burden of the Present: The Liberal-Radical Controversy over Southern African History.* Cape Town: D. Philip; London: R. Collings, 1977. 137p.

Local and District Histories

Beach, David N. "Afrikaner and Shona settlement in the Enkeldoorn area, 1890–1900," *Zambezia,* 1, 2 (1970), 25–34.

Blick, G. A. B. *The History of Shamva.* Shamva: Rural Council, 1972. 50p.

Bourdillon, Michael F. C. "Peoples of Darwin," *Nada,* X, 2 (1970), 103–14.

Cherer-Smith, R. *Avondale to Zimbabwe: a collection of cameos of Rhodesian towns and villages.* Borrowdale, Harare: Mardon Printers, 1978. 314p.

Edwards, J. A. "The Lomahundi District: an historical sketch," *Rhodesiana,* 7 (1962), 1–21.

Hodder-Williams, Richard. *White Farmers in Rhodesia, 1890–1965: a history of the Marandellas district.* London: Macmillan, 1983. 256p.

Meredith, L. C. "Melsetter District—history of native tribes and chiefs," *Nada,* XI, 3 (1976), 338–44.

Morris, E. W. "Marondella's district—history of native tribes and chiefs," *Nada,* XI, 4 (1977), 436–42.

Ransford, Oliver. *Bulawayo: Historic Battleground of Rhodesia.* Cape Town: A. A. Balkema, 1968. 182p.

Robinson, K. R. "A history of the Bikita District," *Nada,* 34 (1957), 75–87.

Sinclair, Shirley. *The Story of Melsetter.* Salisbury: M. O. Collins, 1971. 197p.

Tanser, George Henry. *A Scantling of Time: The Story of Salisbury, Rhodesia (1890–1900).* Salisbury: Stuart Manning, 1965. 278p. (Rep., 1975.)

_____. *A Sequence of Time: The Story of Salisbury, Rhodesia, 1900 to 1914.* Salisbury: Pioneer Head, 1974. 299p.

von Sicard, Harald. "The origin of some of the tribes in the Belingwe Reserve," *Nada,* 25 (1948), 93–104; 27 (1950), 7–19; 28 (1951), 5–25; 29 (1952), 43–64; 30 (1953), 64–71; 32 (1955), 77–92.

White, J. D. "Some notes on the history and customs of the Urungwe District," *Nada,* X, 3 (1971), 33–72.

Wild, N. C. "A question of succession: Maribeha T.T.L.: Matobo District," *Nada,* XI, 4 (1977), 415-27.

Stone Age

Clark, John Desmond. *The Prehistory of Southern Africa.* Harmondsworth, England: Penguin, 1959. 341p.

Cooke, Cranmer Kenrick. "Evidence of human migrations from the rock art of Southern Rhodesia," *Africa,* XXXV, 3 (1965), 263–85.

Cooke, Herbert Basil Sutton, Roger Summers, and K. R. Robinson. "Rhodesian prehistory re-examined," pt. I: "The Stone Age," *Arnoldia,* II, 12 (1966).

Inskeep, R. R. "The late Stone Age in Southern Africa," in W. S. Bishop and J. D. Clark (eds.), *Background to Evolution in Africa* (Chicago, 1967), 557–82.

Jones, Neville. *The Prehistory of Southern Rhodesia: An Account of the Progress of the Research from 1900 to 1946.* Cambridge, England: Cambridge UP, 1949. 77p.

_____. *The Stone Age in Rhodesia.* London: OUP, 1926. 120p. (Rep., New York: NUP, 1969.)

Sampson, C. Garth. *The Stone Age Archaeology of Southern Africa.* New York: Academic Press, 1974. 518p.

Walker, N. J. *Late Pleistocene and Holocene Hunter-Gatherers of the Matopos: An Archaeological Study of Change and Continuity in Zimbabwe.* Uppsala: Archaeological Society of Uppsala Univ., 1995. 284p.

———. "Later Stone Age research in the Matopos," *So. Afr. Arch. Bul.,* 35, 131 (1980), 19–24.

Willoughby, Pamela. *Spheroids and Battered Stones: A Case Study of Technology and Adaptation in the African Early and Middle Stone Age.* Los Angeles: Univ. California Press, 1985. 360p.

Iron Age: General

Bent, James Theodore. *The Ruined Cities of Mashonaland: Being a Record of Excavation and Exploration in 1891.* London: Longmans, Green, 1892. 427p. (Reps. of 3rd ed., 1895; Bulawayo: BOR, 1969; London: Cass, 1975.)

Bernhard, F. O. "Notes on the pre-ruin Ziwa culture of Inyanga," *Rhodesiana,* 11 (Dec. 1964), 22–30.

Cooke, Cranmer Kenrick, Roger Summers, and K. R. Robinson. "Rhodesian prehistory re-examined," pt. II: "The Iron Age," *Arnoldia,* II, 17 (Feb. 1966), 11p.

———. "Wooden and bone artefacts: Pomongwe Cave, Matobo district, Zimbabwe," *So. Afr. Arch. Bul.,* 35, 131 (1980), 25–29.

Crawford, J. R. "The Monk's Kop ossuary," *Jnl. Afr. Hist.,* VIII, 3 (1967), 373–82.

Fagan, Brian M. *Southern Africa During the Iron Age.* New York: Praeger, 1965. 222p.

Garlake, Peter S. "Rhodesian ruins—a preliminary assessment of their styles and chronology," *Jnl. Afr. Hist.,* XI, 4 (1970), 495–513.

———. "The value of imported ceramics in the dating and interpretation of the Rhodesian Iron Age," *Jnl. Afr. Hist.,* IX, 1 (1968), 13–33.

Hall, Richard N. *Prehistoric Rhodesia: An Examination of the Historical, Ethnological and Archaeological Evidences as to the Origin and Age of the Rock Mines and Stone Buildings . . . .* London: Unwin, 1909. 488p.

———, and W. G. Neal. *The Ancient Ruins of Rhodesia (Monomotopae Imperium).* London: Methuen, 1902. 396p. (Reps., 2nd ed., 1904; Bulawayo: BOR, 1972; New York: NUP.)

Huffman, Thomas N. *The Leopard's Kopje Tradition.* Salisbury: Nat. Museums and Monuments of Rhod., 1975. 155p.

———. "The linguistic affinities of the Iron Age in Rhodesia," *Arnoldia,* VII, 7 (1974), 1–11.

Jaffey, A. J. E. "A reappraisal of the history of the Rhodesian Iron Age up to the fifteenth century," *Jnl. Afr. Hist.,* VII, 2 (1966), 189–95.

Lancaster, C. S., and A. Pohorilenko. "Ingombe Ilede and the Zkimbabwe culture," *Internat. Jnl. Afr. Hist. Studies,* X, 1 (1977), 1–30.

Mtetwa, R. M. G. "Myth or reality: the 'cattle complex' in Southeastern Africa, with special reference to Rhodesia," *Zambezia,* 6, 2 (1978), 23–35.

Prendergast, M. D. "Iron Age settlement and economy in part of the Southern Zambezian Highveld," *So. Afr. Arch. Bul.,* 34, 130 (1979), 11–119.

Pwiti, G. "The Iron Age in Northern Zimbabwe," *Mohlomi,* 6 (1990), 165–174.